196 nations* in
the world, 196
illustrations on this
cover. All generated
by code, in a place
where technology
and creativity
meet. The designer
created these
illustrations based
on each country's
data, to evoke the
diversity of D&AD's
global community.
Horizon lines are
determined by
latitude; colours
by time and
meteorological
data. You can see
the UK's northerly
latitude and cooler
blue green colours
on the right. And
the illustrations
on the following
pages represent
the 42 nations with
winning work in
this book.

Be part of a living,
user-created,
global design.
Create your own
horizon, specific
to your location, at
www.dandad.org/
globalhorizons

—
Cover and book
design by Fleur
Isbell.

Fleur Isbell is a
designer at Wolff
Olins, London.
A 2011 Bath
Spa University
graduate, she was
helped in her career
by D&AD's work for
students and young
creatives. Fleur
was chosen to
design this book
as part of D&AD's
commitment to
champion great
young talent.

D&AD13

*Number of official
independent countries
in the world

D&AD13

TASCHEN

GBR 54°0'N 2°0'W 7° 12:00

CONTENTS

President's Introduction

Discovering and nurturing new creative talent is at the heart of what D&AD does. All the revenue from our Awards programmes and sponsorships is reinvested to help us discover and support the creative superstars of the future.

In the UK we're currently facing a crisis in creative education. Students are being made to invest in this nation's future, which is an absurd situation. We haven't had the benefit of 50 years of US educational history – a country where the industry knows it has to create endowments and give gifts. It's not been a phased handover. It's just been a sudden culture shock, and we've all been pushed off the cliff and told to swim.

Through the D&AD Foundation we're trying to lead the way with new models of support for young creative people. But we can only do so much. Industry must take up the considerable slack left by a deficit in investment in creative people that could severely weaken our future prosperity, as a business and as a society.

Neville Brody
D&AD President

Einleitung des Präsidenten

Die Entdeckung und Förderung kreativer Nachwuchstalente steht bei D&AD im Mittelpunkt. So werden alle bei Preisverleihungen und Sponsoren gesammelten Gelder in die Suche und Unterstützung der kreativen Superstars von morgen investiert.

In Großbritannien erleben wir im Bereich der künstlerischen Ausbildung derzeit eine Krise. Die Studierenden sollen in die Zukunft des Landes investieren – eine absurde Situation. Wir verfügen nicht über das 50 Jahre währende Know-how eines US-Systems, wo die Industrie ganz selbstverständlich durch Stiftungen und Stipendien Talente fördert. Statt einer allmählichen Entwicklung haben wir einen Kulturschock erlebt, bei dem wir einfach ins kalte Wasser geworfen wurden.

Mit der D&AD Foundation versuchen wir als Vorbild für die Unterstützung junger Kreativer voranzugehen. Jedoch können wir nicht alles alleine erreichen. Die Industrie muss nun das riesige Loch stopfen, das durch mangelnde Förderung unseres kreativen Nachwuchs entstanden ist – und das die Zukunft unserer Wirtschaft und Gesellschaft gefährden könnte.

Neville Brody
Präsident des D&AD

Introduction du Président

La raison d'être de D&AD est de découvrir et de stimuler de nouveaux talents créatifs. Toutes les recettes obtenues de nos prix et de nos sponsors sont réinvesties en vue de découvrir et de soutenir les futures stars de la création.

Le Royaume-Uni traverse actuellement une crise en matière d'enseignement créatif. On demande aux étudiants d'investir dans l'avenir de la nation, ce qui est absurde. Nous n'avons pas eu la chance de vivre 50 années d'histoire éducative comme aux États-Unis, pays où l'industrie sait qu'elle doit encourager les contributions et les dons. Nous n'avons pas eu droit à une prise en main progressive de la situation. Le choc culturel a été brusque : on nous a jetés du haut de la falaise et demandé de nous mettre à nager.

La mission de la Fondation D&AD vise à marquer le chemin à suivre pour soutenir les jeunes créateurs selon de nouveaux modèles. Mais ce que nous pouvons faire est limité. L'industrie doit combler l'écart de taille dû au manque de soutien économique apporté aux créateurs. La prospérité du secteur et de la société dans son ensemble pourrait s'en voir sinon fortement diminuée.

Neville Brody
Président de D&AD

D&AD dropped the 'British' from its name 25 years ago. We are proud to be a truly global show and a worldwide measure of creative excellence in advertising and design.

This year 98 of our distinguished jury women and men were from outside the UK; that's 54%. As was 75% of the work that was entered and 67% of the pieces that made it into the Annual.

We know that some of our British members regret the passing of 'British D&AD'. It was a cosier world back then. But the reality is that we work in a global industry for increasingly globalised clients. All of us need to test ourselves against the best. And the best is what the book you have in your hands contains.

The money D&AD makes from the Awards and its commercial operations – membership, events, training and professional development – goes to support creative education in arts universities and our New Creatives programme – the Student Awards themselves, New Blood and Graduate Academy; all designed to help the brightest and best creative students to transition into the industry successfully and productively.

There's plenty of international participation in the New Creatives programme, with frequent international Student Award winners. But we have plans to advance this further. Already we have partnerships and representation in Brazil, Japan, China and India. There are plans to extend further – to Australia, South Africa and Thailand.

The next part of D&AD's journey is to begin to replicate the New Creatives programme in other parts of the world, extending opportunities to talented young creatives and continuing the quest – to support, stimulate and award creative excellence.

Tim Lindsay
D&AD CEO

Vor 25 Jahren strich D&AD das Wort „British" aus seinem Namen. Wir sind stolz auf unsere globale Ausrichtung und unsere Rolle als internationaler Maßstab für Exzellenz in Werbung und Design.

In diesem Jahr kommen 98 unserer angesehenen Jurymitglieder (also 54%) sowie 75% der Einsendungen und 67% der ins Jahrbuch aufgenommene Arbeiten von außerhalb Großbritanniens.

Einige unserer britischen Mitglieder trauern den alten Zeiten des „British D&AD" nach, als die Welt noch übersichtlich war. Heute sind wir jedoch auf einem internationalen Markt für global arbeitende Kunden tätig. Wir müssen uns mit den Besten der Branche messen können. Und das Buch in Ihren Händen enthält dieses Beste.

Das Geld, das D&AD durch die Preisverleihung und seine kommerziellen Aktivitäten – Mitgliedschaften, Veranstaltungen, Schulungen und berufliche Weiterbildung – einnimmt, fließt in die kreative Ausbildung an Kunstuniversitäten und in unser „New Creatives Programme": die „Student Awards", „New Blood" und „Graduate Academy". Mit diesem Angebot möchten wir die besten Studierenden im Kreativbereich beim Einstieg in ein erfolgreiches und produktives Berufsleben unterstützen.

Bei dem „New Creatives Programme" und den „Student Award"-Gewinnern gibt es zahlreiche internationale Teilnehmer, wir möchten unsere internationale Ausrichtung jedoch weiter stärken. Wir haben bereits Partnerschaften und Vertretungen in Brasilien, Japan, China und Indien, und es sind weitere in Australien, Südafrika und Thailand geplant.

Der nächste Meilenstein in der Geschichte von D&AD ist die Einführung des „New Creatives Programme" in anderen Teilen der Welt. So können wir noch mehr kreative Nachwuchstalente fördern und exzellente Leistungen weiter unterstützen und auszeichnen.

Tim Lindsay
D&AD CEO

Voilà déjà 25 ans que D&AD a éliminé le mot « British » de son nom. Nous sommes fiers de notre envergure internationale et d'être une référence mondiale de l'excellence créative dans le monde de la publicité et du design.

Cette année, 98 de nos éminents membres du jury (hommes et femmes confondus) n'étaient pas originaires du Royaume-Uni, soit 54%, tout comme 75% des travaux présentés et 67% des œuvres incluses dans cet album.

Nous sommes conscients qu'une partie de nos membres britanniques regrettent le feu « British D&AD », témoin d'un monde alors plus confortable. Mais la réalité est que nous évoluons dans une industrie mondiale pour des clients chaque fois plus internationaux. Nous devons nous référer à ce qu'il se fait de mieux, et c'est précisément le contenu de l'ouvrage que vous avez entre les mains.

Les recettes de D&AD issues des prix décernés et des opérations commerciales (adhésions, événements, formations et développement professionnel) servent à soutenir l'enseignement de disciplines créatives dans les universités. Elles financent aussi notre programme New Creatives (Student Awards, New Blood et Graduate Academy) conçu pour aider les étudiants les plus brillants et créatifs à mettre un pied dans l'industrie et à s'y faire une place.

La participation internationale est très élevée pour le programme New Creatives, et les lauréats des Student Awards sont souvent de differents pays. Notre intention est d'aller plus loin dans cette direction. Nous avons déjà des partenariats et une représentation au Brésil, au Japon, en Chine et en Inde ; nous visons aussi l'Australie, l'Afrique du Sud et la Thaïlande.

Le voyage de D&AD se poursuivra dans l'optique de reproduire le programme New Creatives dans d'autres parties du monde, en offrant une reconnaissance à de jeunes créateurs doués et en poursuivant notre objectif : soutenir, encourager et récompenser l'excellence créative.

Tim Lindsay
D&AD CEO

Interaction
Seiichi Saito

Postscript
Mark Porter

Editor
Lynda Relph-Knight

Graphics
Sue Walsh

Multimedia
John Maeda

Education
John Warwicker

Design
Wayne Hemingway

CONTRIBUTORS

President's Perspective
Neville Brody

In Context
Lynda Relph-Knight

Overview
Sir Christopher Frayling

Advertising
Nick Gill

THERE IS A PRESSING URGENCY TO ADDRESS EDUCATION FOR THE SURVIVAL, GROWTH AND GLOBAL SUCCESS OF THE CREATIVE INDUSTRIES.

Britain, for example, is a nation of inventors and we have successfully convinced the government of our engineering prowess with the ability to cut across boundaries. What is critical in the UK now is to break down the barrier between creative thinking and engineering thinking. But our current geo-industrial landscape means sectors of the country have been disadvantaged by government policy with regard to broader creative education.

In an age of widening inequality, our duty is to ensure access for everyone to the opportunity of creative education and not just the so-called STEM subjects of science, technology, engineering and mathematics. It is the duty of governments to take the creative industries and creativity seriously.

This is a political situation. Many nations have the resources to support creative education, but it depends whether or not their governments are prepared to allocate them. Because creativity isn't quantifiable it loses out, as it's doing in the UK, yet some of our greatest cultural treasures have been vilified at the point of launch. We wouldn't have had David Bowie at London's V&A Museum – or The Beatles – if not for art schools.

The British Government is obsessed with a Victorian model of society that is mechanistic. But the modern world is hybridised. It's about crossing boundaries through people bent on changing society. It shouldn't be about having to choose, but about everyone having access to some form of creative learning.

For developing countries, creative education and the creative industries are, meanwhile, a way to develop trade and culture. The international challenge is to identify what we need for emerging countries on the one hand and for declining nations on the other.

If creative education is broken there are two ways we can approach it: to fix it or to start again. There is a real opportunity to start again. It's worth looking for inspiration at the original free-school idea and models like Montessori or Steiner schools. I have based the School of Communication at the Royal College of Art on that – providing a rigorous foundation coupled with deprogramming graduate students to create a culture of lateral and critical thinking.

One of the biggest challenges for educationalists generally is MOOCs – massive open online courses. How do teachers manage that process and what role do they play in MOOC-based initiatives like FutureLearn, which gives online access to some of the UK's top universities? But open source learning doesn't work for creative education, which involves making and working in teams. That is all about community.

This is a moment of unprecedented opportunity to develop the next revolution in global culture – a creative revolution. There is a lot of work to do, lots of discussions to be had and arguments to be debated. The creative community finds itself at the heart of it.

—
Neville Brody is an internationally renowned designer, typographer, art director, brand strategist and consultant, and the founder of the Research Studios network. He is also the Dean of the School of Communication and Head of the Visual Communication Programme at the Royal College of Art, London.

IDN 5°0'S 120°0'W 30° 19:00

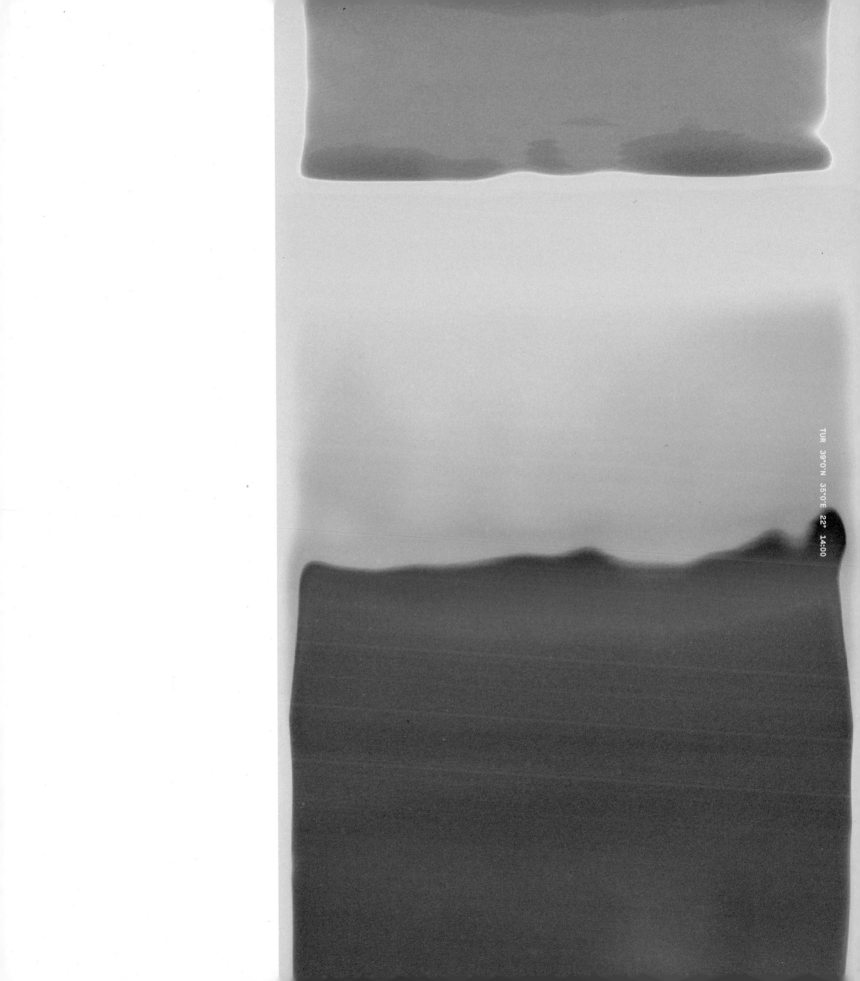

TUR 39°0'N 35°0'E 22° 14:00

ONLY ONE THING IS CERTAIN IN THESE DAYS OF RAPID CHANGE. THE FIGURES SURROUNDING CREATIVE EDUCATION ARE UNRELIABLE.

Data from the West in particular were generally compiled before global economic recession hit and a squeeze on education ensued, particularly in the UK. At best they are contradictory, drawing on different definitions of what constitutes the creative industries, ranging from design and art to music and writing, and at worst so out of date as to be irrelevant.

For example, the UK Government's Higher Education Statistics Agency (HESA) put the number of college students on Design Studies courses as 69,020 in 2011-12. The same year saw 182,085 students studying Creative Art & Design, according to HESA. So which data are correct, what exactly do they include and is there an overlap? No one appears able to say with any degree of conviction.

But while Western figures may raise more questions than they answer, statisticians can hardly keep pace with developing nations and their zeal, not to catch up, but to lead the way to the future. We are told by some sources that the number of design schools in China is 400 plus and rising, with some 10,000 graduates expected a year. But we are also told that the Chinese Government's focus has been on building schools rather than educational programmes, so while the numbers are impressive, they are not necessarily matched by the quality of the student experience or the level of skills they acquire.

This is a generalisation, of course, and much of the 'information' amounts to little more than barbed speculation by Western concerns challenged by a newcomer with the potential to take the market by storm. What we do know though is that while the West is in relative decline and given to navel-gazing, not least in education, developing nations such as Brazil, Russia, India and China are putting design at the heart of that development. Indeed, as far back as 2009 the International Design Scoreboard, a research report from Cambridge University backed by the UK Design Council, surveyed 12 countries and found that the economic well-being of Western nations was under threat from East Asian 'powerhouses'.

These 'powerhouses', the report observed, were increasingly competing through design. Even then they were developing their own design sectors, investing in national design promotion and producing skilled graduates. The notion that the West had the expertise and the East merely the production capacity and cheap labour was coming under scrutiny.

The escalating building programme for universities in China alone is enough to impress. This country means business and it has the population and the facilities to make its point. It has also attracted partnerships with design colleges from Europe, the US and beyond that are keen to cash in on a potentially lucrative new market. Indeed, in October 2011 UK and Chinese Government ministers forged a Higher Education Partnership programme to foster links and exchanges between the two countries. And in the same month the Canadian province of Alberta was among other Western authorities that did the same.

–

But what is China teaching? Western colleges still often maintain that they offer a better standard of tuition, even if the facilities might not be quite up to oriental standards. But the quality of thinking reported from some Far Eastern universities, particularly in Korea and Taiwan, suggests it won't be long before they dominate in more than numbers. They have the rare opportunity to innovate in education to help nurture graduates better equipped than some in the West to meet the needs of the age of connectivity.

We in the West have long prided ourselves as being a 'knowledge economy' – a phrase coined by California-based technology specialist Dr Jeff Conklin in the mid-1990s and bandied about by organisations such as the London-based Work Foundation. Yet it is Korea that pioneered the idea of a government Ministry of Knowledge Economy.

To an extent, though, that is just terminology and we shouldn't whip ourselves too much over it, What we do have is a grasp on what is needed for the future in terms of social and communications strategies, with design leading a charge that is not just about economic prowess on a global stage.

Key to that are graduates who are fleet of mind and can move with ease across more traditional disciplines. These are 'Versationalists', according to Andreas Schleicher of the international Organisation for Economic Co-operation and Development, who runs the OECD Programme of International Student Assessment. His descriptor arguably builds on the notion of 'T-shaped people' first mooted in the 1990s to describe people with a depth of expertise but the breath to interact and share with others of different experience.

There is also a popular belief among innovation activists that art and science need to work more closely together to meet current social and economic needs. This is not new – architects and product designers, for example, have long worked alongside engineers to achieve their objectives. But when Google Executive Chairman Eric Schmidt espouses it it will reach fresh ears.

Sadly, in the UK those ears don't belong to government ministers, who have singularly excluded art and design from the mandatory STEM subjects – science, technology, engineering and mathematics – to be taught in secondary schools. Fortunately, British universities haven't proved so deaf and there have been several examples of 'incubators' that bring students and staff from both disciplines together. Take the Royal College of Art's Design London link up with the neighbouring Imperial College or Edinburgh's Design Informatics Centre that combines the expertise of the university, where computing is a strength, with that of the city's college of art and design.

–

Despite such pockets of excellence, the global picture remains patchy. But with the Far East looking set to take the lead we can be sure that the West will have to try harder if it is to continue to compete. The nations that succeed will be those like Singapore, whose trade development body International Enterprise Singapore maintains that investment in design gives a 26% better return than it would in banking and is 20% better than investment in computing.

If any nation supports such a powerful economic belief with commensurate investment in design education then its future is assured – assuming, that is, that quality of thinking and innovation are at the heart of its brief to educators.

It does though need to bear in mind that design is not just a creator of wealth. It can play a powerful role in addressing social concerns at all levels of society. Any nation that adds that into the educational blend is the one we will all seek to emulate.

CAN 60°0'N 95°0'W -3° 7:00

—
Lynda Relph-Knight is a
design writer and consultant.

PHL 13°0'N 122°0'E 28° 20:00

AUT 47°20'N 13°20'E 10° 13:00

CHE 47°0'N 8°0'E 10° 13:00

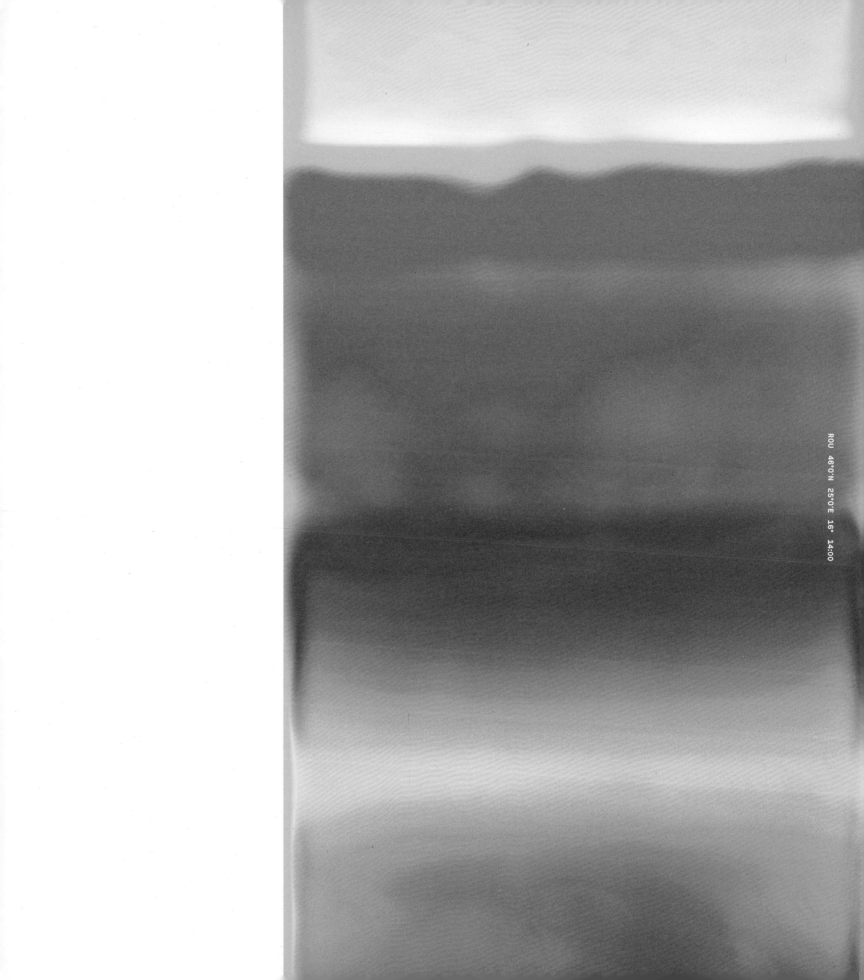

ROU 46°0'N 25°0'E 16° 14:00

SCHOOLS OF THOUGHT: THE FUTURE OF CREATIVE EDUCATION

SITTING IN THE COURTYARD OF LONDON'S V&A MUSEUM, PROFESSOR SIR CHRISTOPHER FRAYLING IS IN HIS ELEMENT.

An eminent cultural historian, Frayling is a research fellow of the museum. He has also curated exhibitions there, including the hugely successful Hollywood Costume show of 2012-13. But he is equally steeped in education. As Rector of London's Royal College of Art for 13 of his 37 years at the college, he had first-hand experience of post-graduate students. But his perspective is broad and he has spoken against UK Government plans to dumb down or omit design teaching in schools.

'These are interesting times', he says of creative education globally. But he takes the long view. 'Since the 1950s, the British art and design avant-garde – which was its strength – has become institutionalised', he says. 'But we have seen the creation of the art student as an abrasive individual with their own voice'. He cites artist David Hockney, who pronounced it a cardinal sin for a teacher not to have a point of view, because creativity lies in the friction between teacher and student.

'In cultures where the avant-garde is problematic it can't be like that', says Frayling. He points to China, where the educational infrastructure develops daily – 'but the bloody-minded avant-garde is a long way off'.

From the Chinese model, 'you will get extra pairs of hands to work at various levels in industry', but can expect little more. He believes that to engender creative thinking, 'collision and abrasion should be at the heart of art education'.

'Conformity is the death of creativity', he says. 'Yet in Britain the avant-garde has become the establishment. In China, at least the idea of studying design has traction and I am deeply impressed by the infrastructure. They get a building in place and then colour it in', whereas in the UK it can take years for a good idea to be adopted and the infrastructure to support it put in place.

The deeply ideological Chinese way is flawed however. 'Confusionism is about sitting at the feet of the master. But I would sooner have a bloody-minded student, with a point of view, though they might not yet know how to express it', he says.

There have been times when the British Government looked to design students for innovation, says Frayling. But the professionalisation of design ended that implicit trust and the pitch to government about the creative industries being a cohesive economic sector has worn thin – even though they account for some 9.7% of the UK's gross domestic product.

'The big issue', says Frayling, 'is how far the creative industries' argument holds up. In Britain we are discovering it is a fiction. What do advertising, fashion, the music industry, games, crafts and the antiques trade really have in common as industrial structures? And if you take computer software out of the bundle, the creative industries lose about 50% of their value. The idea of coherence is false, except they all depend on creativity for their intellectual property'.

Frayling is scathing about how the British creative community has made its case to date. 'It was a lot of rhetoric and bullshit and we have lost ground in design education over the past 15 years', he states. 'We have to regroup to present a fresh argument'. British politicians now talk about 'productive industries' rather than 'creative industries', he says. Productivity has to be at the heart for them – which renders the Chinese approach interesting.

He says that for years a designerly attitude was considered valuable, opening up career opportunities for students. But design is also deemed to be vocational. 'Is design vocational or isn't it?' he asks. 'A lot of educational institutions dangle a carrot of a job in front of students. There's always a muddle about that'.

–

On the effect of globalisation on colleges, Frayling says it's about balance. 'When asked why London art schools are so lively, I used to say it's because they are multicultural. It was seen as an advantage. This isn't new. The potter Bernard Leach went for inspiration to Japan and Pablo Picasso saw moving between different cultures as a positive. When I was at the RCA I didn't think there were enough overseas students. I loved the nourishment we got from each other.'

'But now colleges tend to bring in overseas students to balance the books. It is ignoble to bring students in just because of money. It is also unfair to expect students from radically different educational cultures to behave like their British counterparts.'

'One of the big areas is to build real partnerships, as I tried to do at the RCA. Students came to London, bringing their culture with them, and would then take what they learned back home and temper it to the local culture. Satellites of knowledge would grow in their own countries as they sowed genuine academic seeds.'

'The problem with the ignoble motive for bringing in overseas students is that it is short-term', says Frayling. 'People realise they are not being invited in because of their intrinsic value, but because of their bank balance.'

Is anyone getting it right? 'It is usually okay in pockets', says Frayling. 'It is a matter of institutions deciding how to push the envelope. Complacency is the enemy.'

Frayling is adamant that boosting student numbers will not foster greater creativity. 'Scale is interesting', he says, citing the Bauhaus as only having 250 students. 'In education small is beautiful. A small, but diverse landscape is what is desirable.'

–

Sir Christopher Frayling was speaking to Lynda Relph-Knight.

—
Sir Christoph
historian, wr
He was Rect
Art from 199
the Design (
from 1999
the Arts Co
to 2009.

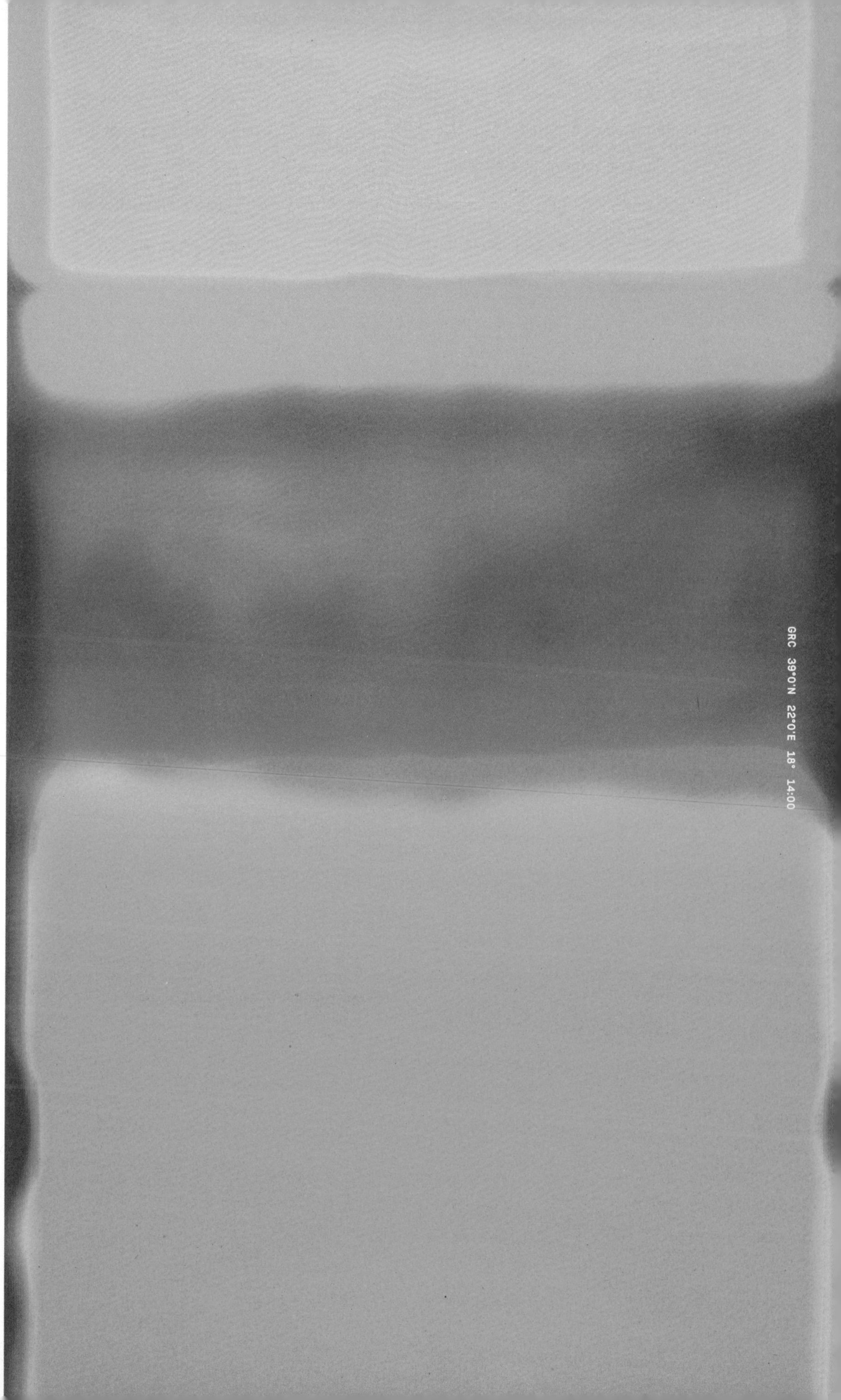

NICK GILL IS A BUSY MAN. BUT HE MAKES TIME TO TALK ABOUT EDUCATION BECAUSE HE BELIEVES PASSIONATELY ABOUT THE FUTURE.

And for him that future – for BBH London where he is Executive Creative Director and for his beloved advertising industry – is firmly in the hands of much younger talents. So much so that he has put bright graduates at the heart of the BBH business.

'The more responsibility they are given, the more they will take it', he says of the new blood he has brought into BBH since he was promoted to Executive Creative Director in 2008. Over the past five years, he has not only continued to foster fresh talent – not least through the agency's Barn initiative to manage placements for aspiring creatives. He has actively involved young creatives in every aspect of agency life.

He has put placement and very junior teams on the biggest briefs and the biggest pitches in the agency, and he reckons that a huge percentage of the best work produced at BBH over the past few years was written by creatives with less than two years' experience.

This commitment to youth is part of a bigger plan hatched by Gill to shake up BBH in the recent recession. He subscribes to the American dictate 'Don't waste a good recession' and his actions bear this out.

'The agency was going through tough times [in 2008]', he says. 'We needed a reaction. I saw the opportunity to work in a different way to embrace change. I didn't want to work in a business with a creative department, but in a creative business.'

This has meant a shift from BBH's old linear structure that Gill likens to the UK Government's Department of Health and Social Security. 'We have mixed people and clients together and literally knocked down walls in the Kingley Street building to encourage a more open approach. We're all on top of each other now.'

The move wasn't popular with everyone at BBH though. 'Some quarters of the creative department didn't want change', Gill admits, 'and we found we had a few jobs to fill. But we took on a couple of great creative directors and flooded the team with kids'.

'Now', he says, 'we are a meritocracy. Everyone gets a crack at a job. The younger creatives 'inspire upwards', in that their brilliance, enthusiasm and open-mindedness had a positive impact on the more senior people at BBH. The approach encourages us to be both young in age and young in outlook. If we're running a pitch we make sure everyone is listened to. The idea can come from anyone'.

_

Gill's own experience has informed this open approach. A designer by inclination, studying Design for Communication media at Manchester Art College placed him firmly in the advertising camp. In a career spanning some 30 years, he spent 13 years at DDB BMP. Following a brief spell at Wieden+Kennedy in London, he joined BBH in 1998.

Gill can be proud of what BBH has achieved on his watch to date and others may emulate the model he has created. But for him there remains a problem. The agency still doesn't have enough women at the creative level. 'A diverse creative department is a more interesting creative department', he says. 'Women are often stronger, but they tend not to stay', he says. There lies his challenge.

So what does Gill look for in recruits of whatever sex? As for most top creatives, good ideas, hunger and open-mindedness head his list. But Gill goes further, adding grit to his agenda.

'I'm a northern lad and I like people who, like me, have had to fight a bit', he says. 'This takes us back to diversity. I've found some great people from tough backgrounds who aren't seduced by the idea of a sexy, wealthy advertising world.'

But he'd also like to see more evidence of craft in graduates – a vital part of creative education that has been eroded by college cuts. As a wordsmith now within BBH, by way of example he harks back to a time when advertising had 'real' writers – novelists and playwrights.

'The reason, I think, there is a lack of craft skills coming out of the colleges isn't about scant resources (although it is a factor)', he says. 'It's about students these days having to focus on so many different channels. The explosion in media and technology, while representing a huge opportunity for all of us, means that students have had to broaden their creative thinking. And the bigger and broader their ideas become the less focus there seems to be on how best to craft those ideas.'

Colleges should, says Gill, encourage students to pick a craft they want to excel in and urge them to go for it. It could be writing to typography to coding. 'Colleges can inspire a love of craft through exposure to it. My ticket out of obscurity was the fact I can draw', he says.

He says that though they may have training budgets, agencies don't have the time to teach crafts. But where the colleges fall short organisations like D&AD could step in and run academies to teach younger creatives craft skills. That learning doesn't have to be part of a college course.

_

Advertising has a big awards culture – and BBH has enjoyed its share of prizes. But Gill views things differently. 'It's about improving your skills, conceptually and crafts-wise. If you come into advertising trying to win awards it's no good. I want people to step forward who want to crack research-based, conservative jobs – the big, tough hard hits of business'.

And the message to his peers? 'Give young people a chance', says Gill. All agencies, especially the big ones, should hire them and give them responsibilities. It will involve mentoring and tutoring, but take a gamble on them.

_

Nick Gill was speaking to Lynda Relph-Knight.

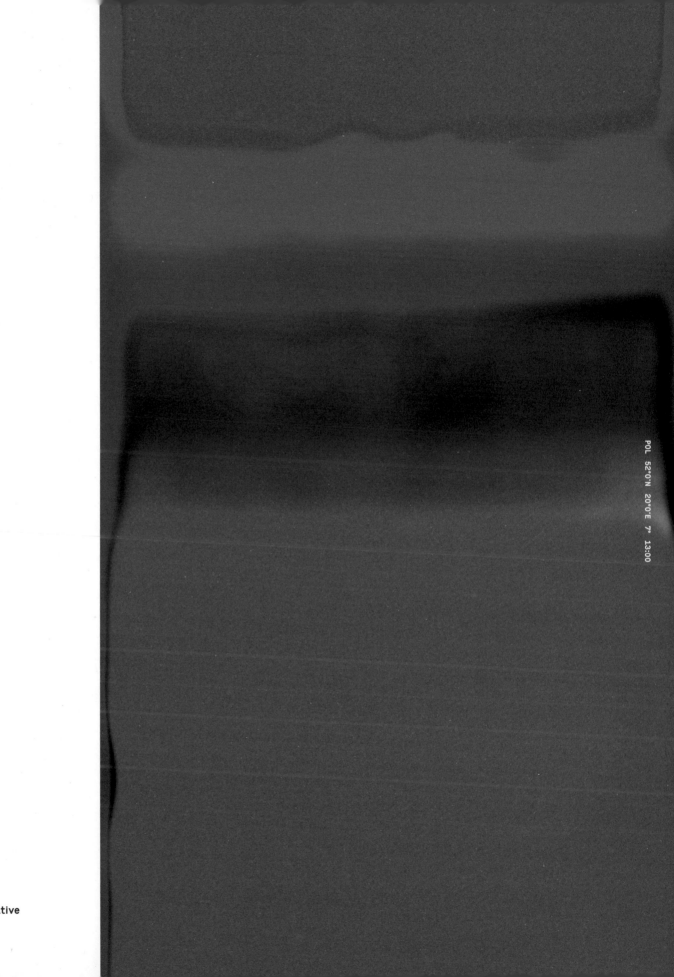

POL 52°0'N 20°0'E 7° 13:00

Nick Gill is Executive Creative
Director at BBH London.

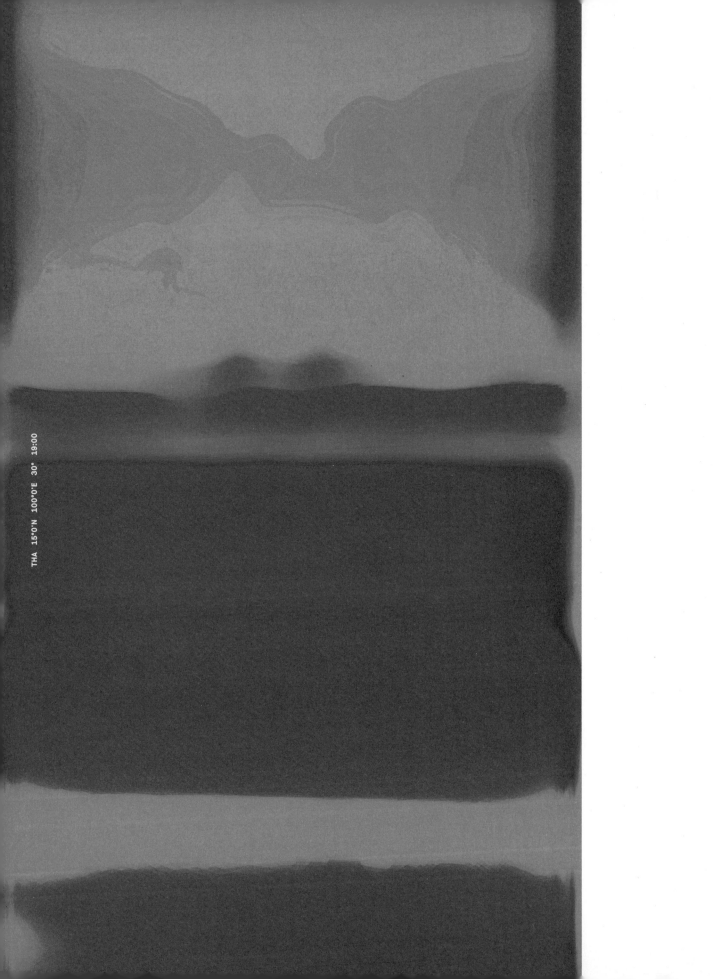

THA 15°0'N 100°0'E 30' 19:00

CHN 35°0'N 150°0'E 18° 20:00

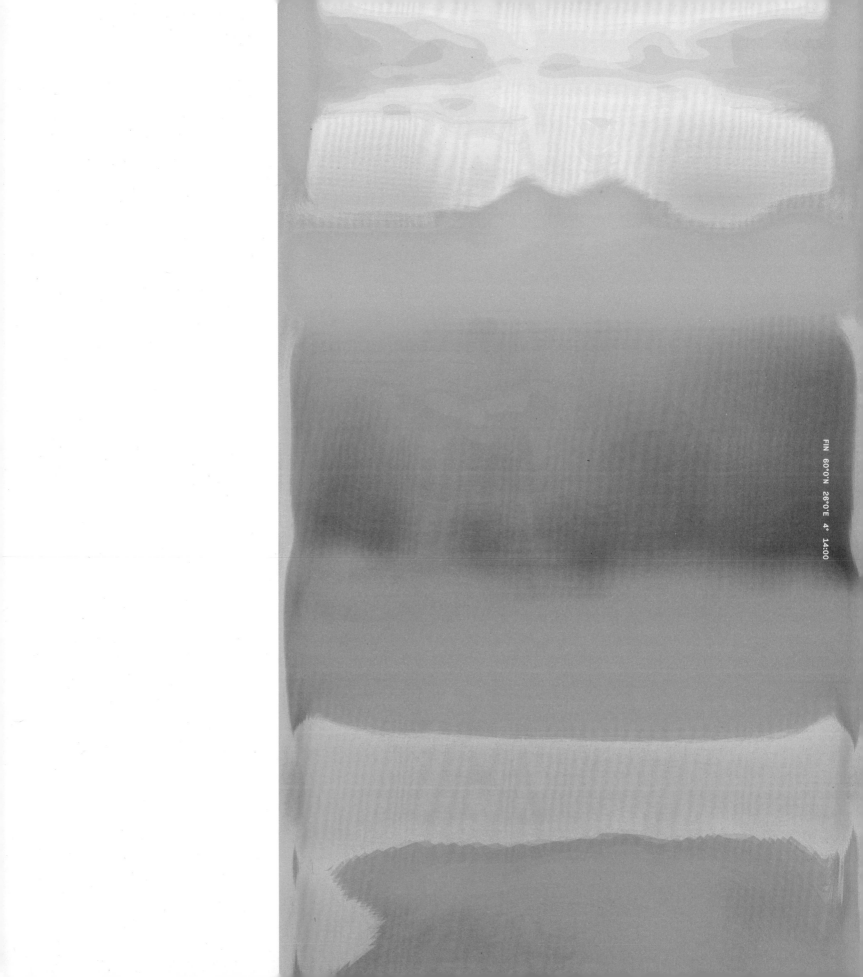

FIN 60°0'N 26°0'E 4° 14:00

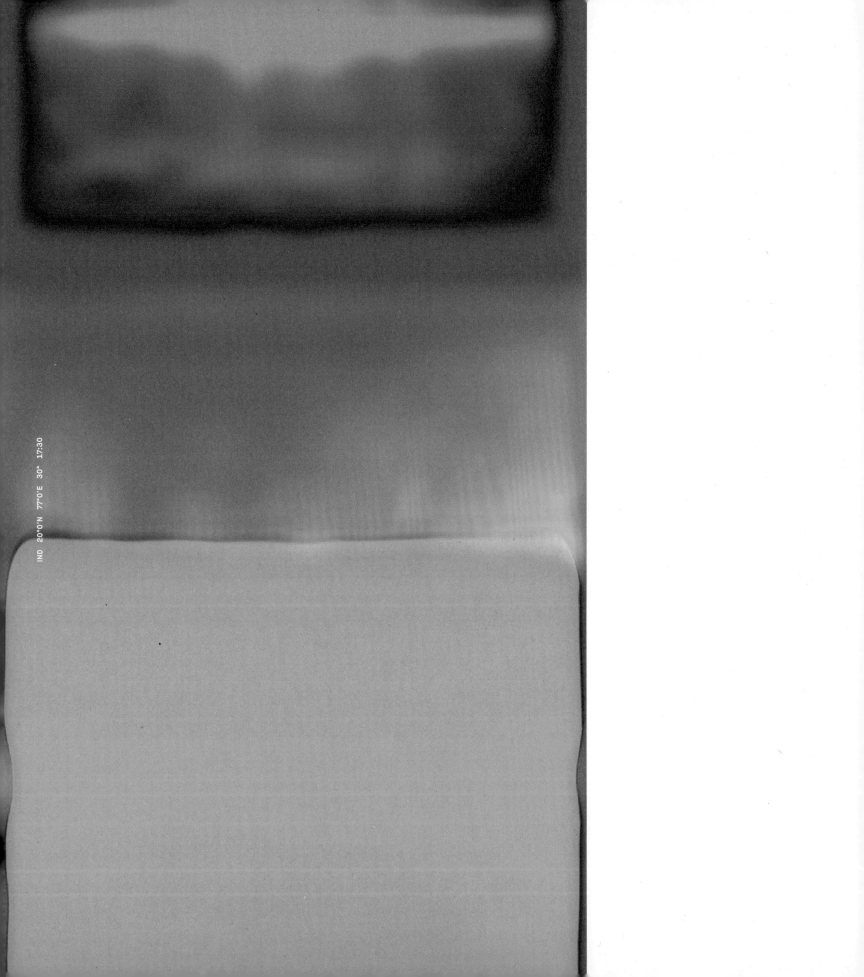

IND 20°0'N 77°0'E 30° 17:30

GTM 15°30'N 90°15'W 16° 6:00

Graphics
Sue Walsh

IT IS SUCH A TRANSITORY TIME IN TERMS OF THE BEST SKILLS EDUCATION CAN PROVIDE BECAUSE OF THE HUGE AMOUNT OF NEW COMMUNICATION FORMS.

As an alumna of the 2006 Master of Fine Arts Design course from Manhattan's School of Visual Arts, I felt like such a grandma after seeing last year's students develop apps for their thesis projects. We didn't even have apps as a form when I was in school and it was only seven years ago. But, regardless of form, the best designers must possess intelligence, open-mindedness and commitment and be able to work well within a team.

The best graduates we see at Milton Glaser show clear intelligence and have a flexible, open mind. Maybe it is because our office is so small – everyone here fills many different roles and there are opportunities to exploit many different skills. It's the opposite of big business, I suppose.

Our connection to my alma mater SVA, where Milton has taught for 50 years and is the Acting Chairman of the Board, leads us to seek out graduates from the MFA Design or Batchelor of Fine Arts Graphic Design programmes at that institution, but we also see talented students from Rhode Island School of Design, Pratt Institute and California College of the Arts, among others.

I don't believe there is a cardinal rule regarding the type of education designers should get, whether they are self-taught, graduate or post-graduate. The whole conversation about 'what educational system works best' seems inconclusive.

I think it's wise to examine the benefits of self-teaching versus formal education, but in the end talent can be found and nurtured in many ways. One defining benefit of formal education is that the student is placed within a community or network, and that is advantageous both professionally and developmentally. But that doesn't guarantee success (whatever that may mean) or development.

Personally, I don't know how I would be where I am now without going to SVA. I learned so much and was plunked directly into a world that I may not have had access to otherwise. People frequently ask me, 'Is it worth it to get your masters degree?' as if I could assess where I am simultaneously with my MFA and without it and then make a decision as to its value. For me, it has been absolutely worth it. But for others, maybe it wouldn't be. I feel it's difficult to give conclusive direction on this topic. Learning is about the individual.

USA 38°0'N 97°0'W 11° 6:00

Sue Walsh is a senior designer
at Milton Glaser.

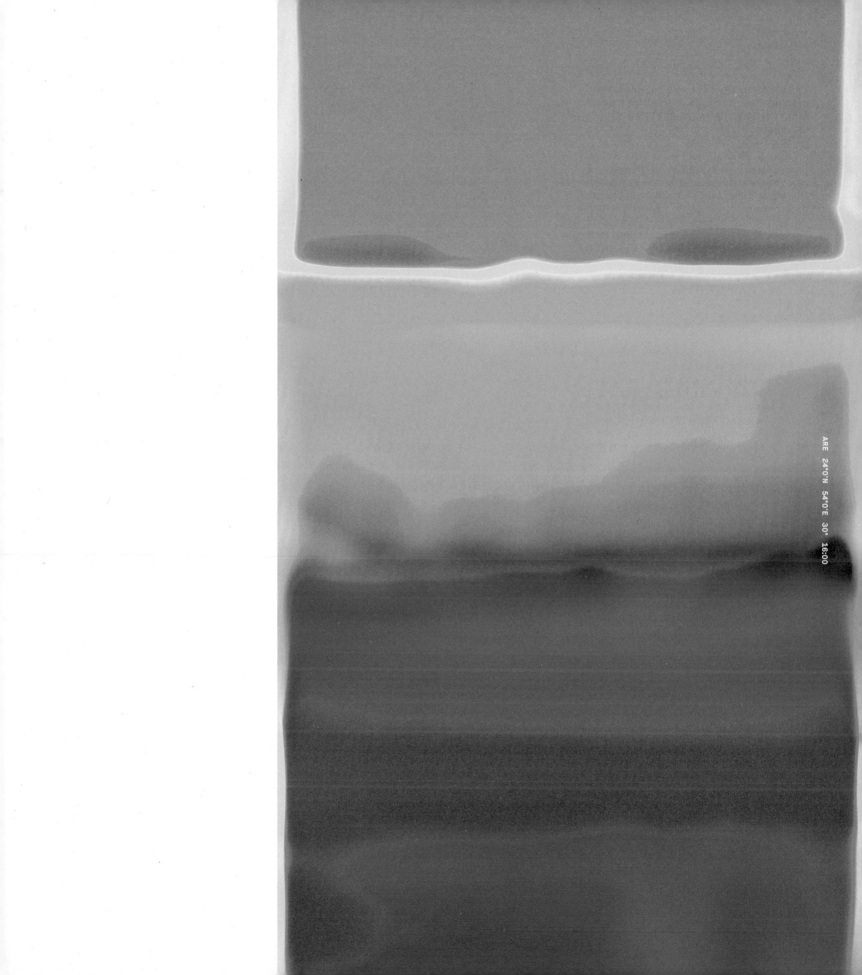

Multimedia
John Maeda

THE STORY IN THE CREATIVE ARENA IS OF DISRUPTION. TRADITIONAL MEDIA ARE BEING DISRUPTED BY THE FRAGMENTATION OF CHANNELS.

I see the traditional creative industries in the product arena getting disrupted by designers' new ability to market directly to the consumer via online platforms; and in the graphics arena they have long been disrupted by desktop publishing.

To meet these challenges creatives must take a new, broader approach. They will need to absorb more skills from fields that are far afield from art and design, be they in computation, neuroscience, psychology – you name it.

They will need to extend their repertoire by taking on more thoughtful, analytical disciplines. Fine art is an important space for design to reconnect with. But, of course, so too are all fields involving how we think, such as psychology and neuroscience, and exploring how we act, in the way anthropology and history do.

These needs are being met in part by colleges through existing programmes. But while I think formal programmes and tuition have always provided a part of the education necessary for students (and teachers) to find new bits of knowledge, expecting the education system to address all needs is unrealistic.

For me, the ideal scenario that would foster creativity at all levels of education would be for us to make it possible for students to have more free time to explore on their own.

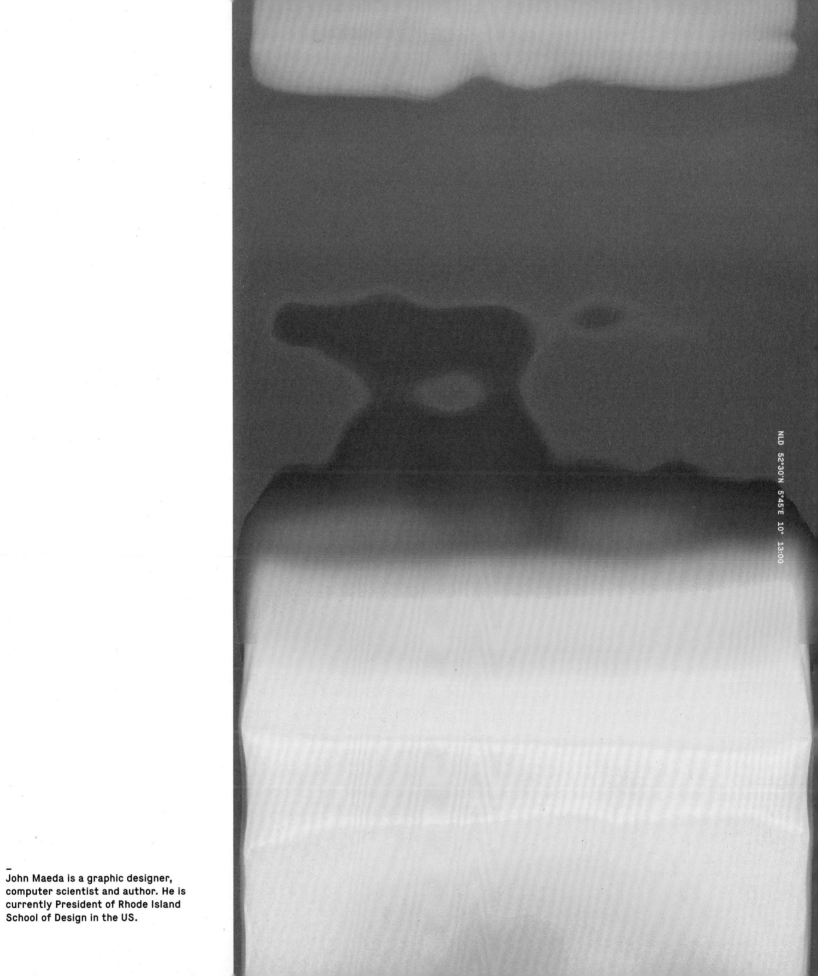

NLD 52°30'N 5°45'E 10° 13:00

John Maeda is a graphic designer,
computer scientist and author. He is
currently President of Rhode Island
School of Design in the US.

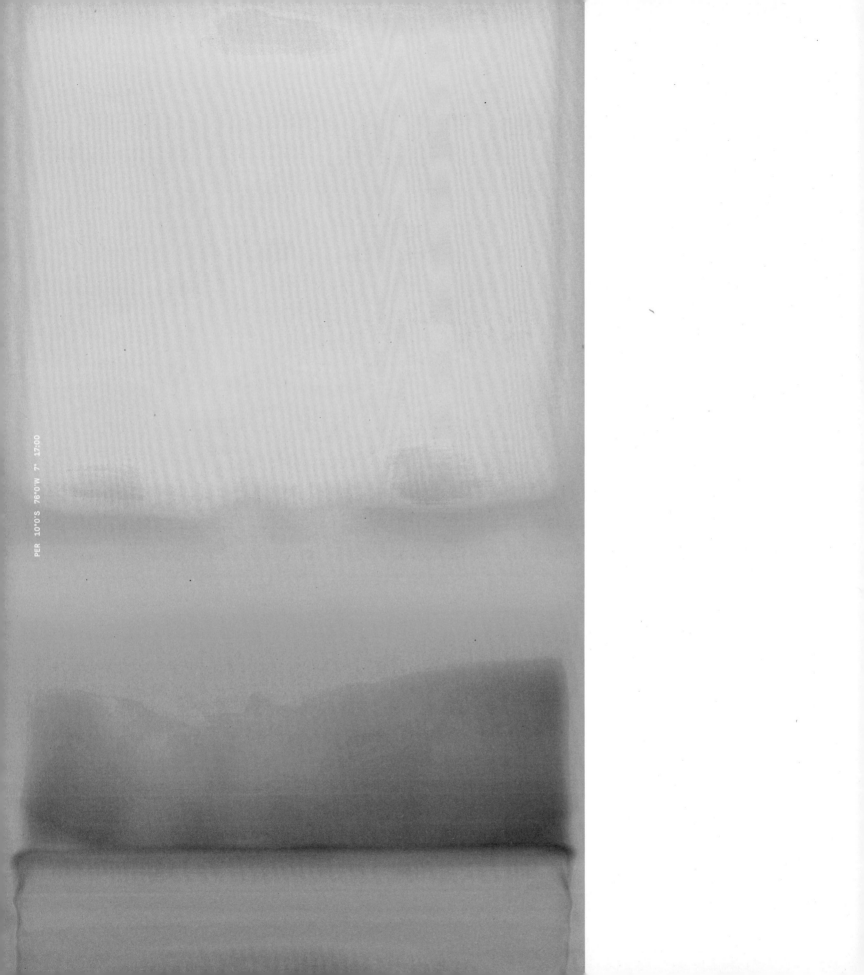

PER 10°0'S 76°0'W 7· 17:00

h
ossi
chan
lex geo
ins
**** to

MYS 2°30'N 112°30'E 27° 20:00

o-founder
of Tomato,
at Monash Art
re, Melbourne,
or of Design
rsity.

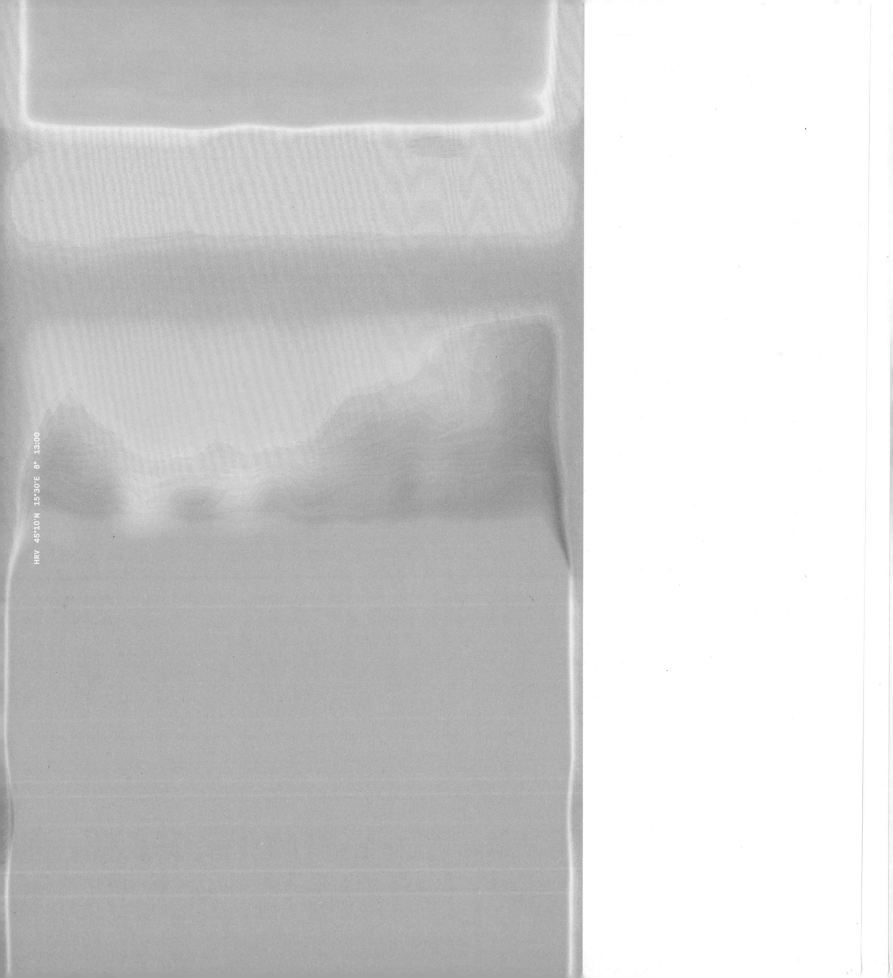

ITA 42°50'N 12°50'E 13° 13:00

I AM A GREAT BELIEVER IN THE POWER OF NURTURE AND A STAUNCH SUPPORTER OF THE IDEA THAT 'PRACTICE MAKES PERFECT'.

With a lot of people who excel at something, you can more often than not trace their expertise back to their childhood. If you do something all your life it becomes second nature, and you can't always pick it up later.

Famously, Andre Agassi learnt his trade at three years old and David Beckham learnt his signature skill of being able to 'land a football on a sixpence' by spending hours practising and not going inside till he had kicked a ball through a tyre hung from a tree ten times consecutively.

I know from families like mine that kids growing up with creativity around them more often than not become creative almost by default. Matthew Syed's book 'Bounce: the Myth of Talent and the Power of Practice' says more than I can say here.

I therefore have a problem with people who go to college at 18 in the expectation of becoming creative. It is extremely difficult to come at it from a standing start. Being creative is in you in some way by adulthood or it's not. You can choose to turn it off, but it won't be easy to develop without nurture early on.

I was brought up in a tremendously creative household. It was a working class family in Morecambe, Lancashire, that wanted to do things. My granddad made all my toys, fishing rods and so on and my mum and gran always had two sewing machines whirring. They even dyed their own fabrics.

Gerardine and I have four kids and they are all very creative. They were brought up surrounded by magazines and books, attended fashion and materials shows when we ran Red or Dead and frequented vintage design shops. And after we sold Red or Dead in 1996, they came to visit housing developments and regeneration schemes around the world with us. We never had time to teach them, but they were immersed in design and creativity.

You can go out and learn things, but you have a better chance if you start that learning early in your life. Our son Jack left college after 18 months, for example, because he felt he was gaining nothing. He just wanted to go out and do it and was ready for that.

This is why primary and junior schools are very important. They give children a chance to indulge their passions early on. It can be too late at 18. I do though have a problem with the lack of creativity in state schools – when we sent our younger two kids to private school they were much happier with their creative schooling.

There has been an increased demand for creative education over recent years. In my generation parents wouldn't have seen it as such a good idea, working in a bank or for Marks & Spencer being seen as better options. That perception has changed, particularly among middle class parents who see design as a viable alternative and one with 'bragging rights'.

In our business we need designers who are fleet of foot and can work across disciplines. For example, our daughter Tilly studied urban design, works with us at Hemingway Design and is equally at home designing G-Plan furniture and uniforms for McDonald's.

If you've got a creative mind you can be flexible, but colleges don't generally allow for that. Design for us is a state of mind rather than a particular course of study.

MEX 23°0'N 102°0'W 11° 6:00

Wayne and Gerardine Hemingway MBE
of Hemingway Design, are hugely
successful, yet neither has formal
design training. They started with a
market stall before founding fashion
brand Red or Dead in 1982. They
sold it on to Pentland in 1996.
www.hemingwaydesign.co.uk

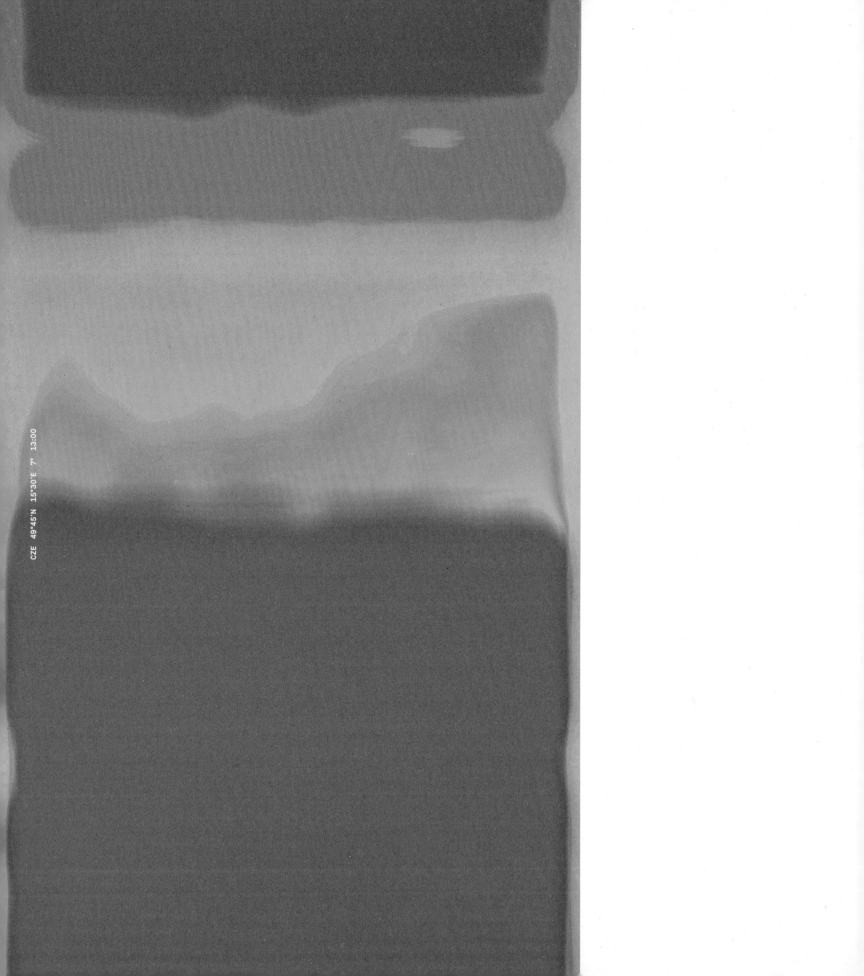

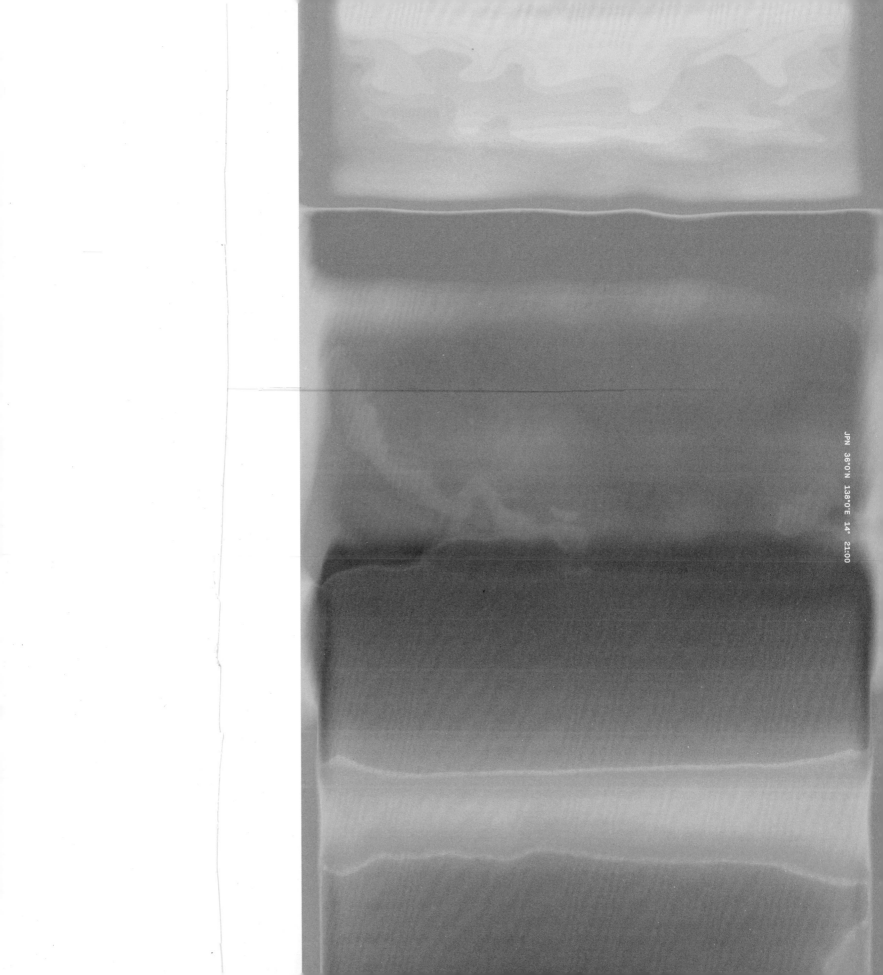

IRL 53°0'N 8°0'W 5° 12:00

SGP 1°22'N 103°48'E 26° 20:00

SCHOOLS OF THOUGHT: THE FUTURE OF CREATIVE EDUCATION

'I'VE ALWAYS SAT OUTSIDE THE DESIGN EDUCATION DEBATE. MINE WAS A TRADITIONAL ACADEMIC SCHOOL AND I STOPPED TAKING ART AT 14.'

British designer Mark Porter is renowned for transforming The Guardian newspaper to the Berliner format in 2005. He subsequently art directed the print title's hugely successful move online through an award-winning website, Guardian Online, and apps. It was he who commissioned Christian Schwartz and Paul Barnes to design the Guardian Egyptian typeface as part of that move. In 2010 he left The Guardian to set up Mark Porter Associates. Since then he has redesigned a host of publications based outside the UK, from Italy's Panorama to Swedish title SVD, building on his international reputation for great newspaper design. Yet he has never studied design in any formal context. He believes that life-long learning, sharing and collaborating are the keys to creative education for the future. Colleges must try harder if they are to remain relevant, he maintains.

'I've always sat outside the design education debate. I went to a traditionally academic school and stopped taking art classes at 14. Afterwards I went up to Oxford to study modern languages. All through school and university I was passionate about design, illustration and photography, and I designed posters and magazines in my own time, but I had no formal design education.

I imagined that this would prevent me from ever working in the creative industries. I also thought that my academic background was irrelevant to design. Happily, it turned out that I was wrong on both counts, and eventually, through a combination of luck and opportunism, I managed to stumble into a design career.

Of course, I did have a design education, but it had nothing to do with school or college.

Initially, I taught myself. I looked at great work, analysed it, and – at the beginning – imitated it. And I read books (there was no internet then) about the technical aspects of typography. I did try an evening course at the London College of Printing, but I gave it up after two visits because it completely failed to engage my attention.

Later, when I started work as a junior designer, I was lucky enough to have a series of jobs with some brilliant art directors and editors, which was the best possible way of learning. Daily one-on-one contact with great professionals was much more valuable to me than any college course could have been.

As I progressed in my career it became clear that my academic background was not as irrelevant as I had thought. Of course, working as a designer requires creativity and visualisation skills. But a surprising amount of my time is devoted to researching and analysing clients' problems, finding logical solutions and presenting the case for my work. As it turned out I was admirably prepared for all those things at school and university.

So when young designers come to me, I'm interested in how their work looks, but also in how they talk about it. Typography and layout skills and visual ideas have limited value for me without an understanding of the context and the ability to explain and justify it.

—

I have seen enormous changes in the industry over the course of my career. The explosion in digital media in the last 15 years has caused massive upheaval. Working in a digital environment forced me to question all my assumptions, and to unlearn many of the ways of working that I had always relied on.

For example, the way we design for print is to start with a fixed canvas and work inwards. Everything has been conditioned by the size and shape of the paper. But in digital design we rarely know the size of the screen, so we are forced to start with the content and work outwards, investigating how it will behave on different platforms. Print has always strived for perfection in the image frozen in ink on the paper. Digital media are always in flux; perfection is never attainable, and every project becomes a series of iterations rather than a single, definitive piece of work.

My field of editorial design has changed completely. I now find myself creating identities and ways of communicating that can function across various media, rather than individual publications.

Some of my colleagues have never got over the shock of this change, and I know many designers who still see digital as a threat. It has not been an easy transition for me, but more than anything I was thrilled by the opportunity to learn something new, and to adapt to change.

The design world is also increasingly international. Globalisation means that we compete for projects with designers from across the globe with very different cultural and educational backgrounds. We have to be open-minded, curious, and ready to see the world through different eyes.

I grew up at a time when your degree subject could set you up for life. Now it is impossible to know what kind of jobs my children will have. We live in an age of technological, economic and cultural destabilisation and we can expect the pace of change to increase. I wonder if the kind of educational institutions that evolved in the 19th and 20th Centuries can keep up. Are they still ideal environments for learning? The technology world is an interesting comparison. Tech people have their own ways of learning — in collaborative workspaces, at conferences, on blogs and Twitter. They share projects and ideas generously and sidestep more traditional forms of education, preferring to educate themselves and each other about technology.

The most valuable parts of my education were, first, training in how to think, and then a kind of apprenticeship, learning from the experts working on real projects. I still learn every day from other designers, and collaboration and mutual sharing of information seem much more inspiring ways of learning than vocational college courses.

I believe that the best a college education can offer is to help students to think for themselves and learn to research and evaluate information. Formal education needs to be flexible, and not based on imparting specialist skills or technical knowledge that are likely to become obsolete.

In the future, we should expect more and more change. We can never assume the skills we have will be required in five years' time. As designers, we need to be open-minded and adaptable and to help each other develop and learn.

The most important skill for designers now is adaptability.'

ESP 40°0'N 4°0'W 14° 13:00

Mark Porter is founder
of Mark Porter Associates.

NOR 62°0'N 10°0'W 5° 13:00

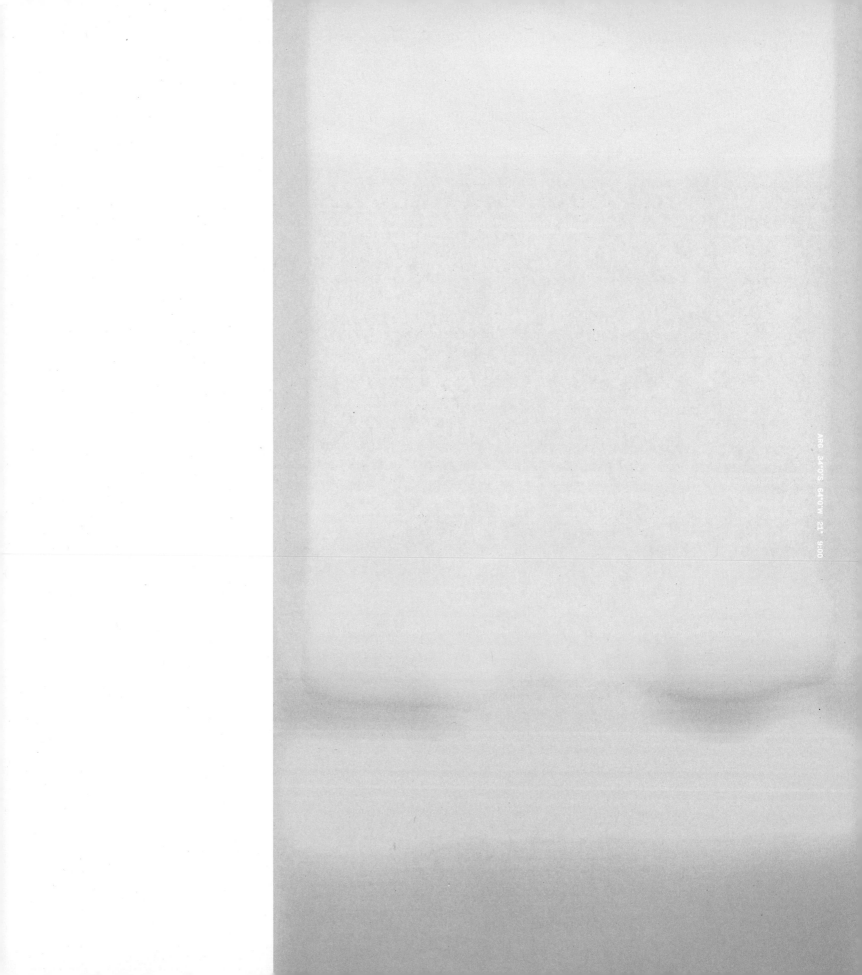

ARG. 34°0'S. 64°0'W. 21° 9:00

DEU 51°0'N 9°0'E 8° 13:00

BEL 50°50'N 4°0'E 11° 13:00

I am proud to be giving this year's President's Award to Alex McDowell. As the person who employed me straight out of college, I also have a lot to thank him for.

Alex's history extends from the early days of punk through magazine design and he is now, in my opinion, Hollywood's finest Production Designer.

Despite his incredible catalogue of work and major effect on the way that we see the world, he's a more or less unknown name. Yet he's extraordinarily influential, and has been present at some of the key moments in the development of our industry. From origins in helping define the aesthetic of punk, he has now progressed to showing us what the future of communication might look like in his major work on Minority Report.

Alex was always a maverick, and you'd never try to predict what you were going to get from him. His background as a fine art painter led to being a radical, sometimes politicised practitioner. His work has been incredibly impactful – sometimes rough and jagged, sometimes slick and entertaining, but always edgy. It mixes constructivism with trashy detective novels; sci-fi with children's toys. He draws inspiration from everywhere.

Alex's contribution has been as a catalyst. He's always been at the right juncture with the right idea, and his associations with key people has led to major developments in their work, from Steven Spielberg to Tim Burton to David Fincher. Yet his consummate professionalism means that he has never sought the limelight. He deserves this award more than anyone for his ideas, his craft and his inspiration to more than one generation of creatives.

Neville Brody
D&AD President

Ich freue mich, den diesjährigen President's Award an Alex McDowell zu vergeben. Ich habe ihm auch viel zu verdanken, denn er hat mich damals direkt nach meinem Abschluss eingestellt.

Alex' Werdegang reicht von den frühen Tagen des Punk bis hin zum Magazindesign – heute ist er in meinen Augen der beste Szenenbildner Hollywoods.

Obwohl sein beeindruckendes Werk unsere visuelle Wahrnehmung stark geprägt hat, ist sein Name relativ unbekannt. Alex hat jedoch als einer der einflussreichsten Szenenbildner weltweit an einigen Meilensteinen unserer Branche mitgewirkt. Während er in seinen Anfängen als Mitgestalter einer Ästhetik des Punk arbeitete, zeigt er uns heute in seinem großen Werk Minority Report, wie die Kommunikation der Zukunft aussehen könnte.

Alex ist seit jeher ein Querdenker, von dem man nie weiß, was er als Nächstes aushecken könnte. Sein Hintergrund als Kunstmaler erklärt seine radikalen, teilweise politisch geprägten Arbeiten. Sein Werk ist unglaublich einflussreich; es zeigt sich mal kantig und unbequem, mal smart und unterhaltsam – jedoch stets unkonventionell. Er verheiratet den Konstruktivismus mit trivialer Krimiliteratur, Science-Fiction mit Kinderspielzeug – und lässt sich dabei von allem Möglichen inspirieren.

Alex McDowell war vor allem ein Katalysator. Er war stets mit der richtigen Idee am richtigen Ort und hat das Werk von Schlüsselfiguren der Filmwelt – von Steven Spielberg über Tim Burton bis David Fincher – stark geprägt. Dennoch suchte er nie das Rampenlicht. Alex hat diesen Preis mehr als verdient – für seine Ideen, sein Können und seinen inspirierenden Einfluss auf mehrere Generationen Kreativer.

Neville Brody
Präsident des D&AD

Je suis fier de décerner le prix du Président de cette année à Alex McDowell. Je lui dois aussi beaucoup pour m'avoir offert un emploi alors que j'étais fraîchement diplômé.

Le parcours d'Alex va des débuts du punk au design de magazines ; il est actuellement, à mon avis, le meilleur chef décorateur de Hollywood.

Son nom reste assez méconnu, en dépit de son incroyable carrière et de son influence sur notre façon de voir le monde. Il est pourtant une immense référence et est intervenu à des moments clés du développement de notre industrie. Il a débuté en travaillant sur l'esthétique punk ; il nous montre maintenant à quoi peut ressembler l'avenir de la communication dans son œuvre magistrale pour Minority Report.

Alex a toujours été un rebelle, et il est impossible d'anticiper ce que vous pouvez attendre de lui. Sa formation de peintre l'a conduit à être un professionnel radical, parfois engagé. Son travail a eu un impact énorme, parce que détonant et corrosif ou parce que simple et amusant, mais aussi parce que toujours audacieux. Il mélange constructivisme et romans policiers de pacotille, science-fiction et jouets. Il puise son inspiration de toutes parts.

La contribution d'Alex a servi de catalyseur. Toujours présent au moment opportun et avec l'idée juste, ses collaborations avec des personnes décisives ont donné des travaux de grande qualité, de Steven Spielberg à Tim Burton en passant par David Fincher. Sa rigueur professionnelle démontre cependant qu'il n'a jamais cherché à être sous les feux de la rampe. Il mérite plus que quiconque ce prix en hommage à ses idées, ses œuvres et son inspiration pour plus d'une génération de créateurs.

Neville Brody
Président de D&AD

Charlie Bucket's house from Charlie and the Chocolate Factory (2005)

House on Paper Street in Fight Club (1999)

The owl ship from Watchmen (2009)

Set design from Minority Report (2002)

Suitcase

The brief was to come up with a fully inclusive concept for the digital future of the BBC. 'Suitcase' is an innovative, user-centred platform that allows you to customise your own unique experience of the BBC. Think of the 'Suitcase' as a vessel for all the sites' content, your own personal case in which you can pack all your favourite programmes and categories. It also automatically updates its contents so you can use it to follow stories and articles as they develop. Whether the content is new or old, the 'Suitcase' lets you engage with the BBC in a style that feels alive and relevant to you.

–
Students
Callum Best
Malin Hassel
Joshua Ogden
Luke Patton
James Smith
Tutors
Sally Hope
Amanda Jackson
College
Arts University
Bournemouth

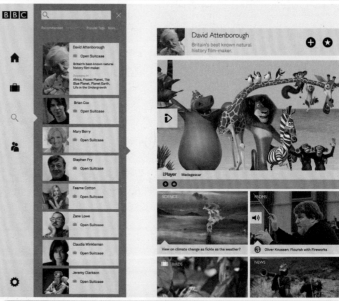

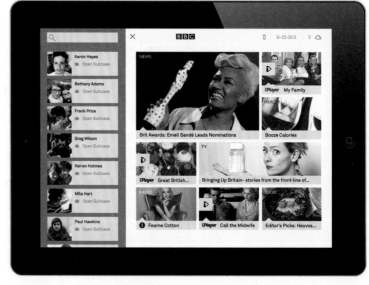

BOURNEMOUTH 50°43'N 1°52'W 9° 12:00

**The Ribbon
of the V&A**

The brief was to
design a hoarding to
be erected around
a new building site
which is part of the
V&A Museum. 'The
Ribbon of the V&A'
showcases the essence
of the museum.
The images work in
harmony with the
ribbon graphic based
on the museum's
marque and brand.
This structure links
subject areas to create
a free flowing visual
that directly relates
to the museum's
approach to their own
exhibition spaces.
The hoarding would
develop throughout
the construction
period, providing
new information and
images each month to
engage the public.

–
Student
Christopher Algar
Tutor
Glen Robinson
College
University of Lincoln

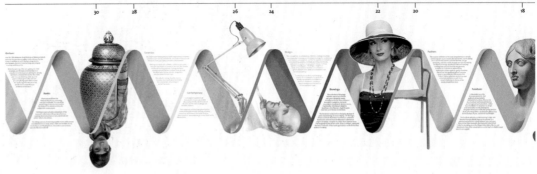

LINCOLN 53°23'N 0°54'W 6° 12:00

STUDENT AWARDS

This is Our Fault

The brief was to introduce the Ted Baker label abroad. While searching for insights into the British, we considered common attributes such as punctuality. The key was to use this quality in a different way. We realised that wherever we took the brand, it would be 25 years late. This idea allowed us to talk about the terrible fashion sense before the arrival of Ted. Making use of the knowledge that everybody harbours an embarrassing old photo of themselves, we introduced the brand by accepting the blame and admitting that it was Ted's fault for being late.

–
Students
Gustavo Crespo
Jara Dominguez
Tutors
Juan Carlos Alonso
Carlos Font
Curro de la Villa
College
Miami Ad
School Madrid

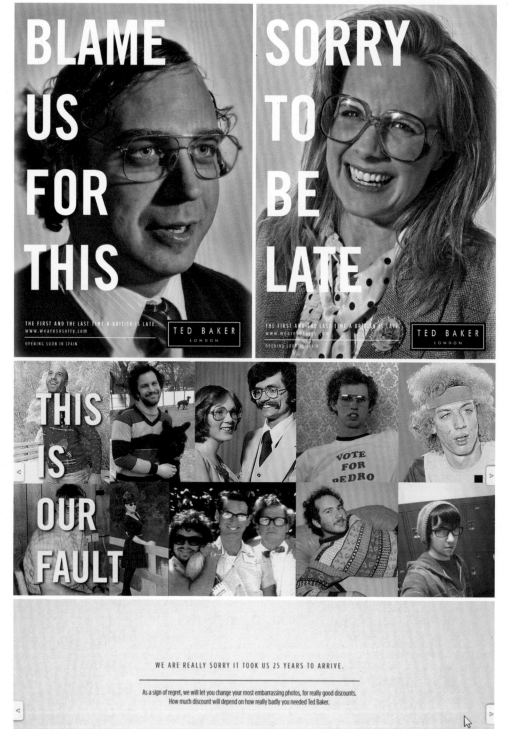

MADRID 40°26'N 3°42'W 14° 13:00

Invisible Crown

The brief was to restyle a limited edition haircare range. I wanted to visually express how using Batiste as a styling product boosts the user's hair and their confidence. I used crowns on the bottle caps that fit nicely over the heads of the models, and high contrast fashion style photography. The models were dressed in plain but contemporary clothing to retain focus on the hair and crowns. The condensed sans serif type reflects the styling of current fashion editorial, with flashes of colour lifting the cans as well as further differentiating between the limited edition fragrances.

—
Student
Morgan Swain
Tutors
Lucy Blazey
Maria Fletcher
College
Norwich University
of the Arts (NUA)

LIMITED EDITION — BOURBON ROSE & POMEGRANATE

LIMITED EDITION — HIBISCUS & INDIAN CRESS

LIMITED EDITION — JAPANESE ROSE & LIME BLOSSOM

LIMITED EDITION — WILD ORCHID & JASMINE

batiste Dry Shampoo

NORWICH 52°37'N 1°17'E 7° 12:00

•
YELLOW PENCIL
COPYWRITING FOR RAB

Awkward

The brief was to sell the power of radio to brand managers, showing how radio adverts can emotionally engage the listener. We created the 'Awkward' campaign, which consisted of two ads, 'Hold Tight' and 'Mixed Up'. Each radio script provokes an emotional reaction in the listener which is then challenged by the addition of sound effects. This flips the scenario in an unexpected way. The scripts create a range of emotional reactions in a short space of time, demonstrating how the ultimate power of radio is its ability to create pictures in the mind.

—
Students
Charli Plant
Michael Venner
Tutors
Chris Hill
Marc Lewis
College
School of
Communication
Arts 2.0

Hold Tight

MVO   Close your eyes. Picture him standing, patiently waiting. She squeezes in to her outfit: snug, shiny leather. Slipping her feet into knee high boots, one by one. Whip in hand, she straddles him.
(Pause)
Feeling awkward?
(Pause)
Let's add some sounds to complete the picture.

SFX   Neigh of a horse and clip-clop of hooves, building to a trot then gradually fading away.

MVO   Now you've heard the difference sound can make, just imagine how hard radio can work for your brand.

To find out more about how you can use the power of radio to bring your campaign to life, visit rab.co.uk. If you're listening via a digital device, simply click on the link appearing now.

Britain loves radio; your brand will too.

LONDON 51°32'N 0°5'W 9° 12:00

BBC Mobius

The brief was to come up with a fully inclusive concept for the digital future of the BBC. We wanted to develop a new product which could deliver all of the BBC's brands and allow users to interact with live events in a new way. With the British living room in mind, we asked ourselves, 'What is the future of the red button?'. We believe connected devices like Smart TVs and tablets will soon enable users to replace their remote controls, providing a richer and more streamlined experience. 'BBC Mobius' helps to enrich live broadcasts. The solution proposes three main elements: an elastic player, live discussion and widgetised interaction.

Students
James Greenaway
Max Seabrooke
Tutor
Louise Prideaux
College
Ravensbourne

Sustainable Sound

The brief was to share the story of Yamaha. Electric motorbikes are not only environmentally friendly, they are also silent. As well as causing problems for traffic safety, the silence also denies motorcyclists that special riding feeling. Yamaha, a brand with expertise in both motors and musical instruments, can define the sound of sustainable riding. 'Sustainable Sound' is a platform where you compose new motor sound effects using 125 years of Yamaha sound. Find all Yamaha's products in the online studio, then try, mix and share so your friends can vote for your creation. People can also sample the sounds and vote in banners. The top rated sound will be installed in the next electric motorbike from Yamaha.

**Students
(Creative Team)**
Emelie Leijon
Pontus Levahn
Fredrick Lewandowski
Andreas Sandberg
Ebba Körlof Sundberg
**Students
(Support Team)**
Peter Hammarberg
Jacob Olofsson
Tutor
Charlotta Rydholm
College
Berghs School of Communication

Yamaha Garage

The brief was to share the story of Yamaha. We wanted to show how Yamaha unites people, despite the wide range of their products, from music to motors. While researching, we found that the uniting location for musicians and motorcyclists is a garage. Amateur musicians usually need a place to rehearse, while motorbike owners often have room to spare in their garage. Our solution was 'Yamaha Garage', a service which would allow motorbike owners to rent their garage space to musicians for band practice, bringing together like-minded Yamaha fans.

Students
Julia Artamonova
Kir Khachaturov
Sergey Pleshkov
Tutor
Anton Yarusov
College
British Higher
School of Art &
Design

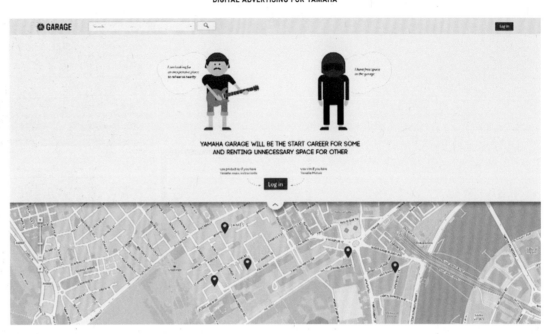

Lost & Sound

The brief was to share the story of Yamaha. Yamaha's 125th anniversary is coming up, and embedded in their brand history lie thousands of consumer stories waiting to be told. We brought these stories forward with 'Lost & Sound', an initiative by Yamaha on eBay. We would collect all Yamaha auctions that are put up on eBay under their own branded channel. And give all sellers the chance to tell their own stories connected to the products. It's a great reminder of the thousands of great products Yamaha have in circulation and proof that they are a force to be reckoned with for hundreds of years to come.

**Students
(Creative Team)**
Filip Callas
Frida Thunholm
Anna Werkell
**Students
(Support Team)**
Ebba Brasch
Frida Karlsson
Emelie Wiberg
Andreas Zannin
Tutor
Charlotta Rydholm
College
Berghs School of
Communication

Come Home Droga

The brief was to make your dream job a reality. 'Come Home Droga' was launched by four Australian students to get the attention of New York-based company founder David Droga. The campaign played on the fact that Droga would feel homesick and winked at some of his famous work. Rather than contact him directly, the group waited for the digital campaign to generate buzz. Droga made contact within days and spoke with the students for over two hours. He described the campaign as 'original' and 'relentless'. Droga5 receives over 300 student folios a day, but 'Come Home Droga' cut through the creative clutter. The team became the first students Droga had contacted in over ten years.

–
Students
Shannon Crowe
Luke Falkland-Brown
Jackson Harper
Millicent Malcolm
Tutor
Cangie Contessa
College
RMIT University

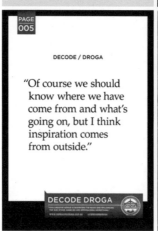

"Of course we should know where we have come from and what's going on, but I think inspiration comes from outside."

Megabus Book

The brief was to make your dream job a reality. Sunderland is 300 miles from London, so industry isn't exactly on our doorstep. Over three years, we've travelled over 9,000 miles for book crits, events and placements. The Megabus has been our link to industry. On 14th March 2013, we made use of the seven hour journey by writing an entire new portfolio on the way down, just before book crits at R/GA. To date, the 'Megabus Book' has earned us six placements in London, including at R/GA. The stunt also landed us onto the Creative Circle Award Show stage, where Ed Morris auctioned us for placements.

–
Students
Callum Prior
Marc Rayson
Tutor
Keith Nevens
College
University of Sunderland

Popkinson's Miniature Marvel

The brief was to make your dream job a reality. I created a twist on the pop up gallery phenomenon: an actual pop up gallery. Busy creatives don't always get a chance to see exhibitions, so I'm bringing the gallery to them; showing examples of my own work and my personal attributes of attention to detail, enthusiasm towards hard work and ability to apply creative concepts to briefs. I produced a run of 15 galleries. Using smooth white card, paper and grey board, parts were die cut then hand assembled and tape bound.

—
Student
Leanne Watkinson
Tutor
Andy Edwards
College
Leeds Metropolitan University

STUDENT AWARDS

Designer with a Unique Perspective

The brief was to make your dream job a reality. Being 6'5"tall gives me, quite literally, a 'unique perspective'. This provided the inspiration for my project which targeted Sagmeister & Walsh, an agency I admire for their playful, hands-on approach to design. With this in mind, I built an anamorphic type installation which reveals a hidden message on increasing the viewer's height. This literal take on my unique aspect looks to inform Sagmeister & Walsh of the fresh diversity I could bring to their studio. I also developed a height chart, which would allow them to interact with my piece from a personal perspective.

—
Student
Calum Middleton
Tutor
Kathryn Coates
College
Nottingham Trent University (NTU)

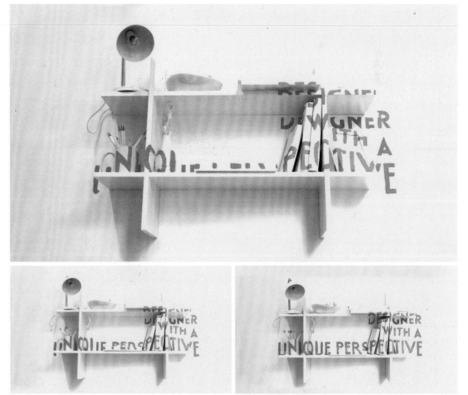

The Simple Steps Campaign

The brief was to use a Unilever brand to make the world a better place. The perfect opportunity to check for breast cancer is in the shower; a time when women are already in close contact with their bodies. With this in mind, we redesigned Simple shower gel packaging so the correct directions for checking signs of breast cancer appear when the bottle becomes wet. The directions are written as song lyrics so women can sing along in the shower: the song having been released during Breast Cancer Awareness Month by celebrities who have been affected by breast cancer.

–
Students
Joshua Cunningham
Thomas
Fenwick-Smith
Tutor
Marc Lewis
College
School of
Communication
Arts 2.0

4seven Loop: Brand & Ident

The brief was to put channel 4seven in motion. 4seven broadcasts a repeat of the Channel 4 shows that have created a critical buzz from the last seven days. The looping relationship between the two channels has shaped the brand's form, identity and ident, where we tried to visualise a continuous process. Considering the importance of viewer interaction with the channel, we integrated social media into onscreen activity allowing people to interact with each other and the programme.

–
Students
Liam Alexander
Campbell
Matthew Hill
Tutor
Marion Morrison
College
Kingston University

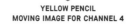
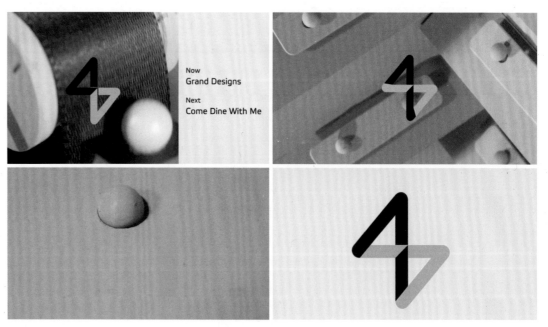

The Nice Screen Tour

The brief was to find new and exciting ways to keep students engaged with It's Nice That. The 'Nice Screen Tour' is a mobile screen-printing workshop that would travel across the UK, stopping at different art colleges and universities. The transport is an icecream van, branded for the event with unique summer treats graphics. Inside the van is a pop up marquee, pop up tables and a selection of ready-made silk screens with unique designs. The students would receive live screen-printing demonstrations of limited edition designs for free, printed on paper, clothing or any other printable material.

–
Student
Thomas Fitzmaurice
Tutor
Alexis Taylor
College
Coventry University

Phrases de L'âme

The brief was to showcase a new range of scents by breaking the rules of conventional perfume packaging. Perfume has, like poetry, long been a way to express oneself. With this in mind, 'Phrases de L'âme' (Expressions from the Soul) was born – a series of scents that invites users to be creative while applying it. Unlike traditional scents, 'Phrases de L'âme' is written onto the skin. The perfume appears as black ink on the skin for a few seconds before vanishing; allowing anyone to express their feelings through both scent and writing.

–
Students
(Creative Team)
Erik Hellquist
Emelie Jinhee Johnsson
Claes Lovén
Carl-Johan Ostrom
Anna Turdell
Students
(Support Team)
Caroline Ernsth
Carl Lundgren
Sara Rehioui
Tutor
Charlotta Rydholm
College
Berghs School of Communication

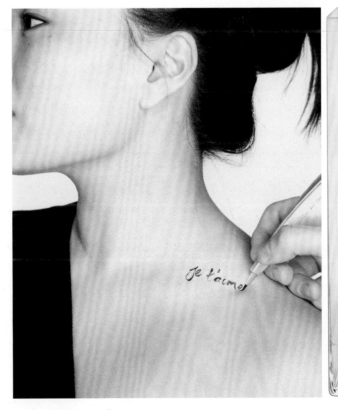

Hidden Performance Cycling Jeans

The brief was to create performance cycle wear. Everyday cyclists want to make their cycling experience as easy as possible. I designed a specialised pair of functional and stylish cycling jeans. Aerodymanics are enhanced with lightweight, flexible denim fabric and adjustable in-built ankle straps. A variety of pockets for essentials such as mobile phones and d-locks are strategically placed in comfortable positions. While for safety, waterproofing and visibilty measures have been integrated into the design, with reflective ankle straps and water resistant fabric protecting the most exposed areas of the garment.

–
Student
Kehan Yu
Tutor
Charlotte Lo
College
Central Saint Martins College of Art and Design

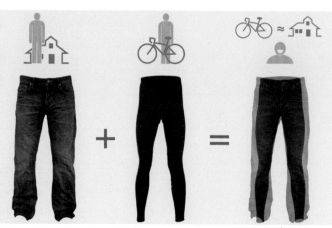

LONDON 51°32'N 0°5'W 9° 12:00

STUDENT AWARDS

Photobooth

The brief was to create a portrait of contemporary youth. After watching people publicly groom, photograph and flaunt themselves online, I stole pictures taken on products in Apple stores to expose and question contemporary youth's lack of privacy in the internet age. The image was left unaltered.

–
Student
Luke Evans
Tutor
Zelda Malan
College
Kingston University

LONDON 51°32'N 0°5'W 9° 12:00

Lev

The brief was to create a portrait of contemporary youth. The photo shows a young boy from a Moscow orphanage sitting in a kitchen. The day the photo was taken he had a scrap with a classmate. His red knuckles were evidence of what had happened.

–
Student
Anastasia Korosteleva
Tutors
Dmitry Karpov
Tim Simmons
College
British Higher School of Art & Design

MOSCOW 55°45'N 37°36'E -2° 16:00

Martyn, Sean and Jacob

The brief was to create a portrait of contemporary youth. This image is part of a project I am working on, focused on the town of Great Yarmouth and its surrounding villages. I approached the three boys because they were representative of an awkward stage of adolescence most of us can relate to. The trio reflects the confused and uncertain identity of the area, once a popular English holiday destination and now a struggling and distorted landscape.

–
Student
William Lakin
Tutor
Paul Duke
College
Middlesex University

LONDON 51°32'N 0°5'W 9° 12:00

STUDENT AWARDS

Most Awarded
Advertising
Agencies

1. McCann Erickson
   Melbourne
2. BBH London
3. Ogilvy & Mather
   London

–

'This is perhaps
the standout
campaign of the
year. The viral video
is extraordinary.
The song, genius.
The art direction
and animation,
mesmerising.
The incongruity of
a happy message
and death, brilliant.
And the poster
executions, just one
part of this brilliant
campaign, are
here because they
deserve recognition
in their own right.'

Nick Worthington
Creative Chairman,
Colenso BBDO

Dumb Ways to Die by McCann Erickson Melbourne

Most Awarded
Digital Agencies

1. R/GA
2. North Kingdom
3. VML

–

'It's hard to tell
where the digital
sports technology
ends and the online
shopping starts.
A great 360° to
online retail and
experience.'

James Greenfield
Creative Director,
DesignStudio

–

'A project of
significant scale
that artfully blends
the aesthetic with
the functional and
commercial. A
digital benchmark.'

Simon Manchipp
Co-Founder and
Executive Creative
Director, SomeOne

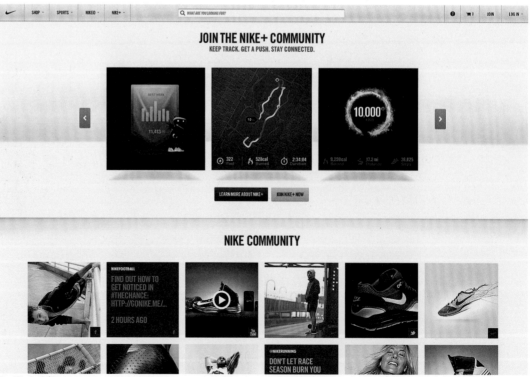

OneNike by R/GA

**Most Awarded
Design Agencies**

1. B-Reel
   Bibliothèque
   MAP
   Tellart
   Universal Design
   Studio

–
'Chrome Web Lab
is the indicator of
the new generation
of digital projects.
It embraces the
crossover of in-
browser digital work
into physical space,
while dealing with
collaboration of
shared audiences on
a global scale. But
more importantly
it's a triumph in
explaining the power
of the internet
by physically
representing its
possibilities.'

Gui Seiz
Creative Director,
Stink Digital

Chrome Web Lab by B-Reel, Bibliothèque, MAP, Tellart and Universal Design Studio

**Most Awarded
Clients**

1. Nike
2. Metro Trains
3. Channel 4

–
'Much of the
industry talks about
making products
and services that
become ongoing
platforms. Very
few succeed. Nike
do it again.'

Iain Tait
Executive Creative
Director, Google

–
'The future of
advertising can
be seen right here.
That's right, it's
not an ad – it's a
brilliant addition to
my life that doesn't
intrude, it just
works.'

Chris Baylis
Executive Creative
Director, Tribal DDB
Amsterdam

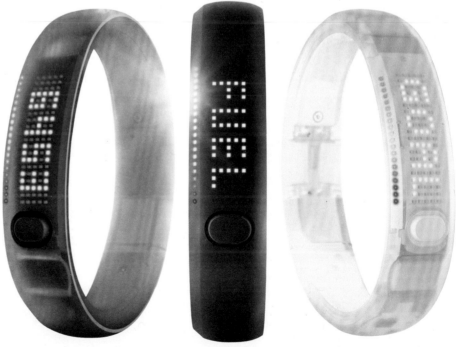

Nike+ FuelBand by R/GA

Dumb Ways to Die

So we wrote a song called 'Dumb Ways to Die', created a music video for it and attributed it to an artist that didn't exist: Tangerine Kitty. We uploaded the video onto YouTube and the song onto iTunes. We pushed the music video on our interactive campaign site, on MTV, in cinema, through outdoors and at stations. The song earned 40 million YouTube views in a month, over 3 million social media shares, was covered by over 750 global news outlets and charted in 28 countries. We also placed posters showing the video's colourful dead guys throughout the Metro network. 'Dumb Ways to Die' is now the third most viral ad of all time – good luck to the campaign that knocks it off.

–
Art Director
Pat Baron
Copywriter
John Mescall
Creative Director
Pat Baron
Executive Creative Director
John Mescall
Producer
Cinnamon Darvall
Senior Producer
Mark Bradley
Illustrator
Julian Frost
Animator
Julian Frost
Music Producer
Oliver McGill
Advertising Agency
McCann Erickson Melbourne
Production Company
McCann Erickson Melbourne
Account Manager
Tamara Broman
Account Director
Alec Hussain
Group Account Director
Adrian Mills
Brand Manager
Leah Waymark
Marketing Manager
Chloe Alsop
Client
Metro Trains

BLACK PENCILS

MELBOURNE 37°47'S 144°58'E 12° 23:00

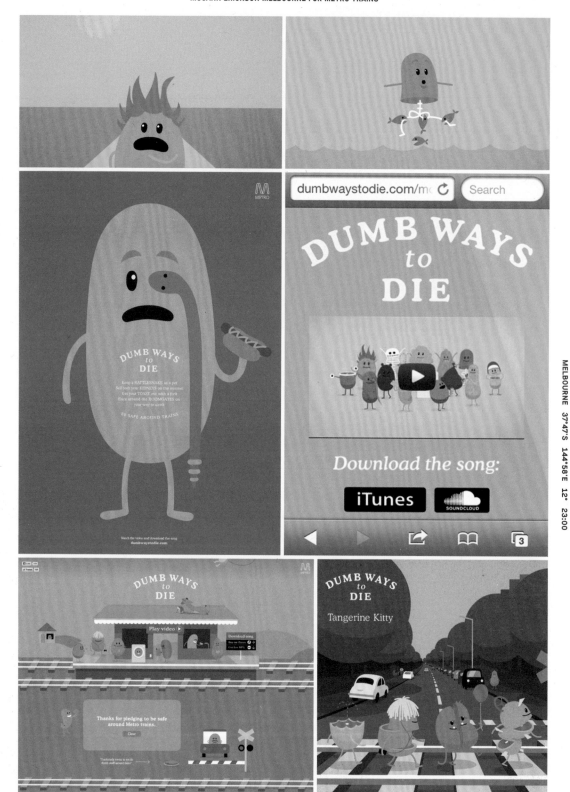

Olympic Cauldron

The Olympic Cauldron incorporated every participating country in its creation and in doing so made a single combined object that only existed for the two weeks of the London 2012 Olympic Games. After this the elements were sent back with each of the national teams to their country. The 204 copper pieces that formed the dramatic flourish of the cauldron were made using new digital technologies and traditional craft techniques. The rising of the cauldron's stems was one of the defining moments of London 2012, as each competing country's copper piece rose upwards and combined into a single surging flame.

—
Executive Producer
Danny Boyle
Architectural Studio
Heatherwick Studio
Contractors
Contour Autocraft
FCT
Stage One
Client
London Organising
Committee of
the Olympic and
Paralympic Games
(LOCOG)

BLACK PENCILS

LONDON 51°32'N 0°5'W 9° 12:00

Meet the Superhumans

Championing alternative voices is at the heart of Channel 4's remit. In promoting the London 2012 Paralympic Games we wanted to get back to the true meaning of 'para' as being 'side by side/alongside' and therefore 'equal to'. Against a background of indifference (only 14% of people said they were looking forward to them), we helped create an atmosphere of excitement building up to the Games that was unprecedented. The Paralympics sold out for the first time ever, and the opening ceremony drew Channel 4's biggest audience in over ten years.

—
Director
Tom Tagholm
Creative Director
Tom Tagholm
Producers
Rory Fry
Gwilym Gwillim
Business Director
Olivia Browne
Director of Photography
Luke Scott
Production Designer
Will Htay
Costume Designer
Wiz Francis
Visual Effects Producer
Tim Phillips
Visual Effects Supervisor
Michael Gregory
Colourist
Jean-Clement Soret
Editor
Tim Hardy
Music Composers
Carlton Douglas Ridenhour
Gary J Rinaldo
Sound Designer
Rich Martin
Casting Director
Julie Tomkins
Production Manager
Simon Maniora
Location Manager
Algy Sloane
Visual Effects Company
The Moving Picture Company
Editing
STITCH
Sound Design
Envy
Marketing Manager
James Walker
Client
Channel 4

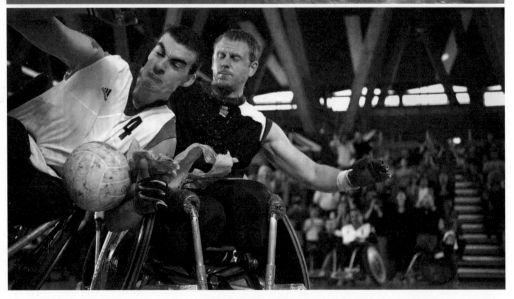

LONDON 51°32'N 0°5'W 9° 12:00

GOV.UK

The Government Digital Service, together with colleagues from departments across government, wanted to have a single domain for government – consolidating hundreds of government websites into one place, redesigning and rewriting information and services to be simpler, clearer and faster, focusing on the needs of users rather than the needs of government. That domain is GOV.UK.

–

Content Lead
Sarah Richards
Head of Design
Ben Terrett
Creative Director
Russell Davies
Writing
Government
Digital Service
HM Government
Design
Government Digital
Service
Client
Her Majesty's
Government
Brand
GOV.UK

BLACK PENCILS

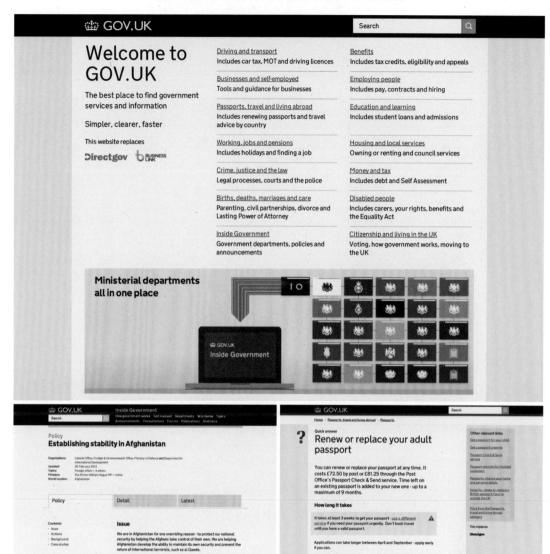

LONDON 51°32'N 0°5'W 9° 12:00

In 2012, D&AD launched a new award, the White Pencil, in partnership with not-for-profit organisation Peace One Day. The challenge to the creative communities was to raise awareness of Peace Day, 21 September, as a global annual day of truce when everyone can take action to end conflict in their lives and the lives of others.

JURY

Jury Foreman
Lord David Puttnam
Rosie Arnold
BBH London
Jan Chipchase
frog
David Droga
Droga5
Jeremy Gilley
Peace One Day

David Jones
Havas
One Young World
Marc Mathieu
Unilever
Ruth Mortimer
Marketing Week
John Mulholland
The Observer

Recipeace

In a world of increasing violence, the D&AD White Pencil brief asked the world's creative communities to help raise awareness for Peace Day, 21 September. In response we created 'Recipeace'; a movement that inspired conflicting people to come together over food. Because nothing allows two people to bury the hatchet, settle their differences and create understanding better than a shared meal. The campaign elements were designed to unite people at the dinner table. It started with the Recipeace olive oil bottle, which invited people to break bread together. From there, the idea spread, ultimately reaching a global audience, one meal at a time.

–

Art Director
Kate Harding-Jackson
Copywriter
Adam Ferguson
Designer
Casey Martin
Senior Designers
Kelly Dorsey
Kyle Poff
Peter Ty

Creative Directors
Phil Jungmann
Matt Miller
Executive Creative Director
Jeanie Caggiano
Chief Creative Officers
Susan Credle
Mark Tutssel
Design Director
Alisa Wolfson
Producers
Richard Blanco
Mark Phan
Steve Tabor
Executive Producers
Vincent Geraghty
Rob Tripas
Senior Producer
Laurie Gustafson
Production Designer
Chris Apap
Editor
Joe Clear
Photographers
Chris Cassidy
Jason McKean
Advertising Agency
Leo Burnett Chicago
Production Companies
Giannini Creative
Rider-Dickerson
Creative Resource Manager
Joe Maggiore
Account Executives
Riley Bernardin
Dane Gunderson
Account Directors
Nina Abree
Karla Flannery
Josh Raper
Client
Peace One Day

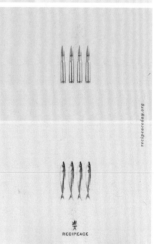

CHICAGO 41°52'N 87°37'W 3° 07:00

Blood Relations

Our aim was to bring Israeli and Palestinian citizens closer together. Instead of spilling blood, people from both sides could share it, starting with those who have the most reason to hate – bereaved Israeli and Palestinian families. The Israeli national blood bank the Al-Makassed Islamic Charitable Society Hospital for Palestinians in East Jerusalem agreed to accept blood donations so they could be shared with those on the opposite side. People across the world who couldn't donate blood physically showed their support by donating virtual blood on facebook, reaching an estimated 250 million people worldwide.

–

Art Director
Nathan Freifeld
Copywriter
Shachar Aylon
Concept
Jean-Christophe Royer
Creative Directors
Tomer Gidron
Eran Nir
Nadav Pressman

Digital Creative Director
Eddie Goldenberg
Executive Creative Director
Yoram Levi
Director
Guy Michael
Producer
Bosmat Marmarely
Editor
Guy Dagan
Cinematographer
Benjamin Hiram
Digital Artist
Steve Reiches
Music Arranger
Tomer Beran
Programmer
Leonid Angarov
Head of Production & Content
Dorit Gvili
Advertising Agency
Baumann Ber Rivnay Saatchi & Saatchi Israel
Media Agency
Zenith Optimedia
Senior Planner
Guy Gordon
Strategic Planner
Rachel Friend
Account Executive
Noa Sharf
Group Account Director
Nir Federbush
Clients
Peace One Day
The Peres Center for Peace

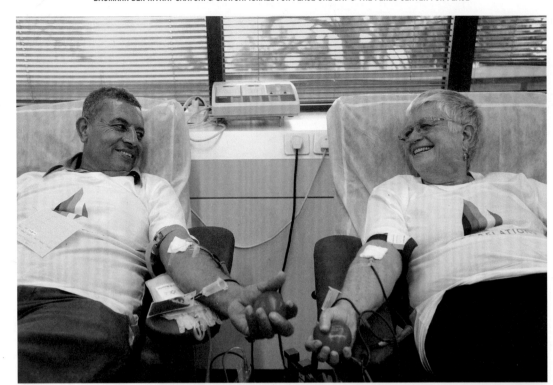

TEL AVIV 32°8'N 34°80'E 29° 14:00

The Peace Flag

'The Peace Flag' is a name, which unites all flags rendered white on white and raised on International Peace Day 21 September. While there are various peace symbols – the olive branch, the dove – there is no official flag of peace adopted by the United Nations. Our idea is to institutionalise the world's first official flag of peace through a formal UN ratification and propose for national embassies to adopt this concept. The principle behind the design will work across any flag – whether it's sports teams or corporations. The campaign seeks to create a symbol that communicates national and individual observance of Peace Day.

—

Art Directors
Leong Darren Abriel
Tadas Maksimovas
Copywriters
Leong Darren Abriel
Will Awdry
Giles Montgomery
Designer
Andy Breese
Flag Artist
Aaron Fein
Photographers
Linas Justice
Neringa Rekasuite
Editor
Tadas Vidmantas
Programmer
Marius Sprunskas
Web Developers
Petras Navickas
Rapolas Vosylius
Client
Peace One Day

WHITE PENCIL 2012

LONDON 51°32'N 0°5'W 9° 12:00

WHITE PENCIL 2012

Israel Loves Iran

One evening of 2012, as the governments of Israel and Iran renewed their calls to war, Ronny Edry and Michal Tamir uploaded a poster to their facebook page, along with a personal message to the people of Iran. The poster had a photo of Ronny with his daughter holding the Israeli flag. Within hours, similar posters were being posted by Iranians and Israelis alike. Within days, news of the images had reached the press, and facebook conversations between the people of the two nations grew deeper. Years of hate propaganda were stripped away message by message – all by starting a simple conversation and getting to know the other side.

–
Concept
Ronny Edry
Michal Tamir
Graphic Designers
Dorit Shohat
Tamar Yadin
Project Manager
Sarah Gaudron
Client
Peace One Day

TEL AVIV 32°8'N 34°80'E 29° 14:00

Peaceful Countries

Knowledge is the first step towards global peace. Our campaign highlights the fact that many of the world's most peaceful countries arm the world's least peaceful countries, exporting deadly weapons every single day.

–
Art Director
Kathrin Laser
Copywriter
Chris Colliton
**Executive
Creative Directors**
Ted Royer
Nik Studzinski
Creative Chairman
David Droga
Producer
TJ Ryan
**Executive Digital
Producer**
Lindsey Slaby
Developer
Doug Pfeffer
**Head of Integrated
Production**
Sally-Ann Dale
Advertising Agency
Droga5 NY
Researcher
Emily Mulvey
Client
Peace One Day

WHITE PENCIL 2012

NEW YORK 40°40'N 73°56'W 8° 8:00

Peace Star

We wanted to find a way to communicate with the whole world on Peace Day. Our idea was to launch a satellite into space, equipped with powerful LED lighting, illuminating the night sky like a bright star. The lights would be switched on remotely once a year on 21 September, connecting everyone on earth through a shared spectacle. For the special event, we would encourage people to get together to see the peace star, as they would to spot an eclipse or enjoy a fireworks display, making it the perfect occasion to reflect on world issues.

—
Senior Copywriter
Stuart Turner
Executive Creative Director
Damon Stapleton
Editor
Iain Nealie
Advertising Agency
Saatchi & Saatchi Sydney
Client
Peace One Day

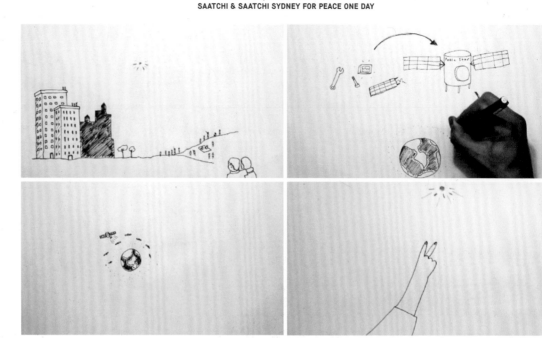

Cease Fire

On Peace Day, 21 September, we teamed up with facebook's largest shoot 'em up game UBERSTRIKE. We gave its seven million players a choice to throw down their weapons and raise the Peace One Day flag. For 24 hours players were unable to kill each other. Instead, they were encouraged to use their avatars to create and share images of peace, spreading the Peace One Day message to a community normally surrounded by violence. As a result, we got 24 hours of peace on facebook's most violent game with thousands of participants. Hundreds of thousands of virtual lives were saved.

—
Creative Directors
Fiona Chen
Nad Chishtie
Executive Creative Director
Francis Wee
Associate Creative Director
Martin Latham
Chief Creative Officer
Graham Fink
Project Director
Ludovic Bodin
Advertising Agency
Ogilvy & Mather Shanghai
Game Design
CMUNE
Project Manager
Nad Chishtie
Digital Consultant
Sascha Engel
Client
Peace One Day

Peace Baby

A baby born on 21 September is special. Wherever they are in the world Peace Day babies are born without the sound of gunfire in their ears on a day when medical supplies aren't threatened by bombs. We think that makes them different. Perhaps it makes them capable of helping the world find peace every day of the year. We created a global microsite where people could register their babies, nominate others and be part of a network of peace. We contacted current peace babies (from rock stars to former Prime Ministers) and even got retweeted by Ricki Lake. As there was a generation of war babies, let's create a generation of Peace Babies.

—
Creative Director
James de Zoete
Executive Creative Director
Charlie Mawer
Producer
Sarah Caddy
Editor
Richard McCormack
Programmer
Richard Najdowski
Interactive Programmer
Giles Wright
Production Manager
Jita Mitra
Production Company
Red Bee Media
Social Media Executive
Becky Emmott
Researcher
Uzma Iqbal
Planner
Tim Whirledge
Account Director
Richard Stuart
Client
Peace One Day

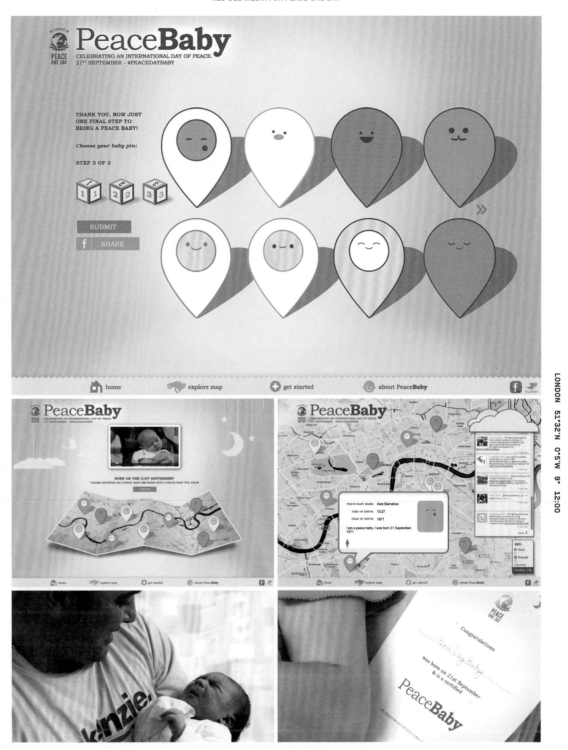

In 2013, the White Pencil evolved into a unique category that recognises the power of creativity to make the world a better place. It is awarded for work that results in positive social change or has purpose beyond profit, regardless of whether the client is a neighbourhood charity or global commercial brand. All types of creative work are welcome, from communications to community programmes to product and service innovations.

JURY

Jury Foreman
Michael Conrad
Berlin School of
Creative Leadership
Kathleen Enright
OgilvyEarth
Simon Higby
DDB Copenhagen
Nat Hunter
Royal Society of Arts (RSA)

Harry Pearce
Pentagram Design London
Paul Priestman
Priestmangoode
Walter Susini
Unilever
Ailsa Wolfson
Leo Burnett Chicago

Help I Want to Save a Life

We wanted to add thousands of new names to the Marrow Donor Registry. Our solution was to turn a normal, everyday act into a chance to save a life. We put a simple marrow registry kit into boxes of over-the-counter help bandages. The kit contained a sterilised cotton swab to collect blood and a prepaid envelope. We were able to catch people while they were already bleeding. By making marrow registration part of a common occurrence, as well as part of a mass-produced consumer product, we reached a huge, new audience and reinvented the way marrow registration takes place.

–
Art Director
Alfredo Adan Roses
Copywriters
Graham Douglas
Alberto Portas
Martagon
Creative Director
Nathan Frank
Advertising Agency
Droga5
Clients
DKMS
Help Remedies
Brand
help

NEW YORK CITY   40°40'N   73°56'W   8°   8:00

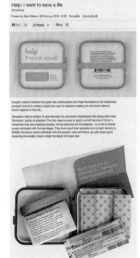

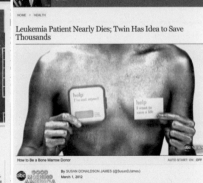

Immortal Fans

Sport Club do Recife is known for having some of football's most passionate fans, who will do anything for their club. What if we could engage the fans and leverage their passion for a truly good cause? For Sport Club do Recife fans, the team is their life. Our strategy was to push this passion even further. We created the first organ donor card for a football team. The donor card keeps a fan's passion alive through the lives of others. And, at the same time, it solves the biggest barrier to organ transplants in Brazil: family authorisation.

—
Art Director
João Coutinho
Copywriter
Paco Conde
Designer
João Coutinho
Executive Creative Directors
Paco Conde
Roberto Fernandez
Chief Creative Officer
Anselmo Ramos
Advertising Agency
Ogilvy Brazil
Client
Sport Club do Recife

ADRIANO
MARCOS
DOS SANTOS
Aguarda transplante
de fígado e pâncreas

"PROMETO QUE SEUS ORGÃOS VÃO CONTINUAR VIVENDO PELO SPORT"

PELO SPORT TUDO. ATÉ DEPOIS DE MORRER.
Faça a sua carteirinha em sportrecife.com ou facebook.com/sportrecife

DOADOR SPORT

Sport Club Recife

immortal fans

The World's Most Valuable Social Network

The Missing Children Society of Canada handles an estimated 50,000 reported cases every year, yet receives no government funding support. As a result, it has limited financial resources for expansive search efforts. Instead of an ad campaign, we created 'The World's Most Valuable Social Network', the first-ever online search party. It worked by getting people to 'donate' their social networks, allowing alerts to be posted on their newsfeeds. This digital innovation helped the search and rescue efforts of the organisation at no additional cost, and was directly responsible for assisting in the rescue of six missing children in the first five months since launch.

–

WHITE PENCIL 2013

Art Directors
Todd Lawson
Yusong Zhang
Copywriter
James Ansley
Chief Creative Officer
Patrick Scissons
Creative Technologists
John Breton
Daryl Brewer
Toby Pilling
Producer
Alice Keith
Advertising Agency
Grey Group Canada
Planner
Malcolm McLean
Account Directors
Patty Moher
Darlene Remlinger
Client
Missing Children Society of Canada

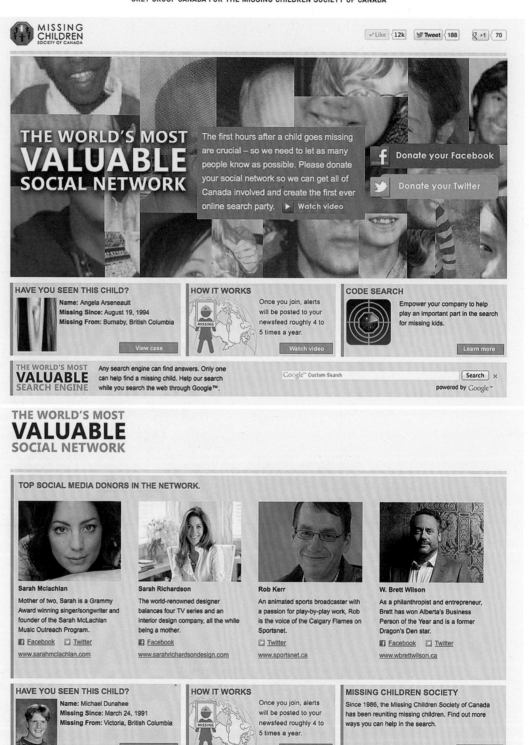

TORONTO   43°42'N   79°24'W   6°   8:00

Dumb Ways to Die

Accidents and deaths among young people on Melbourne's Metro train system had been on the rise for years. The problem is, young people don't listen to public safety messages – especially when they come from authorities. 'Dumb Ways to Die' changed that. It turned a safety message that people needed to hear, into a message people wanted to hear. Along the way the campaign was reducing injuries and saving lives while creating smiles. Of particular note, the 'Dumb Ways to Die' single sold over 77,000 copies on iTunes with money generated being re-invested in further train safety programmes.

–
Art Director
Pat Baron
Copywriter
John Mescall
Creative Director
Pat Baron
Executive Creative Director
John Mescall
Producer
Cinnamon Darvall
Senior Producer
Mark Bradley
Illustrator
Julian Frost
Animator
Julian Frost
Music Producer
Oliver McGill
Advertising Agency
McCann Erickson Melbourne
Production Company
McCann Erickson Melbourne
Account Manager
Tamara Broman
Account Director
Alec Hussain
Group Account Director
Adrian Mills
Brand Manager
Leah Waymark
Marketing Manager
Chloe Alsop
Client
Metro Trains

WHITE PENCIL 2013

MELBOURNE 37°47'S 144°58'E 12° 23:00

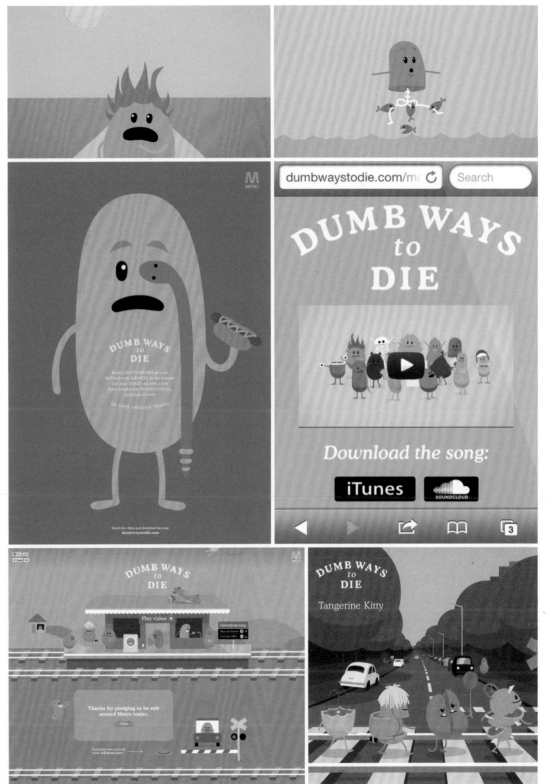

Bridge of Life

A large number of people jump off the Mapo Bridge in South Korea every year. Our idea to prevent further suicides was not simply to install a physical device to hinder the attempts, but to create an interactive bridge that would change people's minds through communication. Lights on the guardrails are activated by sensors as people walk by, illuminating short messages and giving the impression that the bridge is speaking to them personally. They included warm and kind words that appeased the anxious and confused minds of those attempting to end their lives.

—
Art Directors
Jiyeon Choi
Jaeyeon Kim
Minjoo Kim
Chaehoon Lee
Hyungkyun Oh
Jinwoo Ryu
Copywriters
Yongkyu Choi
Yukyung Joo
Youngjun Kim
Jieun Park
Creative Director
Joohoon Lee
Executive Creative Director
Thomas Hongtack Kim
Chief Creative Officer
Jeongkeun Yoo
Advertising Agency
Cheil Worldwide
Account Executives
Kyungtae Kim
Inyoung Lee
Account Director
Jungho Park
Client
Samsung Life Insurance

WHITE PENCIL 2013

SEOUL 37°33'N 126°58'E 5° 21:00

Beggar Broadcast

Johannesburg is inundated with beggars. Yet in their masses they have become invisible. And with a failing education system, the next generation will end up on the streets too. This is something that registered charity One School at a Time plans to change by improving just one school at a time. A solution for the education system can deliver a solution for poverty. Our idea? To give the voiceless a voice. By building a device capable of interrupting any radio frequency, we broadcast the stories of real beggars into the cars of those ignoring them. Their message? Don't give us money; instead donate online to One School at a Time.

–
Art Director
Freda Raubenheimer
Copywriter
Jeanine Vermaak
Executive Creative Director
Xolisa Dyeshana
Chief Creative Officer
Pepe Marais
Agency Producer
Ananda Swanepoel
Sound Engineer
Jo Darling
Advertising Agency
Joe Public Johannesburg
Client
One School at a Time

WHITE PENCIL 2013

It's me on the crutches next to you,

JOHANNESBURG 26°12'S 28°4'E 16° 14:00

ADVERTISING

PHL
BBDO
Guerrero

NZL
Colenso BBDO/
Proximity
New Zealand
DDB New
Zealand
Draftfcb
New Zealand

RUS
Look At Media
Moscow

FRA
CLM BBDO
DDB Paris
Les
Télécréateurs
Marcel
Worldwide

KOR
Cheil
Worldwide

IDN
Lowe
Indonesia

URY
Lowe Ginkgo

ARE
Memac Ogilvy
& Mather
TBWA\RAAD
Middle East –
Dubai

NAM
Advantage
Y&R Namibia

ZAF
DDB
South Africa
FoxP2
Lowe and
Partners
Cape Town
Net#twork
BBDO
Johannesburg
Ogilvy &
Mather
Johannesburg
Ogilvy
Cape Town
TBWA\Hunt\
Lascaris
Johannesburg

BRA
AlmapBBDO
Leo Burnett
Tailor Made
Loducca
Ogilvy Brazil

BEL
Duval
Guillaume
Happiness
Brussels
Publicis
Belgium

SGP
DDB
Singapore
TBWA\
Singapore

GTM
Ogilvy &
Mather
Guatemala

NLD
Havas
WorldWide
Amsterdam
Publicis
Amsterdam

THA
Leo Burnett
Bangkok

USA
72andSunny
Arnold
Worldwide
Boston
Barton F. Graf
9000
BBDO
New York
BBH New York
CP+B
David&Goliath
DDB Chicago
DDB New York
Draftfcb
New York
Droga5
Goodby
Silverstein &
Partners
Grey New York
Johannes
Leonardo
Leo Burnett
Chicago
Pereira &
O'Dell
R/GA
The Martin
Agency
Wieden+
Kennedy
New York
Wieden+
Kennedy
Portland
Y&R New York

DEU
BBDO
Proximity
Düsseldorf
Serviceplan
München

MEX
Ogilvy &
Mather Mexico
Y&R Mexico

AUS
Clemenger
BBDO
Melbourne
DDB Group
Melbourne
DDB Sydney
George
Patterson Y&R
Melbourne
JOY.
M&C Saatchi
Sydney
Marketforce
Advertising
McCann
Erickson
Melbourne
Whybin\TBWA\
DAN Sydney

CAN
BBDO Canada
Dare
Vancouver
Grey Group
Canada
Grip
TAXI Montréal

PER
Mayo Draftfcb

ARG
Del Campo
Nazca Saatchi
& Saatchi

SWE
åkestam.holst
DDB
Stockholm
Forsman &
Bodenfors
North Kingdom
Prime

GBR
4creative
adam&eveDDB
AMV BBDO
BBH London
Beattie
McGuinness
Bungay
CHI & Partners
CP+B London
Google
Creative Lab
Leo Burnett
London
Ogilvy &
Mather London
OgilvyOne
Worldwide
London
Rattling Stick
RKCR/Y&R
Rubber
Republic
Sauna@
Grillifilms
The Assembly
The Brooklyn
Brothers
WCRS
Weapon7
Wieden+
Kennedy
London

CHN
JWT Shanghai
Ogilvy &
Mather
Shanghai

CHN

GBR

SWE

PER CAN AUS

ARG USA THA NLD

MEX DEU

GTM SGP BEL

NAM

ZAF

BRA

ARE

URY IDN

KOR FRA

RUS

NZL PHL

Dumb Ways to Die

Also In Book
in Integrated Digital Campaigns

This catchy little music video epitomises client bravery. Not only did it demonstrate the client's product killing the client's customers, it did so without mentioning the client's brand until the very last breath. A marvellous piece of marketing is the result. As is close to 40 million YouTube views in the first month.

–
Art Director
Pat Baron
Copywriter
John Mescall
Creative Director
Pat Baron
Executive Creative Director
John Mescall
Producer
Cinnamon Darvall
Senior Producer
Mark Bradley
Illustrator
Julian Frost
Animator
Julian Frost
Music Producer
Oliver McGill
Production Company
McCann Erickson Melbourne
Advertising Agency
McCann Erickson Melbourne
Account Manager
Tamara Broman
Account Director
Alec Hussain
Group Account Director
Adrian Mills
Brand Manager
Leah Waymark
Marketing Manager
Chloe Alsop
Client
Metro Trains

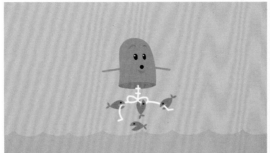

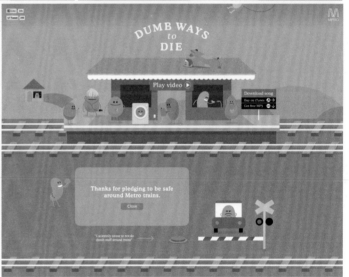

MELBOURNE 37°47'S 144°58'E 12° 23:00

From Love to Bingo

This ad was created using only still images from the Getty archive, shown at sufficient speed to transform the series into a video that tells a beautiful story. This was a powerful way to show that Getty Images' archive is so vast you can even make a film with it.

–
Directors
Marcos Kotlhar
João Simi
Art Director
Marcos Kotlhar
Copywriter
Sophie Shoenburg
Creative Directors
André Kassu
Marcos Medeiros
Renato Simoes
Digital Creative Directors
Luciana Haguiara
Sandro Rosa
Executive Creative Director
Luiz Sanches
Chief Creative Officer
Marcello Serpa
Information Architect
Luis Felipe Fernandes
Production Director
Fernando Boniotti
Sound Designer
Kito Siqueira
Production Companies
Paranoid
Split Filmes
Digital Production Company
Inkuba
Advertising Agency
AlmapBBDO
Project Manager
Rafael Puls
Account Handler
Marina Leal
Brand Manager
Veronica Raad
Client
Getty Images

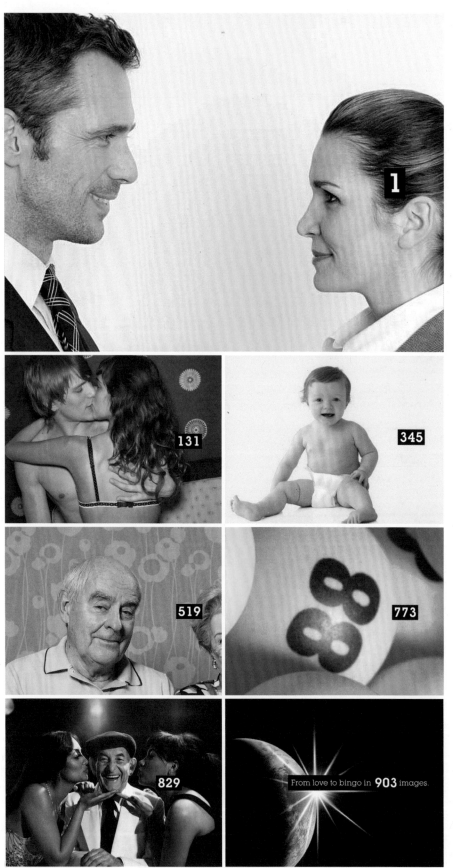

SÃO PAULO 23°31'S 46°31'W 23° 10:00

Nike+ FuelBand

Nike came to us to realise an idea: a wristband device that tracks your daily activity and a common, universal metric called Fuel for every active body out there. They asked us to design the entire user experience. We ensured ease of use: set your goal, and get from red to green. If you meet your goal, animations celebrate your performance. Data graphics show where you were most active daily, weekly, monthly, and beyond. We created Bluetooth sync technology so the results of your day's activities can be transferred to your mobile device and visualised on the FuelBand app.

–
Art Director
Ray Sison
Copywriter
Evan Maranca
Creative Directors
Cesar Marchetti
Kirill Yeretsky
Executive Creative Director
Tara Greer
Associate Creative Directors
Keith Byrne
Gaurabh Mathure
Technical Directors
Nick Coronges
Sune Kaae
Daniel Katz
Designer
Ellen Pai
Senior Software Engineers
Robert Carlsen
Fernando Mazzon
Niall McCormack
Executive Producer
Avery Holden
Senior Producers
Alan Donnelly
Guy Helson
Michael Klimkewicz
Head of Product
Ian Spalter
Quality Assurance Manager
Leslie Chong
Digital Agency
R/GA
Managing Director
Jennifer Allen
Client
Nike
Brand
Nike+

The Liberation

ONLY is a Danish fashion brand targeting girls between 15 and 25. They wanted to manifest the product DNA of the brand, interacting directly with consumers and making it easy for them to buy, like, pin, tweet and create more traffic to the website. 'The Liberation' is an online interactive film experience and the world's first on-demand video retail environment. The campaign spread to thousands of sites and blogs, increasing traffic to only.com by over 500%.

–
Director
Christoffer Von Reis
Art Directors
Charlotte Boysen
Kenneth Graupner
Mia Lykkegaard
Katrine Jo Madsen
Digital Art Director
Daniel Nicolajsen
Senior Art Director
Jakob Nylund
Creative Directors
Jimmy Blom
Daniel Ilic
Creative Technologist
Karsten Loewe Kirkegaard
Producers
Mia Wallmark
Kristina Wibom
Editor
Stefan Ström
Director of Photography
Niklas Johansson
Sound Designers
Johan Belin
Erik Brattlöf
Artist
Lune
Developer
Einar Öberg
Technical Director
Daniel Isaksson
User Experience Designer
Ana Cecilia Martins
Digital Agency
North Kingdom
Advertising Agency
Uncle Grey Copenhagen
Sound Design
DinahMoe
Strategist
Lars Samuelsen
Account Director
Charlotte Porsager
Client
ONLY Jeans

ADVERTISING   DIGITAL ADVERTISING

SKELLEFTEÅ 64°45'N 20°57'E 5° 13:00

Build With Chrome

'Build with Chrome'
is the world's biggest
Lego set, a mash-up
of Google Maps
and Lego bricks,
that lets you build
anywhere in Australia
or New Zealand.
It demonstrates
the power of the
Chrome browser
and its support for
rich, interactive
3D through Web
Graphics Library.
The site received
over 500,000
visitors within 48
hours, spending the
equivalent of over
four years building,
all before any paid
media. Nearly a year
on, people continue
to build online.

—
Digital Agencies
M&C Saatchi/Mark
Sydney
North Kingdom
Clients
Google Australia
LEGO
Brand
Google Chrome

ADVERTISING DIGITAL ADVERTISING

SYDNEY 34°0'S 151°0'E 22° 20:00

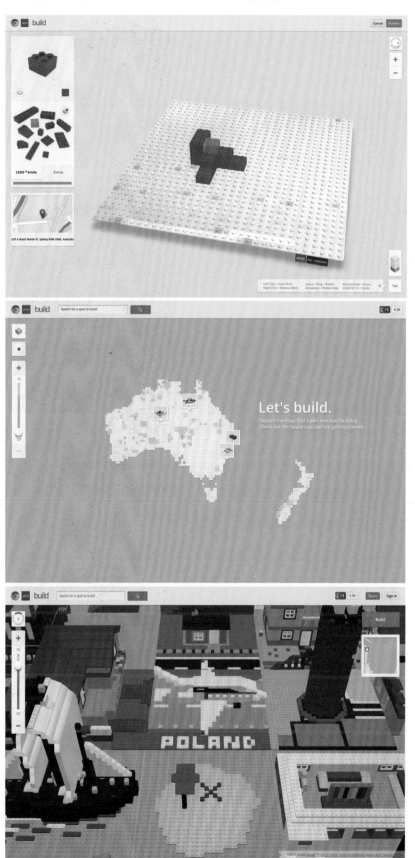

Faktum Hotels

Gothenburg has about 3,400 homeless people. Most of them find a roof over their heads with a friend or at a refuge, but some sleep in the open air. We chose ten of the places where they might spend the night and made it possible for visitors of this website to book them just like they would book a hotel room online. The money goes to Faktum's work for homeless and socially vulnerable people.

–
Art Directors
Staffan Forsman
Staffan Lamm
Copywriter
Martin Ringqvist
Designers
Staffan Håkansson
Christoffer Persson
Interactive Producer
Stefan Thomson
Photographer
Håkan Ludwigsson
Advertising Agency
Forsman &
Bodenfors
**Production
Companies**
F&B Factory
Thomson Interactive
Media
Sound Design
Plan8
Account Managers
Åsa Pedersen
Linda Tiderman
Marketing Managers
Sara Erkhagen
Åse Henell
Client
Faktum

ADVERTISING DIGITAL ADVERTISING

GOTHENBURG 57°42'N 11°58'E 9° 13:00

Hashtag Killer

The 'Hashtag Killer' campaign set out to eradicate the ironic #FirstWorldProblems meme, in which people tweet about frivolous life burdens. For the anthem commercial, we gathered real 'First World Problems' tweets and then approached people in Haiti to recite them. But perhaps even more effective was the series of personalised response videos, in which various Haitians consoled those using the hashtag on Twitter.

—

Art Director
Sam Shepherd
Copywriter
Frank Cartagena
Executive Creative Director
Menno Kluin
Chief Creative Officer
Matt Eastwood
Designers
Zeynep Aydogmus
Gina Lin
Juan Carlos Pagan
Producer
Lindsey Hutter
Executive Producer
Ed Zazzera
Director
Alec Helm
Editors
Alec Helm
Melanie Meditz
Advertising Agency
DDB New York
Client
Water is Life

Dan Jordan
@DanJordan2001 - New York City

There really isn't anything worse than leaving your headphones at home.
#FirstWorldProblems

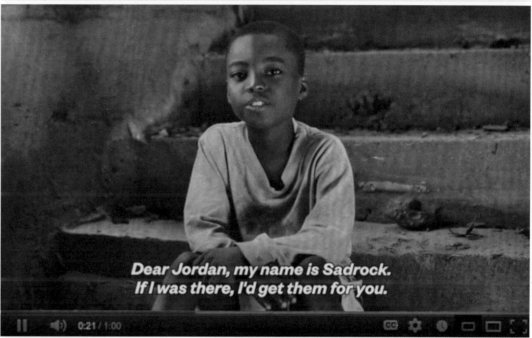

Dear Jordan, my name is Sadrock.
If I was there, I'd get them for you.

0:21 / 1:00

NEW YORK CITY   40°40'N   73°56'W   8°   8:00

I hate when my phone charger won't reach my bed.

iQ Street View

The Toyota iQ completed Google Street View in Belgium by filming all the streets Google couldn't get into. A PR strategy and making-of video led people to our version of the street view site. There people could tag their streets to invite the street view crew. When their street was filmed, a direct mailing was sent to all people living in the street with a promotional message and an invite to check out their street on iQstreetview.be.

—
Art Director
Naim Baddich
Copywriter
Patrick Glorieux
Creative Director
Peter Ampe
Executive Creative Director
Karen Corrigan
Graphic Designer
Jeremy Vandenbosch
Agency Producer
Bart Vande Maele
Interactive Producer
Stijn Van Velthoven
Director of Photography
Bob Jeusette
Head of Art
Cecilia Azcarate Isturiz
Digital Agency
BLISS interactive
Advertising Agency
Happiness Brussels
Strategist
Joris Joosten
Account Manager
Mehdi Sel
Group Account Director
Pascal Kemajou
Client
Toyota Belgium
Brand
Toyota iQ

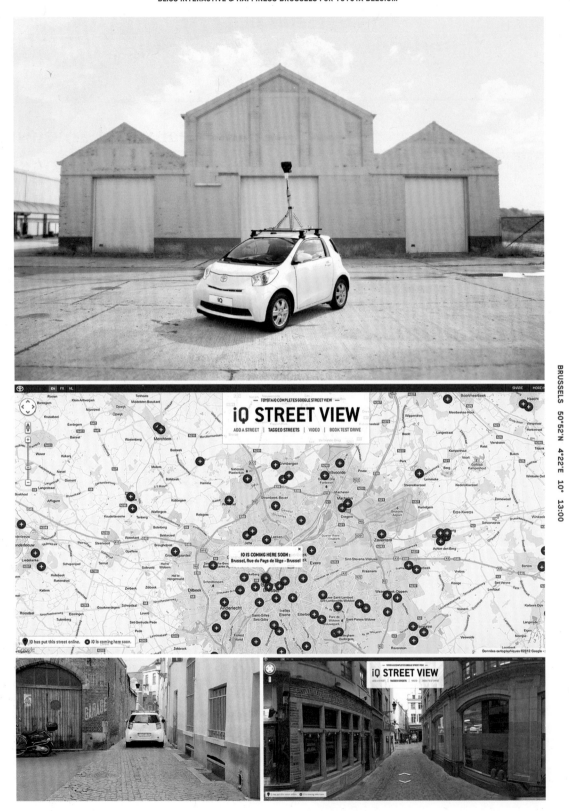

Oreo Daily Twist

Born in 1912, Oreo was celebrating its 100th year. The brand had developed a traditional image, which we wanted to rejuvenate. We created 100 ads in 100 days. Each morning we identified trending news stories, gave them a playful Oreo twist and pushed the ad to our social networks. The results: 433 million facebook views with a 280% increase in shares; and 231 million media impressions – making Oreo the brand with the highest buzz increase in 2012 (up 49%).

–
Art Director
Mike Lubrano
Senior Art Directors
Jackie Anzaldi
Jared Isle
Senior Copywriter
Noel Potts
Creative Director
Megan Sheehan
Group Creative Director
Jill Applebaum
Digital Agency
360i
Advertising Agency
Draftfcb New York
Media Agency
Mediavest
Public Relations
Weber Shandwick
Strategic Director
Auro Trini-Castelli
Account Director
Lori Johnson
Group Account Director
Susan Polachek
Brand Manager
Danielle Brown
Marketing Manager
Cindy Chen
Client
Mondelēz International
Brand
Oreo

ADVERTISING DIGITAL ADVERTISING

NEW YORK CITY 40°40'N 73°56'W 8° 8:00

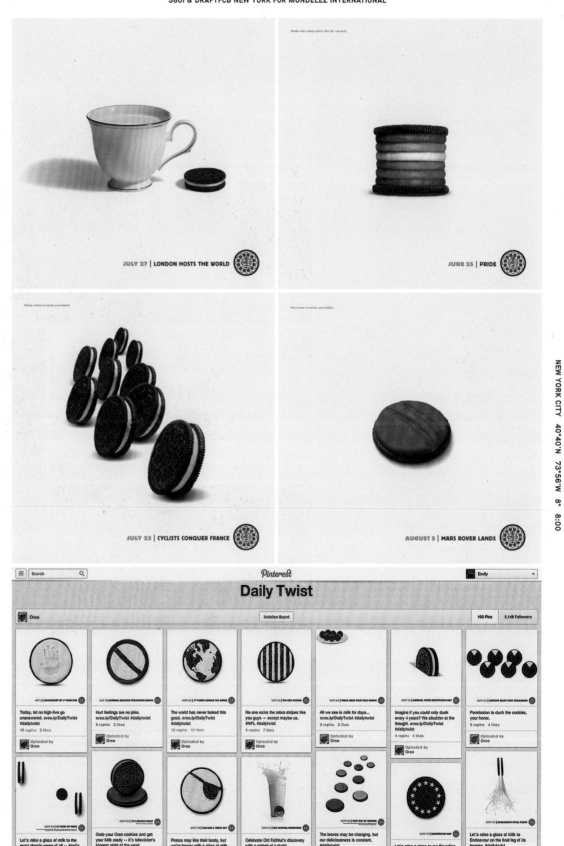

Call of Duty: Black Ops II

After nine iterations, gamers thought they'd seen everything Call of Duty had to offer. So we positioned Call of Duty: Black Ops II as a game of wholesale innovation, rewriting the game launch playbook with a six-month story of near-future warfare and weaponry. First, we put a future weapon in the hands of YouTube hero FPSRussia. Then hijacked an NBA playoff game with a chilling, category-breaking documentary and created an app with Bad Robot to showcase future weapons. Everything culminated in a global launch campaign featuring a surprising cast of gamer icons.

–

Senior Art Director
Rey Andrade
Senior Copywriter
Josh Fell
Creative Directors
Matt Murphy
Jason Norcross
Peter Novosel
Chief Creative Officer
Glenn Cole

Designer
Geovanny Panchame
Producers
Erin Goodsell
Eric Rasco
Dan Ruth
Interactive Producer
Shoni Gustafson
Production Director
Sam Baerwald
Head of Interactive Production
Heather Wischmann
User Experience Architect
Jessica Rudzewicz
Advertising Agency
72andSunny USA
Production Companies
Ant Farm
Bad Robot
Interactive
Logan
Reset
The Mill Los Angeles
Strategist
Mike Jacobson
Strategic Directors
Matt Jarvis
Bryan Smith
Account Managers
Jen Marvin
John Moloney
Group Account Director
Mike Parseghian
Client
Activision Publishing
Brand
Call of Duty

THERE'S A SOLDIER IN ALL OF US

SURPRISE

OLIVER NORTH
LIEUTENANT COLONEL, USMC. RET.

LOS ANGELES   34°3'N   118°15'W   15°   5:00

YouTube Space Lab

The number of children studying science subjects has dropped in recent years, and with the decline of NASA's shuttles, the world seems less interested in space now than it did for the latter half of the 20th Century. Through the wonder of space we challenged 14 to 18-year-olds to dream up an experiment to be carried aboard the International Space Station and streamed live on YouTube. In partnership with Lenovo, NASA and other space agencies, YouTube revealed to the world a new initiative to capture the imagination of students and teachers, and reinvigorate the study of space and space science.

–
Creative Agencies
Google Creative Lab
Toaster
Digital Production Companies
Psycle
WEIR+WONG
Production Company
Across the Pond
Clients
Google
YouTube

AUCKLAND   36°52'S   174°45'E   15°   1:00

Driving Dogs

In New Zealand, shelter dogs were seen as second rate compared to store bought animals, so finding them homes was a daily challenge for the SPCA. As a longstanding SPCA sponsor, MINI wanted to help. Our strategy was to demonstrate just how smart these dogs really are and to dispel the idea that they're damaged, despite their abusive or difficult pasts. So, we taught three of them to drive a MINI and showed them, in a never-before-seen event, live on national TV. To build anticipation for the event, we released an online video with footage of the dogs in training, and seeded over 800 pieces of content across digital and social platforms. In one week, over 200 million saw the dogs driving. The campaign received more than $20 million in PR across over 70 countries. New Zealand saw a positive shift in attitudes toward shelter dogs, adoption interest increased by 590% and, most importantly, every SCPA dog was adopted.

_

Copywriters
Peter Vegas
Matt Williams
Executive Creative Directors
Tony Clewett
Regan Grafton
James Mok
Interactive Designer
Catherine Chi
Designer
Nick McFarlane
Producer
Sarah Yetton
Cinematographer
Marco Siraky
Photographer
Stephen Langdon
Retoucher
Anton Mason
Editor
Blair Walker
Advertising Agency
Draftfcb New Zealand
Digital Strategist
Harri Owen
Planner
Steph Pearson
Media Managers
Rachel Leyland
Sarah McEwen
Simon Teagle
Account Managers
Eloise Hay
Stephanie Hueber
Account Director
Sally Willis
Group Account Director
Toby Sellers
Public Relations Manager
Angela Spain
Communications Director
Rufus Chuter
Clients
MINI New Zealand
SPCA New Zealand

CAN YOU TEACH A DOG TO DRIVE?

FIND OUT MONDAY 7PM ON CAMPBELL LIVE

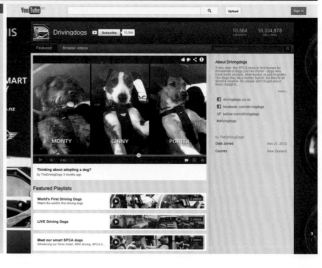

Who Cares?

The Swedish Armed Forces need to recruit young people to an occupation that requires you to give up your own comfort in order to help others. To highlight this aspect we created a digitally integrated event in Stockholm to see how far people are willing to go for one another. A person agreed to be locked inside in a box until someone volunteered to replace them. The person's fate depended on the sympathy of others. To encourage potential recruits, footage of the hostage was streamed live on our campaign site. Those with the right response would be mobilised to come over and take the person's place.

–
Art Directors
Lisa Granberg
Daniel Mencák
Copywriters
Martin Lundgren
Jeffrey Salomonsson
Creative Directors
Magnus Jakobsson
Fredrik Simonsson
Digital Designer
Robin Karlsson
Graphic Designer
Patrik Pagréus
Developer
Sebastian Ross
Digital Producer
Elisabet Halming
Advertising Agency
DDB Stockholm
Production Companies
Atomgruppen
B-Reel
Planners
Adam Sandahl
Cornelia Wangel
Account Manager
Tina Munck
Account Director
Sandra Kaludjercic Bergman
Business Director
Johan Dannemann
Client
Swedish Armed Forces

Muscle Music

We partnered with Vimeo to create an embeddable interactive player that allowed guys to play custom musical creations using Terry Crews' muscles. Guys shared their muscular symphonies on various social networks.

–

Director
Tom Kuntz
Art Director
Max Stinson
Copywriter
Andy Laugenour
User Experience Designer
Jake Doran
Interactive Designer
Billy McDermott
Creative Directors
Craig Allen
Jason Bagley
Mark Fitzloff
Matt O'Rourke

Executive Creative Director
Susan Hoffman
Executive Producer
Ben Grylewicz
Interactive Producers
Mike Davidson
Pierre Wendling
Advertising Agency
Wieden+Kennedy Portland
Production Company
Morton Jankel Zander
Editing
Mackenzie Cutler
Music Composer
Daedalus
Sound Design
The Mill Los Angeles
Account Handler
Jessica Monsey
Client
Procter & Gamble
Brand
Old Spice

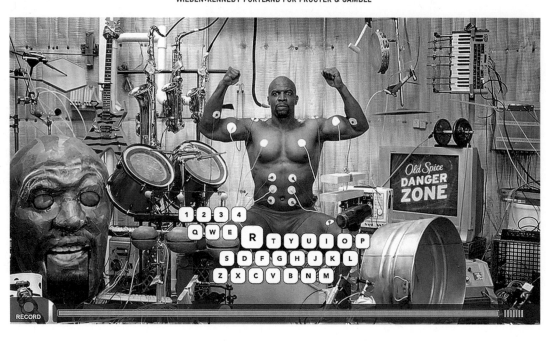

ADVERTISING   DIGITAL ADVERTISING

Golden Chains

ALB is an emerging French musician who's planning to release his second album in 2013. Like many other artists, ALB isn't supported by a major label yet. So, to promote and finance his upcoming album, ALB came up with 'Golden Chains', a participative music video in which the artist took up the challenge of selling his personal everyday items – for real. The plan was to use the revenue gained to fund the production of his next album.

–

Director
Johnatan Broda
Art Director
Julien Boissinot
Copywriter
Kevin Salembier

Creative Directors
Matthieu Elkaim
Olivier Lefebvre
Benjamin Marchal
Producer
Willy Morence
Agency Producer
Jean-Gabriel Saint-Paul
Interactive Technical Director
Anthony Hamelle
Production Company
Carnibird
Digital Agency
ACNE Production
Advertising Agency
CLM BBDO
Sound Design
Green United Music
Music Supervision
Green United Music
Public Relations Manager
Lauren Weber
Client
ALB

The Ballerina Stunt

This spectacular stunt documentary was filmed to spark interest in the launch of the new Volvo FH series. High liner Faith Dickey crossed a tight rope between two speeding FH trucks to demonstrate the vehicles' control and precision. As a result 'The Ballerina Stunt' was featured on 75,000 news sites and blogs in 225 countries, reaching more than 162 million people.

–
Director
Henry Alex Rubin
Art Directors
Anders Eklind
Sophia Lindholm
Copywriters
Björn Engström
Martin Ringqvist

Designer
Jerry Wass
Producer
Ray Leaky
Agency Producer
Alexander Blidner
Editor
Spencer Ferszt
Production Company
Smuggler
Advertising Agency
Forsman & Bodenfors
Post Production
Absolute Post
Planner
Tobias Nordström
Account Managers
Alison Arnold
Jenny Edwardsson
Britta Malmberg
Account Directors
Cilla Glenberg
Olle Victorin
Client
Volvo Group Sweden
Brand
Volvo FH

Bodyform Responds: The Truth

A light-hearted post on Bodyform's facebook page, accusing the brand of misrepresenting the joys of periods, went viral. We seized this opportunity to retort with a playful spoof video response, in which fictional CEO Caroline Williams addresses 'Richard', the disappointed facebook user, with an apology for the flagrant use of metaphors in the company's advertising. The web film clocked nearly three million views in its first week. It generated over 82,000 facebook actions, over 6,000 tweets and 98% YouTube likes. It was featured in more than 200 pieces of editorial across some of the most influential media worldwide.

–
Director
Matt Golding
Copywriters
Rory Ahern
Tiffany Maddox
Tom Wainwright
Producer
Oli Kendall
Editor
Matt Golding
Director of Photography
Lindsey Hopkinson
Advertising Agency
Rubber Republic
Media Agency
Carat
Digital Strategist
Coral Baker-Hoummady
Planner
Rachael Lake
Account Director
Rachael Clark
Brand Manager
Yulia Kretova
Marketing Director
Nicola Coronado
Public Relations Manager
Vanessa Munnings
Client
Bodyform

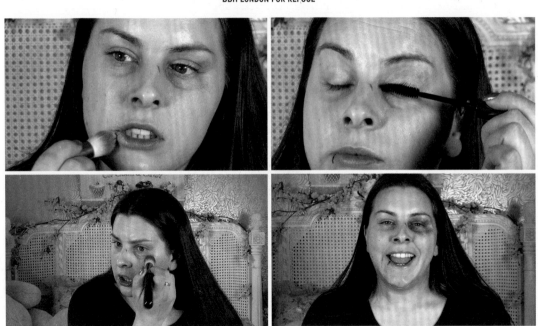

Don't Cover it Up

Fearing there is nowhere they can turn for help, 65% of domestic abuse victims routinely cover up their emotional and physical scars. Refuge challenged us to raise awareness among this audience. Lauren Luke is a YouTube makeup artist. With over 125 million views from young women, her channel gave us a way to talk directly to victims. In the style of her makeup tutorials, a bruised Lauren showed how to cover up signs of abuse. Caught off guard, her young fans began a global discussion about an unspoken problem.

—
Directors
Wesley Hawes
Gary McCreadie
Art Directors
George
Hackworth-Jones
Stephen Noble

Copywriter
Jack Smedley
Creative Director
Pablo Marques
Executive Creative Director
Nick Gill
Agency Producers
Bryony Dellow
Jeremy Gleeson
Interactive Producer
Richard Atkins
Production Company
The Mill London
Digital Agency
Addictive Pixel
Advertising Agency
BBH London
Sound Design
Factory Studios
Content Strategist
Claire Coady
Strategic Director
Simon Robertson
Account Handler
Carly Herman
Brand Manager
Lisa King
Client
Refuge

Clouds Over Cuba

This campaign site shows 'Clouds over Cuba', an interactive multimedia documentary commemorating the 50th anniversary of the Cuban Missile Crisis. The feature begins with Castro's overthrow of Batista in 1959, and follows on until the missiles were removed in October 1962. Features include 15 expert interviews, 200 related documents and images linked to the film's timeline, mobile sync, tablet optimisation, and calendar integration so you can attend JFK's secret meetings 'live', 50 years on.

—
Art Director
Brian Williams
Copywriter
Wade Alger
Creative Director
Joe Alexander

Design Director
Matt Gase
Technical Director
Bartek Drozdz
Agency Producers
Nicole Hollis-Vitale
Kristen Little
Executive Producers
Dustin Callif
Oliver Fuselier
Steve Humble
Brian Latt
Interactive Producer
Kristen Koeller
Directors
Erich Joiner
Ben Tricklebank
Head of Interactive Production
Joy Kuraitis
Advertising Agency
The Martin Agency
Production Company
Tool
Editing Company
STITCH
Music Production
Plan8
Client
The JFK Presidential Library & Museum

ADVERTISING DIGITAL ADVERTISING

The Science of Imitation Milk

The site invites participants to interact with a quirky educational experience, exploring the ingredients in imitation milk. Syncing your phone or tablet to create a remote control for the experiment allows you to perform a variety of actions, from shelling soya beans to shaking a beaker of imitation milk.

–

Art Director
Maggie Bradshaw
Copywriter
Carter Debski
Executive Creative Director
Christian Haas
Chief Creative Officer
Jeff Goodby
Creative Technologist
Mike Newell
Producer
Leila Seghrouchni
Executive Producer
Alex Burke
Interactive Producer
Maribel Arellano

Director
David Shane
Editor
Jim Hutchins
Head of Broadcast
Cindy Fluitt
Advertising Agency
Goodby Silverstein & Partners
Interactive Production Company
Silk Tricky
Project Manager
Mallory Frye
Strategists
Nancy Jeng
Krista Miyashiro
Henrietta Probert
Alina Schabashevich
Fiona Su
Strategic Directors
Christine Chen
Bonnie Wan
Account Managers
Krista Kelly
Meredith Williams
Account Director
Kelly Johnson
Managing Partner
Robert Riccardi
Client
California Milk Processor Board
Brand
got milk?

Create the Rainbow

For Christmas 2012, we gave people the opportunity to make their own Skittles commercial. 'Create the Rainbow' is a DIY Skittles holiday commercial maker: a video based toolbox where people can choose dialogue, music, characters, settings and even a Christmas miracle. They can also finish the spot off with their own name.

–

Art Director
Jeff Cheung
Writer
Michael Clowater
Creative Director
Michael Clowater
Digital Creative Director
Pablo Vio
Executive Creative Directors
Peter Ignazi
Carlos Moreno
Creative Technologist
Jeff Vermeersch
Developers
Mikko Haapoja
Sunil John

Producer
Greg Benedetto
Digital Producer
Michael Dobell
Agency Producer
Beatrice Bodogh
Director
Matt Eastman
Director of Photography
Ian MacMillan
Visual Effects
Rafael Ludwig
Advertising Agency
BBDO Canada
Production Companies
Jam3
Thelonious Films
Editing
Jam3
Music Production
RMW Music
Project Managers
Mark Carpenter
Matt Dewaal
Account Manager
Saloni Wadehra
Group Account Director
Chitty Krishnappa
Client
Wrigley Canada
Brand
Skittles

SAN FRANCISCO 37°47'N 122°25'W 15° 5:00

TORONTO 43°42'N 79°24'W 6° 8:00

Recipe Receipt

Most people still think mayonnaise is only good for sandwiches. And even though Hellmann's has been successfully teaching new uses to consumers, one challenge still remained: the point of sale. We came up with a digital solution that would inspire shoppers to integrate Hellmann's mayonnaise into their daily cooking routine. When a consumer buys Hellmann's at the supermarket, the software in the cash register detects it and starts matching it with other purchased products, printing a personalised recipe on the receipt itself.

–
Art Directors
Raphael Lucone
Guilherme Nobrega
Rafael Rizuto
Copywriters
Ricardo Lins
Eduardo Marques
Creative Directors
Rubens Filho
Eduardo Marques
Executive Creative Directors
Claudio Lima
Fred Saldanha
Chief Creative Officer
Anselmo Ramos
Producers
Nana Bittencourt
Juscelino Vieira
Advertising Agency
Ogilvy Brazil
Project Manager
Paula Santana
Client
Unilever
Brand
Hellmann's

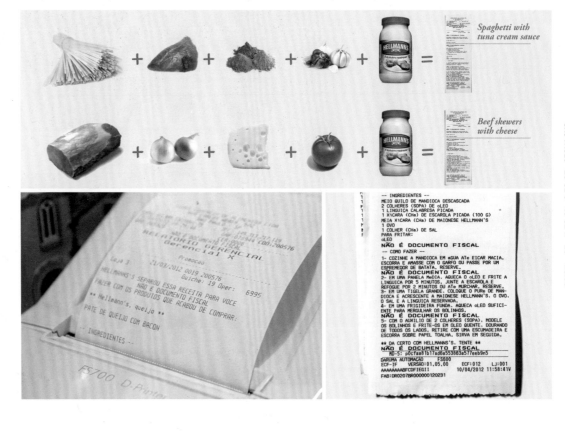

Spaghetti with tuna cream sauce

Beef skewers with cheese

Easy Way Subtitles

For the many international students and professionals living in Brazil, we created captioning technology combined with Google Translate to provide subtitles for Brazilian TV in any language.

–
Copywriter
Raphael Franzini
Creative Directors
Guga Ketzer
Cassio Moron
Sergio Mugnaini
Fabio Saboya
Programmers
Raphael Franzini
Vitor Manfredini
Designer
Gustavo De Lacerda
Advertising Agency
Loducca
Account Handler
Wilson Negrini
Client
Easy Way Language Center
Brand
Easy Way

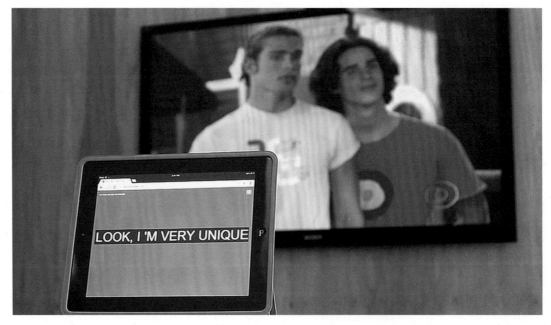

LOOK, I'M VERY UNIQUE

ADVERTISING DIGITAL ADVERTISING

SÃO PAULO 23°31'S 46°31'W 23° 10:00

SÃO PAULO 23°31'S 46°31'W 23° 10:00

**Red Tomato VIP
Fridge Magnet**

All the big pizza players with their big budgets are in Dubai. So how can a small pizzeria compete on a limited budget? With a local insight: over 200 nationalities and subsequent language barriers make ordering a pizza more frustrating than convenient. We turned this into an opportunity. The VIP Fridge Magnet is no ordinary fridge magnet – it doubles up as a pizza emergency button. This first ever one-touch delivery system refreshed the delivery business and inspired pizza passions around the world. It helped customers feel valued and set our client apart from the big brands.

–
Digital Creative Director
Preethi Mariappan
Associate Creative Directors
Melanie Clancy
Rafael Guida
User Experience Designer
Jerome Conde
Producer
Kishore Ramachandran
Technical Delivery Manager
Navin Chauhan
Creative Agency
TBWA\RAAD Middle East – Dubai
Account Executives
Weam Elhila
Mohammad Khan
Client
Red Tomato Pizza

One small fridge magnet.
One giant leap to banish your hunger forever!

Hello Isabela,

This Red Tomato fridge magnet is designed for Very Important Pizza lovers only... and that means you! So next time you're hungry, just open the box, push the button and we'll bring your Red Tomato favorite, the glorious Pianta e Frutto Classic (with triple cheese) direct to your door, lickety-split.

Get the sauce!

First, you need to power up your fridge magnet. Next, turn it on by holding the button down for ten seconds. Don't forget to count!

Easy-Cheesy!

You've got one last step – connecting with your mobile! Turn your Bluetooth® on and pair the device with your mobile phone by searching for Red Tomato.

Hot and Hungry

...or just feeling peckish? Whatever your appetite, if your fridge magnet is blinking blue, you know what to do! Push the button, and enjoy your pizza in minutes.

Your registered mobile is 050-551 6708. Set-up your magnet ONCE and you're hands-free forever! Questions? Wanna change your favorite pizza? Visit www.redtomato.biz/Magnet or call 800 TOMATO

DUBAI 25°15'N 55°18'E 30° 16:00

Chrome Web Lab

Chrome 'Web Lab'
is a first-of-its-kind
open exhibition that
can be accessed from
anywhere in the
world. It features five
physical interactive
experiments that
bring the magic of
the internet to life.
The exhibition is
available online and at
the Science Museum,
London. By creating
tangible versions
of invisible web
technologies,
the public were able
to get their hands on
them and learn how
the web works. In
July 2012 'Web Lab'
launched in beta,
a world first for a
physical exhibition,
and it continued 24
hours a day, seven
days a week until
summer 2013.

–
Creative Agency
Google Creative Lab
**Computational
Designer**
Karsten Schmidt
**Digital Production
& Design**
B-Reel
**Graphic Design
Agency**
Bibliothèque
Experience Design
Tellart
Branding Agency
B-Reel
**Production
Company**
WEIR+WONG
Engineering Agency
Tellart
**Project &
Construction
Managers**
Fraser Randall
**Spatial & Industrial
Design**
MAP
**Spatial & Exhibition
Design**
Universal Design
Studio
Sound Design
Shroom
Music Production
Shroom
Client
Google
Brand
Google Chrome

ADVERTISING DIGITAL ADVERTISING

LONDON 51°32'N 0°5'W 9° 12:00

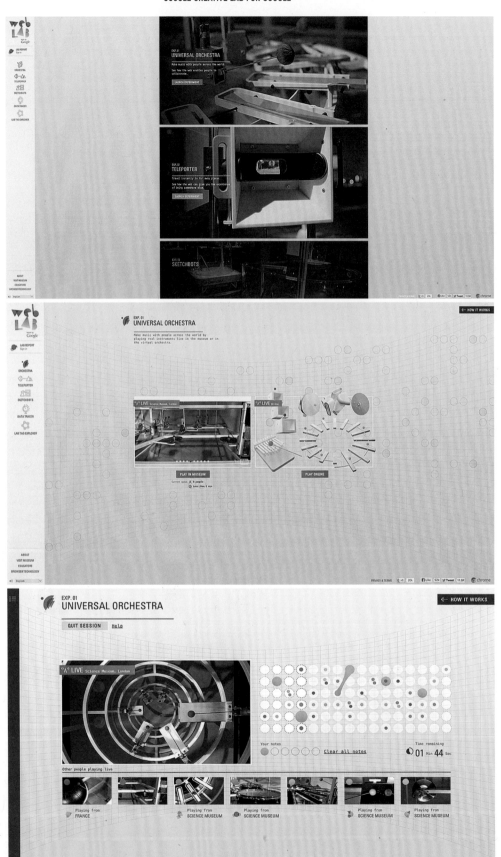

Swedish Radio Plus

We invented a completely new way to consume radio. We made radio visual, interactive, and very shareable. And we made sharing personal. 'Swedish Radio Plus' is a visual experience with a central timeline. As you listen to a programme, and hear something interesting, you can comment on that specific subject, at that exact part of the programme. You can add a comment, picture, video, link or poll. You can also see other people's contributions and interact with them. You can share that same post on facebook, with a direct link to the exact part of the programme where the post was made. So as people start discussions and add interesting content, they are also sharing the programmes.

–
Art Director
Ted Mellström
Copywriter
Marcus Hägglöf
Designer
Axel Söderlund
Agency Producer
Magnus Kennhed
Interactive Producer
Stefan Thomson
Advertising Agency
Forsman & Bodenfors
Production Companies
FLX
Society 46
Account Manager
Nicole van Rooij Ekström
Account Director
Andreas Engstrand
Public Relations Manager
Lina Thomsgård
Client
Sveriges Radio

ADVERTISING   DIGITAL ADVERTISING

GOTHENBURG 57°42'N 11°58'E 9° 13:00

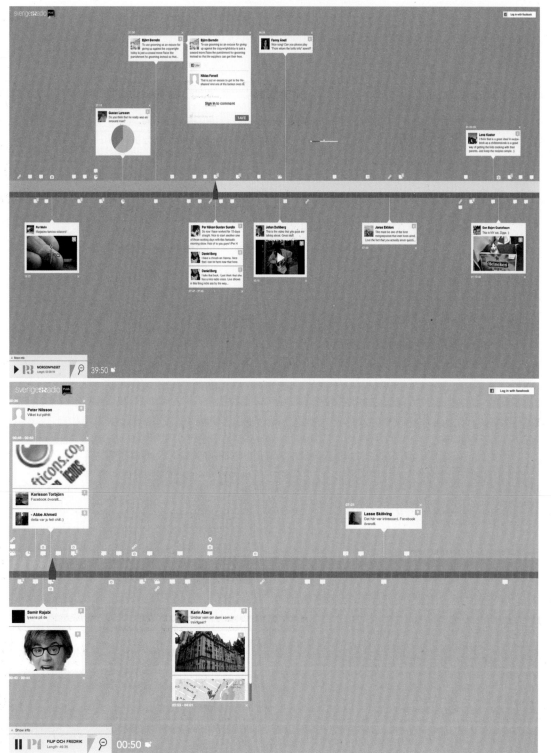

Civil Rights Captcha

CAPTCHAs are used daily around the web to protect websites from spam, making users decipher letters that spam robots can't read. But what really separates us from robots is empathy, which is also the foundation for promoting civil rights. To prove this, Civil Rights Defenders developed a CAPTCHA based on empathy. Instead of visually interpreting words the user has to take a stand on a current human rights case, before being able to comment. The CAPTCHA is available to download and implement through an open source wiki. The project sparked a global debate involving over 700 million people.

Copywriter
Louise Sallander
Creative Directors
Tom Beckman
Olle Thunberg
Developer
Pär Thunberg
Creative Agency
Prime
Marketing Manager
Natasha Esbjörnson
Client
Civil Rights Defenders

STOCKHOLM 59°17'N 18°3'E 16° 13:00

Parcel Memory

The brief was to promote the Swedish Post's pre-franked parcels and encourage people to post more Christmas gifts in December. Our solution was 'Parcel Memory' – an online match-making game challenging the nation to keep parcels in mind. If you found a matching pair of parcels, you won both. But as the parcels were identical, so was their content. Because giving and receiving are just as fun, the gifts were delivered free of charge to two different recipients. In December 2012 over 1% of Sweden's population spent an average of 16 minutes memorising the Swedish Post's pre-franked parcels.

Art Director
Lars Holthe
Copywriter
Joakim Labraaten
Creative Director
Andreas Ullenius
Graphic Designer
Olov Oqvist
Interactive Producer
Johan Eklund
Digital Agency
From Stockholm with Love
Advertising Agency
åkestam.holst
Production Company
It's Showtime
Planner
Lars Friberg
Account Handler
Jacob Stjarne
Account Manager
Katarina Johansson
Brand Manager
Jonas Brodén
Client
Swedish Post

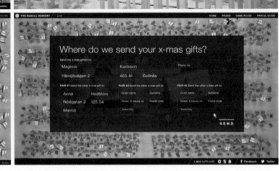

STOCKHOLM 59°17'N 18°3'E 16° 13:00

ADVERTISING   DIGITAL ADVERTISING

Dikembe Mutombo

According to the Mayans, the world was going to end on 21 December 2012. In order to stop this prophecy from happening, Old Spice created an eight-bit online video game featuring the best defender of all time, NBA legend Dikembe Mutombo. With Dikembe's help, Old Spice fans engaged in a four-and-a-half week battle against numerous evil forces based on topical and cultural news stories, in an attempt to save the world from ruin. — **Art Director** Max Stinson **Copywriter** Andy Laugenour **Creative Directors** Craig Allen Jason Bagley Sam Deats Mark Fitzloff Susan Hoffman Matt O'Rourke	**User Experience Designer** Jake Doran **Executive Producer** Ben Grylewicz **Interactive Producers** Mike Davidson Ben Kendall Pierre Wendling **Animators** Chris Beaver Ed Booth Willis Bulliner Frank Gabriel Brad Graeber Louie Granda Stephanie McCrea Kellan Stover Bruce Tinnin **Advertising Agency** Wieden+Kennedy Portland **Development** Driftlab **Animation** Powerhouse Animation Studios **Account Handlers** Liam Doherty Jessica Monsey **Client** Procter & Gamble **Brand** Old Spice

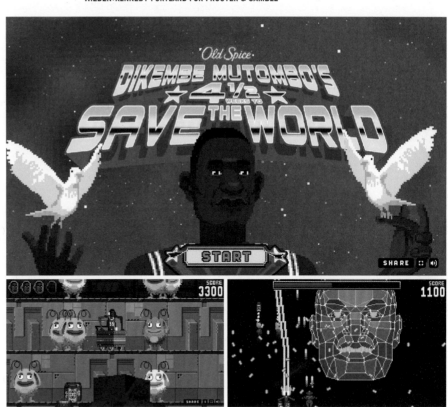

The Smallest IKEA Store in the World

To demonstrate IKEA's commitment to saving space, we built an entire IKEA store in a 10.5 x 8.8 cm web banner. We targeted people looking for small apartments by placing our tiny stores in the property section of community websites. The banner allows you to browse by department, click on any item and buy it straight from the IKEA website. With over 2,000 products available on the banner, it's definitely the smallest and smartest IKEA store in the world. — **Art Director** Gary Rolf **Copywriters** James Bisset Sascha Kuntze Gary Rolf	**Creative Directors** Ben Knight Robin Smith **Technical Directors** Hamza Afaq Niv Baniahmad Jens Steffen **Designer** Gary Rolf **Developers** Fouad Abdel-Latif Ali Mokdad Nadia Rahman Lina Safstrom **Advertising Agencies** Memac Ogilvy & Mather OgilvyOne Worldwide Frankfurt **Account Executive** Farnoush Pourebrahim **Marketing Manager** Katja Sottmeier **Business Director** Claus Adams **Client** IKEA

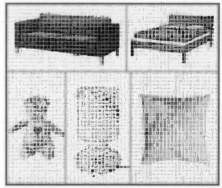

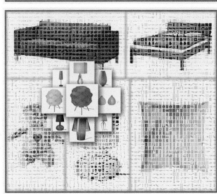

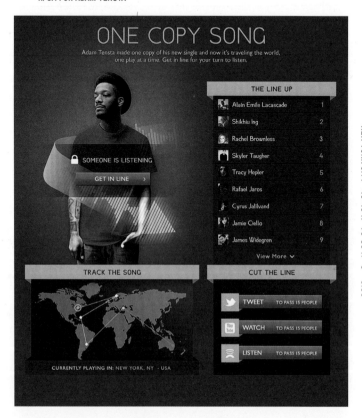

The Dove Ad Makeover

Also In Book in Use of Social Media

Negative online ads reinforce women's insecurities about their bodies. We empowered women to replace such ads with positive messages.

–
Art Directors
Trevallyn Hall
Stephanie Symonds
Copywriters
Laura Rogers
Margo Young
Creative Director
Ivan Pols
Executive Creative Director
Gerry Human
Chief Creative Officer
Gerry Human
Creative Technologist
Craig Blagg
Designer
Simone Zharadka
Developer
Martin Robertson
Information Architect
Anthony Butterfield

Producer
Carl Phillips
Agency Producer
Fiona Renfrew
Digital Producer
Sasha Dunn
Animation Director
Carl Addy
Editor
James Mortner
Advertising Agency
Ogilvy & Mather London
Digital Strategist
Giles Rhys-Jones
Planner
Michael Hines
Account Manager
Lucy Luo
Account Director
Emily Creek
Brand Manager
Kathleen Ryan
Brand Director
Fernando Machado
Brand Communications Director
Steve Miles
Marketing Director
Stacie Bright
Managing Partner
Stephane Orhan
Client
Unilever
Brand
Dove

Sponsored — Create an Ad

Muffin Top? ✕
It could get worse! Lose it with these spa tips.

Sponsored — Create an Ad

Jelly Rolls? ✕
Reduce your belly fat with this one old trick.

Sponsored — Create an Ad

Need a bigger bust? ✕
This miracle cream will enhance what you want.

Sponsored — Create an Ad

The perfect bum is the one you're sitting on ✕
Tessa and Dove displaced a feel-bad ad with this positive message. Send yours.

Sponsored — Create an Ad

Every body is beautiful ✕
Elena and Dove displaced a feel-bad ad with this positive message. Send yours.

Sponsored — Create an Ad

Think of your cups as half full ✕
Sarah and Dove displaced a feel-bad ad with this positive message. Send yours.

LONDON 51°32'N 0°5'W 9° 12:00

One Copy Song

We helped Adam Tensta release his new single as just one – and only one – copy. 'One Copy Song' is a facebook app that allows only one person to listen to a song at a time before passing it to the next person in line. Fans signed up to listen on Adam's facebook page. Once in line, they could 'cut the line' by tweeting, watching his videos or listening to his other songs on Spotify. Once it was their turn, fans had only one hour to listen and could only play the song once, before it was passed to the next person in line.

–
Writers
Joanna Crean
Mark Moll
Executive Creative Directors
Chuck Tso
Taras Wayner
Chief Creative Officer
Nick Law
Creative Technologist
Alex Swidersky
Design Director
Rasmus Wangelin
Designers
Morten Halvorsen
Rasmus Keger
Music Composer
Adam Tensta
Digital Agency
R/GA
Client
Adam Tensta

NEW YORK CITY 40°40'N 73°56'W 8° 8:00

ADVERTISING DIGITAL ADVERTISING

Mariachi Doritos

To make English parties better you need to add a bit of the Mexican flavour of Doritos. We launched a band 'Mariachi Doritos' that brought Mexican fun to parties everywhere by playing Mariachi versions of tired English classics. Through the brand's facebook page you could book them for a live gig at your party or for a virtual gig over the web. In effect it was the first ever facebook tour. We did 70 gigs in all, and thanked the party host with a bespoke Mariachi song composed from their facebook profile.

–

Art Directors
Thiago de Moraes
Jeremy Tribe
Prabhu Wignarajah
Copywriters
Mark Fairbanks
Jeremy Tribe
Prabhu Wignarajah

Creative Directors
Mark Fairbanks
Thiago de Moraes
Executive Creative Director
Paul Brazier
Producers
Dickie Jeffares
Rebecca Mitchell
Trish Russell
Digital Producers
Angela Meier
James Rowley
Directors
Sniper Twins
Editor
Jinx Godfrey
Advertising Agency
AMV BBDO
Digital Design
AMV LAB
Production Company
Independent Films
Post Production
AMV LAB
The Mill London
Editing
Marshall Street Editors
Audio
AMV LAB
Client
PepsiCo
Brand
Doritos

The Beauty Inside

We auditioned fans for the lead role of Alex in our ongoing social film 'The Beauty Inside'. Alex wakes up each morning with a new physical appearance, so anyone could play the part; both in the film and by participating in his facebook timeline.

–

Art Director
Chaz Whitworth
Copywriter
Neil Ramanan
Creative Director
Jason Apaliski
Executive Creative Director
Jaime Robinson
Chief Creative Officer
PJ Pereira
Agency Producer
Jeff Ferro
Interactive Producer
Erin Davis
Head of Integrated Production
Elisa Moore
Screenwriter
Richard Greenberg

Director
Drake Doremus
Music Composer
Dustin O'Halloran
Sound Designer
Robert Feist
Production Company
B-Reel
Advertising Agency
Pereira & O'Dell
Animation
Laundry
Visual Effects Company
NTROPIC
Editing
Lost Planet Editorial
Strategist
Justin Cox
Strategic Director
Nick Chapman
Media Managers
Dan Beer
Joshua Brandau
Account Director
Henry Arlander
Public Relations Manager
Molly Parsley
Business Director
Xandra Ess
Client Services Director
Gary Theut
Clients
Intel
Toshiba

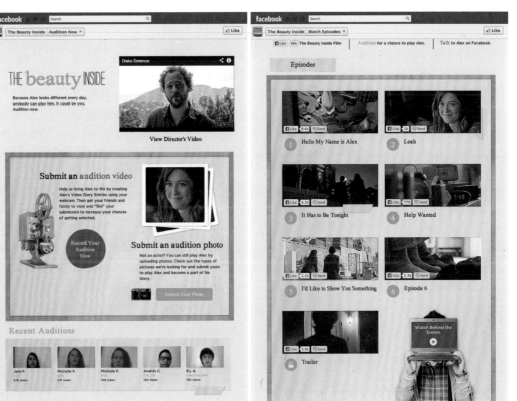

Gang Up For Good

We created an anti-bully kit for schools, with goodies that imparted important life lessons. It ended with blue nail polish and a pledge against bullying driving girls to meanstinks.com. There they could find thousands of tips from a community of 1.2 million supporters.

–
Art Directors
Emma Arnold
Angela Paris
Jon Wyville
Copywriters
Charlotte Haynie
Dave Loew
Creative Directors
AJ Hassan
Diane Magid
Executive Creative Director
Susan Treacy
Chief Creative Officers
Susan Credle
Mark Tutssel
Creative Technologist
Kevin McGlone
Executive Producer
Rob Tripas

Producers
Bobby Gruenberg
Steve Tabor
Senior Producer
Laurie Gustafson
Digital Producers
Andrea Lyons
Rachelle Sartini Garner
Digital Development Director
Mark Renshaw
Advertising Agency
Leo Burnett Chicago
Production Company
Haus Interactive
Media Agency
Starcom MediaVest Group
Public Relations
Marina Maher Communications
Strategic Director
Jason Parker
Account Supervisor
Kristin Ware
Account Manager
Martha Friedner
Account Director
Cindy Blikre
Client
Procter & Gamble
Brand
Secret

YNYWYH Twitter Campaign

For the UK launch of Snickers' global campaign 'You're Not You When You're Hungry' we used Twitter. We asked five celebrities to post a series of out-of-character tweets. As we'd hoped, this produced widespread confusion, with numerous replies and retweets. Each celebrity then tweeted a picture of themselves eating a Snickers together with the campaign line. In all, just 25 tweets were posted, but the campaign received significant coverage online, in newspapers, on radio and TV – and was even mentioned during a debate in the House of Commons.

–
Copywriter
Tim Riley
Creative Directors
Alex Grieve
Adrian Rossi
Executive Creative Director
Paul Brazier
Advertising Agency
AMV BBDO
Production Company
Nomadic Films
Social Community Manager
Naomi Martin
Social Community Director
Paul McCrudden
Account Manager
Bobbie Gannon
Business Affairs Manager
Michelle Holmes
Client
MasterFoods
Brand
Snickers

Metropole Tweetphony

The Metropole Orchestra's subsidy and existence were under threat. We asked the Dutch audience to 'Let the Metropole Orchestra play'. Using our special online keyboard, participants composed a musical tweet. The best tweets were arranged into scores and played live by the orchestra in an eight-hour concert streamed live. A video of each Tweetphony was sent back to its composer. Thousands composed a Tweetphony and 33 were performed. All major media picked up on the story, and after Tweetphony parliament granted the orchestra's funding until 2017.

–
Digital Production Company
Perfect Fools
Advertising Agency
Havas WorldWide Amsterdam
Client
Metropole Orchestra

The Society of Good Taste

Grey Poupon has always preferred quality over quantity. So we launched 'The Society of Good Taste' app – the first facebook page that deletes fans who do not exemplify good taste. To determine those most worthy, the society scanned prospective fans' facebook profiles for check-ins, status updates, grammar and spelling. If a fan proved to be classy enough, they would be accepted. If not, the society would be forced to remove their 'Like' and point them to the nearest finishing school.

–
Art Directors
Tushar Date
Patricia Ortiz
Copywriters
Rachel Carlson
Jamie Toal
Creative Directors
Robin Fitzgerald
Cameron Harris

Executive Creative Directors
Jason Gaboriau
Tom Markham
Associate Creative Directors
Mike Kohlbecker
Alexandra Sann
Chief Creative Officer
Rob Reilly
Creative Technologist
Dan Fox
Technical Director
Brian Wigginton
Designer
Douglas Menezes
Interactive Designer
Anders Svensson
Digital Designers
Sabrina Fraley
Brett Reiland
User Experience Designers
Alex Riegelman
Matt Walsh
Graphic Designer
Eduardo Santiesteban
Advertising Agency
CP+B
Client
Kraft Foods
Brand
Grey Poupon

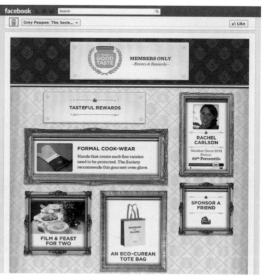

JURY

Jury Foreman
Emma de la Fosse
OgilvyOne London
Ian Bates
Indicia
Nigel Clifton
EHS4D
Christoph Everke
Serviceplan Campaign

Alain Janssens
Publicis Brussels
André Rabanea
TORKE+CC
Jason Williams
Leo Burnett Melbourne

Donation Glasses

Every year, the Pedigree Adoption Drive offers support to thousands of abandoned and mistreated dogs across New Zealand. While the numbers of abandoned dogs hadn't dropped, public interest had. We needed to find a new way to connect. Cinema goers saw two entirely different films on the same screen: one of a mistreated dog who gets rescued; the other of the same mistreated dog who tragically never gets found. Before the movie, viewers were asked to choose between two pairs of glasses: a free pair and a donation pair. That choice decided the fate of the dog on screen.

–

Director
Nic Finlayson
Art Director
Jae Morrison
Copywriter
Levi Slavin
Creative Director
Levi Slavin
Chief Creative Officer
Nick Worthington
Producer
Phil Liefting
Executive Producer
Rob Galluzzo
Digital Producer
Serena Fountain-Jones

Agency Producers
Rob Linkhorn
Jen Storey
Designer
Kate Slavin
Cinematographer
Crighton Bone
Gaffer
Grant McKinnon
Creative Technologist
Emad Tahtouh
Editor
David Coulson
Advertising Agencies
Colenso BBDO/
Proximity New Zealand
FINCH
Post Production
Digital Sparks
Sound Design
Franklin Road
Music Production
Mushroom Records
Round Trip Mars
Planner
Hayley Pardoe
Account Executive
Courtney Herbert
Account Manager
Dave Munn
Group Account Director
Scott Coldham
Brand Manager
Aurelia Moly
Marketing Manager
Oliver Downs
Marketing Director
Pete Simmons
Client
Mars Petcare
Brand
Pedigree

Donation Glasses   Free Glasses

AUCKLAND 36°52'S 174°45'E 15° 1:00

iQ Street View

The Toyota iQ completed Google Street View in Belgium by filming all the streets Google couldn't get into. A PR strategy and making-of video led people to our version of the street view site. There people could tag their streets to invite the street view crew. When their street was filmed, a direct mailing was sent to all people living in the street with a promotional message and an invite to check out their street on iQstreetview.be.

–
Art Director
Naim Baddich
Copywriter
Patrick Glorieux
Graphic Designer
Jeremy Vandenbosch
Creative Director
Peter Ampe
Executive Creative Director
Karen Corrigan
Head of Art
Cecilia Azcarate Isturiz
Agency Producer
Bart Vande Maele
Interactive Producer
Stijn Van Velthoven
Director of Photography
Bob Jeusette
Advertising Agency
Happiness Brussels
Digital Agency
BLISS interactive
Strategist
Joris Joosten
Account Manager
Mehdi Sel
Group Account Director
Pascal Kemajou
Client
Toyota Belgium
Brand
Toyota iQ

ADVERTISING DIRECT

BRUSSELS 50°52'N 4°22'E 10° 13:00

I Have Already Died

The aim was to increase donations to the ALS Foundation Netherlands. ALS (also known as Lou Gehrig's disease) is an incurable and deadly disease of the nervous system, which makes your muscles stop one by one. On average, patients die within three years after being diagnosed. It's cynical, but it's the reason why the pharmaceutical industry doesn't invest in finding a cure. To make people aware of this unknown disease and increase willingness to give, we chose a confrontational strategy. Participating patients made campaign statements, which were aired after they died.

–

Art Director
Jeroen van Zwam
Copywriter
Marcel Hartog
Designer
Dave Fransen
Digital Designers
Jeroen Hessing
Kelly Kouw
**Executive
Creative Directors**
Marcel Hartog
Jeroen van Zwam
Director
Olaf van Gerwen
Producers
George Goudsblom
Remco Roohe
Agency Producers
Marja Borkus
Ron Townsend
Editors
Kim Hinrichs
Michael Horvers
Francisco Rodriguez Bouzas
Photographer
Lukas Göbel
Sound Designer
Robin Schlösser
Retoucher
Jan Hibma
Advertising Agency
Publicis Amsterdam
Production Company
In Case of Fire
Planner
Gertjan Hafkamp
Account Handlers
Marcella van Holten-Beekman
Michiel van der Linden
Client
ALS Foundation Netherlands

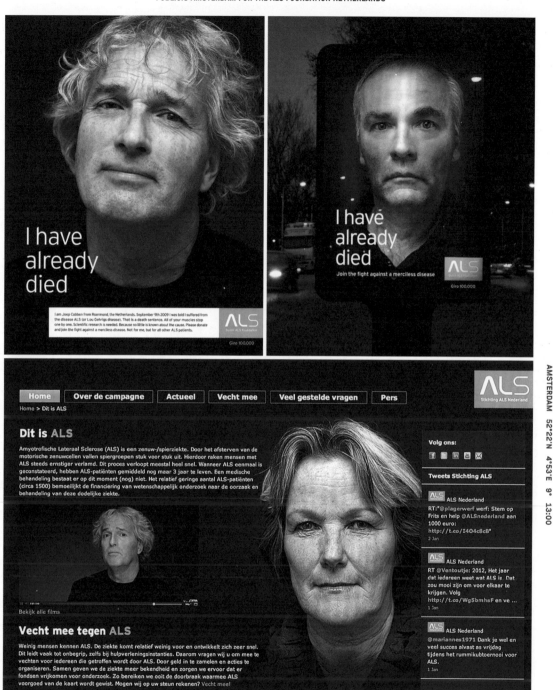

One Copy Song

We helped Adam Tensta release his new single as just one – and only one – copy. 'One Copy Song' is a facebook app that allows only one person to listen to a song at a time before passing it to the next person in line. Fans signed up to listen on Adam's facebook page. Once in line, they could 'cut the line' by tweeting, watching his videos or listening to his other songs on Spotify. Once it was their turn, fans had only one hour to listen and could only play the song once, before it was passed to the next person in line.

—
Writers
Joanna Crean
Mark Moll
Design Director
Rasmus Wangelin
Creative Technologist
Alex Swidersky
Designers
Morten Halvorsen
Rasmus Keger
Executive Creative Directors
Chuck Tso
Taras Wayner
Chief Creative Officer
Nick Law
Music Composer
Adam Tensta
Digital Agency
R/GA
Client
Adam Tensta

ADVERTISING DIRECT

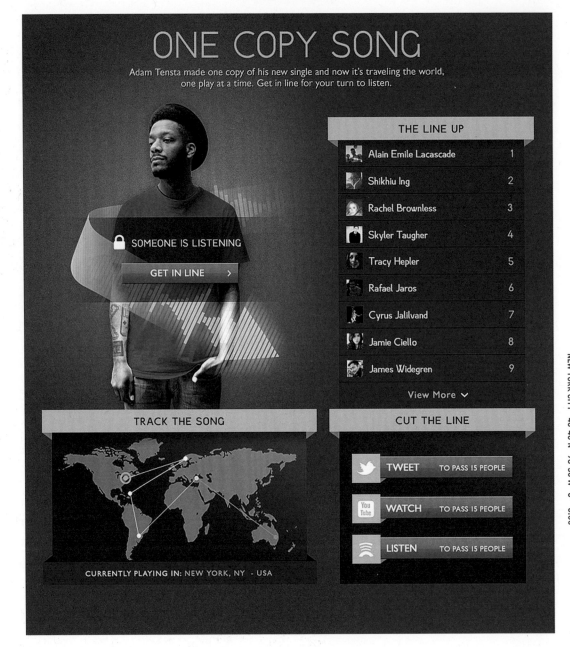

NEW YORK CITY 40°40'N 73°56'W 8° 8:00

My Blood is Red and Black

For Hemoba blood bank to meet the demand of the population during holiday season, it was necessary to increase its supply of donated blood by 25%. As people are only motivated to donate blood when someone they like is in need, we invited them to donate blood for their greatest passion: their football club. We removed the red from Vitória's centenary jersey, leaving it monochrome. Only with the direct participation of the fans, through blood donations, would the colour return, stripe by stripe as blood was being donated. Flyers were distributed at the football stadium and an endorsement by actor Wagner Moura was screened. This was followed by the launch of a TV spot, facebook page and print ads. There was an increase of 46% in blood donations. Approximately 130 million people were impacted, with more than one billion page views on the web and 935 minutes of TV exposure.

—
Art Directors
Rodolfo Fernandes
Guilherme Jahara
Alexandre Pagano
Copywriters
João Caetano Brasil
Erick Mendonça
Creative Directors
Guilherme Jahara
Rodrigo Jatene
Marcelo Reis
Executive Creative Director
Guilherme Jahara
Chief Creative Officer
Marcelo Reis
Agency Producers
Camila Aquino
Celso Groba
Rafael Messias
Maria Fernanda Moura
Advertising Agency
Leo Burnett Tailor Made
Planners
Manuela Gambagorte
Tiago Lara
Marcello Magalhães
Media Managers
André Massuda
Fernando Sales
Account Executive
Anelene Putini
Account Manager
Junior Bottura
Account Director
Pablo Arteaga
Clients
Esporte Clube Vitória
Hemoba

ADVERTISING DIRECT

SÃO PAULO 23°31'S 46°31'W 23° 10:00

A Message from Jennifer

Parkinson's Victoria funds research into Parkinson's disease. It needed to turn what had been an unreliable trickle of donations into a steady flow. Thirty captains of industry were handpicked to receive a CD. Each watched Jennifer, a young woman with Parkinson's, write a name – their name – on an envelope and struggle out into the world. They then saw Jennifer making a painful journey to their office door just for them. Even something as simple as asking for support is difficult for someone with Parkinson's disease.

–
Art Directors
Ruben Cirugeda
Glen Dickson
Copywriters
Ruben Cirugeda
Glen Dickson
Director
Jake Robb
Creative Directors
Ruben Cirugeda
Glen Dickson
Grant Rutherford
Digital Creative Director
Steven Skrekovski
Producer
Jackie Fish
Director of Photography
Garry Richards
Editor
Jake Robb
Sound Engineer
Dylan Stephens
Sound Supervisor
Kate Reynolds
Head of Broadcast
Simon Thomas
Advertising Agency
DDB Group Melbourne
Music Supervision
Level Two Music
Account Manager
Richie Taaffe
Managing Partner
Tess Doughty
Client
Parkinson's Victoria

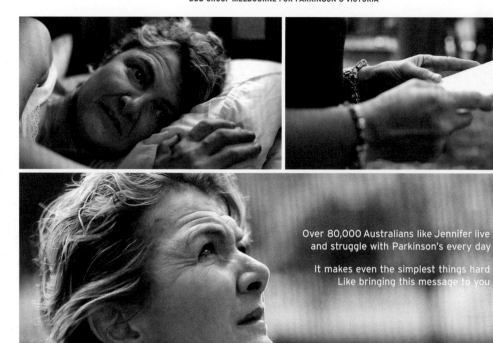

Over 80,000 Australians like Jennifer live and struggle with Parkinson's every day

It makes even the simplest things hard Like bringing this message to you

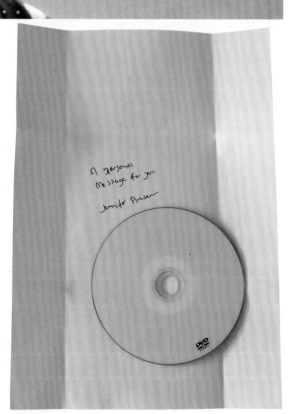

A personal message for you
Jennifer Parker

The Gnome Experiment

Also In Book
in Direct Integrated
Campaigns

Kern & Sohn wanted to become famous for precision scales throughout the world's schools and laboratories. So it carried out a global experiment to prove a little-known phenomenon: gravity varies slightly wherever you go. Kern & Sohn mapped these fluctuations by circulating a gnome and set of scales among scientists around the world. Participants simply recorded the gnome's weight then sent him on his way. The story reached over 355 million people in 152 countries. There was a TED talk about the gnome's adventure. The experiment has become part of the teaching curriculum in several countries.

–
Art Directors
Nick Hearne
Graham Jenks
Copywriter
James Nester
Creative Directors
Graham Jenks
James Nester
**Executive
Creative Directors**
Emma de la Fosse
Charlie Wilson
Producer
Aphrodite Paxinou
Advertising Agency
OgilvyOne Worldwide
London
**Public Relations
Manager**
Blair Metcalfe
Client
Kern & Sohn

ADVERTISING DIRECT

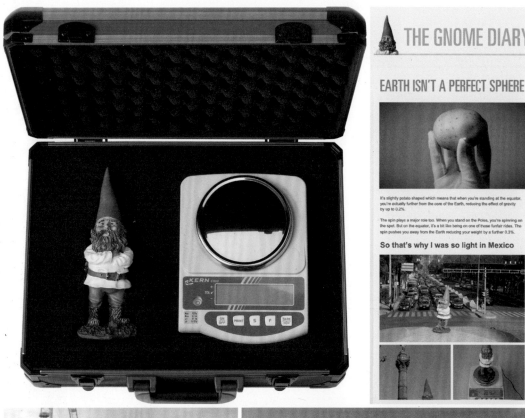

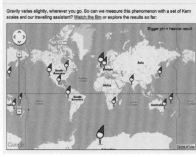

LONDON 51°32'N 0°5'W 9° 12:00

ADVERTISING DIRECT

NRMA Car Creation

NRMA Insurance discovered that there are thousands of parts on Australian cars that it covers, but its competitors won't. So many in fact, that you could build an entire working car out of them. So that's exactly what they did. A car made from over 52 different models and 30,000 parts. A fully integrated campaign launched the idea and NRMA invited people to guide the mechanics building the car by submitting uninsured parts from their own cars. When complete, it was launched like a real car and Top Gear Australia presenter Shane Jacobson gave it a review and took it for a test drive.

–

Art Director
Craig Brooks
Copywriter
Tammy Keegan
Creative Director
Gavin McLeod
Digital Creative Director
Russ Tucker
Executive Creative Directors
Dave Bowman
Matty Burton
Associate Creative Directors
Dave Brady
Asheen Naidu
Direction
The Glue Society
(Matt Devine &
James Dive)

Digital Producer
Evan Clements
Executive Digital Producer
Rebecca Merrifield
Creative Technologists
Lewis Benge
Danny Mcgillick
Photographer
Andreas Smetana
Head of Broadcast Production
Honae MacNeill
Advertising Agency
Whybin\TBWA\DAN
Sydney
Production Companies
Revolver
Will O'Rourke
Editing
The Editors
Planner
Cam Deague
Executive Planning Director
Hristos Varouhas
Account Directors
Bridget Cleary
Bryony Marks
Digital Account Director
Serena Ryan
Client Services Director
Peter Fitzhardinge
Public Relations Managers
Rob Lowe
Sydney Spagnoletti
Client
Insurance Australia
Group
Brand
NRMA Insurance

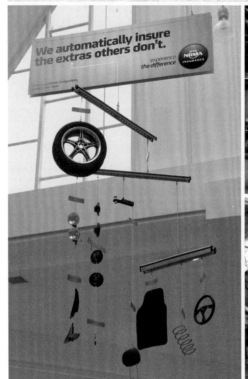

Demand Equal Pay

On average, women in New Zealand are paid 10% less than their male counterparts. To draw attention to this imbalance, we decided to charge men 10% more than women. All our communication encouraged New Zealanders to visit the website and show their support for the Pay Equality Bill. It sparked debate in both national and international media. Launch month saw visitors to the site increase by 9,000% and donations by 22% compared to the previous month. Most importantly, we received all the signatures we needed and the Pay Equality Bill has now been put forward to Parliament to become an Act.

–
Art Directors
Ben Barnes
Lisa Fedyszyn
Toby Morris
Copywriters
Simone Louis
Jonathan McMahon
Matt Webster
Designer
Amanda Summersby
Interactive Designer
Sam Schrey
Creative Director
Steve Kane
Digital Creative Director
Aaron Goldring
Executive Creative Director
Andy Fackrell
Agency Producers
Jane Mill
Rebecca Rassie
Developers
Robbie Boyd
Jarrad Edwards
Print Producer
Andy Robilliard
Advertising Agency
DDB New Zealand
Account Directors
Sean Brown
Jenny Travers
Group Account Director
Bob Glancy
Business Director
Paul Pritchard
Client
YWCA Auckland

ADVERTISING DIRECT

AUCKLAND 36°52'S 174°45'E 15° 1:00

133

Mobile Medic

The brief was to recruit medical students worthy of a Defence Force University Sponsorship. To find the best we created medically diagnosable advertising, which doubled as an entrance exam. 'Mobile Medic' allowed students to use a range of diagnostic techniques to identify and treat medical conditions using their smartphones. Visual and audio augmentation immersed them in the role of Medical Officer, on real Defence Force scenarios. Students entered their details and received their results instantly. Those who performed best were offered a Defence Force University Sponsorship application.

Art Director
Jake Barrow
Copywriter
Matt Lawson
Designers
Marcus Byrne
Janna Mamar

Creative Director
Chris Northam
Chief Creative Officer
Ben Coulson
Photographer
Hugh Peachy
Digital Producer
Carrie Burman
Audio Producer
Katherine Muir
Sound Engineer
Paul Baxter
Developer
Chuck Brandt
User Experience Architect
Luke Tellefson
Retoucher
Mal Stark
Advertising Agency
George Patterson Y&R Melbourne
Digital Agency
VML
Strategist
Tom Ward
Account Handler
Jason Bass
Account Executives
Chris Bush
Daniel Smith
Account Director
Janet Proposch
Group Account Director
Julian Bell
Client
Defence Force Recruiting

ADVERTISING DIRECT

MELBOURNE 37°47'S 144°58'E 12° 23:00

Hashtag Killer Case

The 'Hashtag Killer'
campaign set out to
eradicate the ironic
#FirstWorldProblems
meme, in which
people tweet about
such life burdens as
non-heated leather
seats or forgetting
their maid's last
name. In the process,
it aimed to raise
awareness about
serious developing
world issues. For the
anthem commercial,
we gathered real
'First World Problem'
tweets and then
approached people in
Haiti to recite them.
But perhaps even
more effective was the
series of personalised
response videos, in
which various Haitians
consoled those using
the hashtag on Twitter.

—
Art Director
Sam Shepherd
Copywriter
Frank Cartagena
Director
Alec Helm
**Executive Creative
Director**
Menno Kluin
**Chief Creative
Officer**
Matt Eastwood
Designers
Zeynep Aydogmus
Gina Lin
Juan Carlos Pagan
Producer
Lindsey Hutter
Executive Producer
Ed Zazzera
Editors
Alec Helm
Melanie Meditz
Advertising Agency
DDD New York
Client
Water is Life

ADVERTISING   DIRECT

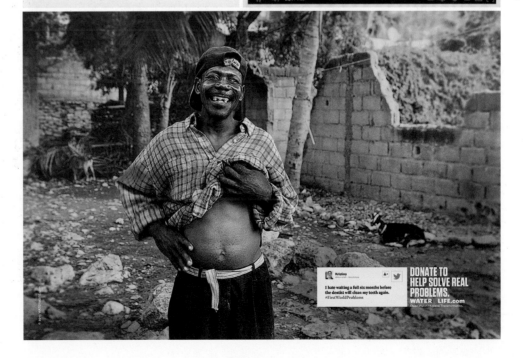

NEW YORK CITY   40°40'N   73°56'W   8°   8:00

ADVERTISING DIRECT

The Dove Ad Makeover

Negative online ads feed women's insecurities by targeting their beauty anxieties. We helped empower women to displace negative ads with positive messages.

–
Art Directors
Trevallyn Hall
Stephanie Symonds
Copywriters
Laura Rogers
Margo Young
Creative Director
Ivan Pols
Executive Creative Director
Gerry Human
Chief Creative Officer
Gerry Human
Creative Technologist
Craig Blagg
Designer
Simone Zharadka
Developer
Martin Robertson
Information Architect
Anthony Butterfield
Producer
Carl Phillips

Digital Producer
Sasha Dunn
Agency Producer
Fiona Renfrew
Animation Director
Carl Addy
Editor
James Mortner
Advertising Agency
Ogilvy & Mather London
Digital Strategist
Giles Rhys-Jones
Planner
Michael Hines
Account Manager
Lucy Luo
Account Director
Emily Creek
Brand Manager
Kathleen Ryan
Brand Director
Fernando Machado
Brand Communications Director
Steve Miles
Managing Partner
Stephane Orhan
Marketing Director
Stacie Bright
Client
Unilever
Brand
Dove

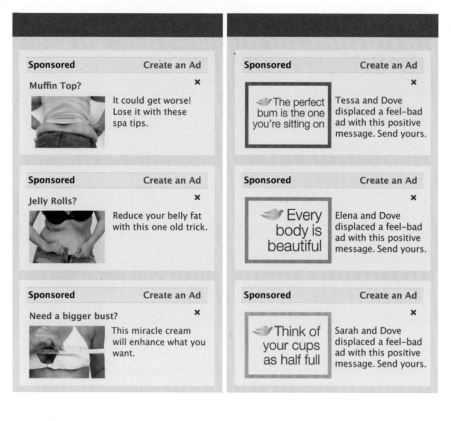

LONDON 51°32'N 0°5'W 9° 12:00

Golden Chains

ALB is an emerging French musician who's planning to release his second album in 2013. Like many other artists, ALB isn't supported by a major label yet. So, to promote and finance his upcoming album, ALB came up with 'Golden Chains', a participative music video in which the artist took up the challenge of selling his personal everyday items – for real. The plan was to use the revenue gained to fund the production of his next album.

–
Art Director
Julien Boissinot
Copywriter
Kevin Salembier
Creative Directors
Matthieu Elkaim
Olivier Lefebvre
Benjamin Marchal
Director
Johnatan Broda
Interactive Technical Director
Anthony Hamelle
Producer
Willy Morence
Agency Producer
Jean-Gabriel Saint Paul
Digital Agency
ACNE Production
Advertising Agency
CLM BBDO
Production Company
Carnibird
Sound Design
Green United Music
Music Supervision
Green United Music
Public Relations Manager
Lauren Weber
Client
ALB

PARIS 48°48'N 2°20'E 10° 13:00

○

IN BOOK IN DIRECT, DIRECT RESPONSE/TV & CINEMA ADVERTISING
GEORGE PATTERSON Y&R MELBOURNE AND THE CAMPAIGN PALACE FOR THE NEW SOUTH WALES GOVERNMENT

Planning to Make a Plan: Computer / TV / Car

Australia has suffered some of the most devastating bush fires in history because of its dry climate. But after two wet seasons and growth in rural New South Wales, what fire fighters feared more than the driest summer in decades was, in fact, apathy. The people of rural New South Wales needed to know how to protect themselves, their families and their property more than ever. That having a bush fire survival plan was essential. And not something that could wait till later.

–
Director
Dave Klaiber
Art Director
John Koay
Copywriter
Karl Fleet
Chief Creative Officer
Reed Collins
Producers
Rach Paget
Vicky Rhedey
Designer
Helen Sham
Editor
Danny Tait
Advertising Agencies
George Patterson
Y&R Melbourne
The Campaign Palace
Planner
Karen Dwyer
Account Directors
Sari De
Holly McDavitt
Group Account Director
Toby McKinnon
Client
New South Wales Government

ADVERTISING DIRECT

Computer

TV

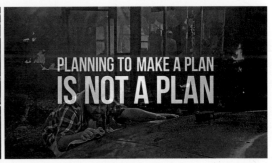

Car

MELBOURNE 37°47'S 144°58'E 12° 23:00

Half of HBO for Free

Claro, Guatemala's largest cable provider, teamed up with HBO to increase subscriptions to the premium channel. It decided to take down the usual blank screen that non-subscribers see and replace it with half of the HBO picture. Suddenly, viewers could see what they were missing – getting half of a great story is even worse than not getting the story at all.

–
Director
Edgar Ramirez
Copywriter
Ronald Arriola
Creative Director
Herberth Monterroso
Chief Creative Officer
Ramiro Eduardo
Production Company
16mm
Advertising Agency
Ogilvy & Mather Guatemala
Post Production
Magnetico
Account Handlers
Gustavo Alejos
Mariana Morales
Marketing Manager
Ana Rena Garcia Salas
Client
Claro

ADVERTISING DIRECT

GUATEMALA CITY 14°37'N 90°31'W 16° 6:00

Radio Ghosts

One in eleven deaths caused by car accident involves drink driving. To raise awareness we installed small radio stations in the shape of wooden crosses throughout Hamburg, at actual locations where car accidents caused by drink happened. Through these, we played radio spots describing the accident by the deceased victims: 'radio ghosts'. While stationary, a driver's attention was drawn to the cross by a personal address from the radio ghost. 'Sorry. I'm talking to all drivers on this corner. Because I died here. Right there at the railing, that's my death cross'. These small radio stations aired the story of the victims directly to the traffic stopping nearby.

–
Copywriter
Andreas Schriewer
Creative Director
Marc Vosshall
Executive Creative Director
Till Diestel
Chief Creative Officer
Alexander Schill
Creative Producer
Florian Panier
Producers
Philipp Feit
Eduardo Garcia
Advertising Agency
Serviceplan München
Production Company
German Wahnsinn
Account Managers
Kristian von Elm
Ines Herbold
Client
Johanniter-Unfall-Hilfe

ADVERTISING DIRECT

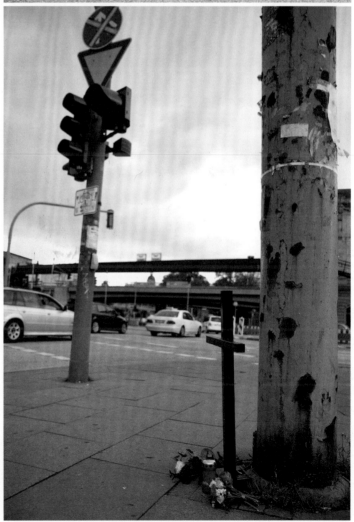

MUNICH 48°8'N 11°35'E 10° 13:00

Builders of Sound

The brief was to promote LEGO Star Wars sets in cinemas for the release of 'Star Wars 3D – Episode 1'. So we let LEGO play music – with a gigantic barrel organ made from LEGO Star Wars. On it, over 20,000 bricks were arranged so that they played the Star Wars main theme. Fans could play the organ in cinemas all over Germany and order the built sets via a QR code. Fans from around the world could also play the organ on a microsite. We achieved 60,000 contacts in cinemas, and articles in major international blogs. Five of the sets were among the best selling toys in Germany.

–
Art Directors
Andreas Balog
Marijo Sanje
Copywriters
Nicolas Becker
Lorenz Langgartner,
Designers
Axel Al-Rubaie
Rene Hoffmeister
Graphic Designer
Anna Tracy Wodera
Creative Directors
Oliver Palmer
Alexander Rehm
Digital Creative Director
Markus Maczey
Executive Creative Director
Matthias Harbeck
Chief Creative Officer
Alexander Schill
Producer
Florian Panier
Advertising Agency
Serviceplan
München
Sound Design
Westpark Studios
Account Directors
Monika Klingenfuss
Denise Mancinone
Client
LEGO

ADVERTISING DIRECT

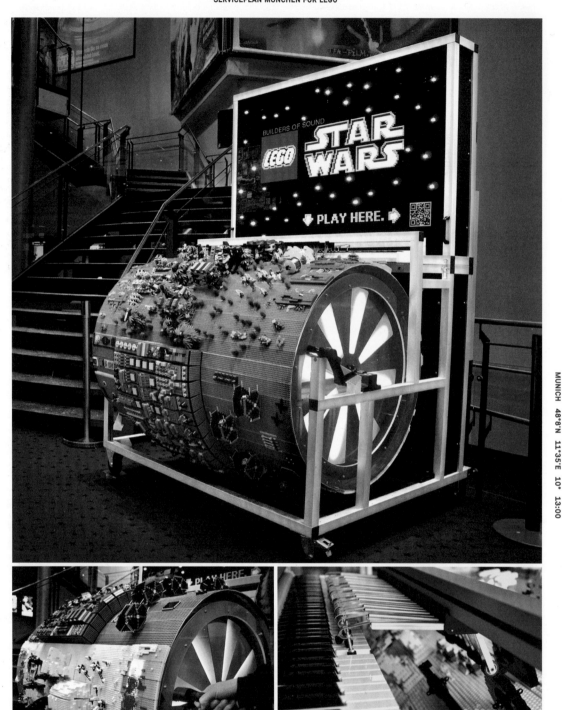

MUNICH 48°8'N 11°35'E 10° 13:00

Bridge of Life

A large number of people jump off the Mapo Bridge in South Korea every year. Our idea to prevent further suicides was not simply to install a physical device to hinder the attempts, but to create an interactive bridge that would change people's minds through communication. The sensors on the guardrails switched the lights on when people walked by and short messages appeared as if the bridge was speaking to passers-by. They included warm and kind words that appeased the anxious and confused minds of those attempting to end their lives.

–
Art Directors
Jiyeon Choi
Jaeyeon Kim
Minjoo Kim
Chaehoon Lee
Hyungkyun Oh
Jinwoo Ryu
Copywriters
Yongkyu Choi
Yukyung Joo
Youngjun Kim
Jieun Park
Creative Director
Joohoon Lee
Executive Creative Director
Thomas Hongtack Kim
Chief Creative Officer
Jeongkeun Yoo
Advertising Agency
Cheil Worldwide
Account Executives
Kyungtae Kim
Inyoung Lee
Account Director
Jungho Park
Client
Samsung Life Insurance

ADVERTISING DIRECT

SEOUL 37°33'N 126°58'E 5° 21:00

Recipe Receipt

Most people still think mayonnaise is only good for sandwiches. And even though Hellmann's has been successfully teaching new uses to consumers, one challenge still remained: the point of sale. We came up with a digital solution that would inspire shoppers to integrate Hellmann's mayonnaise into their daily cooking routine. When a consumer buys Hellmann's at the supermarket, the software in the cash register detects it and starts matching it with other purchased products, printing a personalised recipe on the receipt itself.

–
Art Directors
Raphael Lucone
Guilherme Nobrega
Rafael Rizuto
Copywriters
Ricardo Lins
Eduardo Marques
Creative Directors
Rubens Filho
Eduardo Marques
Executive Creative Directors
Claudio Lima
Fred Saldanha
Chief Creative Officer
Anselmo Ramos
Producers
Nana Bittencourt
Juscelino Vieira
Advertising Agency
Ogilvy Brazil
Project Manager
Paula Santana
Client
Unilever
Brand
Hellmann's

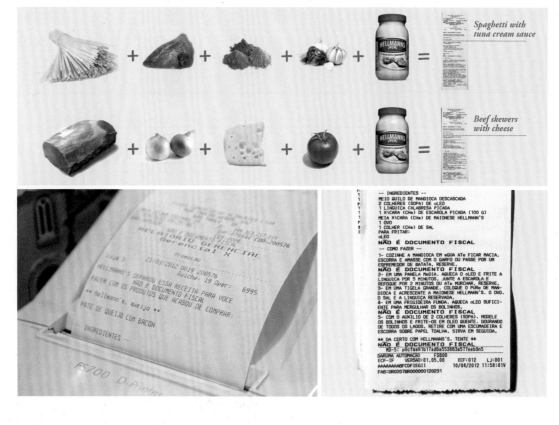

Spaghetti with tuna cream sauce

Beef skewers with cheese

The BlueMotion Label

BlueMotion is the eco-conscious Volkswagen range. So we asked a simple question: can a print ad help save paper, not waste it? We created The BlueMotion Label – a small insert with prepaid postage on it that could be used to recycle magazines. The idea turned the network of South African post boxes into neighbourhood recycling bins. By December 2012, we had a 14% response rate (nearly three times the projected 5%), and as a result rolled out nationwide by the second quarter of 2013. The smallest VW ad we've ever made has the potential to make the biggest difference.

–
Art Director
Prabashan Gopalakrishnan Pather
Copywriter
Sanjiv Mistry
Creative Directors
Sanjiv Mistry
Prabashan Gopalakrishnan Pather
Executive Creative Director
Chris Gotz
Print Producer
Lara Bothma
Advertising Agency
Ogilvy Cape Town
Project Manager
Cathy Day
Account Handlers
Lauren Baker
Greg Tebbutt
Jason Yankelowitz
Client
Volkswagen
Brand
BlueMotion

Hangman

Some countries like Iraq, Egypt, Eritrea and Sudan are still practising capital punishment by hanging. The decision of life or death is frequently based on the arbitrariness of state leaders. The international print campaign 'Hangman' by The International Society for Human Rights aims to raise awareness of these grievances with striking posters at major airports. Using the principle of the popular game Hangman, the campaign makes it clear how easy it can be to help. Each observer will be challenged to finish the Hangman game before it's too late, by donating $, €, £ or ¥ via text message.

–
Art Directors
Nicoletta Kiermanszek
Sven Knaebel
Copywriter
Dominique Becker
Photographer
Robert Eikelpoth
Creative Directors
Sebastian Hardieck
Christian Mommertz
Michael Plueckhahn
Chief Creative Officer
Wolfgang Schneider
Agency Producer
Bernhard Burg
Advertising Agency
BBDO Proximity Düsseldorf
Account Directors
Judith Hillebrand
Liselotte Schwenkert
Art Buyer
Birgit Paulat
Client
International Society for Human Rights

ADVERTISING DIRECT

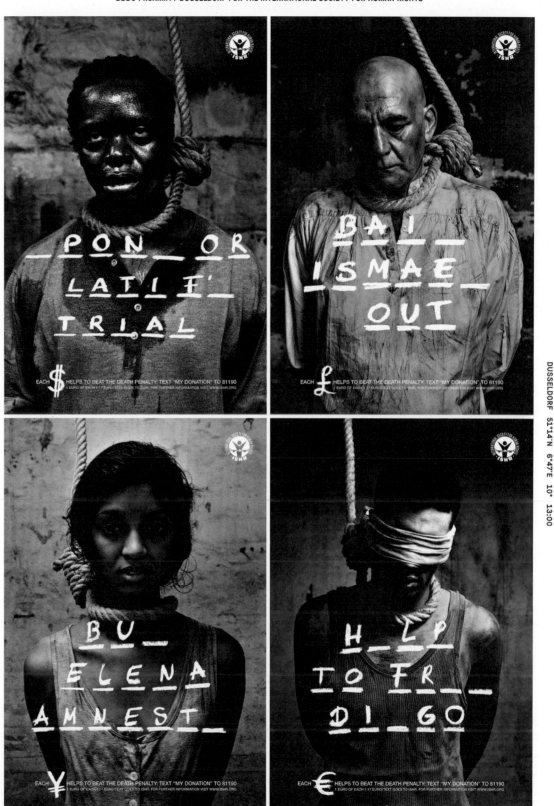

DÜSSELDORF 51°14'N 6°47'E 10° 13:00

**Women's Aid
Campaign**

In association with
the Metropolitan
Police, this campaign
encourages the public
to stop domestic
violence by calling
the police whenever
they hear it. The
radio ads feature the
horrifying sounds of
domestic abuse.
A voiceover explains
that, while the sounds
are distressing, they
will continue until
listeners dial a given
number to have them
stopped, 'just as in
real life, making a
call can make it stop'.

–
Copywriter
Martin Loraine
Art Director
Steve Jones
Creative Director
Paul Brazier
**Executive
Creative Director**
Paul Brazier
Director
Dominic Savage
Producers
Stephen Gash
Rebecca Scharf
Recording Engineer
Ben Gulvin
Sound Designer
Ben Gulvin
Advertising Agency
AMV BBDO
**Production
Company**
QI Commercials
Client
The London
Metropolitan Police
Service
Women's Aid

ADVERTISING   DIRECT

Call to Stop

Sounds are loud but muffled and indistinct, as if heard through a wall. The overall impression is chaotic disorder and destruction.

FVO Women's Aid want the public to help stop domestic violence by calling the police if they hear it. We want people to get used to the idea that making a call stops the sounds of domestic abuse. The following sounds are typical. This is a woman being punched in the face.

SFX Muffled argument and something crashing to the floor

FVO This is a woman's fingers being trapped in a door.

SFX Muffled slamming door and shout of pain

FVO This is a woman's jaw being broken.

SFX Muffled scuffle and woman's scream

SFX Man shouting angrily as a woman cries

FVO (over SFX)
The sounds are distressing. We'd understand if you never want to hear them again. In fact, we'd welcome it. To stop the sounds, call 0800 5877 332. Until someone calls, the sounds will continue. This is a woman being pushed down stairs.

SFX Muffled banging and screaming

FVO This is her being choked.

SFX Muffled man's voice shouting and furniture toppling

SFX Fade

FVO To stop the sounds, call 0800 5877 332.
Just as in real life, making a call can make it stop.
WomensAid.org.uk

Sounds in this commercial are loud but muffled, as if heard through a wall.

FVO Women's Aid are asking the public to help stop domestic violence by calling the police if they hear it. We want people to get used to the idea that making a simple call can stop the sounds of such violence. So recently, we've been playing the horrifying sounds of domestic abuse.

SFX Muffled argument and something crashing to the floor

FVO We said we'd continue until someone calls a given number to make it stop.

SFX Muffled scuffle and woman's scream

FVO As yet, no one has. So, as with real domestic violence, until someone calls, it will go on. To make it stop, call 0800 5877 332.

This is a woman being dragged by her hair.

SFX Muffled man shouting and woman whimpering

SFX Fade

FVO To stop the sounds, call 0800 5877 332. Just as in real life, making a call can make it stop. Women's Aid.

FVO During recent commercial breaks, Women's Aid have been playing the sounds of domestic violence. We said we'd play the sounds until someone called to make it stop.

Encouragingly, we received our first call within minutes, so now, it's stopped.'

And it's just like that in real life. If you hear the horrifying sounds of domestic violence, call the police.

Making a call can make it stop. Women's Aid.

LONDON 51°32'N 0°5'W 9° 12:00

145

Pencils Equal Profits

**Also In Book
in Writing for Direct**

Every year the
Australasian Writers
and Art Directors
Association
(AWARD) needs
a call for entries to
drive the submission
of creative advertising
work into its award
show. And every year
that call for entries
targets those who
win the awards – the
advertising creatives.
But the truth is, with
so many awards out
there competing for
the agency 'entry
dollar', we needed
to reach a different
audience. Those
who actually control
the agency awards
budget. So we decided
to target and hero the
finance directors
of ad agencies. We
also knew we had to
hero what they care
about – profits.

–
Art Director
Brett Colliver
Copywriter
Nick Kelly
Graphic Designer
Jake Turnbull
Creative Directors
Tom Martin
Julian Schreiber
**Executive
Creative Director**
Ant Keogh
Creative Chairman
James McGrath
Retoucher
Mike McCall
Post Producer
Mary Darzi
Advertising Agency
Clemenger BBDO
Melbourne
Account Manager
Kate McCarthy
Client
Australasian Writers
and Art Directors
Association

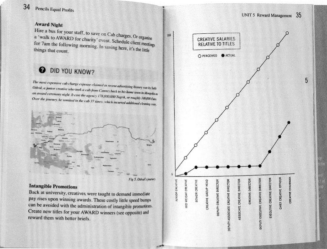

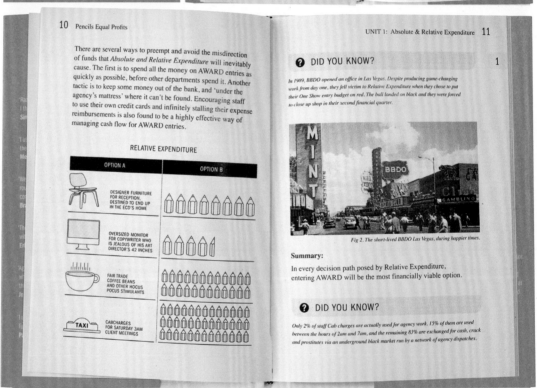

ADVERTISING DIRECT

MELBOURNE 37°47'S 144°58'E 12° 23:00

Stop the Debt
Starter Pack

The task for QM Financial was to warn Indonesians about the risk of having too many credit cards and the dangers of accumulating debt. We parodied a typical pre-approved credit card starter pack and sent it from a fictitious bank. Proper financial advice was strategically plastered throughout the direct mail, educating the financially illiterate recipient. It also contained invites to QM Financial seminars. The large attendance allowed QM Financial to make personal connections with people and shattered the stereotypes of financial planners as being intimidating and money-sucking.

–
Senior Art Director
Tania Huiny
Senior Copywriter
Adra Gesza
Photographer
Woko
Creative Director
Bondan Eko
Executive
Creative Director
Ferly Novriadi
Chief Creative
Officer
Din Sumedi
Agency Producer
Anastasia Nova
Advertising Agency
Lowe Indonesia
Account Manager
Ferry Antono
Account Director
Rachma Devi
Client
QM Financial

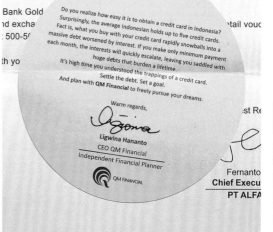

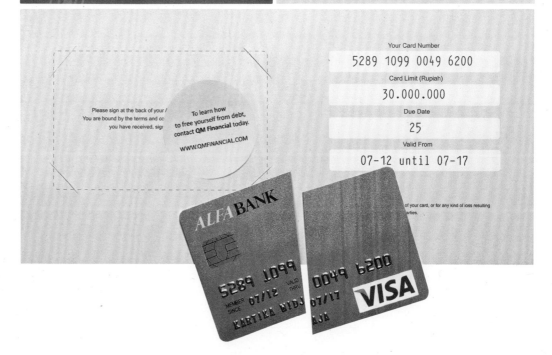

The Daily Abuse

Also In Book
in Art Direction
for Direct

'The Daily Abuse' is
a 48-page newspaper
filled with nothing but
the names of 241,095
children. Produced by
Innocence in Danger,
it comprised 210
articles, diagrams
and ads filled with
names that represent
the children who are
abused on one single
day. The final sentence
of each article reported
what had been done to
them. The newspaper
was published on
19 November 2012 –
the International Day
Against Child Abuse
– in nine languages,
across 23 cities, with
720,000 copies and
over one million
readers. The message:
it's the attention of
every one of us that
will bring on change.

–
Art Directors
Robin Lorentschat
Iliés Terki-Hassaine
Copywriter
Angeliki Karnoupaki
Graphic Designers
Christopher
Hanebuth
Christoph Klasen
**Executive
Creative Directors**
Maik Kaehler
Christoph Nann
Chief Creative Officer
Alexander Schill
Creative Producer
Florian Panier
Agency Producer
Sven Simon
Advertising Agency
Serviceplan München
Account Managers
Anna Hacker
Florian Klietz
Client
Innocence in Danger

ADVERTISING   DIRECT

MUNICH   48°8'N   11°35'E   10°   13:00

The Wine List

Research showed that DB Export Dry's target market of young males didn't like wine, but they drank it to fit in. So we set out to save them from Sauvignon and get them a beer. We created an ad disguised as a wine list. Instead of a long list of elaborate, hard-to-pronounce vintages, the wine list talked men through all the reasons they should stop playing pretend and order an Export Dry instead.

—

Copywriters
Levi Slavin
Simon Vicars
Art Director
James Tucker
Designer
Kate Slavin
Creative Director
Levi Slavin
Chief Creative Officer
Nick Worthington
Producer
Sheriden Derby
Advertising Agency
Colenso BBDO/
Proximity New
Zealand
Strategist
Stacey Stephenson
Planners
James Hurman
Hayley Pardoe
Account Managers
Stefanie Robertson
Patrick Rowley
Group Account Director
Tim Ellis
Marketing Managers
Russell Browne
Clare Morgan
Client
DB Breweries
Brand
Export Dry

ADVERTISING DIRECT

AUCKLAND 36°52'S 174°45'E 15° 1:00

THE WINE LIST

It's just been handed to you.
DEAR GOD, WHAT DO YOU DO NOW?
JUST STARE AT THE PAGE.

Can they tell your eyes aren't moving?
MAYBE.
TRY READING A FEW LINES.

Is it too soon to look up?
PROBABLY.
RUB YOUR CHIN FOR A BIT.

That's long enough. Time to pick one.
SEE IF YOU CAN SPOT ANY NAMES YOU KNOW.
NO. NO. NO. NO. NO. NO.

Right, that's not working.
SEE IF YOU CAN SPOT ANY WORDS IN ENGLISH.
NOPE.

Time to pick the second cheapest.
WOW. YOU'D PROBABLY NEED A SECOND MOUTH TO PRONOUNCE THAT.
MAYBE JUST POINT.

Then it's; swirl, sniff, sip, and say, "Mmm, very nice thanks."
MAYBE THIS TIME TRY, "MMM, THAT TASTES NICE AND OLD."
YEAH, THAT WORKS.

How did it get to this?
WINE ISN'T YOU.
BEER IS YOU.

That's why Morton Coutts, Head Brewer at DB Breweries, created Export Dry.
A SOPHISTICATED LAGER THAT'S CRISP, REFRESHING AND FULL OF FLAVOUR.
PERFECT FOR ANY OCCASION. ESPECIALLY OCCASIONS LIKE THIS.

So it looks like you've made your selection.
IN A MOMENT YOU ARE GOING TO SIT UP STRAIGHT,
HAND BACK THE WINE LIST AND SAY PROUDLY, "I'LL HAVE AN EXPORT DRY."

OK, you can look up now.

We Sent Their Briefs Back

We needed to introduce our clients to our newly formed design department. We decided to be proactive and intercept existing above-the-line briefs. We created intricate pieces of paper art, transforming our clients' briefs into multi-dimensional design pieces. We then sent our clients' briefs back to them, proving that TBWA \ Design can do amazing things with their briefs. The design studio received its first new brief from a client just five days later. Even more notably, new design work in the agency rose by 450% within the first six weeks.

—
Director
Brett de Vos
Art Directors
Jade Manning
Ilze Venter
Copywriter
Vincent Osmond
Designers
Jason Fieldgage
Grame van Jaarsveld
Katleho Mofolo
Leigh-Anne Salonika
Sacha Traest
Creative Directors
Mike Groenewald
Sacha Traest
Executive Creative Directors
Matthew Brink
Adam Livesey
Agency Producer
Craig Walker
Editor
Brett de Vos
Advertising Agency
TBWA\Hunt\Lascaris
Johannesburg
Art Buyer
Simone Allem
Client
TBWA\Hunt\Lascaris
Johannesburg

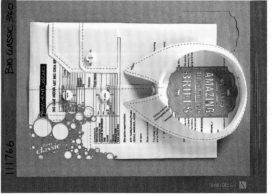

Pantone Queen

For 60 years, Her
Majesty has colour
matched her hats,
dresses and coats
perfectly, as any
queen should.
So we created
'Pantone Queen';
a Pantone colour
guide celebrating
60 of her iconic
single colour outfits,
painstakingly
matching the exact
Pantone reference
to the exact date and
location she wore
them throughout her
60-year reign. The
book was loved so
much by the Royal
Family, it was made
official Diamond
Jubilee memorabilia,
royally endorsing
'Pantone Queen'.
The queens were
numbered from
one to 60, and
right now resting in
Buckingham Palace
is number one, the
Queen's very own
Pantone Queen.

–
Art Director
Will Thacker
Copywriter
Blake Waters
**Executive
Creative Director**
Justin Tindall
Producer
Janice Capewell
Print Producer
Chris Dale
Advertising Agency
Leo Burnett London
Art Buyer
Leah Mitchell
Client
Pantone

ADVERTISING DIRECT

LONDON 51°32'N 0°5'W 9° 12:00

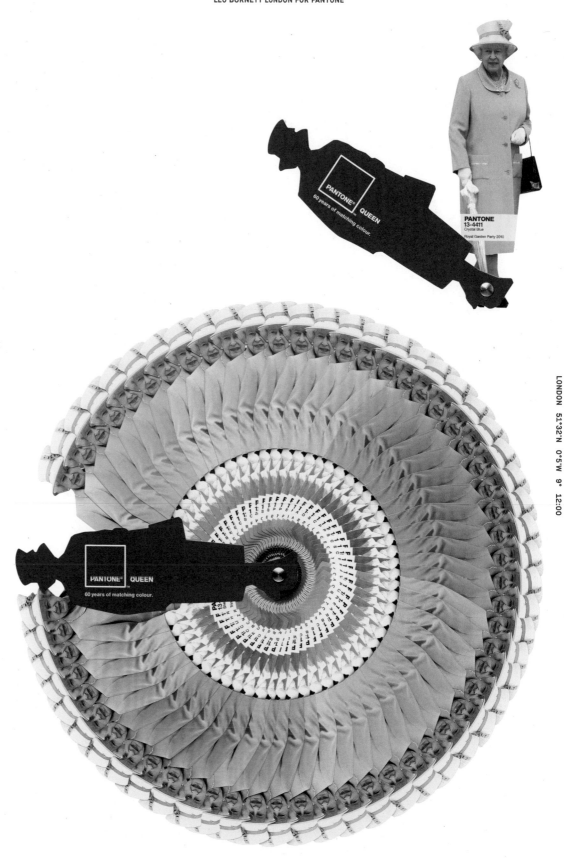

Nike+ FuelBand

Nike came to us to realise an idea: a wristband device that tracks your daily activity and a common, universal metric called Fuel for every active body out there. They asked us to design the entire user experience. We ensured ease of use: set your goal, and get from red to green. If you meet your goal, animations celebrate your performance. Data graphics show where you were most active daily, weekly, monthly, and beyond. We created Bluetooth sync technology so the results of your day's activities can be transferred to your mobile device and visualised on the FuelBand app.

–

Art Director
Ray Sison
Copywriter
Evan Maranca
Designer
Ellen Pai
Creative Directors
Cesar Marchetti
Kirill Yeretsky
Executive Creative Director
Tara Greer
Associate Creative Directors
Keith Byrne
Gaurabh Mathure
Executive Producer
Avery Holden
Senior Producers
Alan Donnelly
Guy Helson
Michael Klimkewicz
Technical Directors
Nick Coronges
Sune Kaae
Daniel Katz
Senior Software Engineers
Robert Carlsen
Fernando Mazzon
Niall McCormack
Digital Agency
R/GA
Head of Product
Ian Spalter
Quality Assurance Manager
Leslie Chong
Managing Director
Jennifer Allen
Client
Nike
Brand
Nike+

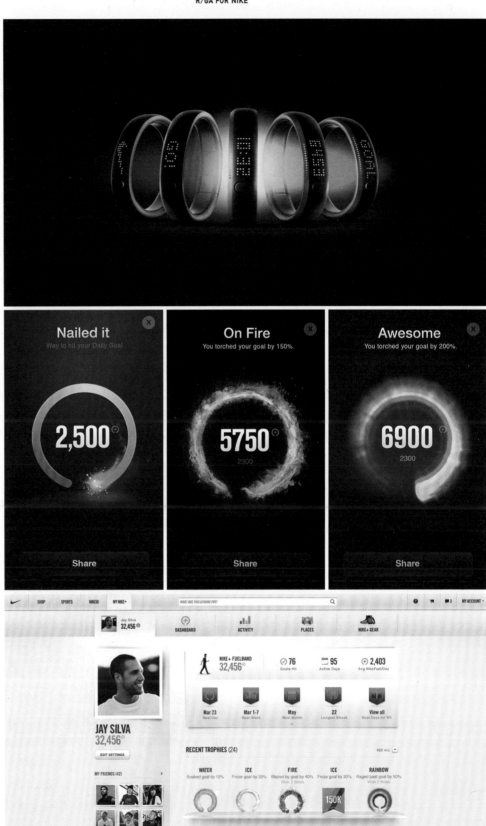

● ●

YELLOW PENCIL IN INTEGRATED & EARNED MEDIA, EARNED MEDIA CAMPAIGNS
LEO BURNETT TAILOR MADE FOR ESPORTE CLUBE VITÓRIA & HEMOBA

My Blood is
Red and Black

Also a Nomination
in Integrated

For Hemoba blood
bank to meet the
demand of the
population during
holiday season, it was
necessary to increase
its supply of donated
blood by 25%. As
people are only
motivated to donate
blood when someone
they like is in need,
we invited them to
donate blood for their
greatest passion: their
football club. We
removed the red from
Vitória's centenary
jersey, leaving it
monochrome. Only
with the direct
participation of the
fans, through blood
donations, would the
colour return, stripe
by stripe as blood was
being donated. Flyers
were distributed at the
football stadium and
an endorsement by
actor Wagner Moura
was screened. This
was followed by the
launch of a TV spot,
facebook page and
print ads. There was
an increase of 46%
in blood donations.
Approximately 130
million people were
impacted, with more
than one billion page
views on the web and
935 minutes of TV
exposure.

–
Art Directors
Rodolfo Fernandes
Guilherme Jahara
Alexandre Pagano
Copywriters
João Caetano Brasil
Erick Mendonça
Creative Directors
Guilherme Jahara
Rodrigo Jatene
Marcelo Reis
Executive
Creative Director
Guilherme Jahara
Chief Creative
Officer
Marcelo Reis
Agency Producers
Camila Aquino
Maria Fernanda
Moura
Celso Groba
Rafael Messias
Advertising Agency
Leo Burnett Tailor
Made
Media Managers
André Massuda
Fernando Sales
Planners
Manuela
Gambagorte
Tiago Lara
Marcello Magalhães
Account Executive
Anelene Putini
Account Manager
Junior Bottura
Account Director
Pablo Arteaga
Clients
Esporte Clube
Vitória
Hemoba

YNYWYH Twitter Campaign

For the UK launch of Snickers' global campaign, You're Not You When You're Hungry, we used Twitter. We asked five celebrities to post a series of out-of-character tweets. As we'd hoped, this produced widespread confusion, with numerous replies and retweets. Each celebrity then tweeted a picture of themselves eating a Snickers, together with the campaign line. In all, just 25 tweets were posted, but the campaign received significant coverage online, in newspapers, on radio and TV – and was even mentioned during a debate in the House of Commons.

–
Art Director
Tim Riley
Copywriter
Tim Riley
Creative Directors
Alex Grieve
Adrian Rossi
Executive Creative Director
Paul Brazier
Advertising Agency
AMV BBDO
Production Company
Nomadic Films
Client
MasterFoods
Brand
Snickers

 Katie Price/Jordan @MissKatiePrice
Great news about China's latest GDP figures!!

 Katie Price/Jordan @MissKatiePrice
Large scale quantitative easing in 2012 could distort liquidity of govt. bond market. #justsayin

 Robert Peston @Peston
Hard to disagree RT @MissKatiePrice: OMG!! Eurozone debt problems can only be solved by true fiscal union!!! #comeoneguys

The Telegraph

HOME NEWS WORLD SPORT FINANCE COMMENT BLOGS CULTURE TRAVEL LIFE FASHION
Technology News | Technology Companies | Technology Reviews | Video Games | Technology Video

HOME » TECHNOLOGY » TWITTER

Twitter users angered by Rio Ferdinand's Snickers 'adverts'

A Snickers Twitter advertising campaign, fronted by celebrities including Rio Ferdinand, Ian Botham and Cher Lloyd could face investigation for ignoring OFT guidelines.

Image 1 of 3
Rio Ferdinand promoting Snickers on Twitter.

 By Emma Barnett, Digital Media Editor
7:00AM GMT 25 Jan 2012
Follow | 23.2K followers

91 Comments

Yesterday the footballer Ferdinand starting posting odd tweets about knitting and 'needing more wool' much to the bemusement of his fans.

 rioferdy5 Rio Ferdinand
Can't wait 2 get home from training and finish that cardigan
About one year ago via UberSocial for BlackBerry ☆ Favorite ⟲

Print this article
Share 192
Facebook 21
Twitter 171
Email
LinkedIn 0
+1 0

 Katie Price/Jordan @MissKatiePrice
You're not you when you're hungry @snickersUk #hungryspon lockerz.com/s/177408824

 Ian Botham @BeefyBotham
You're not you when you're hungry @ snickersUK #hungry#spon pic.twitter.com/pzI6qV7o
Hide photo

powered by Photobucket   Flag this media

2 RETWEETS   3 FAVORITES

12:55 PM - 21 Jan 12 via Twitter for iPhone · Details
Reply Retweet Favorite

 Ian Botham @BeefyBotham   21 Jan
The cello is, of course, derived from other C18 bowed instruments like the viola de gamba and the smaller, squarer viola de braccio. <3!!!

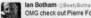 **Ian Botham** @BeefyBotham   21 Jan
OMG check out Pierre Fournier. This dude ROCKS !!! Great bowing technique !!!

 Ian Botham @BeefyBotham   21 Jan
Lovin that Haydn Concerto in D Major !!! #profound

 Ian Botham @BeefyBotham   21 Jan
The cello can convey a depth of feeling and sensitivity that few other instruments can summon. Dontcha think ?

 Ian Botham @BeefyBotham   21 Jan
Decided to learn the cello.

LONDON 51°32'N 0°5'W 9° 12:00

Mobile Medic

The brief was to recruit medical students worthy of a Defence Force University Sponsorship. To find the best we created medically diagnosable advertising, which doubled as an entrance exam. 'Mobile Medic' allowed students to use a range of diagnostic techniques to identify and treat medical conditions using their smartphones. Visual and audio augmentation immersed them in the role of Medical Officer, on real Defence Force scenarios. Students entered their details and received their results instantly. Those who performed best were offered a Defence Force University Sponsorship application.

–
Art Director
Jake Barrow
Copywriter
Matt Lawson
Designers
Marcus Byrne
Janna Mamar

Creative Director
Chris Northam
Chief Creative Officer
Ben Coulson
Photographer
Hugh Peachy
Retoucher
Mal Stark
Digital Producer
Carrie Burman
Developer
Chuck Brandt
User Experience Architect
Luke Tellefson
Audio Producer
Katherine Muir
Sound Engineer
Paul Baxter
Advertising Agency
George Patterson Y&R Melbourne
Digital Agency
VML
Strategist
Tom Ward
Account Handler
Jason Bass
Account Executives
Chris Bush
Daniel Smith
Account Director
Janet Proposch
Group Account Director
Julian Bell
Client
Defence Force Recruiting

Nike Olympics: Find Your Greatness

'Find Your Greatness' was Nike's campaign around the London 2012 Olympics. The convention says greatness is reserved for superstars, for the ones who are participating in the big event in the chosen city. But greatness is a bit bigger than that. It's not just in one special place; it's not just on TV or in elite athletes. Greatness can also be found in London, Ohio and London, Norway and East London, South Africa and Little London, Jamaica and Small London, Nigeria and the London Hotel and London Road. Greatness can be found anywhere someone is trying to find it.

Art Directors
Sezay Altinok
Aramis Israel
Sara Phillips
Copywriters
Caleb Jensen
Brock Kirby
Creative Directors
Ryan O'Rourke
Alberto Ponte
Executive Creative Directors
Susan Hoffman
Joe Staples
Directors
Lance Acord
Seb Edwards
Agency Producers
Jennifer Dennis
Erika Madison
Editors
Robert Duffy
Patrick Murphee
Advertising Agency
Wieden+Kennedy Portland
Production Company
Park Pictures
Editing
Spot Welders
Media Agency
Mindshare
Planner
Rebecca Stambanis
Global Brand Communications Manager
David Reti
Global Brand Communications Director
Ean Lensch
Client
Nike

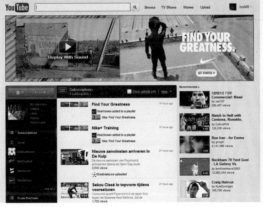

Grazed on Greatness

M. J. Bale is a new Australian men's fashion brand and the Australian Cricket Team's smallest sponsor; the official tailors. It found the field where the Australian Cricket Team had its most victories, the Sydney Cricket Ground, took grass from there, replanted it on a Merino sheep farm, fed it to its sheep, sheared them and used their wool to handcraft suits for the Australian Cricket Team and then the public. It brought the 'Grazed on Greatness' story to life in a documentary which garnered over $3.5 million in PR and saw the brand stocked in 38 new stores.

—

Art Director
Peter Galmes
Copywriter
John Mckelvey
Designer
Chris Mawson
Creative Directors
Peter Galmes
John Mckelvey
Executive Creative Directors
Dave Bowman
Matty Burton
Director
Stephen Oliver
Photographer
Gerrard Needham
Director of Photography
Hugh Miller
Retoucher
Nick Mueller
Music Composer
Scott Langley
Sound Engineer
Simon Lister
Advertising Agency
Whybin\TBWA\DAN
Sydney
Post Production
Method Studios
Sydney
Sound Design
Nylon Studios
Public Relations
Eleven PR
Public Relations Managers
Rob Lowe
Sydney Spagnoletti
Account Director
Bryony Marks
Business Director
Paul Bradbury
Client
M.J. Bale

SYDNEY 34°0'S 151°0'E 22° 20:00

Clouds Over Cuba

'Clouds over Cuba' is an interactive multimedia documentary commemorating the 50th anniversary of the Cuban Missile Crisis. The feature begins with Castro's overthrow of Batista in 1959, and continues on until the missiles were removed in October 1962. Features include 15 expert interviews, a dossier of 200 related documents and images linked to the film's timeline, mobile sync, tablet optimisation, and calendar integration so you can attend JFK's secret meetings 'live', 50 years later. Finally, a 'What If?' short film depicts an alternate 2012 in which the crisis had escalated into nuclear war.

–
Art Director
Brian Williams
Copywriter
Wade Alger
Creative Director
Joe Alexander
Design Director
Matt Gase
Directors
Erich Joiner
Ben Tricklebank
Executive Producers
Dustin Callif
Oliver Fuselier
Steve Humble
Brian Latt
Interactive Producer
Kristen Koeller
Agency Producers
Nicole Hollis-Vitale
Kristen Little
Head of Interactive Production
Joy Kuraitis
Technical Director
Bartek Drozdz
Advertising Agency
The Martin Agency
Production Company
Tool
Editing
STITCH
Music Production
Plan8
Client
The JFK Presidential Library & Museum

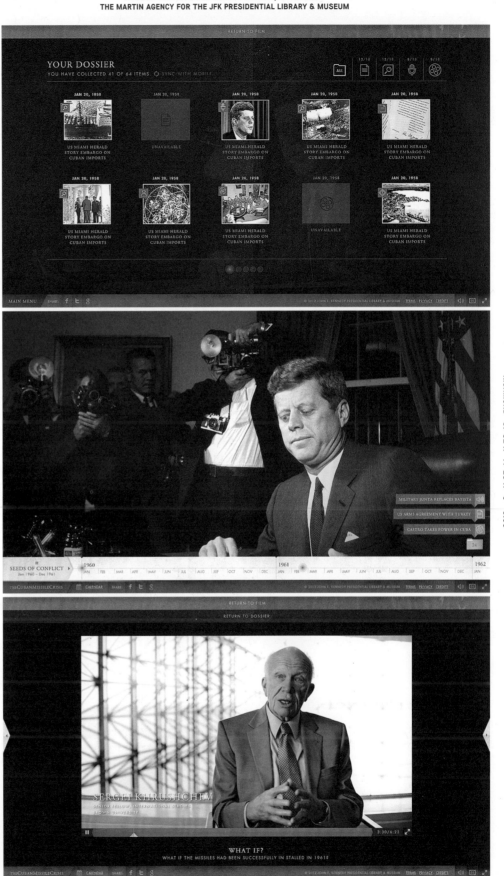

RICHMOND 37°32'N 77°25'W 6° 8:00

ADVERTISING INTEGRATED & EARNED MEDIA

iQ Street View

The Toyota iQ completed Google Street View in Belgium by filming all the streets Google couldn't get into. A PR strategy and making-of video led people to our version of the street view site. There people could tag their streets to invite the street view crew. When their street was filmed, a direct mailing was sent to all people living in the street with a promotional message and an invite to check out their street on iQstreetview.be.

—

Art Director
Naim Baddich
Copywriter
Patrick Glorieux
Graphic Designer
Jeremy Vandenbosch
Creative Director
Peter Ampe
Executive Creative Director
Karen Corrigan
Agency Producer
Bart Vande Maele
Director of Photography
Bob Jeusette
Head of Art
Cecilia Azcarate Isturiz
Interactive Producer
Stijn Van Velthoven
Advertising Agency
Happiness Brussels
Digital Agency
BLISS interactive
Strategist
Joris Joosten
Account Manager
Mehdi Sel
Group Account Director
Pascal Kemajou
Client
Toyota Belgium
Brand
Toyota iQ

Susan Glenn

Axe has always told memorable stories about guys getting girls. Lots of girls. But what about THE girl? We gave THE girl a name: Susan Glenn. With an ambitious seeding programme, we secretly embedded the name in pop-culture. Then with a single film Axe took credit for this phenomenon. This led to a digital/mobile experience allowing guys to declare their own Susan Glenns. Not only did the campaign turn around the at-times perceived chauvinism of Axe, it turned around the brand's sales numbers, beating its goals for the year. Proving anything is possible when you Fear No Susan Glenn.

—
Art Director
Nate Able
Copywriter
Peter Rosch
Executive Creative Director
Ari Weiss
Associate Creative Director
Nate Able
Chief Creative Officer
John Patroulis
Director
Ringan Ledwidge

Executive Producer
Jennifer Barrons
Agency Producer
Calleen Colburn
Computer Graphics Artist
Isaiah Palmer
Editor
Rich Orrick
Director of Photography
Matthew Libatique
Line Producer
Pat Frazier
Music Composer
Phil Kay
Sound Designer
Brian Emrich
Sound Engineer
Rohan Young
Colourist
Fergus McCall
Head of Broadcast
Lisa Setten
Advertising Agency
BBH New York
Production Company
Rattling Stick
Visual Effects Company
The Mill New York
Editing
Work
Strategist
Eric Fernandez
Strategic Directors
Griffin Farley
John Graham
Account Director
Mandy Dempsey
Business Director
Armando Turco
Client
Unilever
Brand
Axe

ADVERTISING   INTEGRATED & EARNED MEDIA

NEW YORK CITY   40°40'N   73°56'W   8°   8:00

161

Project Re: Brief

Despite almost two decades of innovation online, display ads are still seen by the advertising industry as a periphery medium; a space too small for big ideas. So we put display to the ultimate test. We took some of America's greatest ads, dating as far back as 1962, and partnered with the legendary creatives behind them to re-imagine them for mobile. Even advertising's biggest ideas can fit in advertising's smallest spaces.

–
**Executive
Creative Directors**
Howie Cohen
Harvey Gabor
Amil Gargano
Paula Green
Bob Pasqualina
Advertising Agency
Johannes Leonardo
Digital Agency
Grow Interactive
**Production
Companies**
@radical.media
Nexus Productions
Oil Factory
Rebolucion
RSA Films
**Digital Production
Company**
Fake Love
Post Production
Katabatic Digital
Editing
Cosmo Street
Rock Paper Scissors
Music Arrangement
Beacon Street
Studios
House of Hayduk
Human
Mixing
Penny Lane
Studio Center
Client
Google
Brand
Google Display

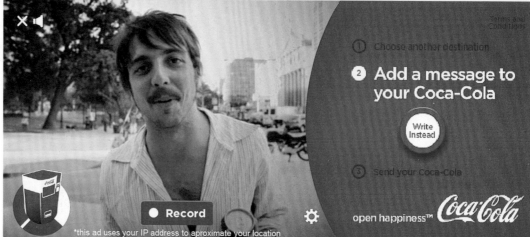

Help I Want to Save a Life

We wanted to add thousands of new names to the Marrow Donor Registry. Our solution was to turn a normal, everyday act into a chance to save a life. We put a simple marrow registry kit into boxes of over-the-counter help bandages. The kit contained a sterilised cotton swab to collect blood and a prepaid envelope. We were able to catch people while they were already bleeding. By making marrow registration part of a common occurrence, as well as part of a mass-produced consumer product, we reached a huge, new audience and reinvented the way marrow registration takes place.

–
Art Director
Alfredo Adan Roses
Copywriters
Graham Douglas
Alberto Portas
Martagón
Creative Director
Nathan Frank
Advertising Agency
Droga5
Clients
DKMS
Help Remedies
Brand
help

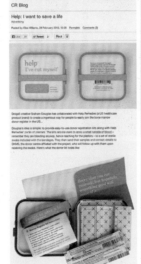

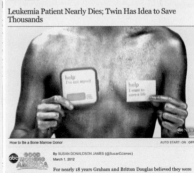

Driving Dogs

In New Zealand, shelter dogs were seen as second rate compared to store bought animals, so finding them homes was a daily challenge for the SPCA. As a longstanding SPCA sponsor, MINI wanted to help. Our strategy was to demonstrate just how smart these dogs really are. So, we taught three of them to drive a car and showed them, in a never-before-seen event, live on national TV. In one week, over 200 million saw the dogs driving. The campaign received more than $20 million in PR across over 70 countries. New Zealand adoption interest increased by 590% and, every SCPA dog was adopted.

–
Copywriters
Peter Vegas
Matt Williams
Designer
Nick McFarlane
Interactive Designer
Catherine Chi
Executive Creative Directors
Tony Clewett
Regan Grafton
James Mok
Producer
Sarah Yetton
Editor
Blair Walker
Photographer
Stephen Langdon
Cinematographer
Marco Siraky
Retoucher
Anton Mason
Advertising Agency
Draftfcb New Zealand
Digital Strategist
Harri Owen
Planner
Steph Pearson
Media Managers
Rachel Leyland
Sarah McEwen
Simon Teagle
Account Managers
Eloise Hay
Stephanie Hueber
Account Director
Sally Willis
Group Account Director
Toby Sellers
Public Relations Manager
Angela Spain
Communications Director
Rufus Chuter
Clients
MINI New Zealand
SPCA New Zealand

Honorary Islander

The challenge was to grow tourism in Iceland outside peak summer months through global PR that inspired 'enlightened tourists' to visit Iceland during winter and talk about their experiences. Winter visitors to Iceland were treated as 'honorary islanders' not just tourists. As honorary islanders they had access to special experiences offering a personal insight into the life of Iceland, as islanders opened their homes and invited them in. It was the most successful winter in Iceland's history, with the campaign making the news in 57 countries and 1.18 billion global impressions, and increasing revenue by £34 million.

—
Creative Agencies
The Brooklyn Brothers
Islenska
Client
Promote Iceland
Brand
Inspired by Iceland

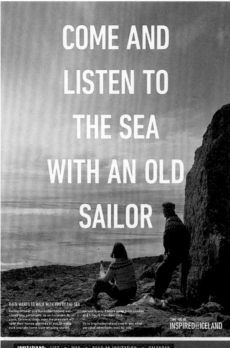

○

IN BOOK IN INTEGRATED & EARNED MEDIA, EARNED MEDIA CAMPAIGNS
DUVAL GUILLAUME FOR TURNER BROADCASTING SYSTEM EUROPE

Push to Add Drama

We were asked to launch the American TV channel TNT in Belgium. The tagline: We know drama; the promise: TV worth talking about. So our assignment was to develop a launch campaign worth talking about. Triggering the unstoppable curiosity of people, we placed a big push button in the average square of an average town. The sign and button invited people to 'push to add drama'. People who dared to push were confronted with a fast sequence of dramatic and crazy events occurring in front of their eyes, all referring to the TNT series.

–
Art Director
Ad Van Ongeval
Copywriter
Dieter De Ridder
**Executive
Creative Directors**
Katrien Bottez
Geoffrey Hantson
Director
Koen Mortier
Producers
Birgit D'Hont
Matthias Schellens
Executive Producer
Eurydice Gysel
Agency Producer
Marc Van
Buggenhout
Advertising Agency
Duval Guillaume
Account Handlers
Jana Vervoort
Marc Wellens
Client
Turner Broadcasting
System Europe
Brand
TNT

News

GO1

Drama at the push of a button

Wacky stunt to promote Belgian TV channel

Flabbergasted ... onlookers watch amazed as actors play out mock-shootout

By MATT QUINTON *Published: 11th April 2012*

👍 Like 65   Tweet 12   +1

5

THESE curious passers-by got a lot more than they bargained for after pressing a button labelled "Push to add drama".

Video of the hilarious stunt, to promote TV channel TNT in Belgium, shows a red button placed on a podium in the middle of a town square.

Bystanders are seen wandering past, before some eventually choose to push the trigger — causing a group of actors to suddenly play out an action-packed scene.

First an ambulance pulls into the square with sirens wailing, but as paramedics go to load the casualty into the back, they drop his stretcher and him on the floor.

They quickly load him into the vehicle, but he tumbles out as soon as it pulls away and soon a cyclist crashes into the van door.

The bike-rider goes to punch one of the paramedics, who easily knocks him away, ripping off his own shirt to reveal his hulking physique.

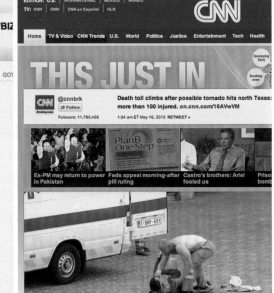

Stuntmen participate in an unusual ad campaign in Belgium.

April 12th, 2012
10:59 AM ET

Gotta Watch: Extreme ad stunts gone viral

Every once in a while, an ad campaign is so creative or unusual that it stands out from all the other commercials we're bombarded with every day. A lot of times these cool ads go viral, such as one fun promotion in Belgium that caught our eye. You've Gotta Watch these memorable ad stunts.

  Pushing buttons

This inventive ad campaign in Belgium invites passers-by to push a button to "add drama" to a town square. Hidden cameras catch the participants getting more than they bargained for. The mini show starts with an ambulance, gunshots, and a woman in lingerie and escalates from there. You've got to see how it ends. This viral ad is for CNN's sister network TNT

Bungay vs Bungay

Bungay Town FC had a problem: no one had ever heard of it. This was hampering crowd attendance, financial support and player acquisition. The club needed a big idea to make them famous on literally no budget. The idea was a game of football between two teams called Bungay, with 22 players called Bungay played at Bungay Town FC, Bungay, Suffolk. Even the professional referee, linesmen, physio, doctor and mascot were Bungays. The game featuring the biggest number of players with the same surname played in any sport anywhere in the world created huge impact, and the most amusing live commentary.

–
Art Director
Bil Bungay
Copywriter
Bil Bungay
Designers
Phil Appleton
Dan Forde
Creative Director
Bil Bungay
Directors
Bil Bungay
Jack Masterson
Scott Newstead
Josh Stack
Daniel Stockmann
Producer
Bil Bungay
Editors
Bil Bungay
Jack Masterson
Scott Newstead
Josh Stack
Daniel Stockmann
Photographer
Laura Bungay
Print Producers
Lol Keen
Ian King
Advertising Agency
Beattie McGuinness
Bungay
Marketing Manager
Shaun Cole
Client
Bungay Town FC

BUNGAY 6 - BUNGAY 6 AND THE SCORERS WERE BUNGAY, BUNGAY, BUNGAY, BUNGAY, BUNGAY, BUNGAY, BUNGAY, BUNGAY, BUNGAY AND BUNGAY

BBC NEWS SUFFOLK

News   Sport   Weather   iPlayer   TV   Radio

Home   World   UK   **England**   N. Ireland   Scotland   Wales   Business   Politics   Health   Education   Sci/E

8 May 2012 Last updated at 14:06

31   Share   f   ✉   🖶

Bungay scores a hat-trick as Bungay draw with Bungay

About 70 people with the surname Bungay travelled to the Suffolk town of the same name to take part in a charity football match.

Two teams of players, the officials, the mascots and a doctor, all called Bungay, were involved in the match at Bungay Town's ground in Bungay.

Players ranged in age from four to 68 and the match finished level, at 6-6.

Organiser Shaun Cole said: "Keiran Bungay scored two penalties to complete his hat-trick and make it a draw."

Mr Cole, part of the Bungay Town FC committee, said: "The pitch was full of Bungays and the stand was full of Bungays.

"One chap came from Queensland, Australia, to play."

The match between Bungay and Bungay ended 6-6

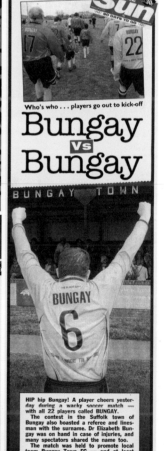

THE Sun

Who's who . . . players go out to kick-off

Bungay
vs
Bungay

BUNGAY TOWN

HIP hip Bungay! A player cheers yesterday during a wacky soccer match — with all 22 players called BUNGAY.
The contest in the Suffolk town of Bungay also boasted a referee and linesman with the surname. Dr Elizabeth Bungay was on hand in case of injuries, and many spectators shared the name too.
The match was held to promote local team Bungay Town FC — and at least 70 Bungays came, some from Australia and the US, after seeing invites online.
Radio commentator Sam Delaney said: "It is the easiest job I have ever done."

Hashtag Killer Case

The 'Hashtag Killer' campaign set out to eradicate the ironic #FirstWorldProblems meme, in which people tweet about such life burdens as non-heated leather seats or forgetting their maid's last name – and, in the process, raise awareness about serious developing world issues. For the anthem commercial, we gathered real 'First World Problem' tweets and then approached people in Haiti to recite them. But perhaps even more effective was the series of personalised response videos, in which various Haitians consoled those using the hashtag on Twitter.

—
Art Director
Sam Shepherd
Copywriter
Frank Cartagena
Designers
Zeynep Aydogmus
Gina Lin
Juan Carlos Pagan
Executive
Creative Director
Menno Kluin
Chief Creative Officer
Matt Eastwood
Director
Alec Helm
Producer
Lindsey Hutter
Executive Producer
Ed Zazzera
Editors
Alec Helm
Melanie Meditz
Advertising Agency
DDB New York
Client
Water is Life

ADVERTISING   INTEGRATED & EARNED MEDIA

NEW YORK CITY   40°40'N   73°56'W   8°   8:00

Dan Jordan
@DanJordan2001 - New York City

There really isn't anything worse than leaving your headphones at home.
#FirstWorldProblems

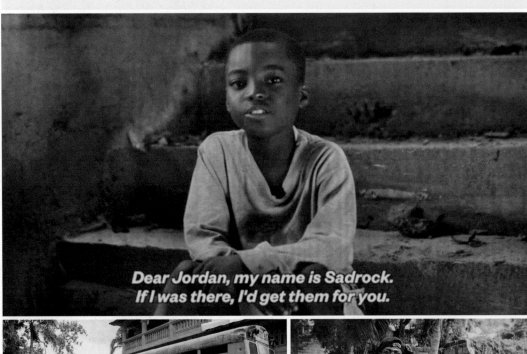

Dear Jordan, my name is Sadrock. If I was there, I'd get them for you.

I hate when my phone charger won't reach my bed.

Don't Cover it Up

Fearing there is nowhere they can turn for help, 65% of domestic abuse victims routinely cover up both their emotional and physical scars. Refuge challenged us to raise awareness among this hard to reach audience. Lauren Luke is a YouTube makeup artist. With over 125 million views, her channel gave us a way to talk directly to victims. In the style of her makeup tutorials, a bruised Lauren showed how to cover up signs of abuse. Caught off guard, her young fans began a global discussion about an unspoken problem.

—

Art Director
George Hackworth-Jones
Art Director
Stephen Noble
Copywriter
Jack Smedley
Creative Director
Pablo Marques
Executive Creative Director
Nick Gill
Directors
Wesley Hawes
Gary McCreadie
Agency Producers
Bryony Dellow
Jeremy Gleeson
Interactive Producer
Richard Atkins
Advertising Agency
BBH London
Digital Agency
Addictive Pixel
Production Company
The Mill London
Sound Design
Factory Studios
Content Strategist
Claire Coady
Strategic Director
Simon Robertson
Account Handler
Carly Herman
Brand Manager
Lisa King
Client
Refuge

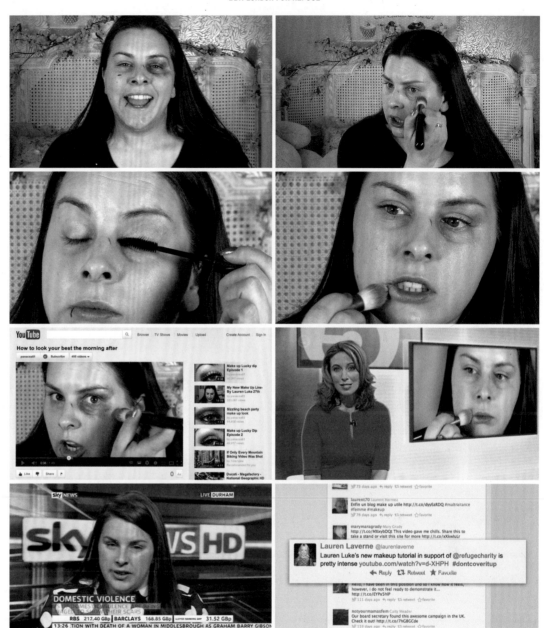

JURY

Jury Foreman
Morihiro Harano
Mori
Tom Eslinger
Saatchi & Saatchi New York
Jackie Jantos
The Coca-Cola Company
Gustav Martner
CP+B Europe

Murat Mutlu
Mobile Inc
Priya Prakash
Design for Social Change
James Temple
R/GA London

Nike+ FuelBand

**Also a Nomination
in Integrated
Mobile Campaigns**

Nike came to us to
realise an idea: a
wristband device
that tracks your
daily activity and a
common, universal
metric called Fuel for
every active body out
there. They asked us
to design the entire
user experience. We
ensured ease of use:
set your goal, and get
from red to green. If
you meet your goal,
animations celebrate
your performance.
Data graphics show
where you were most
active daily, weekly,
monthly, and beyond.
We created Bluetooth
sync technology
so the results of your
day's activities can
be transferred to
your mobile device
and visualised on the
FuelBand app.

–
Creative Directors
Cesar Marchetti
Kirill Yeretsky
**Executive Creative
Director**
Tara Greer
**Associate Creative
Directors**
Keith Byrne
Gaurabh Mathure
Technical Directors
Nick Coronges
Sune Kaae
Daniel Katz
Art Director
Ray Sison
Copywriter
Evan Maranca
Designer
Ellen Pai
**Senior Software
Engineers**
Robert Carlsen
Fernando Mazzon
Niall McCormack
Executive Producer
Avery Holden
Senior Producers
Alan Donnelly
Guy Helson
Michael Klimkewicz
Head of Product
Ian Spalter
**Quality Assurance
Manager**
Leslie Chong
Digital Agency
R/GA
Managing Director
Jennifer Allen
Client
Nike
Brand
Nike+

NEW YORK CITY   40°40'N   73°56'W   8°   8:00

Parking Douche

We created a free app to combat the epidemic of douche parking in Russia. Take photos of a badly parked car and the app identifies its number plate, model, colour and location. The car's profile is stored in the app while the data is streamed live to banner ads that are targeted through an IP address – so people who are in the area are likely to see them. The ads show the offending car. When you scroll over the banner a message appears, saying that this car is annoying people in a nearby street right now. The only way to close the banner ad is to share the photo of the parking douche on social media.

—
Creative Directors
Katya Bazilevskaya
Grisha Sorokin
Technical Director
Alexander Rybyakov
Flash Developer
Alexander Redinger
Art Director
Vladimir Shreyder
Creative Agency
Look At Media
Moscow
Strategist
Alexey Artyukhov
Project Manager
Alya
Gabdurakhmanova
Client
The Village

MOSCOW 55°45'N 37°36'E -2° 16:00

Pothole Season

In Montreal, the return of spring means the return of potholes. To help address the situation and make driving easier for Montrealers, we developed 'Pothole Season', an iPhone app that tracks and shares the locations of these annoying road hazards.

–
Creative Director
Jean-François Houle
Executive Creative Director
Dominique Trudeau
Art Director
Frederic Roux

Copywriters
Martin Charron
Jean-François
DaSylva-LaRue
Web Producer
Maxime Boivin
Head of Integrated Production
Jacques Latreille
Advertising Agency
TAXI Montréal
Mobile Production Company
The Barn & Co.
Digital Production Company
QuatreCentQuatre
Project Manager
Nada Debay
Client
TAXI Montréal

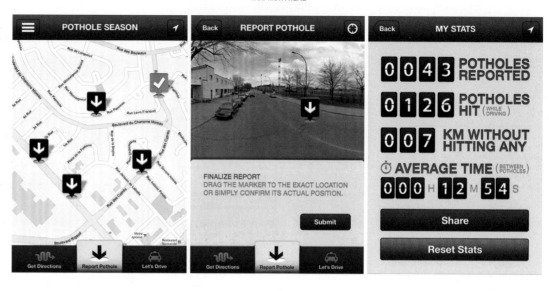

Secret Fishing Spots

Hutchwilco is New Zealand's oldest maker of lifejackets. But its customers keep drowning, because fishermen don't like to reveal their favourite fishing spots – and so are hard to locate if they get in trouble. The app 'Secret Fishing Spots' allows fishermen to log their secret spots without sharing them. Then if they don't come home, a loved one can access their account, see where they like to go and send coordinates to rescue services.

–
Creative Directors
Regan Grafton
Steve Kane
Chris Schofield
Executive Creative Director
Andy Fackrell
Digital Creative Director
Aaron Goldring

Lead Developer
Cameron Crosby
Developer
Jarrad Edwards
Art Directors
Damian Galvin
Adam Thompson
Copywriter
Rory McKechnie
Designer
Renee Lam
Digital Designer
Jason Vertongen
Director
Andy Fackrell
Producer
Dov Tombs
Photographer
Lewis Mulatero
Retoucher
Kevin Hyde
Editors
Sam Arden
Steve Gulik
Advertising Agency
DDB New Zealand
Account Managers
Jonathan Rea
Nisa Solipo
Group Account Director
Scott Wallace
Client
Hutchwilco

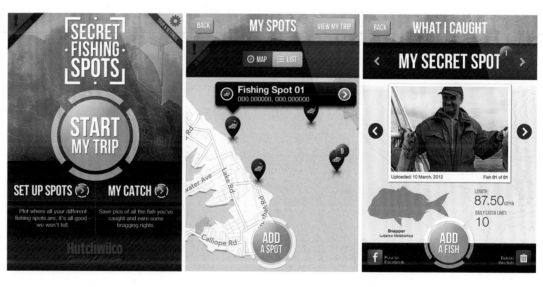

Easy Way Subtitles

For the many international students and professionals living in Brazil, we created captioning technology combined with Google Translate to provide subtitles for Brazilian TV in any language. The site can be accessed on mobile devices for ease of use, and invites users to book a Portuguese language lesson with Easy Way.

–
Creative Director
Guga Ketzer
Creative Directors
Cássio Moron
Sergio Mugnaini
Fabio Saboya
Programmers
Raphael Franzini
Vitor Manfredini
Copywriter
Raphael Franzini
Designer
Gustavo De Lacerda
Advertising Agency
Loducca
Account Handler
Wilson Negrini
Client
Easy Way
Language Center
Brand
Easy Way

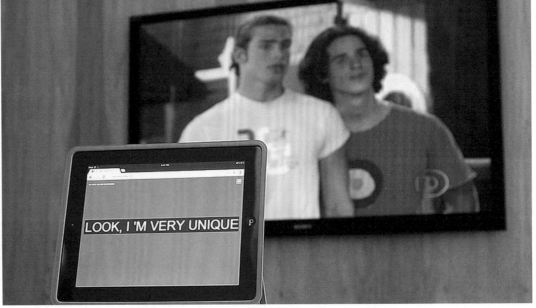

SÃO PAULO 23°31'S 46°31'W 23° 10:00

ADVERTISING MOBILE MARKETING

Clouds Over Cuba

'Clouds over Cuba' is an interactive multimedia documentary commemorating the 50th anniversary of the Cuban Missile Crisis. The feature begins with Castro's overthrow of Batista in 1959, and continues on until the missiles were removed in October 1962. Features include 15 expert interviews, a dossier of 200 related documents and images linked to the film's timeline, mobile sync, tablet optimisation, and calendar integration so you can attend JFK's secret meetings 'live', 50 years on.

–

Creative Director
Joe Alexander
Technical Director
Bartek Drozdz
Art Director
Brian Williams

Copywriter
Wade Alger
Design Director
Matt Gase
Directors
Erich Joiner
Ben Tricklebank
Interactive Producer
Kristen Koeller
Executive Producers
Dustin Callif
Oliver Fuselier
Steve Humble
Brian Latt
Agency Producers
Nicole Hollis-Vitale
Kristen Little
Head of Interactive Production
Joy Kuraitis
Advertising Agency
The Martin Agency
Production Company
Tool
Music Production
Plan8
Editing
STITCH
Client
The JFK Presidential Library & Museum

RICHMOND   37°32'N   77°25_W   6°   8:00

VIP Fridge Magnet

All the big pizza players with their big budgets are in Dubai. So how can a small pizzeria compete on a limited budget? With a local insight: over 200 nationalities and subsequent language barriers make ordering a pizza more frustrating than convenient. We turned this into an opportunity. The VIP Fridge Magnet is no ordinary fridge magnet – it doubles up as a pizza emergency button. This first ever one-touch delivery system refreshed the delivery business and inspired pizza passions around the world. It helped customers feel valued and set our client apart from the big brands.

–

Associate Creative Directors
Melanie Clancy
Rafael Guida
Digital Creative Director
Preethi Mariappan
Technical Delivery Manager
Navin Chauhan
User Experience Designer
Jerome Conde
Producer
Kishore Ramachandran
Creative Agency
TBWA\RAAD Middle East – Dubai
Account Executives
Weam Elhila
Mohammad Khan
Client
Red Tomato Pizza

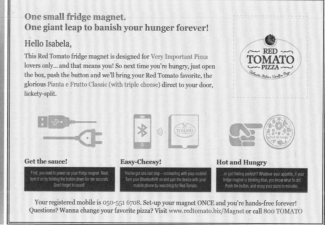

DUBAI   25°15'N   55°18_E   30°   16:00

Happiness Refill

Coke wanted to engage with the young, emerging middle-class consumers who love their mobile phones, but can't afford a generous data plan. In Brazil most Wifi spots aren't free. So we created 'Happiness Refill': a dispenser with a built-in computer and Wifi network. Instead of dispensing soda, it fills up mobile phones with a Coke browser and free data credits for surfing the internet. The browser features three buttons: Coke FM radio to listen to music, social network links including facebook and Twitter, and the weather forecast.

—
Creative Directors
Rubens Filho
Edu Garretano
Eduardo Marques
Executive Creative Directors
Claudio Lima
Fred Saldanha
Chief Creative Officer
Anselmo Ramos
Digital Integration Director
Daniel Tartaro
Art Directors
Raphael Lucone
Guilherme Nobrega
Rafael Rizuto
Copywriters
Ricardo Lins
Eduardo Marques
Flavio Tamashiro
Producers
Nana Bittencourt
Juscelino Vieira
Motion Graphics Artist
Guilherme Todorov
Advertising Agency
Ogilvy Brazil
Project Manager
Paula Santana
Marketing Manager
Adriana Knackfuss
Client
The Coca-Cola Company
Brand
Coca-Cola

ADVERTISING   MOBILE MARKETING

SÃO PAULO   23°31'S   46°31'W   23°   10:00

Project Re: Brief

Despite almost two decades of innovation online, display ads are still seen by the advertising industry as a periphery medium, a space too small for big ideas. So we put display ads to the ultimate test. We took some of America's greatest ads, dating as far back as 1962, and partnered with the legendary creatives behind them to re-imagine them for mobile. Even advertising's biggest ideas can fit in advertising's smallest spaces.

–
**Executive Creative
Directors**
Howie Cohen
Harvey Gabor
Amil Gargano
Paula Green
Bob Pasqualina
Advertising Agency
Johannes Leonardo
Digital Agency
Grow Interactive
**Digital Production
Company**
Fake Love
**Production
Companies**
@radical.media
Nexus Productions
Oil Factory
Rebolucion
RSA Films
Post Production
Katabatic Digital
Music Arrangement
Beacon Street
Studios
House of Hayduk
Human
Editing
Cosmo Street
Rock Paper Scissors
Mixing
Penny Lane
Studio Center
Client
Google
Brand
Google Display

JURY

Jury Foreman
Nick Worthington
Colenso BBDO
Carl Broadhurst
BBH London
Catalin Dobre
McCann Erickson Bucharest
Simon Learman
adam&eveDDB
Carlos Rodriguez
Lowe/SSP3

Gavin Simpson
Ogilvy & Mather Malaysia
Kate Stanners
Saatchi & Saatchi London
Guillermo Vega
Wieden+Kennedy São Paulo
Dave Woods
JWT London
Amanda Yang
Leo Burnett Shanghai

Dumb Ways to Die

How do you reach young commuters who think they will outlive religion? Why not start by breaking every single rule of public safety messaging one could find? A key part of a broader campaign, these cute little dead guys ended up on people's cameras, hashtagged all over Instagram and cheerfully etched in the consciousness of a segment of risk hungry young Melbournians, hard wired to do dumb stuff when and where they shouldn't.

–
Art Director
Pat Baron
Copywriter
John Mescall
Illustrator
Julian Frost
Creative Director
Pat Baron
Executive Creative Director
John Mescall
Advertising Agency
McCann Erickson Melbourne
Account Manager
Tamara Broman
Account Director
Alec Hussain
Group Account Director
Adrian Mills
Brand Manager
Leah Waymark
Marketing Manager
Chloe Alsop
Client
Metro Trains

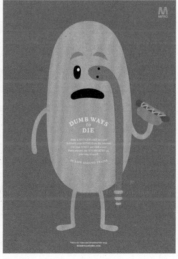

MELBOURNE 37°47'S 144°58'E 12° 23:00

Everyday

To a Parkinson's sufferer, everyday tasks such as making a cup of tea or tying a tie are incredibly difficult. Because Parkinson's is a neurological condition, the brain mixes up the messages it sends to the body, making the actions confused. To dramatise this, we similarly depicted a simple act and 'muddled up' the messaging, leaving the viewer the task of reassembling the images and messages for themselves.

—
Art Director
Alexandra Taylor
Copywriter
Sean Doyle
Photographer
Alexandra Taylor
Typographers
Stuart
Harrington Gill
Alexandra Taylor
Executive Creative Director
Steve Dunn
Advertising Agency
The Assembly
Planner
Trevor Hardy
Account Handler
Tina Woods
Brand Manager
Lily Dwek
Client
Parkinson's UK

ADVERTISING OUTDOOR ADVERTISING

Push to Add Drama

We were asked to launch the American TV channel TNT in Belgium. The tagline: We know drama; the promise: TV worth talking about. So our assignment was to develop a launch campaign worth talking about. Triggering the unstoppable curiosity of people, we placed a big push button in the average square of an average town. The sign and button invited people to 'push to add drama'. People who dared to push were confronted with a fast sequence of dramatic and crazy events occurring in front of their eyes, all referring to the TNT series.

–
Art Director
Ad Van Ongeval
Copywriter
Dieter De Ridder
Executive Creative Directors
Katrien Bottez
Geoffrey Hantson
Producers
Birgit D'Hont
Matthias Schellens
Executive Producer
Eurydice Gysel
Agency Producer
Marc Van Buggenhout
Advertising Agency
Duval Guillaume
Account Handlers
Jana Vervoort
Marc Wellens
Client
Turner Broadcasting System Europe
Brand
TNT

ADVERTISING OUTDOOR ADVERTISING

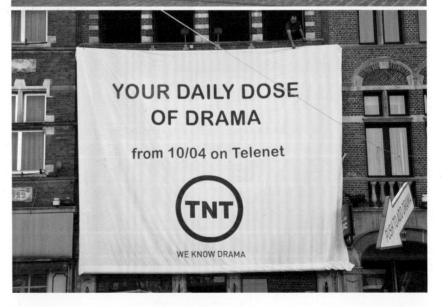

ANTWERP 51°13'N 4°24'E 11° 13:00

Potable Water Generator

The University of Engineering and Technology believes the world can be changed through engineering. To demonstrate this, they started with their own city, Lima. It's the second largest desert capital in the world and potable water is scarce. UTEC and the agency built the first billboard in the world to produce potable water out of air. Machines inside the billboard condense atmospheric moisture to obtain bulk water. The water is then purified and stored in a tank where it can be drawn as drinking water. The billboard also served to attract students to the university during the application period.

—
Art Director
Juan Donalisio
Copywriter
Alejandro Aponte
Creative Directors
Alejandro Aponte
Juan Donalisio
Executive Creative Director
Humberto Polar
Advertising Agency
Mayo Draftfcb
Media Agency
MediaConnection BPN
Account Executive
Cesar Centurion
Account Director
Ines Lertora
Cost Consultant
Juan Christmann
Marketing Manager
Jessica Ruas
Client
The University of Engineering and Technology

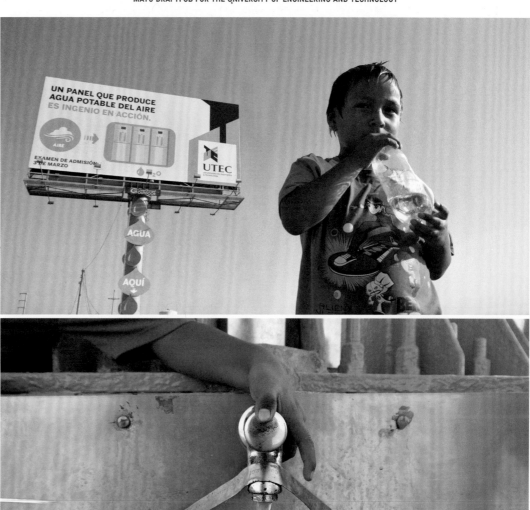

LIMA 12°0'S 77°2'W 17° 7:00

Wsh Ewe Wre Ere

There are 9,000 airports around the world and every one has its own three-letter code. Instead of the usual travel clichés, we used these humble but iconic codes that we're all familiar with to promote a wide range of offers and specials for the Expedia brand.

–
Art Director
Mike Watson
Copywriter
Jon Morgan
Typographer
Mark Osborne
Designer
Mark Osborne
Executive Creative Director
Gerry Human
Associate Creative Directors
Mark Harrison
Paul Mason
Chief Creative Officer
Gerry Human
Retoucher
Trevor Qizilbash
Advertising Agency
Ogilvy & Mather London
Project Manager
Grant Mason
Account Executive
Jessica Wilkinson
Brand Communications Director
Andrew Warner
Business Director
Stephen Hillcoat
Client
Expedia

ADVERTISING OUTDOOR ADVERTISING

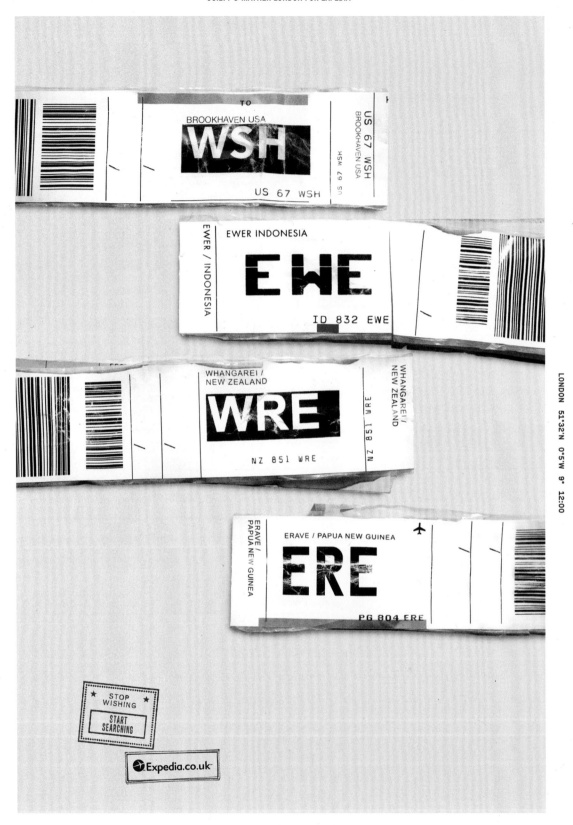

LONDON 51°32'N 0°5'W 9° 12:00

Coke Hands

Our idea was to bring friendship and Coke closely together in an iconic fashion that would be easily understood by anybody from tier one, two and three cities in China.

–
Art Director
Jonathan Mak Long
Illustrators
Eno Jin
Jonathan Mak Long
Designer
Jonathan Mak Long
Executive Creative Director
Francis Wee
Chief Creative Officer
Graham Fink
Advertising Agency
Ogilvy & Mather Shanghai
Planner
Mark Sinnock
Content & Marketing Director
Stephen Drummond
Managing Director
Martin Murphy
Client
The Coca-Cola Company
Brand
Coca-Cola

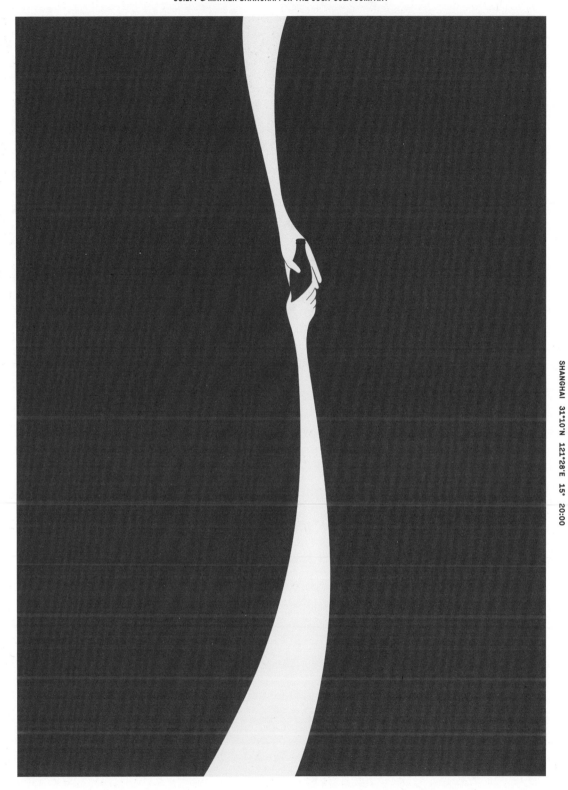

ADVERTISING   OUTDOOR ADVERTISING

SHANGHAI 31°10'N 121°28'E 15° 20:00

Sport

'The Sunday Times Rich List' is a list of the 1,000 wealthiest people or families in the UK, updated annually in April and published as a magazine supplement. 'The Sunday Times Rich List' has become an annual event that drives huge newspaper sales for The Sunday Times. It's one of the key events in the marketing calendar that attracts both loyal and casual readers. We therefore took famous partnerships and rescaled images of them so that the person's size within the advert was proportional to their wealth. This created adverts that challenged our perception of fame and success.

–
Art Director
Richard Brim
Copywriter
Daniel Fisher
Designers
Rob Swainson
David Turfitt
Creative Director
Jonathan Burley
Executive Creative Director
Jonathan Burley
Advertising Agency
CHI & Partners
Art Buyer
Emma Modler
Client
News International
Brand
The Sunday Times

Next Stop, McDonald's

Our objective was to remind drivers that a McDonald's drive-thru is a convenient service. From one of the many restaurants dotted around London, you can get food and drink delivered directly from a drive-thru window to your vehicle window. Observing that the stem of a bus T-side would be at the same height as a passing motorcycle, car or van window, the media allowed us to get up close with our target audience. The buses travelled along major routes all over London, passing thousands of vehicles every day.

–
Art Director
Ed Tillbrook
Copywriter
Richard Ince
Executive Creative Director
Justin Tindall
Advertising Agency
Leo Burnett London
Client
McDonald's

LONDON 51°32'N 0°5'W 9° 12:00

Dragons' Den

'The Sunday Times Rich List' is a list of the 1,000 wealthiest people or families in the UK. This promotional poster shows the wealth of each Dragon in proportion to their rivals. The Dragons, who we tend to consider on an even playing field, are depicted in a new light.

–
Art Director
Richard Brim
Copywriter
Daniel Fisher
Designers
Rob Swainson
David Turfitt
Creative Director
Jonathan Burley
Executive Creative Director
Jonathan Burley
Advertising Agency
CHI & Partners
Art Buyer
Emma Modler
Client
News International
Brand
The Sunday Times

LONDON 51°32'N 0°5'W 9° 12:00

ADVERTISING   OUTDOOR ADVERTISING

Sky Tweets

Paddy Power's 'We Hear You' campaign saw the bookmaker responding to sports fans' social media comments in a variety of mischievous ways. For the 2012 Ryder Cup golf tournament, the bookmaker took its activity to the next level – into the skies above the course at Medinah. Paddy Power encouraged its Twitter followers to send pro-Europe messages of support using #goeurope. A fleet of planes then used sky writing to relay the best tweets and distract Team USA. With Paddy Power providing support from above, Team Europe went on to record a memorable and unlikely final day victory over Tiger and co.

–
Art Director
Christen Brestrup
Copywriter
Bertie Scrase
Creative Directors
Matt Gooden
Ben Walker
Director of Integrated Production
Anthony Ganjou
Agency Producer
Joe Bagnall
Advertising Agency
CP+B
Interactive Production Company
Curb Media
Public Relations
Taylor Herring
Brand Manager
Conor McIntyre
Marketing Manager
Ken Robertson
Client
Paddy Power

Driving Dogs

In New Zealand, shelter dogs were seen as second rate compared to store bought animals, so finding them homes was a daily challenge for the SPCA. As a longstanding SPCA sponsor, MINI wanted to help. Our strategy was to demonstrate just how smart these dogs really are. So, we taught three of them to drive a car and showed it, in a never-before-seen event, live on national TV. In one week, over 200 million saw the dogs driving. New Zealand adoption interest increased by 590% and, most importantly, every SCPA dog was adopted.

–
Copywriters
Peter Vegas
Matt Williams
Photographer
Stephen Langdon
Designer
Nick McFarlane

Interactive Designer
Catherine Chi
Executive Creative Directors
Tony Clewett
Regan Grafton
James Mok
Digital Strategist
Harri Owen
Advertising Agency
Draftfcb New Zealand
Planner
Steph Pearson
Media Managers
Rachel Leyland
Sarah McEwen
Simon Teagle
Account Managers
Eloise Hay
Stephanie Hueber
Account Director
Sally Willis
Group Account Director
Toby Sellers
Public Relations Manager
Angela Spain
Communications Director
Rufus Chuter
Clients
MINI New Zealand
SPCA New Zealand

Kia Optima Panoramic Sunroof: Cat

The Kia Optima comes equipped with a class-exclusive panoramic sunroof – which in layman's terms means it's the only car in its class with a really, really big glass roof. This poster was part of an integrated campaign which highlighted the Optima's key features.

–
Art Director
Joseph Danluck
Copywriter
Noah Phillips
Photographer
Toby Pederson
Creative Directors
John Battle
Eron Broughton

Executive Creative Director
Colin Jeffery
Associate Creative Director
Joseph Danluck
Chief Creative Officer
David Angelo
Retoucher
Gabriel Apodaca
Advertising Agency
David&Goliath
Account Directors
Brook Dore
Brian Dunbar
Art Buyer
Andrea Mariash
Marketing Managers
Tim Chaney
Michael Sprague
Client
Kia Motors America
Brand
Kia Optima

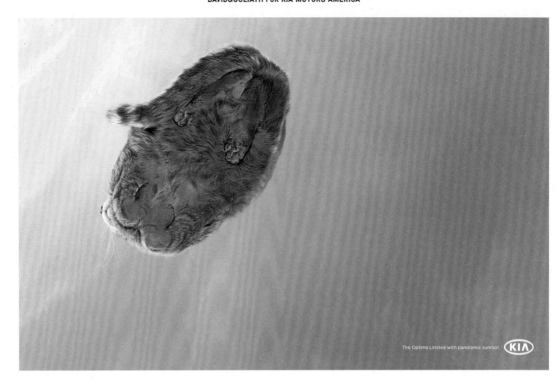

The Optima Limited with panoramic sunroof. **KIA**

Mum Dad IOU

There are 9,000 airports around the world and every one has its own three-letter code. Instead of the usual travel clichés, we used these humble but iconic codes that we're all familiar with to promote a wide range of offers and specials for the Expedia brand.

–
Art Director
Mike Watson
Copywriter
Jon Morgan
Typographer
Mark Osborne
Designer
Mark Osborne
Executive Creative Director
Gerry Human

Associate Creative Directors
Mark Harrison
Paul Mason
Chief Creative Officer
Gerry Human
Retoucher
Trevor Qizilbash
Advertising Agency
Ogilvy & Mather London
Project Manager
Grant Mason
Account Executive
Jessica Wilkinson
Brand Communications Director
Andrew Warner
Business Director
Stephen Hillcoat
Client
Expedia

The World Without Billionaires

There's only one thing bigger than billionaire's bank accounts: their egos. To give an insight into our magazine's financial content, we decided to show how the world would be completely different without them. OK – that's bulls**t. In fact, we just forgot some Photoshop layers were turned off and 'wow', the idea came to us.

–
Art Directors
Arthur d'Araujo
Fernando Reis
Copywriter
Marcelo Lima
Photographer
Ale Catan
Creative Director
Eduardo Marques
Executive Creative Directors
Claudio Lima
Fred Saldanha
Chief Creative Officer
Anselmo Ramos
Advertising Agency
Ogilvy Brazil
Account Director
Carolina Rocha
Art Buyer
Nanci Bonani
Marketing Manager
Antonio Camarotti
Client
Forbes Brasil
Brand
Forbes Magazine

ADVERTISING OUTDOOR ADVERTISING

SÃO PAULO 23°31'S 46°31'W 23° 10:00

**Park Assist
Technology**

We've all been there:
you're searching for
a parking spot and
the only space is
between a rock
and a hard place.

—
Art Directors
Nick Pringle
Steve Wakelam
Photographer
Andreas Bommert
Creative Directors
Nick Pringle
Steve Wakelam
**Executive Creative
Director**
Dylan Harrison
Retoucher
Matt Bright
Producer
Grant Navin
Advertising Agency
DDB Sydney
Art Buyer
Leesa Murray
Brand Managers
Loren Elsegood
Peter Stewart
Marketing Manager
Jutta Friese
Business Director
Dave Murphy
Managing Partner
Nicole Taylor
Client
Volkswagen Group
Australia

ADVERTISING OUTDOOR ADVERTISING

Park Assist technology from Volkswagen.

Park Assist technology from Volkswagen.

SYDNEY 34°0'S 151°0'E 22° 20:00

Road Letters

After we came up with the concept 'One letter is all it takes', we worked on visual solutions that could represent the damage that a simple letter can have on a driver's life and the people surrounding them. We experimented with every letter of the alphabet to see which letters looked like a road when put in perspective. Then we gave the letters a slight texture similar to asphalt. The tree and human elements were all made in 3D. Graphic, but realistic enough to evoke danger. The posters are very minimalist so that the eye of the viewer travels from the letter base to the potential accident.

–
Art Director
Diego Machado
Copywriter
Hugo Veiga
Designer
Diego Machado
Creative Director
Andre Kirkelis
Executive Creative Directors
Claudio Lima
Fred Saldanha
Chief Creative Officer
Anselmo Ramos
Advertising Agency
Ogilvy Brazil
Marketing Manager
Erik Fernandes
Client
Claro

ADVERTISING OUTDOOR ADVERTISING

SÃO PAULO 23°31'S 46°31'W 23° 10:00

Break the Circle

In Mexico child abuse is a big problem. Statistics show that child abuse is a behaviour that is repeated if not tackled early on. Our campaign focused on raising social awareness of this issue, provoking change from the very centre of the problem: the home. We expressed this as a cycle, showing the evolution of a child victim to a parent offender in a single character.

–
Art Directors
Oscar Chávez
José Muñoz
Ana Segurajauregui
Copywriters
Gumaro Davila
Salvador Lara
Photographer
Ale Burset
Creative Director
Francisco Ferro
Associate Creative Director
Auber Romero
Chief Creative Officers
Rafael Barthaburu
Esteban Sacco
Producers
Chon Alatorre
David Alatorre
Agency Producers
Ivonne Cortes
Adrian Ramos
Advertising Agency
Y&R Mexico
Production Company
Circo Films
Account Director
Alvaro Dopico
Art Buyers
Rodolfo Fernandez
Diego Speroni
Client
Save the Children
Mexico

Mobile Medic

The brief was to recruit medical students worthy of a Defence Force University Sponsorship. To find the best we created medically diagnosable advertising, which doubled as an entrance exam. 'Mobile Medic' allowed students to use a range of diagnostic techniques to identify and treat medical conditions using their smartphones. Visual and audio augmentation immersed them in the role of Medical Officer, on real Defence Force scenarios. Students entered their details and received their results instantly. Those who performed best were offered a Defence Force University Sponsorship application.

–

Art Director
Jake Barrow
Copywriter
Matt Lawson
Photographer
Hugh Peachy

Designers
Marcus Byrne
Janna Mamar
Creative Director
Chris Northam
Chief Creative Officer
Ben Coulson
Retoucher
Mal Stark
Digital Producer
Carrie Burman
Developer
Chuck Brandt
User Experience Architect
Luke Tellefson
Audio Producer
Katherine Muir
Sound Engineer
Paul Baxter
Advertising Agency
George Patterson Y&R Melbourne
Digital Agency
VML
Strategist
Tom Ward
Account Handler
Jason Bass
Account Executives
Chris Bush
Daniel Smith
Account Director
Janet Proposch
Group Account Director
Julian Bell
Client
Defence Force Recruiting

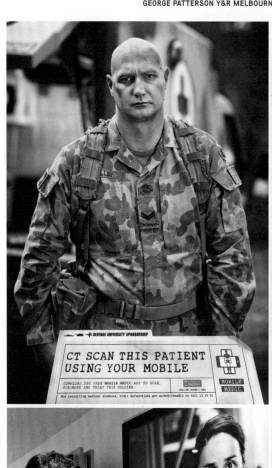

CT SCAN THIS PATIENT USING YOUR MOBILE

PERFORM AN ANGIOGRAM USING YOUR MOBILE

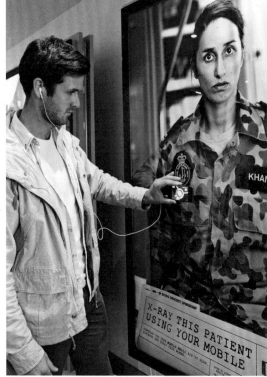

X-RAY THIS PATIENT USING YOUR MOBILE

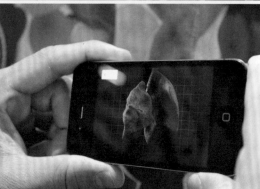

ADVERTISING   OUTDOOR ADVERTISING

MELBOURNE 37°47'S 144°58'E 12° 23:00

Anarchy

This is a press campaign to promote the new Axe Anarchy variants 'For Him' and 'For Her'. The campaign depicts a world where attraction reigns and chaos ensues. Shot by Jean-Yves Lemoigne in his trademark colour-rich, hyper-real style, the executions show the moment just before increasingly crazed behaviour causes utter mayhem.

—

Art Director
Szymon Rose
Copywriter
Daniel Schaefer
Photographer
Jean-Yves Lemoigne
Typographer
Szymon Rose
Creative Directors
Dominic Goldman
David Kolbusz
Executive Creative Director
Nick Gill
Head of Art
Mark Reddy
Retoucher
Gary Meade
Advertising Agency
BBH London
Planners
Jonathan Bottomley
Tim Jones
Account Manager
Jennifer Omran
Account Director
Keir Mather
Art Buyer
Jeremy Gleeson
Brand Managers
Ali Kashani
Tomas Marcenaro
Client
Unilever
Brand
Axe

ADVERTISING   OUTDOOR ADVERTISING

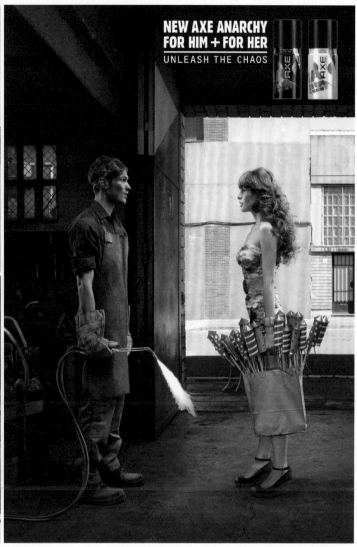

LONDON   51°32'N   0°5'W   9°   12:00

Fight for Literacy

The ANLCI is a French organisation fighting against illiteracy. We wanted to remind everyone that in 2012, 10% of French people were still illiterate, and to push people to sign the online petition to make illiteracy a national cause for 2013. The posters were mainly displayed in pedestrian areas, so they could be read in detail. At first glance, you see an ordinary ad for a computer, a movie or mascara. Then, because you can read, you quickly detect the disguised message. The campaign was a success: in February 2013, Prime Minister Jean-Marc Ayrault announced that illiteracy was the new national cause.

–
Art Director
Emmanuel Courteau
Copywriter
Jean-François Bouchet
Executive Creative Director
Alexandre Hervé
Advertising Agency
DDB Paris
Planner
Sébastien Genty
Account Handlers
Pierre Beffa
Jean-Jacques Sebille
Art Buyers
Justine Bruneau
Quentin Moenne Loccoz
Client
ANLCI

ADVERTISING OUTDOOR ADVERTISING

PARIS 48°48'N 2°20'E 10° 13:00

75 Years of Legend

Ray-Ban is a brand that believes people should ignore trends and be themselves. The brand's 75th anniversary was a perfect opportunity to celebrate the timelessness of this belief. The campaign told stories of individuals defining themselves in different time periods throughout Ray-Ban's storied history: a bold soldier, dancers breaking free of convention and dresses that were shorter. Love in the midst of chaos, freedom and fun, an unexpected artist; moments in time where people chose to be themselves and never hide. Online we told true stories of real people who conveyed the spirit of our print executions for further engagement.

–
Art Directors
Anais Boileau
Bastien Grisolet
Souen Le Van
Copywriter
Martin Rocaboy
Photographer
Mark Seliger
Creative Directors
Dimitri Guerassimov
Eric Jannon
Erik Vervroegen
Executive Creative Director
Erik Vervroegen
Chief Creative Officer
Erik Vervroegen
Head of Art
Jean-Luc Chirio
Print Producers
Thomas Geffrier
Ruth Levy
Advertising Agency
Marcel Worldwide
Strategic Director
Rob Klingensmith
Account Director
Shannon Eddy
Group Account Director
Alberto Scorticati
Art Buyer
Lauriane Dula
Communications Director
Erika Ferzt
Client
Luxottica
Brand
Ray-Ban

ADVERTISING OUTDOOR ADVERTISING

JURY

Jury Foreman
Alexandre Gama
NEOGAMA/BBH
Dan Beckett
CHI & Partners
Eugene Cheong
Ogilvy & Mather Asia Pacific
Cosimo Möller
Serviceplan

Alexandra Taylor
Mrs McGuinty
Alice Tonge
4creative
Yang Yeo
JWT Shanghai

Sport

**Also In Book
in Press Advertising
Campaigns:**
Sunday Times Rich
List Campaign

**Also In Book
as single
executions:**
Dragons' Den
Harry Potter

'The Sunday Times
Rich List' is a list of
the 1,000 wealthiest
people or families
in the UK, updated
annually in April
and published as a
magazine supplement.
'The Sunday Times
Rich List' has
become an annual
event that drives
huge newspaper
sales for The Sunday
Times. It's one of
the key events in the
marketing calendar
that attracts both loyal
and casual readers.
We therefore took
famous partnerships
and rescaled images
of them so that
the person's size
within the advert
was proportional to
their wealth. This
created adverts
that challenged our
perception of fame
and success.

–
Art Director
Richard Brim
Copywriter
Daniel Fisher
Designers
Rob Swainson
David Turfitt
Creative Director
Jonathan Burley
**Executive Creative
Director**
Jonathan Burley
Advertising Agency
CHI & Partners
Art Buyer
Emma Modler
Client
News International
Brand
The Sunday Times

LONDON 51°32'N 0°5'W 9° 12:00

Mother's Favourites

It may be called French Polony but this lunch meat is actually a South African classic. And in 2012 Enterprise released it in a 200 g, bigger pack. Good news for those who love it on their sandwiches and salads; even better news for Mum. The question is, what will she do with it?

—
Art Director
Shelley Smoler
Copywriter
Raphael Basckin
Photographer
Clive Stewart
Creative Director
Mike Groenewald
Executive Creative Directors
Matthew Brink
Adam Livesey
Advertising Agency
TBWA\Hunt\Lascaris Johannesburg
Account Executive
Claire Peters
Art Buyer
Simone Allem
Client
Tiger Brands
Brand
Enterprise

Selfies

Every journalist knows the key to a great story is getting it, as they say, straight from the horse's mouth. A first-hand account. Not from bystanders but from the people who are at the heart of the story. In this way journalists are able to provide much more detailed, in-depth and insightful accounts, which consequently means readers are better informed. We applied the style of selfies to famous journalistic shots of important historical figures to express how close the Cape Times gets to the source of the news. Every story feels like a first-hand account.

—
Art Director
Dane Alexander
Copywriter
Natalie Rose
Photographer
David Prior
Executive Creative Director
Kirk Gainsford
Advertising Agency
Lowe and Partners Cape Town
Art Buyer
Tenille Abrahams
Client
Independent Newspapers
Brand
Cape Times

CAPE TOWN   33°55'S   18°22'E   29°   14:00

Break the Circle

**Also In Book
in Press
Advertising:**
Living Room
Kitchen

In Mexico child
abuse is a big
problem. Statistics
show that child
abuse is a behaviour
that is repeated if
not tackled early
on. Our campaign
focused on raising
social awareness of
this issue, provoking
change from the
very centre of the
problem: the home.
We expressed this as
a cycle, showing the
evolution of a child
victim to a parent
offender in a single
character.

–
Art Directors
Oscar Chávez
José Muñoz
Ana Segurajauregui
Copywriters
Gumaro Davila
Salvador Lara
Photographer
Ale Burset
Creative Director
Francisco Ferro
**Associate Creative
Director**
Auber Romero
**Chief Creative
Officers**
Rafael Barthaburu
Esteban Sacco
Producers
Chon Alatorre
David Alatorre
Agency Producers
Ivonne Cortes
Adrian Ramos
Advertising Agency
Y&R Mexico
**Production
Company**
Circo Films
Account Director
Alvaro Dopico
Art Buyers
Rodolfo Fernandez
Diego Speroni
Client
Save the Children
Mexico

ADVERTISING   PRESS ADVERTISING

MEXICO CITY   19°26'N   99°8'W   11°   6:00

Obama

This is one in a series
of adverts focussing
on the state of the
US in mid 2012,
as global markets
fluctuated wildly
due to Eurozone
uncertainty
and an energy
revolution gripped
the imagination of
financial analysts
across the globe.
'Obama' commented
on how a Eurozone-
led recession in the
US could affect
Obama's chances
of re-election in
an intelligent,
witty, thought-
provoking way.

—
Art Director
Aaron McGurk
Copywriter
Chris Lapham
Creative Directors
Pete Heyes
Matt Lee
**Executive Creative
Director**
Ben Priest
Advertising Agency
adam&eveDDB
Account Manager
Flemming Lerche
Client
Financial Times

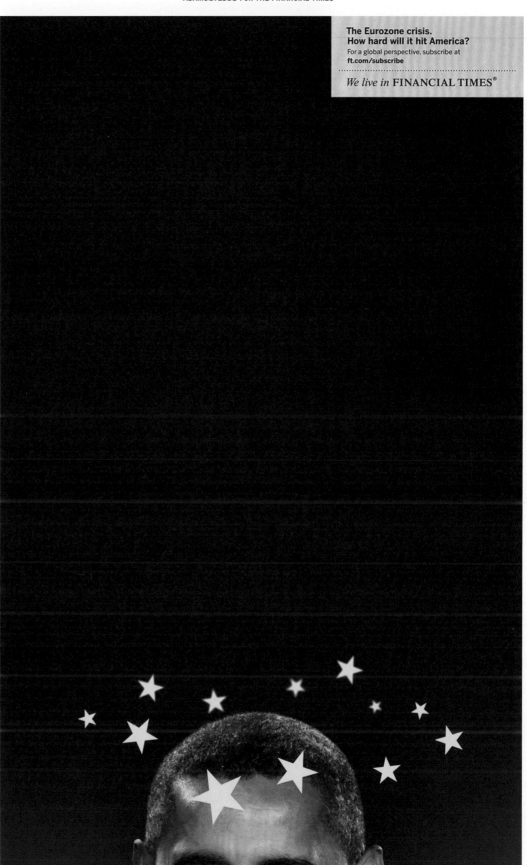

LONDON 51°32'N 0°5'W 9° 12:00

**It Never Goes Away:
A Girl / A Boy**

The Center for the Protection of Children's Rights Foundation began its crusade to protect children's rights in 1981. It was initially focused on assisting children who had been neglected, abandoned, physically abused or exploited through child labour. Lately, its area of involvement expanded and it has become involved in fighting the commercial sexual exploitation of children. It now also assists young sexual abuse victims. We announced this in our latest communication campaign.

–
Art Directors
Sanpathit Tavijaroen
Wantaya Thitipaisal
Sompat Trisadikun
Copywriter
Chanwit Nimcharoen

Photographer
Chub Nokkaew
Creative Director
Sanpathit Tavijaroen
Executive Creative Director
Keeratie Chaimoungkalo
Chief Creative Officer
Sompat Trisadikun
Agency Producer
Sarawut Lertkittipaporn
Advertising Agency
Leo Burnett Bangkok
Production Company
Chubcheevit Studio
Account Executive
Nattanan Arriyavat
Account Director
Purita Usnabhiraks
Client
The Center for the Protection of Children's Rights Foundation

Bookshelf

The Land Rover Defender can take you 'above and beyond'. To portray these limitless capabilities, we used a variety of travel, outdoor and adventure related books to reflect the Defender 90's iconic shape.

–
Art Director
Steffen List
Creative Director
Patrick Held
Advertising Agency
Advantage Y&R Namibia
Account Handler
Truda Meaden
Client
Land Rover
Brand
Defender

Civilization: Egypt

If you don't want
germs to settle
and develop a whole
civilization inside
your tooth, use
Maxam toothpaste.

–
Art Directors
Danny Li
Haoxi Lv
Copywriter
Chanfron Zhao
Photographers
Kingkong
Surachai
Puthikulangkura
Illustrators
Surachai
Puthikulangkura
Supachai U-Rairat
Creative Director
Hattie Cheng
**Executive Creative
Directors**
Elvis Chau
Yang Yeo
Print Producer
Anotai Panmongkol
**Production
Managers**
Liza Law
Isaac Xu
Joseph Yu
Advertising Agency
JWT Shanghai
**Production
Company**
Illusion
Account Handler
Carol Ma
Art Buyer
Chivel Miao
Client
Maxam

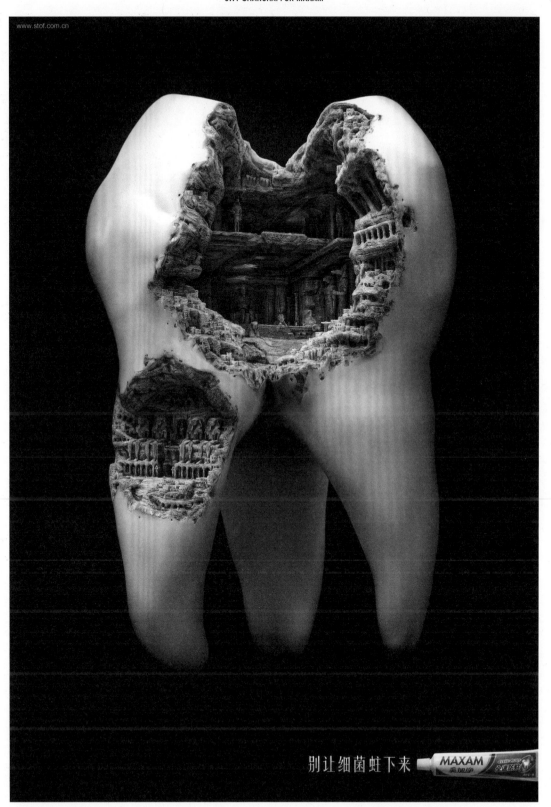

Anarchy:
Fireworks / Petrol

This is a press campaign to promote the new Axe Anarchy variants 'For Him' and 'For Her'. The campaign depicts a world where attraction reigns and chaos ensues. Shot by Jean-Yves Lemoigne in his trademark colour-rich, hyper-real style, the executions show the moment just before increasingly crazed behaviour causes utter mayhem.

–
Art Director
Szymon Rose
Copywriter
Daniel Schaefer
Photographer
Jean-Yves Lemoigne
Typographer
Szymon Rose
Creative Directors
Dominic Goldman
David Kolbusz
Executive
Creative Director
Nick Gill
Retoucher
Gary Meade
Head of Art
Mark Reddy
Advertising Agency
BBH London
Planners
Jonathan Bottomley
Tim Jones
Account Manager
Jennifer Omran
Account Director
Keir Mather
Art Buyer
Jeremy Gleeson
Brand Managers
Ali Kashani
Tomas Marcenaro
Client
Unilever
Brand
Axe

ADVERTISING PRESS ADVERTISING

LONDON 51°32'N 0°5'W 9° 12:00

Monsters

McDonald's isn't just a fast food chain, it's also the perfect venue for kids' parties. Parents needed to know that. To convince them to have their child's party at McDonald's, we highlighted a child's potential for destruction – destruction that could take place in your beloved home. So why not have the party at McDonald's instead?

–
Art Director
Hital Pandya
Copywriter
Andre Vrdoljak
Executive Creative Director
Grant Jacobsen
Advertising Agency
DDB South Africa
Photography
Carioca
Account Handler
Tsitsi Dhlamini
Client
McDonald's
South Africa

Luggage Labels

There are 9,000 airports around the world and every one has its own three-letter code. Instead of the usual travel clichés, we used these humble but iconic codes that we're all familiar with to promote a wide range of offers and specials for the Expedia brand.

–

Art Director
Mike Watson
Copywriter
Jon Morgan
Typographer
Mark Osborne
Designer
Mark Osborne
Executive Creative Director
Gerry Human
Associate Creative Directors
Mark Harrison
Paul Mason
Chief Creative Officer
Gerry Human
Retoucher
Trevor Qizilbash
Advertising Agency
Ogilvy & Mather London
Project Manager
Grant Mason
Account Executive
Jessica Wilkinson
Brand Communications Director
Andrew Warner
Business Director
Stephen Hillcoat
Client
Expedia

YNYWYH Press Campaign

This campaign is based on the idea that you're really not yourself when you're hungry. We launched a campaign of press ads showing what famous people through the ages might have said if they had been hungry.

–
Art Director
Alan Wilson
Copywriter
Diccon Driver
Typographers
Sebastien Delahaye
Alison Greenway
Aaron Moss
Alan Wilson
Creative Directors
Alex Grieve
Adrian Rossi
Executive Creative Director
Paul Brazier
Advertising Agency
AMV BBDO
Client
MasterFoods
Brand
Snickers

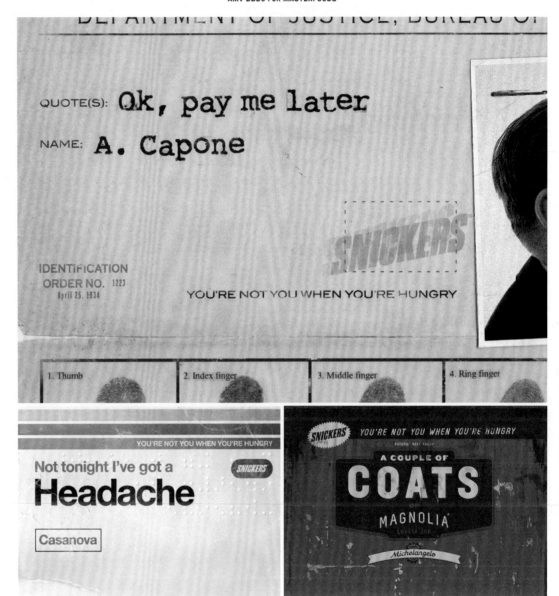

Park Assist
Technology

We've all been there:
you're searching for
a parking spot and
the only space is
between a rock
and a hard place.

–
Art Directors
Nick Pringle
Steve Wakelam
Photographer
Andreas Bommert
Creative Directors
Nick Pringle
Steve Wakelam
**Executive Creative
Director**
Dylan Harrison
Retoucher
Matt Bright
Producer
Grant Navin
Advertising Agency
DDB Sydney
Art Buyer
Leesa Murray
Brand Managers
Loren Elsegood
Peter Stewart
Marketing Manager
Jutta Friese
Business Director
Dave Murphy
Managing Partner
Nicole Taylor
Client
Volkswagen
Group Australia

ADVERTISING   PRESS ADVERTISING

Park Assist technology from Volkswagen.

Park Assist technology from Volkswagen.

Park Assist technology from Volkswagen.

SYDNEY 34°0'S 151°0'E 22° 20:00

Life Cycle

City dwellers spend much of their day cooped up inside. Yet there's so much more out there to explore and discover. And the best way to do that is on the saddle of a bike. Cycling offers an individual perspective: a city looks and feels completely different when riding on a bike. To dramatise this idea, we created compositions of maps and landscapes from a variety of bicycle parts, encouraging people to break free of their daily routine, and to look at their surroundings in a completely different light.

–
Art Directors
Chris Soh
Thomas Yang
Copywriter
Andrew Hook
Photographer
Allan Ng
Typographer
Celeste Anning
Designers
Chris Soh
Thomas Yang
Creative Directors
Andrew Hook
Thomas Yang
Executive Creative Director
Joji Jacob
Chief Creative Officer
Neil Johnson
Advertising Agency
DDB Singapore
Retouching
Digitalis
Account Manager
Sandy Lee
Client
Life Cycle

ADVERTISING   PRESS ADVERTISING

SINGAPORE   1°17'N   103°50'E   26°   20:00

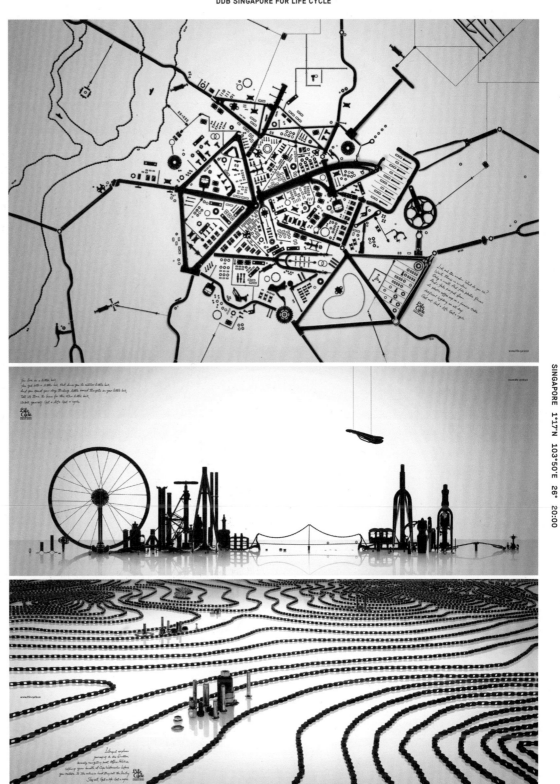

Omar / Roberto

This campaign reminds us of the people who were persecuted and tortured, as well as those who disappeared, under the military dictatorships in Uruguay, Argentina and Chile. It was released in commemoration of 40 years of democracy in the region and as a reminder of Amnesty's ongoing fight for justice for those still missing.

—
Art Directors
Agustín Acosta
Álvaro Díaz
Luis Meyer
Copywriters
Camila De Simone
Mateo Vidal
Photographer
Gustavo Germano
Creative Directors
Gonzalo López
Baliñas
Diego Román
Executive Creative Directors
Fernando De Clemente
Jorge González
Sebastián Mir
Chief Creative Officer
Gabriel Román
Advertising Agency
Lowe Ginkgo
Account Managers
Marcelo Bonomi
Victoria Martin
Brand Managers
Maria García
Mariana Labastie
Client
Amnesty International

Omar Dario and Mario Alfredo Amestoy

Roberto Sorba, Jorge Cresto and Azucena Sorba

MONTEVIDEO 34°53'S 56°10'W 19° 10:00

ADVERTISING PRESS ADVERTISING

○

IN BOOK IN PRESS ADVERTISING, INSERTS & WRAPS FOR PRESS ADVERTISING
OGILVY & MATHER JOHANNESBURG FOR PEOPLE OPPOSING WOMEN ABUSE

A Shoe Brochure in Case of Emergency

In South Africa, abuse of women is seen as the issue of low income groups, despite high rates of abuse in upper income groups. The challenge was to reach these women and communicate life-saving information to them in a relevant way, without arousing the abusers' suspicions. We disguised POWA pamphlets as high-end Nine West shoe brochures, placed inside niche publications, targeting wealthy areas. Even if the brochure didn't reach a victim directly, it could be passed on, in front of a man, or slipped under a door, with the knowledge that a woman would look at it but a man would ignore it.

–
Art Directors
Alexa Craner
Michelle McKenna
Copywriter
Taryn Scher
Creative Director
Mariana O'Kelly
Executive Creative Director
Fran Luckin
Retouchers
Ryan Greig
Neil Webb
Print Producers
Shirley Wagner
Quintin Wright
Advertising Agency
Ogilvy Johannesburg
Photography
Nine West
Planner
Candice Blumenthal
Account Handler
Shera Eshmade
Client
People Opposing Women Abuse

ADVERTISING   PRESS ADVERTISING

JOHANNESBURG   26°12'S   28°4'E   16°   14:00

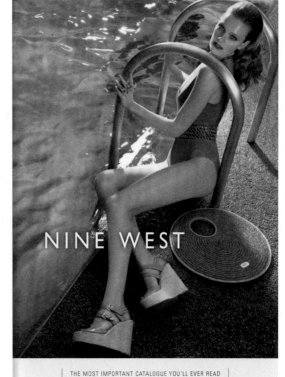

NINE WEST

| THE MOST IMPORTANT CATALOGUE YOU'LL EVER READ |

THIS IS NOT WHAT YOU THINK IT IS. PLEASE KEEP READING. THIS CATALOGUE IS DESIGNED TO GET INFORMATION TO **WOMEN IN ABUSIVE RELATIONSHIPS,** WITHOUT AROUSING THE SUSPICIONS OF THE ABUSER.

213

ADVERTISING   RADIO ADVERTISING

JURY

Jury Foreman
Rui Alves
Y&R Johannesburg
Tim Craig
Radioville
Fabian Frese

Jenny Glover
Network BBDO Johannesburg
Richard Muntz
JWT Melbourne
Kelvin Tillinghast
Wunderman

Call Girl

DJs love to talk. So to promote the season premiere of TV show 'Secret Diary of a Call Girl' we gave them something well worth talking about: a high-class, S&M savvy call girl working from a bedroom directly opposite their studio window. Of course they couldn't help but broadcast their saucy observations to the world and as predicted other stations immediately picked up on the story. Then on premiere night with public interest at its peak, our actress slowly closed the blinds on her eager audience and revealed this message: 'Secret Diary of a Call Girl. 9:35 Tonight on Prime'.

–
Senior Copywriters
Hywel James
Kelly Lovelock
Executive Creative Directors
Tony Clewett
Regan Grafton
James Mok
Producer
Kelly Gillard
Advertising Agency
Draftfcb New Zealand
Media Manager
Nicole Earnshaw
Account Manager
Jess Sheffield
Account Director
Sally Willis
Group Account Director
Toby Sellers
Client
Prime Television

AUCKLAND 36°52'S 174°45'E 15° 1:00

Poetry

Also In Book
in Writing for
Radio Advertising

When it comes to
bridging the gap
between feuding
mother and daughter,
nothing comes
close to the gift
of Campbell's
Chunky Soup.

—
Copywriter
Robert Rooney
Creative Director
Robert Rooney
Executive Creative
Director
James Caporimo
Chief Creative
Officer
Jim Elliott
Producer
Jona Goodman
Advertising Agency
Y&R New York
Client
Campbell's Soup
Company
Brand
Chunky Soup

ADVERTISING RADIO ADVERTISING

SFX Sounds of obsessive cleaning

Mom Sara, I'm going to obsessively clean this window until I blurt out that I can't believe you chose Elizabethan poetry as your major.

Daughter I'm going to look at you for several moments without saying anything.

SFX Clock ticking

Daughter Then go into another room and slam a door.

SFX Slam

Mom I'm going to keep pretending to clean while I fume!

Daughter I will now slam another door...

SFX Slam

Daughter Twice!

SFX Slam

Mom I am now completely unhinged because I hate door slamming just slightly less than Elizabethan poetry!

Daughter I am now going to the pantry!

Mom I'm following you.

SFX Door opening
Rummaging sounds

Daughter I'm taking every can of Campbell's Chunky Soup back with me to school because it's delicious and I'm poor!

Mom And I will choke down my outrage at that new tattoo I just noticed for the first time because I want you to have decent meals!

Daughter And I love you for letting me!

Mom And you'll always be my little girl!

Daughter Let's both storm off in opposite directions!

Mom OK!

MVO Campbell's. It's amazing what soup can do.

NEW YORK CITY 40°40'N 73°56'W 8° 8:00

Frank

When life is good, you dream big – winning the lottery or driving a fancy car. But when you are homeless, your dreams are much smaller – eating a hot meal or having something warm to wear. The Salvation Army, as the biggest non-governmental provider of social services in Canada, makes the small dreams of those in need come true. The story of 'Frank' demonstrates just how small some of those dreams actually are and what a difference their fulfillment could make. No dream is too small when you are in need.

Copywriter
James Ansley
Art Director
Yusong Zhang
Chief Creative Officer
Patrick Scissons
Producer
Sam Benson
Audio Producer
Adam Damelin
Recording Engineer
Matt Gautier
Advertising Agency
Grey Group Canada
Production Company
The Eggplant Collective
Planner
Malcolm McLean
Account Manager
Alix Myers
Account Director
Stephanie Nerlich
Client
The Salvation Army

SFX   City noise up and under

MVO   Broke, with no place to live, left wandering the cold city streets while he waits for the shelter to open, Frank daydreams that he is broke, with no place to live, left wandering the cold city streets while he waits for the shelter to open… with a warm coat to wear.

No dream is too small when you're in need. The Salvation Army. Give generously at salvationarmy.ca.

Death Doesn't Try Very Hard: Chocolate Bar

Death doesn't have to try very hard; thankfully, with life cover from Frank.Net, neither do you.

Copywriters
Heidi Kasselman
Simon Lotze
Saf Sindhi
Creative Director
Justin Gomes
Agency Producer
Katherine Searle-Tripp
Voice Over Artist
Adam Behr
Recording Engineer
Stephen Webster
Advertising Agency
FoxP2
Account Handler
Catherine Kawitzky
Client
Frank.Net

MVO   Death is a nut in a nut-free chocolate bar. Death is a gust of wind at a scenic viewpoint. Death is an air traffic controller with a weak bladder, a misidentified mushroom or an absent 'Slippery When Wet' sign on a floor that's slippery when wet. Death doesn't have to try very hard. But thankfully, with Frank Life Cover, neither do you.

Just SMS 'Frank' to 43002, we'll call you right back and you can have up to R10 million life cover by the end of the call. That's 'Frank' to 43002. SMS rates and Ts and Cs apply. Frank.Net is a licensed financial services provider.

Knock, Knock

Also In Book
in Writing for
Radio Advertising

Letting your college-bound child raid the pantry for Campbell's Chunky Soup is the greatest act of parental kindness.

—
Copywriter
Robert Rooney
Creative Director
Robert Rooney
Executive Creative Director
James Caporimo
Chief Creative Officer
Jim Elliott
Producer
Jona Goodman
Advertising Agency
Y&R New York
Client
Campbell's Soup Company
Brand
Chunky Soup

SFX Sound of knocking on door

Dad I'm knocking to respect your privacy Son, but I'm walking in without waiting for an answer to assert my authority while you're home for the weekend.

Son Well, I'm pretending to text someone rather than make eye contact, thereby undermining your pathetic attempt to assert your authority.

Dad I'm not mentioning your grade point average, because I promised your mother I wouldn't ruin the weekend.

Son I'm storming out of the room and going to the pantry.

Dad I'm following you, because I don't want to let you have the last word.

SFX Rummaging sounds

Son I'm violently rummaging through the pantry in search of something.

Dad I'm now openly seething. You are ruining my obsessively organised pantry!

Son I'm taking this whole case of Campbell's Chunky Soup with me to school because it's delicious and the dining hall is gross!

Dad I'm going to let you because even though I'm steeped in disappointment at you, I don't want you going hungry.

Son You giving me this soup is the greatest show of affection you ever gave me! I love you!

Dad I'm tearing up! So I will withdraw in a huff!

Son Fine!

Dad Fine!

SFX Doors slamming

MVO Campbell's. It's amazing what soup can do.

NEW YORK CITY 40°40'N 73°56'W 8° 8:00

Dumb Ways to Die

In 2012, 77,000 people paid to own this radio ad. In fact, it charted in 28 countries reaching a peak of number three in Hong Kong. This is all despite the fact that the song was available for free download on Soundcloud and also available on all self-respecting illegal download sites. While radio advertising was purchased in Melbourne, stations around the world played it for free, as a pop song. Not bad.

—

Music Composer & Producer
Oliver McGill
Copywriter
John Mescall
Art Director
Pat Baron
Creative Director
Pat Baron
Executive Creative Director
John Mescall
Producer
Cinnamon Darvall
Senior Producer
Mark Bradley
Advertising Agency
McCann Erickson Melbourne
Production Company
McCann Erickson Melbourne
Account Manager
Tamara Broman
Account Director
Alec Hussain
Group Account Director
Adrian Mills
Brand Manager
Leah Waymark
Marketing Manager
Chloe Alsop
Client
Metro Trains

ADVERTISING   RADIO ADVERTISING

SFX   Jolly musical intro
on guitar

Singer   Set fire to your hair
Poke a stick at a
grizzly bear
Eat medicine that's
out of date
Use your private parts
as piranha bait.

Dumb ways to die,
so many dumb ways
to die.

Get your toast out
with a fork
Do your own
electrical work
Teach yourself
how to fly
Eat a two-week old
unrefrigerated pie.

Dumb ways to die,
so many dumb ways
to die.

Invite a
psycho killer inside
Scratch your drug dealer's
brand new ride
Take your helmet off
in outer space
Use a clothes dryer
as a hiding place.

Dumb ways to die,
so many dumb ways
to die.

Keep a rattlesnake
as a pet
Sell both your kidneys
on the internet
Eat a tube of superglue
'I wonder, what's this
red button do?'

Dumb ways to die,
so many dumb ways
to die.

Dress up like a moose
during hunting season
Disturb a nest of wasps
for no good reason
Stand on the edge of
a train station platform
Drive around the boom
gates at a level crossing
Run across the tracks
between the platforms
They may not rhyme but
they're quite possibly

Dumbest ways to die
Dumbest ways to die
Dumbest ways to die
So many dumb
So many dumb ways
to die.

FVO   Be safe around trains.
A message from Metro.

MELBOURNE   37°47'S   144°58'E   12°   23:00

ADVERTISING RADIO ADVERTISING

Distance to Danger

When driving, the greater your following distance, the safer you are. Conversely, the closer you are, the greater the danger. These spots tell stories of increasing danger the closer the driver gets to the vehicle ahead, and demonstrate precisely why Mercedes-Benz Collision Prevention Assist with following distance control is so vital for your personal safety.

–

Copywriters
Jenny Glover
Brent Singer
Creative Directors
Jenny Glover
Brent Singer
Executive Creative Director
Robert McLennan
Agency Producer
Natalie Sutton
Sound Designer
David Law
Advertising Agency
Net#work BBDO Johannesburg
Client
Mercedes-Benz

Virus

FVO The van on the road in front of me appeared to be enveloped in a soupy black smoke, but as I moved closer I saw it to be an entourage of adoring flies. The bumper was collaged with a collection of stickers from countries with voweless names, their national flags depicting scenes of revolution and meat products. Unfazed, I accelerated. I could see the driver now. The angry red welts on his neck so much like whole-fruit jam. I pull in closer. I can hear him. He makes the kind of distressed noises best associated with water births. A smell wafts in the window. 'Mortuary gravy' are the first words that pop into my head. I'm right on the van's tail. I see a dangling key ring. 'Free hugs' it reads. I inch forward. It's then that I spot a mosquito taking a long bloody sip from the driver's pale flesh. Instantly, it falls to its back with its legs in the air. Dead. And that's when I hear the beeping of my Mercedes-Benz Collision Prevention Assist with following distance control. Reminding me that the closer I get, the more dangerous things are bound to become.

Scooter

MVO It pulled into the road ahead of me. One of those swell little obesity scooters. Manned by a fellow whose body type could best be demonstrated by stuffing a mattress with pork scratching. I accelerated forward. I could now just make out the roast chicken clutched like a meaty posy in the driver's massive fist. Bits of fatty skin and bone floated in on the breeze towards me. Still, I edged closer. Our eyes met. It was a look that succinctly screamed, 'I make children's toys out of asbestos siding and discarded syringes and I'd like to pluck your nails to make printers-tray nick-nacks'.

Despite this I pulled in closer. I could smell his breath now. It smelt of the ink from the pages of 'Knife Enthusiast'. And deserted caravan. The stench turned my wedding ring green. Still I pulled closer. I could just make out the lettering on the driver's pinkie ring: 'Society... for... the... sterilisation... of redheads' it read. My ginger eyebrows shoot up just as I hear the all-knowing beep of my Mercedes-Benz Collision Prevention Assist with following distance control. Reminding me that the closer I get, the more dangerous things are bound to become.

Lawyer

MVO The car ahead had the kind of gleam that could only be achieved by a team of menservants with seal cub chamois. I pull my car closer. The driver I see has the mocha skin of a small Mauritian child. Literally. And cheekbones that you could shave fancy ham on. He wears the bat-like robes of a blood sucking viscount... or lawyer. I guess lawyer and accelerate forward. On the console I see a doll of the 'show us where he touched you on this anatomical replica' kind. I notice several dog hairs on the driver's jacket. Shed by a small jewellery-wearing terrier owned by his high maintenance wife.

Again I move in a tad closer. I spot the heavy cufflinks engraved with the two jauntily crossed crutches and neck brace that make up the driver's prestigious family crest. I inhale his car fumes, which smell of filet mignon and orphan tears. I edge closer. Our gazes meet. I lock eyes with a man who laughed in 'Ol' Yella'. He mouths the words 'Cha-ching' just as I hear the cautionary beep of my Mercedes-Benz Collision Prevention Assist with following distance control. Reminding me that the closer I get, the more dangerous things are bound to become.

JOHANNESBURG 26°12'S 28°4'E 16° 14:00

New Shoes

Our campaign idea stemmed from a simple truth: students are at a stage where they seek the freedom to control their lives. Unfortunately, that's impossible to do with their current bank: The First National Bank of Mom and Dad. Every transaction with mom and dad comes with strings attached. The scrutiny is endless. It's time for students to break free from mom and dad's oversight and approval. It's time to switch to student banking at Fifth Third Bank.

–
Copywriter
John Deignan
Executive Creative Directors
Dave Loew
Jon Wyville
Chief Creative Officer
Susan Credle
Agency Producer
Stephen Clark
Sound Engineer
John Binder
Advertising Agency
Leo Burnett Chicago
Production Company
Another Country
Account Directors
Marie Bubendorff-Gomez
Lauren Gibbs
Client
Fifth Third Bank

SFX **Phone rings**

Mom **First National Bank of Mom and Dad, the answer is probably no, Mom speaking.**

Daughter **Hi Mom.**

Mom **Oh, hi honey. What is it?**

Daughter **Well, I have this formal coming up.**

Mom **Yeah.**

Daughter **I could use some money for new shoes.**

Mom **Well, what about your black heels? They go with everything.**

Daughter **Mom.**

Mom **Let me talk to my colleague. Please hold.**

SFX **Sound of call going on hold. Bad music plays. A promo in Mom's voice plays: 'Ask about our Constantly Checking Up on You Checking Account'.
Sound of call coming off hold**

Mom **Your father said sorry, we're not an ATM machine. Thanks for calling. We miss you.**

MVO **It's time for a new bank. Find out more at 53.com/students. Fifth Third Bank. The curious bank. Member FDIC.**

CHICAGO 41°52'N 87°37'W 3° 7:00

Laugh Track: Sitcom

Rottofest is an annual comedy festival held on Rottnest – an island 18 km off the coast of Perth, Western Australia. Rottofest asked us to create a campaign that encouraged people to turn off their TVs and enjoy some real comedy, rather than watch sitcoms at home.

–
Copywriter
Guy Hamilton
Howlett
Art Director
Neil Martin
Creative Directors
Pat and Beans
Recording Engineer
Brad Habib
Advertising Agency
Marketforce
Post Production
Soundbyte
Client
Vulture Culture
Brand
Rottofest

MVO1 **This is a laugh track.**

SFX **Laugh track**

MVO1 **You've heard this sound effect a million times during sitcoms. It was recorded in the 50s, so most of these people are dead. And we disrespect their memory by using their laughter in shows like this:**

SFX **Theme song sung like the 'Two and a Half Men' theme: Males, males, males, males**

MVO2 **I can't believe you did it with my son's Spanish teacher, Mrs Rodriguez. Then you stank up my toilet!**

MVO3 **You know what happens after I eat Mexican.**

SFX **Laugh track**

MVO1 **Those are people's dead mothers, fathers, grandmas and grandpas being forced to laugh at crass innuendo!**

SFX **A loud fart followed by a laugh track**

MVO1 **There's nothing funny about laugh tracks. Get some real laughs at Rottofest this weekend. Two days of stand up on Rottnest Island.**

PERTH 31°57'S 115°52'E 15° 22:30

Universe

A narrator takes you on a journey through human history, describing the unlikelihood of your existence and the responsibility that comes with that.

—
Copywriter
James Holman
Writers
Reggie Ocampo
Nuno Teixeira
Creative Directors
Gary Steele
Hagan de Villiers
Executive Creative Director
Mel du Toit
Agency Producer
Haydn Evans
Voice Over Artist
Hugh Barford
Sound Designer
Damian Waddell

Production Manager
Ian Lew
Advertising Agencies
TBWA\Singapore
The Integer Group Singapore TBWA
Production Companies
Six Toes
Song Zu Singapore
Account Executive
April Tan
Account Manager
Sophia Hung
Account Director
Dan Paris
Head of Brand Marketing
Kerensa Ang
Client
Lend Lease Retail Investments
Brand
313@Somerset

MVO Imagine the cosmic improbability of your existence. The miraculous unlikelihood that here, on one blue planet out of countless trillions, you were lucky enough to be born. You're the sum of every single one of your ancestors having avoided artillery, avalanches, dysentery, drunk drivers, polar bears, polio and the plague. And they all lived long enough to find the right partner, at the right time, in the right mood to pass on one bit of genetic material. All this continued on and on and on until you beat over 30 million other sperm to an egg, and finally began the miracle that is your life. It took all that to get you here.

The least you can do is put on a nice shirt.

For the latest trends in fashion, visit 313@Somerset.

SINGAPORE 1°17'N 103°50'E 26° 20:00

ADVERTISING RADIO ADVERTISING

When Will it End?

Embarrassing moments seem to go on and on and on. Stimorol Infinity's long-lasting flavour, however, actually does last forever.

—
Copywriter
Anthony Walton
Art Director
Justin Enderstein
Executive Creative Director
Chris Gotz
Agency Producer
Jo Weiss
Voice Over Artist
Adam Behr
Recording Engineer
Graham Merrill
Advertising Agency
Ogilvy Cape Town
Production Company
We Love Jam
Account Manager
Alexis Leih
Account Director
Awie Erasmus
Client
Kraft Foods South Africa
Brand
Stimorol Infinity

MVO Dad says that I should sit down; that we need to talk. So I do. Mom's sitting already. She's holding a banana. Menacingly. Dad says that I've reached the age where I should have questions about my body. Mom starts to cry. Dad tells me that I'm full of raging hormones. We stare at each other. Somewhere, I can hear a dog barking. Mom pulls out a small square of shiny foil. It says 'Knight Rider' on it. And that it's ribbed for extra pleasure. She opens the packet with her teeth. Dad puts his hand on my shoulder as Mom slips the condom over the banana in one smooth, practised movement.

VO Some things feel like they last forever. Others actually do. Stimorol Infinity. It goes on and on.

CAPE TOWN 33°55'S 18°22'E 29° 14:00

Rescue Radio

In Lebanon, there are 200,000 foreign domestic workers, mostly from countries like the Philippines and Sri Lanka. As they try desperately to support families back home, the reality is that thousands are physically and sexually abused. Often they are locked up and prevented from leaving their employers' homes, making it impossible for charities like our client, Sawa Mninjah, to reach them. We found a way in. We created radio ads in languages only the domestic workers could understand and played them on popular Lebanese stations. Disguised as typical retail ads, they broke into homes, delivering our secret message of hope.

–
Copywriters
Logan Allanson
Dylan Kidson
Sascha Kuntze
Ali Mokdad
James Purdie
Art Director
Christian Louzado
Creative Directors
Ben Knight
Ramzi Moutran
Executive Creative Director
Steve Hough
Agency Producer
Diana Jebaly
Advertising Agency
Memac Ogilvy & Mather
Production Company
BKP Music
Client
Sawa Mninjah

SFX   Water park music

FVO   If you're a domestic worker, please listen to this message. We've disguised it as a water park ad so your employer doesn't catch on.

SFX   Water park sounds, water splashing, people screaming

FVO   As an organisation that fights for domestic workers' rights, we can't mention our name, but if you are a victim of physical or sexual abuse, and you're too scared to talk to anyone, we want you to know we're here to help. So if you, or anyone you know, has been subjected to beatings or unwanted sexual advances please call us, any time, on 76 573 842.

SFX   Water park sounds, water splashing, people screaming

FVO   Remember, you can call us any time on 76 573 842. We will help.

SFX   Water park music

Christine's Flavour Tip

Everyone knows that smoking kills. But few think about what it's like living with a tobacco-related disease. The 'Tips' campaign used the voices of real victims to demonstrate the potential consequences of tobacco on their lives. From experience, they give helpful 'tips' on dealing with your life if smoking leaves you in the same condition. 'Christine's Flavour Tip' offers a bleak image of life on a liquid diet, with nauseating sound effects to really put things in context.

–
Copywriter
Bill Girouard
Creative Directors
Bill Girouard
John Kearse
Associate Creative Director
Steve Tom
Chief Creative Officer
Pete Favat
Agency Producer
Katie Harris
Advertising Agency
Arnold Worldwide Boston
Planner
Kelleen Peckham
Account Executive
Paul Nelson
Client
Centers for Disease Control and Prevention

Christine   I'm Christine. I'm here to give you a tip on how to eat if smoking gives you oral cancer and you have to have your jaw removed. Like I did. Since chewing is kind of difficult without a jaw – and if you're like me, without any teeth too – you'll be on a liquid diet. OK, I'm pouring it into my feeding bag. In case you're wondering, it looks pretty much like how it sounds. Here we go…

SFX   Grinding of a feeding machine

Christine   That sound you're hearing is the sound of your dinner from now on. And your lunch. And your breakfast. My tip for you is, don't get too hung up on choosing the flavour of your liquid diet. They all really taste the same once you put them in your feeding tube.

MVO   Smoking causes immediate damage to your body. You can quit. For free help call 1800–QUIT–NOW. A message from the US Department of Health and Human Services and CDC.

Vincent

To showcase its extraordinary new Ecoboost engine and highlight the impossible-sounding benefit of increased power but reduced size, Ford ran a national radio campaign for the new Focus. The Ecoboost engine is a triumph of contradiction, delivering more power from a smaller engine, so to tell this intriguing story the ads are written as a series of contradictions.

–

Copywriters
Jason Mendes
Giles Montgomery
Andy Wyton
Creative Director
Andy Dibb
Executive Creative Director
Gerry Human
Chief Creative Officer
Gerry Human
Agency Producer
Ruth Darsow
Recording Engineer
Graeme Elston
Advertising Agency
Ogilvy & Mather London
Account Manager
Emma Forsyth
Client
Ford of Britain
Brand
Ecoboost

ADVERTISING   RADIO ADVERTISING

Stephen Fry (talking in a breezy, conversational style) I was driving with Vincent, my tall short friend, who was regaling me with the most hilariously tragic stories while the rain pelted down out of a clear blue sky.

'Great car, this', said Vincent with disgust. 'You're right', I disagreed. 'And I do hate the lovely colour', continued Vincent. 'It's a sort of midnight sunrise'.

'Yes', I said. 'But you know the most interestingly dull thing is the engine, which is both big and small'.

'I don't understand', nodded Vincent. 'Well', I said, 'it gives the power of a large engine with the fuel efficiency of a small one'.

Vincent frowned. 'That makes perfect sense', she said.

FVO The new Ecoboost engine in the Ford Focus – a triumph of contradiction.

Ford. Go further.

LONDON   51°32'N   0°5'W   9°   12:00

Courtesy Day:
Chivalry

Renault and Dacia, two brands of the Renault Group, wanted to pay special attention to bad behaviour on the road on 22 March, European Road Courtesy Day. We aired this commercial during rush hour in the week before 22 March, showing drivers how ridiculous impolite and aggressive road behaviour is. Renault and Dacia fought for the same media space, just like drivers would fight for the same parking space. On 22 March, they finally understood, and ended their dispute in a courteous manner.

–
Copywriters
Wim Corremans
Alex Gabriëls
Executive Creative Director
Paul Servaes
Associate Creative Directors
Tom Berth
Geert De Rocker
Producer
Raf de Braekeleer
Agency Producer
Katie Kelly
Audio Producers
Christophe Cossement
Tim Leitner
Sound Engineer
Joe Barone
Advertising Agency
Publicis Brussels
Production Companies
Bar1
Cobra
Strategists
Henk Ghesquière
Annemie Goegebuer
Tom Theys
Account Managers
Julie Oostvogels
Jonas De Wit
Account Director
Francis Lippens
Brand Communications Director
Xavier Laporta
Client
Renault Group
Brand
Dacia
Renault

SFX Music for a Renault ad begins

FVO The Renault Clio with interior styling…

SFX Music for a Dacia ad

MVO The Dacia Duster, a 4x4 that…

FVO Excuse me, but I was here first.

MVO Yeah? Whatever, I reserved this spot before you sweetheart.

FVO And they say chivalry is dead.

MVO I think it killed itself when it saw you coming.

FVO Funny.

MVO Women selling cars. (he imitates her) Renault Cliooo…

FVO I do not sound like that!

MVO Let me show you how it's done sugar. (he begins to read his script again) The Dacia Duster, a 4x4 that…

FVO The Dacia Duster, blah blah blah.

MVO Grow up!

FVO You grow up!

MVO Go bleach your moustache!

FVO At least I have one.

MVO I've got one! (arguing continues)

FVO2 (calm) Remember, 22 March is Road Courtesy Day. Supported by the Renault Group.

FVO Why don't you ask for directions because this isn't your commercial!

ADVERTISING RADIO ADVERTISING

BRUSSELS 50°52'N 4°22'E 10° 13:00

Radio Ghosts

One in eleven deaths caused by car accident has to do with driving after drinking. To raise awareness we created radio spots describing the accident by the deceased victim himself: a radio ghost. We installed small radio stations in the shape of wooden crosses in Hamburg, at real places where car accidents caused by drink driving happened. These small radio stations aired the story of the deceased as a radio spot directly to the cars stopping nearby.

—
Copywriter
Andreas Schriewer
Creative Director
Marc Vosshall
Executive Creative Director
Till Diestel
Chief Creative Officer
Alexander Schill
Creative Producer
Florian Panier
Producers
Philipp Feit
Eduardo Garcia
Advertising Agency
Serviceplan München
Production Company
German Wahnsinn
Account Managers
Kristian von Elm
Ines Herbold
Client
Johanniter-Unfall-Hilfe

ADVERTISING RADIO ADVERTISING

Die Johanniter, Radio Ghost – Milena

Woman (talks imploringly)
Hello. I'm Milena.
Or rather, was. Because where you stand now, we stood last Saturday night. At the traffic lights, right at the snack bar. The death cross has been hung up by my girls. Of course, we were already a little drunk and I was a bit close to the road. But I'm dead only because of this drunk idiot trying to turn up the volume of his stereo and then going off the road.

MVO Don't drink and drive.
Die Johanniter.
Because we love life.
www.johanniter.de

Die Johanniter, Radio Ghost – Child

Girl (talks frankly)
Hello. Please stop driving when you have been drinking. Because I have been run over here. Right over there at the tree is my death cross. I came from the Moorweide; I played on the lawn with my friends. Then I had to hurry home. And here on the corner I was waiting for the traffic light to turn green. I did not see the car coming. He came from an office party. He had drunk one champagne and three beers.

MVO Don't drink and drive.
Die Johanniter.
Because we love life.
www.johanniter.de

Die Johanniter, Radio Ghost – Holger

Man (talks desperately)
Sorry. I'm talking to all drivers on this corner. Because I died here. Right there at the railing, that's my death cross. I was here on the left in the Wagenbau, celebrating with friends. My girlfriend was on the other side. At about 1am I wanted to meet her. I was already pretty tipsy and didn't look properly. But the guy who killed me had a blood alcohol level of two parts per thousand and drove at 80 km/h.

MVO Don't drink and drive.
Die Johanniter.
Because we love life.
www.johanniter.de

MUNICH 48°8'N 11°35'E 10° 13:00

JURY

Jury Foreman
Mick Mahoney
Havas Worldwide London
Amber Casey
TBWA\London
Andy Cheetham
CHEETHAMBELL\JWT
Manchester
Phil Cockrell
DLKW Lowe
Magnus Jakobsson
DDB Stockholm

Paul Malmström
Mother New York
Sean Thompson
Arnold Amsterdam
Gustavo Victorino
DDB Brasil
Micah Walker
The Monkeys
Francis Wee
Ogilvy & Mather Shanghai

Beach

'Beach' is one of the ads of the 'Whatever's Comfortable' campaign. Much like the Southern Comfort brand, it was created to celebrate and inspire the awesome attitude of people who are completely comfortable with themselves.

–
Director
Tim Godsall
Art Director
Jeff Dryer
Copywriter
Nick Kaplan
Executive Creative Directors
Ian Reichenthal
Scott Vitrone
Executive Producers
Shawn Lacy
Holly Vega
Agency Producer
Alison Hill
Line Producer
Rick Jarjoura
Head of Content Production
Lora Schulson
Director of Photography
Eduard Grau
Editor
Gavin Cutler
Production Company
Biscuit Filmworks
Advertising Agency
Wieden+Kennedy New York
Editing
Mackenzie Cutler
Digital Strategist
Marshal Ball
Brand Strategist
Ben Alter
Head of Brand Strategy
Stuart Smith
Account Handler
Karla Stewart
Client
Brown-Forman
Brand
Southern Comfort

NEW YORK CITY 40°40'N 73°56'W 8° 8:00

Three Little Pigs

Also a Nomination in Cinema Commercials 61-120 Seconds

Newspapers are facing an uncertain future. As print circulation and sales continue to fall, more and more people are turning to the internet for information. Our task was to promote The Guardian's new model of 'open journalism' and demonstrate the brand's multi-media credentials as it evolves from a newspaper to a digital-first organisation. The film imagines how The Guardian might cover the tale of the 'Three Little Pigs' in print and online, following the story from the paper's front page headline, through a social media discussion and finally to an unexpected conclusion.

–
Director
Ringan Ledwidge
Art Director
Matt Fitch
Copywriter
Mark Lewis
Creative Director
David Kolbusz
Executive Creative Director
Nick Gill

Producer
Chris Harrison
Agency Producer
Davud Karbassioun
Assistant Agency Producer
Genevieve Shepherd
Production Designer
Simon Davis
Director of Photography
Franz Lustig
Editor
Rich Orrick
Music Composer
Phil Kay
Sound Designers
Sam Brock
Will Cohen
Production Manager
Patrick Bailey
Production Company
Rattling Stick
Advertising Agency
BBH London
Post Production
The Mill London
Editing
Work
Strategists
Lynsey Atkin
Ida Siow
Strategic Business Lead
Ngaio Pardon
Head of Strategy
Jason Gonsalves
Account Director
Alex Monger
Marketing Director
David Pemsel
Head of Sales & Marketing
Richard Furness
Client
The Guardian

Dumb Ways to Die

This catchy little music video epitomises client bravery. Not only did it demonstrate the client's product killing the client's customers, it did so without mentioning the client's brand until the very last breath. A marvellous piece of marketing is the result. This campaign entertained both cinema audiences and the young'uns watching at home on MTV.

–
Art Director
Pat Baron
Copywriter
John Mescall
Creative Director
Pat Baron
Executive Creative Director
John Mescall
Producer
Cinnamon Darvall
Senior Producer
Mark Bradley
Illustrator
Julian Frost
Animator
Julian Frost
Music Producer
Oliver McGill
Production Company
McCann Erickson Melbourne
Advertising Agency
McCann Erickson Melbourne
Account Manager
Tamara Broman
Account Director
Alec Hussain
Group Account Director
Adrian Mills
Brand Manager
Leah Waymark
Marketing Manager
Chloe Alsop
Client
Metro Trains

ADVERTISING   TV & CINEMA ADVERTISING

MELBOURNE 37°47'S 144°58'E 12° 23:00

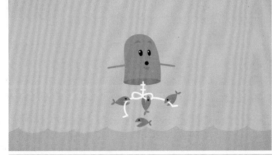

It's Not Crazy, it's Sports: The Name

Whenever anyone hears the name Michael Jordan, they can't help but think of the greatest basketball player and arguably the most famous athlete of all time. However, there happen to be 3,024 other people in the United States who are also named Michael Jordan and who are not the most famous basketball player of all time. In this spot, we focus on one of the other Michael Jordans: an ordinary man, saddled with a legendary name.

–
Director
Tim Godsall
Art Director
Cyrus Coulter
Copywriters
Dave Canning
Lauren Costa
Creative Directors
Brandon Henderson
Stuart Jennings
Executive Creative Directors
Ian Reichenthal
Scott Vitrone
Executive Producers
Shawn Lacy
Holly Vega
Agency Producers
Kelly Dage
Temma Shoaf
Line Producer
Rick Jarjoura
Head of Content Production
Lora Schulson
Production Company
Biscuit Filmworks
Advertising Agency
Wieden+Kennedy New York
Account Executive
Mark Williams
Account Supervisor
Brian D'Entremont
Account Director
Casey Bernard
Group Account Director
Brandon Pracht
Brand Strategist
Jason Gingold
Client
ESPN

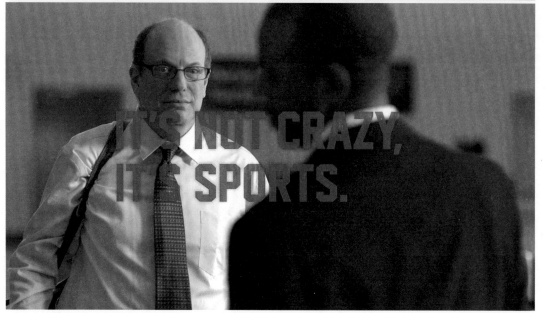

NEW YORK CITY   40°40'N   73°56'W   8°   8:00

○○○

NOMINATION IN TV & CINEMA ADVERTISING, TV COMMERCIALS 41-60 SECONDS
DEL CAMPO NAZCA SAATCHI & SAATCHI FOR BGH AIR CONDITIONERS

Dads in Briefs

**Also In Book
in TV Commercial
Campaigns:**
Dads in Briefs

**Also In Book
in Cinema
Commercials
21-40 Seconds:**
Friends

The campaign
comprises three spots
depicting different
situations which
show that, with
the arrival of the
summer heat, nothing
causes families more
suffering than dads
in briefs. And each of
the spots ends with
the perfect solution:
get them dressed
with a BGH Silent
Air Conditioner.

–
Directors
Nico & Martin
Art Director
Ezequiel De Luca
Copywriter
Nicolás Diaco
Creative Directors
Juan Pablo Lufrano
Ariel Serkin
**Executive Creative
Directors**
Maxi Itzkoff
Mariano Serkin
Advertising Agency
Del Campo Nazca
Saatchi & Saatchi
Client
BGH Air
Conditioners

Dads in Briefs

Friends

No Signal

Susan Glenn

Axe has always told memorable stories about guys getting girls. Lots of girls. But what about THE girl? We gave THE girl a name: Susan Glenn. With an ambitious seeding programme, we secretly embedded the name in pop culture. Then with a single film Axe took credit for this phenomenon. The spot is shown from the point of view of a high school boy who has fallen for Susan Glenn. Over fantastical sequences, the boy's recollection of his dream girl is narrated by Kiefer Sutherland, describing how his adoration stopped him getting the girl. Then, referring to how he feels emboldened with the help of Axe, he confides 'If I could do it again, I'd do it differently'.

–
Director
Ringan Ledwidge
Art Director
Nate Able
Copywriter
Peter Rosch
Executive Creative Director
Ari Weiss
Associate Creative Director
Nate Able

Chief Creative Officer
John Patroulis
Line Producer
Pat Frazier
Executive Producer
Jennifer Barrons
Agency Producer
Calleen Colburn
Director of Photography
Matthew Libatique
Computer Graphics Artist
Isaiah Palmer
Editor
Rich Orrick
Colourist
Fergus McCall
Music Composer
Phil Kay
Sound Designer
Brian Emrich
Sound Engineer
Rohan Young
Head of Broadcast
Lisa Setten
Production Company
Rattling Stick
Advertising Agency
BBH New York
Visual Effects Company
The Mill
Editing
Work
Strategist
Eric Fernandez
Strategic Directors
Griffin Farley
John Graham
Account Director
Mandy Dempsey
Business Director
Armando Turco
Client
Unilever
Brand
Axe

Meet the Superhumans

Championing alternative voices is at the heart of Channel 4's remit. In promoting the London 2012 Paralympic Games we wanted to get back to the true meaning of 'para' as being 'side by side/alongside' and therefore 'equal to'. Against a background of indifference (only 14% of people said they were looking forward to them), we helped create an atmosphere of excitement building up to the Games that was unprecedented. The Paralympics sold out for the first time ever, and the opening ceremony drew Channel 4's biggest audience in over ten years.

—
Director
Tom Tagholm
Creative Director
Tom Tagholm
Producers
Rory Fry
Gwilym Gwillim
Business Director
Olivia Browne
Director of Photography
Luke Scott
Production Designer
Will Htay
Visual Effects Producer
Tim Phillips
Visual Effects Supervisor
Michael Gregory
Editor
Tim Hardy
Music Composers
Carlton Douglas
Ridenhour
Gary J Rinaldo
Colourist
Jean-Clement Soret
Costume Designer
Wiz Francis
Sound Designer
Rich Martin
Casting Director
Julie Tomkins
Production Manager
Simon Maniora
Location Manager
Algy Sloane
Production Company
4creative
Visual Effects Company
The Moving Picture Company
Editing
STITCH
Sound Design
Envy
Marketing Manager
James Walker
Client
Channel 4

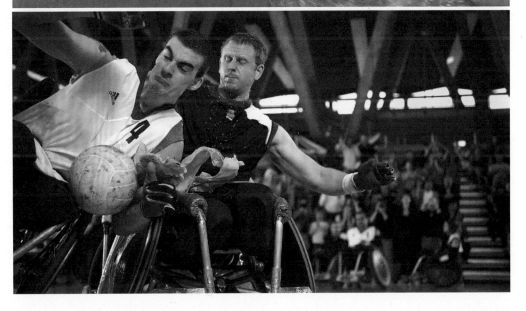

Kayak.com
Television Campaign

Also a Nomination
in TV Commercials
21-40 Seconds:
Brain Surgeon

Also In Book
in TV Commercials
21-40 Seconds:
Roommates

Because Kayak.com
searches hundreds of
travel sites in seconds
to find the best deal
on flights and hotels,
there's no need to
make compromises.
This campaign
humorously illustrates
the measures people
take to research
their vacations
before realising they
should have used
Kayak.com.

–
Director
Harold Einstein
Art Directors
Eric Dennis
Joey Ianno
Molly Jamison
Matt Rogers
Matty Smith
Copywriters
Eric Dennis
Joey Ianno
Molly Jamison
Matt Rogers
Matty Smith
Executive
Creative Director
Eric Kallman
Creative Chairman
Gerry Graf
Producer
Eric Liney
Executive Producer
Amanda Revere
Editor
Gavin Cutler
Colourist
Tim Massick
Advertising Agency
Barton F. Graf 9000
Client
Kayak.com

Roommates

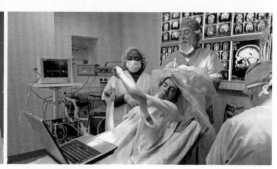

Brain Surgeon

Pupils

Cable Effects

To highlight the problems people have with cable TV – high prices, poor customer service, unreliable signals – we show the consequences of these issues and offer DIRECTV Satellite as the better alternative.

–
Director
Tom Kuntz
Art Director
Doug Fallon
Copywriter
Steven Fogel
Creative Directors
Doug Fallon
Steven Fogel
Executive Creative Director
Dan Kelleher
Chief Creative Officer
Tor Myhren
Producer
Emily Skinner
Executive Producers
Scott Howard
David Zander
Agency Producers
Andrew Chinich
Lindsay Myers
Director of Photography
Chris Soos
Editors
Nick Divers
Erik Laroi
Sound Designer
Sam Shaffer
Production Company
Morton Jankel
Zander
Advertising Agency
Grey New York
Visual Effects Company
Method Studios
New York
Editing
Mackenzie Cutler
Project Manager
Joanne Peters
Planner
Melanie Wiese
Account Manager
Kristen Stahl
Account Directors
Beth Culley
Chris Ross
Marketing Manager
Pamela Duckworth
Client
DIRECTV

Platoon

Wig Shop

House

Funeral

Needing/Getting

In a first for both the car and music worlds, OK Go used a Chevy Sonic to play their song 'Needing/Getting'. The car was modified with seven robotic arms and driven around a desert track covered with 1,157 precisely placed instruments. The band activated the car's arms from inside it as singer Damian belted out the lyrics.

–
Director
Brian L Perkins
Art Director
Joakim Borgstrom
Copywriter
Brian L Perkins
Creative Director
Joakim Borgstrom
Executive Creative Directors
Jamie Barrett
Hunter Hindman
Associate Creative Directors
Andrew Bancroft
Niklas Lilja
Chief Creative Officer
Jeff Goodby
Executive Producers
Tracy Coleman
Jon Ettinger
Michael Sagol
Jasper Tomlinson
Agency Producer
Dan Watson
Line Producer
Luke Ricci
Director of Photography
Yon Thomas
Production Designer
Bill Horbury
Editor
Doug Walker
Music Composer & Arranger
Damian Kulash
Music Producer
Dave Fridmann
Production Company
Caviar LA
Advertising Agency
Goodby Silverstein & Partners
Editing
Beast
Sound Design
Kickstand LA
Account Managers
Julie Evans
Molly McLafferty
Noah Polsky
Group Account Directors
Todd Grantham
Grace Kao
Client
Chevrolet
Brand
Sonic

ADVERTISING TV & CINEMA ADVERTISING

SAN FRANCISCO 37°47'N 122°25'W 15° 5:00

Hospital Ward

An optical illusion was used to demonstrate the BC Children's Hospital's dire lack of space. As a nurse walks from one side of the room to another, she appears to grow very large within the space. The set was built like an Ames room and shot in-camera without special effects.

–

Director
Miles Jay
Art Directors
Addie Gillespie
Mia Thomsett
Copywriters
Addie Gillespie
Mia Thomsett
Creative Directors
Bryan Collins
Rob Sweetman
Producer
Tony Di Marco
Executive Producers
Donovan Boden
Harland Weiss

Agency Producer
Mike Hasinoff
Director of Photography
Andre Pienaar
Editor
Mark Paiva
Production Company
OPC
Advertising Agency
Dare Vancouver
Post Production
Alter Ego
Crush
PosterBoy Edit
Editing
PosterBoy Edit
Sound Design
Adelphoi Music
Mixing
GGRP
Koko Productions
Planner
Catherine Piercy
Account Supervisors
Marcel Da Silva
Natalie Wu
Client
BC Children's
Hospital Foundation

WE'VE RUN OUT OF SPACE.

HELP US BUILD A NEW CHILDREN'S HOSPITAL.

BC CHILDREN'S HOSPITAL FOUNDATION
GiveSpace.ca

I Will Return

'I Will Return' brought emotion to the category of self-storage. The creative idea was brought to life with a heart-rending story about that most tender of relationships: a boy and his teddy bear. About to be separated amid a growing cacophony of driving rain and stormy weather, the boy reassures his teddy that he'll be 'safe' at Safestore with a rousing speech. The TV spot, directed by award-winning Dougal Wilson and shot with cinematic flair and big orchestral soundtrack, ends with the campaign line: 'Safestore the things you love'.

–

Director
Dougal Wilson
Art Director
Ross Neil
Copywriter
Billy Faithfull
Creative Director
Tim Robertson

Producer
Ben Link
Agency Producer
Eileen Stevens
Director of Photography
Eduard Grau
Visual Effects
Adam Crocker
Editor
Amanda James
Production Company
Blink Productions
Advertising Agency
WCRS
Post Production
The Moving Picture Company
Editing
Final Cut London
Sound Design
Factory Studios
Media Agencies
Engine
The 7 Stars
Planner
James Stevens
Media Planner
Pete Edwards
Account Handlers
Rick Hirst
Alanna McGill
Marketing Managers
Dave Cox
Tracey Makepeace
Client
Safestore

safestore
self storage

safestore the things you love

Candidates Affair

In this spot, as two candidates prepare for their local election, the only things that are coming out clean, elegant and professional are the campaign materials created by FedEx Office.

–
Director
Jim Jenkins
Art Director
Nick Klinkert
Copywriters
Chris Beresford-Hill
Tom Kraemer
Creative Directors
Chris Beresford-Hill
Nick Klinkert
Tom Kraemer

Executive Creative Directors
Greg Hahn
Mike Smith
Chief Creative Officer
David Lubars
Senior Producer
Tricia Lentini
Director of Photography
Mott Hupfel
Editors
Nick Divers
Ian Mackenzie
Production Company
O Positive
Advertising Agency
BBDO New York
Editing
Mackenzie Cutler
Client
FedEx

Planning to Make a Plan: TV

Australia has suffered some of the most devastating bush fires in history because of its dry climate. But after two wet seasons and growth in rural New South Wales, what fire fighters feared more than the driest summer in decades was, in fact, apathy. In the lead up to summer 2013, the people of rural New South Wales needed to know that having a bush fire survival plan was essential. And not something that could wait till later.

–
Director
Dave Klaiber
Art Director
John Koay
Copywriter
Karl Fleet

Chief Creative Officer
Reed Collins
Producers
Rach Paget
Vicky Rhedey
Designer
Helen Sham
Editor
Danny Tait
Advertising Agencies
George Patterson
Y&R Melbourne
The Campaign Palace
Planner
Karen Dwyer
Account Directors
Sari De
Holly McDavitt
Group Account Director
Toby McKinnon
Client
New South Wales Government
Brand
NSW Rural Fire Service

If You Could See Yourself

During a house party a boy and girl enter a bedroom looking for a mobile. They're having fun and start to kiss before the girl breaks away, wanting to return to the party. The boy is indignant at being rejected; he's convinced they came upstairs for sex. He ignores her protests and forces her onto the bed. We see an exact double of the boy looking on, desperately trying to stop himself. End frame reads: If you could see yourself, would you see rape?

–
Director
Yann Demange
Art Director
Richard Barrett
Copywriter
James Manning
Executive Creative Directors
Astrid Edwards
Toby Talbot
Producers
Astrid Edwards
Fiona Plumstead

Director of Photography
Rob Hardy
Editor
Dan Robinson
Sound Engineer
Nick Angell
Production Manager
Astrid Edwards
Production Company
Stink
Advertising Agency
RKCR/Y&R
Post Production
The Moving Picture Company
Editing
Cut+Run London
Sound Design
Angell Sound Studios
Music Production
Mcasso Music
Planner
Colwyn Elder
Account Manager
Camilla Cramsie
Account Director
Nick Fokes
Business Director
Graham Smith
Client
Home Office

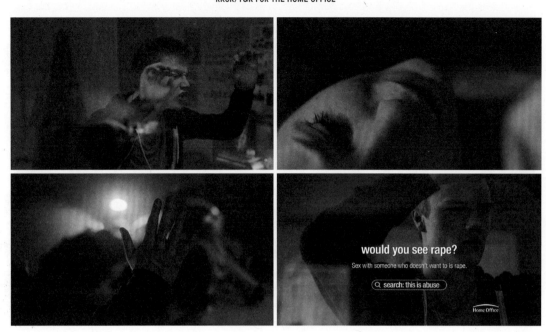

Yeah, That Kind of Rich: Writers' Room

This spot shows that when you win New York Powerball's jackpot you're more than just wealthy, you're the kind of rich that hires Andy Richter and a team of comedy writers to sit in a room all day feeding you jokes through an earpiece. 'Yeah, that kind of rich.'

–
Director
David Shane
Art Director
Sean Labounty
Copywriter
Scott Cooney
Group Creative Directors
Richard Sharp
Mike Sullivan

Chief Creative Officer
Matt Eastwood
Executive Producers
Walter Brindak
Ed Zazzera
Production Company
O Positive
Advertising Agency
DDB New York
Editing
Cutting Room
Account Director
Leo Mamorsky
Client
NY Lottery
Brand
Powerball

ADVERTISING TV & CINEMA ADVERTISING

Rainbow

The 60-second TV spot is a dance between the senses – a visual bombardment of colour, movement and textures. The viewer moves through a rainbow showing the exciting world of healthy food with Lurpak Lightest Spreadable at the heart of it. Several camera and animation techniques were used, allowing ingredients to be seen in a new, joyful light – travelling through the heart of red cabbage and following the dollop of Lurpak as it bounces with corn on the cob in a saucepan. A song provides the spine of the spot, with Rutger Hauer lending his distinctive tones, and is accompanied by a really tight sound design track, all recorded live as Foley that fits seamlessly with the lyrics.

–
Director
Dougal Wilson
Creative Directors
Dan Norris
Ray Shaughnessy
Executive Creative Directors
Tony Davidson
Kim Papworth
Producer
Ben Link
Post Producer
Tom Harding
Agency Producer
Anna Smith
Editor
Joe Guest
Music Composer
Michael Russoff
Artist
Rutger Hauer
Sound Designer
Aaron Reynolds
Production Company
Blink Productions
Advertising Agency
Wieden+Kennedy London
Media Agency
Carat
Planner
Theo Izzard-Brown
Client
Arla
Brand
Lurpak Lightest

From Love to Bingo

This ad was created using only still images from the Getty archive, shown at sufficient speed to transform the series into a video that tells a beautiful story. This was a powerful way to show that Getty Images' archive is so vast you can even make a film with it.

–
Directors
Denis Cisma
Marcos Kotlhar
Art Director
Marcos Kotlhar
Copywriter
Sophie Schoenburg
Creative Directors
Andre Kassu
Marcos Medeiros
Luiz Sanches
Renato Simoes

Executive Creative Director
Luiz Sanches
Chief Creative Officer
Marcello Serpa
Agency Producers
Gabriel Dagostini
Vera Jacinto
Animator
Marcos Kotlhar
Editor
Marcos Kotlhar
Sound Designer
Kito Siqueira
Production Company
Paranoid
Advertising Agency
AlmapBBDO
Post Production
Split Filmes
Animation
Split Filmes
Sound Design
Satelite Audio
Client
Getty Images

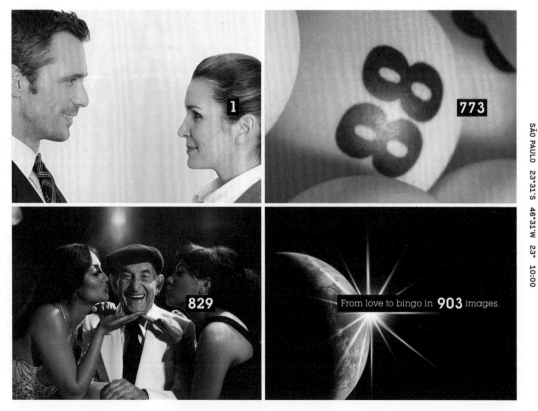

Fragile Childhood: Monsters

For a child a monster can be real. One in four children in Finland experiences harm during their childhood caused by parental alcohol abuse. The 'Monsters' campaign aimed to make all parents and media talk about the child's point of view, and by doing so, drive behavioural change in the nation. The campaign received over 9,000 media hits in the month after launch, and PR worth millions of euros. It was in the top ten most talked about topics in the political and social category in 2012, based on the Viral Video Chart.

–
Director
Mikko Lehtinen
Art Directors
Tina Fratnik
Marko Vuorensola
Copywriters
Paul Earl
Annu Terho
Creative Director
Marko Vuorensola
Producer
Hana Kovic
Executive Producer
Petteri Lehtinen
Digital Producer
Barabra Oy

Director of Photography
Jure Verovsek
Production Designer
Spela Kropusek
Flame Artist
Sakari Raappana
Editor
Anders Meinander
Colourist
Marko Terävä
Music Composer
Tuomas Kallio
Sound Designers
Timo Anttila
Anders Meinander
Production Coordinators
Mia Ekman
Urska Vardijan
Production Manager
Tina Pungartnik
Production Companies
Sauna@Grillifilms
Studio Arkadena
Advertising Agencies
Euro RSCG Helsinki
Havas Worldwide Helsinki
Post Production
Post Control
Project Coordinator
Janne Takala
Planner
Muusa Salminen
Account Director
Nina Myllyharju
Client
Lasinen Lapsuus
Brand
Fragile Childhood

HELSINKI 60°10'N 25°0'E 4° 14:00

Find Your Greatness: Jogger

This is Nathan. He is 12 years old. He's from London, Ohio. Greatness is not beyond his reach, nor is it for any of us. Nike was built on the belief that if you have a body you are an athlete. Our message for the London 2012 Olympic Games was simple: greatness can be found anywhere someone is trying to find it.

–
Director
Lance Acord
Art Director
Aramis Israel
Copywriter
Caleb Jensen
Creative Directors
Ryan O'Rourke
Alberto Ponte
Executive Creative Directors
Mark Fitzloff
Susan Hoffman

Agency Producers
Shelley Eisner
Erika Madison
Editor
Catherine Bull
Production Company
Park Pictures
Advertising Agency
Wieden+Kennedy Portland
Editing
Spot Welders
Media Agency
Mindshare
Planner
Rebecca Stambanis
Account Handlers
Karrelle Dixon
Alyssa Ramsey
Catherine Wolpe
Global Brand Communications Manager
David Reti
Global Brand Communications Director
Ean Lensch
Client
Nike

Team Spirit

Also In Book in Long Form Branded Content

People say when you're a fan, you're a fan for life, but that may be a little shortsighted. These are the stories of fans who don't just dedicate their lives to their team; they dedicate their deaths as well. In this short film we examine a subculture of fans that has team-related funerals, burials and cremations. They're die-hard fans in the truest sense.

–
Director
Errol Morris
Art Director
Cyrus Coulter
Copywriter
Dave Canning
Creative Directors
Brandon Henderson
Stuart Jennings

Executive Creative Directors
Ian Reichenthal
Scott Vitrone
Executive Producer
Robert Fernandez
Agency Producers
Temma Shoaf
Jesse Wann
Head of Content Production
Lora Schulson
Production Company
Moxie Pictures
Advertising Agency
Wieden+Kennedy New York
Account Executives
Alex Scaros
Mark Williams
Account Supervisors
Brian D'Entremont
Katie Hoak
Account Director
Casey Bernard
Group Account Director
Brandon Pracht
Client
ESPN

Helpless

This ad tells the distressing story of a cancer survivor who dies as a result of choking. It highlights the fact that first aid could prevent up to 140,000 deaths each year – the same number of people that die of cancer – and demonstrates that basic first aid techniques can be the difference between life and death.

_

Director
Benito Montorio
Art Director
Charlene Chandrasekaran
Copywriter
Dan Morris
Creative Directors
Matt Doman
Ian Heartfield
Executive Creative Director
Nick Gill
Producer
Joshua Barwick
Agency Producer
Matthew Towell
Cinematographer
Fede Alfonzo

Production Designer
Anna Rhodes
Editor
Andy McGraw
Colourist
Jean-Clement Soret
Sound Designer
Will Cohen
Production Managers
Mavreen Brown
Beatrice Warren
Production Company
Blink Productions
Advertising Agency
BBH London
Post Production
The Moving Picture Company
Editing
STITCH
Sound Design
Factory Studios
Planner
Carl Mueller
Account Coordinator
Katie Beevers
Account Director
Emma Brooker
Marketing Director
Scott Jacobson
Business Director
Ann-Marie Costelloe
Client
St John Ambulance

Skate Fortwo

We were asked to celebrate the fact that a smart fortwo only has two seats. Which makes it a lot of fun for two people. So, we set out to film something that had never been attempted before. We asked two world-class skaters if it was possible for them to perform tricks on the same board simultaneously. Then we captured the result.

_

Director
Ben Newman
Art Director
Anthony McGinty
Copywriter
Jason Cascarina

Creative Directors
Jason Cascarina
Anthony McGinty
Executive Creative Director
Jeremy Garner
Producer
Oliver Roskill
Agency Producer
Adam Walker
Editor
Thomas Carter
Production Company
Pulse Films
Advertising Agency
Weapon7
Planner
Dan Bowers
Account Director
Richard Maloney
Client
Mercedes-Benz
Brand
smart

The Journey

This acclaimed spot for John Lewis tells the story of a snowman and snowwoman. One morning the snowman mysteriously disappears. We follow him on an epic journey across river, mountain, road and city, until he returns just in time with a Christmas present. The spot shows the extra lengths we go to find the perfect gift for someone we love.

—
Director
Dougal Wilson
Art Director
Frank Ginger
Copywriter
Shay Reading
Executive Creative Directors
Ben Priest
Emer Stamp
Ben Tollett
Producer
Ben Link
Executive Producer
James Bland

Agency Producer
Lucie Georgeson
Director of Photography
Edward Grau
Post Producer
Sam Davidson
Editor
Joe Guest
Music Composers
Peter Gill
Holly Johnson
Brian Nash
Mark O'Toole
Artist
Gabrielle Aplin
Sound Designer
Anthony Moore
Production Company
Blink Productions
Advertising Agency
adam&eveDDB
Post Production
The Moving Picture Company
Music Supervision
Leland Music
Planner
David Golding
Account Director
Sarah Collinson
Marketing Managers
Craig Inglis
Lloyd Page
Client
John Lewis

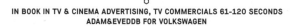

Give a little more love this Christmas

Dad

This 90-second spot tracks the evolving relationship, from the moment a protective father first brings his daughter home from hospital, sheltering her and her mother from the rain under his jacket, to the day she finally leaves home, when he hands her the keys to a shiny new Polo – ensuring she 'stays in safe hands'.

—
Directors
Will Lovelace
Dylan Southern
Art Director
Luke Flynn
Copywriter
Tom Chancellor

Executive Creative Director
Jeremy Craigen
Producer
Mark Harbour
Agency Producers
Sarah Browell
Natalie Hill
Production Company
Pulse Films
Advertising Agency
adam&eveDDB
Editing
Speade
Sound Design
Wave Studios
Business Director
Paul Billingsley
Client
Volkswagen
Brand
Polo

Best Job

In Procter & Gamble's ongoing effort to support the mums of the world, we wanted to create a spot for the London 2012 Olympic Games that honours the amazing mothers behind Olympic athletes. We also wanted to make all mums feel proud of their own accomplishments. The spot shows the dedication and hard work mums put in to give their children the best start in life. Their lives turn into a cycle of chauffeuring their kids around, washing their clothes, providing meals on the run and supporting them at practices and competitions. Mums do all this to see their children succeed. The hardest job in the world is the best job in the world.

Director
Alejandro Gonzalez Inarritu
Art Director
Ollie Watson
Copywriter
Kevin Jones
Creative Directors
Danielle Flagg
Karl Lieberman
Producer
John Benet
Executive Producers
Jeff Baron
Dave Morrison
Eric Stern
Agency Producers
Matt Hunnicutt
Erika Madison
Director of Photography
Rodrigo Prieto
Editor
Peter Wiedensmith
Colourist
Adam Scott
Advertising Agency
Wieden+Kennedy Portland
Account Handlers
Eric Gabrielson
Jesse Johnson
Francine Li
Client
Procter & Gamble

Push to Add Drama

We were asked to launch American TV channel TNT in Belgium. The tagline: We know drama; the promise: TV worth talking about. Our assignment was to develop a launch campaign worth talking about. We placed a big push button on the average square of an average town and triggered the unstoppable curiosity of people with a sign and button inviting them to 'push to add drama'. As soon as they hit the button, onlookers were confronted with a fast sequence of dramatic and crazy events occurring in front of their eyes, all referring to the TNT series. We filmed the reactions of those who dared to push and made them into a TV spot.

Director
Koen Mortier
Art Director
Ad Van Ongeval
Copywriter
Dieter De Ridder
Executive Creative Directors
Katrien Bottez
Geoffrey Hantson
Producers
Birgit D'Hont
Matthias Schellens
Executive Producer
Eurydice Gysel
Agency Producer
Marc Van Buggenhout
Advertising Agency
Duval Guillaume
Account Handlers
Jana Vervoort
Marc Wellens
Client
Turner Broadcasting System Europe
Brand
TNT

Beer Chase

Using over the top Hollywood car chases, this ad highlights men's unhappiness to part with their beer. It's part of the 'Made from Beer' campaign which makes light of popular culture, like big budget ads and super slow motion footage, to reinforce that Carlton Draught doesn't take itself too seriously; it's just 'Made from Beer'.

–
Director
Steve Ayson
Art Director
Anthony Phillips
Copywriter
Richard Williams
Executive Creative Director
Ant Keogh
Creative Chairman
James McGrath
Producer
Cindy Kavanagh
Executive Producers
Sonia von Bibra
Wilf Sweetland
Director of Photography
Greig Fraser

Production Designer
Robbie Freed
Editors
Jack Hutchings
Nicholas Ponzoni
Edel Rafferty
Music Producer
Karl Ritcher
Sound Designers
Byron Scullin
Cornel Wilczek
Production Company
The Sweet Shop
Advertising Agency
Clemenger BBDO Melbourne
Post Production
Fin Design & Effects
Editing
The Butchery
Planners
Michael Derepas
Sam Mackisack
Account Manager
Brendan Taylor
Account Director
Nick Cohen
Brand Manager
Alastair McCausland
Managing Partner
Paul McMillan
Client
Carlton & United Breweries
Brand
Carlton Draught

Donation Glasses

We played two films about an abandoned dog simultaneously on the same screen. Only viewers who had paid for donation glasses at the door saw a happy ending to the story.

–
Director
Nic Finlayson
Art Director
Jae Morrison
Copywriter
Levi Slavin
Creative Director
Levi Slavin
Chief Creative Officer
Nick Worthington
Producer
Phil Liefting
Executive Producer
Rob Galluzzo
Digital Producer
Serena Fountain-Jones
Agency Producers
Rob Linkhorn
Jen Storey
Designer
Kate Slavin
Cinematographer
Crighton Bone
Creative Technologist
Emad Tahtouh

Editor
David Coulson
Gaffer
Grant McKinnon
Advertising Agencies
Colenso BBDO/ Proximity New Zealand
FINCH
Post Production
Digital Sparks
Sound Design
Franklin Road
Music Production
Mushroom Records
Round Trip Mars
Planner
Hayley Pardoe
Account Executive
Courtney Herbert
Account Manager
Dave Munn
Group Account Director
Scott Coldham
Brand Manager
Aurelia Moly
Marketing Manager
Oliver Downs
Marketing Director
Pete Simmons
Client
Mars Petcare
Brand
Pedigree

Red Glasses

Yellow Glasses

Persistent
Headaches

Also In Book
in TV Commercials
1-20 Seconds:
Pound

Saridon is a pill that
treats persistent
headaches. The TV
spots show such
headaches coming
to life in the form of
'headache doubles'
and attacking people
while they work, non-
stop. The headaches
are usually aggravated
by their tough
working conditions.
A powerful remedy
is therefore essential
for them to get back
on track.

–
Director
Joel Limchoc
Art Directors
Gary Amante
JP Palileo
Copywriters
David Guerrero
Red Ollero
Rey Tiempo
Creative Directors
Gary Amante
Rey Tiempo
**Executive Creative
Director**
David Guerrero
Agency Producer
Aldous Pagaduan
**Director of
Photography**
J A Tadena
**Production
Company**
Revolver
Advertising Agency
BBDO Guerrero
Post Production
Post Manila
Sound Design
Hit Productions
Planner
Cristina
Buenaventura
Account Manager
Iking Uy
Account Director
Cindy Evangelista
Brand Managers
Christian Galvez
Jay Lopez
Client
Bayer Philippines
Brand
Saridon

ADVERTISING TV & CINEMA ADVERTISING

MAKATI CITY 14°33'N 121°2'E 28° 20:00

Stamp

Wash

Pound

Skittles Campaign:
Treadmill /
Bleachers

Also In Book
in TV Commercials
21-40 Seconds:
Bleachers

These TV spots
for the 'Taste the
Rainbow' campaign
take a surreal
approach to the idea of
afflictions. Fantastical
afflictions involving
sweated or sprouted
skittles prove too
irresistible to ignore.

–
Director
Rodrigo Garcia Saiz
Creative Directors
Bart Culberson
Brad Morgan
**Executive Creative
Director**
Mark Gross
**Associate Creative
Directors**
Pat Burke
Chris Carraway
Frank Oles
Mike Porritt
**Chief Creative
Officer**
Ewan Paterson
Agency Producer
Will St Clair
Production Manager
Scott Terry
**Production
Company**
Boxer Films
Advertising Agency
DDB Chicago
Post Production
Filmworkers Club
Editing
Whitehouse Post
Clients
Mars
Wm. Wrigley Jr.
Company
Brand
Skittles

Treadmill

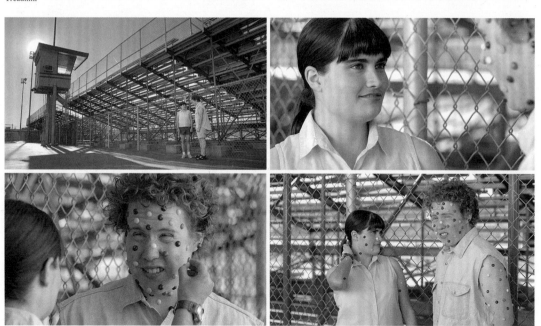

Bleachers

Gandhi TV
Campaign

Also In Book
in Cinema
Commercials
41-60 Seconds:
Executed

When people read,
they get so absorbed
in their books
that everyday life
disturbances remain
on the periphery of
their imagination.
This campaign shows
the power of books.
Dramatic peaks in a
story are punctuated
by little interruptions,
like a child requesting
help to open a jar,
but the reader never
strays far from the
world of their novel.

–
Directors
Rodrigo García
Luis Lance
Copywriters
Gastón Bigio
Lee Galvez
Manuel Vega
Gonzalo Villegas
Creative Director
Manuel Vega
Creative Chairmen
José Montalvo
Miguel Angel Ruiz
Producer
Juan Pablo Osio
**Production
Companies**
Catatonia
Central Films
Advertising Agency
Ogilvy & Mather
Mexico
Marketing Manager
Alberto Achar
Client
Gandhi Bookstores

ADVERTISING   TV & CINEMA ADVERTISING

MEXICO CITY   19°26'N   99°8'W   11°   6:00

Woods

Buried

Executed

Sensories

All girls expect guys to put in a little effort to keep them happy, but some girls are in a different league. They don't care if you're hungover, tired or whatever, they expect 100% of you 100% of the time. The Axe coloured shower gels have sensory properties that help guys keep up with these girls physically, emotionally and mentally. There are different shower gels corresponding to the different girls in the ads. In each film we hero a guy who is able to keep up with the demands of his girl thanks to the Axe coloured shower gel that he uses.

–
Director
Tim Godsall
Art Directors
Charlene
Chandrasekaran
Rob Ellis
Emmanuel Saint
M'leux
Copywriters
Dan Morris
Simon Pearse
Creative Director
David Kolbusz
Producer
Rick Jarjoura
Executive Producers
Holly Vega
Orlando Wood
Agency Producer
Rachel Hough
**Director of
Photography**
Stephen Keith-Roach
Editor
Rich Orrick
**Production
Company**
Biscuit Filmworks
Advertising Agency
BBH London
Post Production
Framestore CFC
Sound Design
Factory Studios
Phaze UK
Planner
Tim Jones
Account Manager
Nic Manser
Account Directors
Richard Lawson
Keir Mather
Brand Director
Giovanni Valentini
Client
Unilever
Brand
Axe

Brainy

Maintenance

Sporty

Guitar Man

The campaign
shows guitarists
playing classic riffs
on guitar people.

—
Director
Dulcidio Caldeira
Art Directors
Alexandre Amaral
Gregory Kickow
Copywriters
Patrick
Matzenbacher
Marcelo Rosa
Creative Directors
Andre Faria
Guga Ketzer
Cassio Moron
Producer
Egisto Betti
Agency Producers
Ana Luisa Andre
Karina Vadasz
**Director of
Photography**
Ted Abel
**Production
Company**
ParanoidBr
Advertising Agency
Loducca
Post Production
Sindicato VFX
Sound Design
A9 Audio
Account Handler
Sabrina Spinelli
Client
MTV Brasil

Miguel

Ramirez

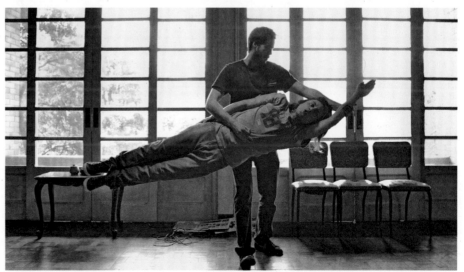

Fabricio

**Channel 4
Documentary
Sponsorship Idents**

Honda's engineers approach problems with a curiosity and lateral thinking process that can be surprising. They take their inspiration from places you wouldn't expect. The Channel 4 Documentaries sponsorship was the perfect opportunity to demonstrate this approach to innovation, while also reminding people why documentaries can be so inspiring. We created a series of idents under the theme 'The more we look the more we learn'. Using match cuts, they demonstrate how Honda product innovations are inspired by the world around us.

—
Director
James Caddick
Art Director
Ben Shaffery
Copywriter
Max Batten
Creative Directors
Chris Groom
Sam Heath
Jon Matthews
**Executive Creative
Directors**
Tony Davidson
Kim Papworth
Producer
Aly Moffat
Post Producer
Paul Wilmot
Agency Producer
Michelle Brough
**Lighting
Cameraperson**
Ollie Downey
Editor
Owen Oppenheimer
Sound Engineer
Dan Beckwith
**Production
Company**
2am Films
Advertising Agency
Wieden+Kennedy
London
Post Production
Finish
Sound Design
Factory Studios
Account Director
Laura McGauran
**Head of Brand
Marketing**
Olivia Dunn
Client
Honda

ADVERTISING TV & CINEMA ADVERTISING

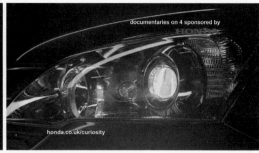

Adaptive Headlights

Magic Seats

Windscreen Wipers

Lane Keep Assist

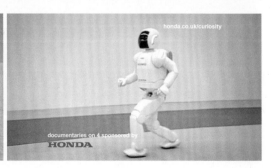

Asimo

LONDON 51°32'N 0°5'W 9° 12:00

The Movie Out Here

Kokanee is a western Canadian beer with a history of engaging consumers in unconventional ways. 'The Movie Out Here' is a 90-minute film, created with the help of Kokanee fans, from acting and music to prop making and location scouting. The film was released in cinemas across Canada and drew in audiences of beer lovers.

–
Director
David Hicks
Art Director
Catherine Allen
Interactive Art Directors
Joel Holtby
Hiten Patel
Copywriter
Ian Simpson
Junior Copywriter
Naeem Ghafari
Screenwriters
David Chiavegato
Rich Pryce-Jones
Creative Directors
Scott Dube
Randy Stein

Agency Producer
Laurie Maxwell
Designer
Andy Slater
Editor
Griff Henderson
Production Company
Infinity Films
Advertising Agency
Grip
Post Production
Finale
Section Eight
Visual Effects Company
Axys
Editing
PosterBoy Edit
Sound Design
Jingle Punks
Post Modern
Account Coordinator
Matthew Yip
Account Manager
Brendon Sargent
Account Director
Martin McClorey
Client Services Director
John Miller
Client
Labatt Breweries of Canada
Brand
Kokanee

I Want to Say

'I Want to Say' is a documentary short that chronicles the lives of children living with autism, including their challenges and the breakthroughs they achieve using touch technology. The documentary is centred on students in Silicon Valley at the Hope Technology School (an inclusive programme with both typical and special needs students learning together), and features Temple Grandin, a hero in the autism community.

–
Director
Peter Sorcher
Art Director
Tim Semple
Copywriter
Jody Horn
Executive Creative Director
Rich Silverstein
Producer
Emily Petit
Executive Producer
Clint Goldman

Agency Producer
Whitney Ferris
Agency Executive Producer
Todd Porter
Directors of Photography
Steve Condiotti
Peter Sorcher
Editor
Ian Montgomery
Music Producer
Todd Porter
Production Company
Bodega
Advertising Agency
Goodby Silverstein & Partners
Design Agency
Picture Mill
Post Production
Northern Lights
Sound Design
SuperExploder
Strategists
Heather Lewis
Nam Nguyen
Account Manager
Danielle Gard
Group Account Director
John Coyne
Client
Autism Speaks

ADVERTISING TV & CINEMA COMMUNICATIONS

JURY

Jury Foreman
Chris Bovill
Channel 4
Julien Chavepayre
Les Télécréateurs
Graham Jones
venturethree

Loïc Lima Dubois
Lobo
Lucy Powell
JWT London
Joanna Sheppard
BBC Worldwide

France 5 Idents: 2012 Rebranding

We worked on a concept that would epitomise knowledge and also act as a clear link to the France 5 multidisciplinary identity. A multitude of things move in the same direction, one following the other, like a chain reaction between completely different worlds. The underlying meaning: knowledge is derived from making new links. Each shot is just long enough for you to grasp what you're watching, but not too long that it bores you. This is about moving forward, striving, exploring, pushing the limits and developing. It symbolises what makes humanity prosper; what fascinates us in life.

–
Directors
Marcus Linnér
Daniel de Viciola
Creative Directors
Julien Chavepayre
Eric Nung
Producer
Nathalie Cohen
Executive Producer
Eric Nung
Director of Photography
Hannes Isaksson
Editor
Fredrik Åkerström
Sound Designer
Fredrik Åkerström
Production Company
Aspekt
Branding Agency
Les Télécréateurs
Direction
Alphabetical Order®
Head of Broadcast
Bruno Patino
Strategist
Julien Chavepayre
Head of Creative Services
Eric Rinaldi
Client
France 5

Movement

Aerial

Solid Fluid

PARIS 48°48'N 2°20'E 10° 13:00

**Amanda: Emotions
on Demand**

This work is part
of a campaign that
uses the power of
human emotions to
communicate the
benefits of the SBS
On Demand service.

–
Director
Mark Molloy
Art Director
Matt Ryan
Copywriter
Nick Marzano
**Executive
Creative Director**
Christy Peacock
Producer
Alice Grant
Agency Producer
Trelise Caughey
**Director of
Photography**
Jeremy Rouse
Special Effects
Colin Renshaw
Editor
Graeme Pereira
Sound Designer
Byron Scullin
**Production
Company**
Exit Films Melbourne
Post Production
ALT VFX
The Butchery
Advertising Agency
JOY.
Sound Design
Electric Dreams
Music Production
Level Two Music
Account Handlers
Tim Stuart
Alex Tracy
Marketing Director
Katherine Raskob
Client
SBS
Brand
SBS On Demand

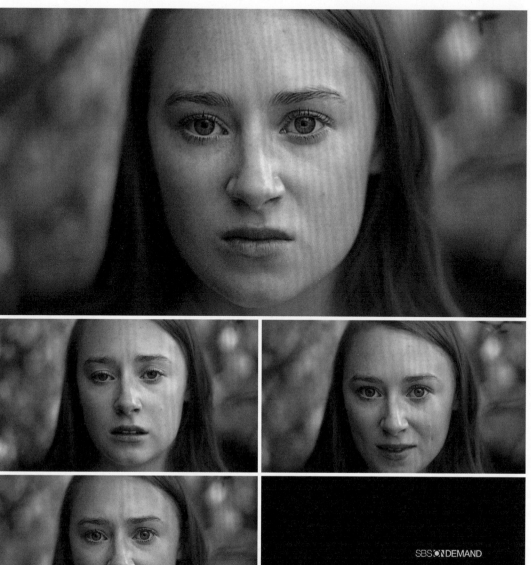

ADVERTISING   TV & CINEMA COMMUNICATIONS

SYDNEY 34°0'S 151°0'E 22° 20:00

Stadium UK

Also In Book
in TV Title
Sequences

As sole broadcaster
for London 2012,
the BBC wanted
marketing, titles and
programming that
showed it was making
the 2012 Olympic
Games accessible
to everyone,
everywhere. To
dramatise this, we
created an animated
world in which the
British Isles was one
venue, big enough
for everyone to be
invited: 'Stadium
UK'. Within these
epic surroundings,
we see a whole host of
Olympians (including
sprinters on London
streets, cyclists in
quarries, weightlifters
in dockyards and
swimmers in Scottish
lochs) preparing,
then performing
throughout the land.

—
Director
Pete Candeland
Art Directors
Paul Angus
Jules Chalkley
Nick Simons
Rick Thiele
Mario Ucci
Copywriter
Ted Heath
Creative Director
Damon Collins
**Executive Creative
Director**
Damon Collins
Producers
Sarah Caddy
Lottie Hope
Anna Lord
Executive Producers
Michael Adamo
Hugo Sands
**Computer Graphics
Artist**
Jason Nicholas
**Visual Effects
Supervisor**
Neil Riley
Editors
Jamie Foord
Anne Monnehay
Artist
Elbow
Production Manager
Jane Hunt
Post Production
Blueprint
Advertising Agency
RKCR/Y&R
Account Executive
Claudia Newman
Account Directors
David Pomfret
Charlie Smith
Business Director
Jo Bacon
Client
BBC
Brand
BBC Sport

ADVERTISING   TV & CINEMA COMMUNICATIONS

LONDON   51°32'N   0°5'W   9°   12:00

4seven

New channel 4seven features the best of Channel 4 from the last seven days. The marque features a '7' within the existing Channel 4 marque, revealed as you pan around a corner. This corner became the visual signature for our idents, created using an innovative mix of angled camera work and CG augmentation and resulting in eye-catching, logic-defying scenes, reminiscent of mathematical artist M.C. Escher.

–
Directors
Mike Alderson
Tim Swift
Alice Tonge
Art Directors
Mike Alderson
Tim Swift
Alice Tonge
Designer
James Greenfield
Creative Directors
Alice Tonge
Chris Wood
Producer
Louise Oliver
Production Designers
Patrick Lyndon-Stanford
Adam Zoltowski
Directors of Photography
Olivier Cariou
Bob Pendar-Hughes
Motion Graphics Artists
Douglas Bowden
Rupert Burton
Simon Holmedal
Visual Effects
Jim Radford
Visual Effects Producer
Julie Evans
Visual Effects Supervisors
Chrys Aldred
Tim Civil
Colourist
George K
Editors
Nick Armstrong
Alex Lee
Sound Designer
Gavin Little
Sound Engineer
Chris Turner
Post Production
The Moving Picture Company
Design Agency
Magpie Studio
Product Manager
Caroline Greig
Marketing Managers
Ros Godber
James Walker
Client
Channel 4
Brand
4seven

ADVERTISING   TV & CINEMA COMMUNICATIONS

Allotment

LONDON   51°32'N   0°5'W   9°   12:00

Pool

Supermarket

Day to Night

More4 Rebrand

The focus of More4 has shifted over the years. It was felt that the time had come to redress the gap between the channel branding and its more lifestyle focused content. The new logo is the hero of the new look. On the on-screen presentation, end and beginning of programmes, it sits on clean backgrounds while the logo flips, flops and spins to form and reveal its palette of colours. For the idents we wanted to take the key elements of the logo and break it out into the real world, so instead of spending hours in post-production, we created 400 special mechanical flippers.

—

Directors
Mike Alderson
Daniel Chase
Chris Wood
Tim Swift
Creative Directors
Daniel Chase
Chris Wood
Producer
Louise Oliver
Post Producers
Sarah Antrobus
Pete Winslett
Directors of Photography
Martin Hill
Daniel Trapp
Visual Effects
Marcus Dryden
Dan Wyles
Telecine
Mark Horrobin
Editors
Nick Armstrong
Jamie Foord
Sound Designers
Ian Hargest
Rich Martin
Production Design
Jason Bruges Studio
Marketing Manager
James Walker
Client
Channel 4
Brand
More4

ADVERTISING   TV & CINEMA COMMUNICATIONS

LONDON 51°32'N 0°5'W 9° 12:00

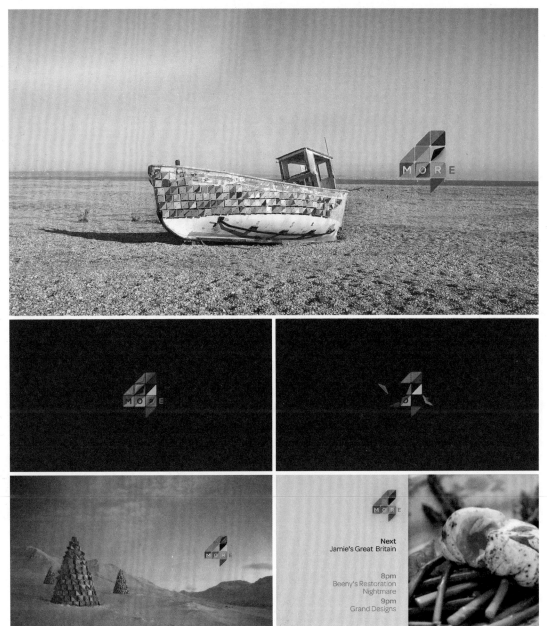

Skyfall

'Skyfall' is the 23rd film in the James Bond series, released by Eon Productions for the 50th anniversary of the franchise. The 'Skyfall' titles mark the sixth sequence created by series veteran Daniel Kleinman. Following a shoot that captured footage of Daniel Craig, Javier Bardem, a number of models and a range of elements, the titles were developed and assembled at Framestore CFC over four months. They reflect the film's narrative in a captivating and striking manner, and are accompanied by an anthemic soundtrack written by Adele and Paul Epworth, resulting in a suitably iconic sequence.

–
Director
Daniel Kleinman
Art Director
John Ebden
Producer
Johnnie Frankel
Line Producer
James Alexander
Director of Photography
John Mathieson
Stunt Coordinator
Gary Powell
Visual Effects Producer
Helen Hughes
Visual Effects Supervisors
William Bartlett
Russell Dodgson
Diamid Harrison-Murray
Editor
Daniel Kleinman
Music Composers
Adele
Paul Epworth
Production Manager
Chris Harrison
Production Company
Rattling Stick
Post Production
Framestore CFC
Client
Eon Productions

Funny Fortnight

Our aim was to promote Channel 4's 'Funny Fortnight', a season of classic and brand new comedy on Channel 4. It featured both up-and-coming talent and big names from 30 years of British comedy on Channel 4. We wanted to strip comedy back and let our audience get closer, so we paired up top Channel 4 comedians and filmed conversations between them in interesting couples. Creating an environment where they could riff off each other gave a wonderfully frank, personal and hilarious insight into them as people and comedians. The campaign popularity led us to make a 20-minute programme, which aired on 4OD.

—
Directors
Alex Boutell
Molly Manners
Art Director
Molly Manners
Copywriters
Alex Boutell
Molly Manners
Creative Director
Chris Wood
Producers
Rory Fry
Shananne Lane
Production Designer
Adam Zoltowski
Director of Photography
Matt Fox
Editor
Kel McKeown
Sound Designer
Rich Martin
Post Production
Moving Picture Company
Advertising Agency
4creative
Business Director
Olivia Browne
Marketing Manager
Charlie Palmer
Client
Channel 4

ADVERTISING TV & CINEMA COMMUNICATIONS

LONDON 51°32'N 0°5'W 9° 12:00

Gregg and Sharon

Simon and Jessica

Noel and Vic

Jimmy and Morgana

28 NATIONS

NZL
Alt Group
Colenso BBDO/
Proximity
New Zealand
Draftfcb
New Zealand

HRV
Bruketa&Zinic

FRA
CLM BBDO

ROU
Spotlight

KOR
601BISANG

IND
Leo Burnett
Mumbai

CHE
Jung von
Matt/Limmat
Ludovic
Balland
Typography
Cabinet

ARE
Memac Ogilvy
& Mather
Y&R Dubai

AUT
brand unit

CZE
Ogilvy &
Mather Prague

ZAF
Fishgate
Advertising
Joe Public
Johannesburg

BRA
AlmapBBDO
Loducca
Ogilvy Brazil

POL
Leo Burnett
Warsaw

DESIGN

SGP
DDB
Singapore
WORK

DEU
BBDO
Proximity
Berlin
Factor Product
gürtler-
bachmann
Süddeutsche
Zeitung

NLD
Lava Design
Momkai
Part of a
Bigger Plan
Studio Dumbar
WE ARE Pi

THA
Leo Burnett
Bangkok

ESP
Ena Cardenal
de la Nuez
Errea
Comunicación
Lighting
Design
Collective
Moruba
Sánchez/
Lacasta

AUS
Alaskan Rock
Bear Meets
Eagle on Fire
Clemenger
BBDO Sydney
Container
Frost* Design
Sydney
George
Patterson Y&R
Melbourne
Mash Design
Re
The Monkeys/
MAUD

JPN
6D-K
arctik
Bascule
cosmos
Dentsu Nagoya
Dentsu Tokyo
Drawing and
Manual
Erotyka
Hakuhodo
KIGI
Nippon Design
Center
PARTY
Taku Satoh
Design Office

SWE
Bedow
BVD
Family
Business
Forsman &
Bodenfors
North Kingdom

FIN
358
Project 999
Tuomas
Siitonen

GBR
& SMITH
4creative
aberrant
architecure
AKQA London
Alphabetical
Arthur
Steen Horne
Adamson
B&B Studio
Barber-
Osgerby
BBC
BBH London
Blood Creative
Brighten the
Corners
Cartledge
Levene
Casson Mann
Crystal CG
Dare London
DesignLSC
DesignEdge
Cambridge
Designers
Anonymous
dn&co.
Fieldwork
Facility
Frieze
FutureBrand
GBH
Google
Creative Lab
Heatherwick
Studio
Here Design
Human After
All
IMAGES&Co
Jason Bruges
Studio
KVGD
Laurence King
Publishing
Leo Burnett
London
Lloyd
Northover
Lypiatt Designs
MAP
MR PORTER
Music
Mytton
Williams
Native Design
NB
Ogilvy &
Mather London
PearsonLloyd
Design

CAN
Leo Burnett
Toronto
lg2boutique
Lowe Roche
MacLaren
McCann
TAXI Montréal
Trigger
WAX
Partnership

USA
A+B
AKQA
Washington DC
Ammunition
Apple
BBDO Atlanta
Bloomberg
Businessweek
Bould Design
DDB New York
Draftfcb
Chicago
Draftfcb
New York
Google
Google
Creative Lab
Hungry Man
Johannes
Leonardo
Landor
Associates
Cincinnati
Leo Burnett
Chicago
Leo Burnett
New York
Local Projects
Mullen
New York
Magazine
Non-Format
Office: Jason
Schulte Design
Ogilvy &
Mather
Chicago
PRETTYBIRD
R/GA
Sandstrom
Design
Snibbe Studio
The Martin
Agency
Turner
Duckworth
San Francisco

NOR
Yokoland

ITA
Il Sole 24 Ore
Leftloft

CHN
84000
Communications
EOQ
Ogilvy & Mather
Shanghai

GBR (cont'd)
Penguin Books
Pentagram
Phaidon Press
Random
International
RM&CO
Royal Mail
SEA
Somewhat_
Studio
Myerscough
Tayburn
TBWA\London
The
Gentlewoman
The Gild
The Times
There Is
This is Real Art
Toaster
Turner
Duckworth
London
Universal
Design Studio
Universal
Everything
venturethree
Wallpaper*
Wayward
Plants
WPA Pinfold

JURY

Jury Foreman	Jamie Keenan
Carin Goldberg	Robert Klanten
Carin Goldberg Design	Gestalten
John Gall	Roy Poh
Abrams Books	Beautiful
Julia Hasting	Robert Violette
Phaidon Press	Violette Editions

In the Shadow of the Tree and the Knot of the Earth

This catalogue was designed for Anish Kapoor's exhibition 'In the shadow of the tree and the knot of the earth' at the Lisson Gallery in London. Instead of representing the sculptures in a traditional catalogue style, the artist's drawings (absent from the exhibition itself) are used to set the mood of the publication. The dark and atmospheric drawings form the main content of the 320-page book, pre-empting the sculptural forms present in the exhibition space which emerge as loosely inserted, full-colour photographs of the work.

—
Art Directors
Billy Kiosoglou
Frank Philippin
Print Producer
Richard Foenander
Design Agency
Brighten the
Corners
Clients
Anish Kapoor
Lisson Gallery

**Let's Make Some
Great Fingerprint Art**

Deuchars takes
mankind's oldest
and most universal
way of mark making,
the fingerprint, and
shows how anyone
can build an endlessly
inventive universe
around it. The book
demonstrates different
and surprising ways
to create art from
fingerprints and
hand printing in
combination with other
art techniques. With
subjects ranging from
aliens and monsters
to Native American
totem poles, the book
encourages young
artists to have fun,
but at the same time
learn to be innovative
and creative.

–
Art Director
Angus Hyland
Illustrator
Marion Deuchars
Publishing Company
Laurence King
Publishing
Client
Laurence King
Publishing
Brand
Let's Make

DESIGN   BOOK DESIGN

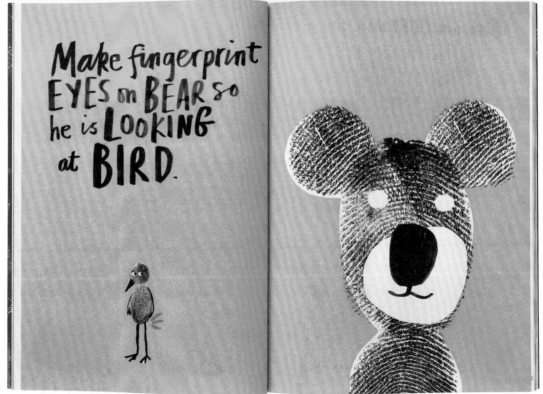

LONDON 51°32'N 0°5'W 9° 12:00

Buchner Bründler Buildings

This monograph provides an insight into the building practice of Basel-based architects Buchner Bründler. A selection of buildings is presented with extensive picture sequences. The images are edited focusing on materials, details, urban context and temporal developments. As a supplement, an index of small works and unrealised projects completes the overall view on Buchner Bründler's practice. A table of contents, consisting of keywords, cross-links the chapters and directs the reader to specific aspects of the projects.

–
Designers
Ludovic Balland
Gregor Schreiter
Editors
Andreas Bründler
Daniel Buchner
Design Agency
Ludovic Balland
Typography Cabinet
Client
Buchner Bründler
Architekten

DESIGN   BOOK DESIGN

BASEL   47°34'N   7°36'E   10°   13:00

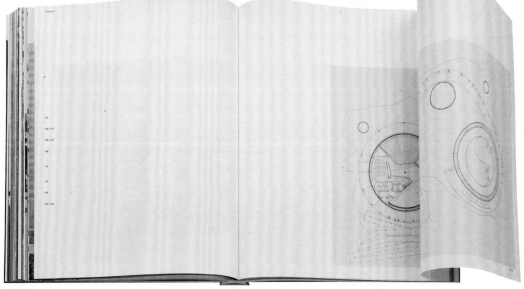

Planning the Bothnian Sea

The book presents the Plan Bothnia spatial plan for the Bothnian Sea, a part of the Baltic Sea between Sweden and Finland. It includes analysis of the characteristics, uses and future developments in the region. This initiative was carried out by ministries and institutions from Finland and Sweden under the leadership of the intergovernmental Helsinki Commission (HELCOM). Visual presentation was emphasised to help politicians and citizens form their own opinions about the offshore areas, as well as to highlight the sea as a source of identity and inspiration.

–
Designers
Johannes Nieminen
Tuomas Siitonen
Illustrator
Jukka Pylväs
Artworker
Kyösti
Saaren-Seppälä
Editors
Hermanni Backer
Manuel Frias Vega
Publishing Company
Baltic Marine
Environment
Protection
Commission
**Production
Managers**
Hermanni Backer
Manuel Frias Vega
Clients
Baltic Marine
Environment
Protection
Commission
Boverket

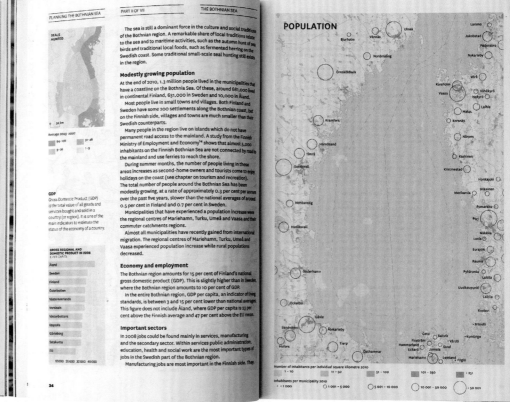

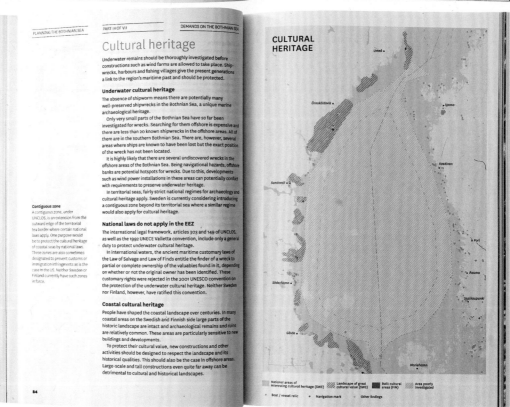

Fäviken

Fäviken Magasinet restaurant is located in a remote area of Sweden and only serves food that can be sourced locally. The biggest challenge was to convey the restaurant's individual location and identity. This was achieved by drawing inspiration from Swedish folk art: the red house in the landscape on the cover is a stylised interpretation of the restaurant, but also captures the essence of Sweden and evokes a sense of how remote Fäviken is. The typefaces in the book are all Swedish too, which subtly reflect the restaurant's strict policy of sourcing home-grown materials.

Designers
Espen Friberg
Aslak Gurholt
Rønsen

Illustrators
Espen Friberg
Aslak Gurholt
Rønsen

Author
Magnus Nilsson

Publishing Company
Phaidon Press

Client
Phaidon Press

DESIGN BOOK DESIGN

Wild trout roe in a warm crust of dried pigs' blood

A STRANGE STORY

LONDON 51°32'N 0°5'W 9° 12:00

Ronan & Erwan Bouroullec: Works

This is a monograph on the work of product designers Ronan and Erwan Bouroullec. The book includes previously unpublished images and drawings from their archive, plus a catalogue section detailing every project they have ever produced. The designer worked very closely with the two brothers during the design process – from image selection to the choice of paper. Full-page photographs, drawings and double-page spreads showcase their work. The textured art paper on the case ensures that this is a sleek and tactile object in keeping with the Bouroullecs' design philosophy.

–
Art Director
Sonya Dyakova
Designer
Sonya Dyakova
Author
Anniina Koivu
Publishing Company
Phaidon Press
Client
Phaidon Press

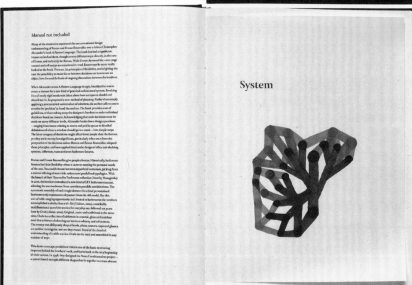

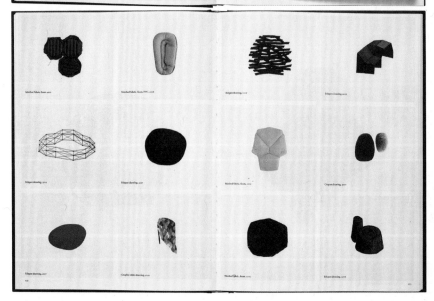

History of Jazz

'History of Jazz' by Ted Gioia is a bestseller from Turner Publishers. There is a paperback edition and this is the hardcover version, conceived as a gift book. The brief was to design a lively and dynamic cover, with rhythm and movement. We chose a typographical design in which the word 'Jazz' is the protagonist. The letters, in vibrant colours, move in one direction on the cover and in the opposite direction on the back cover and the spine.

–
Designer
Ena Cardenal de la Nuez
Author
Ted Gioia
Publishing Company
Turner Publishers
Client
Turner Publishers

DESIGN   BOOK DESIGN

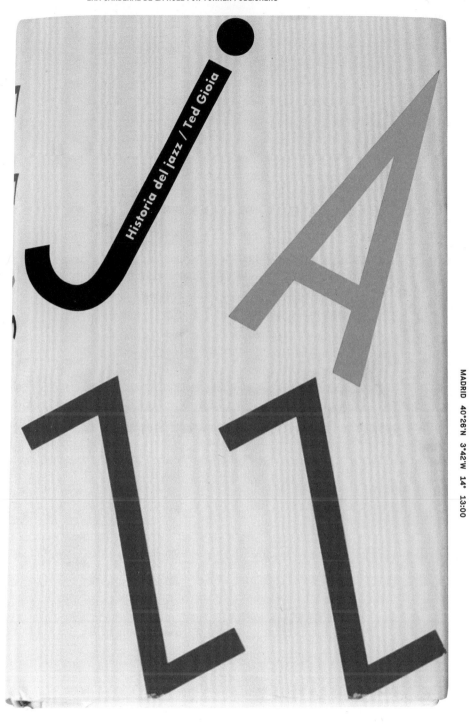

MADRID   40°26'N   3°42'W   14°   13:00

Sticky Notes Annual

Why is the 'Sticky Notes Annual' so useful? In Japan, almost every creative writes notes directly onto annuals and dog-ears pages when they study. This usually results in the precious annual becoming damaged too quickly. We've solved this problem by adding sticky notes to the cover. There are three special features to the 'Sticky Notes Annual': notes and memos can be written onto the annual without damaging the pages; sticky notes will never get lost; the variety of colours creates a bright design.

—
Art Director
Michihito Dobashi
Designers
Masao Shirasawa
Koji Tanaka
Masatsugu Yano
Creative Director
Yoshihisa Ozaki
**Sticky Notes
Producer**
Toshiya Yamada
Copywriters
Kotoha Tanaka
Yoshiki Toya
Yosei Urushibata
Photographer
Yoshihiro Ozaki
Retouchers
Osamu Sato
Makoto Tobita
Print Directors
Norio Kito
Satoru Ozawa
Advertising Agency
Dentsu Nagoya
Japan
Translator
Yunosuke Kunimoto
Client
Copywriters Club
Nagoya

DESIGN BOOK DESIGN

NAGOYA 35°7'N 136°56'E 13° 21:00

The Art Directors Club 91st Annual

In the Art Directors Club's 91st call for entries, DDB New York coined the 'Keep fighting' battle cry as a nod to the pain and suffering endured on the path to creating great work. In the 91st Award Annual, we continued to encourage creatives in every discipline via our 'Keep fighting the good fight' theme. We called out the different obstacles each medium deals with via our colourful illustrated page dividers, because, in the end acknowledgement and an ADC Cube award make it all worthwhile.

—
Art Director
Joao Unzer
Graphic Designers
Brian Gartside
Juan Carlos Pagan
Executive Creative Director
Menno Kluin
Associate Creative Directors
Aron Fried
Carlos Wigle
Chief Creative Officer
Matt Eastwood
Copywriter
Rodgrigo de Castro Silva
Typographers
Juan Carlos Pagan
Brian Gartside
Illustrator
Rami Niemi
Advertising Agency
DDB New York
Art Buyer
Carol Brandwein
Client
Art Directors Club

DESIGN   BOOK DESIGN

NEW YORK CITY   40°40'N   73°56'W   8°   8:00

JURY

Jury Foreman
Paula Scher
Pentagram New York
Alan Dye
Apple
Vanessa Eckstein
Blok Design
James Greenfield
DesignStudio

Jo Jackson
Protein®
Simon Manchipp
SomeOne
Mike Smith
The Allotment Brand Design
Sue Walsh
Milton Glaser

JA Minds Identity

JA stands for Japan Agricultural Cooperatives, the nation's largest cooperative in its category; JA Minds is an agricultural union responsible for the Tama district in Tokyo. JA was struggling with the reality that people viewed it as somewhat conservative and it had difficulty communicating the distinctive services it offers. Our solution was a new visual identity incorporating pictograms, which demonstrate the diversity of its business as well as build affinity among a wide audience including children, senior citizens and those engaged with agriculture.

—
Designers
Shogo Kishino
Nozomi Tagami
Art Director
Shogo Kishino
Illustrator
Ichio Otsuka
Design Agency
6D-K
Brand Director
Yasuhiro Kondo
Client
Minds Agricultural Cooperative
Brand
JA Minds

TOKYO 35°40'N 139°45'E 15° 21:00

**Louis Vuitton
Yayoi Kusama Book**

We created this book to celebrate the 2012 collaboration between Louis Vuitton and Japanese artist Yayoi Kusama. The book is inspired by Kusama's symbolic polka dots that represent the self-obliteration of one's ego. Aside from silkscreen and die-cut production methods, the three-fold cover uses three different materials, including a paper that resembles the Louis Vuitton paper bag, and also a canvas material. The latter depicts the art canvas that Kusama uses for her drawings.

—
Designers
Geraldine Chua
Ernest Ho
MAA
Farah Siman
Design Director
Theseus Chan
Photographers
Bruno Asselot
Jean Marc Cedile
Kishin Shinoyama
Design Agency
WORK
Publishing Company
Louis Vuitton Japan
Printers
AlsOdoMinie
Producers
ASHU NAKANISHIYA
Client
Louis Vuitton Japan

DESIGN BRANDING

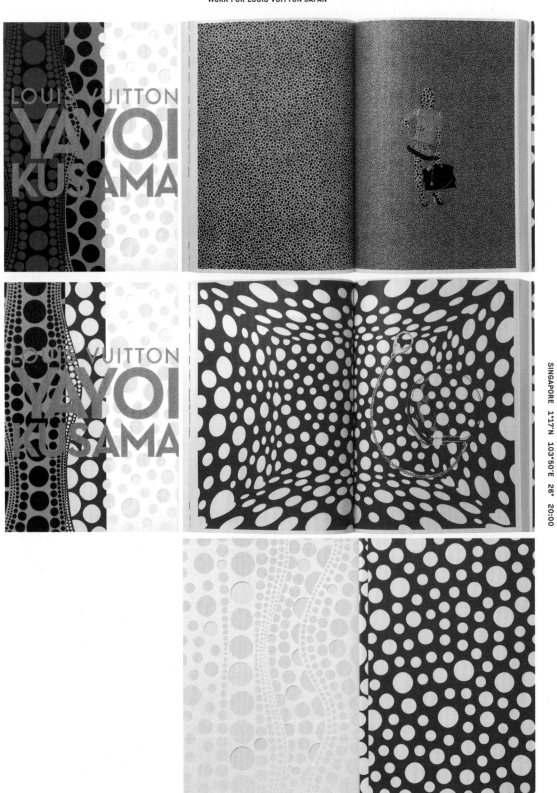

SINGAPORE 1°17'N 103°50'E 26° 20:00

Pantone Queen

For 60 years, Her Majesty has colour matched her hats, dresses and coats perfectly, as any queen should. So we created 'Pantone Queen'; a Pantone colour guide celebrating 60 of her iconic single colour outfits, painstakingly matching the exact Pantone reference to the exact date and location she wore them throughout her 60-year reign. The book was loved so much by the Royal Family, it was made official Diamond Jubilee memorabilia, royally endorsing 'Pantone Queen'. The queens were numbered from one to 60, and right now resting in Buckingham Palace is number one, the Queen's very own 'Pantone Queen'.

–
Art Director
Will Thacker
Copywriter
Blake Waters
Executive Creative Director
Justin Tindall
Producer
Janice Capewell
Print Producer
Chris Dale
Advertising Agency
Leo Burnett London
Art Buyer
Leah Mitchell
Client
Pantone

DESIGN BRANDING

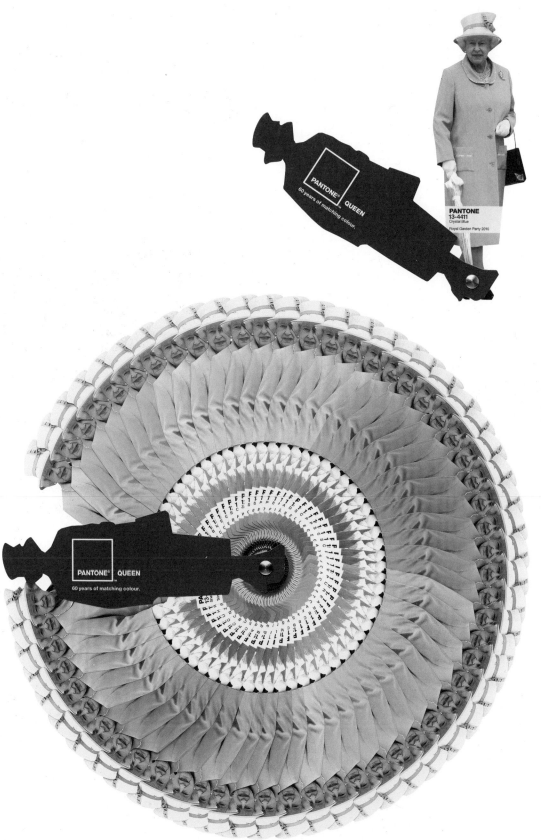

LONDON 51°32'N 0°5'W 9° 12:00

OneNike

Nike has always stood for one principle: empowering athletes to reach their full potential. However, online Nike had over 70 different digital properties that weren't consistent or in concert. Brand and sport category destinations weren't integrated with ecommerce, and visitors often were unable to view content on their phones and tablets. We reimagined the entire Nike digital ecosystem streamlining products, services, and brand inspiration, all under one roof. The new nike.com is based on athletes' behaviours, both on and offline.

–
Designers
Erik Herrstrom
Augusto Paiva
Rumiana Williams
Art Director
Matt Schreiber
Interactive
Designers
Evinn Quinn
Caitlin Robinson
Rahul Sen
Creative Directors
Xavier Gallego
Tim Hutchison
Hoshi Ludwig
Executive Creative
Directors
Fura Johannesdottir
Mark Laughlin
Technical Directors
Patricia Choi
Christian Rauh
Technical Architects
Lamar Hines
Adam Housman
Producers
Elizabeth Bell
Emily Fare
Agency Executive
Producer
Mark Norris
Digital Agency
R/GA
Client
Nike

DESIGN BRANDING

NEW YORK CITY 40°40'N 73°56'W 8° 8:00

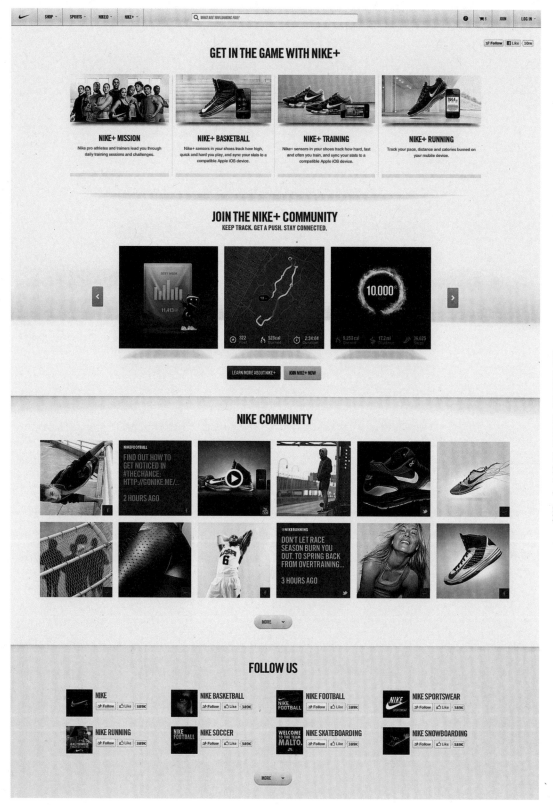

Ugokidase Tokyo

In 2012, Nike+ launched its most innovative digital products to date. And we wanted Japanese consumers to experience them all before they came to market. To reach our audience, we took inspiration from a Japanese obsession – gaming. In central Tokyo, we created a pop-up arcade at the Ugokidase station for the everyday athlete, open throughout the 2012 Olympic Games. Players could compete with friends in five new sporting challenges, each powered by Nike+. Their results fed live into global leader boards, testing performance like never before.

–
Senior Designer
Neil Gurr
Art Director
Nick Bastian
Senior Copywriter
Guy Bingley
Creative Director
Masaya Nakade
Executive Creative Director
Duan Evans
Associate Creative Director
Max Chanan
Executive Producer
Daniela Michelon
Advertising Agency
AKQA London
Digital Production Companies
amana
Rhizomatiks
Taiyo Kikaku
Project Manager
Lauren Ivory
Account Director
Ross Winterflood
Group Account Director
Gareth Nettleton
Client
Nike Japan
Brand
Nike+

DESIGN BRANDING

LONDON 51°32'N 0°5'W 9° 12:00

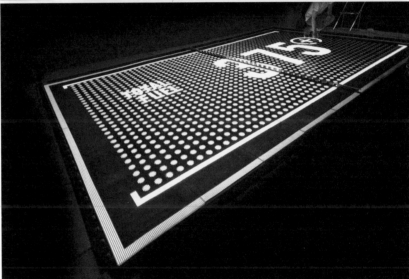

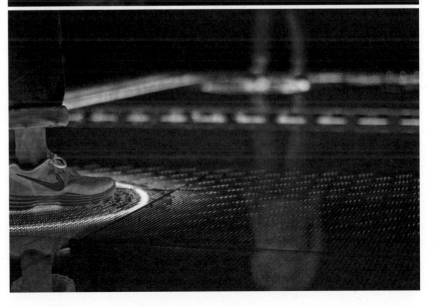

DESIGN BRANDING

Chrome Web Lab

Chrome 'Web Lab' is a first-of-its-kind open exhibition that can be accessed from anywhere in the world. It features five physical interactive experiments that bring the magic of the internet to life. The exhibition is available online and at the Science Museum, London. We created tangible versions of invisible web technologies, so the public were able to get their hands on them and learn how the web works. In July 2012 'Web Lab' launched in beta, a world first for a physical exhibition, and it continued 24 hours a day, seven days a week until summer 2013.

–
Branding Agency
B-Reel
Experience Design
Tellart
Computational Designer
Karsten Schmidt
Creative Agency
Google Creative Lab
Graphic Design Agency
Bibliothèque
Spatial & Exhibition Design
Universal Design Studio
Spatial & Industrial Design
MAP
Production Company
WEIR+WONG
Digital Production & Design
B-Reel
Engineering Agency
Tellart
Project & Construction Managers
Fraser Randall
Sound Design
Shroom
Music Production
Shroom
Client
Google
Brand
Google Chrome

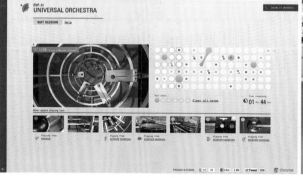

LONDON 51°32'N 0°5'W 9° 12:00

Run Jozi

South Africans aren't safe to run where they want, and certainly not in the streets of the world's crime capital, Johannesburg. In 2012, Nike marked one of South Africa's most commemorated public holidays – Human Rights Day – with a sponsored ten-kilometre race. Nike could help reclaim the streets by organising the race in the city centre, a place few dare to drive, let alone run. To be bolder still, the race was scheduled at night. All communication rallied the city to our cause. We reached our target of 10,000 runners two weeks before the deadline. Our facebook fan base grew by 4,792%. #RunJozi trended on Twitter within 40 minutes of the launch, and stayed at number one for over a week. The results: 350,000 spectators; over R10 million in PR and a growing number of Nike running clubs.

Designers
Christo Kruger
Peter Ringelmann
Art Directors
Christo Kruger
Freda Raubenheimer
Peter Ringelmann
Copywriters
Antoinette Fourie
Johnson
Collin Makhubela
Senior Copywriter
Jeanine Vermaak
Creative Director
Gustav Greffrath
Executive Creative Directors
Xolisa Dyeshana
Maciek Michalski
Chief Creative Officer
Pepe Marais
Agency Producers
Marc Ratcliffe
Annelie Rode
Ananda Swanepoel
Editor
Christopher Pinto
Sound Engineer
Louis Enslin
Advertising Agency
Joe Public Johannesburg
Digital Agency
Trigger Isobar
Strategists
Madelaine Keyser
Laurent Marty
Mmaphuthi Morule
Uno de Waal
Client
Nike
Brand
Nike Running

DESIGN BRANDING

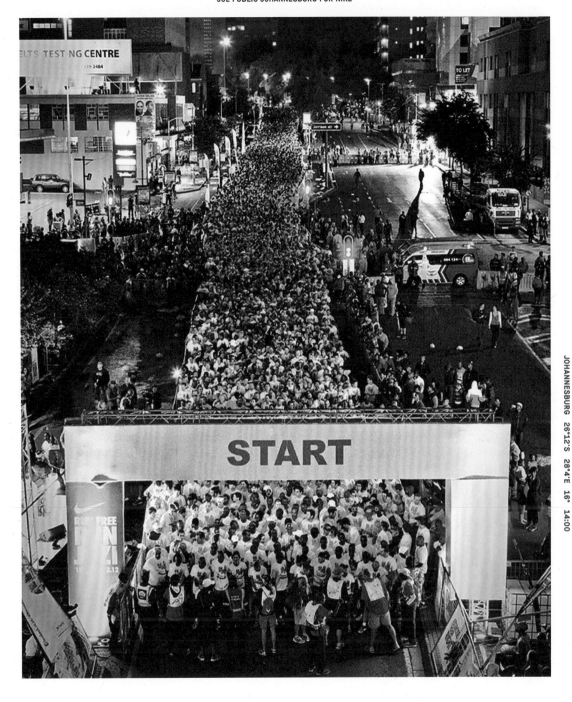

JOHANNESBURG 26°12'S 28°4'E 16° 14:00

Silo Theatre Identity

The Silo logo mark was made by arranging the letters of the name to conjure an image of a face. As a symbol it references the Greek comedy and tragedy masks, which have become the universal symbol for theatre. The logo is a facial expression of surprise and shock, synonymous with the company's ambition to perform challenging contemporary theatre. To launch the Silo 2012 season, a series of physical collages were constructed to hint at the underlying themes of each play. The art direction of the images references the soft forms of surrealism and the preoccupation with dismembered limbs.

—
Designers
Aaron Edwards
Emma Hickey
Kris Lane
Anna Myers
Dean Poole
Alan Wolfgramm
Creative Director
Dean Poole
Photographer
Toaki Okano
Design Agency
Alt Group
Digital Agency
Sons & Co
Client
Silo Theatre

DESIGN   BRANDING

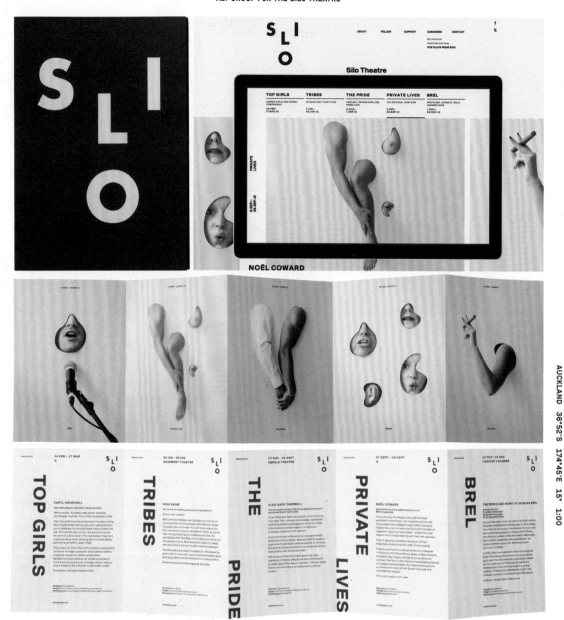

AUCKLAND 36°52'S 174°45'E 15° 1:00

Shrewsbury Identity

Could a brand sum up what's special about Shrewsbury? That was our brief. We came up with 'The original one-off': a brand to showcase all the town's one-offs, big (Darwin was born there) and small (you can get a great loaf of bread near the station). To make sure we involved local people, businesses and organisations, we did away with the usual top-down way of running projects like this and handed over the brand to everyone in the town. We created a toolkit with logos, typeface, taglines and tips, along with a 'one-off' stamp that everyone could use – even with next to no budget.

–
Designer
Jo Jones
Creative Directors
Dan Bernstein
Molly Mackey
Rob Mitchell
Branding Agencies
& SMITH
We All Need Words
Client
Destination
Shrewsbury

DESIGN BRANDING

LONDON 51°32'N 0°5'W 9° 12:00

DESIGN BRANDING

4seven Idents

4seven is a new channel featuring the best of Channel 4 from the last seven days. The channel marque features a '7' within the existing Channel 4 marque, revealed as you pan around a corner. This corner became the visual signature for our idents, which feature ordinary, everyday environments wrapped around a right-angle, with the marque at the heart of each scene. The idents were created using an innovative mix of angled camera work and CG augmentation, resulting in eye-catching, logic-defying scenes, reminiscent of mathematical artist M.C. Escher.

—

Designer
James Greenfield
Directors
Mike Alderson
Tim Swift
Alice Tonge
Art Directors
Mike Alderson
Tim Swift
Alice Tonge
Creative Directors
Alice Tonge
Chris Wood

Producer
Louise Oliver
Production Designers
Patrick Lyndon-Stanford
Adam Zoltowski
Directors of Photography
Olivier Cariou
Bob Pendar-Hughes
Motion Graphics Artists
Douglas Bowden
Rupert Burton
Simon Holmedal
Visual Effects
Jim Radford
Visual Effects Producer
Julie Evans
Visual Effects Supervisors
Chrys Aldred
Tim Civil
Colourist
George K
Editors
Nick Armstrong
Alex Lee
Sound Designer
Gavin Little
Sound Engineer
Chris Turner
Post Production
The Moving Picture Company
Design Agency
Magpie Studio
Product Manager
Caroline Greig
Marketing Managers
Ros Godber
James Walker
Client
Channel 4
Brand
4seven

LONDON 51°32'N 0°5'W 9° 12:00

Allotment

Pool

Supermarket

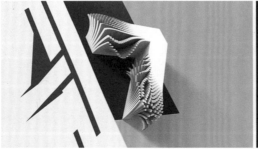

Day to Night

Recipeace Identity

In a world of increasing violence, Peace One Day along with the D&AD White Pencil competition asked us to raise awareness for Peace Day, 21 September. This led us to create 'Recipeace', a movement that brings conflicting people together over food. It's over food that we sit down together to settle our differences, bury the hatchet and create understanding. 'Recipeace' raised awareness for Peace Day by generating over 3.5 million media impressions (with no media weight), thousands of tweets worldwide and, with the help of hundreds of restaurants, countless peace dinners throughout Chicago.

–
Designer
Casey Martin
Senior Designers
Kelly Dorsey
Kyle Poff
Peter Ty
Art Director
Kate
Harding-Jackson

Copywriter
Adam Ferguson
Design Director
Alisa Wolfson
Creative Directors
Phil Jungmann
Matt Miller
Executive Creative Director
Jeanie Caggiano
Chief Creative Officers
Susan Credle
Mark Tutssel
Producers
Richard Blanco
Mark Phan
Steve Tabor
Executive Producers
Vincent Geraghty
Rob Tripas
Senior Producer
Laurie Gustafson
Production Designer
Chris Apap
Photographers
Chris Cassidy
Jason McKean
Editor
Joe Clear
Advertising Agency
Leo Burnett Chicago
Production Companies
Giannini Creative
Rider-Dickerson
Account Executives
Riley Bernardin
Dane Gunderson
Account Directors
Nina Abnee
Karla Flannery
Josh Raper
Client
Peace One Day

DESIGN BRANDING

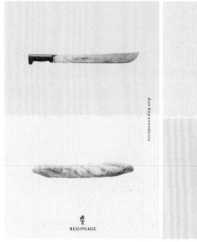

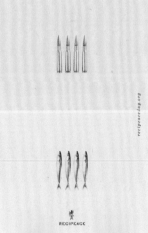

CHICAGO 41°52'N 87°3'W 3° 7:00

09/21/12

COME
TOGETHER
OVER
FOOD

World Chess Identity

We came up with an identity, promotional campaign and game environment for the redesigned World Chess organisation. The identity was created using only black and white, the colours of chess pieces, but also the purest colours of opposition. It features a symbol for the absorbing complexity of the game, a 'chess world' in hexagonal form that presents a trompe-l'oeil three dimensional board in which many different permutations can be seen.

–
Designer
Joe Stephenson
Director
Steven Qua
Graphic Designer
John Rushworth
Illustrator
Christian Montenegro
Writers
Tom Edmonds
Naresh Ramchani
Product Designer
Daniel Weil
Interior Designer
Daniel Weil
Design Agency
Pentagram Design
Client
World Chess

DESIGN   BRANDING

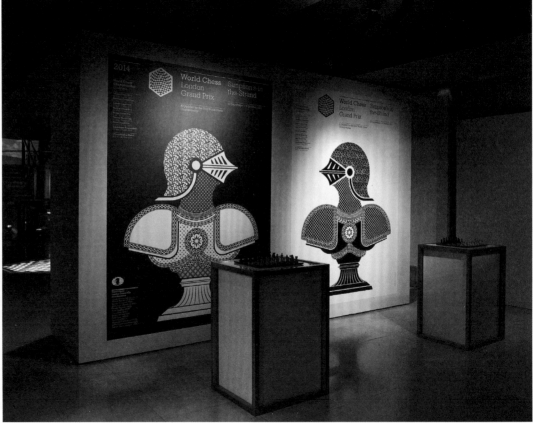

LONDON 51°32'N 0°5'W 9° 12:00

Art in Miniature

We curated a London-wide exhibition of stamps as part of the London Design Festival. We wanted to celebrate the work of the Royal Mail and also to commend designers for solving the problem of creating graphic art for the smallest of canvasses. Around 150 actual size stamps went on show at over 30 venues around London, from the V&A Museum to Homerton Hospital. We provided branded magnifying glasses, while QR codes on caption panels took you to a blog where images could be uploaded and a map of the trail downloaded. Each stamp was framed in laser-cut acrylic, shaped to echo its perforations.

–
Designers
Rory Brady
Gareth Howat
Jim Sutherland
Copywriter
Nick Asbury
Design Directors
Gareth Howat
Jim Sutherland
Design Agency
hat-trick design
Brand Managers
Ben Evans
Marcus James
Philip Parker
Manufacturer
Richard Smart
Clients
London Design
Festival
Royal Mail
Brand
Royal Mail Stamps
and Collectibles

DESIGN BRANDING

LONDON 51°32'N 0°5'W 9° 12:00

**No Two Mamas
Are Alike**

Mama Shelter is a
rapidly growing hotel
brand positioned as
'affordable luxury'.
The Mama way is
an intriguing mix
of friendliness and
community, wrapped
in style, eclecticism
and a drop of surreal
humour; qualities
that are very much
reflected in Mama's
brand identity
and touchpoints.
While the logo
is used sparingly
within hotels as
not to over-brand,
there is a wealth
of ever changing
visual surprise, wit
and seductiveness
across touchpoints,
reminding guests
that this is a creative
experience to be
treasured.

—
Designer
Ross Goulden
Creative Directors
Mark Bonner
Jason Gregory
Peter Hale
Photographer
Jill Greenberg
Design Agency
GBH
Post Production
Tapestry
Client
Mama Shelter

DESIGN   BRANDING

LONDON   51°32'N   0°5'W   9°   12:00

F. Ménard Identity

F. Ménard is a family business involved in the pork production trade. Its new identity draws from tradition and is inspired by the very first logo of this 50-year-old company, yet it displays a very modern look. The platform blends genuine old photos with contemporary shots, proving in one glance that, to guarantee top quality meat, innovation truly is the company's top priority.

–
Designers
Serge Côté
Andrée Rouette
Art Director
Serge Côté
Copywriter
Sophie Bordes
Creative Directors
Claude Auchu
Serge Côté
Photographer
Martin Girard
Video Producer
Simon Lavoie
Design Agency
lg2boutique
Print Production
lg2fabrique
Planner
Pénélope Fournier
Account Handlers
Marion Haimon
Catherine Lanctôt
Johanna Lessard
Florence
Morin-Laurin
Client
F. Ménard

DESIGN BRANDING

MONTREAL 45°30'N 73°34'W 7° 8:00

○

IN BOOK IN BRANDING, BRANDING SCHEMES/LARGE BUSINESS
FUTUREBRAND FOR THE LONDON ORGANISING COMMITTEE OF THE OLYMPIC AND PARALYMPIC GAMES (LOCOG)

London 2012

As part of McCann Worldgroup, FutureBrand developed the look of 'London 2012' and an identity system that worked across every touchpoint. The core idea was to use the lines and shards that the logo emanates, creating a burst of energy. The joy of the graphic device was that it could be adapted across lots of different platforms yet remain clearly recognisable and consistent. This meant we could tell a single design story, from the seating bowl designs to the patterning on the concourse. The ensuing look was provocative, unexpected, distinctive and bursting with life.

—
Designers
Giovanni Rodolfi
Lou Swaine
Design Director
Adam Savage
Creative Director
Matt Buckhurst
Executive Creative Director
Shane Greeves
Branding Agency
FutureBrand
Client
London Organising Committee of the Olympic and Paralympic Games (LOCOG)
Brand
London 2012

DESIGN BRANDING

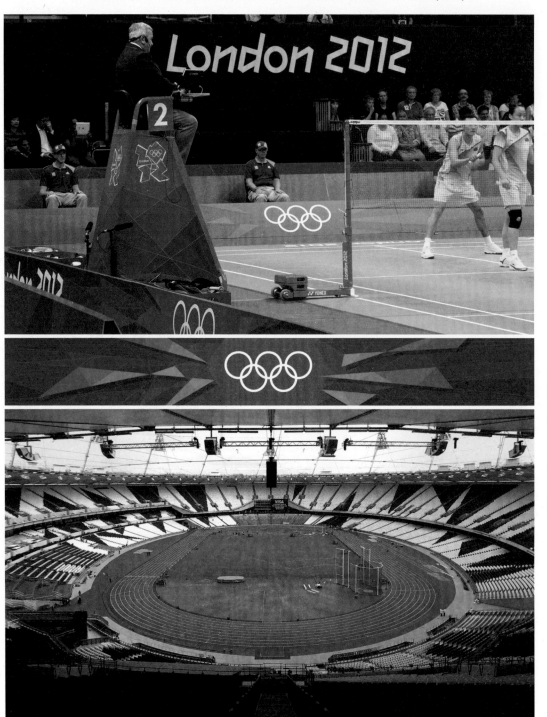

LONDON 51°32'N 0°5'W 9° 12:00

Take the Stage
Newspaper Wraps

In the UK's largest print advertising deal, we commissioned illustrations for 17 cover wraps of London newspaper Metro, one for each day of the London 2012 Olympic Games. They were part of the adidas 'Take the Stage' campaign. The acclaimed campaign was later extended to include T-shirts and commemorative illustrations, and was used in adidas print advertising.

—
Designers
Anna Dunn
Victoria Talbot
Creative Director
Rob Longworth
Illustrator
Paul Willoughby
Advertising Agency
Sid Lee
Creative Agency
Human After All
Project Managers
Ailsa Caine
Danny Miller
Andy Tweddle
Client
adidas

DESIGN   BRANDING

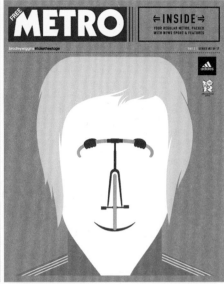

LONDON   51°32'N   0°5'W   9°   12:00

Penguin English Library Covers

The Penguin English Library first appeared in 1963 promoting English language literary masterpieces from the last 500 years. The design brief was to reinvent and rebrand this classic series, reimagining and modernising the cover designs and the branding, and to incorporate Penguin orange on the spines, which was a distinctive element of the original series.

—
Art Director
Coralie Bickford-Smith
Concept Visualiser
Becky Stocks
Creative Director
Jim Stoddart
Illustrators
Alex Allden
Benjamin Anslow
Coralie Bickford-Smith
Imogen Boase
Mick Brownfield
Antonio Colaco
Despotica
Matt Dorfman
Mark Ecob
Neil Gower
Richard Green
Jenny Grigg
Tom Johnson
Emma King
Joji Koyama
Yeti Lambregts
David Mackintosh
Viki Ottewill
Anna Salmane
Jim Tierney
David Wardle
Sara Wood
Matt Young
Artworker
Viki Ottewill
Publishing Company
Penguin Books
Client
Penguin Classics
Brand
Penguin English Library

DESIGN BRANDING

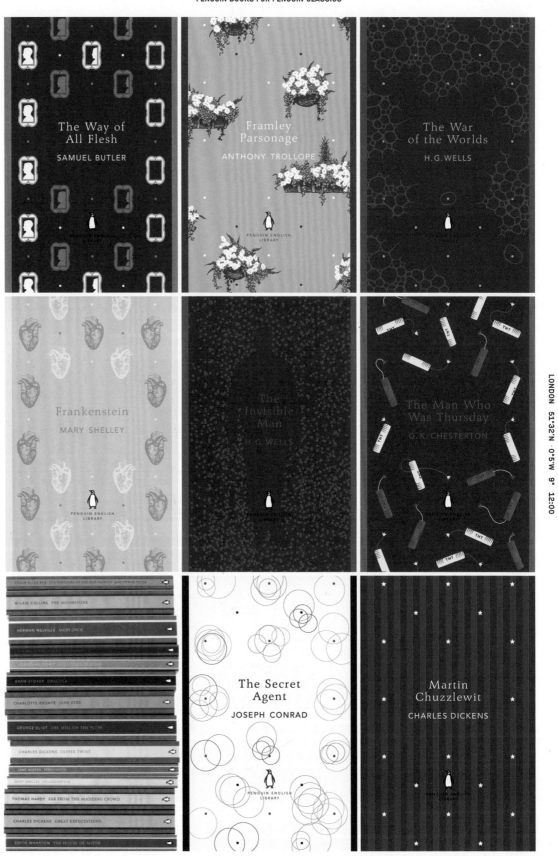

LONDON · 51°32'N · 0°5'W · 9° · 12:00

Wrapple Identity

A shop selling gift wrap and related products was preparing to open its first branch in Tokyo. We were asked to develop the branding and came up with a name that was both playful and relevant to the store's content. For Wrapple's logo we used a red apple to give charm and character to the brand. As a symbol, the apple is iconic and well received across generations through its association with Adam & Eve, Snow White, William Tell, Newton, The Beatles and Apple. However, the logo is distinguished by the apple's coat, designed as a peeling ribbon – a strong and simple graphic to communicate the shop's message.

–
Designers
Natsumi Nakako
Serina Shiota
Art Director
Ryosuke Uehara
Creative Director
Kao Kanamori
Design Agency
KIGI
Client
Shimojima

DESIGN BRANDING

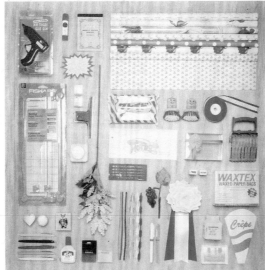
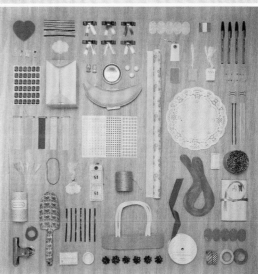

TOKYO 35°40'N 139°45'E 15° 21:00

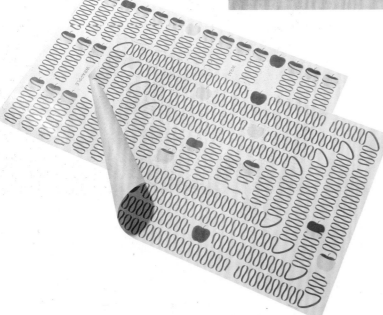

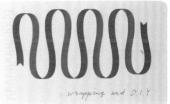

New York Writes Itself

The Village Voice newspaper asked us to prove its position as the real, uncensored voice of New York, and re-establish the brand as a go-to source of arts and culture. The solution was to bring real stories of New Yorkers to life as arts and culture. We began by creating NewYorkWrites Itself.com – a simple destination inviting New Yorkers to write down the funny, weird or crazy things they experience everyday on the street. In 2012, we brought the best stories to life on stage, in a first of its kind crowd sourced show called '8 Million Protagonists'.

–
Designer
Steven Jordao
Senior Art Director
Stian Ward Bugten
Copywriter
Simen Braathen
Executive Creative Directors
Kieran Antill
Michael Canning
Chief Creative Officer
Jay Benjamin
Agency Executive Producer
Jeremy Fox
Agency Producer
Shaina Stigler
Curator
Max Goodwin
Director
Stephen Bishop
Seely
Artist
Sofie Zamchick
Choreographer
Jimmy Burgio
Writer
Caitlin Gallo
Editor
Tom Pina
Publisher
Josh Fromson
Advertising Agency
Leo Burnett
New York
Production Company
LB Entertainment
Interactive Production Company
Avant LLC
Sound Design
Heard City
Music Production
Big Foote
Mophonics
Motive
Account Executive
Emily Brau
Business Director
Tom Flanagan
Client
The Village Voice

DESIGN BRANDING

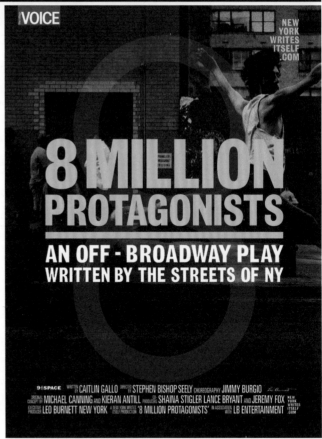

NEW YORK CITY 40°40'N 73°56'W 8° 8:00

Vision Hall

We were invited by the Hyundai Motor Group to create a series of video artworks for the world's highest resolution screen. The films had to simply 'inspire' – allowing leaders, engineers, scientists, workers and designers to learn, think and collaborate in new ways. The films mix a myriad of animation styles and live action, building upon Universal Everything's trademark ethos of 'maximum innovation'. Abstraction is pitted against familiarity to engage all types of viewer, while themes such as nature, technology and man's relationship with them feature heavily.

–
Designer
Chris Perry
Art Director
Dylan Griffith
Design Director
Matt Pyke
Creative Directors
Dylan Griffith
Matt Pyke
Peter Schreyer
Executive Producer
Philip Ward
Director of Photography
Tobia Sempi
Director
Mark Cumming
Animation Director
Chris Perry
Sound Designer
Simon Pyke
Advertising Agency
Innocean Worldwide
Creative Agency
Universal Everything
Project Manager
Karsten Thoms
Client
Hyundai Motor Group
Brands
Hyundai
KIA

DESIGN BRANDING

SHEFFIELD 53°23'N 1°28'W 5° 12:00

DESIGN BRANDING

The V Motion Project

In April 2012, V Energy Drink assembled a team and challenged them to create a piece of music using only the body's movement. 'The V Motion Project' was born. The team developed a piece of technology, combining motion tracking and audio production software, to transform the body's movements into sounds. On 16 June, The V Motion Project showcased the new technology with an unexpected live event in downtown Auckland. The entire project was filmed to create a series of webisodes, TV ads and a music video. The project culminated in a number one hit single on iTunes.

–

Art Directors
Jae Morrison
Lachlan Palmer-Hubbard
Copywriter
Graeme Clarke
Creative Director
Aaron Turk
Chief Creative Officer
Nick Worthington
Directors
Jonny Kofoed
Zoe McIntosh
Matt von Trott

Producers
Nik Beachman
Amanda Chambers
Paul Courtney
Rob Linkhorn
Creative Technologist
Mat Tizard
Lead Developers
Jeff Nusz
Paul Sanderson
Developer
Mike Delucchi
Editor
Mike Hammond
Music Producer
Joel Little
Sound Designer
James Hayday
Advertising Agency
Colenso BBDO/
Proximity New Zealand
Planner
Andy McLeish
Account Executive
Eileen Cosgrove-Moloney
Account Manager
Stefanie Robertson
Account Director
Samantha Parsons
Group Account Director
Tim Ellis
Senior Brand Manager
Cormac Van Den Hoofdakker
Marketing Manager
Luke Rive
Client
Frucor Beverages
Brand
V Energy Drink

AUCKLAND 36°52'S 174°45'E 15° 1:00

Tree Concert

The city of Berlin loses thousands of trees every year. Friends of the Earth Germany aims to stop this trend. Our idea was a one-of-a-kind charity concert, with a chestnut tree as the musician. We built a special set of instruments at the base of the tree. Each instrument consisted of a steel frame, encompassed by polymer membranes. Internal sensors registered any impact on the membrane and converted the vibration into an artistic composition of sound and light. As leaves and chestnuts fell, the tree could play for its companions and collect donations. 'Tree Concert' gained massive media coverage and led to a new donation record for the preservation of trees.

DESIGN BRANDING

–
Art Director
Daniel Schweinzer
Copywriter
Lukas Liske
Creative Directors
Jan Harbeck
David Mously
Chief Creative Officer
Wolfgang Schneider
Producers
Mat Neidhardt
Friederike Seifert
Agency Producer
Michael Pflanz
Sound Designer
Philipp Toegel
Advertising Agency
BBDO Proximity Berlin
Account Executive
Monika Groewe
Account Managers
Joris Jonker
Mia Luecker
Client
BUND Friends of the Earth Germany

BERLIN 52°30'N 13°25'E 6° 13:00

Driving Dogs

In New Zealand, shelter dogs were seen as second rate compared to store bought animals, so finding them homes was a daily challenge for the SPCA. As a longstanding SPCA sponsor, MINI wanted to help. Our strategy was to demonstrate just how smart these dogs really are. So, we taught three of them to drive a car and showed them, in a never-before-seen event, live on national TV. In one week, over 200 million saw the dogs driving. The campaign received more than $20 million in PR across over 70 countries. New Zealand adoption interest increased by 590% and, most importantly, every SCPA dog was adopted.

—
Designer
Nick McFarlane
Interactive Designer
Catherine Chi
Copywriters
Peter Vegas
Matt Williams
Executive Creative Directors
Tony Clewett
Regan Grafton
James Mok
Producer
Sarah Yetton
Photographer
Stephen Langdon
Cinematographer
Marco Siraky
Retoucher
Anton Mason
Editor
Blair Walker
Advertising Agency
Draftfcb New Zealand
Digital Strategist
Harri Owen
Planner
Steph Pearson
Media Managers
Rachel Leyland
Sarah McEwen
Simon Teagle
Account Managers
Eloise Hay
Stephanie Hueber
Account Director
Sally Willis
Group Account Director
Toby Sellers
Public Relations Manager
Angela Spain
Communications Director
Rufus Chuter
Clients
MINI New Zealand
SPCA New Zealand

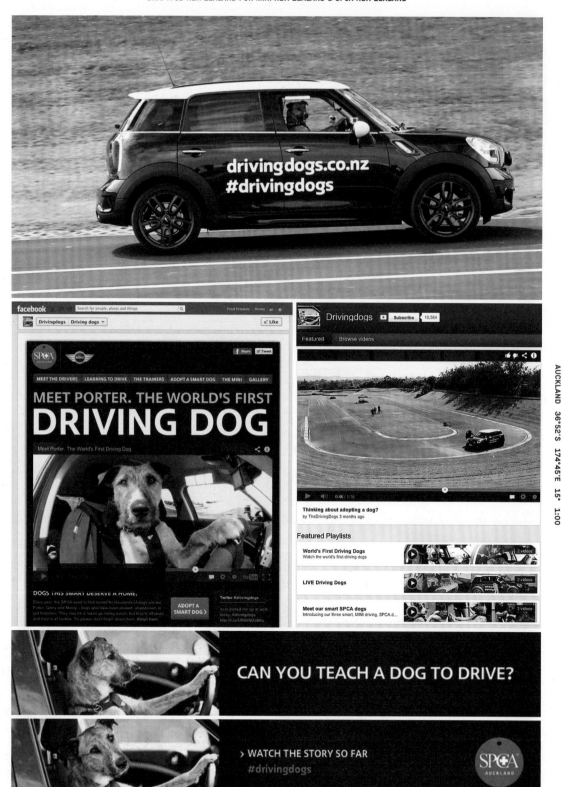

Human Arabesque

TEDxSummit was the first Middle Eastern TED conference and a one-week global TED gathering. The goal: to define the future of 'Ideas Worth Spreading'. The summit united 700 TEDx organisers from 120 countries in Doha, Qatar. We set about finding the 'x' within traditional arabesque patterns to mashup TEDx and Middle Eastern culture. We fused architecture, dance, maths and magic into a bespoke 18m high-mirrored structure that hovered over a multi-colour moving floor to create the world's first human arabesque. The experiment resulted in a kaleidoscope of infinite arabesque patterns choreographed to a soundtrack composed by Yasmine Hamdan.

Directors
Körner Union
Creative Directors
Richard Chant
Barney Hobson
Agency Producer
Jamie Kim
Artist
Yasmine Hamdan
Dance Choreographers
I COULD NEVER BE A DANCER
Music Producer
Michael Kneebone
Production Company
Big Productions
Post Production
Mikros Image
Advertising Agency
WE ARE Pi
Planner
Alexander Bennett Grant
Marketing Manager
Jim Stolze
Clients
Doha Film Institute
TED Conferences
Brand
TED

Golden Chains

ALB is an emerging French musician who's planning to release his second album in 2013. Like many other artists, ALB isn't supported by a major label yet. So, to promote and finance his upcoming album, ALB came up with 'Golden Chains', a participative music video in which the artist took up the challenge of selling his personal everyday items – for real. The plan was to use the revenue gained to fund the production of his next album.

–
Art Director
Julien Boissinot
Copywriter
Kevin Salembier
Creative Directors
Matthieu Elkaim
Olivier Lefebvre
Benjamin Marchal

Interactive Technical Director
Anthony Hamelle
Director
Johnatan Broda
Producer
Willy Morence
Agency Producer
Jean-Gabriel Saint-Paul
Digital Agency
ACNE Production
Advertising Agency
CLM BBDO
Production Company
Carnibird
Sound Design
Green United Music
Music Supervision
Green United Music
Public Relations Manager
Lauren Weber
Client
ALB

The Tux

The MR PORTER iPad Magazine is the definitive guide to dressing for the perfect party. This digital magazine is a journey through the glamorous world of the tuxedo. A world of casinos, cars and cocktails, of timeless sophistication and style, 'The Tux' App for iPad features an array of all-original content imaginatively brought to life, with intuitive navigation, shoppable video and still-life images that react to your touch.

_
Digital Designers
Eric Ahnebrink
Daniel Baer
Rik Burgess
Alexandra Hoffnung
Angelo Trofa
Creative Director
Leon St-Amour
Mobile Developer
Sam Dean
Editor
Jodie Harrison
Editor in Chief
Jeremy Langmead
Production Manager
Xanthe Greenhill
In-House Design
MR PORTER
Client
MR PORTER

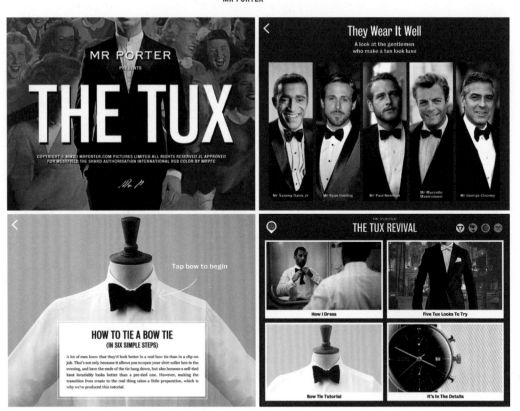

From Love to Bingo

This ad was created using only still images from the Getty archive, shown at sufficient speed to transform the series into a video that tells a beautiful story. This was a powerful way to show that Getty Images' archive is so vast you can even make a film with it.

_
Art Director
Marcos Kotlhar
Copywriter
Sophie Schoenburg
Creative Directors
André Kassu
Marcos Medeiros
Luiz Sanches
Renato Simoes
Executive Creative Director
Luiz Sanches

Chief Creative Officer
Marcello Serpa
Agency Producers
Gabriel Dagostini
Vera Jacinto
Directors
Denis Cisma
Marcos Kotlhar
Animator
Marcos Kotlhar
Editor
Marcos Kotlhar
Sound Designer
Kito Siqueira
Advertising Agency
AlmapBBDO
Production Company
Paranoid
Animation
Split Filmes
Post Production
Split Filmes
Sound Design
Satélite Audio
Client
Getty Images

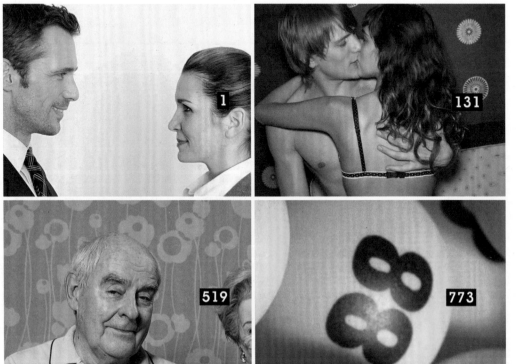

Oreo Daily Twist

Born in 1912, Oreo was celebrating its 100th year. The brand had developed a traditional image, which we wanted to rejuvenate. We created 100 ads in 100 days. Each morning we identified trending news stories, gave them a playful Oreo twist and pushed the ad to our social networks. The results: 433 million facebook views with a 280% increase in shares; and 231 million media impressions – making Oreo the brand with the highest buzz increase in 2012 (up 49%).

–
Art Director
Mike Lubrano
Senior Art Directors
Jackie Anzaldi
Jared Isle
Senior Copywriter
Noel Potts

Creative Director
Megan Sheehan
Group Creative Director
Jill Applebaum
Advertising Agency
Draftfcb New York
Digital Agency
360i
Media Agency
Mediavest
Public Relations
Weber Shandwick
Strategic Director
Auro Trini-Castelli
Account Director
Lori Johnson
Group Account Director
Susan Polachek
Brand Manager
Danielle Brown
Marketing Manager
Cindy Chen
Client
Mondelēz International
Brand
Oreo

Today, let no high-five go unanswered. oreo.ly/DailyTwist #dailytwist

12 repins   5 likes

Uploaded by Oreo

Celebrate Old Faithful's discovery with a splash of a dunk! oreo.ly/DailyTwist #dailytwist

5 repins   1 like

Uploaded by Oreo

The world has never looked this good. oreo.ly/DailyTwist #dailytwist

15 repins   11 likes

Uploaded by Oreo

No one rocks the zebra stripes like you guys — except maybe us. #NFL #dailytwist

5 repins   7 likes

Uploaded by Oreo

Project Re: Brief

Despite almost two decades of innovation online, display ads are still seen by the advertising industry as a periphery medium; a space too small for big ideas. So we put display to the ultimate test. We took some of America's greatest ads, dating as far back as 1962, and partnered with the legendary creatives behind them to re-imagine them for mobile. Even advertising's biggest ideas can fit in advertising's smallest spaces.

–
Executive Creative Directors
Howie Cohen
Harvey Gabor
Amil Gargano
Paula Green
Bob Pasqualina

Advertising Agency
Johannes Leonardo
Production Companies
@radical.media
Nexus Productions
Oil Factory
Rebolucion
RSA Films
Post Production
Katabatic Digital
Digital Agency
Grow Interactive
Digital Production Company
Fake Love
Editing
Cosmo Street
Rock Paper Scissors
Music Arrangement
Beacon Street Studios
House of Hayduk
Human
Mixing
Penny Lane Studio Center
Client
Google
Brand
Google Display

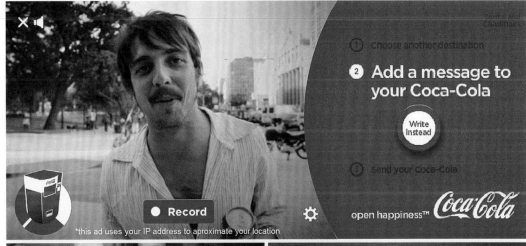

JURY

Jury Foreman	Mike John Otto
Joshua Davis	Hi-ReSI Hamburg
Joshua Davis Studios	Tsubasa Oyagi
Jane Austin	Hakuhodo
Bright North	Leisa Reichelt
Aaron Koblin	Seiichi Saito
Google Creative Lab	Rhizomatiks
A ex Lampe	Gui Seiz
A+B Studio	Stinkdigital London
Esti Landa	Nina Thelberg
Desigual	B-Reel Stockholm

Clouds Over Cuba

**Also In Book
in Interface &
Navigation for
Websites &
Digital Design**

'Clouds over Cuba'
is an interactive
multimedia
documentary
commemorating the
50th anniversary of
the Cuban Missile
Crisis. The feature
begins with Castro's
overthrow of Batista
in 1959, and
continues on until the
missiles were removed
in October 1962.
Features include
15 expert interviews,
a dossier of 200
related documents
and images linked
to the film's timeline,
mobile sync, tablet
optimisation, and
calendar integration
so you can attend
JFK's secret meetings
'live', 50 years later.
Finally, a 'What If?'
short film depicts
an alternate 2012
in which the crisis
had escalated into
nuclear war.

—
Design Director
Matt Gase
Art Director
Brian Williams
Creative Director
Joe Alexander
Technical Director
Bartek Drozdz
Copywriter
Wade Alger
Directors
Erich Joiner
Ben Tricklebank
Interactive Producer
Kristen Koeller
**Head of Interactive
Production**
Joy Kuraitis
Executive Producers
Dustin Callif
Oliver Fuselier
Steve Humble
Brian Latt
Agency Producers
Nicole Hollis-Vitale
Kristen Little
Advertising Agency
The Martin Agency
**Production
Company**
Tool
Editing
STITCH
Music Production
Plan8
Client
The JFK
Presidential Library
& Museum

RICHMOND 37°32'N 77°25'W 6° 8:00

Gallery One

Tasked to cultivate new audiences through technology, Local Projects created 'Gallery One' at the Cleveland Museum of Art, a suite of new interactives that transforms the art museum experience. Visitors can explore high-resolution digital versions of the artworks and see them in their original contexts. These interfaces invite visitors to create their own works of art, and understand art and art-making through intuition, play and creativity.

—

Interactive Designer
Angela Chen
Graphic Designers
Lynn Kiang
Erika Tarte
Art Director
Katie Lee
Technical Director
Ethan Holda
Interactive Director
Ian Curry
Creative Technologists
Eric Mika
Caitlin Morris
Philipp Rockel
David Scharf
Josh Silverman
Motion Graphics Artist
Jen Choi
Technical Architect
Sundar Raman
Content Coordinator
Miriam Lakes
Director
Jake Barton
Design Agency
Local Projects
Sponsor
Cleveland Museum of Art
Project Manager
Keeli Shaw
Client
Cleveland Museum of Art

DESIGN   DIGITAL DESIGN

NEW YORK CITY   40°40'N   73°56'W   8°   8:00

100,000 Stars

'100,000 Stars' is
a Google Chrome
experiment that
uses real data to plot
the position of over
100,000 stars near
the sun. Users may
zoom from our solar
system all the way
out to the Milky
Way galaxy. The
site gives access to
87 clickable star
systems and provides
detailed information,
including a 3D model.
An automated tour
provides a guided
overview of the
visualisation.

—
Creative Agency
Google Creative Lab
Client
Google

DESIGN   DIGITAL DESIGN

SAN FRANCISCO 37°47'N 122°25'W 15° 5:00

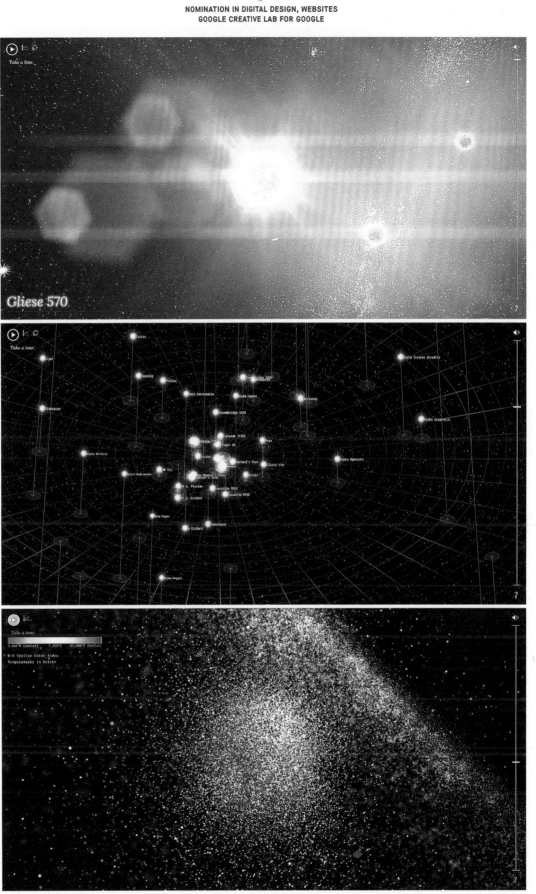

Chrome Web Lab

Chrome 'Web Lab' is a first-of-its-kind open exhibition that can be accessed from anywhere in the world. It features five physical interactive experiments that bring the magic of the internet to life. The exhibition is available online and at the Science Museum, London. We created tangible versions of invisible web technologies, so the public were able to get their hands on them and learn how the web works. In July 2012 'Web Lab' launched in beta, a world first for a physical exhibition, and it continued 24 hours a day, seven days a week until summer 2013.

–
Creative Agency
Google Creative Lab
Computational Designer
Karsten Schmidt
Digital Production & Design
B-Reel
Graphic Design Agency
Bibliothèque
Experience Design
Tellart
Branding Agency
B-Reel
Production Company
WEIR+WONG
Engineering Agency
Tellart
Project & Construction Managers
Fraser Randall
Spatial & Industrial Design
MAP
Spatial & Exhibition Design
Universal Design Studio
Sound Design
Shroom
Music Production
Shroom
Client
Google
Brand
Google Chrome

DESIGN   DIGITAL DESIGN

LONDON   51°32'N   0°5'W   9°   12:00

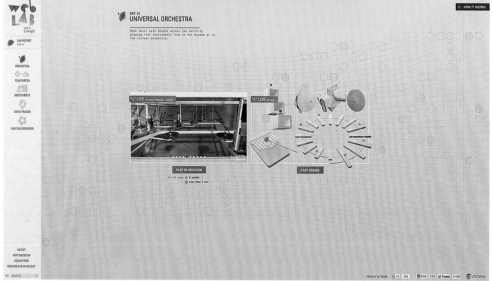

Audience
Pixel Content

We created over 14 hours of moving image content for the London 2012 Olympic and Paralympic Opening and Closing Ceremonies. This was made possible after an intensive period of creative and technical research and development for the 70,500 LED paddles attached to each seat in the Olympic Stadium. The production and implementation required close collaboration with 59 Productions, Treatment Studio and the LOCOG Ceremonies AV team led by Justine Catterall. The resulting immersive experience extended the visual canvas from the field of play up into the stadium audience, making it part of the show and enhancing the broadcast spectacle.

–
Art Directors
Dan Capstick
Kate Dawkins
Creative Director
Will Case
Technical Delivery Manager
Andrew McKinna
Creative Producer
Justine Catterall
Senior Producers
Liberty Dakin
Jayne Hobart
Tom Lowndes
Nina Ludgate
Digital Agency
Crystal CG
Design Agencies
59 Productions
Treatment Studio
Project Director
Ed Cookson
Client
London Organising Committee of the Olympic and Paralympic Games (LOCOG)
Brand
London 2012

DESIGN   DIGITAL DESIGN

LONDON   51°32'N   0°5'W   9°   12:00

Ugokidase Tokyo

In 2012, Nike+ launched its most innovative digital products to date. And we wanted Japanese consumers to experience them all before they came to market. To reach our audience, we took inspiration from a Japanese obsession – gaming. In central Tokyo, we created a pop-up arcade at the Ugokidase station for the everyday athlete, open throughout the 2012 Olympic Games. Players could compete with friends in five new sporting challenges, each powered by Nike+. Their results fed live into global leader boards, testing performance like never before.

—
Senior Designer
Neil Gurr
Art Director
Nick Bastian
Creative Director
Masaya Nakade
Executive Creative Director
Duan Evans
Associate Creative Director
Max Chanan
Senior Copywriter
Guy Bingley
Executive Producer
Daniela Michelon
Advertising Agency
AKQA London
Digital Production Companies
amana
Rhizomatiks
Taiyo Kikaku
Project Manager
Lauren Ivory
Account Director
Ross Winterflood
Group Account Director
Gareth Nettleton
Client
Nike Japan

DESIGN DIGITAL DESIGN

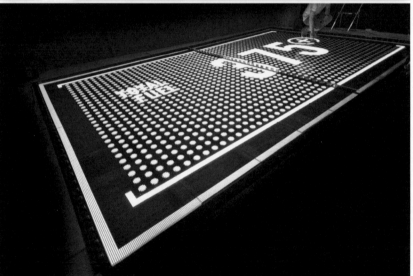

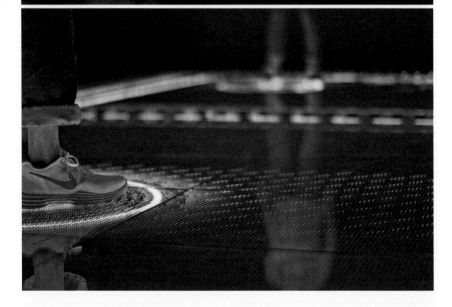

LONDON 51°32'N 0°5'W 9° 12:00

Easy Way Subtitles

For the many
international students
and professionals
living in Brazil, we
created captioning
technology combined
with Google Translate
to provide subtitles
for Brazilian TV in
any language.

–
Designer
Gustavo De Lacerda
Creative Directors
Guga Ketzer
Cassio Moron
Sergio Mugnaini
Fabio Saboya
Programmers
Raphael Franzini
Vitor Manfredini
Copywriter
Raphael Franzini
Advertising Agency
Loducca
Account Handler
Wilson Negrini
Client
Easy Way
Language Center
Brand
Easy Way

DESIGN DIGITAL DESIGN

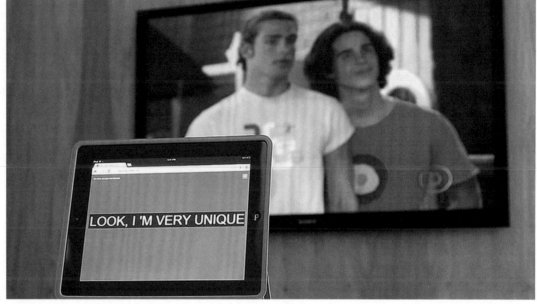

SÃO PAULO 23°31'S 46°31'W 23° 10:00

Nike+ FuelBand

Also In Book
in Interface &
Navigation for
Websites &
Digital Design

Nike came to us to
realise an idea: a
wristband device
that tracks your
daily activity and a
common, universal
metric called Fuel for
every active body out
there. They asked us
to design the entire
user experience. We
ensured ease of use:
set your goal, and get
from red to green. If
you meet your goal,
animations celebrate
your performance.
Data graphics show
where you were most
active daily, weekly,
monthly, and beyond.
We created Bluetooth
sync technology
so the results of your
day's activities can
be transferred to
your mobile device
and visualised on the
FuelBand app.

–
Creative Directors
Cesar Marchetti
Kirill Yeretsky
**Executive Creative
Director**
Tara Greer
**Associate Creative
Directors**
Keith Byrne
Gaurabh Mathure
Technical Directors
Nick Coronges
Sune Kaae
Daniel Katz
Art Director
Ray Sison
Copywriter
Evan Maranca
Designer
Ellen Pai
**Senior Software
Engineers**
Robert Carlsen
Fernando Mazzon
Niall McCormack
Executive Producer
Avery Holden
Senior Producers
Alan Donnelly
Guy Helson
Michael Klimkewicz
Head of Product
Ian Spalter
**Quality Assurance
Manager**
Leslie Chong
Digital Agency
R/GA
Managing Director
Jennifer Allen
Client
Nike
Brand
Nike+

DESIGN   DIGITAL DESIGN

NEW YORK CITY   40°40'N   73°56'W   8°   8:00

The Liberation

ONLY is a Danish fashion brand targeting girls between 15 and 25. They wanted to manifest the product DNA of the brand, interacting directly with consumers and making it easy for them to buy, like, pin, tweet and create more traffic to the website. 'The Liberation' is an online interactive film experience and the world's first on-demand video retail environment. The campaign spread to thousands of sites and blogs, increasing traffic to only.com by over 500%.

—

Art Directors
Charlotte Boysen
Kenneth Graupner
Mia Lykkegaard
Katrine Jo Madsen
Digital Art Director
Daniel Nicolajsen
Senior Art Director
Jakob Nylund
Creative Directors
Jimmy Blom
Daniel Ilic
Technical Director
Daniel Isaksson
Creative Technologist
Karsten Loewe Kirkegaard
Developer
Einar Öberg
User Experience Designer
Ana Cecilia Martins
Director of Photography
Niklas Johansson
Director
Christoffer Von Reis
Producers
Mia Wallmark
Kristina Wibom
Editor
Stefan Ström
Artist
Lune
Sound Designers
Johan Belin
Erik Brattlöf
Digital Agency
North Kingdom
Advertising Agency
Uncle Grey Copenhagen
Sound Design
DinahMoe
Strategist
Lars Samuelsen
Account Director
Charlotte Porsager
Client
ONLY Jeans

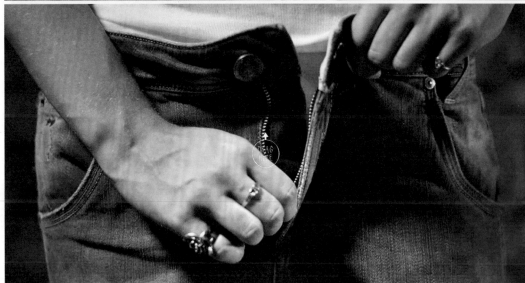

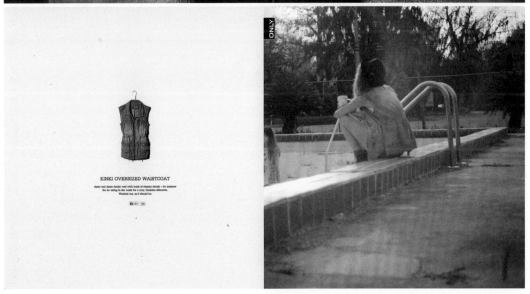

KINKI OVERSIZED WAISTCOAT

SKELLEFTEÅ 64°45'N 20°57'E 5° 13:00

AMSTERDAM 52°22′N 4°53′E 9° 13:00

Lowdi Website

The brief was to create a website for Lowdi, a new portable wireless speaker. Lowdi is a joint venture between Momkai and digital products supplier Linkeet. The site needed to set the tone for the online presence of the speaker, provide all the necessary product details, and make the order process as simple as possible. To create an engaging online experience Momkai designed and built a distinct one pager housing all the information. The top of the site features an animated film that sets the mood, while a subtle colour palette and strong illustration style make Lowdi stand out from other speakers in the market.

–
Designer
Harald Dunnink
Art Director
Harald Dunnink
Creative Director
Harald Dunnink
Developers
Mark Hinch
Pascal Strijbos
Christian de Wit
Illustrators
Martijn van Dam
Cléa Dieudonné
Digital Design Agency
Momkai
Animation
CRCR
Sound Design
Audentity
Client
Lowdi

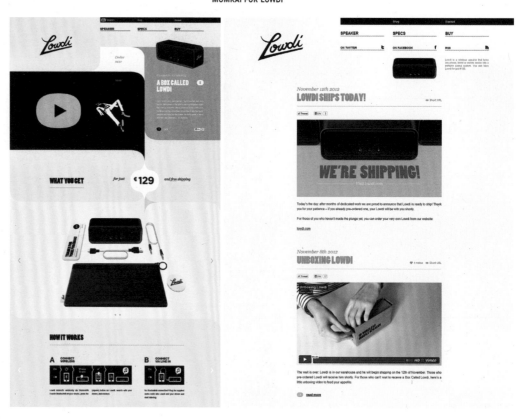

SÃO PAULO 23°31′S 46°31′W 23° 10:00

From Love to Bingo

This ad was created using only still images from the Getty archive, shown at sufficient speed to transform the series into a video that tells a beautiful story. This was a powerful way to show that Getty Images' archive is so vast you can even make a film with it.

–
Art Director
Marcos Kotlhar
Creative Directors
André Kassu
Marcos Medeiros
Renato Simoes
Digital Creative Directors
Luciana Haguiara
Sandro Rosa
Executive Creative Director
Luiz Sanches
Chief Creative Officer
Marcello Serpa

Information Architect
Luis Felipe Fernandes
Copywriter
Sophie Shoenburg
Sound Designer
Kito Siqueira
Production Director
Fernando Boniotti
Advertising Agency
AlmapBBDO
Digital Production Company
Inkuba
Production Companies
Paranoid
Split Filmes
Project Manager
Rafael Puls
Account Handler
Marina Leal
Brand Manager
Veronica Raad
Client
Getty Images

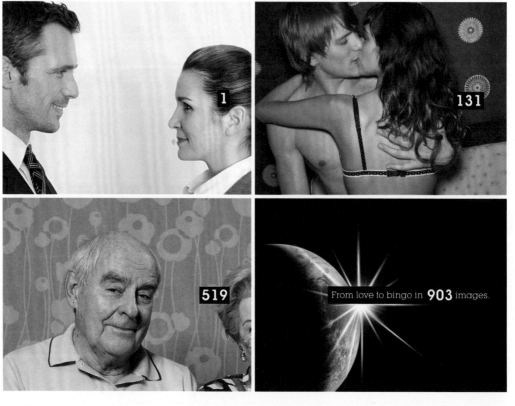

This Exquisite Forest

'This Exquisite Forest' is an interactive installation produced by Google and Tate Modern that lets artists collaboratively create short animations using web-based drawing and music tools. Artists may branch off others' animations as they explore a specific theme, creating tree-like timelines. At Tate Modern, visitors may explore and contribute to life-size animation trees seeded by Tate artists.

–
Creative Directors
Aaron Koblin
Chris Milk
Design Agency
Punk & Butler
Creative Agencies
Google Creative Lab
Tate Modern
Sound Design
DinahMoe
Clients
Google
Tate Modern

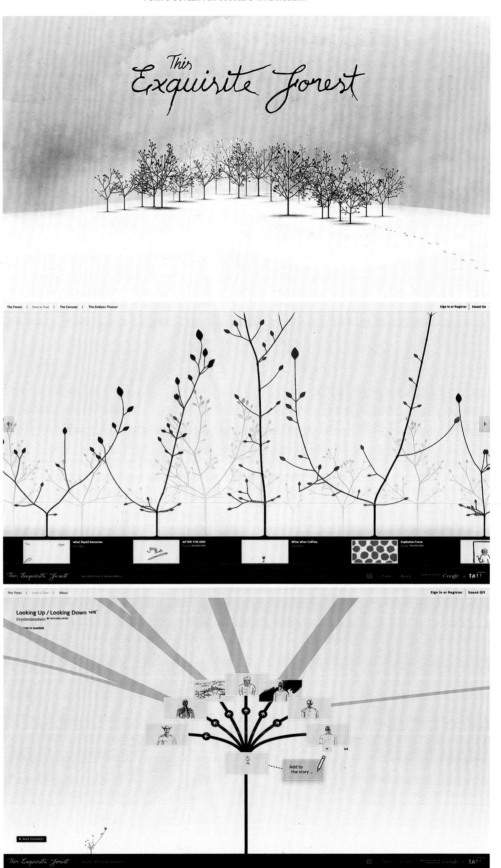

DESIGN   DIGITAL DESIGN

LOS ANGELES   34°3'N   118°15'W   15°   5:00

Tobacco Body

Do you remember the pictures of black lungs from school? 'Tobacco Body' is exactly the same concept for the iPad age. It's a tool for teachers to show how tobacco changes our bodies to help school kids think critically about smoking. To reach the kids we had to highlight something that is relevant to them. Lungs aren't a top priority for teens, so we included other symptoms of smoking more related to appearance and attractiveness, from zits to bad breath. We've taken the age-old shock effect and made it even more shocking with today's technology. And it's all credible science.

–
Art Directors
Maria Fridman
Ville Kovanen
Graphic Designer
Pol Solsona
Creative Director
Erkki Izarra
Copywriters
Anna Lundqvist
Jonathan Mander
Valtteri Väkevä
Agency Producers
Krista Durchman
Peggy Petrell
3D Artists
Kristiina Ojala
Ville Rousu
Photographer
Kimmo Syväri
Advertising Agency
358
**Production
Company**
!NOOB
Client
Cancer Society
of Finland

DESIGN   DIGITAL DESIGN

HELSINKI 60°10'N 25°0'E 4° 14:00

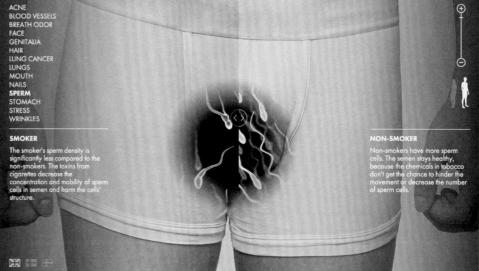

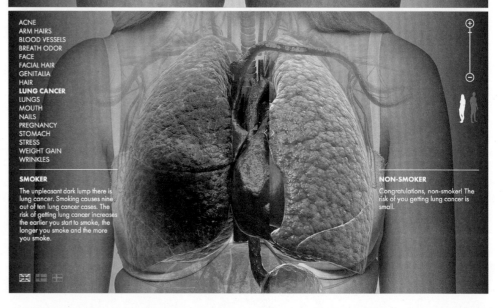

Your Everyday Drive

The Toyota Prius Plug-in Hybrid website takes viewers on a personalised journey to discover how electric and petrol hybrid technology can make a real difference to our everyday drive. Using the latest Google Chrome technology, the captivating experience asks visitors to input the start and end address of an everyday journey they make. It then creates a simulation of their route by cleverly stitching Google Streetview and Maps information together, while simultaneously calculating fuel economy, carbon dioxide emissions and range statistics.

Designers
Tom Dunn
Josh Smith
Art Director
Lorenzo Marri
Creative Director
Aidan Sharkey
Lead Developer
Alberto Giorgi
Developer
André Venâncio
Copywriters
Ollie Kristian
Tom Newman
Producer
Sophie Anderson
Creative Agency
Toaster
Music Production
Aurotone
Strategist
Jesse Basset
Account Executives
Tomomi Kato
Akira Toda
Bert Tomizawa
Client
Toyota
Brand
Prius

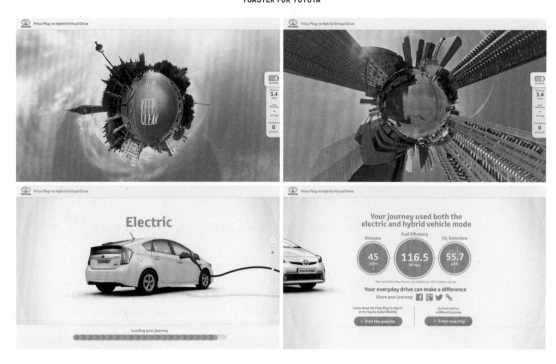

2012 Olympics Digital Portfolio

The Olympics Digital Portfolio project aimed to create a family of products and services across a wide range of platforms and devices. A connected and consistent experience was essential. Our ambition was to show every session of the London 2012 Olympic Games on every device spanning TV, radio, computer, mobile and tablets. We built on the foundation of the recently redesigned BBC Sport website, using the new page layouts and design language to push our coverage to new heights. The Digital Portfolio offered 24 live HD streams on TV, web and via our app, ensuring the entire nation would never have to miss a moment.

Designers
Nick Beese
Martha Chaletlaforet
Joe Fung
Andy Gray
Jessica Rebelo
Kate Shaw-Treseder
Senior Designers
Katherine Aherne
Anne Dahlstrom
David Man
David Wilson
Art Director
Giles Routedge
Creative Directors
Fabian Birgfeld
Scott Byrne-Fraser
Jennifer Crakow
Nick Hailey
Gareth Ingram
Interactive Designer
Ben Gilmore
User Experience Architect
Georgia Muir
Product Manager
Cait O'Riordan
Client
BBC
Brand
BBC Sport

Font Me

Adobe believes that the act of creation will better the world. Upon the launch of Creative Cloud, we aimed to build brand awareness and positive perception within a broader audience, those who were usually 'non-creators'. Our solution was to design an experience where anyone could enjoy creation without knowledge or technique. We created a digital installation that realised live action into fonts. By moving your body, it gave shape to your messages and imagination by creating your own original font. We had live events where anyone could participate and experience the joy of creation.

—
Designer
Masanori Sakamoto
Interactive Designer
Ken Murayama
Technical Designer
Yoshikazu Iida
Art Director
Masanori Sakamoto
Creative Directors
Kampei Baba
Koichi Katsumata
Interactive Director
Tomomi Motose
Lead Developer
Motoi Ishibashi
Developers
Taishi Chihara
Muryo Honma
Hiroyuki Hori
Tsuubito Ishii
Yusuke Kanno
Shojiro Nakaoka
Toshiaki Nakazawa
Shogo Yano
Flash Programmer
Ken Murayama
Copywriter
Seiichi Ookura
Director
Takashi Hirukawa
Producer
Kenichiro Tanaka
Executive Producer
Hitoshi Futami
Interactive Design Agency
Bascule
Brand Manager
Yukiko Iwasa
Marketing Managers
Hisamichi Kinomoto
Akira Nakamura
Client
Adobe Systems
Japan
Brand
Adobe Creative
Cloud

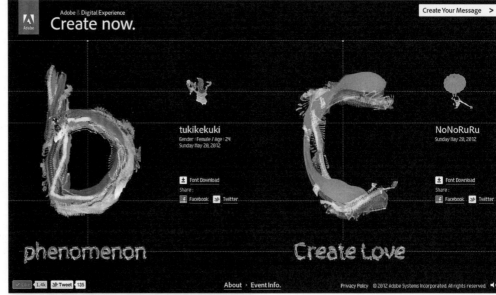

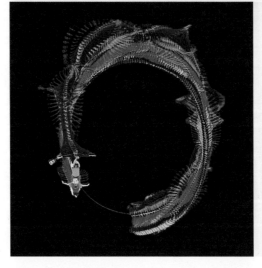

REWORK_

The 'Rework_' app is an interactive tour through the amazing 'Rework_' album that remixes the music of Philip Glass. The app includes eleven interactive visualisations for the remixed songs, along with an interactive 'Glass Machine' that lets people create their own music inspired by Philip Glass's early works using two sliding discs. The 'Rework_' album is a collaboration between Philip Glass and Beck, and includes remixes by Beck, Tyondai Braxton, Amon Tobin, Cornelius, Dan Deacon, Johann Johannsson, Nosaj Thing, Memory Tapes, Silver Alert, Pantha du Prince, My Great Ghost and Peter Broderick.

–
Designer
Graham Plumb
Graphic Designer
Pirate Vereker
Interactive Art Director
Lukas Girling
Programmer
Graham McDermott
Computer Graphics Artist
David Wicks
Colourist
Sean Monroe
Director
Scott Snibbe
Producer
Ahna Girshick
Executive Producer
Hugo Vereker
Media Agency
Snibbe Studio
Clients
Dunvagen Music Publishers
Philip Glass

DESIGN DIGITAL DESIGN

SAN FRANCISCO 37°47'N 122°25'W 15° 5:00

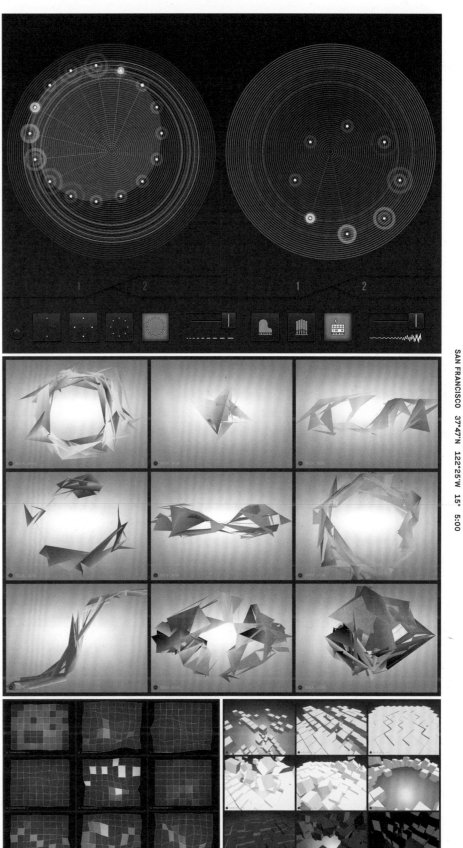

Puppets

'Puppets' is an innovative digital toy that lets you use an iPhone to make an animated puppet walk, wave and jump on your iPad. 'Puppets' isn't a game: there are no levels, tasks to complete, or points to score. Instead, kids can use it to play creatively and express themselves – to tell a story and to put on a show. 'Puppets' reacts to their voice and allows them to record their puppet show so they can share the experience with friends and family. It is part of an experiment by Dare to find better ways for children to interact with screen-based technology.

–
Designers
Ashley Riza
Elly Thompson
Interactive Designer
Simon Baker
Creative Director
Ron Siemerink
Technical Director
Perry Price
Interactive Director
Perry Price
Copywriter
James Maher
Agency Producer
Jade Bisram
Advertising Agency
Dare London
Planner
Roz Thomas
Client
Dare

MTV Under the Thumb

No longer content with living to the schedules of broadcast media, teens of the digital era demand control over their content like never before. MTV 'Under the Thumb' is an app that redefines television for the mobile generation, changing how they see and share their favourite shows wherever they are. The app offers a library of latest MTV episodes and converts into a remote control for viewing on a computer screen.

–
Designer
Hazel Ryalls
Senior Designer
Martina Transtrom
Creative Director
Chris May

Chief Creative Officer
James Hilton
Technical Director
Ben Jones
Creative Developer
Joakim Carlgren
Senior Copywriter
Matt Longstaff
Quality Assurance Managers
Aparna Bajaj
Terry Nweze
Advertising Agency
AKQA Berlin
Senior Project Manager
Lloyd Brazier
Product Strategy Director
Mike Betts
Account Director
Johann Laeschke
Client
Viacom International Media Networks
Brand
MTV

Mobile Medic

To recruit medical students worthy of Defence Force University Sponsorship, we created medically diagnosable posters, which doubled as an entrance exam. 'Mobile Medic' allowed students to use a range of diagnostic techniques to identify and treat medical conditions using their smartphones. Visual and audio augmentation immersed them in the role of Medical Officer, on real Defence Force scenarios. Students entered their details and received their results instantly.

–
Designers
Marcus Byrne
Janna Mamar
Art Director
Jake Barrow
Creative Director
Chris Northam
Chief Creative Officer
Ben Coulson

Developer
Chuck Brandt
User Experience Architect
Luke Tellefson
Copywriter
Matt Lawson
Photographer
Hugh Peachy
Retoucher
Mal Stark
Sound Engineer
Paul Baxter
Digital Producer
Carrie Burman
Audio Producer
Katherine Muir
Digital Agency
VML
Advertising Agency
George Patterson
Y&R Melbourne
Strategist
Tom Ward
Account Handler
Jason Bass
Account Executives
Chris Bush
Daniel Smith
Account Director
Janet Proposch
Group Account Director
Julian Bell
Client
Defence Force
Recruiting

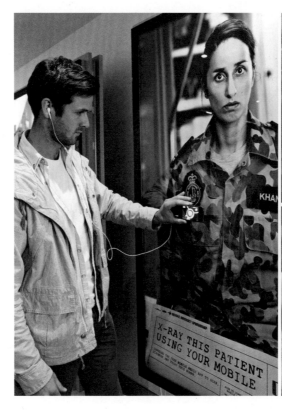

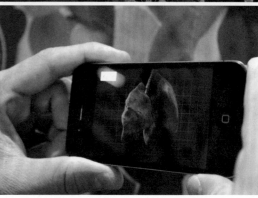

X-RAY THIS PATIENT USING YOUR MOBILE

1440 Project

The '1440 Project' was created to help outdoor enthusiasts share their love of the outside. The core of the site is an interactive minute-by-minute timeline that uses photographs taken by everyday people to represent every single minute spent outdoors. The site is able to read the time stamps embedded in each digital photo and place it precisely on the timeline. Visitors can view a specific point in the day using the clock feature. Our ultimate goal is to fill every single minute of this virtual 24-hour day with photography representing our collective love of the outside.

Interactive Designer
Avery Banguilan
Art Directors
Chris Cavalieri
Alok Nath
Executive Creative Director
Cabot Norton
Copywriter
Scott Biear
Retoucher
Brad Castlen
Digital Producer
Matt Silliman
Advertising Agency
BBDO Atlanta
Production Company
RESN
Project Manager
Lauren Sturla
Strategist
Leslie Turley
Strategic Director
Harley Jebens
Account Director
Peter Bunarek
Client
Recreational
Equipment

WWF Together

To establish a deeper level of engagement between the World Wildlife Fund and its members, we developed an experience in which consumers could personally connect with the organisation's content and brand: the 'WWF Together' iPad app. By sharing the lives and stories of the world's most amazing animals in an original and emotionally engaging way, we enabled the WWF community to get closer to the organisation's mission. The app has had more than 550,000 downloads in over 100 countries resulting in over twelve years' worth of time spent in app; it received a 4.5 star rating and won an Apple Design Award in the App Store.

—
Art Director
Jefferson Liu
Creative Director
Michael Powell
Executive Creative Director
Brendan DiBona
Associate Creative Director
Elizabeth Bieber
Associate Creative Developement Director
Scott Cullum
Motion Graphics Artists
Yi-An Chien
Andy Haynes
Copywriter
Jonathan Lee
Photographer
Morten Koldby
Product Manager
Erin Chandler
Advertising Agency
AKQA Washington DC
Sound Design
Copilot Sound.+ Music
Account Handler
Sarah Cheffy
Client
World Wildlife Fund

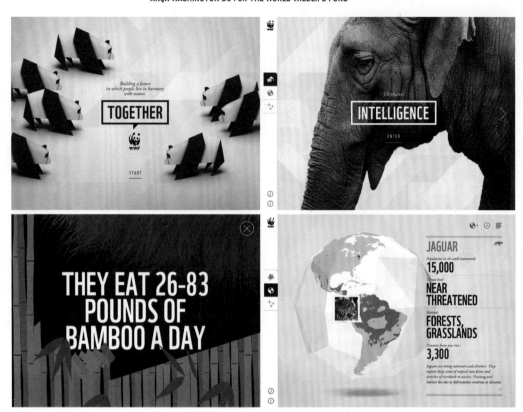

Promillekoll

Our aim was to reduce heavy drinking in Sweden, and so reduce the alcohol-related problems that cost billions of dollars, and cause a lot of suffering every year. We learnt that half of all heavy drinkers actually want to drink less. But changing one's behaviour is hard – almost impossible if you don't have a clear goal. So we gave people who want to drink more moderately a clear goal: keep your blood alcohol content below 0.06% (the point where the positive effects of alcohol reach their peak). The app warns you when you've reached this level by monitoring the number of drinks you log against your personal data.

—
Designer
Joakim Blondell
Interactive Designer
Johan Wingård
Interactive Director
Peter Gaudiano
Art Director
Joakim Blondell
Copywriter
Johan Olivero
Advertising Agency
Forsman & Bodenfors
Production Company
Monterosa
Planner
My Troedsson
Account Manager
Jessica Sjölin
Account Director
Leif Sorte
Marketing Managers
Malin Forman
Åsa Hessel
Anna Larsson
Client
Systembolaget

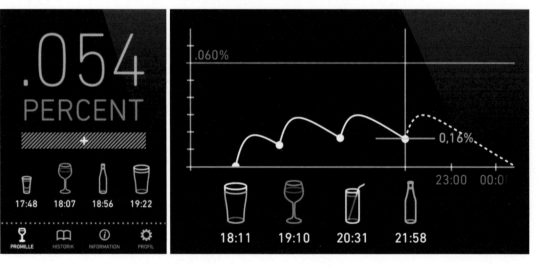

DESIGN   DIGITAL DESIGN

OFFF APPP

In May 2012, Barcelona welcomed 3,000 digital creatives to the ninth OFFF Festival. We were asked to create the official festival guide for smartphones and tablets. The schedule was designed with a new type of interface based on circles and gestures. Each day the festival was accessed from the initial layer of the circle, revealing that day's events represented by the circle's slices. The third layer of information on each event's details was displayed by tapping, holding and dragging the individual event slice.

—
Interactive Designer
Cas Lemmens
Art Director
Matilda Dackevall
Creative Director
Jon Carney
Lead Developer
Cas Lemmens
Copywriter
Thea Frost
Digital Agency
Somewhat_
Planner
Thea Frost
Account Handler
Jon Carney
Brand Manager
Hector Ayuso
Client
OFFF Digital Festival

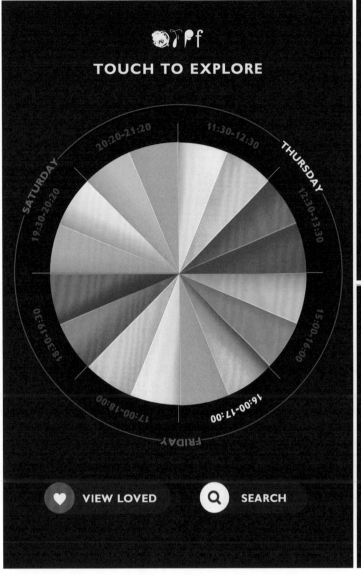

LONDON   51°32'N   0°5'W   9°   12:00

DESIGN GRAPHIC DESIGN

JURY

Jury Foreman
David Hillman
Studio David Hillman
Robert Boon
Inventory Studio
Alex Cowper
EMI Music
Monique Gamache
WAX

Masayoshi Kodaira
FLAME
Amelia Noble
Amelia Noble & Partners
Hector Pottie
Figtree

Kanji City

With exercise programme COG, users can enjoy a 40-minute spinning exercise session in a room where music and an LED light installation are synchronised to the pedalling. There are no instructors in the room, but instead a built-in iPad on each bike gives users effective instructions by showing an animation that is themed to cities around the world. 'Kanji City' is an intermediate programme for COG, designed with original images of Kyoto. Kyoto has tradition, culture and natural beauty. We used Kanji typeface to portray all the virtual landscapes.

–
Designers
Rei Ishii
Chihiro Konno
Art Director
Naoki Ito
Creative Director
Naoki Ito
Director
Kota Iguchi
Typographers
Q Asaba
Chihiro Konno
Animator
Kota Iguchi
Producer
Satoshi Takahashi
Music Producer
Satoshi Murai
Advertising Agency
PARTY
Project Manager
Keita Furusawa
Client
Cafe Company
Brand
COG

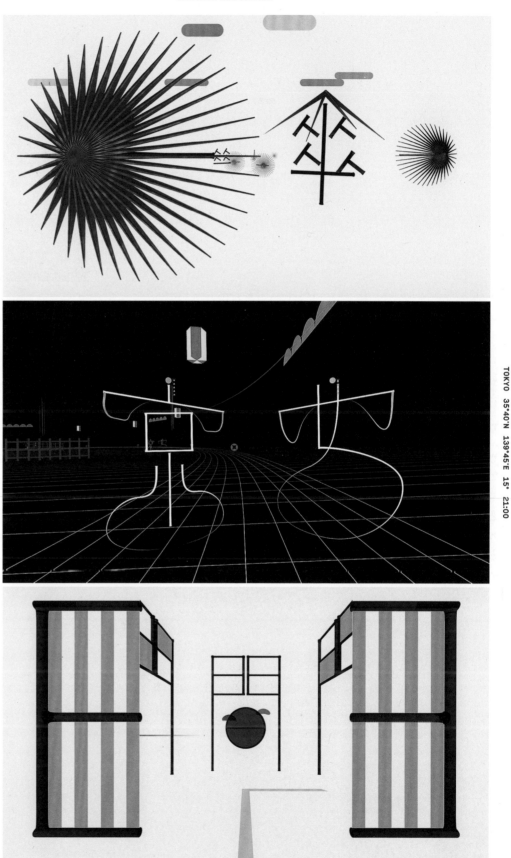

TOKYO 35°40'N 139°45'E 15° 21:00

Zumtobel Group
Annual Report
2011/12

Responding to the theme of light, the annual report for lighting company Zumtobel was separated into two highly contrasting but complementary volumes. The first, a black and white, text-heavy volume containing all the facts and figures for the financial year, typeset exclusively in Courier eight point. The second, a 'silent' publication of pure colour, a graphic reinterpretation of a video work by artist Anish Kapoor into print. The book gutter was used as the source of light, which grows outwards to engulf the book. A total of ten standard and bespoke neon inks blend, overprinting and bleeding.

–
Designers
Billy Kiosoglou
Frank Philippin
Art Directors
Billy Kiosoglou
Frank Philippin
Artist
Anish Kapoor
Print Producer
Richard Foenander
Design Agency
Brighten the
Corners
**Production
Company**
EBS
Marketing Manager
Astrid Kühn
Client
Zumtobel Group
Brands
Ledon
Thorn
Tridonic
Zumtobel

DESIGN   GRAPHIC DESIGN

LONDON   51°32'N   0°5'W   9°   12:00

Edward Hopper, Film and Modern Life

The international 'Edward Hopper, Film and Modern Life' symposium was part of the Hopper exhibition at the Thyssen-Bornemisza Museum. The development of communication elements for the symposium and film cycle (programmes, posters, notebooks, identifiers) is articulated by the play on four shapes and colours borrowed from Hopper's pictorial universe. These correspond to the projections of light in some of his paintings. The shapes and reflections of light on a dark background represent reciprocal influences between Hopper and film, in a game of mirror images.

–
Designers
Paco Lacasta
Sonia Sánchez
Design Agency
Sánchez/Lacasta
Client
Thyssen-Bornemisza
Museum

DESIGN GRAPHIC DESIGN

MADRID 40°26'N 3°42'W 14° 13:00

Recipeace

Also In Book in Posters

In a world of increasing violence, Peace One Day along with the D&AD White Pencil competition asked us to raise awareness for Peace Day, 21 September. This led us to create 'Recipeace', a movement that brings conflicting people together over food. It's over food that we sit down together to settle our differences, bury the hatchet and create understanding. 'Recipeace' raised awareness for Peace Day by generating over 3.5 million media impressions (with no media weight), thousands of tweets worldwide and, with the help of hundreds of restaurants, countless peace dinners throughout Chicago.

—
Designer
Casey Martin
Senior Designers
Kelly Dorsey
Kyle Poff
Peter Ty
Art Director
Kate Harding-Jackson

Design Director
Alisa Wolfson
Creative Directors
Phil Jungmann
Matt Miller
Executive Creative Director
Jeanie Caggiano
Chief Creative Officers
Susan Credle
Mark Tutssel
Photographers
Chris Cassidy
Jason McKean
Copywriter
Adam Ferguson
Producers
Richard Blanco
Mark Phan
Steve Tabor
Executive Producers
Vincent Geraghty
Rob Tripas
Senior Producer
Laurie Gustafson
Production Designer
Chris Apap
Editor
Joe Clear
Advertising Agency
Leo Burnett Chicago
Production Companies
Giannini Creative
Rider-Dickerson
Account Executives
Riley Bernardin
Dane Gunderson
Account Directors
Nina Abnee
Karla Flannery
Josh Raper
Client
Peace One Day

DESIGN GRAPHIC DESIGN

CHICAGO 41°52'N 87°37'W 3° 7:00

Life is Electric

The brief was to globally rebrand an established Japanese electrical appliance manufacturer. Panasonic believes in the power of electricity and its potential to enrich our lives. The advertising uses hand-drawn diagrams of electric circuits to express the fundamental commitment to craftsmanship at the heart of Panasonic's manufacturing philosophy, and to communicate a sense of anticipation and excitement about the company's emerging technologies and products. With Panasonic, 'Life is Electric'.

–
Designers
Daisuke Hatakeyama
Taiji Kimura
Minami Otsuka
Haruko Tsutsui
Yoshihiro Yagi
Art Director
Yoshihiro Yagi
Creative Directors
Hiroyuki Takasu
Yoshihiro Yagi
Creative Producer
Takanori Yasukochi
Illustrator
Philippe Weisbecker
Animator
HORSTON
Copywriter
Haruko Tsutsui
Editor
Tsutomu Motoyama
Producers
Hideyuki Chihara
Jun Katogi
Music Producer
Toru Sasaki
Production Manager
Naotaka Futami
Advertising Agency
Dentsu Tokyo
Artist's Agent
Natsuko Kida
Client
Panasonic

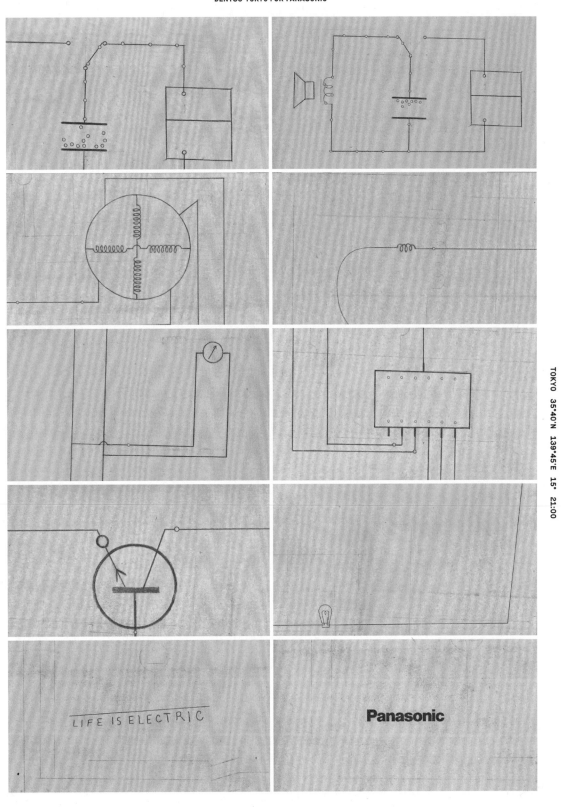

LIFE IS ELECTRIC

Panasonic

Jelly Fish Book

This is a pictorial book that examines the biology of jelly fish, written in imaginary jelly fish language. The blueprint expresses the transparency of jelly fish, and blue metallic squares on some pages represent a sparkle on the surface of the sea. It is an experimental artwork in which the designer wanted to be liberated from existing language and form of text to bring out a beautiful book.

–
Designer
Yasuhide Arai
Art Director
Yasuhide Arai
Print Producer
Kazuhiko Kurohoshi
Design Agency
Nippon Design Center
Client
Recto Verso Gallery

DESIGN GRAPHIC DESIGN

TOKYO 35°40'N 139°45'E 15° 21:00

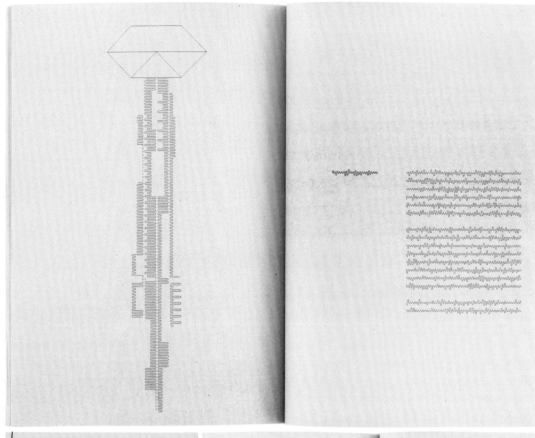

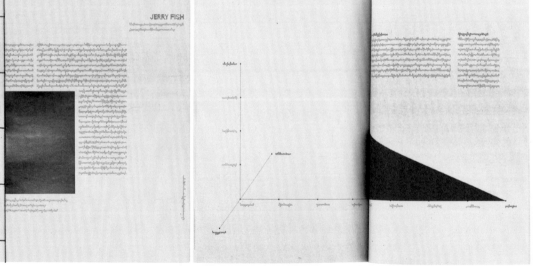

dOCUMENTA (13)
Catalogues

The catalogue for the 'dOCUMENTA (13)' art exhibition consists of three books (plus one extra handbook). Three formats, three tones of green, three different fonts, three chapters. 'The Book of Books' brings together essays and artists' projects, and reproduces the publication series '100 Notes – 100 Thoughts' as facsimiles or in new layouts. 'The Logbook' traces the making of 'dOCUMENTA (13)' through images, correspondence and interviews. 'The Guidebook' provides a map and journey through the artists' works and the project. 'What When', the extra handbook, is a guide to all the exhibition's events.

–
Designer
Francesco Cavalli
Design Agency
Leftloft
Clients
Hatje Cantz
Kunsthalle
Fridericianum
Brand
dOCUMENTA (13)

DESIGN GRAPHIC DESIGN

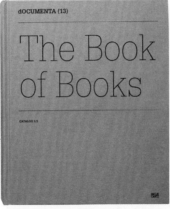
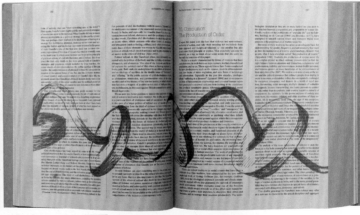

MILAN 45°27'N 9°10'E 13° 13:00

**Great British
Fashion Stamp Set**

Johnson banks was
tasked with creating
ten special stamps
to showcase British
fashion from the
1940s to the present
day. Royal Mail
worked closely with
the V&A Museum
to supply a list of
potential designers
whose work should
be featured. The
set had to include a
mix of classic and
innovative designs.
Sølve Sundsbø
was commissioned
to photograph the
models in dynamic,
period-appropriate
poses. To ensure that
the focus was on the
outfits rather than
the models, johnson
banks came up with a
radical compromise:
the models' faces and
hands were digitally
removed, leaving the
clothes to speak for
themselves.

–
Designers
Michael Johnson
Kath Tudball
Senior Designer
Kath Tudball
Creative Director
Michael Johnson
Design Manager
Dean Price
**Head of Design &
Editorial**
Marcus James
Photographer
Sølve Sundsbø
Design Agency
johnson banks
Client
Royal Mail

DESIGN GRAPHIC DESIGN

LONDON 51°32'N 0°5'W 9° 12:00

**Pleats Please Happy
Anniversary Posters**

We wanted to
celebrate the 20th
anniversary of
traditional fashion
brand Pleats Please
by Issey Miyake,
and to appeal not only
to the loyal fans but
also to a wide range
of customers. The
concept behind these
visuals is 'delicious'.
Pleats Please clothes
evoke an instant
reaction such as:
'Oh, that looks so
delicious!' and 'Oh,
I would love to wear
that!' This inspiration
came while reviewing
the brand's clothes
and guided the
design concept.

–
Designer
Shingo Noma
Art Director
Taku Satoh
Photographer
Yasuaki Yoshinaga
Design Agency
Taku Sotah Design
Office
Client
Issey Miyake
Brand
Pleats Please

DESIGN GRAPHIC DESIGN

TOKYO 35°40'N 139°45'E 15° 21:00

Luggage Labels

There are 9,000 airports around the world and every one has its own three-letter code. Instead of the usual travel clichés, we used these humble but iconic codes that we're all familiar with to promote a wide range of offers and specials for the Expedia brand.

–
Designer
Mark Osborne
Art Director
Mike Watson
Executive Creative Director
Gerry Human
Associate Creative Directors
Mark Harrison
Paul Mason
Chief Creative Officer
Gerry Human
Typographer
Mark Osborne
Copywriter
Jon Morgan
Retoucher
Trevor Qizilbash
Advertising Agency
Ogilvy & Mather London
Project Manager
Grant Mason
Account Executive
Jessica Wilkinson
Business Director
Stephen Hillcoat
Brand Communications Director
Andrew Warner
Client
Expedia

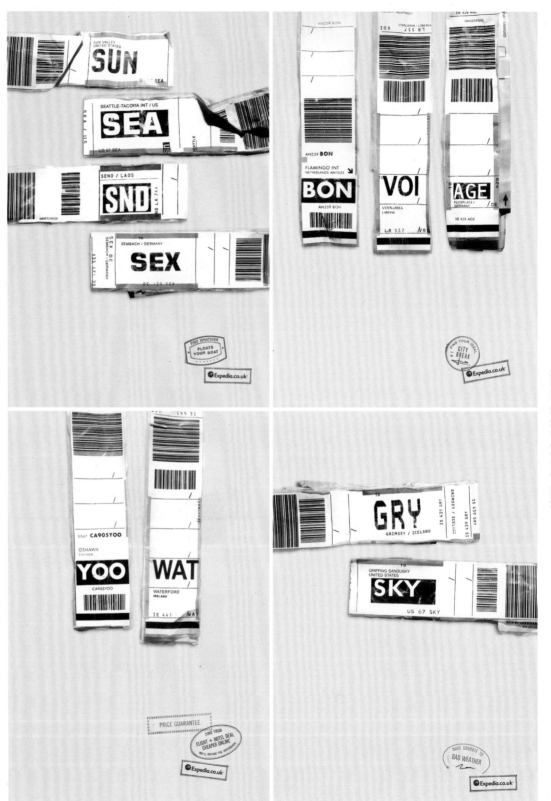

TATAMI

In Japan, the ancient unit of measure 'jō' is still used today for calculating the area of a room. The dimensions of jō are equal to a single Tatami mat. To promote TTN Corporation's Tatami mat outlet Igusa Mono, we wanted to emphasise the beauty of this culturally significant object in the simplest way possible. Using close-up photographs of a black Tatami mat, printed on traditional white Japanese paper (to echo the contrasts in calligraphy), we could accentuate the beauty of its fine, woven handcraft and stitching. The posters present Tatami in its purest form.

–
Designer
Takanari Yoshida
Art Director
Takanari Yoshida
Photographer
Takanori Okuwaki
Copywriter
Ryo Hasumi
Retoucher
Satoshi Ozawa
Producer
Goro Furuzawa
Design Agency
Nippon Design
Center
Client
TTN Corporation
Brand
Igusa-Mono

DESIGN GRAPHIC DESIGN

TOKYO 35°40'N 139°45'E 15° 21:00

**Naruyoshi Kikuchi:
Jazz**

Naruyoshi Kikuchi is one of the most famous jazz musicians in Japan. He needed a poster to decorate Bureau Kikuchi, his new office. We wanted to visualise the dramatic reverberations of Kikuchi's jazz performances. We chose 'ripples of sparkle' as a motif because ripples symbolise sound waves, jazz music suits night time, and the ripples on the black paper look like a loudspeaker. These posters were hung from the ceiling, waving in the wind. They looked different depending on the light around them.

–
Designer
Yusuke Ono
Art Director
Yusuke Ono
Advertising Agency
Hakuhodo
Client
Bureau Kikuchi

DESIGN   GRAPHIC DESIGN

TOKYO 35°40'N 139°45'E 15° 21:00

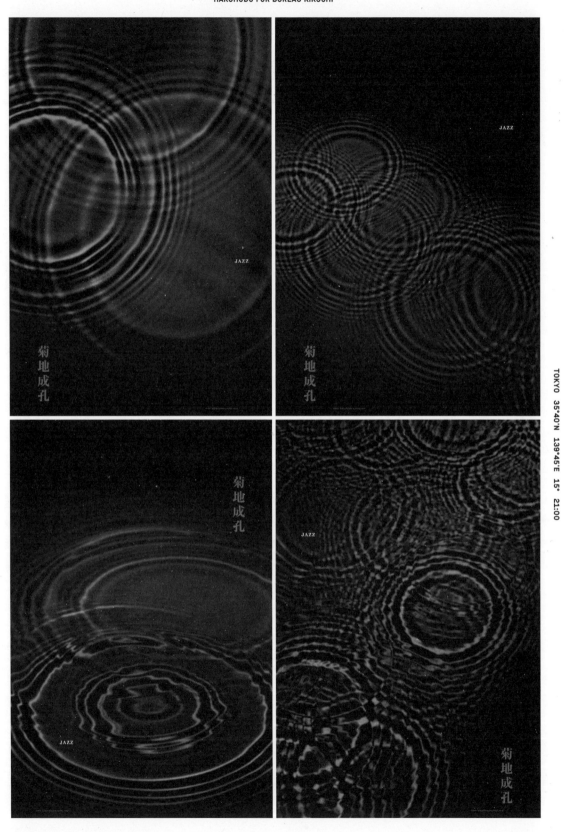

The Street House

Every year Toronto hosts a festival called Doors Open. Hundreds of the city's beautiful and normally private spaces are opened for the public to tour. During the festival we built and opened the doors to 'The Street House', an exhibit that demystified the struggles of homeless people like never before. The goal was to make the public stop and think about the homeless they ignore every day, and put the issue on the map.

—
Designers
Anthony Chelvanathan
Lisa Greenberg
Production Designer
Monika Geresz
Art Director
Anthony Chelvanathan
Creative Directors
Lisa Greenberg
Judy John
Chief Creative Officer
Judy John
Group Creative Directors
Anthony Chelvanathan
Steve Persico
Copywriter
Steve Persico
Print Producer
Kim Burchiel
Producer
Franca Piacente
Advertising Agency
Leo Burnett Toronto
Production Company
OPC FamilyStyle
Account Manager
Jeremy Farncomb
Account Director
Natasha Dagenais
Client
Raising The Roof

A friend's couch.

—

This is a great option. It's comfy. It's warm. It's safe. But can your friend take you in the next night? And the night after that? And the night after that? And the night after that?

—

DESIGN GRAPHIC DESIGN

TORONTO 43°42'N 79°24'W 6° 8:00

IN BOOK IN GRAPHIC DESIGN, INTEGRATED GRAPHICS
STUDIO DUMBAR FOR ALZHEIMER NEDERLAND

Alzheimer Nederland Visual Identity

Alzheimer Nederland works hard to raise awareness and funds for vital research into Alzheimer's disease and other forms of dementia. But times are hard, and competition for donations has never been tougher. With the existing visual style lacking emotion as well as a competitive edge, Studio Dumbar designed a new identity. Having met patients, families and carers to experience the impact of the disease first-hand, we developed an instantly recognisable identity. The new logotype is bold and confident. The 'vanishing points' visualise the effects of dementia, while they can be seen as a source of light and hope.

–
Creative Director
Liza Enebeis
Design Agency
Studio Dumbar
Client
Alzheimer Nederland

ROTTERDAM 51°55'N 4°28'E 10° 13:00

**The Sydney
Pavilion at
The Shanghai
Biennale 2012**

'The Floating Eye' was
the curatorial theme
of the Sydney Pavilion
in the Shanghai
Biennale, the largest
international art
event in mainland
China, attracting
over eight million
visitors. Sydney was
part of the Inter-City
Pavilions, offering
observations of a city's
shifting references
and influences.
The challenge
was to convey the
varied perspectives
of the city's
transforming reality
observed though
its demographics,
environment, history,
geography and society.
We built a visual
language of symbols,
combined and
intertwined by a
shifting graphical
interpretation of the
lens of the viewer.

–
Designers
Samuel Byrnes
Erin Hoffman
Sam McGuinness
Alexis Waller
Design Director
Michael Boston
Creative Director
Jason Little
Artworker
Becca Soons
Design Agency
Re
Client
4A Centre for
Contemporary
Asian Art

DESIGN GRAPHIC DESIGN

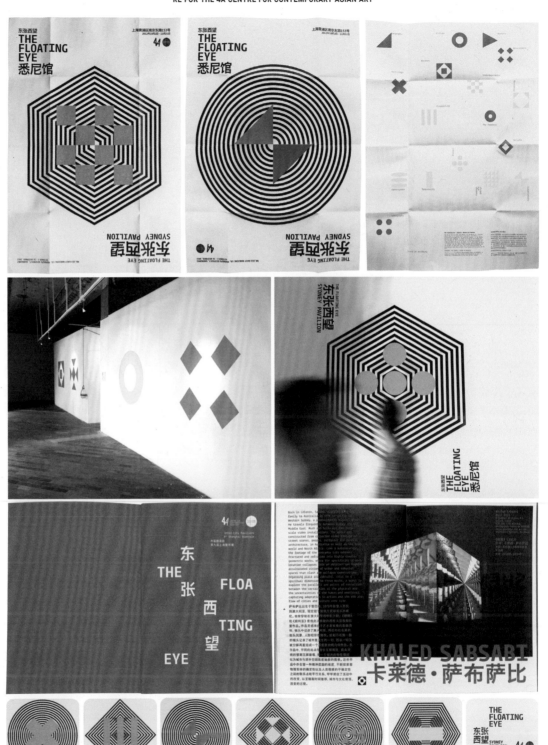

SYDNEY 34°0'S 151°0'E 22° 20:00

Dog Fur

News International's sales and marketing team wanted to reintroduce its five brand values in a memorable way. We found inspiring tales about five people who exemplified each value. For example, Damien Hirst for commercial, and Marie Curie for courageous. And as the main value that sat above the rest was curiosity, we put the stories together in a curious book, using weird phrases from each tale for a headline: 'Pickled Shark' for Hirst, 'X-Ray' for Curie and 'Dog Fur' for George de Mestral. And finally, to make sure people actually read the book, we plastered the headlines all over their offices without explanation to generate curiosity.

—
Designer
George Adams
Creative Director
Stuart Watson
Copywriter
David Milsom
Branding Agency
venturethree
Client
News International

DESIGN   GRAPHIC DESIGN

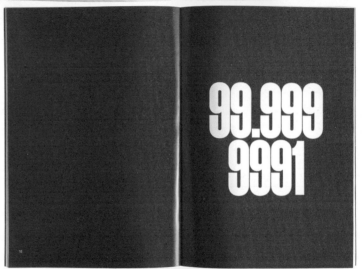

Damien Hirst's art takes its unique flavour from his curiosity in science and natural history, two fields that have inspired his most famous works, including his medicine cabinets and shark suspended in formaldehyde.

But it has been Hirst's commercial skill that turned him from young enfant terrible to Britain's most successful artist. Since his graduate days, he has skilfully managed his career in a notoriously cut throat industry.

In his early years, Hirst developed a hugely profitable relationship with Charles Saatchi, which aside from exposure, gave him the financial backing he needed to make some of his most daring pieces. With increased success, he realised he could unlock his brand equity by getting others to make his work, recruiting young artists to mass produce medicine cabinets and spot paintings.

Hirst's most powerful demonstration of his commercial skill was demonstrated in 2008 when he chose to sell his work through public auction, rather than through a gallery. As creator and salesman, he stage-managed a media frenzy that demonstrated his creativity as a performance artist and brilliance as a businessman. In two days he made over £111 million, a record for a living artist, just a day before the global financial collapse.

DOG FUR

COMMERCIAL

Our products change the way people think, but they only exist because we make the money that makes them happen.

From the biggest retail campaign to the smallest initiative, every penny counts towards our success. And more revenue means we can offer new services, make a bigger impact, and offer better value for our customers.

Where we can't make money, we can save it. We question what we spend and who we spend it to, make sure we're always getting the best return possible. We're as prudent and careful with our company's money as we are with our own.

99.999 9991

PICKLED SHARK

LONDON 51°32'N 0°5'W 9° 12:00

Moscow Design
Museum

The Moscow Design
Museum is very
distinctive. Firstly,
it's the first design
museum in Russia.
Secondly, instead
of a conventional
fixed museum, the
Moscow Design
Museum started out
as a driving pop up
museum – a bus.
The identity is based
on the patterns of
Russian crystal, a
well-known material
in Russian design
history. The glass
is recognisable to
all Russians, which
helps emphasise that
the museum is open
to everyone. The
geometric figures
form the basis for a
dynamic identity that
is easy to apply.

–
Designer
Johan Nijhoff
Art Director
Hans Wolbers
Design Agency
Lava Design
Account Handler
Fleur Greebe
Brand Manager
Alexandra Sankova
Client
Moscow Design
Museum

DESIGN   GRAPHIC DESIGN

AMSTERDAM   52°22'N   4°53'E   9°   13:00

Art is Rubbish

It's official. Art really is rubbish! And that's not just a throwaway line. For our fourth chARiTy event, all of us at WPA Pinfold, along with our creative friends and business partners, scoured the bins and transformed discarded trash and unwanted junk into extraordinary works of art to support Aid to Hospitals Worldwide. The show featured the fruits of those labours: the startling, the seductive and the completely bonkers. It was a perfect opportunity to come along and meet the artists, enjoy the exhibition, and bid for your own work of art.

–
Designer
Patrick Holmes
Art Director
John Atkin
Creative Directors
Richard Hurst
Myles Pinfold
Artists
Trudi Atkin
Joanne Douglas
Pat Glover
Helen Hartley
Simon Henshaw
Elaine Jackson
Kerry Kane
Sue Kirsch
Angela Langlois
Chris McMahon
Nicci McNeil
Andrew Molyneux
Stuart Morey
Darren Pascoe
Brooke Pinfold
Emma Rutherford
Hayley Wall
Artworker
Tom Walshaw
Web Designer
Greg Kirk
Web Producer
Liam Newmarch
Copywriter
Phil Dodd
Branding Agency
WPA Pinfold
Client
Aid to Hospitals
Worldwide
Brand
chARiTy

Boon Jr.

Inspired by their son's
drawings, Boyoung
Lee and Alex Suh
created a whimsical
brand identity for
Boon Jr., a children's
clothing and lifestyle
shop. Child-like
illustrations tell the
story of children who
live in their dreams
and imaginations.
Shoppers create their
own personalised gift
packages by using
rubber stamps and
stickers on the simple
white gift boxes
and shopping bags,
adorned only with
one of several hand-
drawn Boon Jr. logos.
The walls of the
shop are painted as
blackboards covered
with illustrations,
on which children
and adults can also
draw and be part of
the shop.

–
Designer
Ara Ko
Creative Directors
Boyoung Lee
Alex Suh
Illustrator
Jessica Haejeon Lee
Branding Agency
A+B
Architectural Studio
Wonderwall
Contractors
Shinsegae
Clients
Boon The Shop
Shinsegae
Brand
Boon Jr.

DESIGN   GRAPHIC DESIGN

NEW YORK CITY   40°40'N   73°56'W   8°   8:00

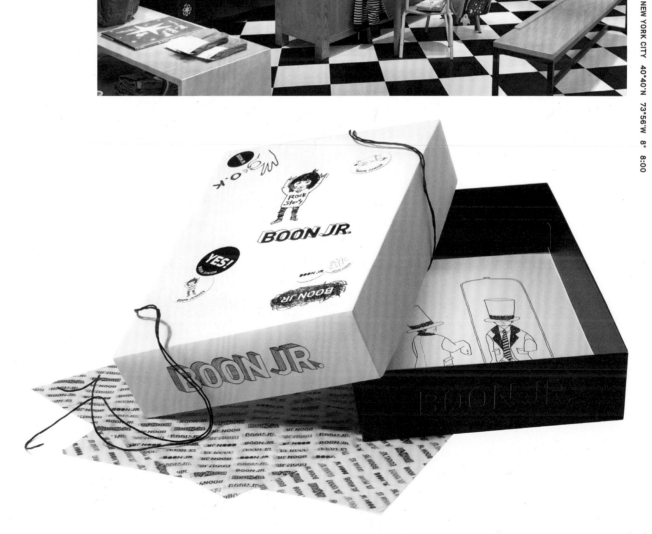

Moorgate Exchange

**Also In Book
in Wayfinding &
Environmental
Graphics**

Moorgate Exchange
is a new development
in the City of London
on the site of the old
Moorgate telephone
exchange. The brand
identity references
old switchboards and
the new building's
distinctive shape.
The identity is
playfully expressed
in large illuminated
signage, an oversized
pegboard display
system, custom
furniture, foil-blocked
half-tone imagery and
a bespoke diagonal
zipper-perforated
brochure envelope.
Our film ident was
shot entirely in
camera and uses fibre
optics to allude to the
site's new guise as a
modern place for the
exchange of ideas
and business.

–
Designers
Richie Clarke
Barry Smith
Stephen Wells
Design Director
Patrick Eley
Digital Designer
Ross Harrington
Creative Director
Ben Dale
Photographer
Robin Gautier
Copywriter
Simon Yewdall
Design Agency
dn&co.
**Production
Company**
Double G Studios
Publishing Company
PUSH Print
Contractors
Standard 8
Account Director
Jenny Whetstone
Managing Director
Joy Nazzari
Client
MGPA
Brand
Moorgate Exchange

DESIGN   GRAPHIC DESIGN

LONDON   51°32'N   0°5'W   9°   12:00

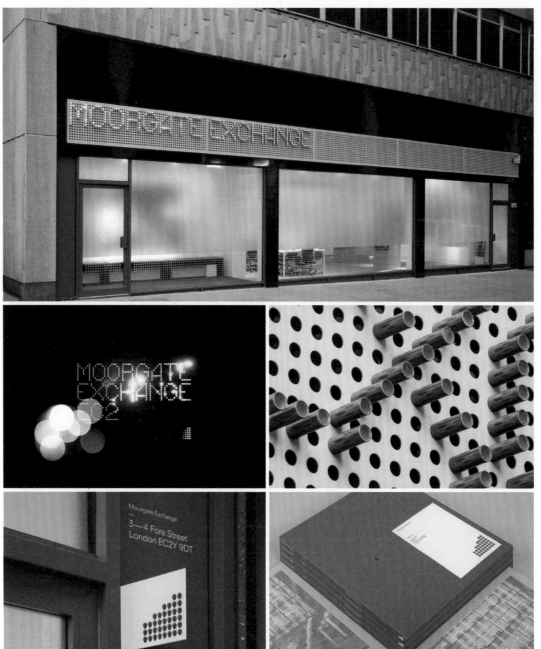

7-Eleven Coffee Concept

By updating the design of the coffee concept, Swedish 7-Eleven wanted to move customer perceptions towards the more modern and urban. The coffee experience is characterised by speed and easy access, and a sense of micropause. Choices of colours, materials and details were made to balance a quick buying process with a comfortable coffee break. Communication and signage were designed to enable easy, as well as inspiring wayfinding and product selection. Cups, bags and packaging were developed where the iconic stripes have been used as starting points for treatments of each identity carrier.

–
Design Agency
BVD
Client
Reitan Convenience Sweden
Brand
7-Eleven

STOCKHOLM 59°17'N 18°3'E 16° 13:00

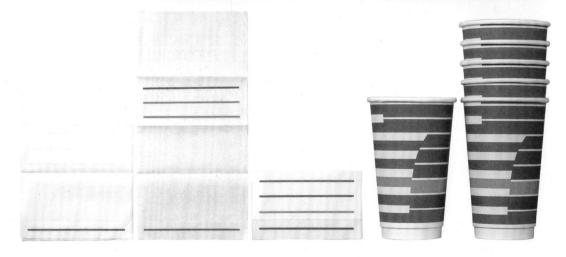

The Democratic
Lecture

'The Democratic
Lecture' is a lecture
initiative led by
designer Craig
Oldham, handing over
the decision of the
lecture content to the
audience. The idea is
very simple: the top
five voted-for topics
(out of a possible 40)
get covered in the
lecture, meaning that
the audience receives
a bespoke lecture
based on its needs,
worries, concerns
and interests. Voting
takes place through
a dedicated website,
and is supported by
bespoke promotional
posters and items,
including a book of
the entire 40 lectures.

—
Designer
Craig Oldham
Artworker
Jon Hatton
Copywriter
John Goddard
Writer
Craig Oldham
**Senior Web
Developer**
David Ashman
Producer
Shelley Wood
Design Agency
Music
Publishing Company
Unified Theory
of Everything
Client
Unified Theory
of Everything

DESIGN   GRAPHIC DESIGN

MANCHESTER 53°30'N 2°15'W 6° 12:00

NEVER MIND THE BALLOTS HERE'S THE DEMOCRATIC LECTURE

THE DEMOCRATIC LECTURE

BUNGS TAKEN. BALLOTS RIGGED. THANK YOU FOR VOTING IN THE DEMOCRATIC LECTURE.

ALL VOTES FROM YOUR GROUP WILL BE COLLATED AND THE TOP 5 VOTED TOPICS WILL FORM YOUR DEMOCRATIC LECTURE.

BOOM!

STYLE IS YEARNING FOR RECOGNITION FROM THE PEER GROUP.

THE DEMOCRATIC LECTURE

POLLING STATION

St James's

St James's is an area of central London. From street level to online, our brief was to present St James's to retailers, offices and a discerning global customer base as the ultimate antidote to the British high street. Our self-imposed graphic structure ties together diverse outcomes with one common thread. Drawing inspiration from St James's heritage, we updated its identity. Old tailoring patterns boldly reinvent street presence; punchy blues pick out illustration and duotone fashion spreads on delicate stocks; traditional newspaper layouts inform the destination website.

–
Designers
Connie Dickson
David McFarline
Barry Smith
John Wynne
Digital Designer
Ross Harrington
Design Director
Patrick Eley
Creative Director
Ben Dale
Illustrator
Emily Robertson
Photographers
Robin Gautier
Lee Mawdsley
Duane Nasis
Jane Wilson
Copywriter
Simon Yewdall
Design Agency
dn&co.
Publishing Company
PUSH Print
Contractors
Standard 8
Project Manager
Jodie McLean
Managing Director
Joy Nazzari
Client
The Crown Estate
Brand
St James's

DESIGN GRAPHIC DESIGN

LONDON 51°32'N 0°5'W 9° 12:00

**Apple Store
Barcelona**

To celebrate the
opening of the Apple
Store in Passeig de
Gràcia, Barcelona, we
paid homage to the
Gaudí mosaics the
city is known for.

–
Design Agency
Apple
Client
Apple

**Apple Store
Amsterdam**

To mark the opening
of the first Apple store
in The Netherlands,
we drew on symbols
of both Holland and
Amsterdam.

–
Design Agency
Apple
Client
Apple

CUPERTINO 37°19'N 122°2'W 15° 5:00

DESIGN GRAPHIC DESIGN

Audience
Pixel Content

Following an intensive period of creative and technical research and development for the 70,500 LED paddles attached to each seat in the Olympic Stadium, Crystal CG created over 14 hours of moving image content for the London 2012 Olympic and Paralympic Opening and Closing Ceremonies. The production and implementation required close collaboration with 59 Productions, Treatment Studio, and the LOCOG Ceremonies AV team. The resulting immersive experience extended the visual canvas from the field of play up into the stadium audience, making it part of the show and enhancing the broadcast spectacle.

–
Art Directors
Dan Capstick
Kate Dawkins
Creative Directors
Will Case
Justine Catterall
Senior Producers
Liberty Dakin
Jayne Hobart
Tom Lowndes
Nina Ludgate
Technical Delivery
Manager
Andrew McKinna
Design Agencies
59 Productions
Treatment Studio
Digital Agency
Crystal CG
Project Director
Ed Cookson
Client
London Organising
Committee of the
Olympic and
Paralympic Games
(LOCOG)
Brand
London 2012

DESIGN GRAPHIC DESIGN

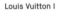

Louis Vuitton I

Louis Vuitton's beginnings in 19th Century Paris are vibrantly animated in this short video, commissioned by NOWNESS for the Louis Vuitton Marc Jacobs exhibition at the Musée des Arts Décoratifs, the Louvre, in Paris. The film celebrates the founder of the world's most recognisable luxury label. The video was presented on a 20 ft-wide wall during the exhibition.

–
Designer
Christian Borstlap
Executive Creative
Director
Christian Borstlap
Creative Agency
Part of a Bigger Plan
Production Company
Glassworks
Clients
Louis Vuitton Paris
Musée des Arts
Décoratifs
NOWNESS

Clouds Over Cuba

'Clouds over Cuba' is an interactive multimedia documentary commemorating the 50th anniversary of the Cuban Missile Crisis. Features include 15 expert interviews, a dossier of 200 related documents and images linked to the film's timeline as well as calendar integration so you can attend JFK's secret meetings 'live', 50 years on. A 'What If?' short film depicts an alternate 2012 in which the crisis had escalated into nuclear war.

–
Designer
Matt Gase
Art Director
Brian Williams
Creative Director
Joe Alexander
Technical Director
Bartek Drozdz

Directors
Erich Joiner
Ben Tricklebank
Copywriter
Wade Alger
Executive Producers
Dustin Callif
Oliver Fuselier
Steve Humble
Brian Latt
Agency Producers
Nicole Hollis-Vitale
Kristen Little
Interactive Producer
Kristen Koeller
Head of Interactive Production
Joy Kuraitis
Advertising Agency
The Martin Agency
Production Company
Tool
Editing
STITCH
Music Production
Plan8
Client
The JFK Presidential Library & Museum

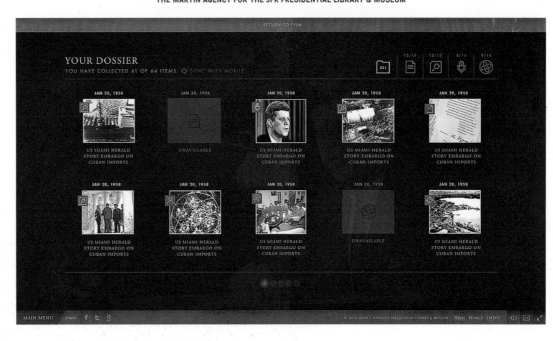

The Smallest IKEA Store in the World

To demonstrate IKEA's commitment to saving space, we built an entire IKEA store in a 10.5 x 8.8 cm web banner. We targeted people looking for small apartments by placing our tiny stores in the property section of community websites. The banner allows you to browse by department, click on any item and buy it straight from the IKEA website. With over 2,000 products available on the banner, it's definitely the smallest and smartest IKEA store in the world.

–
Designer
Gary Rolf
Art Director
Gary Rolf
Creative Directors
Ben Knight
Robin Smith

Technical Directors
Hamza Afaq
Niv Baniahmad
Jens Steffen
Developers
Fouad Abdel-Latif
Ali Mokdad
Nadia Rahman
Lina Safstrom
Copywriters
James Bisset
Sascha Kuntze
Gary Rolf
Advertising Agencies
Memac Ogilvy & Mather
OgilvyOne Worldwide Frankfurt
Account Executive
Farnoush Pourebrahim
Business Director
Claus Adams
Marketing Manager
Katja Sottmeier
Client
IKEA

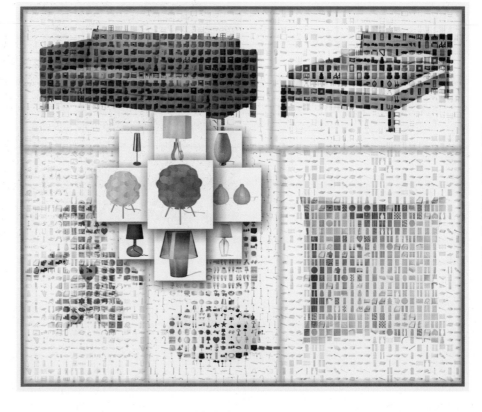

Golden Chains

ALB is an emerging French musician who's planning to release his second album in 2013. Like many other artists, ALB isn't supported by a major label yet. So, to promote and finance his upcoming album, ALB came up with 'Golden Chains', a participative music video in which the artist took up the challenge of selling his personal everyday items – for real. The plan was to use the revenue gained to fund the production of his next album.

–
Designers
Julien Boissinot
Kevin Salembier
Art Director
Julien Boissinot
Creative Directors
Matthieu Elkaim
Olivier Lefebvre
Benjamin Marchal

Interactive
Technical Director
Anthony Hamelle
Director
Johnatan Broda
Copywriter
Kevin Salembier
Producer
Willy Morence
Agency Producer
Jean-Gabriel Saint-Paul
Advertising Agency
CLM BBDO
Digital Agency
ACNE Production
Sound Design
Green United Music
Music Supervision
Green United Music
Production Company
Carnibird
Public Relations Manager
Lauren Weber
Client
ALB

PARIS 48°48'N 2°20'E 10° 13:00

DESIGN   GRAPHIC DESIGN

Promillekoll

The aim was to reduce heavy drinking in Sweden, and so reduce the alcohol-related problems that cost billions of dollars, and cause a lot of suffering every year. We learnt that half of all heavy drinkers actually want to drink less. But changing one's behaviour is hard – almost impossible if you don't have a clear goal. So we gave people who want to drink more moderately a clear goal: keep your blood alcohol content below 0.06% (the point where the positive effects of alcohol reach their peak). The app warns you when you've reached this level by monitoring the number of drinks you log against your personal data.

–
Designer
Joakim Blondell
Interactive Designer
Johan Wingård
Art Director
Joakim Blondell
Interactive Director
Peter Gaudiano
Copywriter
Johan Olivero
Advertising Agency
Forsman & Bodenfors
Production Company
Monterosa
Planner
My Troedsson
Account Manager
Jessica Sjölin
Account Director
Leif Sorte
Marketing Managers
Malin Forman
Åsa Hessel
Anna Larsson
Client
Systembolaget

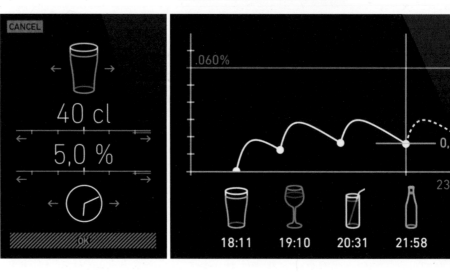

GOTHENBURG 57°42'N 11°58'E 9° 13:00

2011 Visual Report of the Federation of Local Councils in the Pamplona District

This report is the fourth instalment of a collection conceptualised and coordinated by Errea Comunicación. Having previously resorted to basic computer graphics or photographs, this year the report used hand-made drawings to represent its main indicators for the year. Twenty-five views of Pamplona, Barañáin, and other municipalities, together with landscapes from the district, make up a black and white collection, which also features freehand graphs, figures, plants and animals from the Riverside Park, details (bins, refuse collection lorries, buses) and plans based on photographs.

–
Designer
Nerea Armendariz
Creative Director
Javier Errea
Illustrators
Jojo Cruz
Lupe Cruz
Design Agency
Errea Comunicación
Client
Federation of Local Councils in the Pamplona District

DESIGN GRAPHIC DESIGN

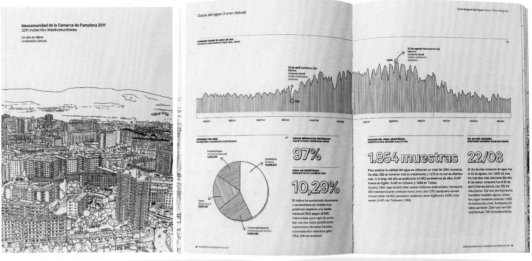

ANSOAIN 42°50'N 1°38'W 15° 13:00

One Page. One Ink. One Goal: Conservation

The Calgary Zoo's 2011 annual report lives and breathes the zoo's conservation values. Printed in one ink on one side of a 100% post-consumer newsprint sheet, the annual saved reams of paper and ink. Plus, the print run was done in just over six minutes. When the Calgary Zoo asked us to design its annual report on a limited budget and time, we used those constraints to our advantage. In just over a week four designers and a writer conceptualised, wrote and designed the 5,000-word annual. The design team divided the space into four, each focusing on a quarter section.

—
Designers
Brian Allen
Todd Blevins
Jonathan Herman
Shauna Luedtke
Production Designer
Andre Pierazzo
Creative Director
Todd Blevins
Associate Creative Director
Jonathan Herman
Copywriter
Jordon Lawson
Product Manager
Cathy Hockenhull
Advertising Agency
Trigger
Account Director
Jill Dewes
Client
Calgary Zoo

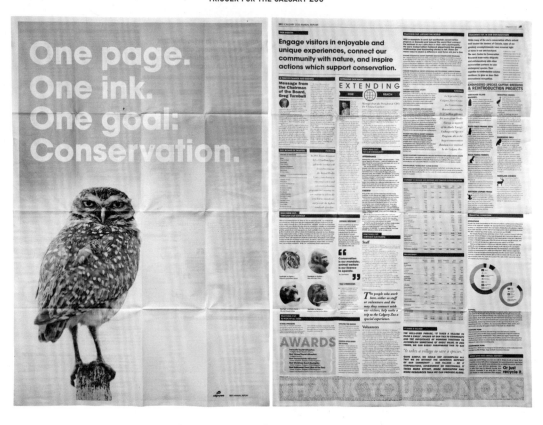

OzHarvest Annual Report 2012

Frost* Design Sydney created a visually impactful annual report for the non-denominational food rescue charity OzHarvest. In the report data is presented as info-graphics with bold pull out quotes and, in an echo of the new identity (created by Frost* and Droga5), text is shown as typographic motifs. In an effort to keep the project as economical as possible, Frost* endeavoured to minimise print costs substantially by designing the document using only black and expressing the brand colours through the use of a bright yellow paper stock. The result is a fluid combination of both functionality and fun.

—
Designers
Vince Frost
Adit Wardhana
Design Director
Carlo Giannasca
Creative Director
Vince Frost
Design Agency
Frost* Design Sydney
Account Handler
Angela Moscoso
Client
OzHarvest

In Good Hands

Adris Group is a successful company in the hands of its hundreds of employees. Good things grow in good hands. Adris Group's annual report entitled 'In Good Hands' reveals floral details when heated with the palms of the hands, metaphorically illustrating how hands can achieve anything. The cover's specially calibrated thermo colour was also used for the inside illustrations. The annual report is filled with short stories in which workers/stockholders share their personal views of the past, future and influence of Adris Group on their lives.

Designer
Nebojsa Cvetkovic
Art Directors
Neven Crijenak
Nebojsa Cvetkovic
Creative Directors
Davor Bruketa
Nikola Zinic
Illustrator
Vedran Klemens
Copywriter
Ivan Cadez
Production Editor
Radovan Radicevic
Production Manager
Vesna Durasin
Advertising Agency
Bruketa&Zinic
Account Executive
Ivana Drvar
Account Director
Zrinka Jugec
Communications Director
Predrag Grubic
Client
Adris Group

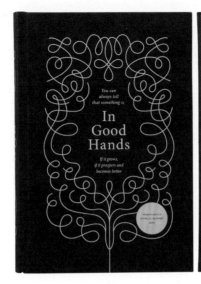
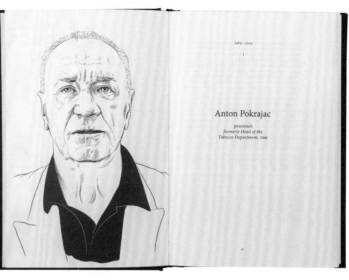

In Pursuit of the Question Mark

We designed this catalogue for George Wyllie MBE's first and last major retrospective 'In Pursuit of the Question Mark'. The overall feel of the catalogue and other related material was closely aligned with his beliefs and processes as an artist, thinker and sculptor, and influenced by his robust use of materials and unfinished approach to his work. The catalogues are limited editions; they include a bespoke hand stamp and are signed by a numbering system.

Designer
Pete Rossi
Photographer
Mark Osborne
Copywriters
Laura Hamilton
Jan Patience
Louise Wyllie
Design Agency
RM&CO
Printers
Kestrel Press
Planner
Lynne Mackenzie
Clients
George Wyllie MBE
Friends of George Wyllie

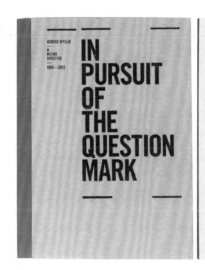
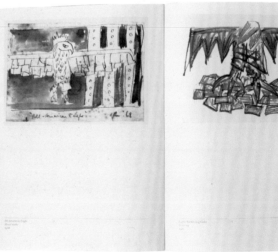

D&AD A–Z: From College to Industry

As part of the 2012 New Blood Festival, D&AD asked us to host an inspirational workshop for graduates. Rather than just showing off our recent work, we wondered how we could create something that might actually help the graduates. We decided to base the workshop around a D&AD Junior Yellow Pages, filled with all the practical advice and tips we think graduate designers will need to call on as they journey from the classroom to the design studio. We structured the content alphabetically using categories from the real Yellow Pages telephone directory, along with sound bites from leading industry professionals.

—
Designer
Jonathan Brodie
Creative Directors
Tommy Taylor
Robert Young
Design Agency
Alphabetical
Client
D&AD

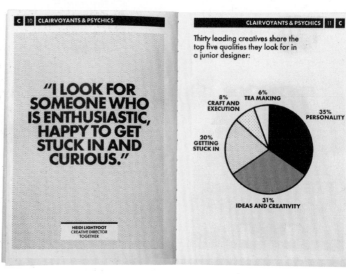

LONDON 51°32'N 0°5'W 9° 12:00

The Ultimate Pencil

In an era of digital advancement where there is an ever-decreasing use of pencils for communication, our brief was to create corporate brand advertising featuring the Mars Lumograph, a product that goes back to STAEDTLER's very origins. We produced two very detailed drawings using only the STAEDTLER pencil to create a level of appeal that exceeds any photography. Drawing a profusion of flowers in bloom conveyed the ability to portray fleeting beauty, while drawing each and every wrinkle on the face of a very old man communicated the ability to portray life.

—
Designers
Kozue Kojima
Hideto Yagi
Art Directors
Kozue Kojima
Hideto Yagi
Creative Directors
Shinya Nakajima
Hideto Yagi
Illustrator
Hideto Yagi
Photographer
Takaya Sakano
Copywriter
Dai Hirose
Retoucher
Yosuke Mochizuki
Producer
Koumei Baba
Advertising Agency
Dentsu Tokyo
Client
STAEDTLER Nippon K.K.
Brand
Mars Lumograph

TOKYO 35°40'N 139°45'E 15° 21:00

Rick Owens
Lookbooks

These are the
lookbooks we designed
for Paris-based fashion
designer Rick Owens.
For the 'DRKSHDW'
and 'RICKOWENS-
LILIES' range,
several types of paper
were used, including
uncoated, coated and
super gloss surfaces,
some trimmed to a
narrower width to
reveal images behind
them. We also used a
black foil logotype.
For 'NASKA', several
types of paper were
also used, including a
wax-coated kraft,
trimmed to varying
heights and widths.
Other finishes include
silkscreen overprinting
with a heavy hit of
white ink; and white
blotter board covers
with blind debossed
logotype.

—
Designers
Kjell Ekhorn
Jon Forss
Art Directors
Kjell Ekhorn
Jon Forss
Design Agency
Non-Format
Brand Manager
Anne Van Den
Bossche
Client
OwensCorp
Brand
Rick Owens

DESIGN   GRAPHIC DESIGN

SAINT PAUL   44°94'N   93°9'W   5°   07:00

Generation 21

This exhibition catalogue displays the work of six influential artist families from a traditional Austrian artists' village, and seeks to break with common reading habits. Six folders have been created with a single sheet per family member that depicts one central piece of work, complemented by biographical details. Each sheet becomes an art print and can be hung up individually. Reserved yet sophisticated, reduced with regard to colour and composition, printed on high-quality paper and varnished, the six folders are held together without binding by a firm carton sleeve.

–
Graphic Designer
Christian Ram
Art Director
Albert Handler
Curator
Petra Schmögner
Branding Agency
brand unit
Clients
Landesgalerie
Burgenland
Brand
Generation 21

VIENNA 48°14'N 16°20'E 10° 23:00

Louis Vuitton
Yayoi Kusama Book

We created this book to celebrate the 2012 collaboration between Louis Vuitton and Japanese artist Yayoi Kusama. The book is inspired by Kusama's symbolic polka dots that represent the self-obliteration of one's ego. Aside from silkscreen and die-cut production methods, the three-fold cover uses three different materials, including a paper that resembles the Louis Vuitton paper bag, and also a canvas material. The latter depicts the art canvas that Kusama uses for her drawings.

–
Designers
Geraldine Chua
Ernest Ho
MAA
Farah Siman
Design Director
Theseus Chan
Photographers
Bruno Asselot
Jean Marc Cedile
Kishin Shinoyama
Design Agency
WORK
Publishing Company
Louis Vuitton Japan
Producers
ASHU NAKANISHIYA
Printers
AlsOdoMinie
Client
Louis Vuitton Japan

SINGAPORE 1°17'N 103°50'E 26° 20:00

The Space Composer

This publication was created for Japan's most famous spatial artist, Junji Tanigawa, to commemorate the tenth anniversary of his company JTQ. To represent the interplay of space, gauze materials and square cut-outs are overlaid on the cover, chosen for their ability to discolour over time, creating an organic feel. The pop ups, clippings and inserts included in this book are design elements inspired by Junji Tanigawa's handmade creations from his childhood diary.

–
Designers
Geraldine Chua
Ernest Ho
MAA
Farah Siman
Design Director
Theseus Chan
Editors
Shogo Hagiwara
Mutsuko Ota
Design Agency
WORK
Publishing Company
JTQ
Producers
ASHU NAKANISHIYA
Printers
AIsOdoMinie
Client
JTQ

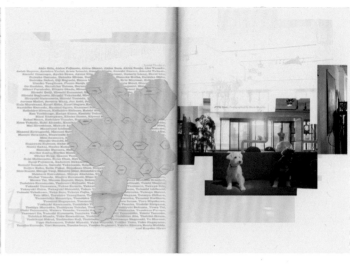

SINGAPORE 1°17'N 103°50'E 26° 20:00

DESIGN GRAPHIC DESIGN

Ink on Paper Brochure

Ink on Paper is a small printing business, competing for work from big companies. It believes what sets it apart isn't just how well it prints on paper or applies production techniques; it's the individual strengths of its people (there are five of them), their honest approach and their willingness to do everything in their power to deliver outstanding work. The brochure uses conversations to illustrate this approach, giving the reader a greater sense of who Ink on Paper are, and what it would be like to work together.

–
Designers
Judith Reid
Michael O'Shea
Design Director
Michael O'Shea
Creative Director
Malcolm Stewart
Production Manager
Nikki West
Branding Agency
Tayburn
Client
Ink on Paper

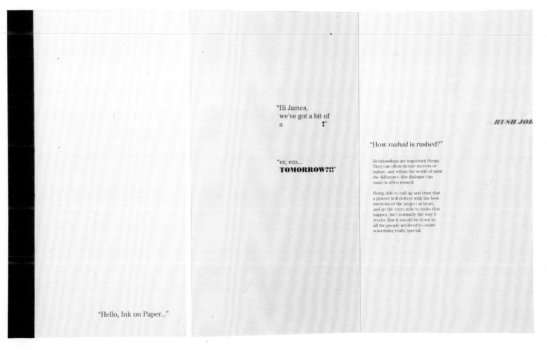

EDINBURGH 55°55'N 3°10'W 5° 12:00

Fedrigoni
Product Guide

Designed and edited
by Design LSC,
this extensive 464
page illustrated
catalogue uses mixed
stocks and various
print techniques to
present the entire
range of papers,
boards, envelopes
and speciality print
products from
Fedrigoni. With each
product displayed
across a double page
spread, specifiers,
printers and designers
are able to access
sheet colour, texture,
size, weight and
price at a glance.
Specifiers can now
find everything that
Fedrigoni offers
in one easy to use
desktop manual.

—
Graphic Designer
Luigi Carnovale
Illustrator
Luigi Carnovale
Editor
Luigi Carnovale
Design Agency
Design LSC
Client
Fedrigoni

DESIGN GRAPHIC DESIGN

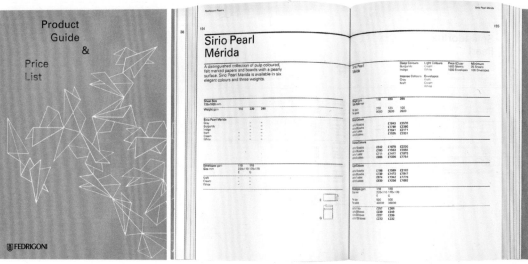

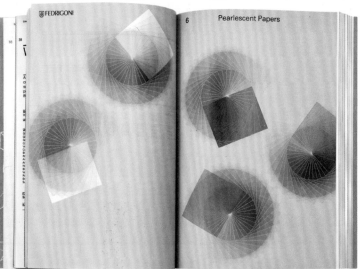

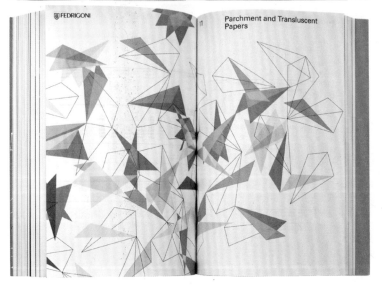

CHORLEY 53°65'N 2°63'W 7° 12:00

dOCUMENTA (13)
100 Notes –
100 Thoughts

'dOCUMENTA (13) 100 Notes – 100 Thoughts' is a series of 100 notebooks published by Hatje Cantz, comprising facsimiles of existing notebooks, commissioned essays, collaborations and conversations of the contributors. The notebooks, representing the cultural background and duration of the documenta exhibition, appear in three different formats (A6, A5, B5) and range from 16 to 48 pages in length. The same cover layout is used for each of them, and the front pieces when arranged together produce a range of images from Kassel and previous exhibitions. Printed and ebook editions are available.

–
Designer
Francesco Cavalli
Design Agency
Leftloft
Clients
Hatje Cantz
Kunsthalle
Fridericianum
Brand
dOCUMENTA (13)

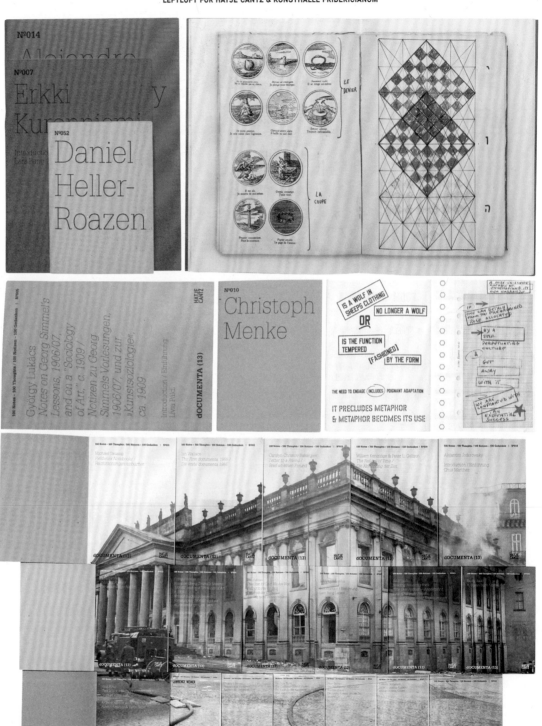

Sirio, The Art of Color

'Sirio, The Art of Color', designed for Italian paper manufacturer Fedrigoni, was conceived as both a visual experience and complete working/specifying tool. Based on French chemist Chevreul's theory of simultaneous colour contrast, its pages are shot through with a bull's eye of concentric circles, showcasing the vivid hues in the Sirio range. 'Sirio, The Art of Color' highlights the endless paper combinations and suggests a new way to use the breadth and depth of the range. Emphasis is placed on the tactility and colour appeal of the physical page.

—
Designers
Bryan Edmondson
Danny McNeil
Creative Director
Bryan Edmondson
Design Agency
SEA
Head of Marketing
Pari Taylor
Client
Fedrigoni

DESIGN GRAPHIC DESIGN

Monotype Collections

No other company does as much with type as Monotype. Monotype designers have created many of the most celebrated and influential typefaces of our time and have developed the technologies that bring type to the screen for millions of consumer products and user interfaces worldwide. The Monotype Libraries are one of the largest and most trusted inventories of type in the world. 'Monotype Collections' brings together personal selections from the vast archive edited by some of Monotype's talented acquaintances.

—
Designers
Alex Broadhurst
Bryan Edmondson
Creative Director
Bryan Edmondson
Design Agency
SEA
Head of Marketing
James Fooks Bale
Client
Monotype

The House of St Barnabas Membership Brochure

The brochure needed to be both inspirational and functional, so was designed to feel like a scrapbook of insights from past attendees of the training academy, with a vision for the charity and a simple application form. As there was little budget, imagery was created from handwritten quotes, illustrations and existing pictures, reinterpreted in a monotone palette to unify the look. The concept came from the desire to stand apart from the rest of the homeless sector, as this is the first of its kind – a not-for-profit members' club, working as a training ground for sustained employment.

–
Designer
Kyle Tolley
Senior Design Director
Alexia Cox
Illustrator
Martina Paukova
Creative Intern
Louise Jones
Branding Agency
The Gild
Printers
Moore Print
Strategist
Stefanie Gilmore
Client
The House of St Barnabas

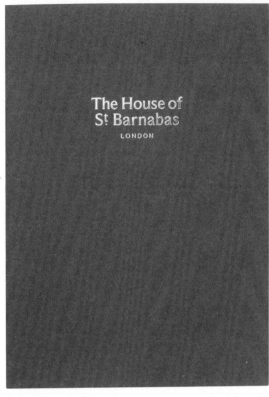

Simon Beattie: Short List 5

'Short List 5' is the fifth catalogue from antiquarian bookseller Simon Beattie. The design was required to be both a celebration of books and an immersive sales catalogue. Beattie has attracted lots of interest from Ivy League schools, which exhibit and research his books. The design played to this by creating an exhibition space for the books with an academic sensibility. The catalogue became an exhibition in its own right; books are celebrated for their tactility and cross-referenced with their descriptions. The acid etched 'exhibition captions' were later repurposed for use at book fairs.

–
Designers
Paul Felton
Robin Howie
Design Agency
Fieldwork Facility
Client
Simon Beattie

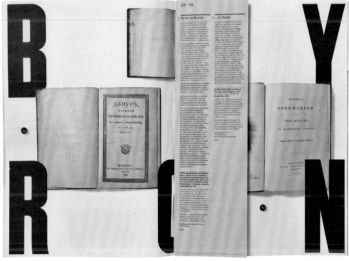

Edible Book

Land Rover owners are adventurers. They believe they are unstoppable, and are not afraid of going deep into the desert. There's a high chance that they might get lost in the middle of nowhere, not knowing what to do or how to get help. This book teaches them the basics of staying alive in the desert, reinforcing what Land Rover stands for in a fun and engaging way. The edible survival guide was made out of edible ink and paper. And it had nutritional value close to that of a cheeseburger, so that in an emergency, they could always eat the book.

–
Designers
Joseph Bihag
Shahir Zag
Art Directors
Joseph Bihag
Khaled Said
Creative Directors
Joseph Bihag
Shahir Zag
Chief Creative Officer
Shahir Zag
Illustrator
Joseph Bihag
Copywriters
Guillaume Calmelet
Shahir Zag
Retoucher
Gitten Tom
Agency Producer
Amin Soltani
Advertising Agency
Y&R Dubai
Account Handler
Pierre Farra
Client
Land Rover

DESIGN   GRAPHIC DESIGN

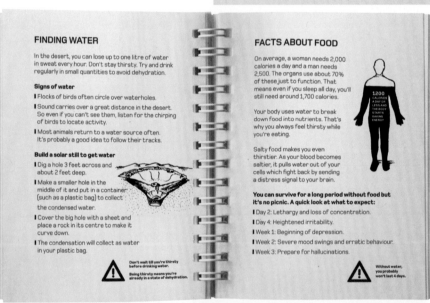

DUBAI 25°15'N 55°18'E 30° 16:00

Privacy International Prospectus

This prospectus outlines the current work and future targets of Privacy International. The perforated cover keeps the content private until physically opened by the reader. It also serves as a mailing envelope.

—
Designers
Paul Belford
Martin Brown
Joseph Carter
Executive Creative Director
Paul Belford
Design Agency
This Is Real Art
Client
Privacy International

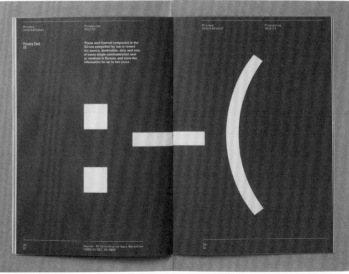

2013 Lucky for Some Calendar

Over the years we have set ourselves the challenge of designing a number of calendars and promotional items to send to our clients and friends. The calendar was inspired by the idea of luck during the year 2013, with 365 raffle style date tickets to tear off, one for each day. We produced a limited run of 365, fully perforated, B2 posters. These were made available initially to our subscribers list, and later via our website.

—
Designers
Keith Hancox
Ed Robin
Creative Director
Bob Mytton
Design Agency
Mytton Williams
Printers
Opal Print
Client
Mytton Williams

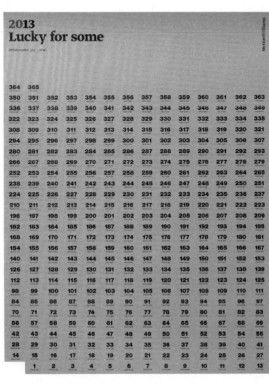

androp: World. Words.Lights./You

'World.Words. Lights.' expresses the power of hope and light that each word can give out in the world. 'You' expresses the light that is in the darkness within. These two themes have opposite meanings to express inner and outer sides of one's self. Since light is the theme of the album, a clear disc and film have been used. Moiré effect is incorporated to let the title on the disc disappear once the case is opened. Lyrics are laid out in a circle on the clear film. 'World.Words. Lights.' is on the outer side and 'You' is on the inner side. A special ink makes it glow in the dark.

–
Designers
Norio Tanaka
Wataru Yoshida
Art Director
Norio Tanaka
Design Agency
arctik
Client
Warner Music
Japan

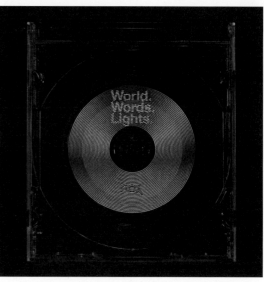

DESIGN GRAPHIC DESIGN

androp: Boohoo/ AM0:40/Waltz

We designed the sleeve for this triple A-side single using the main theme of 'RGB'. The trinity of three songs is shown with three colours on the front side of the three-sided inner-booklet. 'Boohoo' is the passionate light of red; 'AM0:40', the youthful blue light that is eager to see the future; and 'Waltz', the calm green that floats in the sea of lights. Each side of the booklet has its own colour, and when they are folded together, they form a triangle.

–
Designers
Norio Tanaka
Wataru Yoshida
Art Director
Norio Tanaka
Design Agency
arctik
Client
Warner Music
Japan

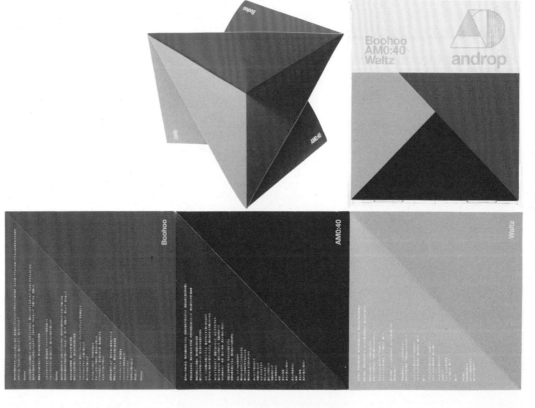

Teleologies

'Teleologies' is a reference to old Greek philosophy and Aristotle: 'A teleology is any philosophical account that holds that final causes exist in nature, meaning that design and purpose analogous to that found in human actions are inherent also in the rest of nature'. By having real leaves cast into the vinyl we wanted to take a physical proof of time and preserve it for the future. Is this the first time anyone has cast organic matter (a readymade from nature) into a vinyl record? We wonder.

—
Designers
Espen Friberg
Aslak Gurholt
Art Directors
Espen Friberg
Aslak Gurholt
Design Agency
Yokoland
Production Company
Optimal Media
Clients
Metronomicon Audio
Now We've Got Members

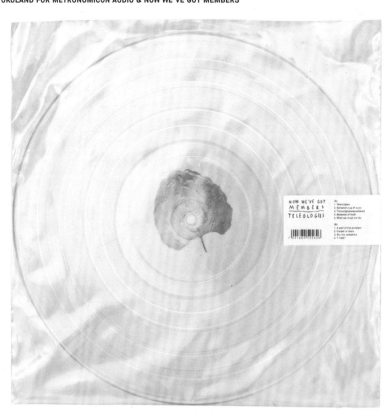

OSLO 59°57'N 10°42'E 5° 13:00

House of Illustrious

'House of Illustrious' contains the entire recorded works of the Illustrious Company over the ten years of its existence in a limited, numbered edition. Ten CDs are bookended by clear acrylic discs, connected by a steel spindle etched with 'Made in Sheffield'. The CD stack is presented in a laser-etched, high-density foam housing. A separate information and authentication sheet, signed by Illustrious Company's founders Martyn Ware and Vincent Clarke, carries details of the origins of the works. The sheet's minimal typographic design ensures the focus remains on the physicality of the CDs and their housing.

—
Designers
Malcolm Garrett
Martyn Ware
Design Agency
IMAGES&Co
Creative Agency
ARTOMATIC
Record Company
Mute
Project Manager
Paul A Taylor
Clients
Illustrious Company
Mute

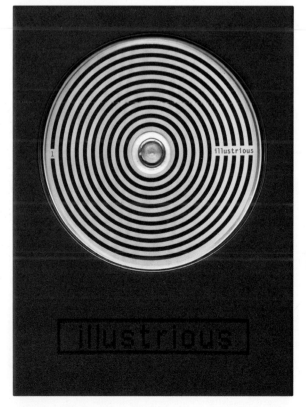

LONDON 51°32'N 0°5'W 9° 12:00

Ask the Dust

The design for Lorn's 'Ask the Dust' record sleeves was inspired by useless, unnecessary and forgotten imagery. The idea was to take a closer look at a selection of found pieces and reshape them to become something meaningful again. Like a puzzle that would find an alternative way to be completed.

–
Designer
Jesse Auersalo
Creative Director
Jesse Auersalo
Creative Studio
Project 999
Clients
Lorn
Ninja Tune

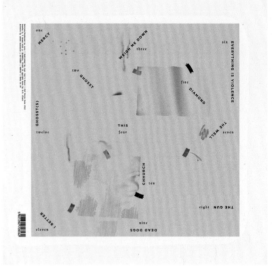

HELSINKI 60°10'N 25°0'E 4° 14:00

DESIGN GRAPHIC DESIGN

Stamping Down on Poaching

The killing of endangered species for trophies or pleasure is unfortunately sometimes overlooked. Pro Wildlife is campaigning against this barbaric sport. We wanted to raise awareness and boost donations in support of this campaign, so we used three different stamps, each with a classic illustration showing an endangered animal. To use the stamp, you have to remove the 'trophy' and thus destroy the animal. The stamps could be ordered online via Pro Wildlife and the private mail service Citykurier. Every stamp sold generated a donation of 50 cents.

–
Designer
Britta Kraina
Art Director
Britta Kraina
Artworker
Christiane Helm
Copywriter
Jana Pütz
Advertising Agency
gürtlerbachmann
Account Manager
Anna Christina Diehl
Brand Manager
Annette Sperrfechter
Client
Pro Wildlife

HAMBURG 53°33'N 10°2'E 6° 13:00

Small Business Card

Bookkeeping is an industry that thrives on lining up, fitting in, and filing away. Sandra Haniak, a bookkeeper who specialises in working with small businesses, needed to stand out a little bit.

–
Designer
Hans Thiessen
Design Director
Monique Gamache
Creative Director
Joe Hospodarec
Design Agency
WAX Partnership
Printers
Studio on Fire
Client
Sandra Haniak

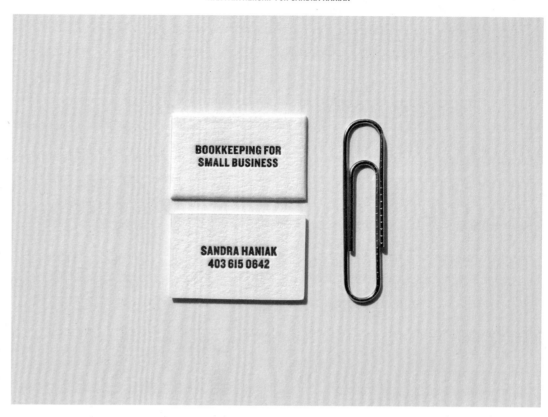

CALGARY 51°3'N 114°4'W -3° 6:00

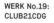

WERK No.19: CLUB21CDG

This was produced in collaboration with luxury fashion retailer Club 21 to commemorate the opening of the Comme des Garçons Singapore boutique. Each cover in the collection is individually handcrafted and assembled with a patchwork made up of editorial spreads from Club 21 magazines, Comme des Garçons hang tags, and pieces of printed graphics and magazine tear sheets. The covers are then finished with graffiti-style numbers and letters. The outcome is unpredictable and original. The content explores what it means to be a woman in a man's world and spotlights the work of nine independent female artists and photographers.

–
Designers
Shermaine Cheong
Geraldine Chua
Design Director
Theseus Chan
Illustrator
Theseus Chan
Photographers
Juli Balla
Lavender Chang
Wen-Li Chen
Mintio
Alecia Neo
Wei Leng Tay
Debbie Tea
Artists
Agathe de Baillencourt
Julie Verhoeven
Printers
AlsOdoMinie
Publishing Company
WORK
Client
WERK Magazine

Digilog 601: Harmony thru Design

In 2012 we were awarded Red Dot: Agency of the Year and invited to showcase our work in Germany. These four exhibition posters reflect the studio's philosophical approach to creativity. The title 'Digilog 601: Harmony thru Design' stands for the fusion of 'digital' and 'analog' while the imagery is filled with symbolic reference to the binding of opposites, such as time and space; east and west; to and from.

–
Designers
Su-jin Jung
Jae-min Park
Kum-jun Park
So-hee Song
Art Directors
Jung-hye Lee
Kum-jun Park
Creative Director
Kum-jun Park
Typographer
Kum-jun Park
Copywriter
Joon-young Bae
Design Agency
601BISANG
Client
601BISANG

DESIGN GRAPHIC DESIGN

SEOUL 37°33'N 126°58'E 5° 21:00

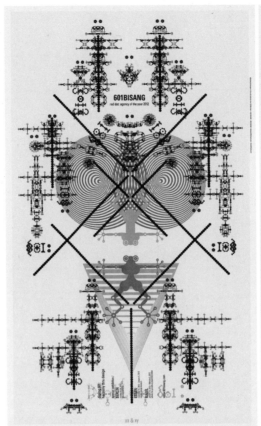

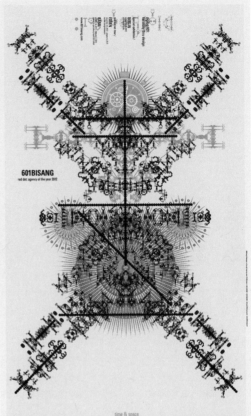

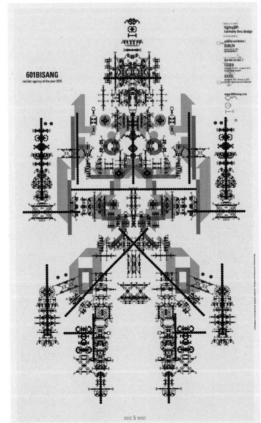

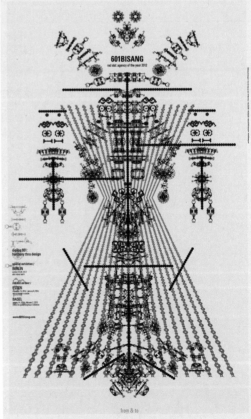

Suicide

Drink driving is still a big problem in Thailand causing large numbers of traffic fatalities every day. We wanted to make people aware of how risky it is, so we made our target audience aware that whenever they chose to drink and drive, they had already chosen to take their own life.

–
Designer
Ariyawat Juntaratip
Art Directors
Ariyawat Juntaratip
Sompat Trisadikun
Sarut Yungcharoen
Creative Director
Ariyawat Juntaratip
Executive Creative Director
Keeratie Chaimoungkalo
Chief Creative Officer
Sompat Trisadikun
Photographer
Chub Nokkaew
Computer Graphics Artist
Chub Nokkaew
Copywriters
Fuad Ahmad
Pathida Akkarajindanon
Retoucher
Chub Nokkaew
Agency Producer
Sarawut Lertkittipaporn
Advertising Agency
Leo Burnett Bangkok
Production Company
Chubcheevit Studio
Account Director
Sipparee Mongkolsri
Client
Don't Drive Drunk Foundation

DESIGN   GRAPHIC DESIGN

BANGKOK 13°45'N 100°30'E 30° 19:00

J'Espère Que Tu Vas Bien in 87 Instagram Posters

'J'espère que tu vas bien' is an 87-minute film that depicts an improvised adventure through the streets of Montreal. To promote it, Instagramers Montréal took an 87-minute walk along the same path taken by the film's actors to create 87 Instagram posters. Translated into English, the film's title means 'I hope you're doing well'.

–
Designer
Isabelle Cote
Digital Designer
Laurent Trudel
Art Director
Nicolas Rivard
Executive Creative Director
Dominique Trudeau
Copywriter
Martin Charron
Head of Integrated Production
Jacques Latreille
Advertising Agency
TAXI Montréal
Photography
Instagramers Montréal
Client
David La Haye (AVIVA Communications)
Brand
AVIVA Communications

DESIGN GRAPHIC DESIGN

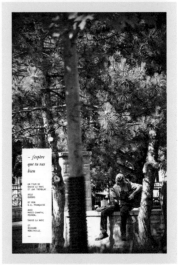

MONTRÉAL 45°30'N 73°34'W 7° 8:00

Mixionary

We created this series of eight limited edition prints for Diageo as part of our 'Mixionary' mixed drinks and cocktails campaign. Each print is one cocktail, screen-printed with proportionate colour blocks that represent the volume of each ingredient. The series includes a Vodka Martini, Cosmopolitan, Bloody Mary, Gin & Tonic, La Primavera, Manhattan and Tom Collins. Metallic inks have been used to highlight Diageo's premium brands in each cocktail, which are printed on a K.W. Doggett Keaykolour craft stock.

—
Designer
Ben Crick
Art Directors
David Park
Kristian Saliba
Creative Director
David Park
Digital Creative Director
Jay Gelardi
Executive Creative Director
Micah Walker
Chief Creative Officer
Justin Drape
Copywriter
Henry Kember
Creative Agency
The Monkeys/MAUD
Content Director
Gini Sinclair
Director of Client Services
Dan Beaumont
Client
Diageo

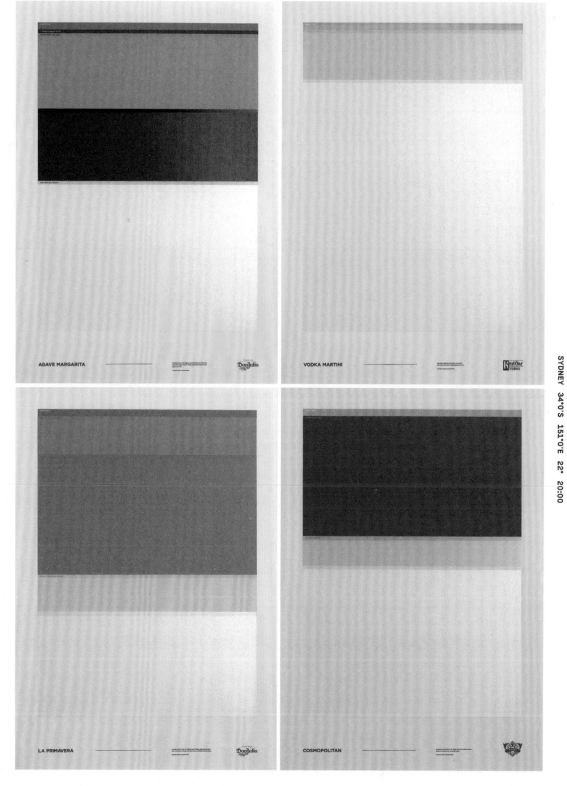

DESIGN   GRAPHIC DESIGN

SYDNEY 34°0'S 151°0'E 22° 20:00

The World's
Smallest Poster

We used things
designers love (Pantone
chips and small type)
to inform them of a
speaking event about
sustainability and the
impact their designs
have on the world.
The AIGA normally
prints over 100 posters
for each event. Our
design consolidated
this excessive number
of posters into one.
A green Pantone chip
was used to evoke a
tree. The poster slowly
disappears after each
designer tears off their
own copy.

–
Designer
Natalie Brown
Senior Designer
Jeff Maurer
Design Directors
Joe Napier
Adam Waugh
Executive Creative
Director
Gerhard Koenderink
Production Designer
Steve Pester
Design Agency
Landor Associates
Cincinnati
Client
AIGA

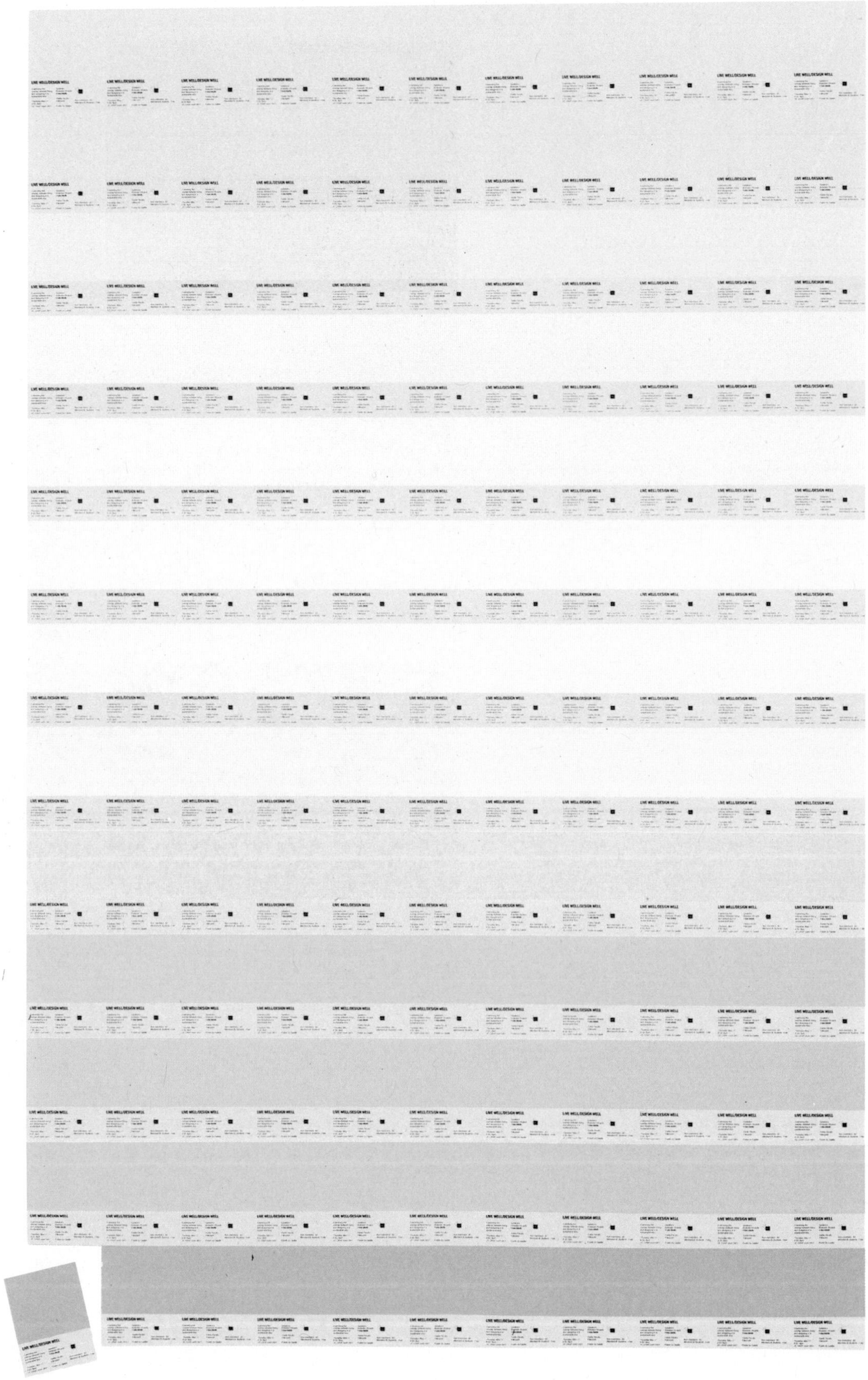

DESIGN   GRAPHIC DESIGN

CINCINNATI   39°6'N   84°31'W   4°   8:00

**I Don't Believe
in You Either: A
Bigfoot-inspired
Art Exhibition**

We conceived,
curated and designed
'I Don't Believe
in You Either', a
Bigfoot-inspired art
exhibition benefitting
826 Valencia
and 826 Boston,
the world's most
inspiring non-profit
writing and tutoring
centres for children.
We searched for
amazingly awful old
landscape paintings,
and then painted new
Bigfoot-inspired art
over them to create
a collection of 38
original framed
paintings, 100
vintage postcards
and a limited
edition four-color
screen-printed
show poster. Why
Bigfoot? Because he
eludes pretty much
everyone, yet we
choose to believe in
him, just a little bit.

–
Designers
Will Ecke
Cecilia Hedin
Jason Schulte
Jon Wong
Creative Director
Jason Schulte
Creative Studio
Office: Jason
Schulte Design
Clients
826 Boston
826 Valencia

DESIGN   GRAPHIC DESIGN

SAN FRANCISCO   37°47'N   122°25'W   15°   5:00

**Cityscapes
Poster Series**

In this series of posters, we show how the transformational power of colour can take you to another place. The colour 'Empire' reveals the power of New York; 'La La Love', the romance of Paris; 'Regal', the majesty of London. The series of prints was made using traditional screen-printing with actual Valspar satin paints.

–
Designer
Kristin Haley
Creative Directors
Gigi Carroll
Drew Donatelle
Michael McGrath
Chief Creative Officer
Todd Tilford
Executive Producer
John Bleeden
Advertising Agency
Draftfcb Chicago
Print Producer
Leslie Burns
Client
Valspar

DESIGN GRAPHIC DESIGN

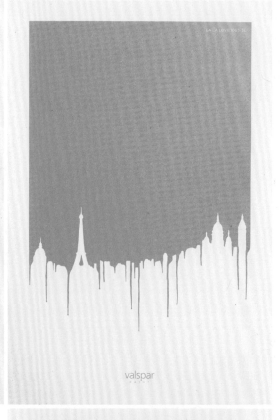

CHICAGO 41°52'N 87°37'W 3° 7:00

Natural

This set of posters was created for a temporary gallery. The idea was to show half of the body, or a part of the animal, in detail, as the core of their vitality. The use of black in drawing the very delicate physical structure particular to each animal reflects the complexity of life.

—
Designer
Junya Maejima
Art Director
Junya Maejima
Illustrator
Junya Maejima
Design Agency
Nippon Design
Center
Client
P.O.M.Y

DESIGN   GRAPHIC DESIGN

TOKYO   35°40'N   139°45'E   15°   21:00

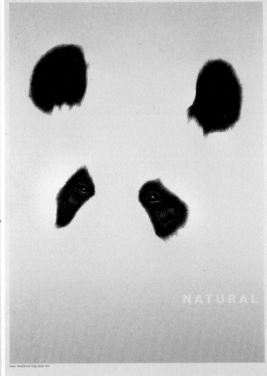

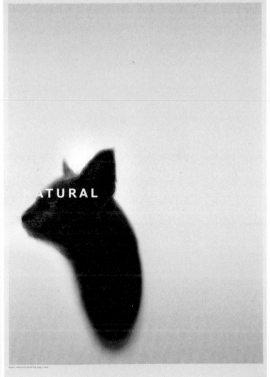

Catch the Moon, Catch the Blossom

We designed these posters to promote a haiku and art exhibition. The aim of the haiku poet is to catch a particular moment in time. To express this idea, a net pattern was chosen as the exhibition's overall visual theme, and the moon and cherry blossoms were used to symbolise the transient beauty and emotion caught by the haiku poet's words. By interpreting tradition in a contemporary context, the creative energy of Japan was on full display.

—
Designers
Daisuke Hatakeyama
Taiji Kimura
Minami Otsuka
Haruko Tsutsui
Yoshihiro Yagi
Art Director
Yoshihiro Yagi
Creative Director
Yoshihiro Yagi
Copywriter
Haruko Tsutsui
Print Director
Shinya Tamura
Advertising Agency
Dentsu Tokyo
Clients
Mitsubishi Estate
Sho Office

DESIGN GRAPHIC DESIGN

TOKYO 35°40'N 139°45'E 15° 21:00

Life is Electric

The brief was to globally rebrand an established Japanese electrical appliance manufacturer. Panasonic believes in the power of electricity and its potential to enrich our lives. The advertising uses hand-drawn diagrams of electric circuits to express the fundamental commitment to craftsmanship at the heart of Panasonic's manufacturing philosophy, and to communicate a sense of anticipation and excitement about the company's emerging technologies and products. With Panasonic, 'Life is Electric'.

–

Designers
Daisuke Hatakeyama
Taiji Kimura
Minami Otsuka
Haruko Tsutsui
Yoshihiro Yagi
Art Director
Yoshihiro Yagi
Creative Directors
Hiroyuki Takasu
Yoshihiro Yagi
Illustrator
Philippe Weisbecker
Creative Producer
Takanori Yasukochi
Copywriter
Haruko Tsutsui
Print Director
Takeshi Arimoto
Producer
Jun Katogi
Advertising Agency
Dentsu Tokyo
Artist's Agent
Natsuko Kida
Client
Panasonic

DESIGN GRAPHIC DESIGN

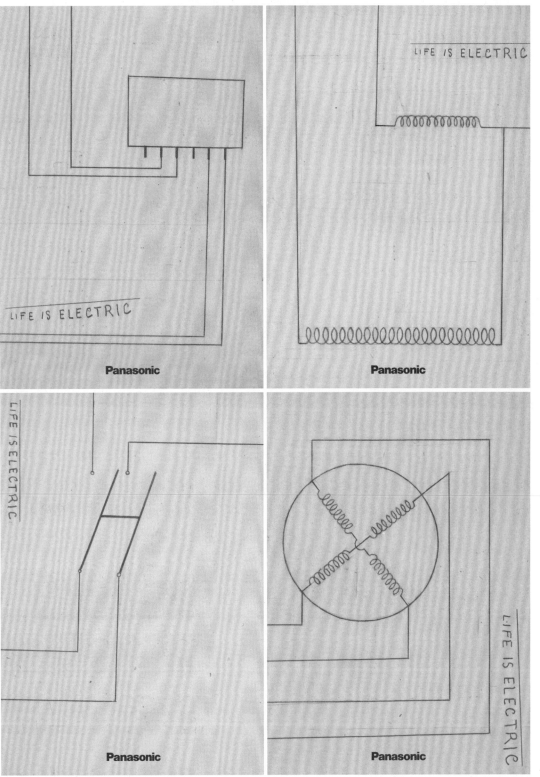

TOKYO 35°40'N 139°45'E 15° 21:00

Migratory Bird

These posters
were created for
Tokyo shop and
gallery Migratory.
Illustrations of
striking migratory
birds were used to
make a strong impact.

–
Designer
Junya Maejima
Art Director
Junya Maejima
Illustrator
Junya Maejima
Design Agency
Nippon Design
Center
Client
Migratory

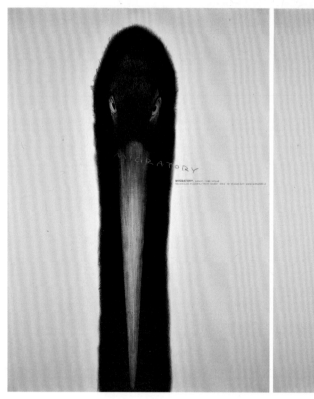

TOKYO 35°40'N 139°45'E 15° 21:00

**Designers
Anonymous
Lecture Poster**

To promote a
lecture by Designers
Anonymous at
Norwich University
of the Arts, we
designed interactive
posters that were
placed around the
university campus in
the weeks preceding
the event. The posters
stated 'reveal all' as
a prompt to remove
the perforated tabs
that hid part of the
poster's headline.
As each tab was
removed, our studio
name was unveiled,
and the heading
changed to 'Designers
Anonymous reveal
all'. Each tab
contained the date,
time and venue of the
lecture on the reverse,
as a handy reminder
to stick in your wallet.

–
Designer
Darren Barber
Creative Directors
Darren Barber
Christian Eager
Creative Agency
Designers
Anonymous
Clients
Designers
Anonymous
Norwich University
of the Arts

LONDON 51°32'N 0°5'W 9° 12:00

Ingenuity. Nature.

'Ingenuity Follows Nature' was a calligraphy exhibition celebrating scripts by artist Tong Yang-Tze. A number of Asian artists and designers were also invited to create posters for the exhibition. These posters have been designed to enjoy the experience of water calligraphy while contemplating the ultimate meaning of life in nature. Water calligraphy is the most meaningful response to the form and emptiness of the Buddhist: everything from absence to presence, and from presence to absence. Form itself is emptiness; emptiness itself is form.

–
Designer
Stanley Wong
Creative Director
Stanley Wong
Typographer
Stanley Wong
Design Agency
84000
Communications
Client
Asian Culture and
Arts Development
Association

DESIGN   GRAPHIC DESIGN

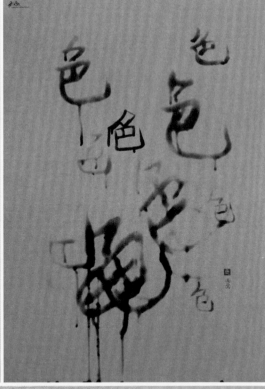

HONG KONG   22°20'N   114°11'E   21°   20:00

Create.

Kyoto, the ancient city in Japan, has been renowned for its traditional handicrafts for over 1,200 years. However, they are now in decline because of cheap, mass-produced goods. Takezasado is a long-established company that brings beautiful wood-block printing to the world. This poster for Takezasado was created under the slogan of the revival of Japanism: 'Re Japon'. The wood-block print highlights Kyoto's traditional crafts heritage.

–
Designer
Yoshiki Uchida
Art Director
Yoshiki Uchida
Print Directors
Yuko Harada
Kenji Takenaka
Design Agency
cosmos
Client
Takezasado

DESIGN   GRAPHIC DESIGN

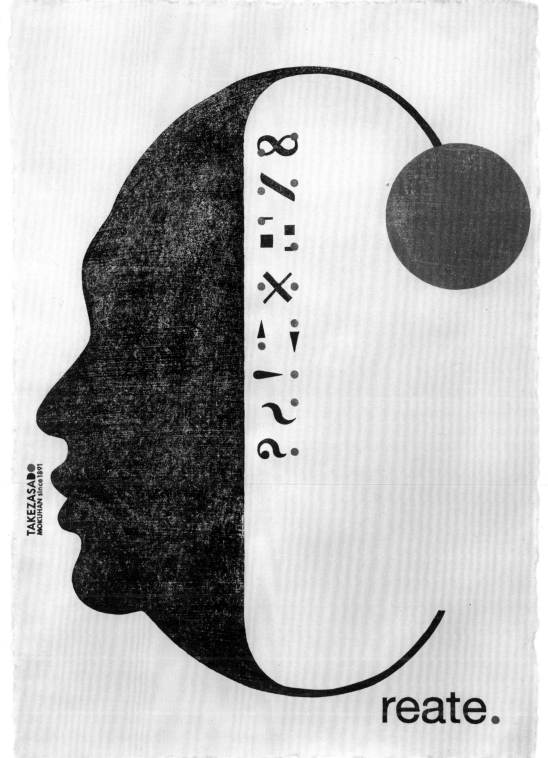

reate.

TAKEZASADO
MOKUHAN since 1891

TOKYO 35°40'N 139°45'E 15° 21:00

Help Feed the Birds

World of Birds in Hout Bay, South Africa, is a bird and monkey sanctuary that relies on donations and money collected from entry fees to feed its animals. We created a series of posters that encourage people to help feed the birds by simply visiting the sanctuary. These posters were made by hand using nothing but bird seeds and non-toxic glue, and were placed in various public spaces to be seen and then shared on social networks. Over time the seeds fell off the posters, making the image disappear and perfectly illustrating how life fades away when food supplies diminish.

–
Designer
Melissa Maloney
Art Director
Herman Venter
Creative Director
Quintes Venter
Printers
Melissa Maloney
Wynand van Staden
Herman Venter
Quintes Venter
Marianne Wende
Copywriter
Wynand van Staden
Advertising Agency
Fishgate Advertising
Client
World of Birds

CAPE TOWN 33°55'S 18°22'E 29° 14:00

DESIGN GRAPHIC DESIGN

Coke Hands

Our idea was to bring friendship and Coke closely together in an iconic fashion that would be easily understood by anybody from tier one, two and three cities in China.

–
Designer
Jonathan Mak Long
Art Director
Jonathan Mak Long
Executive Creative Director
Francis Wee
Chief Creative Officer
Graham Fink
Illustrators
Eno Jin
Jonathan Mak Long
Advertising Agency
Ogilvy & Mather Shanghai
Planner
Mark Sinnock
Content & Marketing Director
Stephen Drummond
Managing Director
Martin Murphy
Client
The Coca-Cola Company
Brand
Coca-Cola

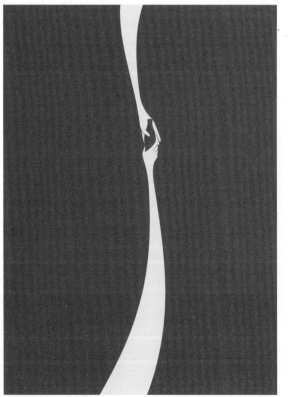

SHANGHAI 31°10'N 121°28'E 15° 20:00

The Whole Picture

The Guardian wanted us to explain its new approach to journalism. Open journalism is where a story can start anywhere. A journalist doesn't have to have the first word, or the last. Instead, a story gets constantly updated with different viewpoints, to provide the whole picture.

–

Designer
James Townsend
Art Director
Carl Broadhurst
Creative Director
David Kolbusz
Executive Creative Director
Nick Gill
Copywriter
Peter Reid
Advertising Agency
BBH London
Client
The Guardian

DESIGN GRAPHIC DESIGN

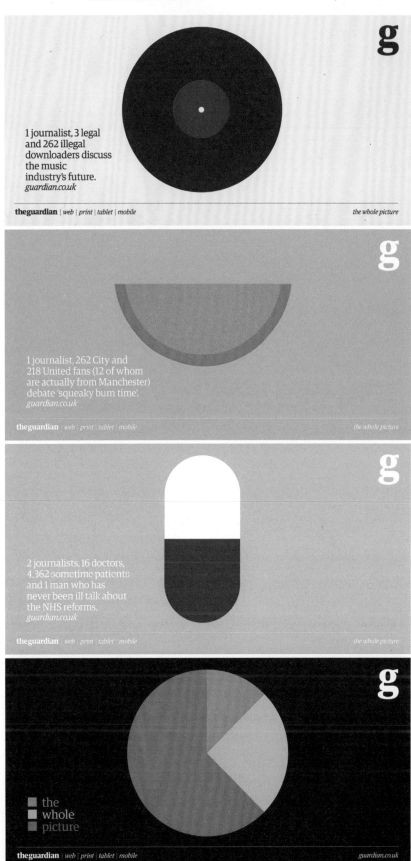

LONDON 51°32'N 0°5'W 9° 12:00

Life Cycle

City dwellers spend much of their day cooped up inside. Yet there's so much more out there to explore and discover. And the best way to do that is on the saddle of a bike. Cycling offers an individual perspective: a city looks and feels completely different when riding on a bike. To dramatise this idea, we created compositions of maps and landscapes from a variety of bicycle parts, encouraging people to break free of their daily routine, and to look at their surroundings in a completely different light.

—
Designers
Chris Soh
Thomas Yang
Art Directors
Chris Soh
Thomas Yang
Creative Directors
Andrew Hook
Thomas Yang
Executive Creative Director
Joji Jacob
Chief Creative Officer
Neil Johnson
Typographer
Celeste Anning
Photographer
Allan Ng
Copywriter
Andrew Hook
Advertising Agency
DDB Singapore
Retouching
Digitalis
Account Manager
Sandy Lee
Client
Life Cycle

DESIGN GRAPHIC DESIGN

SINGAPORE 1°17'N 103°50'E 26° 20:00

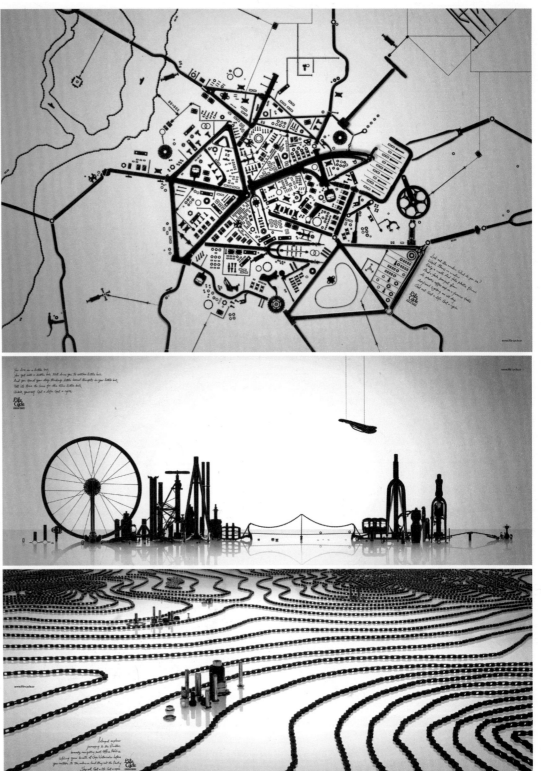

Heroes Wanted

To demonstrate
the role of the Red
Cross, we used two
red tapes to form the
iconic Red Cross
logo, and patched up
the torn pictures of
Red Cross personnel
rescuing helpless
natural disaster
victims, transforming
a heartbreaking
situation into one
filled with hope.

—
Designers
Kalpesh Patankar
Sajesh Pudussery
Art Directors
Kalpesh Patankar
Sajesh Pudussery
Creative Directors
Kalpesh Patankar
Shahir Zag
**Chief Creative
Officer**
Shahir Zag
Copywriters
William Mathovani
Shahir Zag
Retoucher
Gitten Tom
Agency Producer
Amin Soltani
Advertising Agency
Y&R Dubai
Client
Lebanese Red Cross

DESIGN   GRAPHIC DESIGN

DUBAI 25°1'5"N 55°18'E 30° 16:00

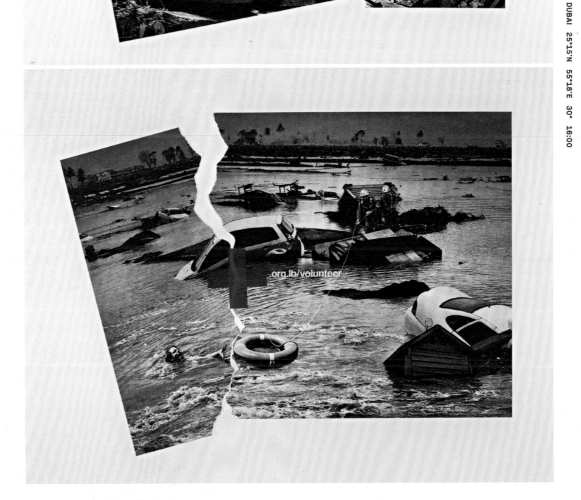

Road Letters

After we came up
with the concept 'One
letter is all it takes',
we worked on visual
solutions that could
represent the damage
that a simple letter
can have on a driver's
life and the people
surrounding them.
We experimented
with every letter of
the alphabet to see
which letters looked
like a road when put in
perspective. Then
we gave the letters a
slight texture similar
to asphalt. The tree
and human elements
were all made in 3D.
Graphic, but realistic
enough to evoke
danger. The posters
are very minimalist
so that the eye of the
viewer travels from
the letter base to the
potential accident.

–
Designer
Diego Machado
Art Director
Diego Machado
Creative Director
Andre Kirkelis
**Executive Creative
Directors**
Claudio Lima
Fred Saldanha
Chief Creative Officer
Anselmo Ramos
Copywriter
Hugo Veiga
Advertising Agency
Ogilvy Brazil
Marketing Manager
Erik Fernandes
Client
Claro

DESIGN   GRAPHIC DESIGN

SÃO PAULO 23°31'S 46°31'W 23° 10:00

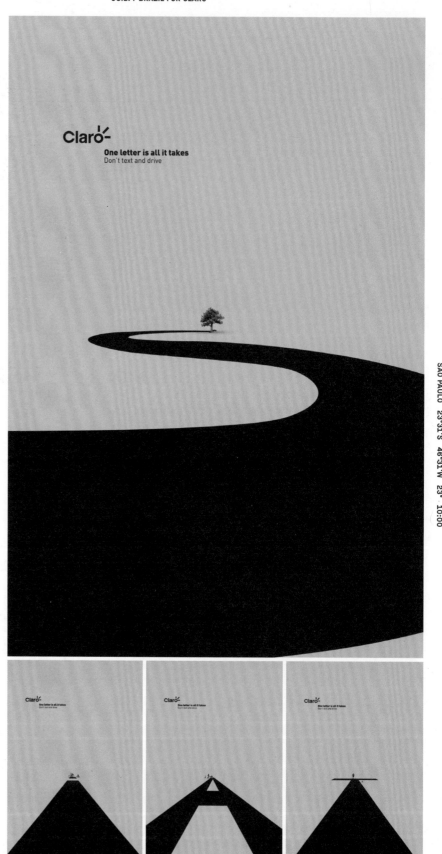

Steppenwolf Series

We created a branded poster series for the Steppenwolf Theatre that tells the story of each play. Each poster should be treated as a piece of art and immediately recognisable as coming from Steppenwolf. As with classic book covers, the challenge was to develop a single key visual that sums up the entire story. We used symbols and metaphors from major themes of each story to create visual intrigue, tension and juxtaposition. The solution focuses on the narrative, rather than the actors, so we reached out to a world-class illustrator to help us create the bold imagery that captures each story.

—
Designer
Rod Hunting
Design Director
Gabe Usadel
Chief Creative Officer
Joe Sciarrotta
Illustrator
Yann Legendre
Advertising Agency
Ogilvy & Mather Chicago
Client
Steppenwolf Theatre

DESIGN GRAPHIC DESIGN

CHICAGO 41°52'N 87°37'W 3° 7:00

Shred-it

Our posters for
Shred-it featured
information
infuriatingly
shredded just before
the interesting bit.

–
Designer
Paul Belford
Art Director
Paul Belford
**Executive Creative
Directors**
Andre Laurentino
Peter Souter
Photographers
Paul Belford
Joseph Carter
Copywriter
Sean Doyle
Advertising Agency
TBWA\London
Account Handlers
Ryan Wain
Tom Wong
Brand Manager
Peter Kadas
Client
Shred-it

DESIGN   GRAPHIC DESIGN

LONDON   51°32'N   0°5'W   9°   12:00

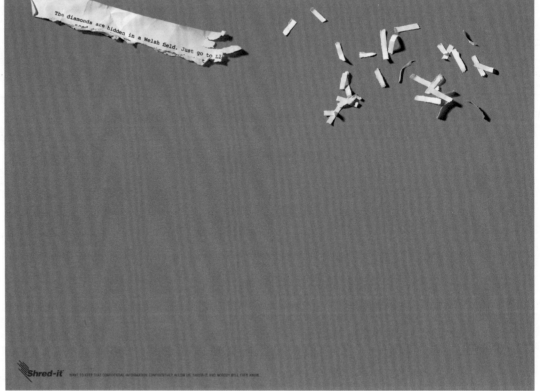

**Five Big Names
in Type**

To advertise a lively
'Any Questions?'
style debate, Bruno
Maag, Henrik Kubel,
Freda Sack, Phil
Baines and Simon
Dixon were invited
to set each of their
names in a typeface
of their creation. The
posters, which came
in five colours, were
signed and given
away on the night.

–
Designer
Jon Rowlandson
Creative Directors
Alan Dye
Nick Finney
Branding Agency
NB
Client
The Typographic
Circle

DESIGN   GRAPHIC DESIGN

LONDON 51°32'N 0°5'W 9° 12:00

Bruno

Set by Bruno Maag in *Plume Ad*. Designed by Dalton Maag in 2007.

Freda

Set by Freda Sack in *Foundry Wilson Book*. Designed by The Foundry in 1995, released in 2011.

Henrik

Set by Henrik Kubel in *Dane ExtraBold*. Designed by A2–Type in 2009, released in 2011.

PHIL

Set & designed by Phil Baines in *Wave Regular*. For the 2004 Tsunami memorial at the Darwin Centre, Natural History Museum, 2011.

SIMON

Set by Simon Dixon in a custom face. Designed by Dixon Baxi, 2010.

Five big names in type
A Typographic Circle debate
Chaired by Lynda Relph-Knight

Thursday 29th March 2012
JWT 1 Knightsbridge Green
London SW1X 7NW

typocircle.co.uk
info@typocircle.co.uk
@typocircle

Poster design by NB
Printed on Colorplan 175gsm
Paper sponsorship by GF Smith
Printed in England by Gavin Martin Associates

Born to Write

Born to Write
is a new project
from Playwright's
Studio Scotland.
It aims to discover,
inspire and mentor
a new generation
of Glaswegian
playwriting talent.
With this logo the
first impression is of
a fountain pen, but
on closer inspection
the pen nib reveals a
sperm approaching
an egg. It works on
multiple levels: I
was born to do this;
writing is in my blood;
it's about bringing
stories to life.

–
Designer
Kerr Vernon
Creative Director
Kerr Vernon
Design Agency
KVGD
Client
Playwrights'
Studio Scotland
Brand
Born to Write

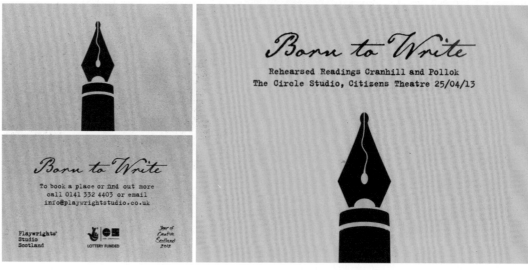

DESIGN GRAPHIC DESIGN

NaturePaint

NaturePaint's
biodegradable
powder-based
products are the
UK's only certified
paints with zero
VOCs – volatile
compounds that
contribute to
pollution and damage
health. B&B's
rebrand disrupts the
conventions of the
chemical-laden paint
category with a black
and white design
that communicates
both purity and
performance. The
logo solution is
deceptively simple:
while it can be
interpreted as a
literal translation
of the brand name –
combining a flower
for nature and a
droplet for paint –
it also echoes the
unusual nature
of the product by
representing the
bucket and water
required to mix it.

–
Designers
Shaun Bowen
Claudia Morris
Design Agency
B&B Studio
Account Handler
Kerry Bolt
Client
NaturePaint

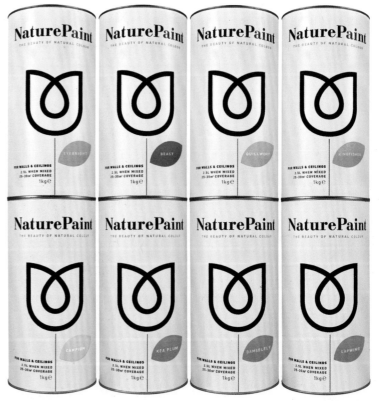

Cactus Kitchens

We designed the logo for Cactus Kitchens, the home of Michel Roux Jr's cooking school. The classic silhouette of a vintage silver fiddleback fork is playfully adapted to become a cactus on the horizon.

–
Designer
Solene Leblanc
Senior Designer
Andrew Giddings
Creative Director
Caz Hildebrand
Design Agency
Here Design
Client
Cactus TV
Brand
Cactus Kitchens

CACTUS KITCHENS

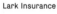

Lark Insurance

A family business founded 60 years ago, Lark offers personal and bespoke products. Many of Lark's clients are private, insuring expensive, bespoke, highly valuable items. Taking cues from the world of tailoring and craftsmanship, we developed an identity that embodied these qualities, captured in the sentiment of 'insurance made to measure'. The master logotype embodies a subtle yet distinctive 'lark' and is further supported by a range of crests for business areas with '1948' to reinforce the brand's heritage.

–
Designers
Chris Greenwood
Liam Lees
Leanne Thomas
Kerry Wheeler
Creative Director
Marksteen Adamson
Deputy Creative Director
Scott McGuffie
Branding Agency
Arthur Steen
Horne Adamson
Client
Lark

LARK

**Andrew Murray
Roofing**

A roofing contractor
from a rural
community, Andrew
Murray needed a
business card that
would stand up to,
out from and above
his competitors.

—
Designer
Arron Isaac
Art Director
Arron Isaac
Creative Directors
Sean Davison
Mike Meadus
**Group Creative
Directors**
Cam Boyd
Troy McGuinness
Copywriter
Natalie Greenspan
Advertising Agency
MacLaren McCann
Client
Andrew Murray
Roofing

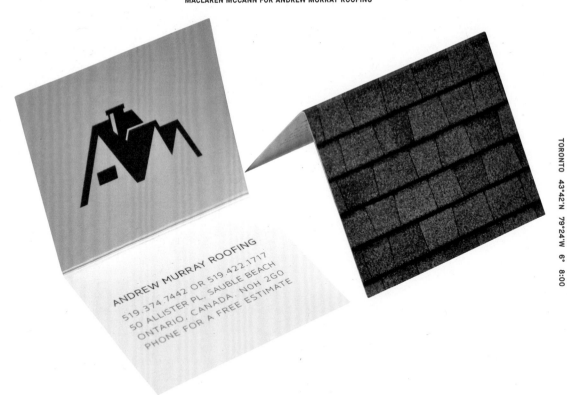

ANDREW MURRAY ROOFING
519.374.7442 OR 519.422.1717
50 ALLISTER PL, SAUBLE BEACH
ONTARIO, CANADA. N0H 2G0
PHONE FOR A FREE ESTIMATE

**London Container
Terminal**

London Container
Terminal provides
a rare combination
of deep sea and
European short
sea trades at the
Port of Tilbury in
London. Following
the acquisition of
Tilbury Container
Services, the business
was renamed
'London Container
Terminal' and Forth
Ports approached
Blood Creative to
create a brand that
would establish
LCT as the most
recognisable place
for containers in the
world. The result was
an iconic mark that
allows Forth Ports
to take ownership
of containers and
sets out LCT as the
container port.

—
Designer
Jon Evans
Design Agency
Blood Creative
Client
Forth Ports
Brand
London Container
Terminal

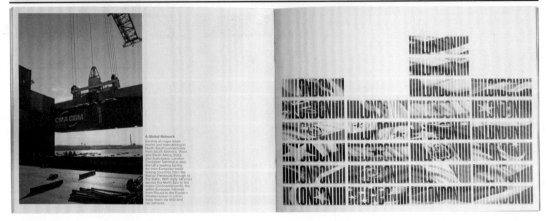

Google Display Logo

Google Display asked us to create an identity to live across all media that leveraged the simplicity and tone of the Google brand. Our challenge was to create a distinct identity for the company's second-highest revenue source that would stand out in a world of B2B clutter. We created a logo that uses its most valuable asset: the Google logo. We then recreated it using the suite of different banner sizes available to advertisers. The banner spaces were designed with a colourful 'Google' take on the traditional 'under construction' pattern, hinting at great things to come.

–
Design Agency
Johannes Leonardo
Advertising Agency
Johannes Leonardo
Client
Google
Brand
Google Display

NEW YORK CITY 40°40'N 73°56'W 8° 8:00

DESIGN GRAPHIC DESIGN

Food for Thought
Thinker Stools

This was part of a wider project organised by the Architecture Foundation and funded by the Mayor of London's Outer London Fund and Brent Council, pairing designers with local businesses to revive shops and bring about a positive change to London's Willesden Green. Taking inspiration from the café's name, we designed bespoke 'Thinker Stools' – a reference to Rodin's famous sculpture 'The Thinker'. They created an amusing point of engagement and a more flexible seating plan. A window display featuring revolving questions acted as a community engagement board giving customers food for thought.

–
Designer
Robin Howie
Creative Director
Robin Howie
Design Agency
Fieldwork Facility
Clients
Food for Thought
The Architecture Foundation

LONDON 51°32'N 0°5'W 9° 12:00

Prostate Cancer UK

Prostate cancer is predicted to become the most common form of cancer by 2030, so Prostate Cancer UK wanted a rebrand to help it reach more men. We needed to raise the profile of the charity for every male, so we created a 'man of men' icon made up from a variety of 'male' symbols. These icons were placed on the walls of the charity's office. A gallery of portraits of iconic men was assembled to communicate that the disease can affect any man. We also created an office clock to serve as a reminder that every 15 minutes a man is diagnosed with prostate cancer.

–
Designers
Rory Brady
Gareth Howat
Jim Sutherland
Design Directors
Gareth Howat
Jim Sutherland
Design Agency
hat-trick design
Manufacturer
Richard Smart
Brand Managers
Olivia Burns
Seamus O'Farrell
Client
Prostate Cancer UK

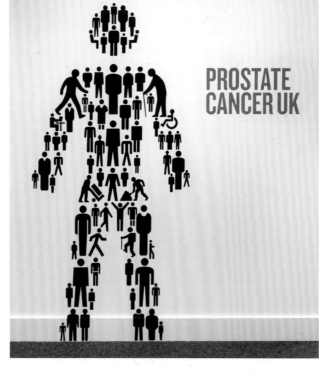

Rambert Dance Company Hoarding

Rambert Dance Company is Britain's flagship contemporary dance company. In 2009, Rambert was given the green light to build a new purpose-built home in the heart of London's Southbank. Along with our appointment to rebrand the company, we were also commissioned to design a series of hoardings for use around this new site. Our approach was to use iconic images of Rambert dancers, but angled so they reflected the idea of movement and broke out of the edge of the hoarding to attract attention.

–
Designers
Rory Brady
Gareth Howat
Jim Sutherland
Design Directors
Gareth Howat
Jim Sutherland
Design Agency
hat-trick design
Manufacturer
Richard Smart
Brand Managers
Nadia Stern
Craig Titley
Client
Rambert Dance Company

DESIGN GRAPHIC DESIGN

LONDON 51°32'N 0°5'W 9° 12:00

The Tanks

The Tanks at
Tate Modern
imaginatively reuses
the underground
space to the south of
the existing building,
which once contained
the oil for Bankside
power station. We
developed a graphic
language and
material application
for the wayfinding
and interpretation
material, to suit
the raw, industrial
aesthetic of the
architecture. Two
simple media were
used for graphic
language: projection
and fly posters. Both
are direct methods
of application which
reveal the raw,
contoured surfaces
of the 'as found'
concrete walls.

–
Designers
Matt Busher
Ian Cartlidge
Morag Myerscough
Melissa Price
Ben Tibbs
Design Directors
Ian Cartlidge
Morag Myerscough
Design Agencies
Cartlidge Levene
Studio Myerscough
Client
Tate
Brand
Tate Modern

DESIGN   GRAPHIC DESIGN

LONDON 51°32'N 0°5'W 9° 12:00

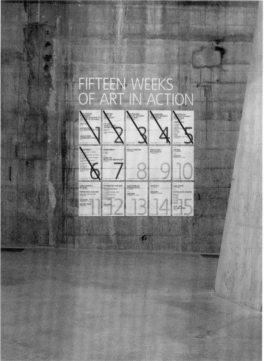

Tate Modern Wayfinding & Signage

Tate Modern is the world's most visited museum of modern art. An eleven-storey extension by architects Herzog & de Meuron is being added to the south side. Our new wayfinding strategy and graphic language will ensure a single, coherent visitor experience. Large scale level numbers and an intuitive building directory orientate the visitor both vertically and horizontally within the space. Listings posters add colour and information at entrances, revealing the diversity of art and activities on offer at Tate Modern.

—
Designers
Matt Busher
Ian Cartlidge
Morag Myerscough
Melissa Price
Ben Tibbs
Design Directors
Ian Cartlidge
Morag Myerscough
Design Agencies
Cartlidge Levene
Studio Myerscough
Client
Tate
Brand
Tate Modern

LONDON 51°32'N 0°5'W 9° 12:00

DESIGN GRAPHIC DESIGN

In Black & White

Having moved into a new studio we wanted to give it a sense of our personality. A vast blank canvas to make our own. We played on the gallery like space and created a series of subtle observational captions that described ready-made objects in a playful way – giving the viewer a glimpse into the way we think and something to smile about.

—
Designer
Jeremy Shaw
Creative Director
Jeremy Shaw
Copywriter
Jeremy Shaw
Design Agency
Lloyd Northover
Client
Lloyd Northover

LONDON 51°32'N 0°5'W 9° 12:00

Empathy Calendars

Every one of us has to measure time. So, why couldn't we do it like prisoners? That was the idea of Empathy Calendars: prison time brought into the world of the free. These calendars are not typical lists of 12 months; they match the terms of prisoners' sentences, even those with no definite period of time set. The calendars we created included the 100 m long mural calendar, 'piece of wall' calendars, and facebook wall calendars. Even the President of Poland has been counting his 'prison time', marking off each day. Week by week. Month by month. More than all year long.

–
Designers
Nina Łupińska
Piotr Zygmunt
Art Directors
Agata Bańkowska
Sebastian Bulski
Małgorzata
Nierodzińska
Andrzej Santorski
Agnieszka
Zajączkiewicz
Creative Director
Paweł Heinze
Illustrator
Artur Wabik
Copywriter
Kamil Kowalczyk
Video Producer
Katka Michalak
Developers
Daniel Kiska
Paweł Kuliński
**Public Relations
Manager**
Agnieszka
Jurkiewicz
Advertising Agency
Leo Burnett Warsaw
Account Manager
Łukasz
Zajączkiewicz
Client
Amnesty
International

DESIGN   GRAPHIC DESIGN

WARSAW 52°14'N 21°0'E 7° 13:00

JURY

Jury Foreman	**Matt Phare**
Mark Porter	ShortList Media
Mark Porter Associates	**Brian Saffer**
Susanna Cucco	How To Spend It
Boiler Corporation	**Richard Turley**
Leo Jung	Bloomberg Businessweek

◆

NOMINATION IN MAGAZINE & NEWSPAPER DESIGN, MAGAZINE & NEWSPAPER FRONT COVERS
JUNG VON MATT/LIMMAT FOR THE NEUE ZÜRCHER ZEITUNG

Binary Code

The Neue Zürcher Zeitung is one of the world's oldest newspapers. Since its founding in 1780, the front page format has only changed a few times, for example in 2005, when it published its first colour picture. In 2012, NZZ faced one of its biggest challenges: going fully digital with its entire content. To inform a broad public about the new digital strategy, NZZ chose to surprise its readers on the newspaper's very own front page, entirely written in binary code – the language of the internet. This is how Switzerland's oldest and most respected newspaper went fully digital.

–
Art Director
Lorenz Clormann
Graphic Designer
Tobias Wirz
Creative Directors
Livio Dainese
Fernando Perez
**Executive Creative
Director**
Alexander Jaggy
Writer
Cyrill Wirz
Programmers
Dominik Brumm
Michael Fretz
Philippe Meier
Advertising Agency
Jung von Matt/
Limmat
Account Executive
Jil Rottmann
Account Directors
Sabrina Arthur
Klara Zürcher
Marketing Manager
Andrea Gallati
Client
Neue Zürcher
Zeitung

ZURICH 47°21'N 8°31'E 10° 13:00

**The City and
the Storm**

We sent photographer
Iwan Baan up in
a helicopter as
Hurricane Sandy
lifted and produced
the image that, for
many New Yorkers,
told its own story.
Because most other air
traffic was grounded,
the controllers allowed
the helicopter a much
higher ceiling than
usual, giving Baan a
far better vantage point
than he'd otherwise
have. We see laid out
before us the familiar
silhouette of lower
Manhattan, inked out;
a visual sinkhole – and
then, to the north,
slicing across as if with
a razor, the dividing
line that demarcates a
city blazing with light.

–
Designer
Thomas Alberty
Design Director
Thomas Alberty
Photographer
Iwan Baan
**Photography
Director**
Jody Quon
Editor in Chief
Adam Moss
Photo Editor
Leonor Mamanna
Senior Photo Editor
Lea Golis
Publishing Company
New York Magazine
Client
New York Magazine

DESIGN MAGAZINE & NEWSPAPER DESIGN

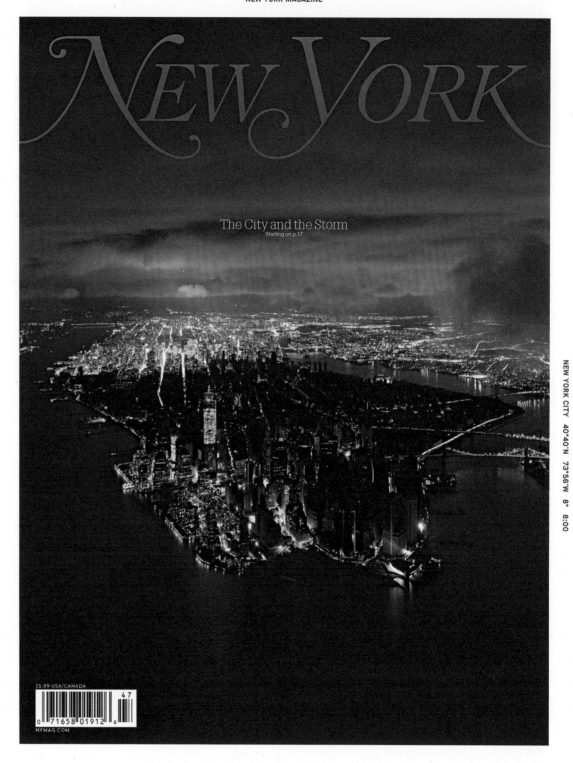

NEW YORK CITY 40°40'N 73°56'W 8° 8:00

Election Issue

We took Ronald Reagan's famous speech in which he asked the American people if they felt better or worse off than four years ago and applied it to Obama's period in office. We open with a black and white shot of the inauguration in 2009 overlaid with facts about the state of the nation then. From there we look at what has since happened in the US; cost of living, employment, security and housing issues are investigated. We conclude with a shot of Washington from the same vantage point, taken two days before we published, with the same set of facts updated to 2012.

–
Art Director
Robert Vargas
Design Director
Cynthia Hoffman
Creative Director
Richard Turley
Publishing Company
Bloomberg
Client
Bloomberg
Businessweek

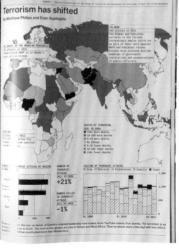

Curves Magazine

Curves is a different kind of travel magazine. Pick up a copy to immediately start a road movie in your head. Curves helps you discover the most beautiful routes through the Italian and Swiss Alps. Spectacular photographs, maps and useful travel information inspire you to actually get on the road and see for yourself. The magazine never shows any vehicles. It's up to you to choose your favourite method of transportation. Because it will be your trip.

—
Design Director
Stefan Bogner
Design Agency
Factor Product
Sponsor
Dunlop Tyres
Client
Curves

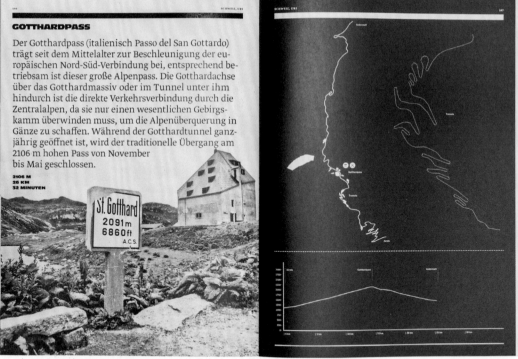

GOTTHARDPASS

Der Gotthardpass (italienisch Passo del San Gottardo) trägt seit dem Mittelalter zur Beschleunigung der europäischen Nord-Süd-Verbindung bei, entsprechend betriebsam ist dieser große Alpenpass. Die Gotthardachse über das Gotthardmassiv oder im Tunnel unter ihm hindurch ist die direkte Verkehrsverbindung durch die Zentralalpen, da sie nur einen wesentlichen Gebirgskamm überwinden muss, um die Alpenüberquerung in Gänze zu schaffen. Während der Gotthardtunnel ganzjährig geöffnet ist, wird der traditionelle Übergang am 2106 m hohen Pass von November bis Mai geschlossen.

2106 M
26 KM
32 MINUTEN

GOTTHARDPASS GORNERGRAT

GOTTHARDPASS (2106 M)
FURKAPASS (2436 M)

129 KM · CA. 3 STUNDEN 30 MINUTEN

Adam bemüht sich um Schadensbegrenzung. Wir sitzen beim Frühstück, und er sülzt nahezu unterbrechungsfrei: Welch sensibler Mensch er doch wäre, wie unterschätzt, ja, vielleicht gar unbekannt doch seine ungemein spirituell empfindsame Seite sei, dass ihn gerade die letzte Nacht im fast mönchischen Ambiente der stillen Zimmer hoch oben, dem Himmel nahe, ganz tief berührt hätte … Ich schaufle ungerührt das exzellente Käseomelette in mich hinein und warte auf die Pointe. Adam kämpft.

The Gentlewoman

The Gentlewoman is a fabulous publication for modern women of style and purpose. It offers a fresh and intelligent perspective on fashion that is focused on personal style – the way women actually look, think and dress. Featuring ambitious journalism and photography of the highest quality, The Gentlewoman celebrates inspirational women through the distinctive combination of glamour, personality and warmth in a collectable biannual magazine.

–
Art Director
Veronica Ditting
Creative Director
Jop van Bennekom
Editor in Chief
Penny Martin
Publishing Company
Fantastic Woman
Client
Fantastic Woman

DESIGN MAGAZINE & NEWSPAPER DESIGN

The Competition Issue

For this special issue of Süddeutsche Zeitung we formed an unlikely alliance: the magazine was produced in collaboration with Zeit magazine, our competitor from Berlin (which ran an issue about the same topic at the same time). We shared the cover idea of Spy v Spy and featured stories that referenced each other. We followed Berlin's anti-motorcycle gang police – and Zeit magazine described how the German Hell's Angels cope with arrests. We had a reporter walk the 600 km from Munich to Berlin, while a reporter from our competitor walked it in the other direction.

–
Art Director
Thomas Kartsolis
Editors in Chief
Michael Ebert
Timm Klotzek
Publishing Company
Süddeutsche
Zeitung Magazin
Clients
Süddeutsche
Zeitung Magazin
Süddeutsche
Zeitung

WERK No.19: CLUB21CDG

This publication was produced in collaboration with luxury fashion retailer Club 21 to commemorate the opening of the Comme des Garçons Singapore boutique. Each cover in the collection is individually handcrafted and assembled with a patchwork made up of editorial spreads from Club 21 magazines, Comme des Garçons hang tags, and pieces of printed graphics and magazine tear sheets. The covers are then finished with graffiti-style numbers and letters. The outcome is unpredictable and original. The content explores what it means to be a woman in a man's world and spotlights the work of nine independent female artists and photographers.

—

Designers
Shermaine Cheong
Geraldine Chua
Design Director
Theseus Chan
Illustrator
Theseus Chan
Photographers
Juli Balla
Lavender Chang
Wen-Li Chen
Alecia Neo
Mintio
Wei Leng Tay
Debbie Tea
Artists
Agathe de Baillencourt
Julie Verhoeven
Publishing Company
WORK
Printers
AlsOdoMinie
Client
WERK Magazine

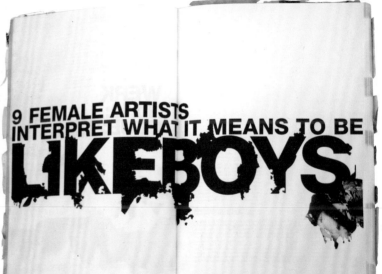

King of Pop

Lemon is pop culture with a twist. An elaborate, one-of-a-kind annual publication staking its claim at the intersection of 60s and 70s pop and 21st Century hyper culture. Illustrated with specially commissioned art, design and photography from celebrated artists and acclaimed talents alike, Lemon is an immersive experience in print. In 'King of Pop', the fifth installment of Lemon, we've checked ridicule at the door and invited an eclectic cast of contributors to celebrate the pure pop magic that Michael Jackson embodied when at his best.

–
Art Director
Tim Young
Designer
Veronica Padilla
Design Director
Kevin Grady
Creative Directors
Kevin Grady
Colin Metcalf
Production Director
AJ Hodgson
Photographer
Kara Kochalko
Editor
Kevin Grady
Retoucher
Nick Carter
Publisher
Colin Metcalf
Print Producer
Bill Noble
Design Agency
Mullen
Project Manager
Chere Furman
Client
Lemon

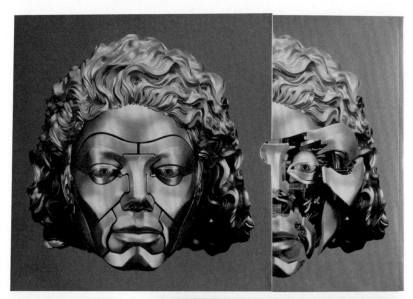

DESIGN MAGAZINE & NEWSPAPER DESIGN

BOSTON 42°21'N 71°3'W 6° 8:00

**Rare Medium
Issue 1**

We like food but we don't like the idea of it being wasted. Rare Medium engages Australian chefs to be more creative with red meat by thinking further than the fillet. It encourages them to use Australian beef, veal, lamb and goat responsibly. The aim: to creatively inspire culinary wizards to do good things with a product that is usually the hero of the menu. Attention to detail and variety makes Rare Medium a pleasure to look through. Each spread is carefully constructed with a variety of typographic layouts and illustrations, and meticulous photography and food styling.

—

Art Director
Darren Song
Designer
Darren Song
Illustrator
Marco Wagner
Photographer
John Laurie
Stylists
Deborah Kaloper
Sonia Rentsch
Design Agency
Mash Design
Project Manager
Clare Rohrsheim
Client
Meat & Livestock
Australia

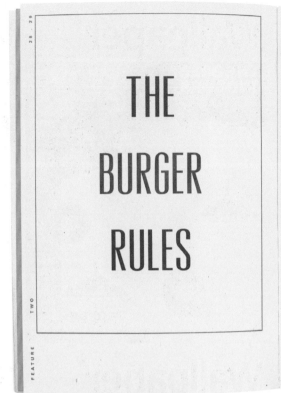

THE
BURGER
RULES

VEAL SLIDER VITELLO TONNATO
CHEF MATT MORAN
· CHISWICK ~ SYDNEY ·

ADELAIDE 34°55'S 138°36'E 13° 22:30

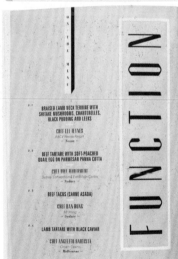

FUNCTION

MENUS

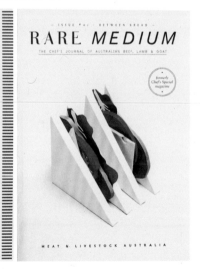

RARE *MEDIUM*
THE CHEF'S JOURNAL OF AUSTRALIAN BEEF, LAMB & GOAT

MEAT & LIVESTOCK AUSTRALIA

Wallpaper*
Cover Series

Wallpaper commissioned Israeli-born graphic designer Noma Bar to create eight different covers for its April 2012 global interiors special. Known for his play on space, usually in 2D, Bar entered a new dimension to create 3D room sets representing Belgium, France, Germany, Italy, Japan, Scandinavia, Spain and the USA. Integrating actual products with his trademark illustrations painted onto the walls, the territory-specific covers generated huge exposure and were distributed to newsstands in the relevant countries. The cover artwork was so popular that prints and posters were sold on Wallpaper's website.

–
Art Director
Meirion Pritchard
Illustrator
Noma Bar
Photographer
Luke Kirwan
Editor in Chief
Tony Chambers
Publishing Company
Wallpaper*
Client
Wallpaper*

DESIGN MAGAZINE & NEWSPAPER DESIGN

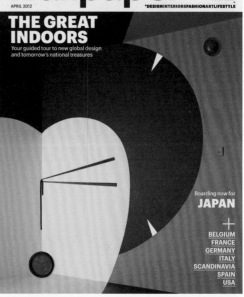

LONDON 51°32'N 0°5'W 9° 12:00

Bloomberg
Businessweek
Cover Series

Our challenge every
week is to try to
make people pick
up a magazine
they wouldn't
necessarily select.

–
Art Director
Robert Vargas
Designer
Tracy Ma
Creative Director
Richard Turley
Director of
Photography
David Carthas
Publishing Company
Bloomberg
Client
Bloomberg
Businessweek

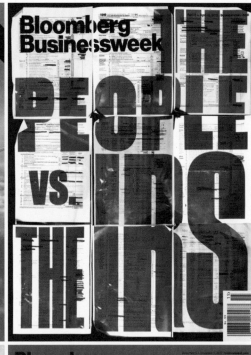

**WERK No.20: GINZA
The Extremities of
the Printed Matter**

We injected a new
energy into the
creation of a set of
publications, with
the aim of heavily
distressing them
to the point of
destruction. Inks
and oils were
collected from the
actual printing
process and later
used to stain the
books, creating
unusual colours,
textures and scents.
We recorded the
techniques and
intricacies explored
in our attempts to
push the boundaries
of print. Details
that are invisible to
the naked eye are
magnified to
reveal the process
of finding the
perfect imperfect balance.
Our motivation is
to find humanity,
permanence and
perfection in a world
that has gone digital.

–
Designers
Geraldine Chua
Ernest Ho
MAA
Farah Siman
Design Director
Theseus Chan
Typographer
Theseus Chan
Photographer
Caleb Ming
Publishing Company
WORK
Printers
AlsOdoMinie
Client
WERK Magazine

DESIGN MAGAZINE & NEWSPAPER DESIGN

SINGAPORE 1°17'N 103°50'E 26° 20:00

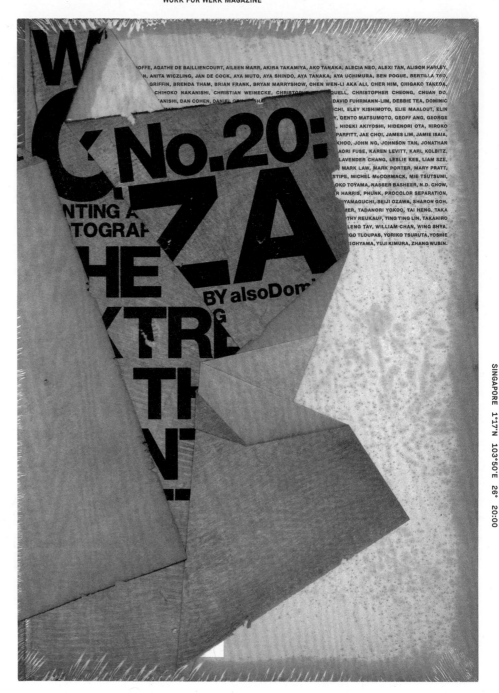

Israel vs Iran

For the 'Israel vs Iran' cover, a war-torn approach was in order, creating the headline in the smouldering remains of the aftermath of conflict. The challenge was to express drama in a rough yet clean aesthetic using raw and evocative materials. Achieving clear legibility while retaining an organic feel to the type was key to creating a bold typographic piece that resonated strongly with the subject.

—
Art Director
Gail Bichler
Design Director
Arem Duplessis
Photographers
Sean Freeman
Julian Wolkenstein
Creative Studio
There Is
Client
The New York
Times Magazine

DESIGN   MAGAZINE & NEWSPAPER DESIGN

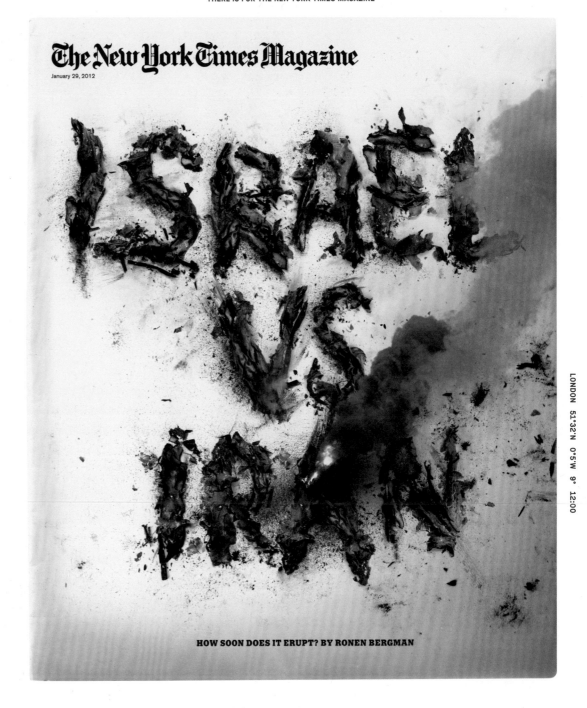

LONDON   51°32'N   0°5'W   9°   12:00

**The Times Wraps
for the Olympics**

These cover wraps
were produced for the
daily edition during
the London Olympics
in 2012.

–
Deputy Art Director
Matt Brown
Design Director
Jon Hill
Picture Editor
Sue Connolly
Publishing Company
The Times
Client
The Times

DESIGN MAGAZINE & NEWSPAPER DESIGN

LONDON 51°32'N 0°5'W 9° 12:00

La Vita Nòva

La Vita Nòva is the digital magazine of Il Sole 24 ORE, conceived and designed specifically for the iPad. The editorial staff has strived to create a native product for the iPad, with the mission to explore in each issue the potential of the new medium. La Vita Nòva presents a truly original and fascinating reading experience through words that generate images, charts that come to life, videos, games and interactive tests, and the chance to share and comment on the articles on the internet and on social networks, with a wide range of access points to services and information.

–
Art Director
Laura Cattaneo
Editors
Antonio Larizza
Pierangelo Soldavini
Editor in Chief
Luca De Biase
Publishing Company
Il Sole 24 ORE
Client
Il Sole 24 ORE

**The Reality Show
No.4**

The Reality Show magazine issue four, 'Beauty is the New Fashion', is a close-up on the magic of makeup and the influential personalities that drive the industry. The iPad application is a motion magazine. The entire issue exclusively features motion photography to create an identical, moving version of the print magazine. This engaging, hypnotic and unparalleled digital magazine ushers in a new era in photography and a high-tech, ultra-modern editorial experience.

–
Art Director
Tomoyuki Yonezu
Designer
Mariko Kobori
Creative Director
Tiffany Godoy
Executive Producer
Tokihiko Tsukamoto
Programmer
Futone
Typographer
Tomoyuki Yonezu
**Director of
Photography**
Koichiro Doi
Visual Effects
Takeshi Yoong
Sound Designers
Jean Marc Fyot
Michel Geubert
Music Composer
Joakim
Copywriter
Tiffany Godoy
Creative Agency
Erotyka
Publishing Company
Erotyka
**Production
Company**
Jitto
Editing
Koichiro Doi Studio
Project Manager
Yukiko Yamazaki
Client
The Reality Show

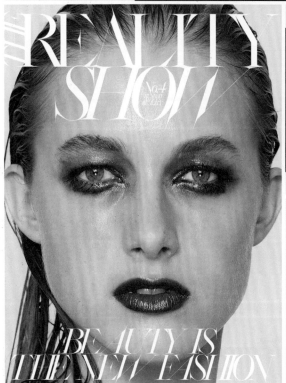

TOKYO 35°40'N 139°45'E 15° 21:00

Frieze Magazine

Frieze, a leading contemporary art magazine, was started in 1991 by Amanda Sharp and Matthew Slotover. The magazine has always prided itself on the standard of its design. In 2012, Atelier Dyakova was commissioned to refresh the look and redefine its contemporary edge. A multi-faceted typographic voice was introduced to create a flexible palette that allows for more expressive opening pages and headlines to respond to the subject matter at hand. Special care went into tactile aspects of the magazine: materials and printing techniques play vital roles in communicating its content.

–
Art Director
Sonya Dyakova
Digital Designer
Sandra Zellmer
Publisher
Anna Starling
Editors
Dan Fox
Jörg Heiser
Jennifer Higgie
Managing Editor
Rosalind Furness
Digital Development Director
Jeremy Leslie
Design Agency
Atelier Dyakova
Publishing Company
Frieze
Client
Frieze

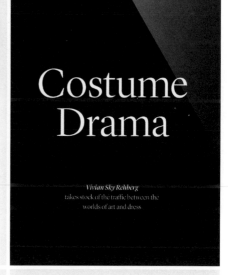

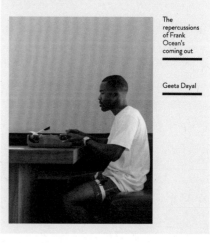

JURY

Jury Foreman
David Turner   Katrin Oeding
Turner Duckworth   Studio Oeding
Shaun Bowen   Taku Satoh
B&B studio   Taku Satoh Design Office
Pascal Duval   Sam Stone
G-Star Raw   Identica
Adam Ellis
Elmwood Design

Absolut Unique

Absolut Vodka has for years led the way in vodka packaging, with limited edition packs like Absolut Disco, Absolut Rock and Absolut Illusion. For 2012, it was time to redefine the concept of limited editions itself. The idea was to make four million unique bottles, so that each and every bottle became a limited edition in itself. We had to rebuild the production line, and use every possible aspect of glass decoration in a new way. The campaign ran globally between September and December 2012, with amazing sales and media coverage.

–
Designers
John Lagerqvist
Fredrik Lindquist
Art Director
Fredrik Lindquist
Creative Directors
Mårten Knutsson
John Lagerqvist
Artworkers
Andy Chong
Anna Jarl
Copywriter
Tove Norström
Creative Agency
Family Business
Project Manager
Cecilia Steenberg
Forsberg
Account Handler
Anna Andrén
Client
The Absolut
Company
Brand
Absolut Vodka

STOCKHOLM 59°17'N 18°3'E 16° 13:00

Long-tongued Animal Shoehorns

Clothing brand Closed wanted to promote its new collection of children's shoes. We needed something that would directly appeal to children. We created this all-rounder – a scary mask, a tidying tool, or just a long-tongued animal shoehorn – to be added as a free gift with every pair of children's shoes. The shoehorn packaging came in three designs: dog, giraffe and chameleon. Each animal fulfilled three functions: product display, scary mask and wall bracket for the child's room. Children loved the colourful creatures with their extra long tongues, which brought their parents' attention to the new shoe collection.

–
Designer
Britta Kraina
Art Director
Britta Kraina
Artworkers
Christiane Helm
Tobias Langkamp
Photo Editor
Tobias Langkamp
Copywriters
Matthias Hardt
Jana Pütz
Advertising Agency
gürtlerbachmann
**Production
Company**
Produktionswerft
Account Manager
Anna Christina Diehl
Brand Manager
Andrea Thiele
Client
Closed

DESIGN   PACKAGING DESIGN

HAMBURG   53°33'N   10°2'E   6°   13:00

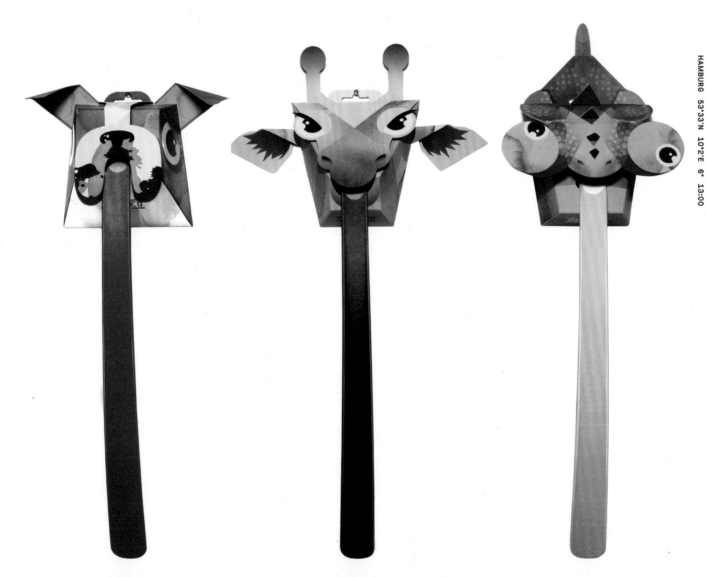

The Balvenie 50

To symbolise The Balvenie's 50 years, this special container was handmade by a Scottish craftsman using 49 strips of Scottish timber (Galloway Ash, Borders Oak, Lothian Walnut, Cherry, Yew, Fife Beech, and Banffshire Elm). The fiftieth strip is a brass band, echoing fittings from traditional spirit safes. Inside the container sits a brass plate certificate, and the whiskey, bottled in hand-blown glass, is labelled with production dates, bottle number and malt master David Stewart's signature.

—
Senior Designer
Andrew Giddings
Creative Directors
Kate Marlow
Mark Paton
Craftsman
Sam Chinnery
Design Agency
Here Design
Client
William Grant
& Sons
Brand
The Balvenie

DESIGN   PACKAGING DESIGN

LONDON   51°32'N   0°5'W   9°   12:00

421

The Erection Blister

Clavin is a hugely
popular over-the-
counter erectile
dysfunction remedy.
Introduced in 1999,
it has been the market
leader in the Czech
Republic since 2006,
yet its customers are
mostly over 40 years
old. We were asked
to use humour and
refocus the product
on a younger target
audience. We used the
well-known box and
logo from the original
design to conceal a
subtle but significant
design change which
perfectly demonstrated
the benefits of the
product.

–
Designer
Daniel Kupr
Art Director
Jiri Langpaul
Creative Directors
Tomas Belko
Will Rust
Copywriter
Jiri Langpaul
Advertising Agency
Ogilvy & Mather
Prague
Client
Clavin

DESIGN   PACKAGING DESIGN

PRAGUE 50°5'N 14°26'E 7° 13:00

**Bulleit Bourbon
Leather Bag**

We were asked to design a custom handcrafted casing for Bulleit Bourbon aficionados that could also be used as company gifts. To respect the brand concept and bottle design, we created a bag made using traditional technology from before 1850. The leathers were hand picked and hand stitched, while the Bulleit Bourbon type on the removable top was drawn through by hand rubbing the leather against the bottle's embossed lettering. Each bag is numbered to mark its traditional formation.

–
Designer
Larry Olmstead
Art Director
Steve Sandstrom
Design Agency
Sandstrom Design
Project Manager
Kay Zerr
Client
Diageo North America
Brand
Bulleit Bourbon

DESIGN PACKAGING DESIGN

PORTLAND 45°31'N 122°40'W 13° 5:00

Smile Makers

Smile Makers is a range of vibrators, designed to sit on pharmacy shelves. The packaging needed to feel accessible and non-threatening, enabling women to place a vibrator in their baskets without anxiety, and also needed to create interest in the product without actually showing it. We employed an illustration style that is playful and seemingly innocent for the category, while being fairly suggestive as well. It had to communicate the nature of the product, its premium quality and its ability to entertain, all without the possibility of a pre-purchase inspection.

—
Designer
Pim Van Nunen
Creative Director
Micah Walker
Copywriter
Justine Armour
Creative Agency
Bear Meets Eagle on Fire
Project Manager
Deanne Constantine
Client
Ramblin' Brands
Brand
Smile Makers

DESIGN   PACKAGING DESIGN

SYDNEY 34°0'S 151°0'E 22° 20:00

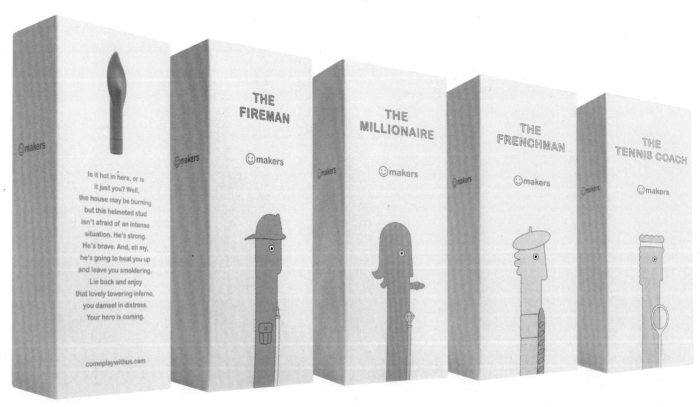

Slamseys Fruit Gins

Slamseys Farm in Essex makes gins each year with fruit handpicked from its own fields and hedgerows. After discovering that famous naturalist John Ray was born near the farm in 1627, B&B Studio created a set of labels for the brand featuring intricate insect illustrations – a nod to his meticulous cataloguing of the local flora and fauna, and to Slamseys' careful gin-making craft.

–
Designer
George Hartley
Creative Director
Shaun Bowen
Design Agency
B&B Studio
Account Handler
Kerry Plummer
Client
Slamseys Drinks
Brand
Slamseys Fruit Gins

DESIGN   PACKAGING DESIGN

LONDON   51°32'N   0°5'W   9°   12:00

Color.Bug

We designed this packaging for coloured hair shadow Color.Bug. The idea for the product was developed from Kevin Murphy's work as a hair stylist, which often had him temporarily colouring the hair of models in fashion shoots. It takes a little while to work out what the product actually does but that's part of the appeal. The ergonomic applicator makes for a striking design that is also easy to hold. Since launching with bright colours, others have been added to the range.

–
Designers
Mark Evans
Brenan Liston
Jonnie Vigar
Design Agency
Container
Client
Kevin Murphy

Travel Bottles

Thanks to a lenticular label applied to their front, these 100 ml shampoo bottles change their appearance at every turn. It's a space saving exercise, allowing for four different information panels, but also helping create an eye-catching package. The technology has been around for many years but is rarely seen within the hair and beauty sector.

–
Designers
Mark Evans
Brenan Liston
Jonnie Vigar
Design Agency
Container
Client
Kevin Murphy

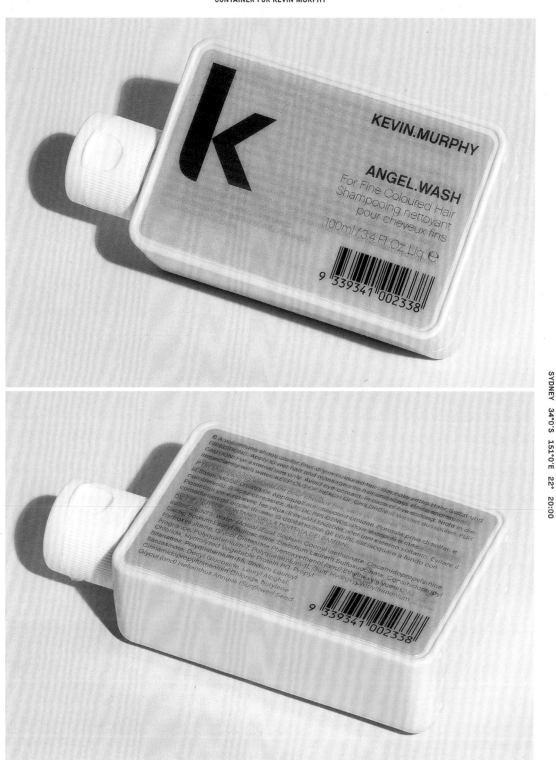

Diet Coke Crop Packaging

Turner Duckworth created a fresh look for autumn with the national release of new Diet Coke packaging. As it was the number two sparkling beverage brand in the US, consumers were already familiar with Diet Coke. The Coca-Cola Company North America challenged us to extend that confidence to packaging. The resulting design provided a bold perspective on this iconic brand by focusing on the union of the 'D' and 'k' as the key recognisable elements of the logo. The crop is at the centre of a visual identity which appears in point of sale and advertising for Diet Coke.

—
Designers
Josh Michels
Rebecca Williams
Creative Directors
Bruce Duckworth
Sarah Moffat
David Turner
Branding Agencies
Turner Duckworth
London
Turner Duckworth
San Francisco
Marketing Managers
Frederic Kahn
Pio Schunker
Vince Voron
Client
The Coca-Cola
Company North
America
Brand
Diet Coke

DESIGN PACKAGING DESIGN

Alaskan Rock Vodka

Alaskan Rock is a small-batch artisanal vodka made in Australia, distilled from malted barley. The bottles have a unique design. With a blackest of black hand-finished Mexican glass, the brands signature 'rock' is embedded in the design by a pronounced punt, crafted to denote an Alaskan mountain range. The raised logo sits astride the bottle's smooth angled corner in a white finish. It's nice vodka in a nice bottle.

—
Designer
Andrew Simpson
Art Director
Nadia Santomaggio
Design Agency
Vert Design
Client
Alaskan Rock

Happy Sparrows

Thousands of sparrows were deserting the city of Mumbai. Their gradual migration was due to reduced green spaces and lack of food and shelter. We came up with an idea: 'Happy Sparrows'. We motivated kids to provide food and shelter for the birds. The resemblance of the McDonald's Happy Meal box to a bird house helped us integrate the brand into the experience. A few alterations transformed our regular Happy Meal box into a make-it-yourself, weather-proof sparrow house. We replaced the existing pack and used kids' favourite character Ronald McDonald to create buzz for the 'Happy Sparrows' project.

—
Designers
Payal Juthani
Nadine Pereira
Art Director
Brijesh Parmar
Creative Directors
Vikram Pandey
KV Sridhar
Nitesh Tiwari
Copywriter
Vikram Pandey
Advertising Agency
Leo Burnett Mumbai
Client
McDonald's India

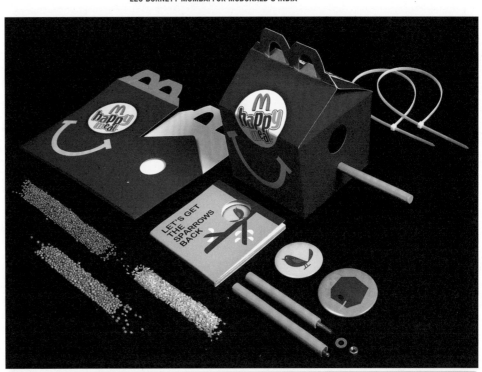

I will show you how, we can turn your happy meal box into a house

HOME SWEET HOME

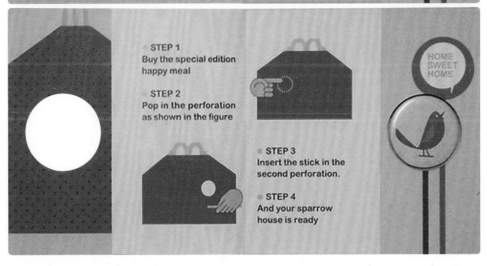

STEP 1
Buy the special edition happy meal

STEP 2
Pop in the perforation as shown in the figure

STEP 3
Insert the stick in the second perforation.

STEP 4
And your sparrow house is ready

HOME SWEET HOME

Rasurado

Rasurado is a Rioja DOC wine. The packaging celebrates La Rioja's barber shop culture. The town's barber shop is like the centre of the world, where mundane chat mingles with ancestral wisdom. The shape of the bottle is a reminder of the striking design of the revolving barber's pole, placing it as the wine of the barber.

–
Designers
Javier Euba
Daniel Morales
Creative Directors
Javier Euba
Daniel Morales
Copywriter
Albert Martinéz
Lopez Amor
Design Agency
Moruba
Client
Arar
Brand
Rasurado

DESIGN PACKAGING DESIGN

LOGROÑO 42°27'N 2°26'W 13° 13:00

Mikkeller + Bedow

The objective was to design the packaging range of four seasonal beers for the Danish brewer Mikkeller. Because of Mikkeller's innovative and experimental approach to brewing, the packaging needed to communicate the four seasons in a progressive way. The idea behind the design was to focus on the transition between the seasons. This was made possible with a heat sensitive ink and two simple symbols. When the beer is cold a symbol representing the previous season is shown, but when the bottle is empty the heat sensitive ink fades away leaving a symbol representing the current season.

—
Designer
Anders Bollman
Creative Director
Perniclas Bedow
Design Agency
Bedow
Client
Mikkeller
Brand
Mikkeller + Bedow

DESIGN   PACKAGING DESIGN

STOCKHOLM 59°17'N 18°3'E 16° 13:00

Mysterium Wine

The concept behind Mysterium originated in the wine's secret blend, which makes the tasting experience a mystery for consumers. This simple and visually exciting bottle was designed to carve a place for Mysterium wine in dark establishments like nightclubs, amongst more traditionally consumed spirits and beers. We achieved this through a labyrinthine design which conceals the disguised typography until it comes under UV light. On the dance floor, the Mysterium logo glows, establishing its strong presence in its new environment.

—
Designer
Ion Barbu
Print Director
Dan Musa
Copywriter
Bogdan Plesa
Production Manager
Dragos Vilcan
Design Group
Spotlight
Project Director
Alina Musat
Client
Jidvei
Brand
Mysterium

DESIGN   PACKAGING DESIGN

BUCHAREST   44°25'N   26°7'E   16°   14:00

Stina

Stina comes from the Adriatic island of Brač, known for its natural beauty and its snow-white stone. The island and its stone have always been a source of inspiration for many sculptors, poets, painters and novelists. Like the island Brač, the wine inspires everyone who tastes it. Stina's label represents a block of stone inviting the sculptor to sculpt, an empty canvas inviting the painter to paint and a piece of paper inviting the poet to write. A drip of wine explored across the label can itself become an artwork.

–
Designers
Davor Bruketa
Sonja Surbatovic
Nikola Zinic
Art Directors
Davor Bruketa
Nikola Zinic
Creative Directors
Davor Bruketa
Nikola Zinic
Copywriters
Anja Bauer Minkara
Maja Bencic
Petra Despot
Production Manager
Vesna Durasin
Production Editor
Radovan Radicevic
Design Agency
Bruketa&Zinic
Branding Agency
Brandoctor
Account Handler
Jelena Mezga
Brand Manager
Ivica Kovacevic
Client
Jako Vino
Brand
Stina

DESIGN   PACKAGING DESIGN

ZAGREB 45°49'N 15°59'E 8° 13:00

JURY

Jury Foreman
Hartmut Esslinger
frog design
Agnete Enga
Smart Design
Matthew Hilton
Dorian Kurz
Kurz Kurz Design

Jay Osgerby
BarberOsgerby
Luke Pearson
PearsonLloyd Design
Kinya Tagawa
Takram Design Engineering

27-inch iMac

With 40% less volume
than its predecessor,
the stunning new
iMac features a
thin 5 mm edge
and a reengineered
laminated display for
brilliant colour and
contrast with 75%
reduced reflection.
Third generation
Intel quad-core
processors, powerful
NVIDIA graphics,
and an innovative
Fusion Drive storage
make this the most
advanced desktop
Apple has ever made.

–
Designers
Jody Akana
Bart Andre
Jeremy Bataillou
Daniel Coster
Daniele De Iuliis
Evans Hankey
Julian Hönig
Richard Howarth
Sir Jonathan Ive
Duncan Kerr
Shin Nishibori
Matthew Rohrbach
Peter Russell-Clarke
Christopher Stringer
Eugene Whang
Rico Zörkendörfer
Design Group
Apple Industrial
Design Team
Client
Apple

CUPERTINO 37°19'N 122°2'W 15° 5:00

London 2012
Olympic Torch

A complex blend of functionality and symbolism, the torch design is imbued with a strong cultural and historical narrative. Its three-sided form cites a pattern of trinities: the third Olympics in London; the Olympic motto 'Faster, Higher, Stronger'; and the three Olympic Values: respect, excellence and friendship. Eight thousand perforations represent the 8,000 torchbearers and their 8,000-mile journey, while making the torch lighter, easy to grip, and allowing heat from the flame to dissipate without conducting down the handle. Rigorously tested in extreme conditions, it had just two 'flame-outs' during the relay – the most reliable Olympic torch on record.

–
Designer
Edward Barber
Designer
Jay Osgerby
Clients
International Olympic Committee
London Organising Committee of the Olympic and Paralympic Games (LOCOG)

DESIGN   PRODUCT DESIGN

LONDON 51°32'N 0°5'W 9° 12:00

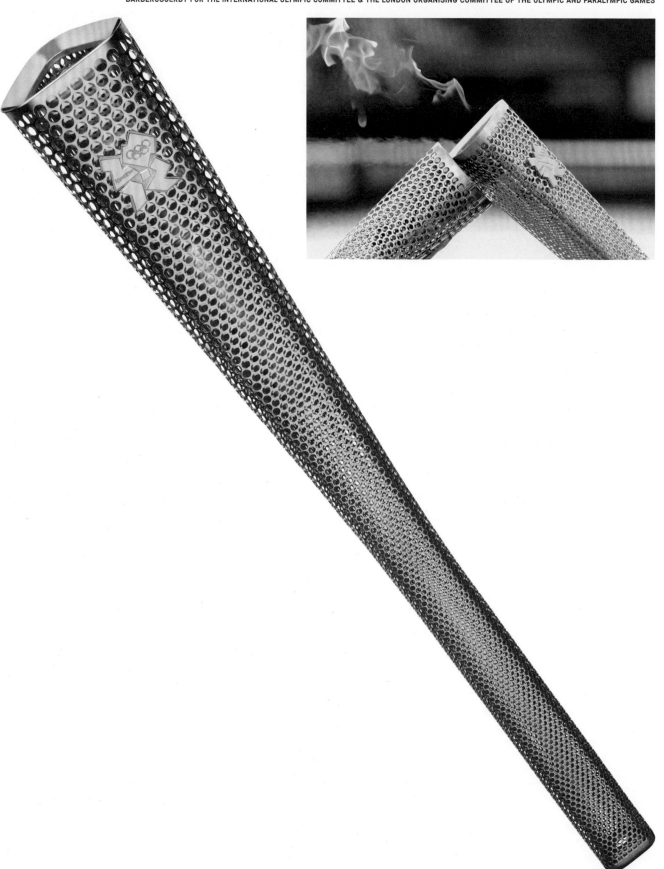

**Nest Learning
Thermostat**

The second generation
Nest Learning
Thermostat is a
significant refinement
of an already very
successful design.
It has all the usability
features of the first
generation product
distilled into a thinner,
sleeker, more elegant
form factor. It still
programmes itself to
keep you comfortable,
save energy, sense
when you are away
and automatically
adjust the temperature
– all while being 20%
thinner. Through
your mobile phone,
you can control the
thermostat from
anywhere. It does
all of this in a more
refined, integrated
form factor that will
maintain its good
looks over time.

–
Designers
Kristen Beck
Fred Bould
Engineer
Ben Filson
Design Agency
Bould Design
Strategic Director
Tony Fadell
Client
Nest Labs

DESIGN   PRODUCT DESIGN

MOUNTAIN VIEW   37°23'N   122°4'W   15°   5:00

HERO3

The GoPro HERO3 is the world's most popular point of view HD photo/ video action camera system. It is sturdy, waterproof, durable, lighter and more compact than its predecessor. The camera design exudes rugged functionality in its simple, logical layout and wrap-around knurl pattern. The water housing is tuned to be more aerodynamic and compact. The HERO3 also introduces a wireless remote. Used together, the camera, water housing and remote control can be used for capturing and sharing adventures and memories whether they are skydiving, scuba diving or your cat's aerial acrobatics.

–
Designers
Kristen Beck
Fred Bould
Engineers
Marvin Balaoro
Karen Baumgartner
Mike Demerjian
David Guasca
Design Agency
Bould Design
Strategic Director
Nicholas Woodman
Project Manager
Meghan Laffey
Client
GoPro

DESIGN   PRODUCT DESIGN

MOUNTAIN VIEW   37°23'N   122°4'W   15°   5:00

The Fireman

The Fireman is a contemporary vibrator designed for first time users, or 'vibrator virgins'. The brand idea behind Smile Makers was to create a range of playful, non-threatening sex toys to sit on pharmacy shelves instead of sex shops. Each vibrator in the range is based on an archetypal fantasy. This informed each product's entire design. Made from high-grade silicon, The Fireman knows his way around a fiery situation and is skilled at cooling things down too. His distinctive, flame-shaped lines are here to rescue damsels in distress, so he's non-threatening, non-invasive, but very effective.

–
Designer
Pim Van Nunen
Creative Director
Micah Walker
Copywriter
Justine Armour
Creative Agency
Bear Meets Eagle on Fire
Project Manager
Deanne Constantine
Client
Ramblin' Brands
Brand
Smile Makers

DESIGN PRODUCT DESIGN

SYDNEY 34°0'S 151°0'E 22° 20:00

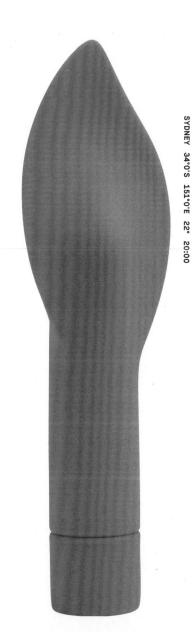

**Lufthansa Business
Class Seat & Cabin**

Lufthansa's first fully
flat business class
seat and cabin was
created for the new
Boeing 747-8i and
fleet retrofit. A V-seat
configuration angles
passengers' feet
towards each other,
creating 1.98 m beds
while maintaining a
high head count and
a quality passenger
space. A modular
shell contains seat
pairs forming calm,
private environments
and a distinct design
identity. The cabin
is light and spacious,
with extended
sightlines across the
space. This efficient,
modular design is
configurable across
a broad aircraft
fleet, maintaining
a consistent brand
offering and identity.

–
Designers
Nick Carpenter
Nathan Matthews
Design Directors
Tom Lloyd
Luke Pearson
Design Agency
PearsonLloyd Design
Client
Lufthansa

DESIGN PRODUCT DESIGN

LONDON 51°32'N 0°5'W 9° 12:00

EndoCuff

EndoCuff is an innovative disposable device that fits various colonoscopes to improve mucosal vision and enhance tip control during a colonoscopy. Using advanced polymer technology, EndoCuff provides a rigid structure with flexible projections to gently open the colon wall. The design language reflects a compact, high quality, technically detailed device for the medical environment; the result of a successful integration between client, designer and manufacturing team. With 60 million procedures worldwide, this innovative product will revolutionise detection rates within cancer screening.

—
Designer
Bruce Hutchison
Design Director
Patrick Axon
Technical Designer
Bruce Hutchison
Design Agency
DesignEdge
Cambridge
Development
Boddingtons Plastics
Client
Arc Medical Design
Brand
EndoCuff

DESIGN   PRODUCT DESIGN

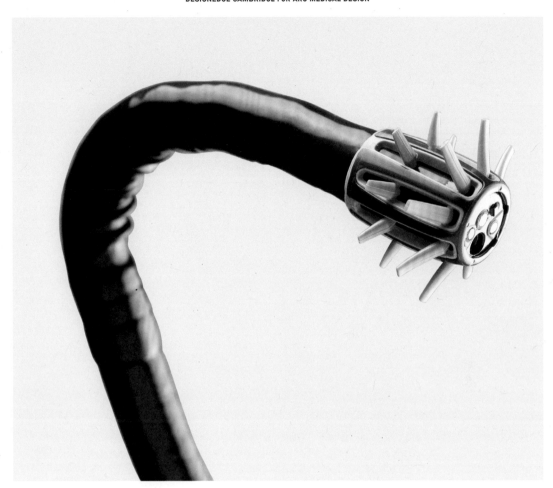

CAMBRIDGE 52°20'N 0°119'E 9° 12:00

Nike+ FuelBand

Nike came to us to realise an idea: a wristband device that tracks your daily activity and a common, universal metric called Fuel for every active body out there. They asked us to design the entire user experience. We ensured ease of use: set your goal, and get from red to green. If you meet your goal, animations celebrate your performance. Data graphics show where you were most active daily, weekly, monthly, and beyond. We created Bluetooth sync technology so the results of your day's activities can be transferred to your mobile device and visualised on the FuelBand app.

—
Creative Directors
Cesar Marchetti
Kirill Yeretsky
Executive Creative Director
Tara Greer
Associate Creative Directors
Keith Byrne
Gaurabh Mathure
Technical Directors
Nick Coronges
Sune Kaae
Daniel Katz
Art Director
Ray Sison
Copywriter
Evan Marcanca
Designer
Ellen Pai
Senior Software Engineers
Robert Carlsen
Fernando Mazzon
Niall McCormack
Executive Producer
Avery Holden
Senior Producers
Alan Donnelly
Guy Helson
Michael Klimkewicz
Head of Product
Ian Spalter
Quality Assurance Manager
Leslie Chong
Digital Agency
R/GA
Managing Director
Jennifer Allen
Client
Nike
Brand
Nike+

DESIGN PRODUCT DESIGN

NEW YORK CITY 40°40'N 73°56'W 8° 8:00

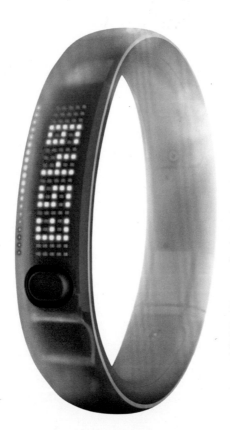

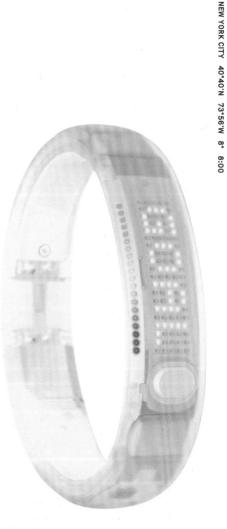

iPhone 5

At a thickness of 7.6 mm, the iPhone 5 is currently the slimmest smartphone on the market. Retaining its black or white casing option, the anodized aluminium housing is 18% thinner and 20% lighter than its predecessor, the iPhone 4S, and is precisely engineered with a diamond-cut bevelled edge around the display. The eight-megapixel camera is crafted of sapphire crystal glass, and the new four-inch Retina Display provides a brilliant 1136 x 640 pixel resolution.

–
Designers
Jody Akana
Bart Andre
Jeremy Bataillou
Daniel Coster
Daniele De Iuliis
Evans Hankey
Julian Hönig
Richard Howarth
Sir Jonathan Ive
Duncan Kerr
Shin Nishibori
Matthew Rohrbach
Peter Russell-Clarke
Christopher Stringer
Eugene Whang
Rico Zörkendörfer
Design Group
Apple Industrial Design Team
Client
Apple

CUPERTINO 37°19'N 122°2'W 15° 5:00

The Chadwick Oven

The Chadwick Oven is a small oven that reaches a temperature of over 500°C for pizzas and flat breads. The device incorporates an airflow system that uses the hot air from a standard gas ring to achieve these temperatures. Combined with a porous stone surface and other novel components, the oven recreates the environment of a wood fired oven. With a typical warm up time of twelve minutes, pizzas can cook in under four minutes. The Chadwick Oven is made in Britain, in stainless steel with a custom chrome finish to outer surfaces.

–
Designers
Guy Adams
Daniel Chadwick
Creative Intern
Hector Henderson
Production Managers
Freja Frosch
Rayner Grant
Design Group
Lypiatt Designs
Communications Director
Annabel Britton
Client
The Chadwick Oven

STROUD 51°74'N 2°21'W 6° 12:00

15-inch MacBook Pro with Retina Display

Featuring a precision-engineered aluminium unibody design and an all-flash storage architecture, the all-new MacBook Pro with Retina Display is the lightest MacBook Pro ever. Nearly as thin as a MacBook Air, the new Pro measures merely 0.71 inches and weighs only 4.46 lb. It features the latest Intel Core i7 quad-core processors, up to 2.7 GHz with Turbo Boost speeds up to 3.7 GHz, NVIDIA GeForce GT 650M discrete graphics, up to 16GB of 1600 MHz RAM, and flash storage up to 768GB. Two Thunderbolt and two USB 3.0 ports allow users to connect to multiple displays and high performance devices.

—
Designers
Jody Akana
Bart Andre
Jeremy Bataillou
Daniel Coster
Daniele De Iuliis
Evans Hankey
Julian Hönig
Richard Howarth
Sir Jonathan Ive
Duncan Kerr
Matthew Rohrbach
Peter Russell-Clarke
Mikael Silvanto
Christopher Stringer
Eugene Whang
Rico Zörkendörfer
Design Group
Apple Industrial Design Team
Client
Apple

Pill

The Pill is a portable Bluetooth speaker built to act not only as a powerful, compact speaker for listening to music but also as an external system for taking calls. The design cleverly mimics the shape of a pill lending to a compact, cylindrical form factor that fits nicely in hand. Behind the prominent metal grill, the cabinet features four one-inch speakers for clear, full-range sound. Tap to pair with NFC technology for easy and instant Bluetooth 2.1 audio or use the Aux input for other MP3 players, phones, PCs, or any device compatible with a 3.5 mm stereo audio cable.

—
Designer
Eric Fields
Creative Director
Robert Brunner
Design Agency
Ammunition
Client
Beats Electronics
Brand
Beats by Dr. Dre

DESIGN PRODUCT DESIGN

Apple EarPods with Remote and Mic

The Apple EarPods with Remote and Mic are designed to rest comfortably and remain inside a variety of ear types. Unlike traditional, circular earbuds, the design of the new Apple EarPods is defined by the geometry of the ear, making them more comfortable for more people than any other earbud-style headphone. The speakers have been engineered to minimise sound loss and maximise sound output and have three microphones. The built-in remote is used to adjust the volume, control the playback of music and video, and answer or end calls.

Designers
Jody Akana
Bart Andre
Jeremy Bataillou
Daniel Coster
Daniele De Iuliis
Evans Hankey
Julian Hönig
Richard Howarth
Sir Jonathan Ive
Duncan Kerr
Shin Nishibori
Matthew Rohrbach
Peter Russell-Clarke
Christopher Stringer
Eugene Whang
Rico Zörkendörfer
Design Group
Apple Industrial
Design Team
Client
Apple

CUPERTINO 37°19'N 122°2'W 15° 5:00

PV1D Subwoofer

PV1D is a compact subwoofer: a perfect balance of acoustic and aesthetic brilliance, designed to expertly complement a home entertainment set up, and blend seamlessly into every environment. The iconic appearance of the PV1D emerged from a mission to deliver exceptional sound. A natural bubble shape is an effective way of containing opposing drive units and dispersing internal pressures, so unwanted vibrations are kept to an absolute minimum. Pushing boundaries further, with an intelligent construction throughout, minimal parts optimise performance and enhance appearance and form.

Designer
Michael Davies
Design Directors
Marcus Hoggarth
Morten Warren
Mechanical Designer
Peter Brook
Industrial Designer
Valérie Pegon
Engineer
Tom O'Brien
Product Manager
Mike Gough
Design Agency
Native Design
Client
Bowers & Wilkins

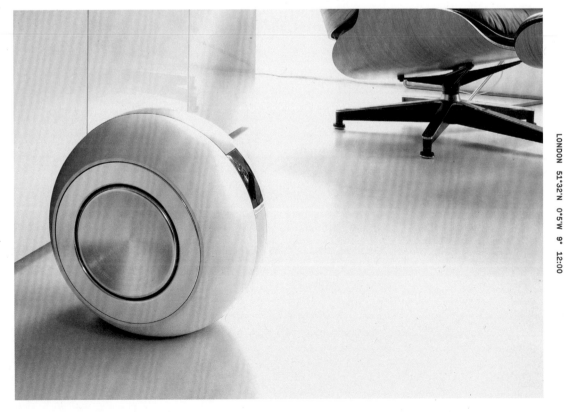

LONDON 51°32'N 0°5'W 9° 12:00

Beats Executive

Beats Executive
are the new, luxury
oriented, premium
headphones from
Beats by Dr. Dre.
With a subtle yet
high-end design,
the Beats Executive
was created
specifically
to attract and invite
a slightly more
mature demographic
into the Beats
audio experience.
Featuring a soft-
brushed aluminium
finish, and leather
feel headband
and ear covers,
the headphones
are extremely
comfortable to wear
and touch. They also
feature active noise
cancellation for
eliminating the
sounds of the office,
home or air travel.

—
Designer
Grégoire
Vandenbussche
Creative Director
Robert Brunner
Design Agency
Ammunition
Client
Beats Electronics
Brand
Beats by Dr. Dre

DESIGN   PRODUCT DESIGN

SAN FRANCISCO   37°47'N   122°25'W   15°   5:00

The Frenchman

The Frenchman is a contemporary vibrator designed for first time users, or 'vibrator virgins'. The brand idea behind Smile Makers was to create a range of playful, non-threatening sex toys to sit on pharmacy shelves instead of sex shops. Each vibrator in the range is based on an archetypal fantasy. This informed each product's entire design. Made from high-grade silicon, The Frenchman is particularly skilled in the art of cunnilingus, leading to an ergonomically shaped electric tongue that knows exactly where to go.

–
Designer
Pim Van Nunen
Creative Director
Micah Walker
Copywriter
Justine Armour
Creative Agency
Bear Meets Eagle
on Fire
Project Manager
Deanne Constantine
Client
Ramblin' Brands
Brand
Smile Makers

DESIGN   PRODUCT DESIGN

SYDNEY 34°0'S 151°0'E 22° 20:00

Bay Chair

The Bay Chair is a shared workplace seating product designed for informal meeting, light task and touchdown work. The circular seat and back supports 360-degree movement, encouraging engagement with surrounding people. A weight sensitive mechanism, concealed within the sculpted seat base, supports multiple body types and only requires height adjustment. As traditional workplace planning is challenged by the growth of shared work settings, Bay provides a comfortable, adaptable and versatile product that establishes a new visual language through a softer, more humane aesthetic.

—
Designers
Tom Lloyd
Luke Pearson
Design Agency
PearsonLloyd Design
Client
Bene

DESIGN PRODUCT DESIGN

LONDON 51°32'N 0°5'W 9° 12:00

Docklands

Docklands delivers compact semi-private enclosures to conduct focused individual work. These acoustically tuned spaces are located close to workplace desking, avoiding the need for individuals to occupy meeting rooms. It's intended as shared, short term usage for visiting guests, or as an alternative work setting within a flexible shared desk environment. The units have integrated power, data, lighting and accessories to meet the needs of users, as well as a flag to signify occupancy. The use of un-technical language and visual softness helps to deliver a sense of professional informality.

—
Designers
Tom Lloyd
Luke Pearson
Design Agency
PearsonLloyd Design
Client
Bene

DESIGN   PRODUCT DESIGN

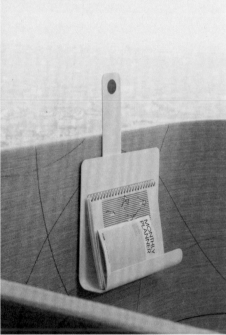

LONDON 51°32'N 0°5'W 9° 12:00

Bramah Pendant

The Bramah Pendant encapsulates the design principles of EOQ – rooted in an industrial context, delivering useful products in a recycled material at an accessible price. After Young spotted components for heat distribution in the factory, the refined details that could be made by extruding a multitude of fins made sense immediately and the Bramah light was created. Each pendant has well over 100 extruded fins delicately drawn out, which create a beautifully effective and unusual way to distribute shards of light within the shade, resulting in an ambient glow.

–
Designer
Michael Young
Client
EOQ

DESIGN PRODUCT DESIGN

HONG KONG 22°20'N 114°11'E 21° 20:00

Google Now

Google Now delivers just the right information at just the right time. There's no digging required. Standing on a train platform, you see when the next train will arrive. Walking down the street, you see reviews of the restaurants you are passing. Throughout the day, the header reflects the current time and your surroundings. Over time you start to rely on Google Now to give you certain critical pieces of information, and can be surprised by its ability to predict and anticipate what you need.

–
Designers
Alex Faaborg
Michael Feldstein
Andy Gugel
Jeromy Henry
Peter Hodgson
Leon Hong
Jonathan Jarvis
Tom Jenkins
Nicholas Jitkoff
Jesse Kaczmarek
Brandon Keely
Jonathan Lee
Michael Leggett
Peter Ng
Hector Ouilhet
Olmos
Helena Roeber
Ede Schweizer
Daniel Shiplacoff
Andy Stewart
Richard The
Simon Tickner
Chris Wiggins
Jon Wiley
Design Director
Matias Duarte
Product Manager
Baris Gultekin
Design Agency
Google
Client
Google

DESIGN PRODUCT DESIGN

MOUNTAIN VIEW 37°23'N 122°4'W 15° 5:00

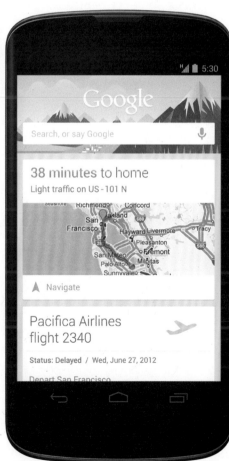

JURY

Jury Foreman
Jason Bruges
Jason Bruges Studio
Jussi Ängeslevä
ART+COM
Kevin Haley
aberrant architecture

Flemming Rafn Thomsen
TREDJE NATUR
Ab Rogers
Ab Rogers Design
Stuart Wood
rAndom International

Chrome Web Lab

The Chrome 'Web Lab' exhibition is open to the world online via 24-hour web cams installed in the Science Museum, London. It brings together museum and website visitors through experiments like 'Universal Orchestra'; an orchestral exhibit that encourages users to collaborate using musical and virtual instruments, or 'Sketchbot'; a camera that converts your portrait into a sand drawing. Designed equally for in-person and online visitors, the exhibition space is easily read online via distinct architectural planes. The graphic floor and bright ceiling grid deliver cabling, expressing the web's data flow. Technology is deconstructed and given material form. A lab aesthetic describes an experimental space and spurs interaction.

—
**Spatial &
Exhibition Design**
Universal
Design Studio
**Spatial &
Industrial Design**
MAP
**Computational
Designer**
Karsten Schmidt
Creative Agency
Google Creative Lab
**Graphic Design
Agency**
Bibliothèque
Experience Design
Tellart
Branding Agency
B-Reel
**Production
Company**
WEIR+WONG
**Digital Production
& Design**
B-Reel
Engineering Agency
Tellart
**Project &
Construction
Managers**
Fraser Randall
Sound Design
Shroom
Music Production
Shroom
Client
Google
Brand
Google Chrome

LONDON 51°32'N 0°5'W 9° 12:00

Rain Room

'Rain Room' is a 100 sqm field of falling water through which it's possible to walk without being drenched in the process. Visitors can choose to simply watch the spectacle or find their way carefully through the rain, putting their trust in the work to the test. Both technical virtuosity and a sculptural rigour made this a successfully choreographed downpour of monumental proportions.

—
Artists
Hannes Koch
Florian Ortkrass
Stuart Wood
Design Engineer
Peter Dalton
Art Studio
rAndom International
Clients
Barbican Centre
Maxine & Stuart
Frankel Foundation
for Art

DESIGN SPATIAL DESIGN

LONDON 51°32'N 0°5'W 9° 12:00

Saatchi & Saatchi 2012 Showcase: Meet Your Creator

For its 22nd showcase at Cannes, Saatchi & Saatchi opened with a live theatrical lightshow performed by a fleet of flying robots. The performance aimed to create ethereal sculptures of light and sound through the use of complex electronics. The dancing UAVs (Unmanned Aerial Vehicles), equipped with LEDs and motorised mirrors, explored deflections and diversions of light, choreographing a spectacle that pushed the anthropomorphism of abstract forms to its limits.

—
Creative Directors
Jonathan Santana
Xander Smith
Developers
Alex Kushleyev
Daniel Mellinger
Directors
Memo Akten
Robin McNicholas
Barney Steel
Producer
Juliette Larthe
Executive Producers
Kerstin Emhoff
Juliette Larthe
Animators
Rob Pybus
Mike Tombeur
Rafael Ziegler
Sound Designer
Daniel Lopatin
Direction
Marshmallow Laser
Feast
**Production
Companies**
Phileog Eleven
PRETTYBIRD
Contractors
KMel Robotics
Vicon Motion
Capture
Record Company
Warp Records
**Executive
Broadcast Director**
Andy Gulliman
Project Executive
Marie De Freitas
Project Director
Norma Clarke
Client
Saatchi & Saatchi
London

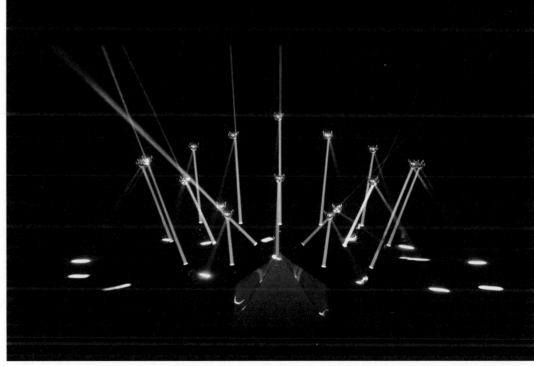

Helsinki Plant Tram

'Helsinki Plant Tram' was a participatory project. It included a mobile garden that travelled throughout Helsinki, identifying potential sites to strengthen the network of growing spaces in the city while collecting passengers' plant donations. The result was an imaginative 100 m long urban garden inspired by the iconic wooden rollercoaster at Helsinki's Linnanmäki Amusement Park. The project was commissioned by the British Council for World Design Capital Helsinki 2012, designed and produced by Wayward Plants and built in partnership with the local Finnish environmental organisation Dodo.

–
Designers
Jarred Henderson
Thomas Kendall
Heather Ring
Urban Gardeners
Petra Jyrkäs
Päivi Raivio
Architectural Studio
Wayward Plants
Environmental Organisation
Dodo
Clients
British Council
World Design Capital
Helsinki 2012

DESIGN   SPATIAL DESIGN

LONDON 51°32'N 0°5'W 9° 12:00

The Small Coal Man's Tiny Travelling Theatre

In 1678, Clerkenwell resident and coal salesman Thomas Britton turned his coal shed into a concert hall called the Small-Coal-Man's Musick Club, which attracted performances ranging from first-time amateur musicians to Handel. The 'Tiny Travelling Theatre' draws on contemporary accounts to replicate the ad-hoc attributes of the original venue. It gave its debut performance at Clerkenwell Design Week 2012. The mobile theatre, towed by a camper van, toured Clerkenwell occupying multiple sites. Inside, an audience of six enjoyed a series of performances, which explored the intense emotion of a micro live concert.

–
Designers
David Chambers
Kevin Haley
Architectural Studio
aberrant
architecture
Client
Clerkenwell
Design Week

LONDON 51°32'N 0°5'W 9° 12:00

aMAZEme

During the London 2012 Olympic Games, Oxfam and Hungry Man Projects set out to build art installation 'aMAZEme' at the London Southbank Centre. The gigantic maze was made of 250,000 books and built in situ with the help of 200 volunteers. Visitors watched it grow over the course of a week. Inspired by Argentinian writer and educator Jorge Louis Borges, the maze forms the shape of his fingerprint. It's a place where people can get lost, have ideas, memories and read books. Projections of literary quotes onto the labyrinth walls helped immerse the audience in a world of literature. Oxfam loaned 150,000 of the books; the rest were gifted by publishing houses from around the UK. All the books went back to Oxfam to raise funds for their work fighting poverty around the world.

DESIGN SPATIAL DESIGN

–
Art Directors
Gualtor Pupo
Marcos Saboya
Technical Director
Paul Denton
Developer
Fran Wheare
Producer
Laia Gasch
Executive Producers
Jack Beardsley
Martin Box
Matt Buels
Alex Mehedff
Production Managers
Sophia Potrz
Konrad Watson
Production Company
Hungry Man
Sponsor
Southbank Centre
Clients
Hungry Man
Projects
Oxfam

LOS ANGELES 34°3'N 118°15'W 15° 5:00

Hollywood Costume

This landmark exhibition explores the role of costume design in cinema storytelling in a backstage environment of stage references, studio lighting, music and animations. Deconstructed costume elements are displayed alongside quotes, images and moving media. Gallery One, 'Deconstruction', explores the art of character construction, showing how the screenplay creates the character. Two, 'Dialogue', examines how the creative collaboration between filmmakers, costume designers and actors contributes to character development. Three, 'Finale', is a celebration of 50 of Hollywood's most iconic characters brought to life.

–
Designer
Virna Di Schiavi
Design Director
Gary Shelley
Creative Director
Roger Mann
Design Agency
Casson Mann
Animation
Squint/Opera
Editing
Picture Production
Company
Client
V&A Museum

DESIGN   SPATIAL DESIGN

LONDON   51°32'N   0°5'W   9°   12:00

Miele Show Haus

Miele asked us to find a way to engage consumers with their brand within the crowded, controlled and often confusing space of a tradeshow. Our solution? The 'Miele Show Haus'. We turned the Miele floor space into a live improv theatre with each show centring on Miele's product range. By casting a mix of theatre and television character actors to perform a variety of comic scenarios, the brand showcased its appliance lines in an attention-grabbing and unexpected way.

–
Creative Directors
Sean Ohlenkamp
Rob Sturch
Architectural Studio
Taylor Group
Advertising Agency
Lowe Roche
Account Handler
Marie-Lise Campeau
Client
Miele

DESIGN SPATIAL DESIGN

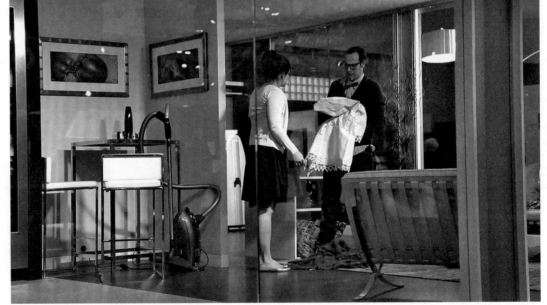

TORONTO 43°42'N 79°24'W 6° 8:00

DESIGN SPATIAL DESIGN

Heatherwick Studio: Designing the Extraordinary

This exhibition took place in the Porter Gallery of the V&A Museum and presented the work of British design agency Heatherwick Studio. The exhibition landscape empowers visitors to explore. Holistic groupings of objects are displayed on single plinths. Clusters of plinths show a particular project and also overlap, evoking the spirit of the studio. Laser engraved exhibit labels, images and audiovisual devices have their own plinths, with equal importance to the 'formal' objects. An interactive gallery guide dispenser was invented. The show received a total of 86,434 visitors, the most successful paid-for contemporary show in the V&A's history.

–
Architectural Studio
Heatherwick Studio
Design Agency
Here Design
Lighting Design Company
DHA Designs
Engraving
Cut Laser Cut
Contractors
Factory Settings
Client
V&A Museum

LONDON 51°32'N 0°5'W 9° 12:00

461

Nature Trail

Jason Bruges Studio completed an inventive project for Great Ormond Street Hospital for children to improve patients' journey to theatre. The brief was to design and install a distraction artwork helping to create a calming yet engaging route that culminates in the child's arrival at the anaesthetic room. Inspiration came from the idea of viewing the patient journey as a nature trail, where the hospital walls become the natural canvas, with digital look-out points that reveal various forest creatures, including horses, deer, hedgehogs, birds and frogs.

–
Designers
Wanju Kim
Miriam Sleeman
Technical Designer
Mike Harrison
Creative Director
Jason Bruges
Engineer
Stefan Dzisiewski-Smith
Interactive Design Agency
Jason Bruges Studio
Contractors
Muraspec
Client
Great Ormond Street Hospital

DESIGN SPATIAL DESIGN

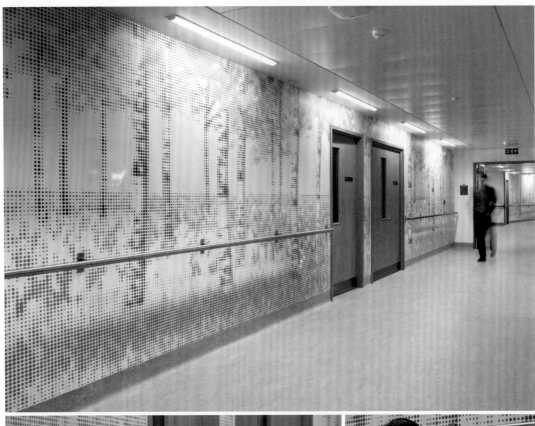

LONDON 51°32'N 0°5'W 9° 12:00

Mimeisthai

Our aim was to engage the audience at TEDx Sydney during the interval and bring to life the event's theme – Real. Live. Now. 'Mimeisthai' is the world's first spoken word trending engine. Think Twitter, without a mobile device; all you need to do to trend a topic, is speak. We turned the TEDx theatre into a giant, real-time emerging topics trending engine by capturing conversations taking place amongst the audience. They were brought to life as graphic art on the main screen via an algorithm, visualising the spread of ideas in the room.

–
User Experience Designer
Claire Alexander
Creative Director
James Theophane

Executive Creative Director
Paul Nagy
Associate Creative Director
Luke Hawkins
Developers
Joshua Brown
John Knutsson
Programmers
Justin James
Claydon
Kyle McDonald
Copywriters
Joel Hauer
Rees Steel
Producer
Jonathan Gerard
Executive Producer
Denise McKeon
Editor
Toby Royce
Sound Designer
Anthony Tiernan
Advertising Agency
Clemenger BBDO Sydney
Visual Effects
Small Multiples
Video Content Management
Viocorp
Client
TEDx Sydney

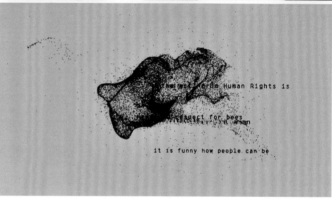

Silo 468

This project saw the conversion of a disused oil silo into a mesmerising light art piece and a public space with the aid of LEDs and natural light. The site sits by the sea in Helsinki, Finland. Prevailing winds have a strong presence. The natural light, wind and the movement of light on water formed the concept. The light art signifies the start of a major urban redevelopment project and draws focus to an unknown district in the city. Bespoke software controls the lights using swarm intelligence and nature simulating algorithms. The patterns are natural in feel and never repeat.

–
Digital Designers
Rodrigo Arcaya
Gorka Cortazar
Lighting Designers
Rodolfo Lozano
Oscar Martin
Tapio Rosenius
Victor Soria
Graphic Designer
Reinaldo Alcala
Design Agency
Lighting Design Collective
Clients
City of Helsinki Planning Department
Helsinki Energy

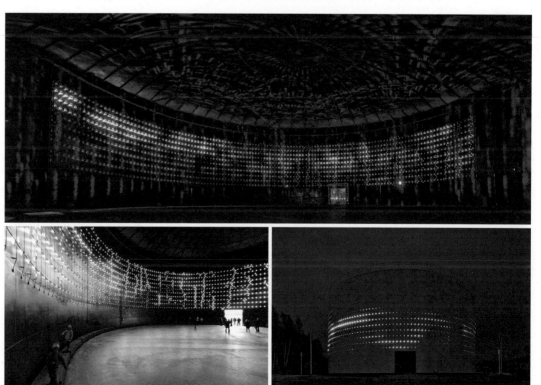

**Elttob Tep Issey
Miyake Ginza
Window Display**

This installation was
created to promote
the 132 5. Issey
Miyake Summer/
Spring 2012
collection. It was
the window display
for the Elttob Tep
Issey Miyake store in
Ginza, Tokyo, for the
month of July. The
brand 132 5. Issey
Miyake has produced
playful clothing
lines, introducing
distinctive folding
shapes in their design.
For the concept,
we focused on the
interesting, dynamic
shapes of the folding
process. The split-flap
display was chosen as
the device to present
moving images of the
design for the season's
window display.

—
Designers
Tomoya Kamiko
Takaharu Shimizu
Art Directors
Yusuke Kobayashi
Tetsuro Tsuji
Technical Director
Tetsuro Tsuji
Programmer
Tetsuro Tsuji
Producer
Takashi Ueno
Design Agency
Drawing and Manual
Client
Issey Miyake
Brand
132 5. Issey Miyake

DESIGN   SPATIAL DESIGN

TOKYO 35°40'N 139°45'E 15° 21:00

The Movement Café

The Movement Café is a café, theatre, local landmark, meeting place and poem. It was designed and built in 16 days to greet locals and visitors arriving at Greenwich DLR station for the London 2012 Olympic events. The café turned a hole in the ground left by demolition into a fabulous community space run by not-for-profit Greenwich Cooperative Development Agency. It exploits the sunken plot to conjure a natural amphitheatre, accessible by ramp and lined with stepped seating – all hand-made and hand-painted including the furniture. The structure is crowned with a tower of scaffolding to hold the words from a tweet by poet Lemn Sissay.

–
Designers
Luke Morgan
Morag Myerscough
Client
Cathedral Group

DESIGN SPATIAL DESIGN

LONDON 51°32'N 0°5'W 9° 12:00

24 NATIONS

GBR
4creative
adam&eveDDB
Alphabetical
AMV BBDO
BBH London
Biscuit
Filmworks
Blink
Productions
CP+B London
Dare London
DLKW Lowe
Draftfcb
London
Factory
Studios
Final Cut
London
Google
Creative Lab
Government
Digital Service
hat-trick
design
Human After
All
Laurence King
Publishing
Leland Music
Leo Burnett
London
McCann
Worldgroup
Ogilvy &
Mather London
Park Pictures
Parlophone
Records
Purpose
Rattling Stick
RSA Films
Saatchi &
Saatchi London
STITCH
The Sweet
Shop
The Workshop
Violette
Editions
Wave Studios
Weapon7
Wieden+
Kennedy
London
Work

IRL
Screen Scene

SWE
Acne
Advertising
Forsman &
Bodenfors
North Kingdom

AUS
BD Network
DDB Sydney
Leo Burnett
Sydney
Mash Design
McCann
Erickson
Melbourne
Naughtyfish
Design
Revolver
The Monkeys/
MAUD

CAN
john st.

NLD
DDB & Tribal
Amsterdam
WE ARE Pi

THA
Leo Burnett
Bangkok
Visionary
Group

JPN
Dentsu Tokyo
I&S BBDO
MR_DESIGN
Peace
Graphics

USA
BBDO Atlanta
Biscuit
Filmworks
Buck
DDB New York
Deutsch LA
Droga5
Goodby
Silverstein &
Partners
Harvest
McCann
Erickson
New York
Morton Jankel
Zander
Q Department
R/GA
Sagmeister &
Walsh
Wieden+
Kennedy
New York
Wieden+
Kennedy
Portland

DEU
BBDO
Proximity
Berlin
FontShop
International

SGP
BBDO
Singapore
DDB Singapore
Kinetic
Singapore
TBWA\
Singapore
WORK

GRC
Beetroot
Design Group

CRAFTS

ZAF
King James
Cape Town
Machine
Velocity Films
Rivonia

BRA
AlmapBBDO
F/Nazca
Saatchi &
Saatchi
JWT Brasil
Loducca
Ogilvy Brazil

ARE
Y&R Dubai

MYS
McCann
Erickson
Malaysia

CHE
KOMET

IND
Ramesh Deo
Production

FRA
DDB Paris
Fred & Farid
Paris
Marcel
Worldwide
TBWA\G1

TUR
TBWA\
ISTANBUL

NZL
Colenso BBDO/
Proximity
New Zealand
String Theory

NOR
Anti &
Grandpeople

ITA
Publicis Italy

CHN
Fred & Farid
Shanghai
Leagas
Delaney
Shanghai
Ogilvy &
Mather
Shanghai

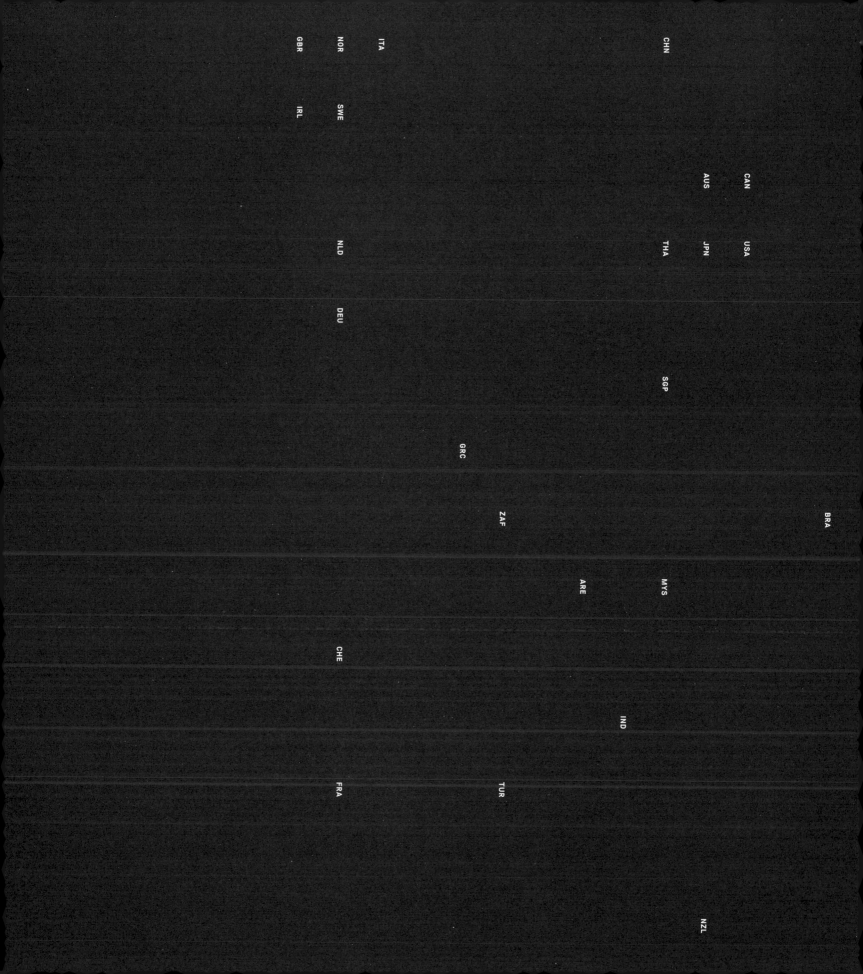

JURY

Jury Foreman
Fred Raillard
Fred & Farid
Axel Chaldecott
JWT London
Tori Fannon
RAPP London
Victoria Gallardo
Creative Orchestra

Alex Lim
EnergyBBDO Shanghai
Nadja Lossgott
AMV BBDO London
Andreas Malm
Forsman & Bodenfors
Antony Nelson
AMV BBDO London

Mixionary

We created this
series of eight
limited edition prints
for Diageo as part of
our 'Mixionary'
mixed drinks
and cocktails
campaign. Each
print is one cocktail,
screen-printed
with proportionate
colour blocks that
represent the volume
of each ingredient.
The series includes
a Vodka Martini,
Cosmopolitan,
Bloody Mary, Gin &
Tonic, La Primavera,
Manhattan and
Tom Collins. Metallic
inks have been used
to highlight Diageo's
premium brands in
each cocktail, which
are printed on a K.W.
Doggett Keaykolour
craft stock.

–
Art Directors
David Park
Kristian Saliba
Designer
Ben Crick
Copywriter
Henry Kember
Creative Director
David Park
**Digital Creative
Director**
Jay Gelardi
**Executive
Creative Director**
Micah Walker
**Chief Creative
Officer**
Justin Drape
Creative Agency
The Monkeys/MAUD
Content Director
Gini Sinclair
**Director of
Client Services**
Dan Beaumont
Client
Diageo

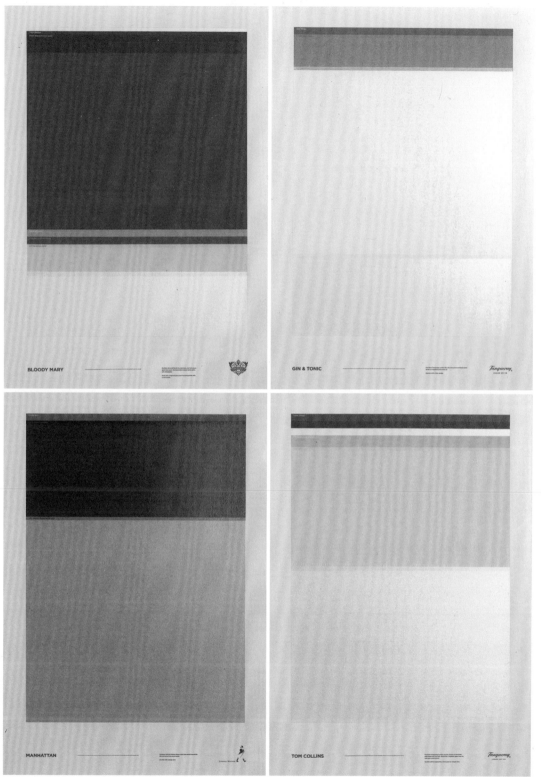

SYDNEY 34°0'S 151°0'E 22° 20:00

Dumb Ways to Die

How do you reach young commuters who think they will outlive religion? Why not start by breaking every single rule of public safety messaging one could find? A key part of a broader campaign, these cute little dead guys ended up on people's cameras, hash tagged all over Instagram and cheerfully etched in the consciousness of a segment of risk-hungry young Melbournians, hard-wired to do dumb stuff when and where they shouldn't.

—
Art Director
Pat Baron
Copywriter
John Mescall
Illustrator
Julian Frost
Creative Director
Pat Baron
**Executive
Creative Director**
John Mescall
Advertising Agency
McCann Erickson
Melbourne
Account Manager
Tamara Broman
Account Director
Alec Hussain
**Group Account
Director**
Adrian Mills
Brand Manager
Leah Waymark
Marketing Manager
Chloe Alsop
Client
Metro Trains

CRAFTS ART DIRECTION

MELBOURNE 37°47'S 144°58'E 12° 23:00

Park Assist Technology

We've all been there: you're searching for a parking spot and the only space is between a rock and a hard place.

—

Art Directors
Nick Pringle
Steve Wakelam
Photographer
Andreas Bommert
Retoucher
Matt Bright
Creative Directors
Nick Pringle
Steve Wakelam
Executive Creative Director
Dylan Harrison
Producer
Grant Navin
Advertising Agency
DDB Sydney
Art Buyer
Leesa Murray
Brand Managers
Loren Elsegood
Peter Stewart
Marketing Manager
Jutta Friese
Business Director
Dave Murphy
Managing Partner
Nicole Taylor
Client
Volkswagen Group Australia

CRAFTS ART DIRECTION

SYDNEY 34°0'S 151°0'E 22° 20:00

Park Assist technology from Volkswagen.

Park Assist technology from Volkswagen.

Dumb Ways to Die

The internet needs feeding. And when you feed it what it wants, it becomes your friend. The 'Dumb Ways to Die' Tumblr site generated huge and immediate viral effect, pushing the campaign onto the front page of the front page of the internet, Reddit.

—

Art Director
Pat Baron
Creative Director
Pat Baron
Executive Creative Director
John Mescall
Illustrator
Julian Frost
Animator
Julian Frost
Copywriter
John Mescall
Producer
Cinnamon Darvall
Senior Producer
Mark Bradley
Music Producer
Oliver McGill
Advertising Agency
McCann Erickson Melbourne
Production Company
McCann Erickson Melbourne
Account Manager
Tamara Broman
Account Director
Alec Hussain
Group Account Director
Adrian Mills
Brand Manager
Leah Waymark
Marketing Manager
Chloe Alsop
Client
Metro Trains

CRAFTS ART DIRECTION

MELBOURNE 37°47'S 144°58'E 12° 23:00

CRAFTS ART DIRECTION

Made of More: Pool

Guinness believes in men who are 'Made of More'. Men who don't believe in luck. Whose success is built on blood, sweat and sheer determination.

–
Art Director
Douglas Goh
Copywriter
Primus Nair
Advertising Agency
BBDO Singapore
Account Handlers
Joe Braithwaite
Fiona Huang
Brand Manager
Bruce Dallas
Clients
Asia Pacific
Breweries
Singapore
Diageo
Brand
Guinness

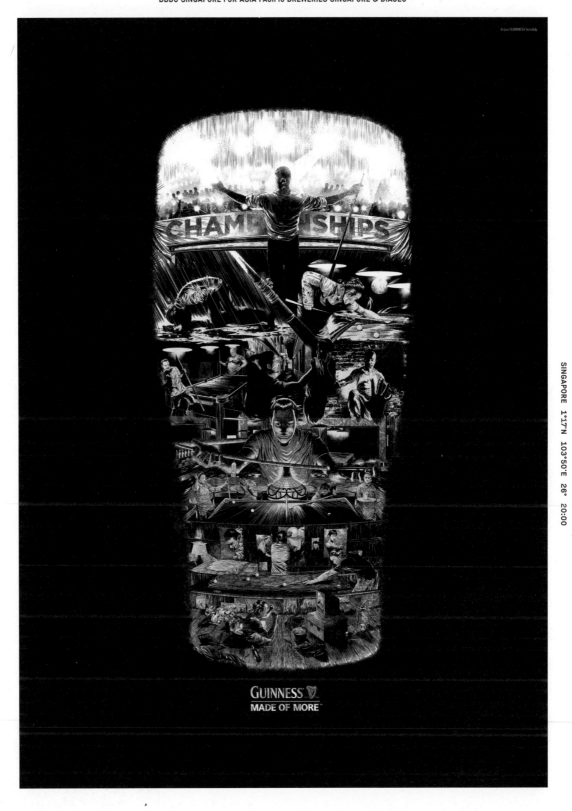

SINGAPORE 1°17'N 103°50'E 26° 20:00

Road Letters

After we came up with the concept 'One letter is all it takes', we worked on visual solutions that could represent the damage that a simple letter can have on a driver's life and the people surrounding them. We experimented with every letter of the alphabet to see which letters looked like a road when put in perspective. Then we gave the letters a slight texture similar to asphalt. The tree and human elements were all made in 3D. Graphic, but realistic enough to evoke danger. The posters are very minimalist so that the eye of the viewer travels from the letter base to the potential accident.

–
Art Director
Diego Machado
Designer
Diego Machado
Copywriter
Hugo Veiga
Creative Director
Andre Kirkelis
**Executive
Creative Directors**
Claudio Lima
Fred Saldanha
**Chief Creative
Officer**
Anselmo Ramos
Advertising Agency
Ogilvy Brazil
Marketing Manager
Erik Fernandes
Client
Claro

CRAFTS   ART DIRECTION

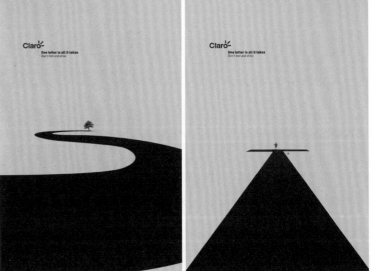

SÃO PAULO   23°31'S   46°31'W   23°   10:00

**Arm Leg /
Mum Dad IOU**

There are 9,000
airports around the
world and every one
has its own three-letter
code. Instead of the
usual travel clichés,
we used these humble
but iconic codes that
we're all familiar
with to promote a
wide range of offers
and specials for the
Expedia brand.

–
Art Director
Mike Watson
Designer
Mark Osborne
Copywriter
Jon Morgan
Typographer
Mark Osborne
Retoucher
Trevor Qizilbash
**Executive
Creative Director**
Gerry Human
**Associate
Creative Directors**
Mark Harrison
Paul Mason
**Chief Creative
Officer**
Gerry Human
Advertising Agency
Ogilvy & Mather
London
Project Manager
Grant Mason
Account Executive
Jessica Wilkinson
**Brand
Communications
Director**
Andrew Warner
Business Director
Stephen Hillcoat
Client
Expedia

CRAFTS ART DIRECTION

LONDON 51°32'N 0°5'W 9° 12:00

JAM With Chrome

'JAM with Chrome' is an interactive website that enables people in different locations to play music together in the Chrome browser on their computers. No matter what level, you can jam together in real-time over the web with up to three other people. Choose one of 19 instruments, from acoustic and bass guitars to drum kits and keyboards. In easy mode, become an instant rock star using pre-recorded arrangements or switch to pro mode to manually play instruments using your keyboard. The project was designed to have a modern aesthetic with a retro touch.

–
Art Directors
Xavier Barrade
Steve Vranakis
Illustrator
Rob Bailey
Creative Agency
Google Creative Lab
Digital Production Company
Tool
Sound Design
Dinahmoe
Client
Google
Brand
Google Chrome

CRAFTS ART DIRECTION

LONDON 51°32'N 0°5'W 9° 12:00

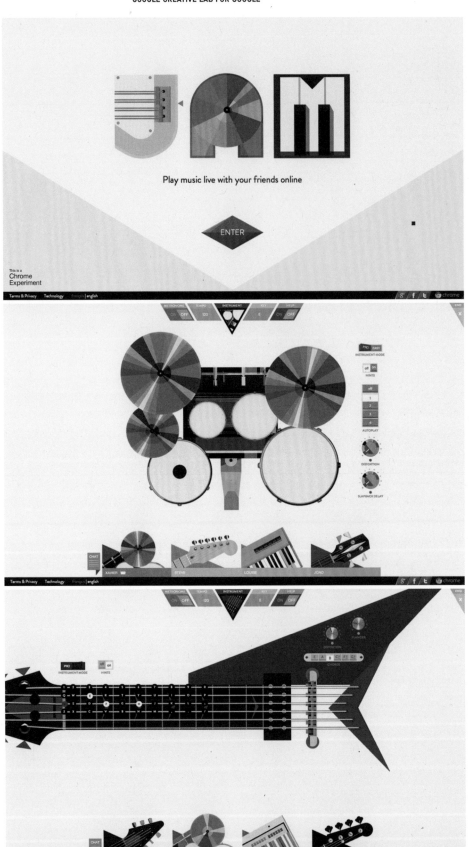

Faktum Hotels

Gothenburg has about 3,400 homeless people. Most of them find a roof over their heads with a friend or at a refuge, but some sleep in the open air. We chose ten of the places where they might spend the night and made it possible for visitors of this website to book them, just like they would book a hotel room online. The money goes to Faktum's work for homeless and socially vulnerable people.

–
Art Directors
Staffan Forsman
Staffan Lamm
Designers
Staffan Håkansson
Christoffer Persson
Photographer
Håkan Ludwigsson
Copywriter
Martin Ringqvist
Interactive Producer
Stefan Thomson
Advertising Agency
Forsman &
Bodenfors
**Production
Companies**
F&B Factory
Thomson
Interactive Media
Sound Design
Plan8
Account Managers
Åsa Pedersen
Linda Tiderman
Marketing Managers
Sara Erkhagen
Åse Henell
Client
Faktum

CRAFTS ART DIRECTION

GOTHENBURG 57°42'N 11°58'E 9° 13:00

CRAFTS CRAFTS FOR ADVERTISING

JURY

Jury Foreman
Tiger Savage King
Tigers Eye
Katherine Hills
Katherine Hills Design
Paul Pateman
Pâté
Adam Springfeldt
Acne Advertising

Pops KV Sridhar
Leo Burnett Mumbai
David Stevanov
Y&R Singapore
Sarah Thomson
Fallon
Tim Vance
AMV BBDO London

●

YELLOW PENCIL IN CRAFTS FOR ADVERTISING, ILLUSTRATION FOR ADVERTISING
OGILVY & MATHER SHANGHAI FOR THE COCA-COLA COMPANY

Coke Hands

Our idea was to bring friendship and Coke closely together in an iconic fashion that would be easily understood by anybody from tier one, two and three cities in China.

–
Illustrators
Eno Jin
Jonathan Mak Long
Art Director
Jonathan Mak Long
Designer
Jonathan Mak Long
Executive Creative Director
Francis Wee
Chief Creative Officer
Graham Fink
Advertising Agency
Ogilvy & Mather Shanghai
Planner
Mark Sinnock
Content & Marketing Director
Stephen Drummond
Managing Director
Martin Murphy
Client
The Coca-Cola Company
Brand
Coca-Cola

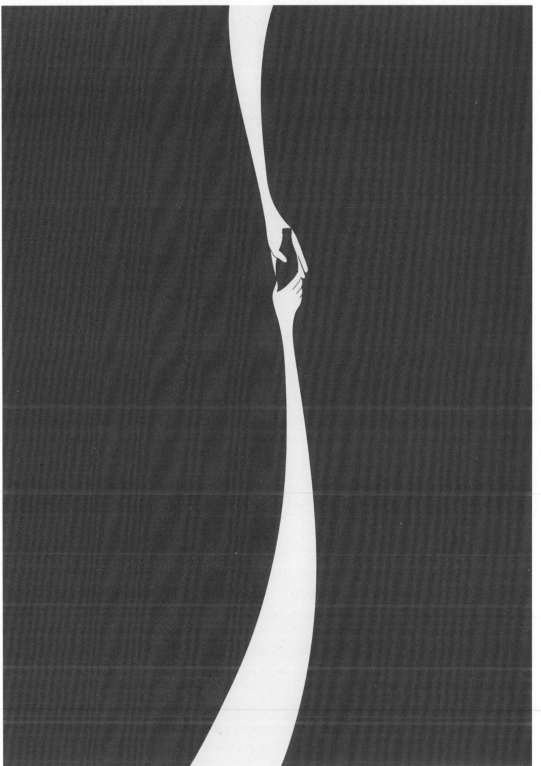

SHANGHAI 31°10'N 121°28'E 15° 20:00

One Copy Song

We helped Adam
Tensta release his new
single as just one –
and only one – copy.
'One Copy Song'
is a facebook app
that allows only one
person to listen to a
song at a time before
passing it to the next
person in line. Fans
signed up to listen
on Adam's facebook
page. Once in line,
they could 'cut the
line' by tweeting,
watching his videos
or listening to his
other songs on
Spotify. Once it was
their turn, fans had
only one hour to listen
and could only play
the song once, before
it was passed to the
next person in line.

–
Music Composer
Adam Tensta
**Executive Creative
Directors**
Chuck Tso
Taras Wayner
**Chief Creative
Officer**
Nick Law
Design Director
Rasmus Wangelin
Designers
Morten Halvorsen
Rasmus Keger
**Creative
Technologist**
Alex Swidersky
Writers
Joanna Crean
Mark Moll
Digital Agency
R/GA
Client
Adam Tensta

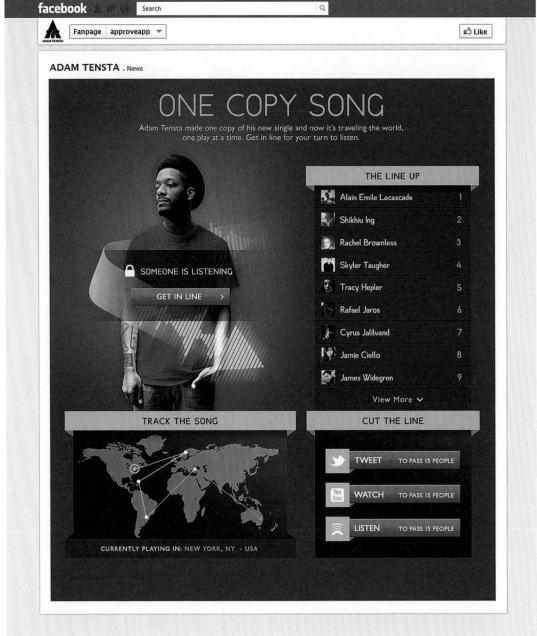

NEW YORK CITY 40°40'N 73°56'W 8° 8:00

CRAFTS CRAFTS FOR ADVERTISING

Dumb Ways to Die

The internet needs feeding. And when you feed it what it wants, it becomes your friend. The 'Dumb Ways to Die' Tumblr site generated huge and immediate viral effect, pushing the campaign onto the front page of the front page of the internet, Reddit.

–
Animator
Julian Frost
Illustrator
Julian Frost
Creative Director
Pat Baron
Executive Creative Director
John Mescall
Art Director
Pat Baron
Copywriter
John Mescall
Producer
Cinnamon Darvall
Senior Producer
Mark Bradley
Music Producer
Oliver McGill
Advertising Agency
McCann Erickson
Melbourne
Production Company
McCann Erickson
Melbourne
Account Manager
Tamara Broman
Account Director
Alec Hussain
Group Account Director
Adrian Mills
Brand Manager
Leah Waymark
Marketing Manager
Chloe Alsop
Client
Metro Trains

CRAFTS   CRAFTS FOR ADVERTISING

MELBOURNE   37°47'S   144°58'E   12°   23:00

Road Letters

**Also In Book
in Illustration
for Advertising**

After we came up
with the concept 'One
letter is all it takes',
we worked on visual
solutions that could
represent the damage
that a simple letter
can have on a driver's
life and the people
surrounding them.
We experimented
with every letter of
the alphabet to see
which letters looked
like a road when put
in perspective. Then
we gave the letters a
slight texture similar
to asphalt. The tree
and human elements
were all made in 3D.
Graphic, but realistic
enough to evoke
danger. The posters
are very minimalist
so that the eye of the
viewer travels from
the letter base to the
potential accident.

–
Typographer
Diego Machado
Art Director
Diego Machado
Copywriter
Hugo Veiga
Illustrator
Diego Machado
Creative Director
Andre Kirkelis
**Executive Creative
Directors**
Claudio Lima
Fred Saldanha
**Chief Creative
Officer**
Anselmo Ramos
Advertising Agency
Ogilvy Brazil
Marketing Manager
Erik Fernandes
Client
Claro

CRAFTS CRAFTS FOR ADVERTISING

SÃO PAULO 23°31'S 46°31'W 23° 10:00

The Ultimate Pencil

In an era of digital advancement where there is an ever-decreasing use of pencils for communication, our brief was to create corporate brand advertising featuring the Mars Lumograph, a product that goes back to STAEDTLER's very origins. We produced two very detailed drawings using only the STAEDTLER pencil to create a level of appeal that exceeds any photography. Drawing a profusion of flowers in bloom conveyed the ability to portray fleeting beauty, while drawing each and every wrinkle on the face of a very old man communicated the ability to portray life.

–
Illustrator
Hideto Yagi
Art Directors
Kozue Kojima
Hideto Yagi
Designers
Kozue Kojima
Hideto Yagi
Copywriter
Dai Hirose
Photographer
Takaya Sakano
Retoucher
Yosuke Mochizuki
Creative Directors
Shinya Nakajima
Hideto Yagi
Advertising Agency
Dentsu Tokyo
Client
STAEDTLER Nippon K.K.
Brand
Mars Lumograph

CRAFTS CRAFTS FOR ADVERTISING

TOKYO 35°40'N 139°45'E 15° 21:00

Corgis

Marmite launched a nationwide outdoor campaign to showcase the limited edition 'Ma'amite' Jubilee jar by playing on the 'Love it or hate it' slogan with the Queen's corgis. The outdoor poster ad featured a twist on the Royal Crest with a pair of corgis reacting to the Marmite and a crown-like rack of toast. The slogan 'One either loves it or one hates it' completes the design, adding a royal twist to Marmite's traditional message. The campaign, which went live on poster sites outside major supermarkets, also benefited from print advertising, experiential activity and digital support.

—
Illustrator
Garry Walton
Art Director
David Mackersey
Designer
Pete Mould
Copywriter
Jonathan John
Artworker
Trevor Slabber
Executive Creative Director
Jeremy Craigen
Illustration Agency
Meiklejohn
Advertising Agency
adam&eveDDB
Client
Bokomo Foods
Brand
Marmite

CRAFTS CRAFTS FOR ADVERTISING

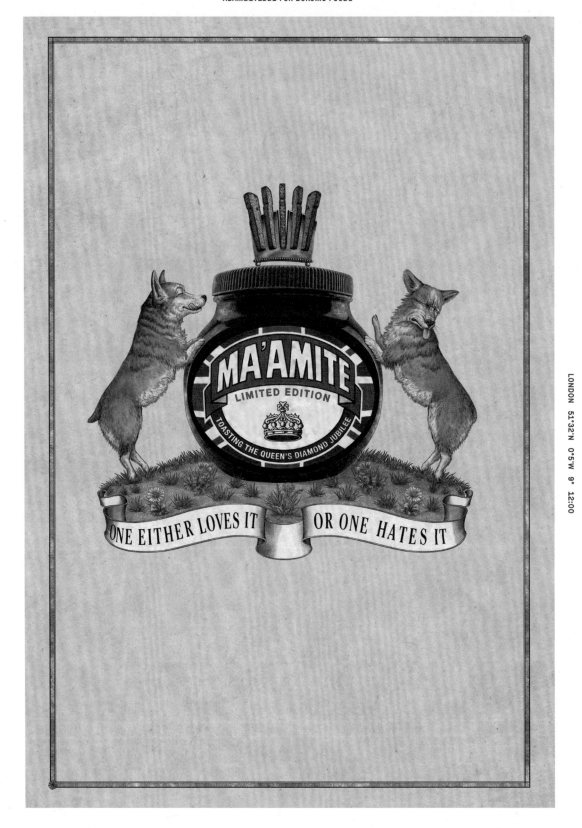

LONDON 51°32'N 0°5'W 9° 12:00

**BlueMotion
Campaign**

**Also In Book
in Typography
for Advertising**

We devised this
campaign to illustrate
how Volkswagen
BlueMotion cars are
designed to use less
petrol, thereby saving
the customer money
on fuel and tax. And
helping the planet
as well.

–
Illustrator
Pete Mould
Art Director
David Mackersey
Copywriter
Jonathan John
Typographer
Pete Mould
**Executive Creative
Director**
Jeremy Craigen
Advertising Agency
adam&eveDDB
Account Manager
Harriet Bates
Account Director
Paul Mitcheson
Client
Volkswagen

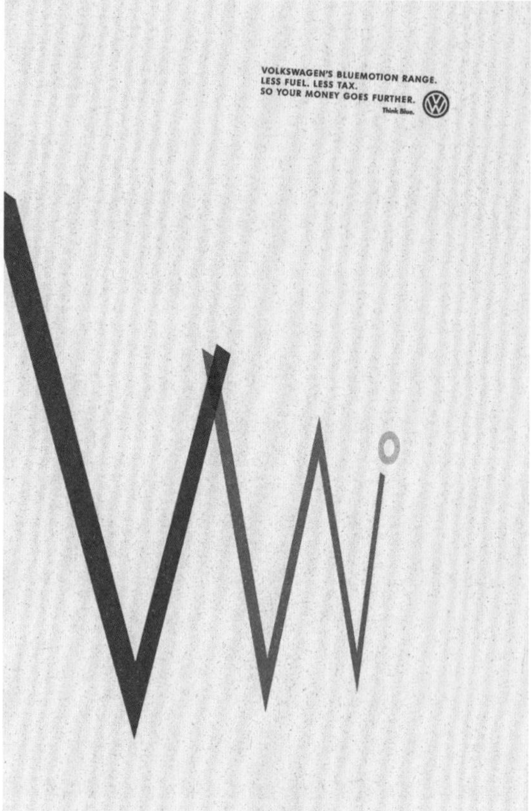

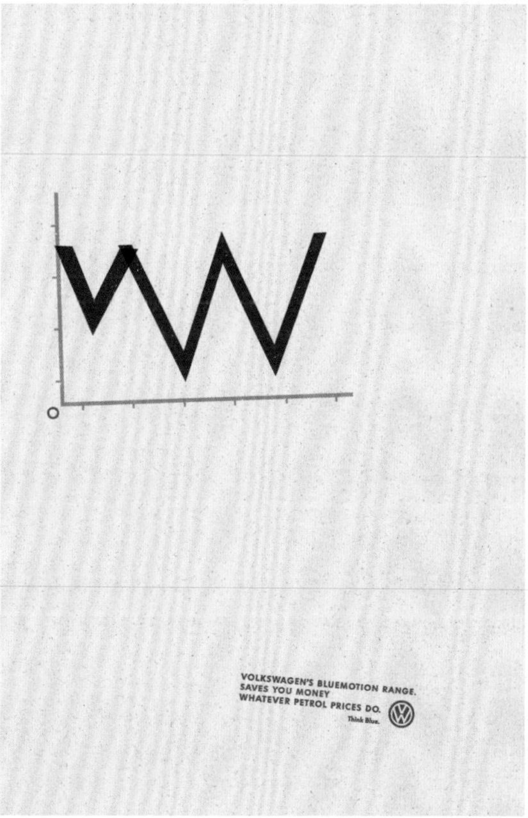

Dumb Ways to Die

How do you reach young commuters who think they will outlive religion? Why not start by breaking every single rule of public safety messaging one could find? A key part of a broader campaign, these cute little dead guys ended up on people's cameras, hash tagged all over Instagram and cheerfully etched in the consciousness of a segment of risk hungry young Melbournians, hard wired to do dumb stuff when and where they shouldn't.

—
Illustrator
Julian Frost
Art Director
Pat Baron
Copywriter
John Mescall
Creative Director
Pat Baron
Executive Creative Director
John Mescall
Advertising Agency
McCann Erickson Melbourne
Account Manager
Tamara Broman
Account Director
Alec Hussain
Group Account Director
Adrian Mills
Brand Manager
Leah Waymark
Marketing Manager
Chloe Alsop
Client
Metro Trains

Say what?!

There's feeling like a foreigner. And there's feeling like something else altogether. When the lines of communication are down, expect the vacant expressions, clumsy gestures, and that uncomfortably awkward moment. This is expressed in our poster campaign for language school Berlitz.

–
Illustrator
KC Chung
Art Director
KC Chung
Copywriter
Eddie Azadi
Creative Directors
Eddie Azadi
KC Chung
Executive Creative Director
Mel du Toit
Advertising Agency
TBWA\Singapore
Account Manager
Joyce Wong
Client
APA Publications
Brand
Berlitz

CRAFTS   CRAFTS FOR ADVERTISING

SINGAPORE   1°17'N   103°50'E   26°   20:00

Japanese

The Museum of Childhood isn't simply a repository for old toys. It lets people understand just how incredible childhood really is, especially that amazing capacity for invention and learning. Through a collaborative process with illustrators, we explored solutions to convey this message on posters. We penned some merry statements that were embellished with vibrant and playful illustrations, and brightened up the streets of London.

–
Illustrators
LouLou & Tummie
Art Director
Thiago de Moraes
Copywriter
Mark Fairbanks
Creative Director
Paul Brazier
Executive Creative Director
Paul Brazier
Advertising Agency
AMV BBDO
Art Buyer
Kirstie Johnstone
Client
V&A Museum of Childhood

CRAFTS CRAFTS FOR ADVERTISING

LONDON 51°32'N 0°5'W 9° 12:00

Axe Anarchy

This is a press campaign to promote the new Axe Anarchy variants 'For Him' and 'For Her'. The campaign depicts a world where attraction reigns and chaos ensues. Shot by Jean-Yves Lemoigne in his trademark colour-rich, hyper-real style, the executions show the moment just before increasingly crazed behaviour causes utter mayhem.

–
Photographer
Jean-Yves Lemoigne
Art Director
Szymon Rose
Copywriter
Daniel Schaefer
Typographer
Szymon Rose
Retoucher
Gary Meade
Creative Directors
Dominic Goldman
David Kolbusz
Executive Creative Director
Nick Gill
Head of Art
Mark Reddy
Advertising Agency
BBH London
Planners
Jonathan Bottomley
Tim Jones
Account Manager
Jennifer Omran
Account Director
Keir Mather
Art Buyer
Jeremy Gleeson
Brand Managers
Ali Kashani
Tomas Marcenaro
Client
Unilever
Brand
Axe

CRAFTS CRAFTS FOR ADVERTISING

LONDON 51°32'N 0°5'W 9° 12:00

**Truck Driver /
Old Lady**

The goal of this
campaign was to
promote Volkswagen
Touareg's Adaptive
Cruise Control, a
feature that ensures
the car automatically
stays at a safe distance
from the vehicle in
front. To show this,
the vehicles were
represented by their
drivers, enacting the
possible results of
a car crash.

—
Photographer
Mauricio Nahas
Art Director
Pedro Rosa
Copywriter
Marcelo Nogueira
Creative Directors
André Kassu
Marcos Medeiros
Creative Directors
Luiz Sanches
Renato Simoes
**Executive Creative
Director**
Luiz Sanches
**Chief Creative
Officer**
Marcello Serpa
Advertising Agency
AlmapBBDO
Client
Volkswagen do
Brasil
Brand
Touareg

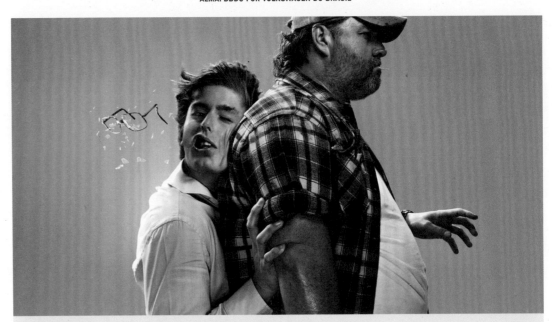

Keep away from the truck driver.
New Touareg with ACC. Maintains a safe distance from the vehicle ahead.

Das Auto.

Keep away from the old lady.
New Touareg with ACC. Maintains a safe distance from the vehicle ahead.

Das Auto.

CRAFTS   CRAFTS FOR ADVERTISING

SÃO PAULO 23°31'S 46°31'W 23° 10:00

**Park Assist
Technology**

We've all been there:
you're searching for a
parking spot and the
only space is between a
rock and a hard place.

—
Photographer
Andreas Bommert
Art Directors
Nick Pringle
Steve Wakelam
Producer
Grant Navin
Retoucher
Matt Bright
Creative Directors
Nick Pringle
Steve Wakelam
**Executive Creative
Director**
Dylan Harrison
Advertising Agency
DDB Sydney
Art Buyer
Leesa Murray
Brand Managers
Loren Elsegood
Peter Stewart
Marketing Manager
Jutta Friese
Business Director
Dave Murphy
Managing Partner
Nicole Taylor
Client
Volkswagen Group
Australia

Park Assist technology from Volkswagen.

Park Assist technology from Volkswagen.

Life Cycle

City dwellers spend much of their day cooped up inside. Yet there's so much more out there to explore and discover. And the best way to do that is on the saddle of a bike. Cycling offers an individual perspective: a city looks and feels completely different when riding on a bike. To dramatise this idea, we created compositions of maps and landscapes from a variety of bicycle parts, encouraging people to break free of their daily routine, and to look at their surroundings in a completely different light.

–
Photographer
Allan Ng
Art Directors
Chris Soh
Thomas Yang
Designers
Chris Soh
Thomas Yang
Copywriter
Andrew Hook
Typographer
Celeste Anning
Creative Directors
Andrew Hook
Thomas Yang
Executive Creative Director
Joji Jacob
Chief Creative Officer
Neil Johnson
Advertising Agency
DDB Singapore
Retouching
Digitalis
Account Manager
Sandy Lee
Client
Life Cycle

CRAFTS   CRAFTS FOR ADVERTISING

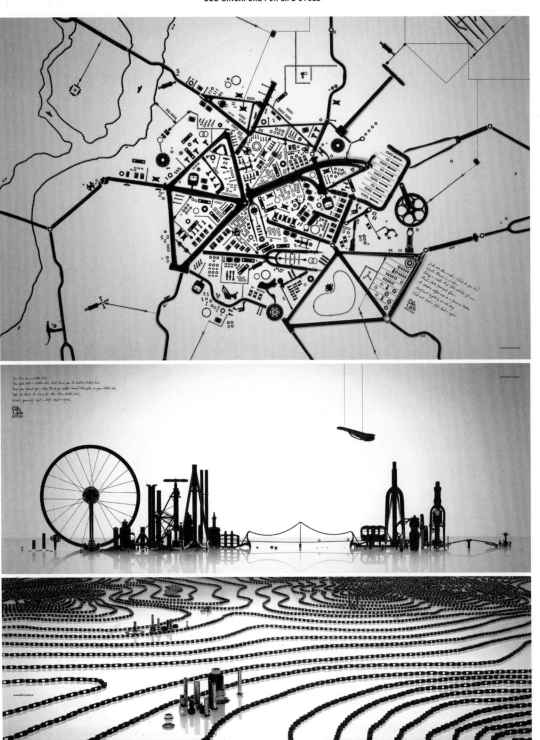

SINGAPORE   1°17'N   103°50'E   26°   20:00

It Never Goes Away

The Center for the Protection of Children's Rights Foundation began its crusade to protect children's rights in 1981. It was initially focused on assisting children who had been neglected, abandoned, physically abused or exploited through child labour. Lately, its area of involvement expanded and it has become involved in fighting the commercial sexual exploitation of children. It now also assists young sexual abuse victims. We announced this in our latest communication campaign.

–
Photographer
Chub Nokkaew
Art Directors
Sanpathit Tavijaroen
Wantaya Thitipaisal
Sompat Trisadikun
Copywriter
Chanwit Nimcharoen
Creative Director
Sanpathit Tavijaroen
Executive Creative Director
Keeratie Chaimoungkalo
Chief Creative Officer
Sompat Trisadikun
Agency Producer
Sarawut Lertkittipaporn
Advertising Agency
Leo Burnett Bangkok
Production Company
Chubcheevit Studio
Account Executive
Nattanan Arriyavat
Account Director
Purita Usnabhiraks
Client
The Center for the Protection of Children's Rights Foundation

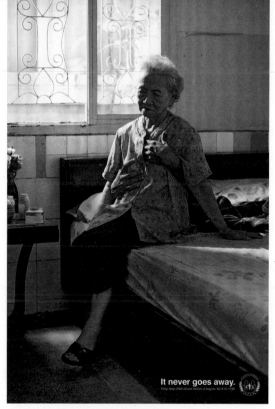

75 Years of Legend

Ray-Ban is a brand that believes people should ignore trends and be themselves. The brand's 75th anniversary was a perfect opportunity to celebrate the timelessness of this belief. The campaign told stories of individuals defining themselves in different time periods throughout Ray-Ban's storied history: two men proudly showing their affection, dancers breaking free of convention and dresses that were shorter. Love in the midst of chaos, freedom and fun, an unexpected artist; moments in time where people chose to be themselves and never hide. Online we told true stories of real people who conveyed the spirit of our print executions for further engagement.

–
Photographer
Mark Seliger
Art Directors
Anais Boileau
Bastien Grisolet
Souen Le Van
Copywriter
Martin Rocaboy
Print Producers
Thomas Geffrier
Ruth Levy
Creative Directors
Dimitri Guerassimov
Eric Jannon
Erik Vervroegen
**Executive Creative
Director**
Erik Vervroegen
**Chief Creative
Officer**
Erik Vervroegen
Head of Art
Jean-Luc Chirio
Advertising Agency
Marcel Worldwide
Strategic Director
Rob Klingensmith
Account Director
Shannon Eddy
**Group Account
Director**
Alberto Scorticati
Art Buyer
Lauriane Dula
**Communications
Director**
Erika Ferzt
Client
Luxottica
Brand
Ray-Ban

The Bronx, 1956

Meet the
Superhumans

We wanted to capture
the Herculean efforts
and extraordinary
achievements of the
Paralympic athletes,
but also the odds
they'd overcome
– emotionally,
physically and
otherwise. 'Meet
the Superhumans'
summed all that
up. The scale and
confidence of the line,
together with the way
it turned any sense of
pity into awe, forced
people to reappraise
what they thought
they knew. The
term 'superhumans'
successfully entered
the vernacular, and
was used to describe
our athletes as heroes.

–
Photographers
The Wade Brothers
Art Director
Pablo González de
la Peña
Creative Director
Tom Tagholm
Business Director
Olivia Browne
Marketing Manager
James Walker
Print Producer
Rory Maclean
Client
Channel 4

Pelicans

The Harvey Nichols Part Sale conjures exciting images of the incredible mayhem that ensues as the collection becomes more affordable. For a fun fresh take on this, we likened it to a plate of freshly poached salmon in the line of sight of hungry pelicans.

—
Photographers
Nok Pipattungkul
Anuchai Secharunputong
Art Director
Kalpesh Patankar
Copywriter
Shahir Zag
Agency Producer
Amin Soltani
Creative Directors
Kalpesh Patankar
Shahir Zag
Chief Creative Officer
Shahir Zag
Advertising Agency
Y&R Dubai
Photography
Remix Studio
Account Handlers
Nazek Fawaz
Zaakesh Mulla
Client
Harvey Nichols

CRAFTS   CRAFTS FOR ADVERTISING

DUBAI 25°15'N 55°18'E 30° 16:00

Arm Leg / Lat Ers /
Mum Dad IOU /
Yoo Wat

There are 9,000
airports around the
world and every one
has its own three-letter
code. Instead of the
usual travel clichés,
we used these humble
but iconic codes that
we're all familiar
with to promote a
wide range of offers
and specials for the
Expedia brand.

–
Typographer
Mark Osborne
Art Director
Mike Watson
Designer
Mark Osborne
Copywriter
Jon Morgan
Retoucher
Trevor Qizilbash
**Executive Creative
Director**
Gerry Human
**Associate Creative
Directors**
Mark Harrison
Paul Mason
**Chief Creative
Officer**
Gerry Human
Advertising Agency
Ogilvy & Mather
London
Project Manager
Grant Mason
Account Executive
Jessica Wilkinson
Business Director
Stephen Hillcoat
**Brand
Communications
Director**
Andrew Warner
Client
Expedia

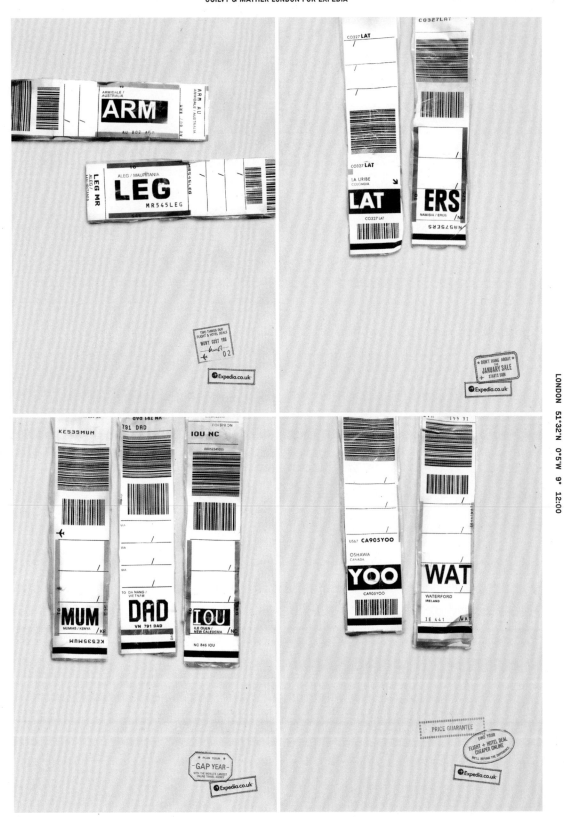

CRAFTS CRAFTS FOR DESIGN

JURY

Jury Foreman
Tom Hingston
Tom Hingston Studio
Noma Bar
Stefan G Bucher
344 Design
James-Lee Duffy
We Are Shadows

Yuri Suzuki
Suzie Webb
SMFB
Ollie Winser
SomeOne

Let's Make Some Great Fingerprint Art

Deuchars takes mankind's oldest and most universal way of mark making, the fingerprint, and shows how anyone can build an endlessly inventive universe around it. The book demonstrates different and surprising ways to create art from fingerprints and hand printing in combination with other art techniques. With subjects ranging from aliens and monsters to Native American totem poles, the book encourages young artists to have fun, but at the same time learn to be innovative and creative.

–
Illustrator
Marion Deuchars
Art Director
Angus Hyland
Publishing Company
Laurence King Publishing
Client
Laurence King Publishing
Brand
Let's Make

LONDON 51°32'N 0°5'W 9° 12:00

Now is Better

'Now is Better' is a series of typographic animations produced for The Happy Show exhibition at the Institute of Contemporary Art in Philadelphia. 'Now is Better' expresses the sentiment that now is the best time to be alive. Indeed, this is the first time in history that large parts of the world population can be in charge of their own destiny. Research also shows that crime – death by the hand of another man – actually decreased in every single century over the last 2000 years. 'Now is better' was created with various materials such as eggs, fish tanks, coffee, and sugar cubes. Typography was captured entirely on camera, with no part of the animation created digitally.

–
Typographer
Stefan Sagmeister
Art Director
Jessica Walsh
Designers
Martin Gnadt
Aline Stieger
Photography Directors
Erik Huber
Matthew Huber
Creative Director
Stefan Sagmeister
Producer
Ben Nabors
Design Agency
Sagmeister & Walsh
Clients
ICA Philadelphia
Sagmeister & Walsh
Brand
Now is Better

CRAFTS CRAFTS FOR DESIGN

NEW YORK 40°40'N 73°56'W 8° 8:00

The Liberation

Danish fashion brand ONLY wanted to interact directly with consumers and make it easy for them to buy, like, pin, tweet and create more traffic to their website. We created 'The Liberation', an online interactive film experience and the world's first on-demand video retail environment. Lune's song 'Let Go' plays throughout the film. At moments when the film is interrupted for user participation, the song blends with a looping soundtrack to create a seamless and tightly synced sound experience. A nice detail is that Lune will always finish the line she is singing even if the user pauses the film.

–
Sound Designers
Johan Belin
Erik Brattlöf
User Experience Designer
Ana Cecilia Martins
Art Directors
Charlotte Boysen
Kenneth Graupner
Mia Lykkegaard
Katrine Jo Madsen
Digital Art Director
Daniel Nicolajsen
Senior Art Director
Jakob Nylund
Creative Directors
Jimmy Blom
Daniel Ilic
Technical Director
Daniel Isaksson
Creative Technologist
Karsten Loewe Kirkegaard
Developer
Einar Öberg
Director of Photography
Niklas Johansson
Director
Christoffer Von Reis
Producers
Mia Wallmark
Kristina Wibom
Editor
Stefan Ström
Artist
Lune
Sound Design
DinahMoe
Record Company
Universal
Digital Agency
North Kingdom
Advertising Agency
Uncle Grey Copenhagen
Strategist
Lars Samuelsen
Account Director
Charlotte Porsager
Client
ONLY Jeans

From Love to Bingo

This ad was created using only still images from the Getty archive, shown at sufficient speed to transform the series into a video that tells a beautiful story. This was a powerful way to show that Getty Images' archive is so vast you can even make a film with it.

–
Animator
Marcos Kotlhar
Art Director
Marcos Kotlhar
Creative Directors
André Kassu
Marcos Medeiros
Luiz Sanches
Renato Simoes
Executive Creative Director
Luiz Sanches
Chief Creative Officer
Marcello Serpa
Copywriter
Sophie Schoenburg
Directors
Denis Cisma
Marcos Kotlhar
Sound Designer
Kito Siqueira
Editor
Marcos Kotlhar
Agency Producers
Gabriel Dagostini
Vera Jacinto
Animation
Split Filmes
Advertising Agency
AlmapBBDO
Production Company
Paranoid
Post Production
Split Filmes
Sound Design
Satélite Audio
Client
Getty Images

CRAFTS CRAFTS FOR DESIGN

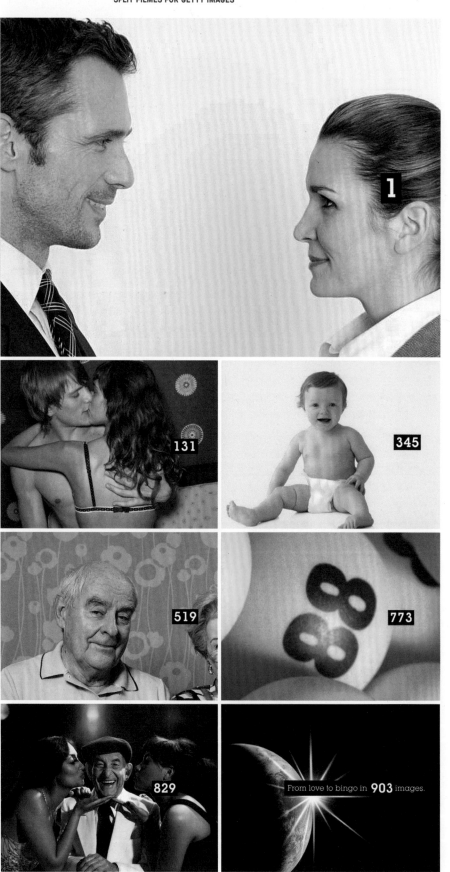

SÃO PAULO 23°31'S 46°31'W 23° 10:00

Toblerone Sculpture

Most people buy
one Toblerone bar
per purchase. We
wanted them to buy
hundreds. So we
created a website
where people could
draw images using
the bar's triangle
shape as a pixel.
When their artwork
was complete, they
could purchase their
designs for a friend
in our online store.
We worked with
a team of local art
students to bring
their illustrations
to life, using actual
Toblerone bars
to build full-scale
models of their digital
drawing. Now,
instead of just one bar,
they were buying
40, 50, or hundreds
at a time.

—
Model Makers
Shanghai Institute
of Visual Art
Art Directors
Kevin Lee
Mike Tay
Zhanglei
Designers
Kevin Lee
Leehom
Tianli Liu
Ling Meng
Rowan Tang
Zhanglei
Copywriters
Ryan Falch
Adams Fan
Photographer
Jason Gao
Typographers
Kevin Lee
Ling Meng
Zhanglei
Visual Effects
Tianli Liu
Programmer
Avenit Software
Editors
Kevin Lee
Tanli Liu
Creative Directors
Adams Fan
Kevin Lee
Producer
Gerald Lee
Agency Producer
Lydia Liu
Advertising Agency
Leagas Delaney
Shanghai
**Production
Company**
Meethepeople
Post Production
LD Post
Sound Design
LD Music
Client
Kraft Foods China
Brand
Toblerone

CRAFTS   CRAFTS FOR DESIGN

SHANGHAI 31°10'N 121°28'E 15° 20:00

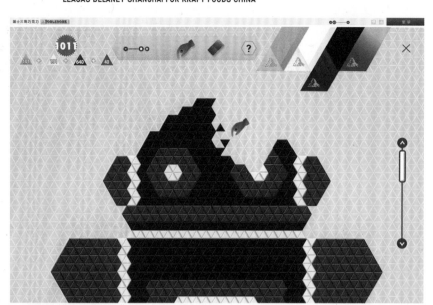

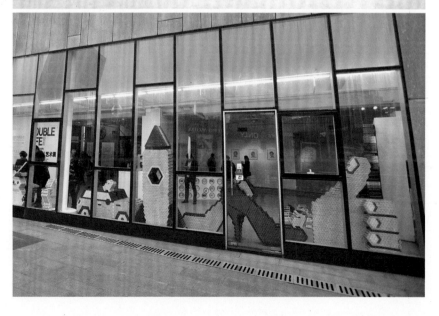

The Mushroom Picker: Penny Bun's Great Escape

'The Mushroom Picker' tells the tale of charismatic mushroom characters thriving in an English wood, and of one heroine in particular, Penny Bun – a rare and spectacular porcini – who evades the mushroom picker's annual autumn harvest. Crafted by a mushroom obsessive, this book reproduces luminograms created by David Robinson in his darkroom using a cameraless process. He arranges hand-cut mushrooms on the plate of his enlarger to create Penny Bun's extraordinary universe. Afterwards, when his luminograms are printed, the fungi are discarded (or eaten), these tableaux never to be recreated.

–
Illustrator
David Robinson
Author
David Robinson
Publishing Company
Violette Editions
Client
Violette Editions

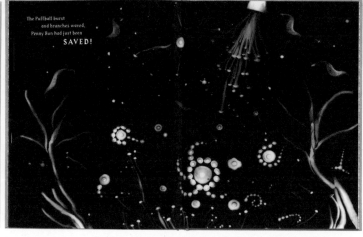

**Advertising
Newspaper Issue 5:
Award Issue**

The Award Issue
of Advertising
Newspaper came out
at roughly the same
time as all the big
advertising prizes
were being awarded
internationally. Its
front cover compares
the advertising award
hunting season to all-
out war. We depicted
award trophies as
militant superheroes
inspired by action
figures from popular
cartoon comics.
The cover came
in three different
colours – gold,
silver, and bronze
– symbolising three
levels of awards.
From observation,
the gold version was
the most popular with
our audience. Many
switched from bronze
to gold once they
realised that a
gold version was
available too.

–
Illustrators
Chootsana
Chotchuang
Thanakrit
Sathirapinitkul
Art Directors
Chutivat Cherdchoo
Wuttikorn
Ekarattanasompop
Graphic Designer
Tanwa Tiammek
Creative Directors
Chutivat Cherdchoo
Thipaporn
Trakulpoonsub
Retoucher
Chutivat Cherdchoo
**Production
Company**
Visionary Group
Client
Advertising
Newspaper

CRAFTS   CRAFTS FOR DESIGN

BANGKOK   13°45'N   100°30'E   30°   19:00

Life is Electric

The brief was to globally rebrand an established Japanese electrical appliance manufacturer. Panasonic believes in the power of electricity and its potential to enrich our lives. The advertising uses hand-drawn diagrams of electric circuits to express the fundamental commitment to craftsmanship at the heart of Panasonic's manufacturing philosophy, and to communicate a sense of anticipation and excitement about the company's emerging technologies and products. With Panasonic, 'Life is Electric'.

—
Illustrator
Philippe Weisbecker
Art Director
Yoshihiro Yagi
Designers
Daisuke Hatakeyama
Taiji Kimura
Minami Otsuka
Haruko Tsutsui
Yoshihiro Yagi
Copywriter
Haruko Tsutsui
Creative Directors
Hiroyuki Takasu
Yoshihiro Yagi
Print Director
Takeshi Arimoto
Producer
Jun Katogi
Creative Producer
Takanori Yasukochi
Advertising Agency
Dentsu Tokyo
Artist Agent
Natsuko Kida
Client
Panasonic

CRAFTS CRAFTS FOR DESIGN

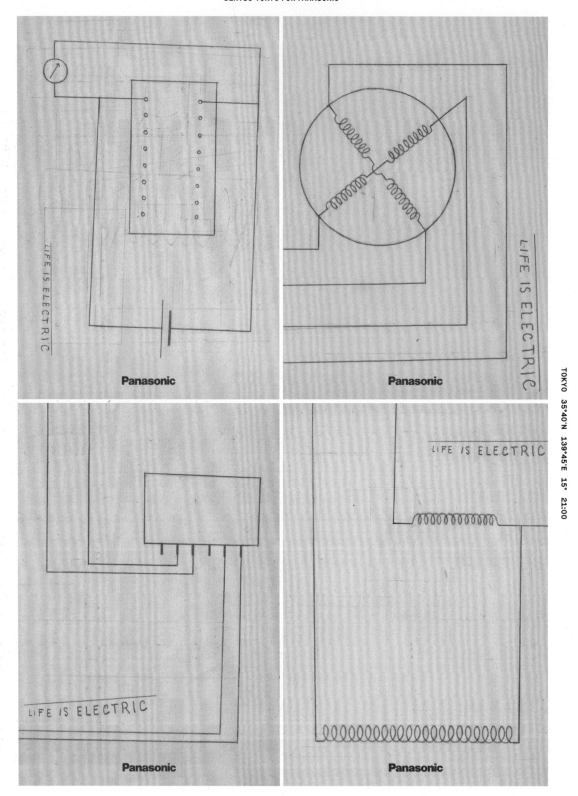

TOKYO 35°40'N 139°45'E 15° 21:00

Onassis Cultural Centre Event Posters

The Onassis Cultural Centre in Athens is a contemporary space for theatre, dance, music and visual arts. This series of posters was commissioned to announce various events in its cultural calendar. The illustrations feature clean-cut single or two-colour gradient coloured shapes as well as black geometric graphic elements such as lines and patterns. These are heavily referenced upon the themes and imagery of each individual show. A rhythm of black lines is used on many of the posters as a nod to the marble lined façade of the Onassis Cultural Centre building.

—
Illustrators
Markos Karellas
Alexandros Nikou
Art Directors
Yiannis
Charalambopoulos
Vangelis Liakos
Alexandros Nikou
Designers
Ilias Pantikakis
Mike Rafail
Design Group
Beetroot Design
Group
Client
Onassis Cultural
Centre

CRAFTS CRAFTS FOR DESIGN

THESSALONIKI 40°65'N 22°9'E 18° 14:00

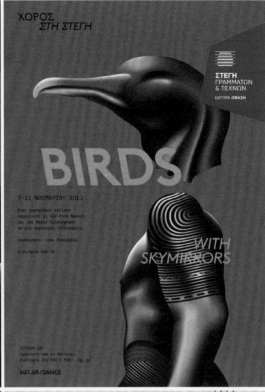

13 Dark Tales

With an aim to re-connect with South African youth culture, our 'Don't be Afraid of the Dark' Halloween campaign for Marmite gave the black spread a twist of horror. We wrote and designed '13 Dark Tales' as part of the campaign. The book featured 13 little-known South African urban legends, illustrated with dark scratchy vintage-style etchings that alluded to characters and scenes from each story.

–
Illustrators
Dani Loureiro
Andrew Ringrose
Designer
Bridget Mclaren
Copywriters
Gisele Human
Craig Walford
Creative Directors
Dani Loureiro
Bridget McLaren
Gareth McPherson
Executive Creative Director
Jake Bester
Advertising Agency
Machine
Client
Bokomo Foods
Brand
Marmite

CRAFTS CRAFTS FOR DESIGN

CAPE TOWN 33°55'S 18°22'E 29° 14:00

The Link
Environmental
Graphics

The Link is a newly opened community centre in South London. It uses an unusual location within the connecting spaces beneath a dual flyover in the heart of Thamesmead. As part of the overall identity for the centre, our brief was to create environmental graphics and wayfinding that would bring this vast concrete space to life in a positive and characterful way. Through workshops with local youth groups we created a series of positive messages that were applied throughout the centre. These expressions established the essence of the project and their playful nature carried on into the wayfinding.

–
Illustrators
Jeffrey Bowman
Denis Carrier
Matt Dent
Andrew Groves
Tommy Taylor
Damien Weighill
Robert Young
Creative Directors
Tommy Taylor
Robert Young
Design Agency
Alphabetical
Client
Trust Thamesmead
Brand
The Link

CRAFTS CRAFTS FOR DESIGN

LONDON 51°32'N 0°5'W 9° 12:00

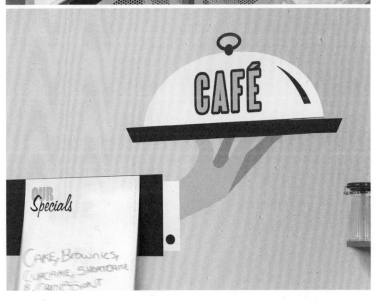

Little White Lies
Issue 42: Lawless

The design ethos for issue 42 was inspired by John Hillcoat's 1920s drama, 'Lawless'. The characters in this film inhabit the mountains of Virginia – a place grappling with the idea of modernity, underpinned by folklore and myth. Little White Lies Creative Director Paul Willoughby explored naive art processes connected with the era and natural elements of the landscape. The decision to hand-carve the images out of plywood was a stylistic and aesthetic one, but the physical action itself was important. It was an exercise in suffering: splinters, blisters, cuts and strains.

—
Illustrator
Paul Willoughby
Designers
Anna Dunn
Fabrizio Festa
Eve Lloyd-Knight
Angus MacPherson
Creative Director
Paul Willoughby
Creative Agency
Human After All
Client
The Church of London Publishing
Brand
Little White Lies

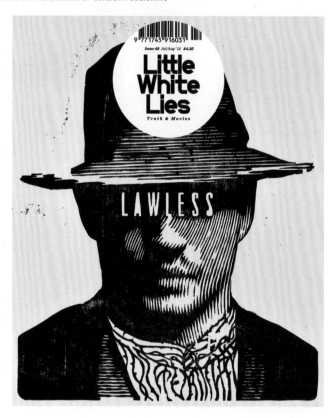

WERK No.19:
CLUB21CDG

This was produced in collaboration with luxury fashion retailer Club 21 to commemorate the opening of the Comme des Garçons Singapore boutique. Each cover in the collection is individually handcrafted and assembled with a patchwork made up of editorial spreads from Club 21 magazines, Comme des Garçons hang tags, and pieces of printed graphics and magazine tear sheets. The covers are then finished with graffiti-style numbers and letters. The outcome is unpredictable and original. The content explores what it means to be a woman in a man's world and spotlights the work of nine independent female artists and photographers.

—
Illustrator
Theseus Chan
Designers
Shermaine Cheong
Geraldine Chua
Design Director
Theseus Chan
Artists
Agathe de Bailliencourt
Julie Verhoeven
Photographers
Juli Balla
Lavender Chang
Wen-Li Chen
Mintio
Alecia Neo
Wei Leng Tay
Debbie Tea
Publishing Company
WORK
Printers
AlsOdoMinie
Client
WERK Magazine

Maki-San

Maki-San is Singapore's first fully customisable sushi store. With a wide selection of ingredients, diners choose precisely what goes into their maki. Using hand-drawn illustrations of mushrooms, avocados, cucumbers and other ingredients, we designed a myriad of patterns which became Maki-San's main visual identity. These motifs were applied throughout the consumer experience – right down to the packaging – to play up the endless and fun options available for diners.

–
Illustrator
Esther Goh
Art Directors
Esther Goh
Gian Jonathan
Pann Lim
Designer
Esther Goh
Copywriters
Joseph Davies
Eugene Tan
Creative Director
Pann Lim
Creative Agency
Kinetic Singapore
Account Handlers
Dennis Lim
Carolyn Teo
Client
Maki-San

SINGAPORE 1°17'N 103°50'E 26° 20:00

Bergen Culture Report 2011

An annual report crammed with numbers and graphs requires an emphasis on legibility and orientation. That's why our goal was to make the reading experience more playful by introducing abstract illustrations to evoke curiosity and wonder. The illustrations are experimentation with techniques that Anti & Grandpeople developed through years of working with creative and cultural clients. The purpose was not to refer directly to the editorial content, rather to represent the wide spectrum of artists and cultural institutions present in the book.

–
Illustrator
Christian Bergheim
Art Director
Magnus Helgesen
Designer
Gaute Tenold Aase
Design Agency
Anti & Grandpeople
Client
The Municipality of
Bergen Norway

CRAFTS **CRAFTS FOR DESIGN**

OSLO 59°57'N 10°42'E 5° 13:00

**Desktop Spine
Totem**

This spine 'Totem' was created to identify publications of desktop, the Australian design magazine, during 2012. The totem graphic is divided into eleven parts, which were rolled out over the months of the year. The totem features were broken down into four parts (forehead/chin, eyes, nose, mouth) so that the spines can be stacked in different ways to create new faces and designs.

—
Illustrator
Paul Garbett
Design Studio
Naughtyfish Design
Clients
Desktop Magazine
Niche Media

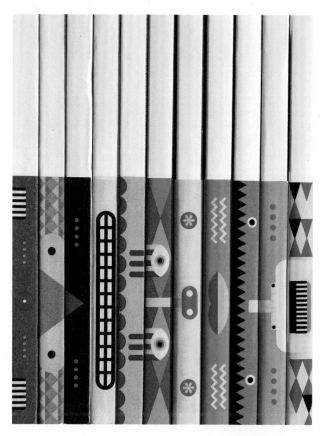

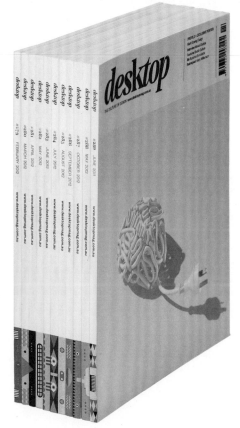

Life is Endless

We wanted to create
an unconventional
poster for funeral
directors Nishinihon
Tenrei. We
represented death
with a skeleton of
pressed flowers. We
rolled out the poster
at venues for funeral
consulting services
and areas near the
funeral homes. Our
client was able to
appeal to customers
with a fresh image
for funeral services.
Customers were
offered a new
perspective
on funerals.

–
Illustrator
Naomi Hou
Art Director
Naomi Hou
Designer
Naomi Hou
Copywriter
Mari Nishimura
Creative Director
Mari Nishimura
**Executive Creative
Director**
Yoshihisa Ogata
Advertising Agency
I&S BBDO
Client
Nishinihon Tenrei

CRAFTS   CRAFTS FOR DESIGN

TOKYO 35°40'N 139°45'E 15° 21:00

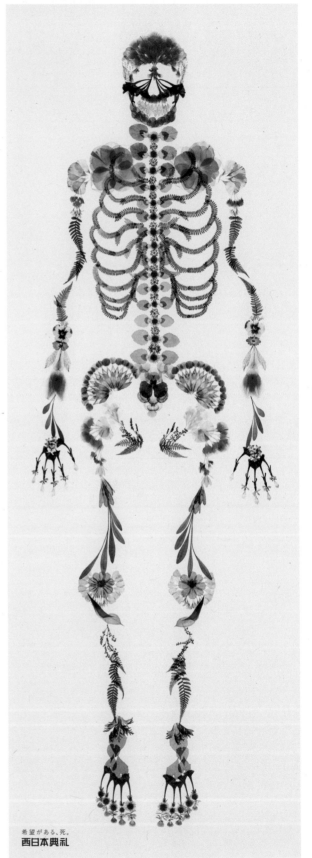

希望がある、死。
西日本興礼

**Bake-off Cake
Posters**

Purpose held an
internal 'bake-off'
competition to judge
the best home-
made cake, with
a prize of limited
edition posters. The
illustrated prints show
a selection of baked
classics including
Battenberg, Tiramisu,
Millionaire's
Shortbread, Cherry
Bakewell and New
York Cheesecake.
The illustrations
were showcased at
the event and were
also used as part of
an internal teaser
campaign.

—
Illustrator
Will Kinchin
Creative Director
Stuart Youngs
Production Manager
Rosie Osborne
Branding Agency
Purpose
Client
Purpose

CRAFTS CRAFTS FOR DESIGN

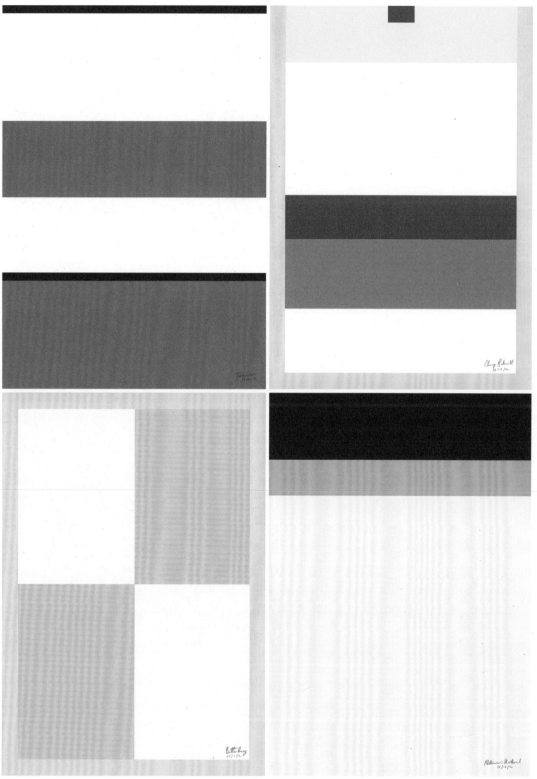

LONDON 51°32'N 0°5'W 9° 12:00

**Louis Vuitton
Yayoi Kusama Book**

We created this book to celebrate the 2012 collaboration between Louis Vuitton and Japanese artist Yayoi Kusama. The book is inspired by Kusama's symbolic polka dots that represent the self-obliteration of one's ego. Aside from silkscreen and die-cut production methods, the three-fold cover uses three different materials, including a paper that resembles the Louis Vuitton paper bag, and also a canvas material. The latter depicts the art canvas that Kusama uses for her drawings.

—
Photographers
Bruno Asselot
Jean Marc Cedile
Kishin Shinoyama
Designers
Geraldine Chua
Ernest Ho
MAA
Farah Siman
Design Director
Theseus Chan
Design Agency
WORK
Publishing Company
Louis Vuitton
Producers
ASHU NAKANISHIYA
Printers
AlsOdoMinie
Client
Louis Vuitton Japan

CRAFTS   CRAFTS FOR DESIGN

SINGAPORE 1°17'N 103°50'E 26° 20:00

Catch the Moon, Catch the Blossom

These catalogues for the 'Catch the Moon, Catch the Blossom' exhibition in London were designed to offer a visual interpretation of its theme: the haiku. The aim of the haiku poet is to catch a particular moment in time. One catalogue explores blossom and the other the moon, using photography and graphics to express the idea of 'catching'.

–
Photographer
Takaya Sakano
Art Director
Yoshihiro Yagi
Designers
Daisuke Hatakeyama
Taiji Kimura
Minami Otsuka
Haruko Tsutsui
Yoshihiro Yagi
Copywriters
Yuko Sugiyama
Haruko Tsutsui
Print Director
Shinya Tamura
Creative Director
Yoshihiro Yagi
Graphic Producer
Hideyuki Chihara
Production Manager
Naotaka Futami
Advertising Agency
Dentsu Tokyo
Clients
Mitsubishi Estate
Sho Office

CRAFTS CRAFTS FOR DESIGN

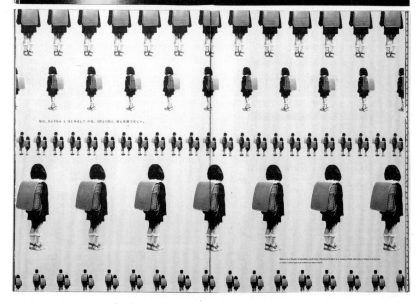

TOKYO 35°40'N 139°45'E 15° 21:00

Shoppyland Logo
Book

Swiss shopping centre
Shoppyland has had its
iconic duck logo since
it opened 35 years ago.
Over the years, the
logo has been used
under different guises
for various ads and
giveaways. Designing
the Shoppyland jubilee
book was a great
opportunity to restage
the logo in a new way.
To show its versatility,
the different ads and
giveaways were
photographed once
again. We invited
more than 30
photographers to shoot
the campaign subject
in their own style, in
order to create a unique
chronicle of the
different faces of
the brand.

—
Photographers
Janosch Abel
Anoush Abrar
Andreas Achmann
Christian Aeberhard
Manuel Archain
Matthias Auer
Sandro Bäbler
Michael Blaser
Croci & du Fresne
Sandro Fiechter
Nathalie Flubacher
Noë Flum
Franziska Frutiger
Daniel Gebhart
Tom Huber
Tamara Janes
Andreas Lux
Pierluigi Macor
Caspar Martig
Sara Merz
Sally Montana
Lea Moser
Stephan Rappo
Tabea Reusser
Regula Roost
Beat Schweizer
Jeroen Seyffer
Cortis Sonderegger
Fabian Unternährer
Fabian von Unwerth
Ulrika Walmark
Ruben Wyttenbach
Yoshi und Annette
Marco Zanoni
Marvin Zilm
Herbert Zimmermann
Manuel Zingg
Ben Zurbriggen
Art Directors
Joel Weber
Roland Zenger
Copywriter
Antonia Bekiaris
Creative Director
Thom Pfister
Advertising Agency
KOMET
Marketing Manager
Karl Gorsatt
Client
Shoppyland
Schönbühl

CRAFTS   CRAFTS FOR DESIGN

BERN 46°57'N 7°27'E 10° 13:00

FABIAN UNTERNÄHRER

MANUEL ZINGG

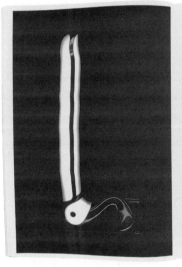
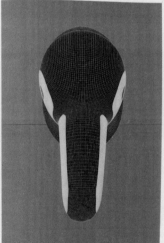

Bat For Lashes:
The Haunted Man

Bat For Lashes' album 'The Haunted Man', in essence, is about love, ancestral bloodlines and heritage. For Natasha Khan (Bat For Lashes), this third album was a long-awaited return to form, so there was a strong sense of stripping away layers of her perceived creative self. New York artist Ryan McGinley was handpicked because of his incredible body of figurative work, its beauty and poetry. Shot in Ryan's studio in May 2012, the man featured in the image was cast from a selection of models whom Ryan works with regularly.

–
Photographer
Ryan McGinley
Art Director
Natasha Khan
Designer
Richard Welland
Illustrator
Zosienka
Record Company
Parlophone Records
Art Buyer
Dan Sanders
Client
Parlophone Records

CRAFTS CRAFTS FOR DESIGN

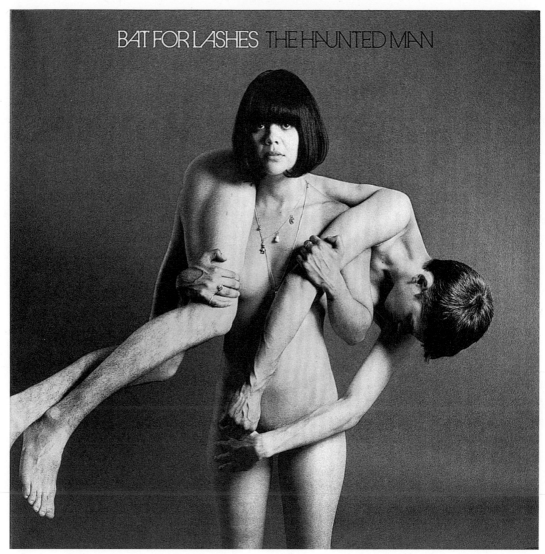

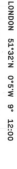

LONDON 51°32'N 0°5'W 9° 12:00

Tamabi

'Tamabi' is a
nickname for the
Tama Art University,
which is one of
the top art schools
in Japan. These
sequential magazine
ads were designed
to demonstrate its
liberalness and the
school's 'Made by
Hands' ethos. A
total of 60 ad designs
helped prospective
candidates imagine
an enjoyable school
career.

–
Typographers
Atsushi Ishiguro
Kenjiro Sano
Designers
Atsushi Ishiguro
Haruna Shibata
Creative Director
Kenjiro Sano
Creative Agency
MR_DESIGN
Client
Tama Art University

CRAFTS   CRAFTS FOR DESIGN

TOKYO   35°40'N   139°45'E   15°   21:00

PechaKucha Night Nagoya

The first PechaKucha Night was held in Tokyo in February 2003 as an event for young designers to meet, network, and show their work in public. Now they are held in close to 600 cities around the world. We were launching PechaKucha Night in Nagoya city. PechaKucha is Japanese for 'chat' so we designed an alphabet using comic-style speech bubbles. The hall was decorated with the posters, and they helped draw a large number of visitors to the event.

—
Typographer
Hidekazu Hirai
Art Director
Hidekazu Hirai
Designer
Hidekazu Hirai
Design Agency
Peace Graphics
Client
Creative Design City Nagoya
Brand
PechaKucha

CRAFTS CRAFTS FOR DESIGN

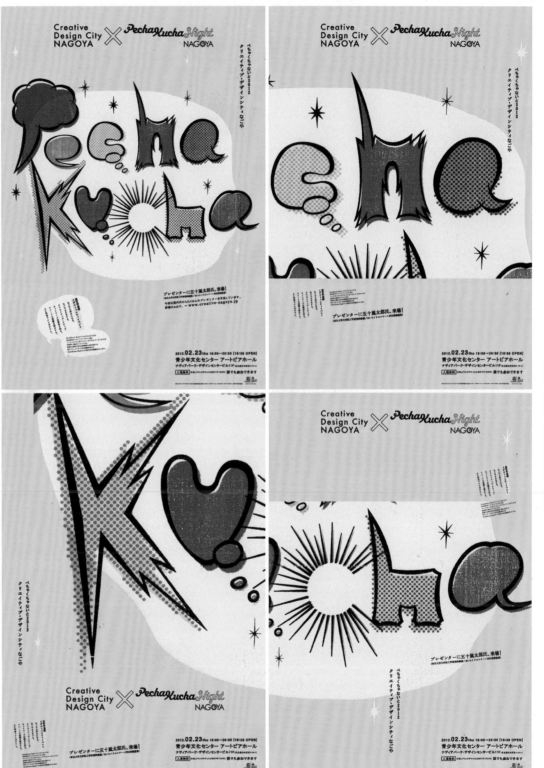

NAGOYA 35°7′N 136°56′E 13° 21:00

WERK No.20: GINZA
The Extremities of the Printed Matter

We injected a new energy into the creation of a set of books, with the aim of heavily distressing them to the point of destruction. Inks and oils were collected from the actual printing process and later used to stain the books, creating unusual colours, textures and scents. We recorded the techniques and intricacies explored in our attempts to push the boundaries of print. Details that are invisible to the naked eye are magnified to reveal the process of finding the perfect imperfect balance. Our motivation is to find humanity, permanence and perfection in a world that has gone digital.

–
Typographer
Theseus Chan
Designers
Geraldine Chua
Ernest Ho
MAA
Farah Siman
Design Director
Theseus Chan
Photographer
Caleb Ming
Publishing Company
WORK
Printers
AlsOdoMinie
Client
WERK Magazine

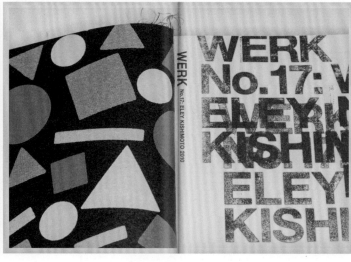

CRAFTS CRAFTS FOR DESIGN

FF Chartwell

Designed by Travis Kochel, 'FF Chartwell' is a fantastic typeface for creating simple graphs. Driven by the frustration of creating graphs within design applications, Kochel saw an opportunity to take advantage of OpenType technology to simplify the process. Using OpenType features, simple strings of numbers are automatically transformed into charts. The visualised data remains editable, allowing for hassle-free updates and styling.

–
Typographer
Travis Kochel
Publishing Company
FontShop International
Client
FontFont

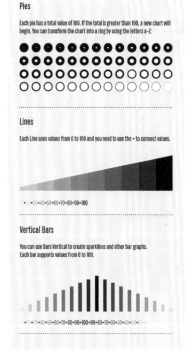
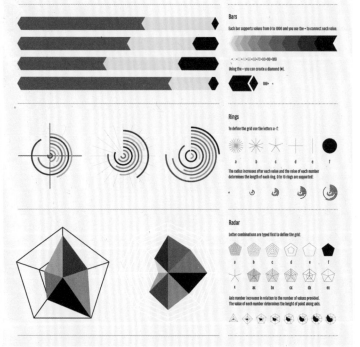

Hairial

This is a custom designed font for an individual campaign. We call it 'Hairial'. It's like Arial went to the salon and got made over all hipster style. Basic crude caps mixed in with a variety of letter details. Down to earth and quirky, this is a font with a whole lot of character (no pun intended).

–
Typographer
Ryan Psaila
Designer
Ryan Psaila
Programmer
Kevin Brown
Creative Director
James Brown
Design Agency
Mash Design
Project Manager
Clare Rohrsheim
Client
Haircare Australia
Brand
evo®

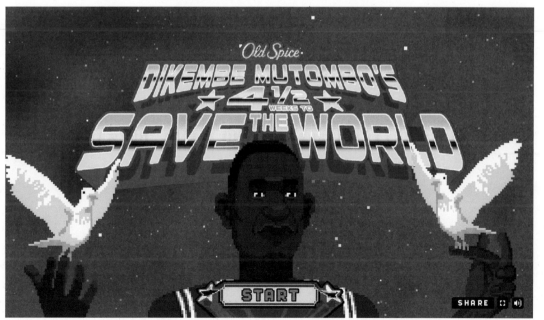

M A S H – HAİRİAL   BOLD

AAAAA-BBB-CCCC
DDD-EEEEÉ-FFFFFF
GGGGGGG-HHHHHH
İİ-JJ-KKKK-LLL
MMMMMM-NN-OOO
PPPP-QQQQ-R-SS-TT
UUU-VV-WWW-XX-Y-Z
† 1234567890 †

! " # $ % & ' ( ) * + , / : ; = ? @ [\ ] ^ _ { } ~ ¡ ¿

M

evo® does not contain: bollox   we: repeat   your: bonus

FOR ALL THAT THE MEEK SHALL İNHERİT, WE CAN AT LEAST HAVE OUR HAİR ●†● GOOD HAİR MEANS GOOD DİET, TİME evo ON YOUR HANDS, A NİCE HAİR-DRESSER, AND EVO® ●†● SO CREAM İT AND THEY WİLL COME ●†● SHOW US THE WAY, BE THE LEAD SWEET EVO® CO. ●†● İF YOU'RE NOT 'İN', WE'LL JUST MUSCLE YOU İN ●†● WELCOME... WE WANT YOU® AND İF YOU® DON'T WANT US WE'LL JUST OUT COOL YOU® SO YOU® WİLL ●†● MOİSTUR-İSER, İT İS JUST VARYİNG DEGREES OF OİL ●†● MEN'S FACİAL CREAM COSTS ON AVER-AGE TWİCE AS MUCH AS WOMEN'S, COS MEN ARE THE NEW SPECİAL! ●†● EVOHAİR.COM ●†●

ADELAIDE 34°55'S 138°36'E 13° 22:30

Dikembe Mutombo

According to the Mayans, the world was going to end on 21 December 2012. In order to stop this prophecy from happening, Old Spice created an eight-bit video game featuring the best defender of all time, NBA legend Dikembe Mutombo. With Dikembe's help, Old Spice fans engaged in a four-and-a-half week battle against numerous evil forces in an attempt to save the world from ruin.

–
Animators
Chris Beaver
Ed Booth
Willis Bulliner
Frank Gabriel
Brad Graeber
Louie Granda
Stephanie McCrea
Kellan Stover
Bruce Tinnin
User Experience Designer
Jake Doran

Art Director
Max Stinson
Creative Directors
Craig Allen
Jason Bagley
Sam Deats
Mark Fitzloff
Matt O'Rourke
Executive Creative Director
Susan Hoffman
Copywriter
Andy Laugenour
Interactive Producers
Mike Davidson
Ben Kendall
Pierre Wendling
Executive Producer
Ben Grylewicz
Animation
Powerhouse Animation Studios
Advertising Agency
Wieden+Kennedy Portland
Development
Driftlab
Account Handlers
Liam Doherty
Jessica Monsey
Client
Procter & Gamble
Brand
Old Spice

'Old Spice'
DIKEMBE MUTOMBO'S 4½ WEEKS TO SAVE THE WORLD
START
SHARE

AUSTIN 30°15'N 97°45'W 15° 7:00

Digital Creativity Guidebook

This interactive pop up book was created to inspire creative professionals with Google's products. Each page of the site displays a beautiful, illustrated metaphor for one of Google's flagship products and services. Navigating through the book reveals complex folding and unfolding interactive elements. Each prop was thought through carefully and designed to fold away in and around dozens of other elements that together make up a single scene. The compositions and transitions were based on real paper folding mechanics to capture the natural and delicate charm of traditional children's pop up books.

–
Illustration
Shotopop
Creative Directors
Emer Stamp
Ben Tollett
Executive Creative Director
Ben Priest
Advertising Agency
adam&eveDDB
Digital Production Company
WeAreHive
Project Director
Mat Agbaba
Account Manager
Justine Deighan
Creative Programme Manager
Reuben Halper
Managing Partner
Alex Hesz
Marketing Managers
Donal Mac Manus
Romain Perrier
Client
Google
Brands
Google+
Google Maps
YouTube

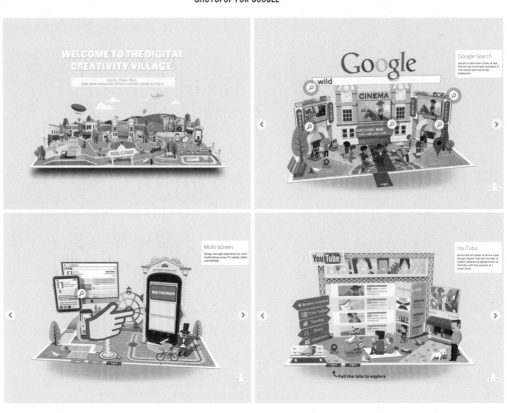

The Sound of Creation

To demonstrate that Philips is 'obsessed with sound' and show music lovers the craftsmanship that goes into making Philips Fidelio audio products, we created 'The Sound of Creation', an interactive musical story. Nine seamless video loops accompanied by a specially composed music loop by American electronic artist Washed Out brought the stories to life. Music visualisations show the amplitude and the number of musical bars in the sound loop.

–
Music Composer
Ernest Greene
Designer
Keith Kornson
Design Director
Robbin Cenijn
User Experience Designers
Joeri Kiekebosch
David Vogel

Creative Directors
Pol Hoenderboom
Bart Mol
Executive Creative Director
Chris Baylis
Director of Photography
Niklas Johansson
Copywriter
Sharon Cleary
Director
Gustav Johansson
Producers
Nikki Haighton
Erik Torell
Fione van Wijk
Agency Producers
Anna Mononen
Bas Muller
Executive Producer
James Britton
Advertising Agency
DDB & Tribal Amsterdam
Project Director
Leon Snelleman
Strategic Director
Peter Hayden
Account Handler
Peter Adams
Client
Philips
Brand
Fidelio

Tree Concert

The city of Berlin loses thousands of trees every year. Friends of the Earth Germany aims to stop this trend. Our idea was a one-of-a-kind charity concert, with a chestnut tree as the musician. We built a special set of instruments at the base of the tree. Each instrument consisted of a steel frame, encompassed by polymer membranes. Internal sensors registered any impact on the membrane and converted the vibration into an artistic composition of sound and light. As leaves and chestnuts fell, the tree could play for its companions and collect donations. 'Tree Concert' gained massive media coverage and led to a new donation record for the preservation of trees.

–
Sound Designer
Philipp Toegel
Art Director
Daniel Schweinzer
Creative Directors
Jan Harbeck
David Mously
Chief Creative Officer
Wolfgang Schneider
Copywriter
Lukas Liske
Producers
Mat Neidhardt
Friederike Seifert
Agency Producer
Michael Pflanz
Advertising Agency
BBDO Proximity Berlin
Account Executive
Monika Groewe
Account Managers
Joris Jonker
Mia Luecker
Client
BUND Friends of the Earth Germany Berlin

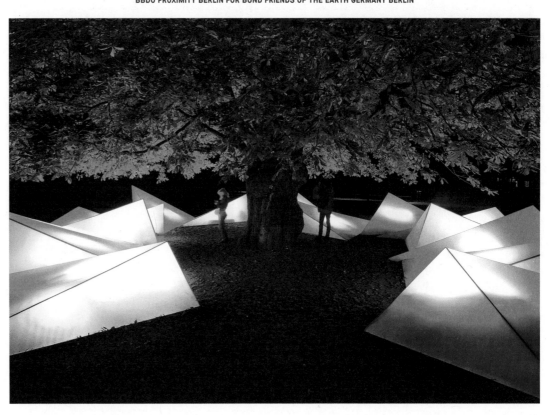

JAM with Chrome

'JAM with Chrome' is an interactive website that enables people in different locations to play music together in the Chrome browser on their computers. No matter what level, you can jam together in real-time over the web with up to three other people. Choose one of 19 instruments, from acoustic and bass guitars to drum kits and keyboards. In easy mode, become an instant rock star using pre-recorded arrangements or switch to pro mode to manually play instruments using your keyboard. Having sampled all original instruments, over ten hours of recordings were edited into 1,200 sound files.

–
Sound Designer
Johan Belin
Art Directors
Xavier Barrade
Steve Vranakis
Illustrator
Rob Bailey
Sound Design
DinahMoe
Digital Production Company
Tool
Creative Agency
Google Creative Lab
Client
Google
Brand
Google Chrome

JURY

Jury Foreman	**Jason Koxvold**
Paul Weiland	**Sergio Lopez**
Weilands	Anomaly
Hugo Allart	**Pedro Pereira**
Mikros image	Sentimental Filme
Gary Cureton	**Sam Robson**
wsd.tv	Factory Studios
Anna Fawcett	**Ezra Xenos**
Filmgraphics Entertainment	Jimmy Lee Amsterdam
Kim Gehrig	
Somesuch & Co	

Metamorphosis

String Theory commissioned Buck to produce and direct 'Metamorphosis' for online bookseller Good Books. The goal of the project was to promote a very good cause: every time a purchase is made from Good Books, all the profit goes directly to fund projects in partnership with Oxfam. We wanted to create an animation that referenced the art associated with the author Hunter S Thompson and the period in which he was prolific, but with a modern and individual approach. The end product is a relentless visual onslaught, a graphic drug-fuelled rant that would, like Thompson's prose, somehow seamlessly hold together to tell the Good Books story.

–
Animation
Buck
Copywriter
Jeremy Taine
Direction
Buck
**Executive
Creative Director**
Jeremy Taine
Executive Producer
Nick Barnes
**Visual Effects
Company**
Buck
**Production
Company**
Buck
Post Production
Buck
Advertising Agency
String Theory
Design Agency
Buck
Sound Design
Antfood
Client
Good Books

LOS ANGELES 34°3'N 118°15'W 15° 5:00

●●

YELLOW PENCIL IN FILM ADVERTISING CRAFTS, CINEMATOGRAPHY FOR FILM ADVERTISING
SENTIMENTAL FILME FOR LEICA STORE SÃO PAULO

Soul

Also a Yellow Pencil in Direction for Film Advertising

We wanted to remind people that some of the greatest photographers in history have used a Leica, and present the Leica M-Monochrom as the reincarnation of those classic cameras from the past. This film tells the story of the life, death and reincarnation of an old Leica III and its owner, a war photographer. The story is told from the camera's point of view.

—
Director of Photography
André Faccioli
Director
Vellas
Art Directors
João Linneu
Bruno Oppido
Copywriter
Thiago Carvalho
Creative Directors
Fabio Fernandes
Eduardo Lima⁺
Head of Art
João Linneu
Compositors
Fernando Rojo
Kito Siqueira
Editor
Talles Martins
Voice Over Artist
Christine Behm
Production Company
Sentimental Filme
Post Production
Sindicato VFX
Advertising Agency
F/Nazca Saatchi & Saatchi
Sound Design
Satélite Audio
Planners
Rafael Paes
José Porto
Media Managers
Sergio Brotto
Lica Bueno
Account Executive
Melanie Zmetek
Account Director
Marcello Penna
Client
Leica Store São Paulo
Brand
Leica

CRAFTS   FILM ADVERTISING CRAFTS

SÃO PAULO   23°31'S   46°31'W   23°   10:00

Prometheus
Viral: David

Also a Yellow Pencil
in Production
Design for Film
Advertising and
In Book in Use
of Music for Film
Advertising

'David' was the
second video to be
released as part of
the online marketing
campaign for Ridley
Scott's feature film
'Prometheus'. In the
style of a corporate
video, the character
of David, as played by
Michael Fassbender,
is introduced to
the world. The aim
was to create online
awareness for the film
by exploring its main
themes and focusing
on a central character.
This gave people a
chance to explore,
share and discuss
without spoiling the
movie. When 'David'
went live it was
hugely successful,
with more than
ten million people
viewing the spot on
the website.

—
Director
Johnny Hardstaff
Art Director
Ridley Scott
Copywriter
Damon Lindelof
Producer
Caspar Delaney
Production Designer
David Lee
**Director of
Photography**
Mark Patten
Visual Effects
Paolo Lonzi
Paul McGeoch
Editor
Ed Cheesman
Music Composer
Drazen Bosnjak
Sound Designer
Joe Mount
Production Manager
James Smith
**Production
Companies**
Black Dog
RSA Films
Music Production
Q Department
Sound Design
Wave Studios
Client
20th Century Fox
Brand
Prometheus

CRAFTS   FILM ADVERTISING CRAFTS

LONDON   51°32'N   0°5'W   9°   12:00

●○

YELLOW PENCIL IN FILM ADVERTISING CRAFTS, DIRECTION FOR FILM ADVERTISING
BIG PRODUCTIONS FOR DOHA FILM INSTITUTE & TED CONFERENCES

Human Arabesque

Also In Book
in Use of Music for
Film Advertising

TEDxSummit
was the first Middle
Eastern TED
conference and a
one-week global
TED gathering.
The goal: to define
the future of 'Ideas
Worth Spreading'.
The summit united
700 TEDx organisers
from 120 countries
in Doha, Qatar. We
set about finding the
'x' within traditional
arabesque patterns
to mashup TEDx
and Middle Eastern
culture. We fused
architecture, dance,
maths and magic into
a bespoke 18 m high-
mirrored structure
that hovered over a
multi-colour moving
floor to create the
world's first human
arabesque. The
experiment resulted
in a kaleidoscope
of infinite
arabesque patterns
choreographed to a
soundtrack composed
by Yasmine Hamdan.

–
Directors
Körner Union
Art Director
Barney Hobson
Writer
Richard Chant
Creative Directors
Richard Chant
Barney Hobson
Agency Producer
Jamie Kim
Artist
Yasmine Hamdan
Music Producer
Michael Kneebone
Choreographers
I COULD NEVER BE A
DANCER
**Production
Company**
Big Productions
Post Production
Mikros Image
Advertising Agency
WE ARE Pi
Planner
Alexander Bennett
Grant
Marketing Manager
Jim Stolze
Clients
Doha Film Institute
TED Conferences
Brand
TED

CRAFTS   FILM ADVERTISING CRAFTS

PARIS   48°48'N   2°20'E   10°   13:00

**Meet the
Superhumans**

**Also a Yellow Pencil
in Editing for Film
Advertising and
Use of Music for
Film Advertising**

Championing
alternative voices
is at the heart of
Channel 4's remit.
This ad captures the
way Paralympians
have triumphed over
adversity to become
elite athletes. We
wanted to jolt people
into seeing the ability
beyond the disability.
Over 90 hours of
footage was cut to
a fine-tuned base of
selects. The powerful
and propulsive Public
Enemy track, 'Harder
Than You Think',
together with the
sound design brings
out the dynamism
of the sport and the
drama of the flashback
sequences.

_

Director
Tom Tagholm
Creative Director
Tom Tagholm
Producer
Rory Fry
Producer
Gwilym Gwillim
Business Director
Olivia Browne
Production Designer
Will Htay

Costume Designer
Wiz Francis
**Director of
Photography**
Luke Scott
**Visual Effects
Producer**
Tim Phillips
**Visual Effects
Supervisor**
Michael Gregory
Colourist
Jean-Clement Soret
Editor
Tim Hardy
Music Composers
Carlton Douglas
Ridenhour
Gary J Rinaldo
Sound Designer
Rich Martin
Casting Director
Julie Tomkins
Production Manager
Simon Maniora
Location Manager
Algy Sloane
**Production
Company**
4creative
Editing
STITCH
**Visual Effects
Company**
The Moving Picture
Company
Sound Design
Envy
Marketing Manager
James Walker
Client
Channel 4

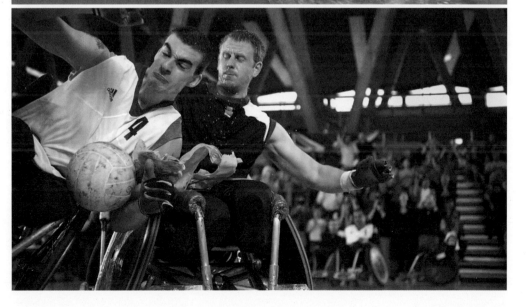

Moreing

Our role was to amp up the little mental-energy kick you get from a boost bar, but our youth audience was difficult to catch and still cynical when caught. So the 'Boosted Inspiration Series' was born; no gratuitous eating shots but loads of tongue in cheek. We made a lot of content. Partnered and co-produced a documentary with MTV. Travelled the world. Created four characters. Invented questionable memes. In part one of the series we meet the inventor of the next big thing – 'Moreing'. In his quest to multiply objects in single spaces, he blurs the lines between art, design, fashion and garden gnomes.

–
Production Designer
James Ting
Director
The Glue Society
(Matt Devine)
Art Director
Cam Blackley
Copywriter
Cam Blackley
Creative Director
Cam Blackley
Executive Creative Director
Duncan Marshall
Creative Chairman
David Nobay
Producer
Alex Kember
Executive Producer
Michael Ritchie
Agency Producer
Paul Johnston
Director of Photography
Stefan Duscio
Editor
David Whittaker
Production Companies
Revolver
Will O'Rourke
Servicing Production Company
ASAP
Post Production
Heckler
Editing
The Editors
Advertising Agency
Droga5 Australia
Client
Kraft Foods
Brand
Boost

4seven

New channel 4seven features the best of Channel 4 from the last seven days. The marque features a '7' within the existing Channel 4 marque, revealed as you pan around a corner. This corner became the visual signature for our idents, created using an innovative mix of angled camera work and CG augmentation and resulting in eye-catching, logic-defying scenes, reminiscent of mathematical artist M.C. Escher.

—
Visual Effects
Jim Radford
Directors
Mike Alderson
Tim Swift
Alice Tonge
Art Directors
Mike Alderson
Tim Swift
Alice Tonge
Creative Directors
Alice Tonge
Chris Wood
Producer
Louise Oliver
Production Designers
Patrick Lyndon-Stanford
Adam Zoltowski
Designer
James Greenfield
Directors of Photography
Olivier Cariou
Bob Pendar-Hughes
Motion Graphics Artists
Douglas Bowden
Rupert Burton
Simon Holmedal
Visual Effects Producer
Julie Evans
Visual Effects Supervisors
Chrys Aldred
Tim Civil
Colourist
George K
Editors
Nick Armstrong
Alex Lee
Sound Designer
Gavin Little
Sound Engineer
Chris Turner
Post Production
The Moving Picture Company
Design Agency
Magpie Studio
Product Manager
Caroline Greig
Marketing Managers
Ros Godber
James Walker
Client
Channel 4
Brand
4seven

CRAFTS FILM ADVERTISING CRAFTS

Allotment

Pool

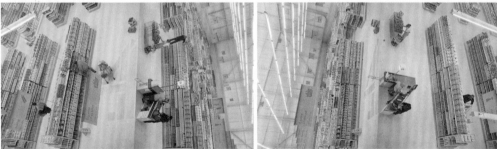

Supermarket

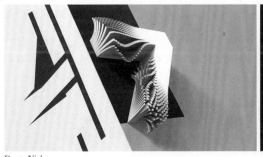 

Day to Night

LONDON 51°32'N 0°5'W 9° 12:00

The Bark Side

In 2012, Volkswagen brought innovation to the Super Bowl once again by creating the first-ever Super Bowl commercial teaser. This set a precedent for consumer engagement that others are now following. Dogs barking the famous 'Star Wars' Imperial March was a viral hit, earning ten million hits by game time and perfectly teeing up 'The Dog Strikes Back' – our 2012 Super Bowl commercial.

–
Music Composers
Jeff Elmassian
Andy Rehfeldt
Director
Keith Schofield
Art Director
Kate O'Connor
Copywriter
Donna Ko
Group Creative Directors
Jerome Austria
Matt Ian
Michael Kadin
Chief Creative Officer
Mark Hunter
Executive Producers
Michael Sagol
Jasper Thomlinson
Agency Producer
Emma Johnson
Director of Integrated Production
Vic Palumbo
Head of Broadcast
Victoria Guenier
Production Company
Caviar LA
Editing
Union Editorial
Advertising Agency
Deutsch LA
Sound Design
Endless Noise
Account Directors
Chris Carter
Rick Schmitz
Group Account Director
Tom Else
Client
Volkswagen

LOS ANGELES   34°3'N   118°15'W   15°   5:00

Beach

Also In Book
in Use of Music for
Film Advertising

'Beach' was the
launch film for
the campaign
'Whatever's
Comfortable' that
debuted online in
summer 2012.
Much like the
Southern Comfort
brand, this campaign
was created to
celebrate and
inspire the awesome
attitude of people
who are completely
comfortable with
themselves.

–
Director
Tim Godsall
Art Director
Jeff Dryer
Copywriter
Nick Kaplan
**Executive Creative
Directors**
Ian Reichenthal
Scott Vitrone
Executive Producers
Shawn Lacy
Holly Vega
Agency Producer
Alison Hill
Line Producer
Rick Jarjoura
**Head of Content
Production**
Lora Schulson
**Director of
Photography**
Eduard Grau
Editor
Gavin Cutler
Music Composer
Odetta
**Production
Company**
Biscuit Filmworks
Editing
Mackenzie Cutler
Advertising Agency
Wieden+Kennedy
New York
Music Arrangement
Good Ear Music
Supervision
Digital Strategist
Marshal Ball
**Head of Brand
Strategy**
Stuart Smith
Brand Strategist
Ben Alter
Account Handler
Karla Stewart
Client
Brown-Forman
Brand
Southern Comfort

CRAFTS   FILM ADVERTISING CRAFTS

LOS ANGELES   34°3'N   118°15'W   15°   5:00

From Love to Bingo

This ad was created using only still images from the Getty archive, shown at sufficient speed to transform the series into a video that tells a beautiful story. This was a powerful way to show that Getty Images' archive is so vast you can even make a film with it.

—
Editor
Marcos Kotlhar
Directors
Denis Cisma
Marcos Kotlhar
Art Director
Marcos Kotlhar
Copywriter
Sophie Schoenburg
Creative Directors
André Kassu
Marcos Medeiros
Luiz Sanches
Renato Simoes
Executive Creative Director
Luiz Sanches
Chief Creative Officer
Marcello Serpa
Agency Producers
Gabriel Dagostini
Vera Jacinto
Animator
Marcos Kotlhar
Sound Designer
Kito Siqueira
Production Company
Paranoid
Post Production
Split Filmes
Animation
Split Filmes
Advertising Agency
AlmapBBDO
Sound Design
Satélite Audio
Client
Getty Images

CRAFTS   FILM ADVERTISING CRAFTS

SÃO PAULO 23°31'S 46°31'W 23° 10:00

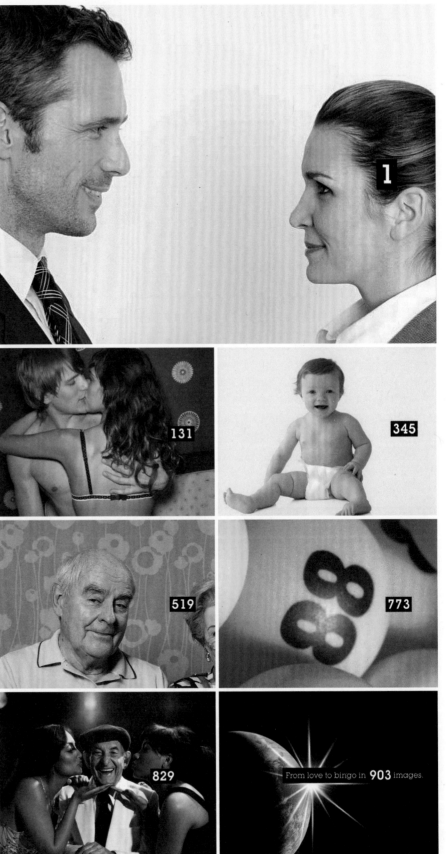

536

Rainbow

**Also In Book
in Editing for Film
Advertising**

Following in the Lurpak saga, 'Rainbow' is a more light-hearted spot to juxtapose with the previous sound design intensity of 'Odyssey'. With the emphasis on fun, but with extremely detailed production values, the trick was to turn cleverly written lyrics into a quality singing performance from Rutger Hauer. Having achieved that, we then created a really tight sound design track, all recorded live as Foley, that would fit seamlessly with the lyrics, until we're left listening to an intense, metronomic and intricate effects composition that acts as the orchestra to Hauer's aria.

—
Sound Designer
Aaron Reynolds
Director
Dougal Wilson
Creative Directors
Dan Norris
Ray Shaughnessy
Executive Creative Directors
Tony Davidson
Kim Papworth
Producer
Ben Link
Agency Producer
Anna Smith
Editor
Joe Guest
Music Composer
Michael Russoff
Artist
Rutger Hauer
Sound Design
Wave Studios
Production Company
Blink Productions
Editing
Final Cut London
Advertising Agency
Wieden+Kennedy London
Planner
Theo Izzard-Brown
Client
Arla
Brand
Lurpak Lightest

CRAFTS FILM ADVERTISING CRAFTS

OUR LOWEST FAT SPREADABLE
MADE WITH REAL BUTTER

LONDON 51°32'N 0°5'W 9° 12:00

Dumb Ways to Die

**Also In Book
in Use of Music for
Film Advertising**

This catchy little
music video
epitomises client
bravery. Not only
did it demonstrate
the client's product
killing the client's
customers, it did so
without mentioning
the client's brand
until the very last
breath. A marvellous
piece of marketing
is the result. As is
close to 40 million
YouTube views.

–
Animator
Julian Frost
Illustrator
Julian Frost
Art Director
Pat Baron
Copywriter
John Mescall
Creative Director
Pat Baron

**Executive Creative
Director**
John Mescall
Producer
Cinnamon Darvall
Senior Producer
Mark Bradley
Music Producer
Oliver McGill
**Production
Company**
McCann Erickson
Melbourne
Advertising Agency
McCann Erickson
Melbourne
Account Manager
Tamara Broman
Account Director
Alec Hussain
**Group Account
Director**
Adrian Mills
Brand Manager
Leah Waymark
Marketing Manager
Chloe Alsop
Client
Metro Trains

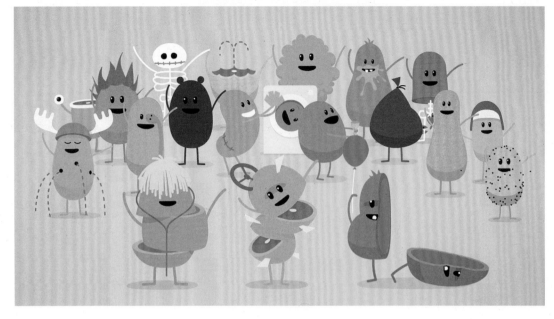

Deaths

This film tells the
stories of how
rock stars like
Rick Nelson, Jimi
Hendrix and Billy
Murcia died in very
unconventional and
'rock 'n' roll' ways.
To tell these stories
we chose a very fluid
and psychedelic style
of animation. The
film ends with the
following message:
'So what about you?
Will you be just
another average car
crash victim? If you
drink, don't drive.
91 Radio Rock.
For a more rock 'n'
roll life. And death'.

–
Animators
Guma
Daniel Semanas
Paulo Stoker
Directors
Guma
Daniel Semanas
Paulo Stoker

Art Director
Rodrigo Adam
Copywriters
Rafael Freire
Leandro Pinheiro
Creative Directors
Rodolfo Amaral
Roberto Fernandez
Ricardo John
Ricardo Marques
**Executive Creative
Directors**
Roberto Fernandez
Ricardo John
Agency Producers
Paula Ferrari
Renata Sayão
**Production
Company**
Paranoid
Advertising Agency
JWT Brasil
Account Handler
Valeria Lopes
Media Manager
Ezra Geld
Client
91 Rock

Made of Imagination

Sony Xperia smartphones are 'made of imagination', so for the global launch we turned to the most imaginative people we know: Wes Anderson and a bunch of eight-year-olds. We asked the kids what was inside Sony phones that makes them special. Then Wes Anderson took one child's story about three tiny robots who record information on themselves, and brought it to life using stop-motion animation.

–
Animator
Mark Gustafson
Director
Wes Anderson
Art Director
Richard Kluver
Copywriter
Ryan Montanti
Creative Directors
Mat Bisher
Jason Schmall
Executive Creative Directors
Sean Bryan
Thomas Murphy
Chief Creative Officer
Linus Karlsson
Producers
Rebecca Bowen
Jeremy Dawson
Agency Producer
Greg Lotus
Editor
Andy Weisblum
Music Composer
Jónsi
Sound Designer
Craig Henighan
Production Companies
LAIKA/house
Moxie Pictures
Advertising Agency
McCann New York
Account Supervisors
Jeff Geisler
Michael Tsang
Account Manager
Jordan Wheeler
Client
Sony Mobile Communications
Brand
Sony Xperia

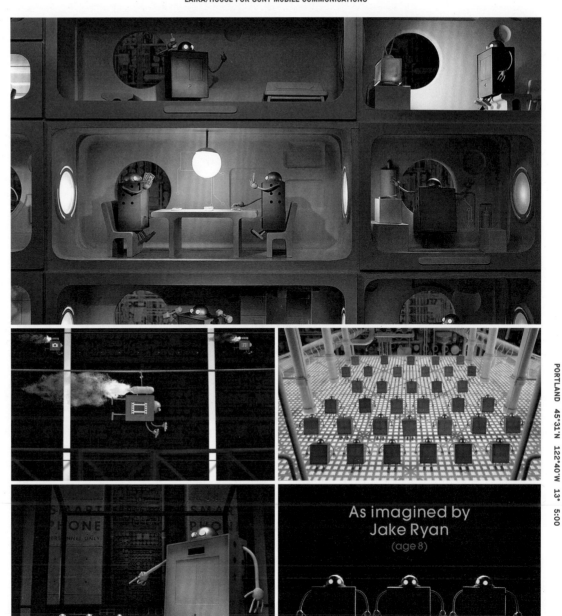

Helpless

**Also In Book
in Direction for
Film Advertising**

This ad tells the
distressing story of a
cancer survivor who
dies as a result of
choking. It highlights
the fact that first aid
could prevent up to
140,000 deaths
each year – the same
number of people
that die of cancer.

–
Cinematographer
Fede Alfonzo
Director
Benito Montorio
Art Director
Charlene
Chandrasekaran
Copywriter
Dan Morris
Creative Directors
Matt Doman
Ian Heartfield
**Executive Creative
Director**
Nick Gill
Producer
Joshua Barwick
Agency Producer
Matthew Towell
Production Designer
Anna Rhodes

Colourist
Jean-Clement Soret
Editor
Andy McGraw
Artist
Sia
Sound Designer
Will Cohen
**Production
Managers**
Mavreen Brown
Beatrice Warren
**Production
Company**
Blink Productions
Post Production
The Moving Picture
Company
Editing
STITCH
Advertising Agency
BBH London
Sound Design
Factory Studios
Planner
Carl Mueller
**Account
Coordinator**
Katie Beevers
Account Director
Emma Brooker
Marketing Director
Scott Jacobson
Business Director
Ann-Marie Costelloe
Client
St John Ambulance

○

IN BOOK IN FILM ADVERTISING CRAFTS, CINEMATOGRAPHY FOR FILM ADVERTISING
SOMESUCH & CO FOR DIAGEO

Paint it Black

'Paint the town red'
is a well-known
English saying,
meaning to go out
on the town and have
a good time. So, to
celebrate Arthur's
Day, the day we
remember the
man who invented
Guinness, we
thought it only right
that we 'Paint the
town black'.

–
**Director of
Photography**
André Chemetoff
Director
Daniel Wolfe
Art Director
Danny Hunt
Copywriter
Gavin Torrance
**Executive Creative
Directors**
Paul Silburn
Kate Stanners
Producer
Dougal Meese

Agency Producer
Rebecca Williams
Editor
Dominic Leung
Production Manager
Madeline Smith
**Production
Company**
Somesuch & Co
Post Production
Framestore CFC
Editing
Trim Editing
Advertising Agency
Saatchi & Saatchi
London
Sound Design
Wave Studios
Planner
Charlie Finnegan
Account Executive
Vinay Chaudhri
Account Director
Miles Burton
Business Director
Andrew Bell
Client
Diageo
Brand
Guinness

Back to Water

Aquatic sports brand Tribord wanted to promote its summer swimwear collection: swimsuits that are designed for practising aquatic sports while making you feel feminine and beautiful at the same time. We used the sea to blur the line between fashion and sport, while giving a more aesthetic dimension to the products and brand. The contrasting conditions of the water reflect that it is the meeting point between sport and sensation.

–
Directors of Photography
Christopher Hewitt
Nicolas Karakatsanis
Director
Christopher Hewitt
Art Directors
Pierre Jouffray
Rayhaan Khodabux

Copywriters
Pierre Jouffray
Rayhaan Khodabux
Creative Directors
Fred & Farid
Producer
Gaspard Chevance
Post Producer
Sacha Adamon
Agency Producer
Karim Naceur
Production Company
Moonwalk Films
Post Production
Nightshift
Advertising Agency
Fred & Farid
Paris-Shanghai
Sound Design
Spock
Account Managers
Alice Lombard
Bérengère Mangin
Brand
Oxylane Group
Client
Tribord

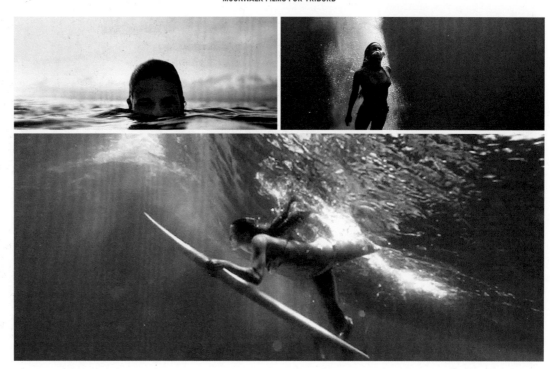

PARIS 48°48'N 2°20'E 10° 13:00

Manny

Hennessy VS and Droga5 set out to introduce the powerful, dark and mysterious 'Wild Rabbit': a metaphor for people's inner drive and ambition. The 'Wild Rabbit' campaign salutes those who never stop and never settle when it comes to reaching success. The 'Manny' ad depicts Manny Pacquiao's personal wild rabbit as a series of subtle shadows and images, which guides him from humble beginnings to boxing glory and a seat in the Philippines Congress.

–
Director of Photography
Linus Sandgren
Director
Johnny Green
Art Director
Alexander Nowak
Copywriter
Feliks Richter

Creative Directors
Maja Fernqvist
Joakim Saul
Executive Creative Directors
David Droga
Ted Royer
Nik Studzinoki
Associate Creative Director
Kim Mok
Executive Producer
Ben Davies
Agency Producer
Sarah Frances Hartley
Head of Integrated Production
Sally-Ann Dale
Designer
Ryan Hoelting
Production Company
Hungry Man
Post Production
The Mill New York
Advertising Agency
Droga5
Strategic Director
Jonny Bauer
Account Director
Steven Panariello
Client
Hennessy USA

NEW YORK CITY 40°40'N 73°56'W 8° 8:00

The Boxer

**Also In Book
in Editing for
Film Advertising**

The old adage 'Time well spent' rings true in this spot for Amstel Lager. Greg Gray and his team went into painstaking detail to craft an epic ad that flows between the past and present, providing a nostalgic slice of life in 1980s South Africa. The final product is an uplifting tale of strength and perseverance, beautifully told.

–
**Director of
Photography**
Paul Gilpin
Director
Greg Gray
Art Director
Martin Sing

Copywriter
Mike Cook
Creative Directors
Mike Cook
Martin Sing
**Executive Creative
Director**
Donovan Bryan
**Chief Creative
Officer**
Felix Kessel
Producer
Helena Woodfine
Executive Producer
Peter Carr
Agency Producer
Helen D'Hotman
Editor
Ricky Boyd
**Production
Company**
Velocity Films
Rivonia
Advertising Agency
OwenKessel
Planner
Erica Gunning
Account Handler
Jesse Rawlings
Client
Amstel

Visions

The film follows four free runners performing incredible stunts in vast and dreamlike sceneries. We see them diving into the ocean, falling through an empty airport, somersaulting across a ballroom, and leaping through a burning building. Or at least, that's how it seems at first. In fact, these backdrops vanish at the switch of a light when someone shuts off the projector and we discover that nothing but their performance has been real. Instead, we've been watching their acts unfold in an abandoned warehouse, which provides the platform for the runners to explore their creative visions. Welcome to the free state of creativity.

–
**Director of
Photography**
Frederik Jacobi
Director
Jaron Albertin
Art Director
Costanza Rossi
Copywriter
Francesco Martini
Creative Directors
Bruno Bertelli
Cristiana Boccassini
Producer
Nick Fewtrell
Agency Producer
Giulia Atzori
**Production
Company**
Smuggler
Advertising Agency
Publicis Italy
Account Handlers
Isabella Rossi
Bela Ziemann
Client
The Coca-Cola
Company
Brand
Burn Energy
Drink

The Stand Up Kid

One in ten young
people have mental
health problems,
and they often suffer
discrimination
from other kids.
Usually this is an
unintentional but
harmful side effect
of kids just trying to
be part of the group.
So we aimed to make
laughing along feel
inappropriate by
making teenagers
aware that friends
with problems aren't
social props – they
are people going
through tough stuff.

–
Director
Tony Barry
Art Director
Robert
Graves-Morris
Copywriter
Dipesh Mistry
Creative Director
Danny
Brooke-Taylor
Executive Producer
Jacob Madsen

Agency Producer
Pete Thornton
Production Designer
Tom Wales
**Director of
Photography**
Theo Garland
Visual Effects
Cath Short
Editor
Rich Orrick
Telecine
Aubrey Woodiwiss
Sound Designer
Jack Sedgwick
Product Manager
Dawn Christy
**Production
Company**
SONNY London
Post Production
The Mill London
Editing
Work
Advertising Agency
Dare London
Sound Design
Wave Studios
Planner
Nick Hirst
Account Handler
Davinia Emberson
Client
Time to Change

CRAFTS FILM ADVERTISING CRAFTS

Skate Fortwo

**Also In Book
in Editing for
Film Advertising**

We were asked to
celebrate the fact that
a smart fortwo city
car only has two seats.
Which makes it a lot
of fun for two people.
So we decided
to film something
that had never been
attempted before.
We asked two
world-class skaters
if it was possible for
them to perform
tricks on the same
board simultaneously.
They set out on
Barcelona's urban
landscape and we
captured the results.

–
Director
Ben Newman
Art Director
Anthony McGinty

Copywriter
Jason Cascarina
Creative Directors
Jason Cascarina
Anthony McGinty
**Executive Creative
Director**
Jeremy Garner
Producer
Oliver Roskill
Agency Producer
Adam Walker
Editor
Thomas Carter
**Production
Company**
Pulse Films
Advertising Agency
Weapon7
Planner
Dan Bowers
Account Director
Richard Maloney
Client
Mercedes-Benz
Brand
smart

Find Your Greatness, Jogger

This is Nathan. He is 12 years old. He's from London, Ohio. Greatness is not beyond his reach, nor is it for any of us. Nike was built on the belief that if you have a body you are an athlete. Our message for the London 2012 Olympic Games was simple: greatness can be found anywhere someone is trying to find it.

–
Director
Lance Acord
Art Director
Sara Phillips
Senior Art Director
Sezay Altinok
Copywriter
Brock Kirby
Creative Director
Alberto Ponte

Global Creative Director
Ryan O'Rourke
Producer
David Mitchell
Executive Producers
Jackie Kelman Bisbee
Mary Ann Marino
Dinah Rodriguez
Senior Agency Producers
Jennifer Dennis
Erika Madison
Director of Photography
Lance Acord
Production Company
Park Pictures
Editing
Spot Welders
Advertising Agency
Wieden+Kennedy Portland
Client
Nike

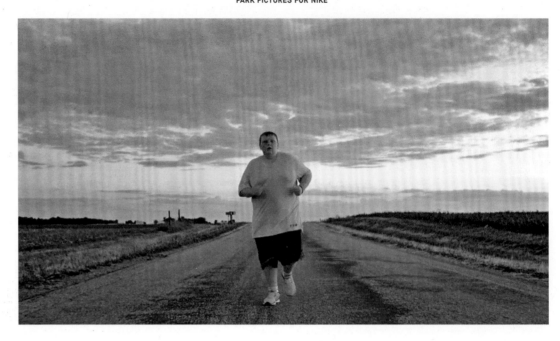

The Truth

This is the Christmas 2012 TV commercial for UK supermarket Morrisons. It aims to engage with the truth that mums in Britain tend to put an awful lot of effort and time into making Christmas perfect for their families. It takes several weeks of hard work for one day of family joy. And is the complete opposite of the perfect, fairytale picture of Christmas that other commercials portray.

–
Directors
Si & Ad
Art Director
Helen Rhodes
Copywriter
Matt Lever
Creative Director
Tom Hudson
Executive Creative Directors
Richard Denney
Dave Henderson

Producer
Lucy Gossage
Agency Producer
Abigail Tarrrant
Production Designer
Nathan Parker
Director of Photography
Alex Barber
Animator
Mark Waring
Editor
Joe Guest
Music Composer
John Debney
Sound Designer
Ben Leeves
Production Company
Academy Films
Post Production
Finish
Advertising Agency
DLKW Lowe
Planner
Alex Huzzey
Account Handlers
James Pool
Alice Tendler
Marketing Director
Rebecca Singleton
Client
Morrisons

Playin' with my Friends

IKEA believes that children are the most important people in the world, and specifically designs products to bring adults and children together. Director Dougal Wilson captures this notion through the imagination of a little girl. Seeing a party through her eyes, the adults are transformed into giant toys. We see the kids and grown-ups use IKEA products and solutions to create the perfect gathering.

–
Director
Dougal Wilson
Art Directors
Danielle Noel
Thom Whitaker
Copywriters
Danielle Noel
Thom Whitaker
Creative Directors
Freddy Mandy
Tim McNaughton
Producer
Ewen Brown

Executive Producer
James Bland
Agency Producer
Craig Keppler
Production Designer
Andy Kelly
Cinematographer
Stephen Keith Roach
Special Effects
Alex Chernogorods
Dan Cowley
Julie Evans
Tom Harding
Colourist
Jean-Clement Soret
Editor
Ed Cheesman
Sound Designer
Sam Ashwell
Production Manager
Beatrice Warren
Production Company
Blink Productions
Post Production
The Moving Picture Company
Editing
Final Cut London
Advertising Agency
Mother London
Sound Design
750mph
Client
IKEA

Three Little Pigs

Also In Book in Editing for Film Advertising and Sound Design for Film Advertising

An ironic retelling of the 'Three Little Pigs' shows how The Guardian remains committed to producing outstanding journalism and giving its readers the whole picture.

–
Director
Ringan Ledwidge
Art Director
Matt Fitch
Copywriter
Mark Lewis
Creative Director
David Kolbusz
Executive Creative Director
Nick Gill
Producer
Chris Harrison
Agency Producer
Davud Karbassioun
Production Designer
Simon Davis
Assistant Agency Producer
Genevieve Shepherd

Director of Photography
Franz Lustig
Editor
Rich Orrick
Music Arranger
Phil Kay
Sound Designers
Sam Brock
Will Cohen
Production Manager
Patrick Bailey
Production Company
Rattling Stick
Post Production
The Mill London
Editing
Work
Advertising Agency
BBH London
Strategists
Lynsey Atkin
Ida Siow
Strategic Business Lead
Ngaio Pardon
Head of Strategy
Jason Gonsalves
Account Director
Alex Monger
Marketing Director
David Pemsel
Head of Sales & Marketing
Richard Furness
Client
The Guardian

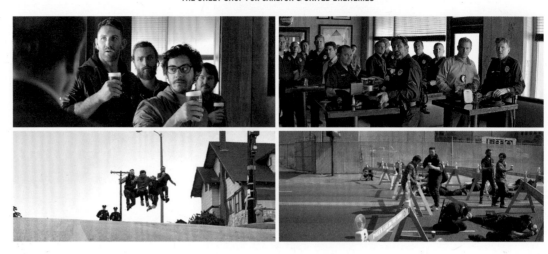

LONDON 51°32'N 0°5'W 9° 12:00

Beer Chase

Building on an already much-loved campaign is no easy task, but Clemenger BBDO Melbourne and director Steve Ayson achieved this with the 'Made from Beer' series. The epic ad uses classic action movie car chases, cops and robbers and a rocking 1980s soundtrack, all with the twist Carlton Draught audiences have come to expect.

–
Director
Steve Ayson
Art Director
Anthony Phillips
Copywriter
Richard Williams
Executive Creative Director
Ant Keogh
Creative Chairman
James McGrath
Producer
Cindy Kavanagh
Production Designer
Robbie Freed
Executive Producers
Sonia von Bibra
Wilf Sweetland

Director of Photography
Greig Fraser
Editors
Jack Hutchings
Nicholas Ponzoni
Edel Rafferty
Music Producer
Karl Richter
Sound Designers
Byron Scullin
Cornel Wilczek
Production Company
The Sweet Shop
Post Production
Fin Design & Effects
Editing
The Butchery
Advertising Agency
Clemenger BBDO
Melbourne
Planners
Michael Derepas
Sam Mackisack
Account Manager
Brendan Taylor
Account Director
Nick Cohen
Brand Manager
Alastair McCausland
Managing Partner
Paul McMillan
Client
Carlton & United
Breweries
Brand
Carlton Draught

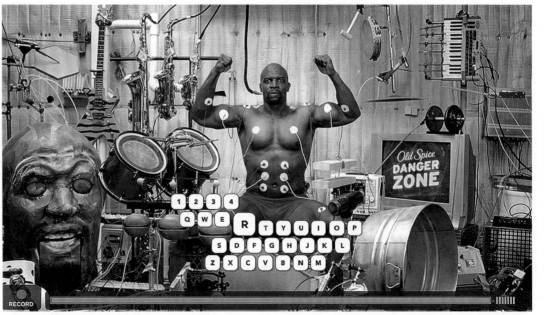

LOS ANGELES 34°3'N 118°15'W 15° 5:00

Muscle Music

Also In Book in Use of Music for Film Advertising

We partnered with Vimeo to create an embeddable interactive player that allowed guys to play custom musical creations using Terry Crews' muscles. These muscular symphonies could then be shared on various social networks.

–
Director
Tom Kuntz
Art Director
Max Stinson
Copywriter
Andy Laugenour
Creative Directors
Craig Allen
Mark Fitzloff
Jason Bagley
Matt O'Rourke
Executive Creative Director
Susan Hoffman

Executive Producer
Ben Grylewicz
User Experience Designer
Jake Doran
Interactive Designer
Billy McDermot
Interactive Producers
Mike Davidson
Pierre Wendling
Production Company
Morton Jankel Zander
Editing
Mackenzie Cutler
Advertising Agency
Wieden+Kennedy Portland
Music Composer
Daedalus
Sound Design
The Mill Los Angeles
Account Handler
Jessica Monsey
Client
Procter & Gamble
Brand
Old Spice

Sensories

All girls expect guys to put in a little effort to keep them happy, but some girls are in a different league. They don't care if you're hungover, tired or whatever, they expect 100% of you 100% of the time. The Axe coloured shower gels have sensory properties that help guys keep up with these girls physically, emotionally and mentally. There are different shower gels corresponding to the different girls in the ads. In each film we hero a guy who is able to keep up with the demands of his girl thanks to the Axe coloured shower gel that he uses.

–
Director
Tim Godsall
Art Director
Charlene Chandrasekaran
Art Directors
Rob Ellis
Emmanuel Saint M'Leux
Copywriters
Dan Morris
Simon Pearse
Creative Director
David Kolbusz
Producer
Rick Jarjoura
Executive Producers
Holly Vega
Orlando Wood
Agency Producer
Rachel Hough
Director of Photography
Stephen Keith-Roach
Editor
Rich Orrick
Production Company
Biscuit Filmworks
Post Production
Framestore CFC
Advertising Agency
BBH London
Sound Design
Factory Studios
Phaze UK
Planner
Tim Jones
Account Manager
Nic Manser
Account Directors
Richard Lawson
Keir Mather
Brand Director
Giovanni Valentini
Client
Unilever
Brand
Axe

High Maintenance

Sporty

Brainy

Flirty

Cable Effects

To highlight the problems people have with cable TV (high prices, poor customer service, unreliable signals) we show the consequences of these issues and offer satellite TV provider DIRECTV as the better alternative.

–
Director
Tom Kuntz
Art Director
Doug Fallon
Copywriter
Steven Fogel
Creative Directors
Doug Fallon
Steven Fogel
Executive Creative Director
Dan Kelleher
Chief Creative Officer
Tor Myhren
Executive Producers
Scott Howard
David Zander
Producer
Emily Skinner
Agency Producers
Andrew Chinich
Lindsay Meyers
Editor
Erik Laroi
Production Company
Morton Jankel Zander
Post Production
Method Studios
New York
Advertising Agency
Grey New York
Planner
Melanie Wiese
Account Manager
Kristen Stahl
Account Directors
Beth Culley
Chris Ross
Client
DIRECTV

CRAFTS   FILM ADVERTISING CRAFTS

LOS ANGELES 34°3'N 118°15'W 15° 5:00

House

Pizzeria

Funeral

Toyota Reinvented

This ad provides a humorous take on potential day-to-day experiences and items that could have been improved: the reinvented couch (that comes in male or female), reinvented rain that makes you lose weight, and the reinvented baby that never requires a nappy change and is also a time machine. The premise of the spot is that good things are always better when reinvented; and the ultimate example is the new Toyota Camry.

–
Director
Tom Kuntz
Art Directors
Verner Soler
Scott Wilson
Copywriters
Marcin Markiewicz
Graham McCann
Copywriters
Scott Model
Matthew Poitras
Creative Director
John Payne

Executive Creative Directors
Chris Adams
Margaret Keene
Associate Creative Director
Jera Mehrdad
Executive Producers
Jeff Scruton
David Zander
Line Producer
Jeff McDougall
Content Producer
Richard Bendetti
Director of Integrated Production
Tanya LeSieur
Editor
Kirk Baxter
Production Company
Morton Jankel Zander
Post Production
The Mill Los Angeles
Editing
Rock Paper Scissors
Advertising Agency
Saatchi & Saatchi Los Angeles
Sound Design
Stimmung
Client
Toyota
Brand
Toyota Camry

The Swan

'The Swan' tells the story of how the cutting-edge Audi concept vehicles of the 1920s have progressed into the stunning and aerodynamically efficient cars of today. Designed by the pioneering Audi engineer Paul Jaray, the prototype car was ahead of its time and its idiosyncratic styling was too futuristic for onlookers. As in the tale of 'The Ugly Duckling', the lonesome Jaray Audi evolves into a confident, sleek, elegant model.

–
Production Designer
Max Gottlieb
Director
Joachim Back
Art Director
Matt Doman

Copywriter
Ian Heartfield
Creative Directors
Nick Kidney
Kevin Stark
Executive Producer
Stephen Brierley
Agency Producer
Ruben Mercadal
Line Producer
Jeremy Barnes
Director of Photography
Jan Velicky
Production Company
Park Pictures
Post Production
The Moving Picture Company
Editing
The White House
Advertising Agency
BBH London
Sound Design
Factory Studios
Head of Brand Marketing
Dominic Chambers
Client
Audi
Brand
Audi A5

Being with You

Over the last few years, condom use among 16 to 24-year-olds has been declining. MTV's Staying Alive Foundation wanted to raise the issue of safe sex and condom use to help reduce the number of new infections. Our strategy was to bring the consequences of having unprotected sex into the moment of pleasure. We show how a young couple, having slept together without using a condom, could have indirectly slept with any number of undesirable characters.

—
Editor
Jinx Godfrey
Director
Neil Harris
Art Director
Andy Bird

Copywriter
Sue Higgs
Executive Creative Director
Gerry Human
Chief Creative Officer
Gerry Human
Producer
Ben Roberts
Agency Producer
Russell Benson
Cinematographer
Nanu Segal
Visual Effects
Franck Lambert
Kamen Markov
Visual Effects Producer
Chris Allen
Production Company
Smuggler
Advertising Agency
Ogilvy & Mather London
Account Executive
Hannah Dale
Account Manager
Hollie Alexander
Client
MTV
Brand
Staying Alive

Night Out

While attitudes to drink driving have transformed in the last ten years, attitudes to driving under the influence of drugs have been slower to change. Habitual cannabis users in particular often feel they can handle the effects without difficulty. That's what this ad sets out to address. Shot like a fly-on-the-wall observation of a night out, the commercial shows how cannabis makes simple things that bit harder to do. And simple mistakes behind the wheel can have terrible consequences.

—
Editor
Jake Walshe
Director
Steve Green
Art Director
Catherine Lennon
Copywriter
Dillion Elliott
Creative Director
Dylan Cotter
Producer
Andy Bradford
Agency Producer
Noel Byrne
Production Company
Sweet Media
Post Production
Screen Scene
Advertising Agency
Irish International BBDO
Client
Road Safety Authority

Jump Rope

Also In Book
In Sound Design for Film Advertising

This film celebrates Californian surfer Kolohe Andino's entry into the surfing world tour. It begins with the rhythmic tick, tick, tick of a jump rope which is Kolohe Andino's signature pre-surfing warm-up. It's a quiet beat that clocks the pace of the film, as layers of Andino's sporting passion unfold with sun-washed and water-soaked glimpses of a young life lived fully.

–
Editor
Mark Hoffman
Directors
The Hoffman Brothers
Executive Producers
Bonnie Goldfarb
Rob Sexton
Line Producer
Chris Berger
Head of Integrated Production
Niko Whelan
Director of Photography
Tim Suhrstedt
Sound Designer
Chip Sloan
Production Company
Harvest
Client
Nike

SANTA MONICA 34°1'N 118°28'W 15° 5:00

Thursday Arvo

Motorcyclists account for just 1% of kilometres travelled in the state of Victoria, but 17% of fatalities. Speeding is the biggest cause of this trauma, so this commercial demonstrates that exceeding the speed limit by a small amount can be fatal. By dissecting a real crash it shows graphically that just 8 km/h is the difference between life and death.

–
Special Effects
Morgane Furio
Scott Hunter
Larry Townsend
Director
Bruce Hunt
Art Director
Peter Becker
Copywriter
Nigel Dawson

Creative Director
Nigel Dawson
Executive Creative Director
Michael Knox
Producer
Catherine Jarman
Executive Producer
Michael Ritchie
Agency Producer
Sandi Gracin
Director of Photography
Danny Ruhlmann
Editor
Seth Lockwood
Production Companies
Revolver
Will O'Rourke
Post Production
Animal Logic
Editing
Method Studios
Advertising Agency
Grey Melbourne
Client
Transport Accident Commission

SYDNEY 34°0'S 151°0'E 22° 20:00

Built to Thrill

'Built to Thrill' conveys the high energy of the Nissan Juke. A motorist's car is built around him while he performs just about every daredevil stunt known to man. The Juke is assembled by a variety of people as it skydives, jumps ramps and scuba dives before emerging out of a tunnel back on to the road. Set to a musical backdrop composed by The Horrors, the spot was shot in South Africa as mostly live action.

–
Special Effects
Antoine Carlon
Laurent Creusot
Christophe Huchet
Julien Meesters
Jean-Lin Roig
Director
Lieven Van Baelen
Creative Directors
Fabio Abram
Braulio Kuwabara
Executive Creative Director
Alasdhair Macgregor-Hastie

Executive Producer
Jean Ozannat
Agency Producer
Maxime Boiron
Line Producer
Louis Saint Calbre
Director of Photography
Nicolas Karakatsanis
Sound Designer
Benoit Dunaigre
Visual Effects Company
Mikros
Production Company
Henry de Czar
Advertising Agency
TBWA\G1
Account Managers
Celina Eude
Eva Gotteland
Gaelle Guillou
Thien-Huong Pham
Account Director
Ewan Veitch
Brand Managers
Arnaud Charpentier
Timothée Gazeau
Elena Karpenko
Bruno Mattucci
Thomas Rodier
Client
Nissan

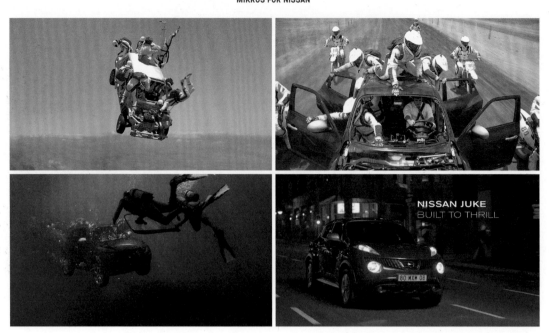

L'Odyssée

'L'Odyssée' tells the story of Cartier's 165-year history. It takes us on an adventure through a dreamscape of legendary inspirations that continue to live through the Maison's creations today. We follow a panther as she encounters various emblems and symbolic locations in seven different tableaux. Each one represents moments from Cartier's origins to the present day, before finally projecting us into the future.

–
Visual Effects Supervisor
Benoit Revillod
Director
Bruno Aveillan
Art Directors
Seyrane Boulekbache
Sébastien Vacherot
Copywriter
Emmanuel Lalleve

Executive Creative Directors
Florent Imbert
Emmanuel Lalleve
Chief Creative Officer
Sébastien Vacherot
Producer
Claudia Traeger
Agency Producers
Pierre Marcus
Patrick Pauwels
Cinematographer
Patrick Duroux
Production Company
Quad Productions
Post Production
Digital District
Advertising Agency
Marcel Worldwide
Account Supervisor
Charles Georges-Picot
Account Manager
Benoit Jehan
Account Directors
Benoit Candelle
Emilie de Saint-Martin
Client
Cartier

PARIS 48°48'N 2°20'E 10° 13:00

CRAFTS FILM ADVERTISING CRAFTS

Spark

'Spark' aimed
to celebrate the
unknown by following
the journey of an idea
from conception to
execution through
the visual medium of
a spark. We follow
the spark across
dramatic landscapes
and see it overcome
the challenges it faces
as it then combines
with other sparks
to culminate in the
conception of the
new Honda Civic.
The challenge was
to give the spark a
plucky character –
the combination of
cold industrial
welding sounds and
warmer, more human
instrumentation
helped give our
spark a voice.

–
Sound Designer
Jack Sedgwick
Director
Martin Krejci
Creative Directors
Toby Allen
Jim Hilson
Sound Design
Wave Studios
**Production
Company**
Stink
Advertising Agency
Wieden+Kennedy
London
Client
Honda
Brand
Honda Civic

Prometheus: Transmission

This is one in a
series of viral shorts
promoting the feature
film 'Prometheus',
showing a
transmission video
of the crew preparing
for their mission.
The sound for
this spot consisted
of snippets of
pre-recorded
transmissions
created by various
characters from the
crew, interspersed
with computational
routines and coded
messages intended
for future alien
encounters. We
therefore had to
strike a fine balance
between cinematic
sound design and
authenticity. Distinct
and believable sonic
styles had to be
realised for each
section, while still
maintaining a
soundscape that
worked on an
aesthetic level
and achieved an
overarching tension
and climactic finale.

–
Sound Designer
Joe Mount
Director
Johnny Hardstaff
Art Director
Ridley Scott
Copywriter
Damon Lindelof
Producer
Caspar Delaney
Production Designer
David Lee
**Director of
Photography**
Mark Patten
Visual Effects
Paolo Lonzi
Paul McGeoch
Editor
Ed Cheesman
Music Composer
Drazen Bosnjak
Production Manager
James Smith
Sound Design
Wave Studios
**Production
Companies**
Black Dog
RSA Films
Music Production
Q Department
Client
20th Century Fox
Brand
Prometheus

Camelot: Heroes Return

Our sound design was created to reflect the abject horror of war as our hero remembers his own experience. The sound design is intended to grow into something unlistenable, something you want to hear ending. Instead of using huge war sounds and explosions, we decided to concentrate on the detail of the smaller, unexpected sounds that are associated with battle and conflict. Soldiers often reference the finer details of sound when remembering a trauma. The final mix solidly conveys the idea of a horrific experience played out from the memory of our hero.

—
Sound Designers
Sean Atherton
Jon Clarke
Anthony Moore
Director
John Hillcoat
Art Director
Adrian Rossi
Copywriter
Alex Grieve
Agency Producer
Olly Chapman
Sound Design
Factory Studios
Production Company
Stink
Advertising Agency
AMV BBDO
Client
National Lottery
Good Causes Fund

LONDON 51°32'N 0°5'W 9° 12:00

Parallel Journeys

This film elevates the everyday journey of India's cricket-crazy youth and athletes committed to reach the playing field on time. Waking up, running, training at the gym, endurance at the nets, hitting the deck harder, chasing the same thing every day, and staying committed to one dream. This journey may be across different landscapes but the destination is the collective soul of every individual pursuit of the ultimate pay-off – the Nike Blue Team India jersey.

—
Music Composers
Dhruv Ghanekar
Taufiq Qureshi
Director
Abhinay Deo
Creative Director
Senthil Kumar
Executive Producer
Apurba Sengupta
Cinematographers
Tapan Basu
Jakob Ihre
Editor
Huzefa Lokhandwala
Production Company
Ramesh Deo
Production
Advertising Agency
JWT India
Client
Nike

MUMBAI 8°58'N 72°49'E 30° 17:30

Guitar Man

This campaign
shows guitarists
playing classic riffs
on guitar people.

–
Music Composers
Geezer Butler
Jimi Hendrix
Tony Iommi
Milton Leeds
Ozzy Osbourne
Nicholas Roubanis
S.K. Russell
Bill Ward
Fred Wise
Artists
Black Sabbath
Dick Dale & His
Del-Tones
Jimi Hendrix
Director
Dulcidio Caldeira
Art Directors
Alexandre Amaral
Gregory Kickow
Copywriters
Patrick
Matzenbacher
Marcelo Rosa
Creative Directors
Andre Faria
Guga Ketzer
Cassio Moron
Producer
Egisto Betti
Agency Producers
Ana Luisa Andre
Karina Vadasz
**Director of
Photography**
Ted Abel
**Production
Company**
ParanoidBr
Post Production
Sindicato VFX
Advertising Agency
Loducca
Sound Design
A9 Audio
Account Handler
Sabrina Spinelli
Client
MTV Brasil

CRAFTS FILM ADVERTISING CRAFTS

Miguel

Ramirez

SÃO PAULO 23°31'S 46°31'W 23° 10:00

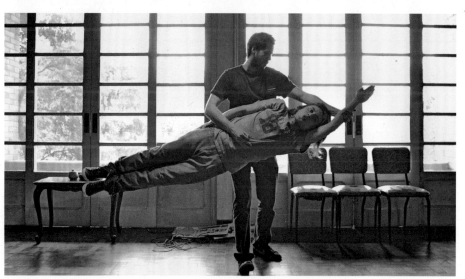

Fabricio

The Journey

This acclaimed spot for John Lewis tells the story of two snowmen. It shows the extra lengths we go to to find the perfect gift for someone we love. The haunting cover of 'The Power of Love' created a national talking point and made the song a number one hit for the second time running exactly 28 years later.

–
Music Composers
Peter Gill
Holly Johnson
Brian Nash
Mark O'Toole
Artist
Gabrielle Aplin
Director
Dougal Wilson
Art Director
Frank Ginger
Copywriter
Shay Reading
Executive Creative Directors
Ben Priest
Emer Stamp
Ben Tollett

Producer
Ben Link
Executive Producer
James Bland
Agency Producer
Lucie Georgeson
Post Producer
Sam Davidson
Production Director
Dougal Wilson
Director of Photography
Edward Grau
Editor
Joe Guest
Sound Designer
Anthony Moore
Music Supervision
Leland Music
Production Company
Blink Productions
Advertising Agency
adam&eveDDB
Post Production
The Moving Picture Company
Planner
David Golding
Account Director
Sarah Collinson
Marketing Managers
Craig Inglis
Lloyd Page
Client
John Lewis

Give a little more love this Christmas

LONDON 51°32'N 0°5'W 9° 12:00

Needing/Getting

In this ad, a Chevy Sonic modified with robotic arms is driven round a desert track lined with 1,157 giant instruments. OK Go singer Damian is singing their song 'Needing/Getting' out loud behind the wheel.

–
Music Composer & Arranger
Damian Kulash
Director
Brian L Perkins
Art Director
Joakim Borgstrom
Copywriter
Brian L Perkins
Creative Director
Joakim Borgstrom
Executive Creative Directors
Jamie Barrett
Hunter Hindman
Associate Creative Directors
Andrew Bancroft
Niklas Lilja
Chief Creative Officer
Jeff Goodby
Music Producer
Dave Fridmann

Executive Producers
Tracy Coleman
Jon Ettinger
Michael Sagol
Jasper Thomlinson
Agency Producer
Dan Watson
Line Producer
Luke Ricci
Production Designer
Bill Horbury
Director of Photography
Yon Thomas
Editor
Doug Walker
Production Company
Caviar LA
Editing
Beast
Advertising Agency
Goodby Silverstein & Partners
Sound Design
Kickstand LA
Account Managers
Julie Evans
Molly McLafferty
Noah Polsky
Group Account Directors
Todd Grantham
Grace Kao
Client
Chevrolet
Brand
Sonic

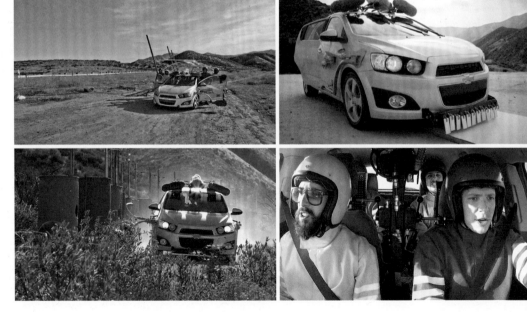

SAN FRANCISCO 37°47'N 122°25'W 15° 5:00

Tesco Christmas 2012

It's the little things that make Christmas special. We wanted to put Tesco and their goods at the heart of the British family Christmas. We took iconic Christmas products and celebrated the moments they enable. In the real world those moments aren't always accompanied by traditional carols and festive jingles. Our bite-sized adverts were driven by music people really play, from T-Rex and Kaiser Chiefs to Lionel Richie and Faithless. Bold, populist and iconic. Just like Tesco.

–
Artists
Adam and the Ants
Faithless
Kaiser Chiefs
Harold Melvin
Queen
Edwin Starr
T Rex
The Crazy World
of Arthur Brown
Directors
James Rouse
Daniel Wolfe
Art Directors
Eddie Fisher
Lisa Jelliffe
Kirsten Rutherford

Copywriters
Charlie Hurst
Lisa Jelliffe
Kirsten Rutherford
Creative Directors
Chris Groom
Stuart Harkness
Executive Creative Directors
Tony Davidson
Kim Papworth
Producers
Marcus Eley
Gemma Knight
Emma Wright
Head of Broadcast
Danielle Stewart
Music Supervision
Leland Music
Production Companies
Outsider
Somesuch & Co
Post Production
The Mill London
Advertising Agency
Wieden+Kennedy London
Sound Design
Wave Studios
Planners
Georgia Challis
Paul Colman
Danni Mohammed
Account Directors
Katja Dienel
Charlotte Evans
Group Account Director
Alex Best
Client
Tesco

Turkey

Hat

Carrot

Party Food

Brandy

Champagne

Pudding

JURY

Jury Foreman
Sean Doyle
TBWA\London
Patrick Collister
Creative Matters
Sue Higgs
Publicis London

Bern Hunter
Wieden+Kennedy Amsterdam
Freddy Mandy
Mother London
Omar Sotomayor
Lápiz Leo Burnett

Dumb Ways to Die

This catchy little music video epitomises client bravery. Not only did it demonstrate the client's product killing the client's customers, it did so without mentioning the client's brand until the very last breath. The result is a marvellous piece of marketing.

–
Copywriter
John Mescall
Art Director
Pat Baron
Creative Director
Pat Baron
Executive Creative Director
John Mescall
Producer
Cinnamon Darvall
Senior Producer
Mark Bradley
Music Producer
Oliver McGill
Illustrator
Julian Frost
Animator
Julian Frost
Production Company
McCann Erickson Melbourne
Advertising Agency
McCann Erickson Melbourne
Account Manager
Tamara Broman
Account Director
Alec Hussain
Group Account Director
Adrian Mills
Brand Manager
Leah Waymark
Marketing Manager
Chloe Alsop
Client
Metro Trains

MELBOURNE 37°47'S 144°58'E 12° 23:00

Sensories

All girls expect guys to put in a little effort to keep them happy, but some girls are in a different league. They don't care if you're hungover, tired or whatever, they expect 100% of you 100% of the time. The Axe coloured shower gels have sensory properties that help guys keep up with these girls physically, emotionally and mentally. There are different shower gels corresponding to the different girls in the ads. In each film we hero a guy who is able to keep up with the demands of his girl thanks to the Axe coloured shower gel that he uses.

—
Copywriters
Dan Morris
Simon Pearse
Director
Tim Godsall
Art Directors
Charlene
Chandrasekaran
Rob Ellis
Emmanuel Saint
M'leux
Creative Director
David Kolbusz
Producer
Rick Jarjoura
Executive Producers
Holly Vega
Orlando Wood
Agency Producer
Rachel Hough
Director of Photography
Stephen Keith-Roach
Editor
Rich Orrick
Production Company
Biscuit Filmworks
Advertising Agency
BBH London
Post Production
Framestore CFC
Sound Design
Factory Studios
Phaze UK
Planner
Tim Jones
Account Manager
Nic Manser
Account Directors
Richard Lawson
Keir Mather
Brand Manager
Giovanni Valentini
Client
Unilever
Brand
Axe

Brainy

Maintenance

Sporty

Metamorphosis

The goal of 'Metamorphosis' was to promote a very good cause: every time a purchase is made from Good Books, all the profit goes directly to fund projects in partnership with Oxfam. Hence, a breathtakingly simple idea: convey the Good Books message in the style of history's most iconic writers. The end product is a relentless visual onslaught, a graphic drug-fuelled rant that would, like Hunter S Thompson's prose, seamlessly hold together to tell the story.

–
Copywriter
Jeremy Taine
Direction
Buck
Executive Creative Director
Jeremy Taine
Executive Producer
Nick Barnes
Production Company
Buck
Advertising Agency
String Theory
Post Production
Buck
Visual Effects Company
Buck
Animation
Buck
Sound Design
Antfood
Client
Good Books

CRAFTS WRITING FOR ADVERTISING

AUCKLAND 36°52'S 174°45'E 15° 1:00

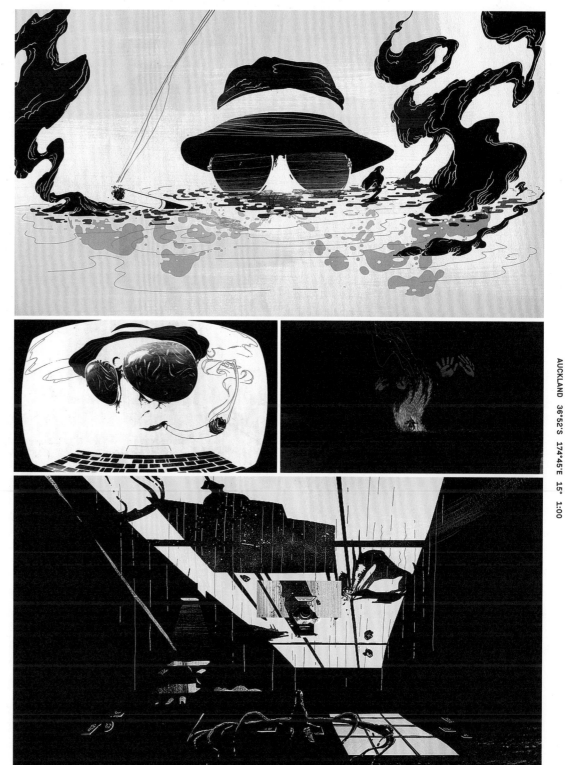

Three Little Pigs

Newspapers are facing an uncertain future. As print circulation and sales continue to fall, more and more people are turning to the internet for information. Our task was to promote The Guardian's new model of 'open journalism' and demonstrate the brand's multi-media credentials as it evolves from a newspaper to a digital-first organisation. The film imagines how The Guardian might cover the tale of the 'Three Little Pigs' in print and online, following the story from the paper's front page headline, through a social media discussion and finally to an unexpected conclusion.

—
Copywriter
Mark Lewis
Director
Ringan Ledwidge
Art Director
Matt Fitch
Creative Director
David Kolbusz
Executive Creative Director
Nick Gill
Producer
Chris Harrison

Agency Producer
Davud Karbassioun
Assistant Agency Producer
Genevieve Shepherd
Production Designer
Simon Davis
Director of Photography
Franz Lustig
Editor
Rich Orrick
Music Arranger
Phil Kay
Sound Designers
Sam Brock
Will Cohen
Production Manager
Patrick Bailey
Production Company
Rattling Stick
Advertising Agency
BBH London
Post Production
The Mill London
Editing Work
Strategists
Lynsey Atkin
Ida Siow
Strategic Business Lead
Ngaio Pardon
Head of Strategy
Jason Gonsalves
Account Director
Alex Monger
Marketing Director
David Pemsel
Head of Sales & Marketing
Richard Furness
Client
The Guardian

LONDON   51°32'N   0°5'W   9°   12:00

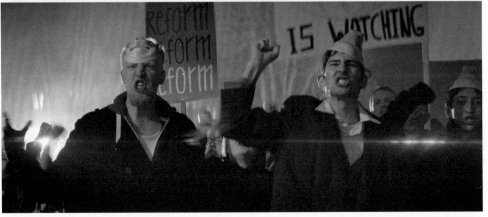

Thanks for the Warm-up

As the London 2012 Olympics came to a close, we launched this cheeky line reminding people that the Paralympic Games were yet to come. The ad appeared in a national poster campaign as well as tactically in papers around news of the Olympic Closing Ceremony.

–
Copywriter
Claire Watson
Designer
Lincoln Grice
Creative Director
Tom Tagholm
Producers
Aymeric Gauvain
Rory Maclean
Business Director
Olivia Browne
Client
Channel 4

The Stand Up Kid

One in ten young people have mental health problems and they often suffer discrimination from other kids. Usually this is an unintentional but harmful side effect of kids just trying to be part of the group. So we aimed to make laughing along feel inappropriate by making teenagers aware that friends with problems aren't social props – they are people going through tough stuff.

–
Copywriter
Dipesh Mistry
Director
Tony Barry
Art Director
Robert Graves-Morris
Creative Director
Danny Brooke-Taylor
Executive Producer
Jacob Madsen

Agency Producer
Pete Thornton
Production Designer
Tom Wales
Director of Photography
Theo Garland
Visual Effects
Cath Short
Editor
Rich Orrick
Telecine
Aubrey Woodiwiss
Sound Designer
Jack Sedgwick
Product Manager
Dawn Christy
Production Company
SONNY London
Advertising Agency
Dare London
Post Production
The Mill London
Editing
Work
Sound Design
Wave Studios
Planner
Nick Hirst
Account Handler
Davinia Emberson
Client
Time to Change

l'il clickers®

Buyral

In 2012, john st. released a video titled 'Buyral' about a professional clicking service you pay to make your videos go viral. The self-promotion poked fun at how far clients and agencies will go to get views. Within days it had gone viral itself. In under a week it had over half a million views, reached number seven on the Global Ads chart and received international coverage – including the LA Times, Huffington Post, Mashable, Buzzfeed and Al Jazeera Europe. We also received 20,000 visits and more than 500 emails at buyral.ca. And we didn't pay for a single click.

–
Copywriter
Kurt Mills
Directors
Will Beauchamp
Jamie Cussen
Art Director
Kyle Lamb

Executive Creative Directors
Stephen Jurisic
Angus Tucker
Agency Producer
Dale Giffen
Web Producer
Marc Cattapan
Production Designer
Yim Hung Kung
Head of Integrated Production
Mavis Huntley
Directors of Photography
Maya Bankovic
Mikhail Petrenko
Editor
Chris Murphy
Production Company
Aircastle Films
Advertising Agency
john st.
Post Production
TOPIX
Visual Effects Company
Alter Ego
Editing
Relish Editing
Sound Design
Vapor Music
Client
john st.

Yeah, That Kind of Rich: Writers' Room

When you win New York Powerball's jackpot you're more than just wealthy, you're the kind of rich that hires Andy Richter and a team of comedy writers to sit in a room all day feeding you jokes through an earpiece. 'Yeah, that kind of rich.'

–
Copywriter
Scott Cooney
Director
David Shane
Art Director
Sean Labounty
Group Creative Directors
Richard Sharp
Mike Sullivan

Chief Creative Officer
Matt Eastwood
Executive Producers
Walter Brindak
Ed Zazzera
Production Company
O Positive
Advertising Agency
DDB New York
Editing
Cutting Room
Account Director
Leo Mamorsky
Client
NY Lottery
Brand
Powerball

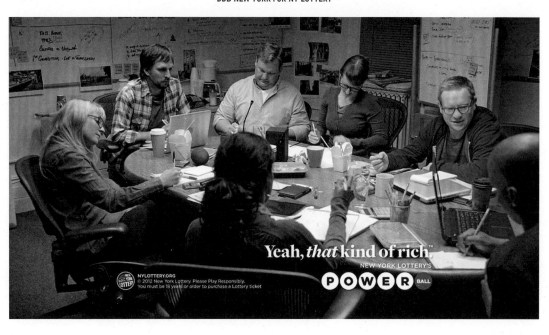

Chav Tranquiliser

The 'We Hear You' campaign saw bookmaker Paddy Power respond to sports fans' facebook comments and tweets in a variety of mischievous ways. One particular fan's facebook worry about troublemakers ruining the world-famous Cheltenham horse racing festival led to this online film featuring a vet using a tranquiliser gun to take down the 'chavs'. The action is encouraged and applauded by a Paddy Power commentator.

–
Copywriter
Bertie Scrase
Directors
Big Red Button
Art Director
Christen Brestrup

Creative Directors
Matt Gooden
Ben Walker
Producer
Barty Dearden
Executive Producer
Dawn Laren
Agency Producer
Joe Bagnall
Director of Photography
Stein Stie
Editor
Ben Harrex
Production Company
Moxie Pictures London
Advertising Agency
CP+B London
Post Production
Absolute Post
Final Cut London
Sound Design
750 MPH
Client
Paddy Power

It's Not Crazy, it's Sports: The Name

Whenever anyone hears the name Michael Jordan, they can't help but think of the greatest basketball player and arguably the most famous athlete of all time. However, there happen to be 3,024 other people in the United States who are also named Michael Jordan and who are not the most famous basketball player of all time. In this spot, we focus on one of the other Michael Jordans: an ordinary man, saddled with a legendary name.

–
Copywriters
Dave Canning
Lauren Costa
Director
Tim Godsall
Art Director
Cyrus Coulter
Creative Directors
Brandon Henderson
Stuart Jennings

Executive Creative Directors
Ian Reichenthal
Scott Vitrone
Executive Producers
Shawn Lacy
Holly Vega
Agency Producers
Kelly Dage
Temma Shoaf
Line Producer
Rick Jarjoura
Head of Content Production
Lora Schulson
Production Company
Biscuit Filmworks
Advertising Agency
Wieden+Kennedy New York
Account Executive
Mark Williams
Account Supervisor
Brian D'Entremont
Account Director
Casey Bernard
Group Account Director
Brandon Pracht
Brand Strategist
Jason Gingold
Client
ESPN

YNWYH Twitter Campaign

For the UK launch of Snickers' global campaign, You're Not You When You're Hungry, we used Twitter. We asked five celebrities to post a series of out-of-character tweets. As we'd hoped, this produced widespread confusion, with numerous replies and retweets. Each celebrity then tweeted a picture of themselves eating a Snickers, together with the campaign line. In all, just 25 tweets were posted, but the campaign received significant coverage online, in newspapers, on radio and TV – and was even mentioned during a debate in the House of Commons.

–
Copywriter
Tim Riley
Creative Directors
Alex Grieve
Adrian Rossi
Executive Creative Director
Paul Brazier
Advertising Agency
AMV BBDO
Production Company
Nomadic Films
Social Community Manager
Naomi Martin
Social Community Director
Paul McCrudden
Account Manager
Bobbie Gannon
Business Affairs Manager
Michelle Holmes
Client
MasterFoods
Brand
Snickers

Katie Price/Jordan @MissKatiePrice
Great news about China's latest GDP figures!!

Katie Price/Jordan @MissKatiePrice
Large scale quantitative easing in 2012 could distort liquidity of govt. bond market. #justsayin

Katie Price/Jordan @MissKatiePrice
You're not you when you're hungry @snickersUk #hungryspon
lockerz.com/s/177408824

Ian Botham @BeefyBotham
You're not you when you're hungry @ snickersUK #hungry#spon
pic.twitter.com/pzI6qV7o
Hide photo

powered by Photobucket   Flag this media

2 RETWEETS   3 FAVORITES

12:55 PM - 21 Jan 12 via Twitter for iPhone · Details
Reply Retweet Favorite

Ian Botham @BeefyBotham   21 Jan
The cello is, of course, derived from other C18 bowed instruments like the viola de gamba and the smaller, squarer viola de braccio. <3!!!

Ian Botham @BeefyBotham   21 Jan
OMG check out Pierre Fournier. This dude ROCKS !!! Great bowing technique !!!

Ian Botham @BeefyBotham   21 Jan
Lovin that Haydn Concerto in D Major !!! #profound

Ian Botham @BeefyBotham   21 Jan
The cello can convey a depth of feeling and sensitivity that few other instruments can summon. Dontcha think ?

Ian Botham @BeefyBotham   21 Jan
Decided to learn the cello.

Work for Will

AT&T launched the sale of the Nokia Lumia 920, a new Windows 8 phone with customisable live tiles providing you with everything you need – like the ultimate personal assistant. 'Work for Will' was the ultimate phone demo disguised as the ultimate job interview. The gig: to be the real assistant of actor Will Arnett. To apply for the position, all you had to do was customise your own virtual Lumia 920. The experience generated a personalised interview, based on your customisation choices. Since the phone is an extension of you, Will used it to decide if you're worthy of the job.

–
Copywriter
Jeremy Postaer
Art Director
Chris Cavalieri
Executive Creative Directors
Heather Gorman
Jeff Spillane
Associate Creative Directors
Rick Williams
Marcel Yunes
Chief Creative Officer
David Lubars
Interactive Designer
Thao Damiano
Digital Producers
Andre Heckstall
Matt Silliman
Agency Producer
Diane Hill
Advertising Agency
BBDO Atlanta
Production Company
Caviar LA
Strategists
Harley Jebens
Rebecca Nadilo
Strategic Director
Mark Himmelsbach
Account Director
Phillip Cantilo
Group Account Director
Doug Walker
Client
AT&T

CRAFTS   WRITING FOR ADVERTISING

ATLANTA 33°45'N 84°23'W 2° 8:00

○

IN BOOK IN WRITING FOR ADVERTISING, WRITING FOR PRESS & POSTER ADVERTISING
COLENSO BBDO/PROXIMITY NEW ZEALAND FOR DB BREWERIES

The Wine List

Research showed that DB Export Dry's target market of young males didn't like wine, but they drank it to fit in. So we set out to save them from Sauvignon and get them a beer. We created an ad disguised as a wine list. Instead of a long list of elaborate, hard-to-pronounce vintages, the wine list talked men through all the reasons they should stop playing pretend and order an Export Dry instead.

–
Copywriters
Levi Slavin
Simon Vicars
Art Director
James Tucker
Designer
Kate Slavin
Creative Director
Levi Slavin
Chief Creative Officer
Nick Worthington
Producer
Sheriden Derby
Advertising Agency
Colenso BBDO/
Proximity New Zealand
Strategist
Stacey Stephenson
Planners
James Hurman
Hayley Pardoe
Account Managers
Stefanie Robertson
Patrick Rowley
Group Account Director
Tim Ellis
Marketing Managers
Russell Browne
Clare Morgan
Client
DB Breweries
Brand
Export Dry

THE WINE LIST

It's just been handed to you.
DEAR GOD, WHAT DO YOU DO NOW?
JUST STARE AT THE PAGE.

Can they tell your eyes aren't moving?
MAYBE.
TRY READING A FEW LINES.

Is it too soon to look up?
PROBABLY.
RUB YOUR CHIN FOR A BIT.

That's long enough. Time to pick one.
SEE IF YOU CAN SPOT ANY NAMES YOU KNOW.
NO. NO. NO. NO. NO. NO.

Right, that's not working.
SEE IF YOU CAN SPOT ANY WORDS IN ENGLISH.
NOPE.

Time to pick the second cheapest.
WOW. YOU'D PROBABLY NEED A SECOND MOUTH TO PRONOUNCE THAT.
MAYBE JUST POINT.

Then it's; swirl, sniff, sip, and say, "Mmm, very nice thanks."
MAYBE THIS TIME TRY, "MMM, THAT TASTES NICE AND OLD."
YEAH, THAT WORKS.

How did it get to this?
WINE ISN'T YOU.
BEER IS YOU.

That's why Morton Coutts, Head Brewer at DB Breweries, created Export Dry.
A SOPHISTICATED LAGER THAT'S CRISP, REFRESHING AND FULL OF FLAVOUR.
PERFECT FOR ANY OCCASION. ESPECIALLY OCCASIONS LIKE THIS.

So it looks like you've made your selection.
IN A MOMENT YOU ARE GOING TO SIT UP STRAIGHT,
HAND BACK THE WINE LIST AND SAY PROUDLY, "I'LL HAVE AN EXPORT DRY."

OK, you can look up now

In Court/On Court

In this ad, the same chapter of a person's life plays out in two very different scenarios. Sported doesn't want to change young people, but tries to shift the focus of their energies to a more positive context. Hence a basketball trial to make the team could mirror the emotions of a courtroom trial. It's your choice as to which path you take in life.

–
Copywriter
James White
Art Director
Henry Finnegan
Photographer
Sharon Chong
Typographer
Sharon Chong
Executive Creative Director
Alistair Ross
Advertising Agency
Draftfcb London
Client
sported

CRAFTS WRITING FOR ADVERTISING

LONDON 51°32'N 0°5'W 9° 12:00

TIME IN COURT

You've been waiting for this day for weeks. Your big trial. Finally spotted after all this time, you never saw it coming. Mom almost burst into tears when you told her. When the neighbours found out, they said you deserved it. Deep down, you never thought you'd find yourself here, all eyes on you. Your heart is beating away. Butterflies fill your stomach. But your family are here for support; they're sat in the second row. Behind them are more people, plenty of them hoping to see you go down. "Good luck, son", says Mom. Let's hope you don't need it.

TIME ON COURT

You've been waiting for this day for weeks. Your big trial. Finally spotted after all this time, you never saw it coming. Mom almost burst into tears when you told her. When the neighbours found out, they said you deserved it. Deep down, you never thought you'd find yourself here, all eyes on you. Your heart is beating away. Butterflies fill your stomach. But your family are here for support; they're sat in the second row. Behind them are more people, plenty of them hoping to see you go down. "Good luck, son", says Mom. Let's hope you don't need it.

SPORT CHANGES LIVES
Help to improve the lives of young people near you by visiting **choosesport.org**

sported.
changing young lives through sport

**Museum of
Childhood**

The Museum of
Childhood isn't
simply a repository
for old toys. It makes
people realise just
how incredible
childhood really
is, especially that
amazing capacity
for invention and
learning. Through a
collaborative process
with illustrators, we
explored solutions to
convey this message
on posters. We
penned some merry
statements that were
embellished with
vibrant and playful
illustrations, and
brightened up the
streets of London.

–
Copywriter
Mark Fairbanks
Art Director
Thiago de Moraes
Illustrators
Lesley Barnes
Till Haffenbrack
Creative Director
Paul Brazier
**Executive Creative
Director**
Paul Brazier
Advertising Agency
AMV BBDO
Art Buyer
Kirstie Johnstone
Client
V&A Museum of
Childhood

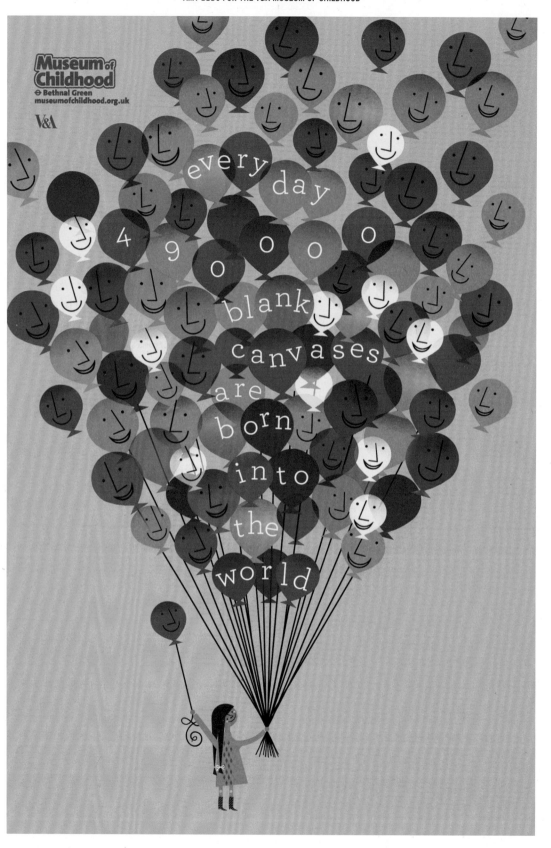

Musée de la Grande Guerre Campaign

Located in Meaux, near Paris, the Musée de la Grande Guerre opened at the end of 2011. To spread its vision of the First World War, we ran this campaign in Paris around Remembrance Day 2012, which coincided with the museum's first anniversary. Some posters were also shown in Eurostar stations in Brussels and London. The ads show photographs of wall-mounted exhibits containing messages of grave truth about our history of war. Each ad conveys the idea that war is not only about strategic plans and military strategies, but also about men suffering and dying in mud-sodden trenches.

–
Copywriter
Jean-François Bouchet
Art Director
Emmanuel Courteau
Typographer
Sonia Presne
Executive Creative Director
Alexandre Hervé
Advertising Agency
DDB Paris
Account Handlers
Marlene Bertranine
Jean-Luc Bravi
Art Buyer
Quentin Moenne Loccoz
Client
Musée de la Grande Guerre

Indispensable Paper

The Cape Argus,
Cape Town's
biggest-selling daily
newspaper, asked us to
create a print campaign
that championed the
newspaper as still
being an indispensable,
credible and objective
news source in an
increasingly digital
and social media-
driven world.

–
Copywriter
James Armstrong
Art Director
Dan Berkowitz
Creative Director
Dan Berkowitz
**Executive Creative
Directors**
Devin Kennedy
Alistair King
Advertising Agency
King James
Cape Town
Project Manager
Vicki Hey
Planner
Megan Clausen
Art Buyer
Samantha Wentzel
Brand Manager
Michael Vale
Client
Independent
Newspapers
Brand
Cape Argus

CRAFTS WRITING FOR ADVERTISING

It was the most beautiful fairytale. A hero defeated the demon of disease to become the greatest man on a saddle the world had ever seen. He courted his princess of pop, started a global movement and gave benevolently back to the people. An immaculate inspiration in yellow, for those who craved the hope that only stories of good can inspire. A tale of triumph about a legend of our own lifetime. A true story we loved to follow, until the truth came along and turned it all into fiction.

In the end, the truth always comes first. Get the latest in the Morning and Afternoon editions of the Cape Argus.

CAPE TOWN 33°55'S 18°22'E 29° 14:00

On 13th September 2011, Nelson Mandela died. The news came from a credible source. Someone knew someone in the hospital who was there to see it happen. The news travelled like a tsunami through Twitter. Within minutes the media had surrounded his home. Within hours millions had heard about it. The country went into a state of shock. Even the stock market wobbled at the news. News that wasn't news at all. News that was an untruth better left untold.

The source of your information is everything. Get the latest in the Morning and Afternoon editions of the Cape Argus.

Butterfly / Catfish

To elaborate on the campaign tag line 'A rum as smooth as life is rough', we told the sad, ironic tales of the catfish and the butterfly; two creatures with a huge capacity for taste, who can't enjoy Bundaberg Red. The animals are personified visually through vintage-style portraits where their heads are superimposed onto human bodies. This stirs empathy in the viewers who, confronted with such plight, develop a renewed appreciation for their own taste buds.

–
Copywriter
Mike Felix
Art Director
Matt Swinburne
Creative Directors
Tim Green
Vince Lagana
Grant McAloon
Executive Creative Director
Andy DiLallo
Advertising Agency
Leo Burnett Sydney
Client
Diageo Australia
Brand
Bundaberg Red

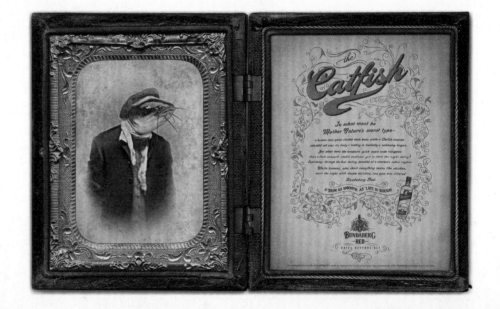

CRAFTS WRITING FOR ADVERTISING

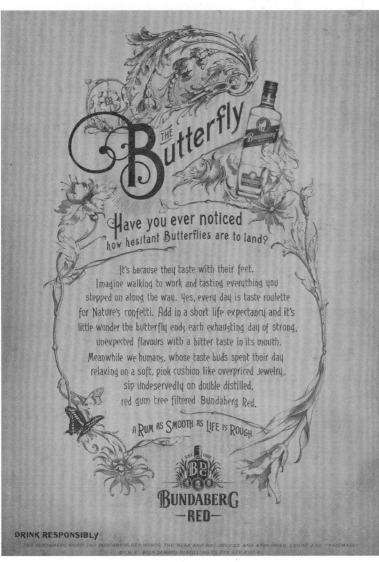

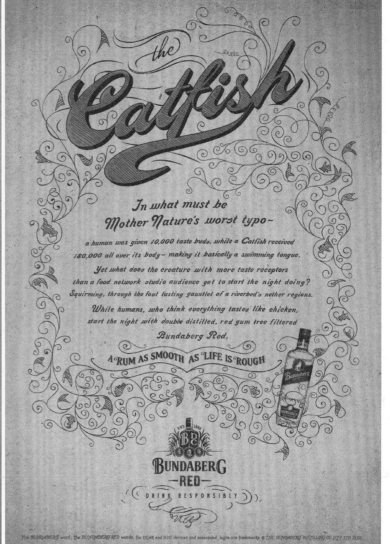

Untouchable Covers

Full of the very best advertising, design, illustration and photography, it's no wonder Lürzer's Archive is known as the world's most stolen magazine. This set of free anti-theft 'Untouchable Covers' turned copies of Lürzer's Archive into publications so dull, unpleasant or controversial that no one would want to touch them, let alone steal them.

–
Copywriters
Mark Denton
Ben Gough
Art Directors
Mark Denton
Ben Gough
Photographer
Fern Berresford
Typographer
Kate Henderson
Designers
Mark Denton
Kate Henderson
Creative Directors
John Jessup
Garry Munns
Executive Creative Director
Justin Tindall
Head of Art
Lance Crozier
Advertising Agency
Leo Burnett London
Production Company
Coy! Communications
Client
Lürzer's Archive

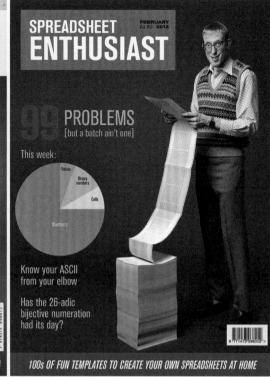

CRAFTS WRITING FOR ADVERTISING

Just Don't F*** it Up

We wanted to make it easier for our audience to understand why we make the kind of content we do. As Channel 4 headed towards its 30th birthday, the media landscape was growing more fragmented and complex. As a not-for-profit, publicly owned corporation, Channel 4's public service remit is at the heart of why it exists. A long copy advert ran in all the major broadsheets to coincide with Channel 4's 30th birthday, telling the story of the channel. The advert had an interactive element where users could download the Aurasma app and be fed all the content referred to in the ad.

–
Copywriter
Indra Sinha
Art Director
Neil Godfrey
Designer
Lincoln Grice
Producer
Edward Webster
Business Director
Kuba Wieczorek
Client
Channel 4

LONDON 51°32'N 0°5'W 9° 12:00

Just don't f*** it up.

Legend has it that in 1987 when Jeremy Isaacs, the outgoing Chief Executive of Channel 4, bumped into his successor Michael Grade, he shoved him up against a wall and hissed in his ear the words quoted above.

Sorry to disappoint, but he didn't.

Apart from the fact that bleeping out expletives, off-air or on, isn't Channel 4's style, Jeremy did not say the word we're here asked not to spell out.

What he *actually* said as he grabbed the amazed Michael by his (bright red) braces and pinned him to the wall was, 'I am handing you a sacred trust. If you screw it up – if you betray it – I'll come back and throttle you.'

The f-word has its impact but if anything this was more passionate and more shocking. Channel 4 is a TV channel, not a crusade.

What's to f*** up or betray?

'**We want to give voice to communities that face discrimination, people with disabilities, gays, lesbians and transgender people.**'

Can you picture Margaret Thatcher saying this? You're right. She didn't. (We lifted it from our 2011 Annual Report.)

Who will forget Oliver Reed, 'sitting there like a burst sofa' (to quote a mesmerised viewer) enlivening a high-minded debate about violence with aperçus such as 'cogito c*** c***'? (Unable to pronounce mouthfuls of asterisks, he uttered the dreadful word unencrypted.)

At one point the show abruptly went off-air to be replaced with a film about Welsh coal mining.

A few minutes later it equally mysteriously reappeared just in time to catch Reed going 'off for a slash'. On his return, he fell over the sofa on to a militant feminist and subjected her to inappropriate simian caresses.

We're trying out revolutionary ways to bring viewers and programme makers together to come up with radical ideas, brave projects that take the sort of risks others daren't.

In the last 18 months about six million people, including one third of all people aged 16-24, have signed up to engage directly with us in all sorts of innovative ways. Find out more by visiting *www.channel4.com*, meanwhile here's something you can do right now.

Think of this ad as a personal interactive invitation to join our 30th birthday party.

First you need the free Aurasma Lite app. You can download it for free. Now point your mobile device at the man being throttled on the other page and all the other pictures, sit back and enjoy what happens next.

From every one of us at Channel 4, and on behalf of every one who has been part of our first 30 years, thank you for watching. Will our next 30 years live up to the sacred trust? Tune in (or better still, join in) and see for yourself.

Claudia Ruane
Abel & Cole
Elise Valmorbida
word-design
Joe Weir
venturethree

Games Maker

By redefining the language of the volunteering sector, we succeeded in mobilising an apathetic nation gripped by recession. Renaming volunteers 'Games Makers' reminded people they could play an active role in making the London 2012 Olympic Games happen. This prompted over 250,000 applications. The effectiveness of the Games Makers encouraged Riò 2016 and the Tour de France to adopt the name. A recent survey revealed that 44% of UK adults (around 20 million people) wished they had been Games Makers. 'Games Maker' is now part of our everyday language and has entered the Oxford English Dictionary.

—
Lead Copywriter
Simon Learman
Copywriter
Chloe Grindle
Art Director
Michael Tomason
Executive
Creative Directors
Brian Fraser
Simon Learman
Advertising Agency
McCann Worldgroup
Account Handler
Simon Hill
Brand Manager
Greg Nugent
Client
London Organising
Committee of
the Olympic and
Paralympic Games
(LOCOG)
Brand
London 2012

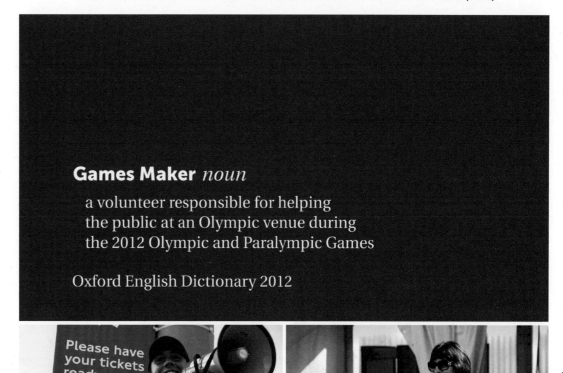

Games Maker *noun*

a volunteer responsible for helping the public at an Olympic venue during the 2012 Olympic and Paralympic Games

Oxford English Dictionary 2012

LONDON 51°32'N 0°5'W 9° 12:00

Disappointments Diary 2013

'Disappointments Diary 2013' is a week-to-view appointments diary with a series of disappointing twists. Each week has a demotivational proverb, including 'Genius is 99% perspiration and you've mastered that bit', 'Everything happens for a terrifyingly random reason', 'What doesn't kill you makes you wish it had' and 'Crappe diem'. The diary includes contact pages for 'People Who Never Call', reminders of notable deaths, and blank pages for 'Ideas You'll Never Follow Up'. The pages get darker as the year progresses to reflect a sense of encroaching doom.

–
Copywriter
Nick Asbury
Designers
Sue Asbury
Jim Sutherland
Design Directors
Gareth Howat
Jim Sutherland
Design Agency
hat-trick design
Client
Asbury & Asbury

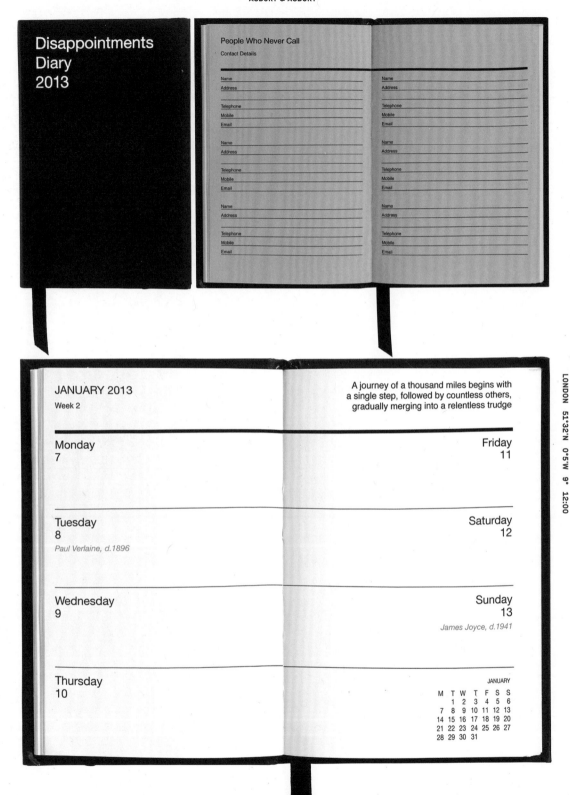

Disappointments Diary 2013

People Who Never Call
Contact Details

Name
Address

Telephone
Mobile
Email

Name
Address

Telephone
Mobile
Email

Name
Address

Telephone
Mobile
Email

JANUARY 2013
Week 2

A journey of a thousand miles begins with a single step, followed by countless others, gradually merging into a relentless trudge

Monday
7

Friday
11

Tuesday
8
Paul Verlaine, d.1896

Saturday
12

Wednesday
9

Sunday
13
James Joyce, d.1941

Thursday
10

JANUARY
M T W T F S S
      1 2 3 4 5 6
7 8 9 10 11 12 13
14 15 16 17 18 19 20
21 22 23 24 25 26 27
28 29 30 31

LONDON   51°32'N   0°5'W   9°   12:00

Best of Britain

The brief was to educate Australians about the UK's favourite sauce. HP Sauce is a staple condiment in its homeland, but most Australians had no idea what it was, let alone how to use it. To tell the story of HP Sauce in a memorable way, we tapped into something Aussies love – poking fun at the Poms. This cheeky booklet was distributed to establishments selling or serving HP Sauce. The pages of the 'passport' celebrate the worst things to come out of Britain, while offering a royal nod to one of its finest, positioning HP Sauce as 'The Best Thing to Come Out of Britain Since Forever'.

–
Copywriter
Tim Pashen
Art Director
Brett Edwards
Creative Director
David Ponce de Leon
Advertising Agency
BD Network
Marketing Manager
Jamie Chater
Client
Heinz Australia
Brand
HP Sauce

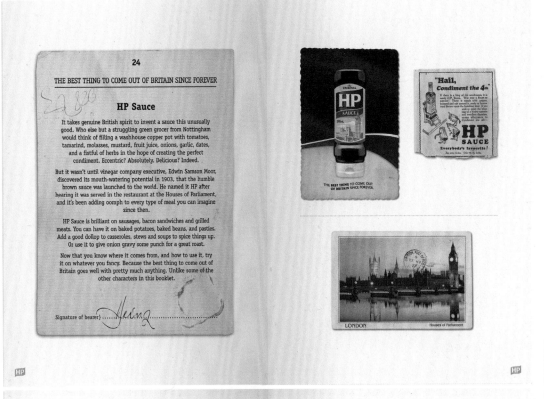

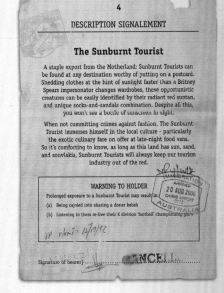

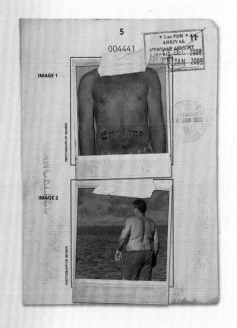

**Attention
All Shipping:
Homeware**

'Attention all shipping' are the opening words of BBC Radio's shipping forecast, a much-loved British institution, famous for its hypnotic delivery and evocative place names (Shannon, Rockall, Malin, west four, occasionally five later…). Our work takes the well-known language of the shipping forecast and twists it to suit a series of domestic situations related to homeware items such as tea towels.

—
Copywriter
Roger Horberry
Design Agency
The Workshop
Client
RNLI Homewares

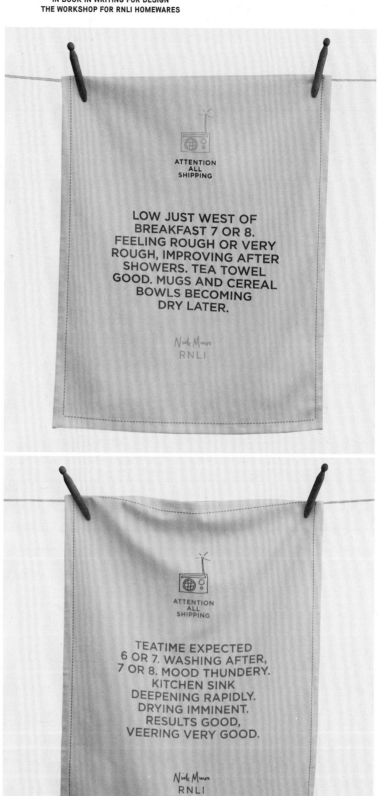

SHEFFIELD   53°23' N   1°28_W   5°   12:00

**The Wine That
Sold Beer**

Research showed
that DB Export Dry's
target market of
young males didn't
like wine, but they
drank it to fit in. So
we decided to save
them from Sauvignon
and get them a beer.
For the first time ever,
DB Breweries made
a wine. It looked like
any other bottle on
the shelf but on closer
inspection it was
actually an ad for
Export Dry in
disguise. The back
label coached men
on how to get out of
buying wine, and into
buying Export Dry.
When the wine bottle
was scanned at the
counter, guys received
$5 off a box of Export
Dry and the wine
bottle was returned
to the display.

—
Copywriters
Levi Slavin
Simon Vicars
Art Director
James Tucker
Designer
Kate Slavin
Creative Director
Levi Slavin
**Chief Creative
Officer**
Nick Worthington
Producer
Sheriden Derby
Advertising Agency
Colenso BBDO/
Proximity New
Zealand
Strategist
Stacey Stephenson
Planners
James Hurman
Hayley Pardoe
Account Managers
Stefanie Robertson
Patrick Rowley
**Group Account
Director**
Tim Ellis
Marketing Managers
Russell Browne
Clare Morgan
Client
DB Breweries
Brand
Export Dry

Lessons in Riding:
Wig / Crotch /
Penny

Grafa is a local cycling lifestyle retail outlet and café, the place to be for fixed gear bicycle enthusiasts and the cycling community. But what about less knowledgeable visitors? To welcome them, we produced 'Lessons in Riding', a series of entertaining posters that educated even Grafa's seasoned regulars. The posters featured an introduction to the fixed gear bicycle; health benefits of cycling; and cycling safety tips. The design approach paid tribute to everything that the fixed gear bicycle stands for: a minimalist design made up of all the right parts and assembled (or in our case, printed) by hand.

Copywriter
John Dorairaj
Art Director
Jerome Ooi
Designer
Chang Chun Boon
Executive Creative Directors
Ean-Hwa Huang
Szu-Hung Lee
Advertising Agency
McCann Erickson Malaysia
Client
Grafa

CRAFTS   WRITING FOR DESIGN

RIDE LIKE A SENIOR (Sorry, Gran.)

Under no circumstance should motorists assume you're a two-wheeled wonder. So yes, take a lesson from wobbly, shaky, unpredictable Gran. But for heaven's sake, be clever about it. While riding, glance back quickly. If you see a car 3 to 4 seconds away veering a little too close, don't ride closer to the road's edge. Your right of space is equally important, so give your bicycle a bit of a wiggle or swerve. An unsteady cyclist gives plenty of reason for the driver to be more careful when passing you.

GET A STRAP-ON. REALLY.

Cycling helmets: At their worst, they look like salad bowls. At their best, pistachio shell halves. Regardless of how they look, you need one to stay alive, so bear with it. Always check for size. If you're between sizes, pick the smaller one so that in the event a ditch jumps out of nowhere, your helmet and noggin won't part ways. While on the subject of snugness, straps must be worn tightly enough to feel taut when you yawn. As for rigging the straps, make sure they meet just below the ear. Consider non-adjustable straps; they hold better than the usual ones that slack and slip out of adjustment.

RIDE LOUD

Your bicycle may be the quintessence of cool, but the statement you really should be making on the road is:

I have no idea what I'm doing!

And nothing screams that louder than reflectors. They cover a larger area than bicycle lights and work a treat, day or night. More importantly, reflectors identify you as a cyclist. (Or if you're one with an active imagination, a compression suit and plenty of reflector tape to spare; a cyclist from the future.)

The Useful Book

'The Useful Book' has 176 pages that can be torn out and used for something other than reading. Each spread has an idea on the right and the instructions for how to use it on the left. It's more or less the Swiss Army knife of books. It's probably not what Gutenberg had in mind when he invented the printing press, but that's kind of the point, isn't it? The book was advertised with posters of an old lady using different pages of the book. An important thing to note is that she is in fact the grandmother of one of the authors.

–
Copywriter
Erik Bergqvist
Authors
Elin Bäckman
Johan Holmgren
Artworker
Julia Reijs
Print Producers
Malin Andersson
Elin Roslund
Advertising Agency
Acne Advertising
Client
Acne R&D

IF Istanbul
Corporate Identity

The identity for independent film festival IF disrupts the blockbuster film clichés with witty sentences. The word IF is used in sentences indicating a condition to cross the line from a clichéd Hollywood commercial film to an independent film. The sentences define each medium (letterhead, envelope, business cards) with a cliché linked to that medium itself. We also created a poster campaign to follow on from the new identity.

–
Copywriter
Kerem Tuten
Art Director
Zeynep Orbay
Executive
Creative Director
Ilkay Gurpinar
Advertising Agency
TBWA\Istanbul
Client
IF Istanbul

Designer
Fleur Isbell

Senior Artworker
Paul Murphy

Artworkers
Natalie Clay
Daniel Nutter

© 2013 D&AD
Britannia House,
68–80 Hanbury Street,
London E1 5JL
+44 (20) 7840 1111
www.dandad.org

D&AD is a registered
Charity (Charity No 305992)
and a Company limited
by Guarantee registered
in England and Wales
(registered number 883234)
with its registered office
at Britannia House, 68–80
Hanbury Street, London
E1 5JL, UK, phone: +44
(20) 7840 1111.

The D&AD logo and the
pencil are the registered
trademarks of D&AD.

D&AD would like to thank
Wolff Olins, in particular
Rejane Del Bello and Owen
Hughes, for giving Fleur the
resources and support to
design this book; and James
Isbell, for helping with the
coding that generated the
cover illustrations.

Interim Awards Director
Claire Fennelow

Editorial Manager
Jana Labaki

Editorial Executive
Zosia Gibbs

Editorial Assistant
Patrick Thomas

Content Management
Donal Keenan
Katy Koren

Content Collection Team
Jamie Anning
Nathalie Alvang
Ricardo Bessa
Matthew Cox
Ovie Eruero
Katy Moore
Jessica Parry
Hayley Smith

Production Consultant
Martin Lee

ACKNOWLEDGEMENTS

© 2013 TASCHEN GmbH
Hohenzollernring 53,
D-50672 Köln
www.taschen.com

To stay informed about
upcoming TASCHEN titles,
please request our magazine at
www.taschen.com/magazine,
find our app for iPad on
iTunes, or write to TASCHEN,
Hohenzollernring 53,
D-50672 Cologne, Germany;
contact@taschen.com.
We will be happy to send
you a free copy of our
magazine, which is filled
with information about all
of our books.

Editor in Charge
Julius Wiedemann

Editorial Coordination
Daniel Siciliano Bretas

Editorial Assistant
Nora Dohrmann

Production
Tina Ciborowius

German Translation
Katrin Kügler
for Delivering iBooks &
Design, Barcelona

French Translation
Valérie Lavoyer
for Delivering iBooks &
Design, Barcelona

ISBN: 978-3-8365-4527-3

Printed in Italy
by Printer Trento, the first
printer in Italy to have been
awarded the certification
FSC (Forest Stewardship
Council) – Chain of Custody.
Also ISO 14001 certified.

Paper: Recystar Polar
100% recycled, woodfree
uncoated paper made by
Lenzing, Austria.